DELIVERING ★ ★ ★ FOR ★ ★ ★ AMERICA

HOW THE UNITED STATES POSTAL SERVICE BUILT A NATION

JAMES H. BRUNS

MELCHER
MEDIA

This book was produced and published by

124 West 13th Street
New York, NY 10011
melcher.com

Founder and CEO: Charles Melcher
VP, COO: Bonnie Eldon
Editorial Director: Lauren Nathan
Production Director: Susan Lynch
Executive Editor: Christopher Steighner
Senior Editor: Megan Worman
Assistant Editor: Madison Brown

Contributor, editor, photo researcher, and project manager:
Ellen Espinoza-Hale, Senior Licensing Specialist, USPS

Designed by Paul Kepple and Alex Bruce at Headcase Design
headcasedesign.com

Special thanks to Chika Azuma, Alisa Cohen Barney, Laura Cray, Emma Dries, Kevin Dupzyk, David Gray, Charlotte Lamm, Carson Lee, Kevin Li, Jo Ann Liguori, Grace Luckett, Sonia Menken, Carolyn Merriman, Robert Saigh, Kayt Sukel, and Eitan Wolf.

Distributed to the trade by Two Rivers Distribution, an Ingram brand. For ordering information please send inquiries to: ips@ingramcontent.com.

ISBN: 978-1-59591-153-7

Library of Congress Control Number: 2025941318

First Edition

10 9 8 7 6 5 4 3 2 1

Printed in the United States of America

ABCD
CCELERATED USINESS OLLECTION- ELIVERY
Mail Collection Box
PUT IT HERE BY 11 A.M.-GET IT THERE BY 3 P.M.
FOR LOCAL BUSINESS DELIVERY
USE
ZIP CODE
THE
LAST WORD
IN MAIL
ADDRESS
U.S.MAIL

ORK RD.
U.S.MAIL
U.S.
MAIL
U.S.MAIL

CONTENTS

UNITED WE STAND
USA 34

July 26, 2025

When the United States Postal Service set out to do an anniversary book, we quickly realized two things—that we had never before written about our own history, and that 250 years would be difficult to condense into just one volume. While others have written about USPS from an outside perspective, it's our turn to tell our story. This book is both a celebration of and a reflection on the legacy of the United States Postal Service.

Going back to our beginnings, there are two Founding Fathers who had the foresight to ensure safe and secure communication through an American postal system. Benjamin Franklin, the first postmaster general, helped to standardize and build the infrastructure that would allow for swift mail delivery. George Washington, the first president, saw mail not only as the best method to distribute information but also as an important tool for building morale. If not for these two men, the postal service today would probably look very different.

Our rich heritage is inextricably linked to democracy, community, and the American spirit, and it is our privilege to serve the public. Two and a half centuries ago, USPS began building itself and America from the ground up. From turning dirt paths into roads, transforming train cars into sorting facilities, testing new modes of delivery transportation, experimenting with tube and missile mail, inventing the ZIP Code™ system, celebrating Americans on commemorative stamps, managing mail-in election ballots, sending out COVID-19 test kits, and being one of the first agencies to head back into communities after natural disasters, our efforts play a critical role in the growth and prosperity of America.

Today, USPS is 640,000 employees strong, with 31,000 retail centers and 256,000 delivery vehicles, delivering more than 400 million pieces of mail and packages to more than 330 million people daily. This book is dedicated to our community heroes—all USPS employees, past and present—as we continue to deliver for America today and for hundreds of years to come.

Opposite: "United We Stand" stamps being printed at the Bureau of Printing and Engraving in Washington, D.C., a couple of weeks prior to their issuance on October 24, 2001.

AMERICA
HONI SOIT QUI MAL Y PENSE
ONE PENNY
176
177
178
179
185
186
187
188
193
194
195
196
We do hereby Acknowledge
among the other Plates & Dies

A FOUNDING FATHER LAYS AMERICAN MAIL'S FOUNDATION

Long before the birth of the United States Postal Service—before the eagle logo, before Mr. ZIP, before mules in the Grand Canyon, before the United States was even a country—early Americans were already dependent on the mail. Many British colonists were hungry for news from Europe, which was still home. For those growing numbers invested in life on their new continent, correspondence from other settlements—nearby by today's standards, but astonishingly remote in the 17th and 18th centuries—was of increasing importance. As a society distinct to the colonists began to develop, the first newspapers were delivered by postal riders, offering news from both sides of the Atlantic, the shipping notices that businessmen craved, and essays that argued over the great questions that would lead, in time, to revolution.

This seven-foot-tall oil portrait of Benjamin Franklin, the first postmaster general, was commissioned in 1918 and painted by Benedict Anton Osnis. It was a gift from the Pennsylvania Postmasters' Association and resides at the USPS headquarters in Washington, D.C.

The colonial mail system, operated under the British Crown, was chaotic and vulnerable. Riders navigated intimidating wilderness, delivered unpredictably, and dropped the post primarily at taverns and coffeehouses, bustling centers of civic life from which mail was routinely lost or stolen. The job of postmaster was often doled out as a favor to printers or publishers, for whom the job conferred certain, undeniably unfair advantages.

Consider 1730s Philadelphia, where an ambitious young newspaperman found himself on the wrong side of the city's postmaster, a rival publisher. Philadelphia had become the flame-keeper of the colonies' intellectual life, and its postmaster, Andrew Bradford, published *The American Weekly Mercury*, the fourth paper in the colonies and the first outside Boston. The newspaperman, who had in fact written for the *Mercury*, had in 1729 purchased another Philadelphia newspaper, *The Pennsylvania Gazette*. Under his leadership, it became a formidable rival to the *Mercury*. But Bradford guarded his business fiercely, and he used the post to do so. So when the *Gazette* threatened his paper, he made a move that was his right as postmaster: He forbade post riders from carrying it.

Unfortunately for Bradford, he'd underestimated his opponent. Despite being scarcely 30 years old, the publisher of the *Gazette* had been around the newspaper business for half his life, ever since his brother had founded a newspaper in Boston. And he was quite clever. In the course of time, he'd come to be known as America's first Renaissance man, renowned in the colonies and beyond for his brilliance as a publisher, philosopher, philanthropist, and inventor. His name was Benjamin Franklin.

★ ★ ★

Franklin's efforts would standardize, professionalize, and all-around improve the post.

Franklin knew that the post riders, in those days, were not exactly famous for their loyalty to their jobs. So when Bradford sought to cripple the *Gazette* by banning them from carrying it, Franklin bribed them to do the opposite. It worked, and the newspaper survived. More important, the episode drew Franklin into the mail business. In time, Bradford fell out of favor with British North America's deputy postmaster general, Alexander Spotswood, and in 1737 his position as postmaster was offered to Franklin, who readily accepted it.

Franklin's leadership was transformative. He established the first local home-delivery service. He instituted and popularized the penny post, a service in which letters not picked up at the post office on the day of their arrival would be delivered to the recipient's residence for an additional penny. Under Franklin's guidance, Philadelphia's post office became profitable for the first time. With this track record, it was inevitable that he would expand the scope of his efforts beyond his home city. On and off over the next four decades, Franklin led the postal service in colonial America, and much as they had in Philadelphia, his efforts would standardize, professionalize, and all-around improve the post all across the 13 colonies.

Benjamin Franklin birthed the modern United States Postal Service, and the reason is that he understood its purpose and potential, going as far back as 1737. For one, Franklin knew the post ought to be incorruptible. He had made use of bribes to keep his paper alive, but he hated being devious. When he replaced Bradford as postmaster, he disavowed the tactics they had engaged in, especially Bradford's discrimination against the *Gazette*. "I thought so meanly of the practice," Franklin said, "that when I afterwards came into his situation, I took care never to imitate it." Even more important, Franklin understood that an effective mail service could be the foundation on which to build something great. He wrote of his commission in Philadelphia that he "found it of great advantage; for, though the salary was small, it facilitated the correspondence that improved my newspaper, increased the number demanded, as well as the advertisements to be inserted, so that it came to afford me a considerable income."

This is the story of the United States Postal Service. Over the vast sweep of its history, from colonial beginnings to the present day, the infrastructure of the USPS has been to the nation's great profit. It has been America's backbone and scaffolding, its nervous system. The USPS makes it possible for Americans to live in new places. It makes it possible for all of us to talk to each other, to *hear* each other, even as our borders have expanded and our frontiers have become more vast. Today, the USPS makes it possible for anyone to receive just about anything—from a college student's care package to a homesick sibling's birthday presents to an elderly, bedridden parent's groceries—without leaving the house.

Of course, in the middle of the 18th century, much of that was a far-off dream. Groceries by mail! But those early decades were when the work began. At the time, what would become America was served by British colonial post, a system administrated from afar, slow to grow, and inconsistent in its performance. The colonies were wilderness, and mail delivery was lost in the tall grass. But Benjamin Franklin saw a way through.

Benjamin Franklin and his daughter, Sally, riding the post roads.

The strange contraption that whirred on the side of Franklin's carriage during the 1763 tour was an odometer.

In the spring and summer of 1763, wagons full of enormous milestones traversed New York, Pennsylvania, New Jersey, and New England, a platoon of workers in tow to retrieve and place them alongside the road. A young woman, scarcely 20 years of age, rode along on horseback. Accompanying her was a chaise carriage with a strange contraption connected to its wheels. In the chaise was a well-to-do man, getting on in years: Benjamin Franklin. The young woman was his daughter, Sally. They were on official postal-service business: an inspection tour of the colonies' post offices, roads, and practices. Over the course of the year, they would travel 1,600 miles.

Franklin had been appointed deputy postmaster general in North America for the British Crown in 1753. He assumed responsibility for postal records of the colonies north of Annapolis, Maryland, while a second deputy, William Hunter, the former postmaster of Williamsburg, Virginia, oversaw south of Annapolis. (The two men had applied for the job at the same time and were named co-deputy postmasters general. Though they could have been rivals, they were good colleagues, inspecting roads together until Hunter grew ill. He died in 1761.) Franklin's tenure was slow to begin; he focused initially on standardizing delivery, then between 1757 and 1762 left America for Europe, where he sought to represent the interests of Pennsylvanians against the wealthy British family that still held much power over them. Upon his return, Franklin decided to take stock of the system that he was responsible for but had not been acquainted with for half a decade.

There was at least one immediate problem he was trying to solve. Ever since the Queen Anne Act (also known as the British Post Office Act of 1710) had taken effect in North America in 1711, the rate of postage had been based on distance. But local postmasters were constantly quarreling over how much to charge because their calculations differed: What one postmaster gauged as 60 miles another may have gauged as 70 miles. The strange contraption that whirred on the side of Franklin's carriage during the 1763 tour was an odometer—one he had designed himself—that he used to measure distances and establish standard rates.

Below, left to right: 56 miles from Boston along Route 9 in Leicester, Worcester County, Massachusetts; one of the Boston Road Parting Stones, dated 1744, erected by Peter Dudley at the junction of Center and Roxbury streets, the terminus point leading right to Cambridge or left to Providence, Rhode Island; 63 miles from Boston at the East End of Town Common, West Brookfield, Massachusetts.

BENJAMIN FRANKLIN, and WILLIAM HUNTER, Eſqrs. joint Poſt-Maſters-General of all his Majeſty's Provinces and Dominions on the Continent of *North-America.*

To all Governors, Mayors of Corporations, Juſtices of the Peace; and to all other his Majeſty's Officers and Miniſters, Eccleſiaſtical, Civil, or Military, within the ſaid Provinces and Dominions, Greeting.

WHEREAS His Majeſty, by His Royal Letters Patents under the Great Seal of *Great-Britain,* bearing Date the 24th Day of *May,* 1745, and in the Eighteenth Year of His Majeſty's Reign; to the End the Deputies, Agents, and other Officers, employed in the Service of His Majeſty's Revenue of the Poſt-Office might not be impeded or hindered in their reſpective Duties, was thereby pleaſed to declare His Royal Will and Pleaſure, That no ſuch Deputies, Agents, and other Officers, ſhall be compell'd or compellable to ſerve on any Jury or Inqueſt, or to appear or ſerve at any Aſſize or Seſſion, or to bear any public Office or Employment, either Eccleſiaſtical, Civil, or Military.

Theſe are to Certify, That the Bearer hereof Mr Woodward Abraham Gent. is Post Master at Marblehead – which Employment requires at all Times his Perſonal Attendance, and that His Majeſty's Revenue in the Poſt-Office (great Part of which is now ſubjected to the Payment of the public Debts), may ſuffer very much by his being obliged to ſerve in the Train'd-Bands, or any other public Office, Eccleſiaſtical, Civil, or Military: For Notification whereof, We have Signed and cauſed the Seal of our Office to be hereunto affixed, this Tenth Day of Aprill in the Thirty First Year of His Majeſty's Reign. 1758

B Franklin

Wm Hunter

By the Post-Master General's Command
James Parker
Agent and Comptroller.
(Pro Tempore)

But the truth is that Franklin was fighting not just petty squabbles but also more than a century of disorder. The first post office in the British colonies in North America was established in a tavern operated by one Richard Fairbanks, at the end of the long wharf in Boston. A barkeep permitted to sell "wines and strongwater," Fairbanks was appointed by the Massachusetts General Court as postmaster in 1639. The decree ordered "all letters which are brought from beyond the seas, or are to be sent thither, to be left with him; and he is to take care that they are to be delivered or sent according to the directions; and he is allowed for every letter a penny and he must answer all miscarriages through his own neglect in this kind." At that time, Boston consisted of 100 homes and one church. Much of the mail was sent between England—"beyond the seas"—and prominent colonists, as few others could afford the postage. Delivering mail to a tavern, a coffeehouse (one of which hosted New York's first post office), or an inn was a common European practice. It wasn't necessarily ideal.

Coffeehouses of the period were described as "the headquarters of life and action, the pulsating heart of excitement, enterprise, and patriotism." Unfortunately, they weren't great places to leave the post: Little attention was paid to the mail to ensure it wasn't miscarried. The common practices at the time were to dump letters into a basket for everyone to sort through or toss them out onto tables until someone claimed them. Another technique was to tack them onto a "card rack," a simple board nailed up in a conspicuous place. The nail was removed for anyone willing to pay the postage, even if they weren't the intended recipient. This practice led to much mail theft.

Above, left: Benjamin Franklin and William Hunter signed this broadside as joint deputy postmasters general of the American colonies. The document, dated April 10, 1758, was used to excuse Woodward Abraham, postmaster of Marblehead, Massachusetts, from jury duty. As noted in the text, the work of His Majesty's postal employees was never to be impeded or delayed by subjecting them to the other responsibilities that were usually also due the monarch by his citizens.

Above, right: Merchant's Coffee House, at far right, located on the corner of Wall and Water streets in New York City.

Mary Katharine Goddard

William Goddard was one of the most important figures in the early history of the Postal Service in what would become the United States, but he may not even be the most remarkable postal worker in his own family. That honor just might go to Mary Katharine Goddard, William's older sister.

Like many people who were involved in the mail business in those days, Mary Katharine started out as a publisher—a job she wound up in because her brother was busy shaping the American mail service. In 1773, William had established Baltimore's first newspaper, *The Maryland Journal and the Baltimore Advertiser*. A year later, fed up with the Crown's mail service, he established his Constitutional Post. Promoting it to colonial governments as a better alternative often took him on trips away from Baltimore, and eventually, the *Journal* needed other leadership. Mary Katharine took over as publisher. In time, she would stop printing it under her brother's name, instead signing it "M.K. Goddard."

It was only another year before she became postmaster of Baltimore—the first-known female postal worker in the United States—and she didn't get the job because her brother vacated a role. She earned it on her own merits, and she was good at it. Baltimore's post office was the very

This 1783 *Baltimore Almanack* was published by Mary Katharine Goddard; however, the portrait is that of Ann Brunton Merry. It is unknown why this portrait was added.

picture of efficiency and effectiveness. In fact, Mary Katharine was so successful at being a publisher and a postmaster that when the Continental Congress came to Baltimore in December 1776, she became the official printer to the Congress. She printed its various resolutions and notices, including one of the earliest copies of the Declaration of Independence, for circulation to the public.

In 1789, Mary Katharine was abruptly removed from her role as postmaster of Baltimore by Postmaster General Samuel Osgood. Osgood believed a woman was unfit for the evolving role and importance of Baltimore's post office, which was being made a regional headquarters for the postal system. The postmaster was going to have to travel a good deal, Osgood argued, and that wasn't safe for a woman.

Mary Katharine fought back. She went straight to the top: She wrote to President George Washington about how much she had contributed to the success of the colonial cause during the Revolutionary War. She stressed how she had even paid post riders out of her own pocket to keep the mail moving. And she also noted that under her care, Baltimore's post office had been "the most punctual & regular of any upon the Continent." Others agreed: More than 230 Baltimoreans signed a petition stating they wished for Mary Katharine to retain her post. But it was all for naught, as President Washington refused to interfere with Osgood's postal appointments. Then she tried

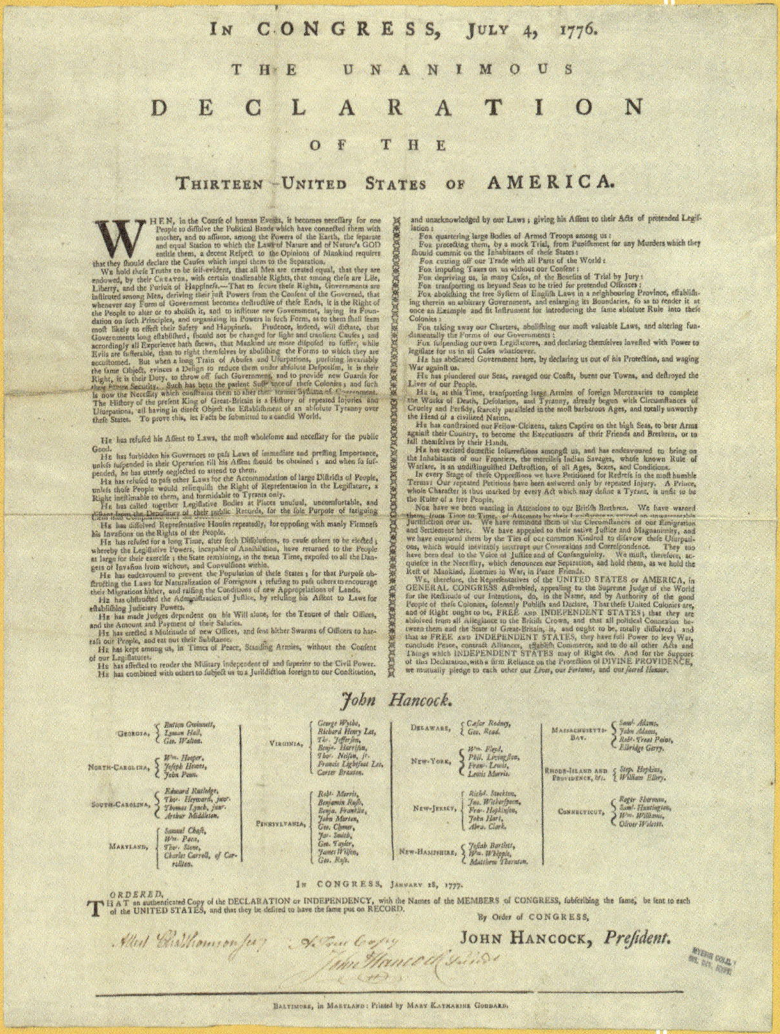
IN CONGRESS, JULY 4, 1776.

THE UNANIMOUS

DECLARATION

OF THE

THIRTEEN UNITED STATES OF AMERICA.

John Hancock.

IN CONGRESS, January 18, 1777.

By Order of CONGRESS,

JOHN HANCOCK, *President.*

BALTIMORE, in MARYLAND: Printed by MARY KATHARINE GODDARD.

A copy of the Declaration of Independence printed by Mary Katharine Goddard.

appealing instead to the Senate, but they didn't want to go against President Washington. An Osgood loyalist named John White was appointed in her place, and Mary Katharine shifted her focus to yet another profession dedicated to the free flow of information, bookselling. She would remain in that industry until her death in 1816.

The Village Tavern, a painting by John Lewis Krimmel created between 1813 and 1814, depicts tavern life where mail is delivered and collected at the local establishment. At left, a man carries in a mailbag for delivery, while the man next to him hails his entrance, announcing to the room that the news has arrived.

In Boston, merchants complained about the level of service they were receiving from Fairbanks, and in 1677 the General Court of Massachusetts replaced him with a man named John Hayward. Initially, Hayward used his house as the post office, but in 1686 he leased space in the town hall, a far more appropriate venue for conducting postal business.

The historical record includes a wealth of disgruntled mail customers well into the 1700s, perhaps none more florid in their complaints than Jonas Green, postmaster of Annapolis and the publisher of *The Maryland Gazette*. In 1753, he lost roughly 200 subscribers' payments when someone walked away with his letters. He advised his readers that "many times sundry evil-minded Persons find Occasion clandestinely to take such Letters out of the Public House, where they are generally left, and break open and conceal the same."

Such losses led many wealthy families, merchants, and newspaper publishers to hire their own horsemen to deliver their mail. This prompted colonies to consider creating their own post offices and post riders. Franklin's 1763 tour exposed even more shortcomings: Colonial roads in many areas were in deplorable condition, post riders were shirking their duties, and ferrymen weren't providing priority treatment for post riders, who were supposed to be transported for free whenever they arrived at a river crossing. Instead, ferrymen waited until there were paying passengers to make it profitable to shuttle post riders across.

With his illustrious history—and the postal system in such poor shape—the least Franklin could do was calculate accurate, standardized distances. Which he did: Following the 1763 survey, Franklin printed a rate chart that clearly set down charges between post offices so that rates were uniformly applied. But of course he did much more. His other projects included accelerating and extending ocean mail with a packet service to the West Indies and Canada, introducing a simplified method of accounting for postmasters, shifting some mail from post riders to wagons, and establishing around-the-clock post riders on selected roads.

Alexander Anderson, often noted as "America's first wood engraver," depicted scenes of colonial life, including this typical passenger wagon.

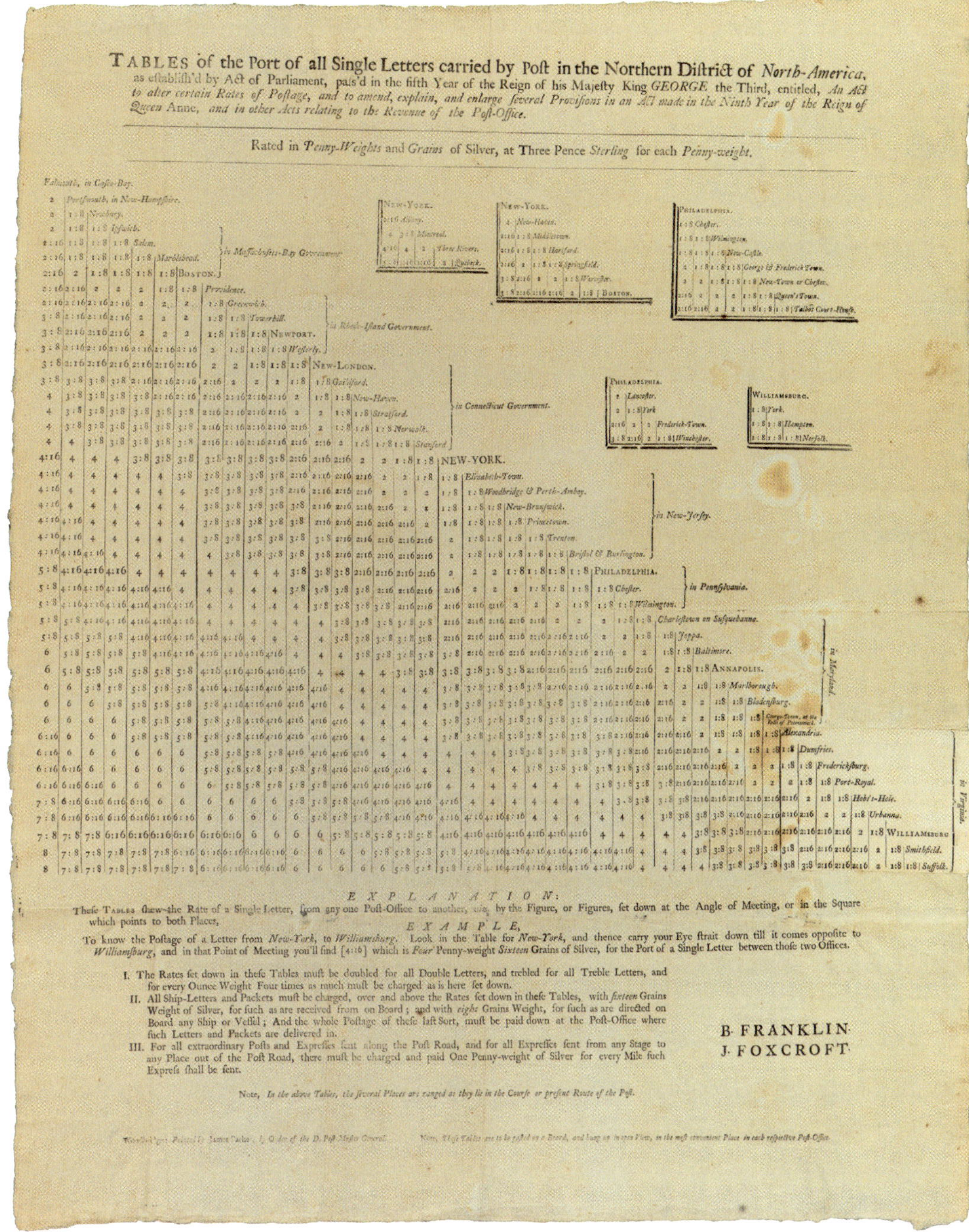

TABLES of the Port of all Single Letters carried by Post in the Northern District of *North-America*, as establish'd by Act of Parliament, pass'd in the fifth Year of the Reign of his Majesty King *GEORGE* the Third, entitled, *An Act to alter certain Rates of Postage, and to amend, explain, and enlarge several Provisions in an Act made in the Ninth Year of the Reign of Queen* Anne, *and in other Acts relating to the Revenue of the Post-Office.*

Rated in *Penny-Weights* and *Grains* of Silver, at Three Pence *Sterling* for each *Penny-weight.*

EXPLANATION:

These TABLES shew the Rate of a Single Letter, from any one Post-Office to another, *viz.* by the Figure, or Figures, set down at the Angle of Meeting, or in the Square which points to both Places,

EXAMPLE,

To know the Postage of a Letter from *New-York*, to *Williamsburg*. Look in the Table for *New-York*, and thence carry your Eye strait down till it comes opposite to *Williamsburg*, and in that Point of Meeting you'll find [4:16] which is *Four* Penny-weight *Sixteen* Grains of Silver, for the Port of a Single Letter between those two Offices.

I. The Rates set down in these Tables must be doubled for all Double Letters, and trebled for all Treble Letters, and for every Ounce Weight Four times as much must be charged as is here set down.

II. All Ship-Letters and Packets must be charged, over and above the Rates set down in these Tables, with *sixteen* Grains Weight of Silver, for such as are received from on Board; and with *eight* Grains Weight, for such as are directed on Board any Ship or Vessel; And the whole Postage of these last Sort, must be paid down at the Post-Office where such Letters and Packets are delivered in.

III. For all extraordinary Posts and Expresses sent along the Post Road, and for all Expresses sent from any Stage to any Place out of the Post Road, there must be charged and paid One Penny-weight of Silver for every Mile such Express shall be sent.

B. FRANKLIN.
J. FOXCROFT.

Note, *In the above Tables, the several Places are ranged as they lie in the Course or present Route of the Post.*

Benjamin Franklin, tasked with standardizing postage rates, did so by surveying mileage from town to town. He and John Foxcroft, his co-postmaster general under British rule, drafted this broadside for display in the 48 colonial post offices to denote the postage rate of a single-sheet letter between various locations between Quebec and Virginia. The table included rates such as "Penny-weights and Grains of Silver, at Three Pence Sterling for each Penny-weight."

Franklin was especially proud of this last feat, writing to the secretary of the British Post Office in London on January 16, 1764: "I will not only mention that we hope in the Spring to expedite the Communication between Boston and New York, as we have already that between New York and Philadelphia, by making the Mails travels by Night as well as by Day, which has never heretofore been done in America." Franklin's post office was doing something remarkable: It was making a big, untamed world smaller.

★ ★ ★

Indeed, the world was changing. As the colonists grew closer to one another, literally and metaphorically, many of them increasingly wanted to put distance between themselves and the Crown. Unrest was growing as those anxious for liberty among them traveled down the path that would lead to the Revolutionary War. In 1764, Franklin was again compelled to travel to Europe to advocate for colonial interests. He would remain for roughly a decade, a tenure during which his revolutionary sentiments would become clear to postal officials in Great Britain. While Franklin wasn't officially dismissed from his role as postmaster until 1774, the time in London would effectively spell his end as a servant of the *British* postal service.

At the same time that revolutionary fervor was causing Franklin to fall from favor in England, the British mail service in North America was losing clout with the colonists, who viewed expensive postage rates as yet another injustice suffered at the hands of the Crown. A British loyalist named Hugh Finlay would see this firsthand on his own tour of the colonial post.

Finlay had worked for the British post since 1763, when he was named by none other than Benjamin Franklin to be postmaster of the colony of Quebec, which the British had just won from the French in the Seven Years' War. Though Finlay would ultimately oversee the collapse of the Crown's postal service in what would shortly be the United States, he was in fact a fantastic postmaster. In Quebec, he mapped new postal routes, initiated service between Canada and New York, and professionalized the job of the post riders, who would now be provisioned with horses at newly established post houses and offered free passage on the region's ferries. Under his leadership, the postal service in Quebec turned a profit.

In 1772, Finlay was appointed to a new role, postal surveyor. In this capacity, he set out the next year on a tour much like Franklin's—but even more extensive. From September 1773 to June 1774, he traveled from Falmouth, Massachusetts (now known as Portland, Maine), to Savannah,

Pages from Hugh Finlay's journal. At left, Finlay records the days and times of delivery and dispatches to Philadelphia, Boston, and Quebec; at right, he illustrates a cut-through road through an island in the Cape Fear River leading to Wilmington, North Carolina.

43

Post days at New York.

Monday	Tuesday	Wednesday
A mail from Philad.a arrives at 8 & goes out at 10 in the morning very regularly. At 12 The Boston Post by way of New Haven New London, Rhode Island & Providence is despatch'd. This is called the lower road.	The Quebec Post by way of Albany arrives at 4 o'clock P.M. he is very regular.	The Boston Mail by way of Hartford called the upper road, is irregular in his arrivals. For reasons assign'd in this Journal under the Boston head, but in Common he arrives between 6 in the evening and 10 at night. The Albany Post which carrys the Canadian Mail is sent off at 11 A.M. A Mail arrives from Philadelphia at 10, & the Post returns at 12. The Packet Mail is made up and despatched from this office the first Wednesday of every month at 12 o'clock at night.
Thursday	**Friday**	**Saturday**
The Post for Boston by New Haven, Hartford and Spring field called the upper road is sent off at Noon.	The Post from Phil.a arrives at 11 o'clock A.M. and returns at one o'clock.	A Post from Boston by the Lower road arrives between 5 and 10 at night, sometimes it is sunday, for reasons assign'd under the Boston head.

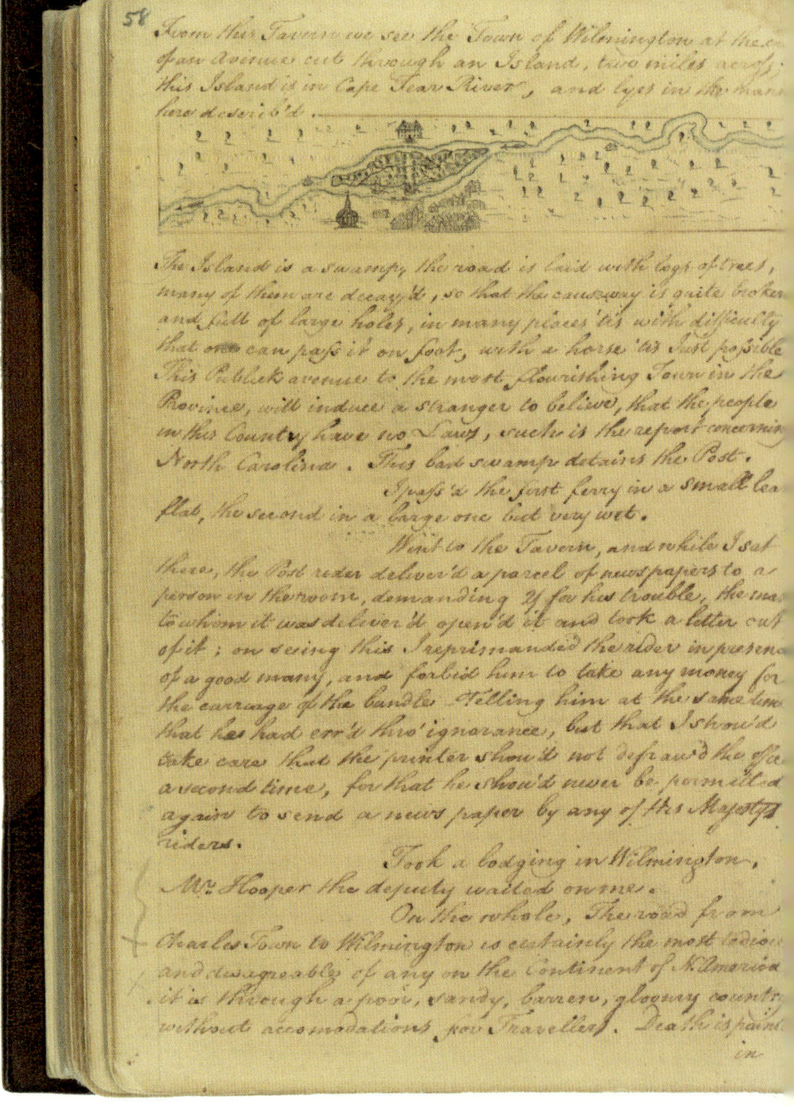

58 From this Tavern we see the Town of Wilmington at the end of an avenue cut through an Island, two miles across; this Island is in Cape Fear River, and lyes in the manner here describ'd.

The Island is a swamp, the road is laid with logs of trees, many of them are decay'd, so that the causeway is quite broken and full of large holes, in many places 'tis with difficulty that one can pass it on foot, with a horse 'tis just possible. This Publick avenue to the most flourishing Town in the Province, will induce a stranger to believe, that the people in this Country have no Laws, such is the report concerning North Carolina. This bad swamp detains the Post.

I pass'd the first ferry in a small flat, the second in a large one but very wet.

Went to the Tavern, and while I sat there, the Post rider deliver'd a parcel of newspapers to a person in the room, demanding 2/ for his trouble, the man to whom it was deliver'd open'd it and took a letter out of it; on seeing this I reprimanded the rider in presence of a good many, and forbid him to take any money for the carriage of the bundle, telling him at the same time that he had err'd thro' ignorance, but that I should take care that the printer shou'd not defraud the office a second time, for that he shou'd never be permitted again to send a news paper by any of His Majesty's riders.

Took a lodging in Wilmington, Mr. Hooper the deputy waited on me.

On the whole, The road from Charles Town to Wilmington is certainly the most tedious and disagreable of any on the Continent of N. America it is through a poor, sandy, barren, gloomy country without accomodations for Travellers. Death is paint-
in-

The Postal Inspection Service

The U.S. Post Office Department Inspector star badge. It appeared on the Chief Inspector's stationery in August 1921, and by 1922 badges were issued to all postal inspectors.

The Continental Congress may have passed over William Goddard when it named Benjamin Franklin postmaster general, but Benjamin didn't make the same mistake. He named Goddard the nation's first surveyor, a role he had created to audit postal accounts and investigate thefts of mail or money. When Goddard took the job on August 7, 1775 (just 12 days after the American Post Office itself was created), it marked the birth of the Postal Inspection Service. The service's primary mission is to protect and secure the mail, ensuring it is delivered unopened and in a timely fashion. The Inspection Service still exists today, and with its own 250 years of history, it ranks as the oldest federal law-enforcement agency in the United States.

Isaac Weld Jr. published a book of his travels through North America during 1795, 1796, and 1797. His mode of transportation was the American stage wagon he took en route between New York City and Philadelphia.

Georgia, keeping a meticulous journal of his findings along the way.

On his tour, Finlay discovered plenty of chaos and lawlessness, beginning in Falmouth, where the postmaster begged Finlay to replace him as soon as possible. According to the postmaster, his patrons barged in at all hours looking for their mail, mindless of the fact that the post office was also his home. Additionally, many of his neighbors never paid the postage on the letters they gave him, leaving him to cover their debts. Even mail just arriving at Falmouth was trouble: When ship captains would reach the port city, they would distribute any letters or newspapers they carried themselves, pocketing the postage. Legally, they were obligated to turn the mail over to the town's postmaster—but they viewed the rules and fees as a way that the Crown was taking their money without their consent. Finlay would write in his journal that "the present act obliging Masters of Vessels to carry their letters to the post office is of no effect in America."

In many places, post riders conducted business on the side, to the detriment of mail delivery. For a fee, some would serve as guides for travelers, escorting them safely to their destinations, even if off the path of the post roads. Around New Haven, Connecticut, Finlay was asked by townsfolk if he'd seen their post rider—because they regularly paid him to drive oxen along his route. Finlay discovered that Peter Mumford, the post rider between Boston and Newport, Rhode Island, was regularly deviating from his mail route to deliver goods for people who paid him a commission. Punctuality mattered less to Mumford than did personal profits. Even worse was a rogue from Guilford, Connecticut, known as "Old Herd." Seventy-two years of age, he had for nearly five decades been delivering the mail—as well as many other things. He would take care of horses, deliver goods, and transport money for people on his route. He "in short refuses no business however it may affect his speed as Post," Finlay wrote in his journal. When Finlay encountered Old Herd, he had been sitting around—waiting for Peter Mumford—for nearly three hours. "'Tis ridiculous to see his Majesty's courier, metamorphos'd to a snail paced Carrier," Finlay wrote.

The postal surveyor was deluged with excuses for why the mail arrived late, including the post rider being delayed at a ferry or his horse losing a shoe. He was particularly taken by riders blaming their lateness on the weather. "They have sometimes said that it was too hot to ride and at other times that it rain'd and they did not chuse (*sic*) to get wet," he noted in his journal.

But there was a greater, more portentous concern than delays and side work. In many communities Finlay visited, not unlike the captains in Falmouth, the colonists were simply circumventing the British mail service. Many post coach drivers carried official mail but also distributed letters outside the postal system, keeping the money. According to Finlay, the coachmen between Boston and Portsmouth, New Hampshire, "hurt the office very much by carrying letters; and they were so artful that the post master cou'd not detect them." One of the gimmicks used by such drivers was to give passengers bundles of letters to hold on to during the trips and, if challenged, have them claim the letters as their own. This practice cut down on the profitability of the local post office to such an extent that the postmaster of Portsmouth told Finlay he wanted to be paid an annual salary instead of the standard commission on the postage he collected. After all, most of his neighbors never paid. Peter Mumford, for his part, wasn't just slow but was found to transport more letters and newspapers *outside* his official mail portmanteau, for personal profit, than

NEWS! NEWS!

AARON OLIVER, *Poſt-Rider,*

WISHES to inform the Publick, that he has extended his Route; and that he now rides thro' the Towns of *Troy, Pittſtown, Hooſick, Mapletown,* Part of *Bennington,* and *Shaftſbury, Peterſburgh, Stephentown, Greenbuſh* and *Schodack.*

All Commands in his Line will be received with Thanks, and executed with Punctuality.

He returns his ſincere Thanks to his former Cuſtomers; and intends, by unabated Diligence, to merit a Continuance of their Favours.

O'er ruggid hills, and vallies wide,
He never yet has fail'd to trudge it;
As ſteady as the flowing tide,
He hands about the NORTHERN BUDGET.

June 18, 1799.

A 1799 woodcut advertisement from *The Northern Budget* of Troy, New York, in which Aaron Oliver offers his services as a post rider.

William Goddard was surveyor of the post as appointed by Benjamin Franklin. Goddard was passed over for Franklin's postmaster-general position for Franklin's son-in-law, Richard Bache.

he held *inside* the Crown's pouch. "In short, I find it is the constant practice of all the riders between New York and Boston to defraud the Revenue as much as they can in pocketing the postage of all way letters," Finlay concluded. The same things were happening in the South.

The undercurrent of this blatant profiteering was disdain or outright hostility toward the British. Whenever Finlay asked sympathetic local postmasters why they hadn't reported such depredations against the government before his visit, the answer was always the same: They feared retribution. The postmaster of Salem, Massachusetts, said he was certain that "an informer would get tarred and feathered." Finlay himself faced increasing antagonism, especially in the northern colonies. The hazards of travel as a British loyalist ultimately played a role in bringing Finlay's tour to an end. So did something else: After Franklin was relieved of his duties as deputy postmaster general for North America, Finlay was given his job. It was February 1774. In just a few months' time, the job would become moot.

★ ★ ★

The United States' colonial forefathers had difficulty starting a suitable mail service. In the earliest days of British North America, the challenges primarily had to do with the geography of the new colonies. Roads had to be carved out of dense forests, leaving them full of stumps, potholes, and stones that impeded travel; methods had to be established for crossing rivers; and settlements were few and far between, with towns big enough to need mail service often spaced hundreds of miles apart. British prices and policies compounded these problems: High postage rates paid by the recipient, rather than the sender, meant that much mail was declined after significant time and energy had been expended in delivering it. But for decades, the British were just that—complications, not a problem in and of themselves. By the 1770s, as Hugh Finlay found out, that had changed. With the colonies careering toward revolution, every penny spent on the Crown's postal service felt to colonists like an affront.

By 1774, publisher William Goddard had had enough. His newspaper, *The Maryland Journal and the Baltimore Advertiser*, featured his rebellious opinions about the British within the colonies. Though he wanted the newspaper delivered by mail between Baltimore and Philadelphia, Thomas Foxcroft, the Philadelphia postmaster and Loyalist, was disinclined to include it in deliveries. So Goddard did something remarkable: He introduced a rival postal system. Known as the Constitutional Post, it quickly took root, establishing service from Portsmouth, New Hampshire, to Williamsburg, Virginia.

Goddard's scheme wasn't perfect. It was based upon subscriptions, which meant that those who couldn't afford it couldn't use it. But it had one overwhelming virtue: Goddard insisted on the sanctity of the seal. The king's colonial representatives were empowered to open any mail suspected of containing seditious writings, but Goddard's system forbade that. The Constitutional Post earned the endorsement of numerous colonial legislatures and committees of correspondence (anti-British communication networks that preceded the Continental Congress, the colonists' governing body in opposition to the Crown). There was a clear revolutionary sentiment among those who favored it. "How cheerfully will every well-wisher to his Country lay hold of the Opportunity to rescue the

As the Crown's control over much of the country evaporated, its post riders were driven from the roads.

Channel of Public and Private Intelligence out of the Hands of a Power, openly inimical to its Rights and Liberties," wrote the *New-York Gazette*.

Naturally, news of Goddard's offering was not well-received in London. In early 1774, the British had named a military general, Thomas Gage, governor of the Province of Massachusetts Bay, and dispatched him across the Atlantic to quell the rebellion in the colonies. Quashing Goddard's planned post was an explicit part of his mandate. But by this point, history's course could not be altered. The First Continental Congress met in September 1774. By the end of the year, the colonists had promulgated a list of demands. In April 1775, the Revolutionary War began. As the Crown's control over much of the country evaporated, its post riders were driven from the roads. The British Post Office ended inland operations in North America forever on Christmas Day 1775 but continued operation aboard a warship in the New York Harbor until 1782.

By the time the British got out of the mail business in North America, the Constitutional Post had long ceased operation—in favor of something more official. On July 26, 1775, the Second Continental Congress had shut it down, taken its rudiments, and created what was then called the General Post Office: the first official mail service homegrown in the colonies, the progenitor of today's U.S. Postal Service. Just as Benjamin Franklin had been there nearly 40 years earlier to begin adapting postal service in Philadelphia to the incipient American identity, so too was he there at the official beginning of what would become today's Post Office. The Continental Congress passed over William Goddard and made Franklin the first postmaster general. His tenure was brief; in 1776, he once again sailed the Atlantic, this time to France, to serve as the rebels' representative for a country that would become a crucial ally in the fight for independence. The revolution was more important than the mail—but then, if Franklin exemplified anything, it is that free and unfettered communication is inseparable from liberty.

America's war for freedom was just beginning, but the mail's war was won. With the help of visionaries like Franklin and Goddard, the colonists had reformed the British post, then usurped it. In 1776, the colonies declared independence. The new General Post Office would help them earn it.

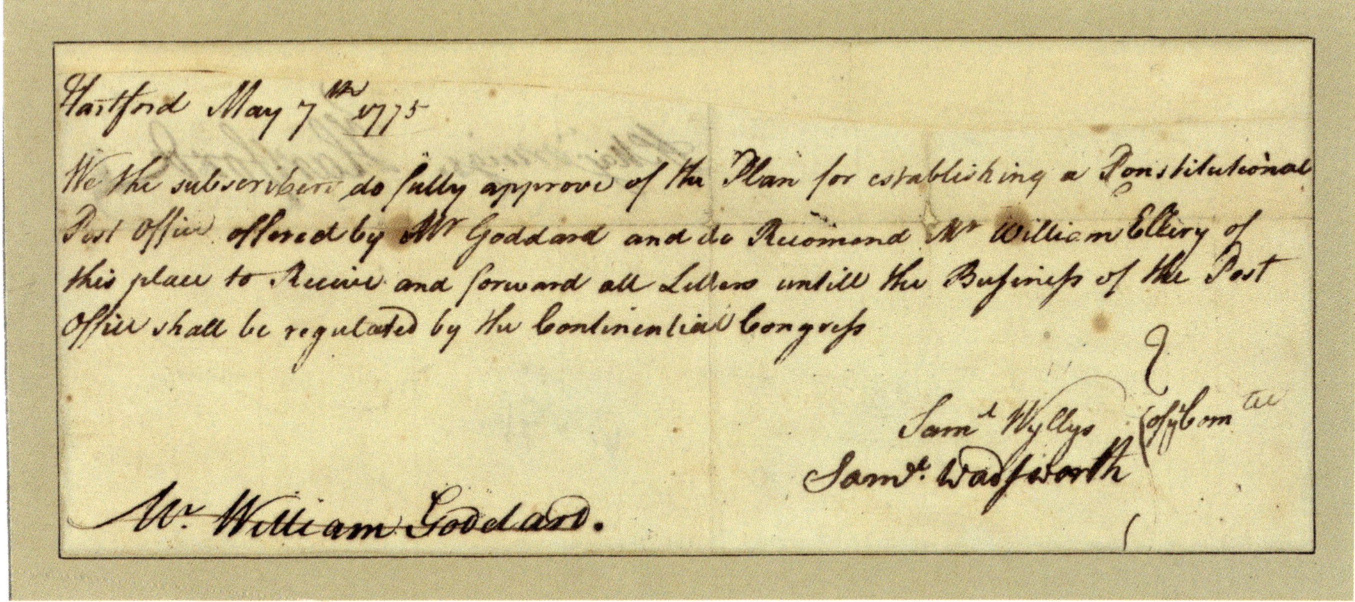
Hartford May 7th 1775

We the subscribers do fully approve of the Plan for establishing a Constitutional Post Office offered by Mr Goddard and do Recomend Mr William Ellery of this place to Receive and forward all Letters untill the Business of the Post Office shall be regulated by the Continential Congress

Saml Wyllys } Comtee
Saml Wadsworth

Mr William Goddard.

An approval letter from committee members Samuel Wyllys and Samuel Wadsworth to William Goddard on his plans for the Constitutional Post stated: "We the subscribers do fully approve of the Plan for establishing a Constitutional Post Office offered by Mr. Goddard and do Recommend Mr. William Ellery of this place to Receive and forward all Letters until the Business of the Post Office shall be regulated by the Continental Congress."

Henry Clay
letter Boston
May 3th 1775

IDENCE
AY 6

3.8 — 10d

A POST OFFICE GROWS IN THE AMERICAS

Ebenezer Hazard served as postmaster general for eight years beginning in 1782.

Ebenezer Hazard didn't even have a horse. Ebenezer Hazard: Princeton-educated man. Bookseller. A man who would one day be remembered as a visionary for his instinct to collect and preserve the records of the early days of the United States. Just a few years before the Declaration of Independence, Hazard had the idea of gathering documents crucial to the history of the colonies, including their break from the British: royal grants, charters for cities, laws, essays, and pamphlets. He reached out to colonist leaders for help, corresponding with Founding Fathers John Adams and Thomas Jefferson, among others. It was a massive project that would take some two decades: It wasn't until the 1790s that Hazard would finally publish *Historical Collections: Consisting of State Papers and Other Authentic Documents; Intended as Materials for an History of the United States of America*, an important record of the new nation. Historically significant projects often take a long time to create, but there was another, quite simple reason that Hazard moved so slowly: He had become involved with the mail.

In September 1775, Ben Franklin commissioned Hazard as deputy-postmaster of New York City. The next year, he unintentionally became "courier of the Army mail." It was a miserable turn of events from his deputy postmaster position. He spent the tail end of 1776 trailing George Washington's Continental Army, fulfilling his patriotic duty with very few resources. Nevertheless, that period would prove influential in the history of the Postal Service. For Washington's part, his experience during the war would shape his views on its value, which would inform his future leadership

Philadelphia, Feb. 5.

On the 28th ult. Congreſs appointed EBENEZER HAZARD, eſquire, poſt-maſter general, and JAMES BRYSON, eſquire, aſſiſtant poſt-maſter general.

as America's first president. As for Hazard, who would come to be the defining figure of American post in the 1780s, his hardships would lead to some of his greatest accomplishments.

Hazard received little compensation to maintain his duties properly—shocking considering how much work they entailed. He soon found himself begging Congress for an increase in salary. At first, they refused; when they eventually granted him his raise, it was paid out in Continental currency, the money used in place of British pounds. The currency was suffering so much inflation that it quickly became worthless.

So it was that Hazard understood something of the economic challenges facing many of the colonists who would soon be Americans.

In any case, with barely any resources, he trailed the soldiers from place to place like a common camp follower, his post supplies carried in a sack by a servant. It was the kind of experience that might make a man realize the value of a network of postal roads, comprehensive and well-maintained: following an army, on foot, unable even to afford a horse.

★ ★ ★

Prior to the Revolutionary War, there was very little official mail to be delivered in the 13 colonies. But when rumblings of war began brewing, suddenly there was a purpose for an organized postal system. At the same time, the pressures of battle and the challenges of setting up a new government (a capital city, currency, and banking, among other things) left little time or thought to be given to any new plans for the Post Office.

The colonists had the new General Post Office, built on the bones of Goddard's Constitutional Post, but during the war years, the mail system emulated many aspects of the British system they previously used, down to the visuals: The Americans readily adopted the use of the "Bishop Mark," a postmark consisting of a circle bisected by a line, with the date of mailing above the line and the abbreviated month below it, devised in 17th-century England under Postmaster General Henry Bishop. The American version of Bishop's date stamp excluded the dividing line, differentiating "American" mail and "British" mail—but, in a symbol of the time, the difference was subtle.

A letter addressed to General Alexander Hamilton with a colonial postmark denoting the date and place from which it originated: March 5, Philadelphia. The Bishop Mark at left shows only the month and date in the circle: April 14.

New York's 1786 schedule for the arrival and departure of mail.

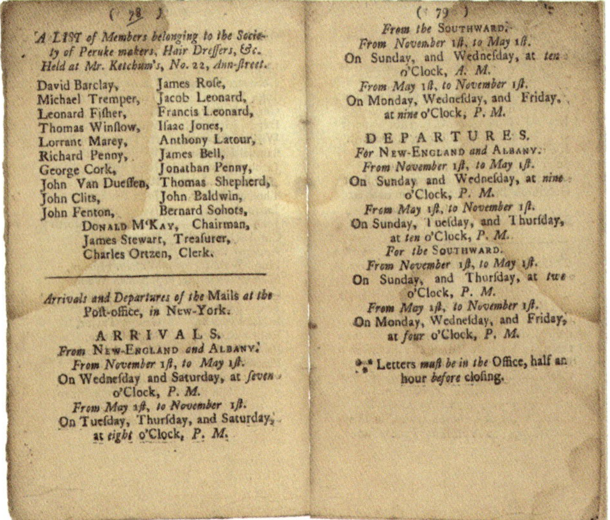

(78)

A LIST of Members belonging to the Society of Peruke makers, Hair Dreſſers, &c. Held at Mr. Ketchum's, No. 22, Ann-ſtreet.

David Barclay, James Roſe,
Michael Tremper, Jacob Leonard,
Leonard Fiſher, Francis Leonard,
Thomas Winſlow, Iſaac Jones,
Lorrant Marey, Anthony Latour,
Richard Penny, James Bell,
George Cork, Jonathan Penny,
John Van Dueſſen, Thomas Shepherd,
John Clits, John Baldwin,
John Fenton, Bernard Sohots,
DONALD M'KAY, Chairman,
James Stewart, Treaſurer,
Charles Ortzen, Clerk.

Arrivals and Departures of the Mails *at the* Poſt-office, *in* New-York.

ARRIVALS.
From NEW-ENGLAND *and* ALBANY.
From November 1ſt, to May 1ſt.
On Wedneſday and Saturday, at *ſeven* o'Clock, *P. M.*
From May 1ſt, to November 1ſt.
On Tueſday, Thurſday, and Saturday, at *eight* o'Clock, *P. M.*

(79)

From the SOUTHWARD.
From November 1ſt, to May 1ſt.
On Sunday, and Wedneſday, at *ten* o'Clock, *A. M.*
From May 1ſt, to November 1ſt.
On Monday, Wedneſday, and Friday, at *nine* o'Clock, *P. M.*

DEPARTURES.
For NEW-ENGLAND *and* ALBANY.
From November 1ſt, to May 1ſt.
On Sunday and Wedneſday, at *nine* o'Clock, *P. M.*
From May 1ſt, to November 1ſt.
On Sunday, Tueſday, and Thurſday, at *ten* o'Clock, *P. M.*
For the SOUTHWARD.
From November 1ſt, to May 1ſt.
On Sunday, and Thurſday, at *two* o'Clock, *P. M.*
From May 1ſt, to November 1ſt.
On Monday, Wedneſday, and Friday, at *four* o'Clock, *P. M.*

⁂ Letters *muſt be in the* Office, half an hour *before* cloſing.

Hazard's reforms, largely incorporated under the Ordinance of October 18, 1782, constituted the first major step toward normalizing mail service and moving away from the royal system.

The similarities ran deeper. British postage rates had been high and were viewed as another unjust tax, prompting colonial Americans to avoid the Royal Post whenever possible. The evolving General Post Office introduced equally high rates, which were needed to support the high start-up costs of a postal system in a frontier nation. Even worse, early postage rates fluctuated unpredictably: By the end of 1779, postal rates were 20 times the 1775 rate, but then by October 1781, they had dropped back to the 1775 rate. The average American had very little money; even when, by the late 1780s, postage rates had dropped to 20 percent *below* the 1775 rate, they were out of reach for most colonists. The mail system primarily served the affluent and merchant classes and was viewed as a privilege of wealth.

Further, under the British system, the sanctity of the mail was nonexistent. Letters could be opened and read by British officials at will. To an extent, the Americans copied these practices. In 1777, Congress created a Dead Letter Office with an appointed inspector. Just as the royal system had before it, it allowed for American mail to be censored; subversive content, such as criticism of the government, was reported back to Congress.

Faith in and reliance on the new American mail system struggled to take root.

As these issues were shaping up to be the big challenges of the 1780s, Hazard was climbing the ranks at the General Post Office. In 1777, he was promoted to surveyor of the post roads, covering what was called the Eastern Department, from Georgia to New England. By the fifth month of that year, his performance was already seen as exemplary by none less than Founding Father and future president John Adams. In a letter to Thomas Jefferson—a rebuttal to Jefferson's complaints that the post office had yet to fulfill the important role it was meant to play, per the Continental Congress, in the spread of information—Adams wrote: "The post is now extremely regular from north to south though it comes but once a week. It is very difficult to get faithful riders to go oftener. And the expense is very high and the profits, so dear is everything, and so little correspondence is carried on except in franked letters [letters some officials were allowed to send without paying postage], will not support the office. Mr. Hazard is now gone southward, in the character of surveyor of the post office, and I hope will have as good success as he had eastward, where he put the office in very good shape." By 1780, Hazard, as post surveyor of the Eastern district, had 12 post riders assigned to him—nearly half of the 31 people employed out of the General Post Office headquarters at that time.

In 1782, Hazard became postmaster general. His reforms, largely incorporated under the Ordinance of October 18, 1782, constituted the first major step toward normalizing mail

Right: The Post Office seal, depicting Mercury, the Roman god of commerce and messengers, was used between 1782 and 1837.

service and moving away from the royal system. Measures included making the colonies' post a monopoly of the federal government; restricting censorship of the mail to times of war or when explicitly directed by Congress or the president; and moderating rates, including extending discounts on newspapers. But though these reforms helped conquer some of the lingering problems rooted in the British system, Hazard had to confront another challenge that was unique to the colonies' geography.

★ ★ ★

The same year Hazard was named postmaster general, the Post Office gained a new seal: Mercury, the messenger of the gods. It was aspirational. In 1780, a letter leaving present-day Charleston, South Carolina, could take 75 days to arrive in New York City—hardly the pace of a winged, fleet-footed messenger. But in the decade ahead, the approval of new mail-carrying contracts began to transform the colonies' network of postal roads, pushing the system more toward speed and efficiency. These contracts covered the main roads between major population centers, particularly in the North—such as from Albany to New York City—as well as "cross-posts" over secondary routes, including to the South along the Mississippi River and into the West, where hopeful new landowners could settle.

At times, these routes continued to struggle with many of the issues mail service had suffered in Franklin's heyday. One that quickly proved problematic for the General Post Office was the Hudson Valley service from New York City to Albany, established in 1785. Isaac Van Wyck, the postmaster and tavern keeper at Fishkill, New York, and his two partners, John Kinney and Talmadge Hall, had been given a 10-year monopoly on the carriage of mail. Anyone unlawfully setting up or carrying mail along this route would pay a penalty of 200 pounds. Van Wyck, Kinney, and Hall wasted no time exploiting their monopoly. Passengers also traveled these routes, which conveniently included stops at taverns owned by the partners along the way. Those departing from Albany breakfasted at Kinney's Tavern in Kinderhook, some 20 miles south, and took dinner and overnight accommodations in Fishkill from Van Wyck. Passengers from New York City had their first meal of the day at Hall's tavern in Washington Heights, at the northern end of the island of Manhattan, and also dined and overnighted at Van Wyck's.

An Aċt to grant to Iſaac Van Wyck, and others, an excluſive right of keeping Stage-Waggons on the Eaſt ſide of Hudſon's River, between the Cities of New-York and Albany, for the term of ten years. Paſſed 4th of April, 1785.

WHereas Iſaac Van Wyck, Talmage Hall, and John Kinney, have by their petition, prayed that on account of great expence and labour attending the undertaking, an excluſive right of carrying on a ſtage from the Cities of New-York and Albany, might be granted them for the term of ten years:

And whereas, the erecting a ſtage as aforeſaid, will tend to promote the eaſe and benefit of the people of this State;

Be it enacted by the People of the State of New-York, repreſented in Senate and Aſſembly, and it is hereby enacted by the authority of the ſame, That the ſaid Iſaac Van Wyck, Talmage Hall, and John Kinney, and their reſpective executors, adminiſtrators and aſſigns, ſhall have, hold, poſſeſs and enjoy, and are hereby given, granted, and allowed the ſole and excluſive right, liberty and permiſſion, for the term of ten years, the ſame to commence on the firſt day of June next, to erect, ſet up, carry on, and drive at all time and times hereafter, during the term aforeſaid, all and every ſuch ſtage-waggon or waggons, from the ſaid Cities of New-York and Albany reſpectively to the other, on the eaſt ſide of Hudſon's River, as they may judge ſufficient for the purpoſe of accommodating ſuch a number of paſſengers as may from time to time apply: And that it ſhall not be lawful for, nor ſhall any other perſon or perſons, upon any pretence whatever, preſume, during the term aforeſaid, to erect, ſet up, carry on, or drive any ſtage-waggon or waggons, or any other carriage or carriages for the like purpoſe, from the ſaid cities reſpectively, under the penalty of two hundred pounds, to be recovered by any perſon or perſons who ſhall proſecute for the ſame, together with coſts, in any court of record having cognizance of the ſame.

The act that granted Isaac Van Wyck and his partners, John Kinney and Talmadge Hall, a 10-year monopoly for the carriage of mail was advertised in *The Poughkeepsie Eagle* on December 22, 1785. This act made it unlawful, with a penalty of 200 pounds, for anyone else to carry mail along the same route.

Literacy Among Colonists and Enslaved People

In many ways, the story of the postal system in the United States is the story of building better and better ways to share information. But what good is that if the American people can't understand the variety of new information they have access to? All of the Post Office's greatest accomplishments, from 250 years ago to today, are worth little if people can't read. It is important to keep in mind from these early years that running alongside the story of the postal system's efforts to build a road network, set postal rates, and establish reliable service is another essential, complementary story: America's journey to becoming a literate nation.

During the development of the mail service in the colonies, the average colonist earned nine pounds per year and was illiterate–they could neither afford to send letters nor read or write them. By 1790, that figure had improved somewhat. That year, about 70 percent of the nation was literate. But hidden in that figure were some shameful realities. Native Americans and indentured servants were illiterate. And there were roughly 690,000 enslaved people in the United States–they were not only unable to read but also forbidden to read, as a means of social control. In the same way that the circulation of newspapers helped spark and spread revolutionary

Thomas Waterman Wood's oil painting *Sunday Morning*, circa 1877, depicts a child, born after emancipation, reading the Bible to a formerly enslaved woman who would not have had the legal right or opportunity to read or worship.

attitudes among colonists, it was feared that literacy could lead enslaved people to rise against their masters. In 1790, *The Columbian Phenix and Boston Review* noted that "no country on the face of the earth can boast of a larger proportion of inhabitants, versed in the rudiments of science, or fewer, who are not able to read and write their names, than the United States of America."

In the decades that followed, literacy rates—for some people—would continue to climb. In 1840, 91 percent of white adults could read. By 1850, the United States—not even 100 years old—had a more literate population than the average European country. A big reason? The mail. Here's another fact about the United States in 1840: It had more newspapers than any other country. By that time, the Post Office had set favorable postage rates for newspapers to make them easier to mail to people. Having all those periodicals in American homes paid off, complementing the young country's growing education system in helping make literacy a reality for most people.

The biggest barrier to universal literacy, or near-universal literacy, was slavery. And that was something the Post Office couldn't do anything about directly. But abolitionists used the mail system to pressure the pro-slavery contingent to end the abhorrent practice. Mass-mailing campaigns in the 1830s brought arguments against slavery to more people than ever before. Of course, it didn't reach most enslaved people themselves: Years of punishment for reading had made them deathly afraid of books, periodicals, and newspapers of any kind. "You better never let master catch you with a book or paper, and you couldn't praise God so he could hear you. If you done them things, he sure would beat you," 95-year-old Albert Jones, a formerly enslaved person, told an interviewer with the Slave Narrative Project of the Works Project Administration in the late 1930s. Eighty-year-old Jane Lassiter agreed. She was held on Kit Council's plantation in the lower edge of Chatham County, North Carolina.

"There was no books or learning of any kind allowed. You better not be catched with a book in your hands. That was something they would get you for," she said.

In 1870, just after the end of the Civil War, the country's literacy rate was 80 percent, as opposed to 20.1 percent for Black Americans. But with slavery abolished, the Black literacy rate rose quickly. By the end of World War II, those figures were at 97.3 percent and 89 percent, respectively. While closing literacy gaps remains an important task in the U.S. today, it is perhaps no coincidence that the postwar period, when almost all Americans could benefit from the information transmitted through the postal system, was a period of incredible innovation—for the mail, and for the country as a whole.

Other routes showed great progress. Travel was established, for example, from Philadelphia to Lancaster, Pennsylvania—a distance of about 62 miles—along what was called the Great Philadelphia Wagon Road. For a long time, it was hardly a road at all.

The route was originally an American Indian pathway that had previously been sufficient only for those on foot, horseback, or packhorse trains. In 1784, a stage line between the towns took almost three days in each direction. A year later, the mail carrier on the route had shaved a day off that time, leaving Philadelphia every Monday morning and reaching Lancaster two days later. These gains in speed and efficiency meant that mail delivery to points west could be more frequent—and points west would shortly become much more important.

In 1781, the Articles of Confederation, a constitution binding together the colonies as 13 sovereign states in common cause, went into effect. The Congress of the Confederation—the governing body established by the Articles—spent some of its time struggling with questions over how to govern the westward expansion of the United States. In 1787, it passed the Northwest Ordinance, establishing a plan for the Northwest Territory, which stretched from the western edge of Pennsylvania to the Mississippi River, and from the Ohio River up to present-day Canada.

The ordinance made rules about how the territory could be divided into new states and defined a process for admitting them to the Union. It also set up a bill of rights for people who settled these lands, including protections for religious freedom and due process. It banned slavery. But

Above: Issued in 1937, this three-cent stamp commemorated the 150th anniversary of the Northwest Ordinance with portraits of Manasseh Cutler, drafter of the ordinance, and William Rufus Putnam, who served as the territory's superintendent of settlement.

Left: A map visualizing the Northwest Ordinance with the 13 original colonies and the area noted for expansion as "the First Colony of the United States": the Northwest Territory.

In 1787, the Congress passed the Northwest Ordinance, establishing a plan for the Northwest Territory.

the big picture was that it opened up huge tracts of land—and the new lands needed post offices.

As the Northwest Ordinance was taking effect, another important document was wending its way through the Congress of the Confederation: The U.S. Constitution. It was presented to the states for ratification in 1787, and in June 1788, New Hampshire became the ninth state to ratify it—making it the law of the land. Among the provisions of this new charter: It clearly allowed Congress the power "To establish Post Offices and post Roads." Mail service could be enhanced and extended further to the west and south, with the full force and support of the new federal government.

With this new government came George Washington's election as the nation's first president. Washington would appoint the country's first postmaster general. It was a role Ebenezer Hazard might have expected to receive as a continuation of his responsibilities before the Constitution became law. It could have been a full-circle moment, harking back to his time trailing Washington and his men in the war years.

But he wasn't impressed with Hazard's performance as postmaster general. During the war, Washington had received complaints of poor service from fellow officers, and charges of irregularities were subsequently brought against Hazard by postmasters and stagecoach operators. Even worse, one of his many financial reforms of the Postal Service, while effective from a practical standpoint, backfired politically: As the Constitution was being debated, Hazard had put in place new rules that made newspapers—previously free to mail—subject to fees if they were sent more than one city away from where they were published.

SAMUEL OSGOOD.

Appointed by George Washington, Samuel Osgood was the first postmaster general to serve under the new U.S. Constitution, from 1789 to 1791. This print is from a painting by John Trumbull, circa 1807.

Though his goal was to limit the amount of mail that failed to produce revenue for the Postal Service, some proponents of the Constitution (Washington among them) interpreted the new rule as a tactic to stifle arguments in its favor. Never mind that Hazard himself was a proponent of the Constitution. When the new government got around to formally starting the Post Office in September 1789, Washington decided to go another way. Samuel Osgood, whose house in New York City was serving as the first executive mansion, was appointed the first postmaster general to serve the United States of America.

Hazard was deeply hurt by being pushed out after all he had been through. He confided in letters that the turn of events felt thankless after all he had risked "in 1776, and afterwards." But the true tragedy of his fate was measured by the mail system. Ebenezer Hazard, the Princeton-educated bookseller who would one day be remembered as a visionary for his instinct to collect and preserve the records of the early days of the United States, wrote to a friend after his dismissal: "Do not write me by post for I can no longer afford to pay postage."

The Franking Privilege

From the beginning of mail in America, some people–typically government officials–have been able to send certain things for free. The practice came to North America with the British: The House of Commons instituted what it called the franking privilege, from the Latin *francus*, meaning "free," in 1660. The notion was that the cost of transmitting information should not be a barrier to the functioning of the government.

In colonial America, the Continental Congress gave its members and some soldiers the right to send things for free. The Articles of Confederation expanded who was eligible, and early postal acts under the newly ratified Constitution continued to refine the rules about who could use the franking privilege and what could be sent–generally, mailings had to be official business, not personal correspondence. Franking was free, and it was easy–those who could take part simply had to sign their name on a letter or parcel rather than affix postage. It was also highly controversial.

Early on, franking was seen as rampantly misused and incredibly wasteful of government funds. (Though those who enjoyed the privilege didn't have to pay postage, there were, of course, still expenses involved in delivering their mailings–and those costs were borne by the government, and by taxpayers.) By the 1820s, franking was so taken advantage of that newspapers were rife with examples of abuse, such as when Representative John Scott of Missouri sent his family Bible from Washington to his wife for free, claiming it was a "public document." In 1822, the *Baltimore Patriot* reported a rumor that members of Congress were franking their shirts home to be washed. The story was corrected but probably not far from the truth, as other stories of items being franked that were clearly not official business showed up in newspapers across the country. It was even reported at one point that a senator had affixed his signature to his horse's bridle and sent the horse home via mail. The abuses prompted the *National Banner and Nashville Whig* in May 1828 to call out Congress, complaining: "The mail coaches intended for the transmission of letters, papers, and pamphlets, for the benefit and information of the people, are converted into baggage wagons for the conveyance of dry goods, groceries, &c., for the accommodation of members of Congress, their families, and friends." These personal effects crowded out legitimate mail, so that "this outrageous abuse is made to impede and almost defeat the very object which alone it was intended to promote," the paper wrote.

In 1873, with abuses out of control, Congress ended the franking privilege...for a time. Over the following years, the practice slowly crept back, restored little by little for certain types of mail and certain senders and recipients. In 1895, franking was officially reinstituted, though with tighter restrictions on its use.

But controversy would return, too. In the 1900s, it was less about abuse and more about politics. Incumbent officeholders who could mail campaign materials to constituents for free were seen as having an unfair advantage in elections. In 1961, a new law allowed members of Congress to send franked mail to people without a specific name or address-in other words, they could send mass mailings indiscriminately to potential voters free of charge. The law also allowed newsletters, surveys, and reports to be sent, expanding what was viewed as "official business." Though the law was quickly repealed, it led to major reforms at roughly the same time that the American mail system was reorganized as the U.S. Postal Service. The Commission on Congressional Mailing Standards, also known as the "Franking Commission," was established by law in 1973. More push and pull would occur in the intervening years, but the same commission still governs the practice today. And though electronic communications technologies have made franking less important than it once was, it remains a key-if controversial-aspect of how the government conducts its business.

To

Mr. Hopkinson

at

Philadelphia

via New York
Packet

B Free Franklin

To reflect his support for the revolutionary cause, Benjamin Franklin altered his franking signature from "Free Benj. Franklin" to "B Free Franklin," as seen on this folded letter mailed from London in 1766.

Boston
FREE

INFORMATION WANTS TO BE FREE

Columbian  Centinel.

Printed and publiſhed, on WEDNESDAYS and SATURDAYS, by BENJAMIN RUSSELL, in *State-Street*, BOSTON, MASSACHUSETTS.

Whole No. 822.] SATURDAY, MARCH 10, 1792. [No. 52, *of* VOL. XVI.

LAWS of the UNITED STATES.

PUBLISHED

By Authority.

SECOND

CONGRESS *of the* UNITED STATES:

AT THE FIRST SESSION,

Begun and held at the City of Philadelphia, in the State of Pennſylvania, on Monday the twenty fourth of October, one thouſand ſeven hundred and ninety-one.

An ACT *to eſtabliſh the* POST-OFFICE *and* POST-ROADS *within the United States.*

BE *it enacted by the* SENATE *and* HOUSE *of* REPRESENTATIVES *of the United States of America, in Congreſs aſſembled,* That from and after the firſt day of June next, the following roads be eſtabliſhed as poſt-roads, namely: From Wiſcaſſet in the diſtrict of Maine, to Savannah in Georgia, by the following rout, to wit; Portland, Portſmouth,

conſidered as poſt-roads, within the terms and proviſions of this act: *Provided,* That no ſuch contract ſhall be made, to the diminution of the revenue of the general poſt-office, and that a duplicate of every ſuch contract, under hand and ſeal, ſhall, within ſixty days, after the execution thereof, be lodged in the office of the Comptroller of the Treaſury of the United States.

And be it further enacted, That there ſhall be eſtabliſhed, at the ſeat of the government of the United States, a general poſt-office. And there ſhall be one Poſtmaſter-General, who ſhall have authority to appoint an aſſiſtant, and deputy poſtmaſters, at all places where ſuch ſhall be found neceſſary. And he ſhall provide for carrying the mail of the United States, by ſtage-carriages or horſes, as he may judge moſt expedient; and as often as he, having regard to the productiveneſs thereof, as well as other circumſtances ſhall think proper, and defray the expenſe thereof, with all other expenſes ariſing

he ſhall have received reſpecting the ſame, in the office of the Comptroller of the treaſury of the United States.

And be it further enacted, That every deputy poſtmaſter ſhall keep an office in which one or more perſons ſhall attend at ſuch hours as the Poſtmaſter General ſhall direct, for the purpoſe of performing the duties thereof. And all letters brought to any poſt-office half an hour before the time of making up the mail at ſuch office, ſhall be forwarded therein.

And be it further enacted, That from and after the paſſing of this act, the Poſtmaſter-General ſhall be allowed, for his ſervices, at the rate of two thouſand dollars per annum, his aſſiſtant, at the rate of one thouſand dollars per annum, to be paid quarterly, out of the revenues of the poſt-office: And no fees or perquiſites ſhall be received by either of them, on account of the duties to be performed in virtue of their appointment.

And be it further enacted, That from and after the firſt day of June next, the

delivered to the poſtmaſter at the port of entry. And it ſhall be the duty of the collector or other officer of the port, empowered to receive entries of ſhips or veſſels, to require from every maſter or commander of ſuch ſhip or veſſel, an oath or affirmation, purporting that he has delivered all ſuch letters, except as aforeſaid.

And be it further enacted, That the poſtmaſters to whom ſuch letters may be delivered, ſhall pay to the maſter, commander, or other perſon delivering the ſame, except the commanders of foreign packets, two cents for every ſuch letter or packet; and ſhall obtain from the perſon delivering the ſame, a certificate ſpecifying the number of letters and packets, with the name of the ſhip or veſſel, and the place from whence ſhe laſt ſailed; which certificate, together with a receipt for the money, ſhall be with his half-yearly accounts, tranſmitted to the Poſtmaſter General, who ſhall credit the amount thereof to the poſt-maſter forwarding the ſame.

The 1792 issue of the *Columbian Centinel* printed the Act to Establish the Post Office and Post Roads within the United States.

It would be too strong a statement to say that George Washington owed his presidency to the newspapers, but it wouldn't be entirely indefensible. After all, Washington's election as the United States' first president was due in part to his renown as a general in the Revolutionary War. And his renown as a general in the Revolutionary War was due in part to newspapers.

Washington was a voracious reader of the news, especially during the war. For one, he knew that a skim of the daily papers could potentially reveal what his opponents, the British, were up to. But perhaps more important, he understood that the newspapers represented the public mood: They showed how people thought the revolutionary fight for independence was going, and how he was doing as the head of the Continental Army. On this count, one paper in particular proved to be indispensable. *The New-Jersey Journal* was founded during the war, on February 16, 1779, and printed in Chatham, a town in northern New Jersey. It covered the exploits of Washington and his comrades from a pro-American point of view, in contrast to the Loyalist newspapers that maintained the idea of a British-run colony. It was absolutely critical for morale—a lesson Washington would carry with him into the presidency.

In his third annual address to Congress on October 25, 1791, Washington outlined four government bodies he believed required legislative attention: the militia, the mint, weights and measures, and the mail. When it came to the Post Office, he was specific about his vision. He remembered the information battle that was part of the Revolutionary War. Congress sought to build out the network of post roads and fortify the postal system, because of its importance for facilitating communication in the young country. By spreading news of the government's operation, Washington told Congress, the post "contributes to the security of the people, [and] serves also to guard them against the effects of misrepresentation and misconception."

Within the year, Congress had gotten the message. In a letter to the House of Representatives, Washington wrote: "The operation of the law establishing the Post-Office, as it relates to the transmission of newspapers, will merit our particular inquiry and attention, the circulation of political intelligence through these vehicles being justly reckoned among the surest means of preventing the degeneracy of a free government, as well as of recommending every salutary public measure to the confidence and cooperation of all virtuous citizens." The law to which Washington was referring was the Post Office Act of 1792, which he signed in February. It created the template for the modern U.S. Postal Service.

Among its many provisions, the act made postage for newspapers just a fraction of the amount charged on letters. Such a law would have cheered Washington back when he was General Washington, leader of the Continental Army, and not simply because he found newspapers so helpful.

No, Washington had a special reason to appreciate low postage for newspapers. *The New-Jersey Journal,* the paper so kind to his cause? With Congress' approval, he had helped fund and publish it.

★ ★ ★

When Samuel Osgood was appointed postmaster general of the United States of America in 1789, the U.S. Constitution freshly in effect, he had a one-room office, one assistant, and one clerk. Beyond that, his full authorities and responsibilities weren't clear even to him. There was no one to train him; His predecessor, Ebenezer Hazard, surely would not; Richard Bache had moved on; and the man with the most knowledge, Benjamin Franklin, was busy helping establish the government. Osgood's most important teacher was Colonel Sebastian Bauman, who was also the postmaster of New York City. This was an important role for a prominent man of the post, as that city hosted one of only 75 post offices serving the nation after the ratification of the Constitution. But Bauman wasn't in it purely because of his capabilities; Washington was constitutionally empowered to select federal postmasters and had given Bauman the job as a form of patronage. He was a friend who had served with him at Valley Forge during the winter of 1778–1789.

Indeed, in the early 1790s, where what was now known as the Post Office would fit within the federal government was initially unclear. The laws of the First Federal Congress had only specified that "the Postmaster General shall be subject to the direction of the President of the United States in performing the duties of his office and in forming contracts for the transportation of the mails," and the Constitution gave Congress the power "to establish Post Offices and post Roads." So while the Post Office would definitely be part of the executive branch, with the growth of the network directed by Congress, everything else was up for debate—debate that embroiled even some of early America's most notable leaders. One key question was whether the Postal Service should fall under the Treasury Department or the State Department, pitting Alexander Hamilton, treasury secretary, against Thomas Jefferson, secretary of state. The two men were already rivals; in this case, Jefferson lost. As a revenue-generating entity that used federal monies to initiate national improvements, the General Post Office was placed under the general supervision of the secretary of the treasury in 1792.

That was a momentous year for the Post Office. In some sense, it was the year today's version began. The Post Office Act of 1792 enacted numerous rules and regulations for the running of the country's information system. The act codified nearly everything the evolving North American post had been working toward for decades. It included an order for private letters to not be opened by mail carriers or postmasters. It established standards for speed and timeliness of mail carriers, down to the minute, and allowed the postmaster general to sign mail carriage contracts, further professionalizing the job. It also included a specific menu of penalties for those who interfered with or delayed the mail. The penalties were remarkably harsh: Anyone who obstructed the flow of the mail in any way was to be fined $100. Ferrymen who refused or neglected to transport the mail upon the arrival of a post rider were subject to a penalty of $10 for every 30-minute delay. If it was found that post riders transported private letters for personal profit, they were fined $50. Stealing, embezzling, or destroying anything related to money would yield a fine of up to $300 (and maybe prison time), and someone who was carrying mail and abandoned it without delivery could be fined up to $500. This was at a time when the average *yearly* salary was $65. In some cases, the applicable penalty was even worse—death—though this was never used and ultimately, and thankfully, rescinded.

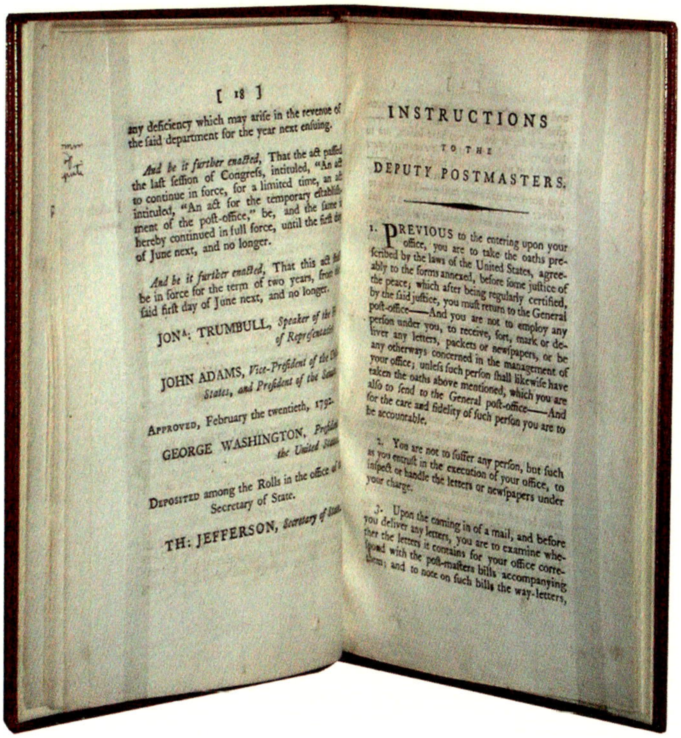

[18]

any deficiency which may arise in the revenue of the said department for the year next ensuing.

And be it further enacted, That the act passed the last session of Congress, intituled, "An act to continue in force, for a limited time, an act intituled, "An act for the temporary establish ment of the post-office," be, and the same is hereby continued in full force, until the first day of June next, and no longer.

And be it further enacted, That this act shall be in force for the term of two years, from the said first day of June next, and no longer.

JONA: TRUMBULL, *Speaker of the House of Representati*

JOHN ADAMS, *Vice-President of the United States, and President of the Sena*

APPROVED, February the twentieth, 1792.

GEORGE WASHINGTON, *Preside the United States*

DEPOSITED among the Rolls in the office of the Secretary of State.

TH: JEFFERSON, *Secretary of State.*

INSTRUCTIONS

TO THE

DEPUTY POSTMASTERS.

1. PREVIOUS to the entering upon your office, you are to take the oaths prescribed by the laws of the United States, agreeably to the forms annexed, before some justice of the peace; which after being regularly certified, by the said justice, you must return to the General post-office—And you are not to employ any person under you, to receive, sort, mark or deliver any letters, packets or newspapers, or be any otherways concerned in the management of your office; unless such person shall likewise have taken the oaths above mentioned, which you are also to send to the General post-office—And for the care and fidelity of such person you are to be accountable.

2. You are not to suffer any person, but such as you entrust in the execution of your office, to inspect or handle the letters or newspapers under your charge.

3. Upon the coming in of a mail, and before you deliver any letters, you are to examine whether the letters it contains for your office correspond with the post-masters bills accompanying them; and to note on such bills the way-letters,

The Post Office Act of 1792 is recorded in this 18-page volume rebound in Moroccan leather.

Perhaps the most visionary, and consequential, element of the act was something Washington had singled out a year prior: special favorability to newspapers. Congress was trying to forge a bond between the free press and the postal system, and the Post Office Act was only half of its efforts. The other half had come a year earlier, in 1791, when the first 10 amendments to the Constitution, known as the Bill of Rights, were passed. At the top of the list was the freedom of the press, codified in the First Amendment. Under this new law of the land, the production of information would be free and unfettered. The Post Office Act ensured that information could travel, setting postage rates for newspapers as their own distinct class of mail. Whereas a single letter cost a minimum of six cents to mail—and up to 25 cents for those bound a great distance away—newspapers cost a maximum of 1.5 cents.

The American experiment—the attempt to design a durable democratic government that would, in Washington's words, "[promote] human happiness"—was new in every respect; therefore, informed citizens took the view that they could never know enough about the workings of the government, even if they didn't always like what they read. At the turn of the 19th century, there were more than 200 newspapers available in the United States. Each had a specific point of view, often aligned with a particular political party. They were frequently critical of the government. This could incense those sympathetic to the president, but at the end of the day, freedom of the press was a cornerstone of American democracy. Though it could be vitriolic, the press was seen as something that could be a counterbalance for partisanship. This unflinching support of freedom of the press—with its potential not to subdue partisanship but rather accelerate it—would be one of the most influential, and contentious, aspects of American history the Post Office would have a hand in. Washington himself shared a warning in his farewell address from the presidency in 1796: "The alternate domination of one faction over another, sharpened by the spirit of revenge, natural to party dissension, which in different ages and countries has perpetrated the most horrid enormities, is itself a frightful despotism."

But that was a question for the long term. In the short term, this bond between the press and the post saw newspapers flourish. The low-cost—and occasionally no-cost—postage allowed the widest circulation of newspapers possible. And

Abraham Bradley created one of the most complete maps, and his first, of the United States in 1796, "...exhibiting the post-roads, the situations, connections and distances of the post-offices, stage roads, counties, ports of entry and delivery for foreign vessels, and the principal rivers."

the new system made it as beneficial as ever for postmasters to double as newspaper editors: They could spot newsworthy items in other publications passing through their post offices and reprint them, sort of like an early Associated Press. They could listen to mail recipients talk about the contents of letters they had just received to pick up publishable tidbits or gossip. Newspapers were the nation's first form of mass communication, and the increased diffusion of knowledge was prized by both Republicans and Federalists alike.

If there was a downside to this situation, it was simply that there were *too many* newspapers. Americans wanted their news—the only avenue of broad public discourse and their treasured reading—in a timely manner. However, because newspapers now made up so much of the mail, their bulk, heft, and volume became a problem. If more lucrative letters came along and there was no space, postal riders had a simple solution: They jettisoned the newspapers.

With the purpose of the Post Office established, the continued expansion of the network of post roads was all the more meaningful. And though the 1780s had seen a great expansion and professionalization of postal routes under Hazard, the 1790s would be a decade of even greater road building. This was utterly crucial: 90 percent of the nation's mail was carried by post riders, with the typical mail route including some combination of horse, coach, and boat. Though the Constitution gave Congress the power to establish post offices and post roads, the 1792 act made clear that it could do so without the approval of the secretary of the treasury, who might opt to constrain expansion to save money.

It wouldn't be Osgood who took this on. At the beginning of the decade, it was decided that the federal government would move to a new national district, Washington, D.C., and that would bring his time atop the Post Office to an end. While the new federal district was being constructed, the seat of government temporarily moved from New York City to Philadelphia, and Osgood opted to stay in the former. In 1791, he resigned as postmaster general. His two immediate successors,

A portrait of Postmaster General Timothy Pickering created by Charles Havens Hunt in 1881.

In the same way that Pickering saw the potential of the rivers, Habersham was interested in transforming rugged frontier paths into passable post roads.

though, were obsessed with expanding the postal network—albeit in different ways.

Postmaster General Timothy Pickering was determined to harness rivers. In 1791, when he was appointed to the position, Pittsburgh was a gateway to the West. Mail would pass from Pittsburgh to Wheeling, Virginia, by way of a rudimentary road; from Wheeling's location on the Ohio River, the post could gain access to the Mississippi. Through those two great rivers, it could reach frontier settlements.

Traffic on the Ohio and Mississippi rivers in 1790 was confined to rafts and flat-bottomed boats, which could navigate shallows but had no way of traveling upstream. These boats were sold for their lumber after a single trip in the direction of the current. A different type of vessel, called a keelboat, was more versatile. Keelboats could travel back upstream: The crew could use long poles to push off the riverbed, against the current, or men onshore could pull them with ropes tied to the mast. Pickering saw an opportunity. He authorized the construction of a few small keelboats, "formed in the best possible manner for ease and expedition in pushing up the stream." The keelboats were expressly for the transport of mail and operated on an efficient circuit: Three men crewed them downstream, which took five days; then a crew of five men poled them back upstream in 10 days.

These keelboats expanded mail delivery—but they were vulnerable to peculiar obstacles that post roads avoided. Periodic floods and ice floes impeded the boats' progress. River pirates infested the waterways. The service ultimately proved unreliable and irregular. By January 1795, Pickering was having doubts about the long-term viability of his keelboats. He expressed his reservations in a letter to the postmaster of Limestone, Kentucky (present-day Maysville), a downstream settlement on the Ohio River. "The great want of regularity and expedition in the conveyance of the mail by the Ohio defeats the object of its establishment," he wrote, "but at the same time is very expensive." Luckily for Pickering, this would no longer be his problem. That month, he was appointed secretary of war.

Pickering's replacement, Joseph Habersham, would serve as postmaster general from 1795 to 1801, closing out the century with a congressional mandate to concentrate on extending the nation's post roads. In the same way that Pickering saw the potential of the rivers, Habersham was interested in transforming rugged frontier paths into passable post roads. This was an indispensable advance. The Post Office's use of its routes was already quite sophisticated; well-choreographed schedules allowed post riders and coaches not only to serve their own routes but also to make timely connections at key intersections to exchange mail that needed to travel even farther. But often the physical landscape of the roads themselves were a barrier to reaching the routes' full potential.

Habersham authorized the creation of the overland mail route on what was called the Wilderness Road in 1797. The Wilderness Road,

Right: A lithograph illustration of a keelboat at the mouth of the Arkansas River by Henry Lewis, from his book *Das Illustrirte Mississippithal*, first published between 1854 and 1858.

The Jolly Flatboatmen, circa 1846, by George Caleb Bingham, depicts life and work on the Missouri and Mississippi rivers.

Habersham Coaches

There was a great deal of ego in the operations of the early postmasters general. (And maybe in the later ones, too.) Pickering and Habersham, the two major route-expanders of the 1790s, exemplified this reality–though perhaps their egotism could be excused in consideration of the fact that they were undertaking the monumental task of wrangling the wilderness into an efficient, modern postal network. Whatever the case, Pickering just had to have his mini armada of postal keelboats. Habersham's ego trip was even more extreme–but it may also have been brilliant. He insisted on a fleet of government-owned post coaches of his own design.

Habersham's specifications were unique for the time, practical, and beautiful. Traditionally, coach passengers faced forward, but he had the novel idea of designing a coach that would hold four passengers more comfortably, in a configuration where two pairs of people faced each other. At the same time, passenger comfort couldn't come at the expense of the post–coaches still needed to be able to carry a large amount of mail. For that, Habersham had a trick up his sleeve: Each seat was a padded chest that could hold mail or baggage. And to allow for travel at night, lamps were mounted on either side of the coachman's seat.

The coaches would also be excellent rolling advertisements for the postal service, thanks to a handsome exterior finish. Habersham called for the coach bodies to be painted green, while the undercarriages and wheel rims were to be bright red. Each coach was to have an eagle painted on the passenger doors. Under the eagle was the proud badging: *United States Mail Stage*.

The first of these new coaches entered into service as a limited test between New York City and Philadelphia in 1799. Habersham hoped that it was just a start; soon, he imagined, he'd have his post coaches operating on every post road in the country.

Then his ingenious idea ran into the buzz saw of Congress.

Congress had no appetite for the expense of maintaining coaches, horses, and drivers, whether Habersham's or a more conventional design. Instead of authorizing a fleet of coaches, they instructed Habersham to issue private-sector contracts for mail carriages and to focus on using contracts to make the mail service more efficient and economical. It was the end of the Habersham coaches and the beginning of a long history of the American post trying to walk a very fine line: between being forward-looking and innovative in delivering an above-and-beyond level of service and being practical and judicious in the use of taxpayer funds. Habersham's ego steered him a little too far toward the former. But as we'll see, the history of the Post Office is full of examples of postmasters general who were able to find the sweet spot right in between.

Daniel Boone Escorting Settlers through the Cumberland Gap, circa 1851, by George Caleb Bingham. This artwork helped establish the myth of Daniel Boone and other folk heroes of western settlement.

Opposite: A standard coach of the time period.

Right: A portrait of Postmaster General Joseph Habersham by R. W. Habersham, circa 1884.

Below: Mile marker 89 on Zane's Trace, Route 22, in Kinderhook, Pickaway County, Ohio.

blazed by Daniel Boone in 1775, was one of the principal routes into Kentucky and Tennessee. It extended from the Cumberland Gap—where three major roads converged at the famous mountain pass through which settlers proceeded to the western side of the Appalachian Mountains—to the Kentucky River, on land purchased from the Cherokee Indians.

Habersham also had his eye on another route, between the federal capital at the time, Philadelphia, and Lexington, Kentucky. The postal route was inaugurated in 1797, with post riders expected to provide service between Philadelphia and Lexington in 19 days. That schedule was overly optimistic. The reality proved to be closer to 30 days, due to the poor condition of the route. In particular, part of the riders' journey traversed Zane's Road, also known as Zane's Trace, a path that had been built by Ebenezer Zane and opened in 1796 to connect Wheeling to Limestone. It was initially little more than a dirt path based upon American Indian trails, turned into a road simply by blazing trees and cutting brush, and when it opened, it was fit only for horse traffic—no wagons could manage the narrow, rugged terrain. But over time, postal workers would have their way with it, and the use of the route for carrying mail would further ensure that it was improved. Though 30 days' travel time was not ideal, Habersham was nonetheless satisfied, telling Edward Tiffin, the postmaster of Chillicothe, Kentucky, in 1799, "I am glad that the mail is now regularly conveyed on Zane's Road agreeable to my schedule, that the present state of the road will admit of travelling during the summer season with the expedition I have contemplated."

Habersham may have been onto something. What's important about a road is not how difficult it is to traverse but whether it serves its purpose. And along the routes Pickering and Habersham developed, a remarkable thing began to happen: People settled. The keelboats promoted the increased rate of settlement in Ohio and Kentucky. From Wheeling, new river routes provided postal service to new settlements springing up in Ohio, Kentucky, and beyond. By 1790, more than 75,000 settlers lived at the western end of the Wilderness Road. And Zane's Road turned out to be not just a trace, nor simply a road, but a 52-mile avenue to the Northwest Territory that prompted the creation of many small hamlets along the way.

When Osgood became the United States' first postmaster general under the Constitution in 1789, he was responsible for supervising mail service on more than 1,075 miles of post roads. A year later, the total was about 1,800 miles. By the end of the decade, there were more than 16,000 miles of mail routes. The country was growing, and mail routes were its circulatory system, carrying the information that was the oxygen of the body politic. In 1797, when Zane's Road was still nearly impassable, a Kentucky newspaper wrote something prophetic about it: "We even flatter ourselves that the period is not very distant, when waggons [*sic*] may by this route transport some part of the various products of this luxuriant soil to our Fellow-Citizens of the Upper Settlements, in exchange for such of theirs as may suit our demands."

One wonders how that newspaper reached its readers.

Master Cha

pr Mail Sunbu

BUILDING THE CAPITOL, BUILDING THE COUNTRY

Rarely do chapters of history align neatly with the calendar, but in 1800, the first year of the second century of America's existence, the new country's federal government officially moved to what would become the United States' permanent capital. Washington, D.C., was founded in 1790, then spent the following decade mired in planning and construction.

Assistant Postmaster General Abraham Bradley Jr. arrived in late May, ready to establish the Postal Service's footprint in the growing city.

The city was not ready for him. Buildings were incomplete; houses were scarce.

On June 2, Bradley wrote to a friend of the conditions he met upon his arrival. "We arrived here on Friday last, having had a pleasant journey as far as we traveled by daylight," he wrote. "Captain Stevenson, with whom I agreed for a house before my arrival, was not ready to give possession, and the house was not convenient for us. I have, therefore, taken a large three-story house within a few roads of Blodget's Hotel which will accommodate the office and my family and the Postmaster's office." This house, which they rented for $600 a year, was advantageously situated on the northwest corner of Ninth and E streets, NW, equally distanced between the Capitol and the President's House. The department's headquarters took up three rooms on the second floor, while Thomas Munroe, the city's postmaster, was allocated a single room on the first floor for his office.

Bradley's fellow governmental officials, arriving in May and June from Philadelphia, found that only the North Wing of the new U.S. Capitol was ready to be occupied. The exterior of the President's House wasn't completed until November—at which point the interior was still under construction. The new federal city had just 372 buildings within about a 10-square-mile area to house the 500 families already living there.

This building served as the first home of the Post Office Department from 1800 to 1801. It was located in Washington City at the northwest corner of Ninth and E streets.

A portrait of Thomas Munroe, the postmaster of Washington City from 1799 to 1829, who was responsible for the locations of the city's post office.

Upon his arrival to the city, Secretary of the Treasury Oliver Wolcott described what he saw in a letter to his wife, Betsy, on July 4, 1790: "There are few houses in any one place, and most of them small, miserable huts, which present an awful contrast to the public buildings...You may look in almost any direction, over an extent of ground nearly as large as the city of New York, without seeing a fence or any object except brick-kilns and temporary huts for laborers."

Washington at that time gave the impression of a city—and, by extension, a country—whose reach exceeded its grasp. But though that could be dispiriting, it could be exciting as well. Bradley, for his part, wrote that "the situation of the city is beautiful."

Bradley may have been reacting to more than just the new capital and the new country. It may also have been exciting to find that the Post Office was immediately very, very busy. Bradley sent an update to Postmaster General Joseph Habersham, who had not yet arrived. On June 11, 1800, he wrote: "We have not been able to open the office and to accommodate business until to-day...We have a flood of business on hand at this time, and our removal has put us a month in arrears." He had two employees already and planned to employ another until Habersham showed up.

Sometimes history aligns with the calendar, and sometimes history merely echoes. Bradley's arrival in Washington, D.C., was in some ways symbolic of the era to come. In just a few years, the country would expand in major ways. Sometimes the Post Office would lead, and sometimes it would lag. There would be growing pains. But where the people of the United States went, so too went the post.

The alternate location Bradley had found managed to serve its purpose for just one year; the ground-floor space proved inadequate for postal business. The federal Post Office and the Washington City Post Office were both relocated to the government's War Office, just west of the President's House. From this two-story brick building with 25 rooms and additional space in the attic, the nation's nerve center would operate. It would remain the postal headquarters until, little more than a decade later, war came to Washington.

One thousand miles away from Washington, D.C., sits the city of Natchez, in present-day Mississippi. As Bradley was setting up shop in the capital, Natchez—which had been an important port for a series of colonial powers for nearly a century—had just come into the possession of the United States. An ancient road, the Natchez Trace, connected it to Nashville.

A watercolor by William Birch depicts a view of the Senate Chamber, the only completed section of the Capitol when the government moved to Washington in 1800.

The Country Postman, an engraving from a painting by George L. Seymour, circa 1884.

In many ways, the Natchez Trace was an unlikely, or at least unassuming, candidate for cracking open the gates of history. The road was rough and rugged; a Presbyterian minister writing about the history of the church in the area noted that it was no more than "a bridle path... an Indian trail from Nashville, which could be traveled only on horseback or on foot. It passed through tangled forests and swamps, through warlike Indian tribes, and was infested by bands of lawless desperadoes, more dreaded than the Indians themselves."

The American Indians were the Chickasaw Tribe, who had used the 500-mile trace for trading purposes. Prior to the 1800s, it was also trafficked by settlers of the Ohio River Valley, who walked it back home after floating their wares down the Mississippi, unable to transit back upstream by boat. And then came the post riders. One of the first was John L. Swaney, who carried mail from Nashville to Natchez for eight years, beginning in 1796 or 1797. Post riders covered about 50 miles per day, making the full one-way journey in 10 days. Swaney often found himself carrying personal letters, government dispatches, and a few newspapers—plus provisions for himself, provisions for his horse, and a tin trumpet to announce the arrival of the mail. The Natchez Trace was a remnant of an older time—but a useful one.

And then in 1801, it became something entirely different: the seam of a new vein of history.

In March 1801, President Thomas Jefferson authorized the Army to improve and widen the Natchez Trace so that it would be suitable for wagon wheels. Jefferson had always had a keen eye for opportunities beyond the 13 original colonies. Prior to becoming the third U.S. president and serving as a delegate to the Congress of the Confederation, he had approached George Rogers Clark in 1783 to lead an expedition to the western coast. He had introduced the Ordinance of 1784, which admitted new western territories as U.S. states. And, finally, he helped sponsor André Michaux in 1793 "to find the shortest and most convenient route of communication between the United States & the Pacific Ocean." In the Natchez Trace, a path to a prominent port, Jefferson saw an opportunity. And by the end of that year, he had done even more to pursue it: On December 17, 1801, the U.S. government signed the Treaty of Fort Adams with the Choctaw Nation, acquiring more than 2.6 million acres of land in what is now the southwest corner of the state of Mississippi.

U.S. control over the land allowed for a more commercial road to be made. Soon the quaint postal route of Swaney's early years was far more professional. A relay station was established halfway along the trace where two post riders could meet, get fresh horses, and exchange mailbags.

Ironically, in just a few decades, the Natchez Trace would cease to be a post road. As the country rapidly expanded, circumstances could change quickly, and by the 1820s more direct routes between Nashville and New Orleans had developed. (Today, the Natchez Trace is a treasured national parkway.) But Jefferson's focus on the route, and on expansion, was an early milestone in three key strands of the historical narrative.

First, the Treaty of Fort Adams was the beginning of a series of treaties that expelled American Indians from their homelands—a conflict not only with the Choctaw Nation but also extended to many other tribes and nations. It was a conflict that would grow in future decades, one that we're still reckoning with today.

Second, the improvement of the route to Natchez was of interest to the federal government in part because of Natchez's importance as a port city that exported large quantities of cotton, especially to Europe. Trade with Europe was becoming more and more important to the country—and would be what ultimately sucked the United States into war in just one decade's time.

And finally, the expansion in 1801 was perhaps a seed of Jefferson's even grander ambitions, which would come to fruition two years later.

Jefferson had always been keen to explore the lands west of the Mississippi, but as the American economy grew, the river itself was proving an enormously vital asset. And it didn't stop at Natchez: A few hundred miles downriver, where the Mississippi emptied into the Gulf of Mexico, was the beginning of shipping routes to markets in Europe. And one city safeguarded access to that port. "There is on the globe one single spot, the possessor of which is our natural and habitual enemy," Jefferson wrote to his ambassador to France, Robert Livingston, in 1802. "It is New Orleans, through which the produce of three eighths of our territory must pass to market."

In the preceding years, the Spanish had controlled New Orleans and the broad swath of land to the west of the river known as the Louisiana Territory. They had given Americans free navigation rights along the Mississippi, allowing for the transfer of goods, mail, and newspapers. But in 1800, just before Jefferson became president, the Spanish and the French secretly signed the Treaty of San Ildefonso, which gave Louisiana to the French. It wasn't until November 1801 that the U.S. government officially got its hands on a copy of the treaty. Jefferson knew that having the imperialistic French leader Napoleon, who wanted to reestablish a colonial empire, at the United States' back door would be the undoing of what the colonists had fought so hard to claim—independence. And sure enough, in October 1802, the port of New Orleans was closed to Americans, all but bringing an end to vital commerce and communication links with Europe.

This section of the Natchez Trace reveals how the footsteps of countless travelers gradually wore down the rough trail into a clearly marked path.

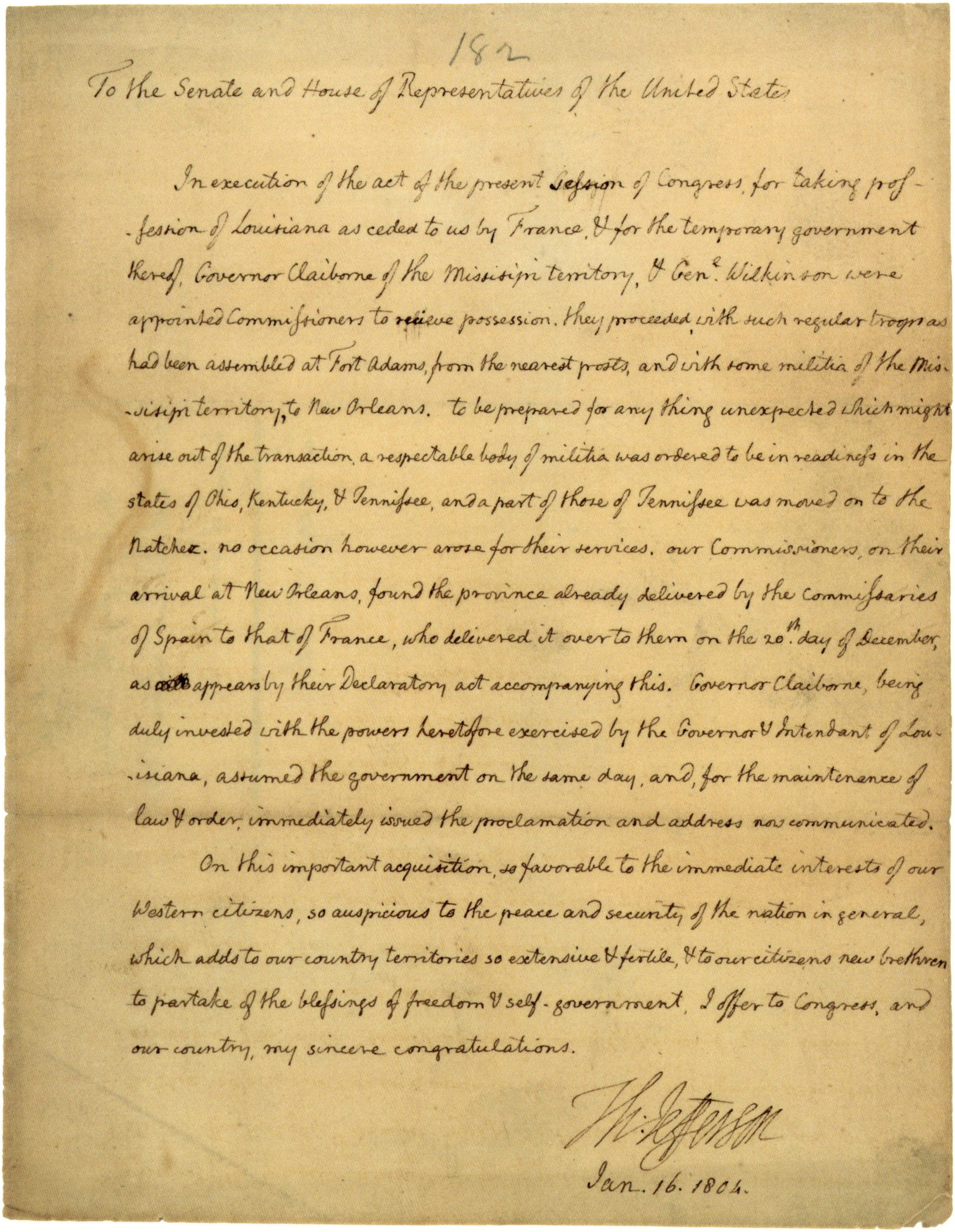

182

To the Senate and House of Representatives of the United States

In execution of the act of the present Session of Congress, for taking possession of Louisiana as ceded to us by France, & for the temporary government thereof, Governor Claiborne of the Missisipi territory, & Genl. Wilkinson were appointed Commissioners to recieve possession. they proceeded, with such regular troops as had been assembled at Fort Adams, from the nearest posts, and with some militia of the Missisipi territory, to New Orleans. to be prepared for any thing unexpected which might arise out of the transaction, a respectable body of militia was ordered to be in readiness in the states of Ohio, Kentucky, & Tennissee, and a part of those of Tennissee was moved on to the Natchez. no occasion however arose for their services. our Commissioners, on their arrival at New Orleans, found the province already delivered by the Commissaries of Spain to that of France, who delivered it over to them on the 20th. day of December, as appears by their Declaratory act accompanying this. Governor Claiborne, being duly invested with the powers heretofore exercised by the Governor & Intendant of Louisiana, assumed the government on the same day, and, for the maintenance of law & order, immediately issued the proclamation and address now communicated.

On this important acquisition, so favorable to the immediate interests of our Western citizens, so auspicious to the peace and security of the nation in general, which adds to our country territories so extensive & fertile, & to our citizens new brethren to partake of the blessings of freedom & self-government, I offer to Congress, and our country, my sincere congratulations.

Th: Jefferson

Jan. 16. 1804.

With war, mail service became even more essential.

Jefferson's audacious response was to try to buy New Orleans from the French. Representatives of the U.S. government went to France to negotiate. And once again, the historical winds shifted quickly. Napoleon's plans for Louisiana and France's Caribbean colonies changed, and the French government offered the United States not just New Orleans but all of the Louisiana Territory. The Louisiana Purchase was signed on April 30, 1803. Jefferson paid $15 million to nearly double the size of the United States.

With the new land came a need for new post offices. The first U.S. Post Office in the Louisiana Territory was opened in New Orleans on February 4, 1804. Two months later, Meriwether Lewis, William Clark, and the Corps of Discovery left on their famous expedition to explore the country's new territory. They departed from just outside St. Louis; some five months later, a post office was opened there. And post offices would continue to open on the newly acquired western side of the Mississippi throughout this era: Cape Girardeau, New Madrid, and Sainte Genevieve in 1804, Saint Charles in 1805, and Tywappity in 1806, all in what is now the state of Missouri.

★ ★ ★

As Lewis and Clark explored the west, back in Washington, D.C., the federal government continued to build its capital city. It could look like business as usual: The federal Post Office and the Washington, D.C., Post Office remained at the War Office building, just west of the President's House, until 1810, when the government purchased Blodgett's Hotel for the Patent Office and the postmaster general, who would occupy the first and second floors. But Lewis, Clark, and the denizens of Washington were all caught in the middle of a larger story, one Jefferson had foreseen back in 1802: There was a brewing trade war between the British and the French. In the second half of the decade, each belligerent nation outlawed trade in ways that hurt American interests, and American attempts at economic retaliation were ineffective.

By December 1810, President James Madison asked Congress to be prepared for either a military or economic war, in the event a conflict with the two countries should unfold. In 1812, the United States declared war on the British.

With war, mail service became even more essential. War news was popular reading. Personal letters or accounts copied from previously published newspapers, delivered by mail, were relied upon as primary sources.

Among the biggest war news came when Washington, D.C., was captured and burned by the British on August 24, 1814. The Capitol and the President's House were among the few large buildings to survive the brief British occupation and rampage throughout the city, although what remained were mere shells of what once stood.

A treaty to end the war was signed not long after the sacking of Washington. In the wake of the destruction, realizing that Congress could opt to move the capital somewhere safer, Washingtonians worked with a new urgency to rebuild the city. And just as the construction of the city was matched by exploration in the West at the beginning of the decade, after the War of 1812, the nation would expedite the building of roads and canals to promote migration and commerce—and the movement of mail.

Right: British Burn the Capitol, 1814, by Allyn Cox, circa 1973. The painting is located in the Hall of Capitols, a corridor in the House side of the United States Capitol.

Opposite: Thomas Jefferson's letter to the Senate and House of Representatives, dated January 16, 1804, discussing the Louisiana Purchase and its importance to the "peace and security of the nation."

Establishing Post Offices

When the Constitution granted Congress the power to establish post offices and post roads, there were only 75 post offices in the original 13 colonies, linked to one another by about 2,400 miles of post roads. In the early 1800s, the two most prominent roads where post offices were established were the Boston Post Road and the Cumberland, or National, Road. By 1806, a third road, the Federal Road, was being built.

So how were town post offices established? First, a settlement had to be formally recognized by the state government as a town with a town charter. Second, a town's citizen had to provide a petition to the Post Office Department. Though having other citizens sign the petition was not necessary, showing the town's support was more likely to get congressional approval than landing a single signature. The request would be submitted by a member of Congress for approval. Before approval, there was the consideration of the distance between an already established post office and the one being requested. For rural areas, the distance between established post offices was at least two miles, barring any natural obstacles such as a hill, mountain, or river that was not easily navigable.

Notifications in newspapers made citizens aware of the requests. One example is a list of petitions outlined in *The North American* on January 31, 1800:

> *Mr. Hanna presented a petition of a number of the inhabitants of the county of Northumberland, in the state of Pennsylvania, praying for the establishment of post offices in certain places therein mentioned; which was referred to the committee appointed on the subject of post offices and post roads.*

Some petitions were even a bit more specific as to post offices, as outlined in the *Virginia Argus* on January 21, 1806:

> *Sundry inhabitants of Augusta, Va., praying that a post office may be established in the town of Greensville, and of sundry inhabitants of Somerset, Penn. Praying that a cross post may be established from Berlin to Fort Cumberland, referred to the post office committee.*

Opposite: A Post Office Department site location report was required for each new post office being established. The report included the post office's location; a land description, such as the closest waterways, roads, and railroads; and the location of the next-closest post office. This report, dated January 1837, was submitted to Amos Kendall, the eighth postmaster general, who was appointed on May 1, 1835, by President Martin Van Buren.

T

POST OFFICE DEPARTMENT,

WASHINGTON, *January* , 1837.

SIR:

To determine with as much accuracy as possible the relative positions of the several Post Offices in the United States, so that they may be correctly delineated on the maps of the Department, you are requested to fill up the spaces and answer the questions below, and return the same to this Department, care of H. A. BURR.

The recent fire having destroyed all the information before obtained on this subject, renders your immediate attention to it necessary.

I am, sir,

Very respectfully,

AMOS KENDALL,

Postmaster General.

The name of my Office is Temperance it is situated ~~in the town~~ at ~~of~~ Temperance County of Amherst and State of Virginia

State the name of the Post Offices nearest to your Office and their distance from it by the mail route. The nearest post office is 4 miles from Temperance, on Piney River Simmons's Mill, from Temperance to N. Glasgow, 7 miles.

If you are on a river, creek, or brook, what is its name, and on which side of it are you?

Ans. Temperance, is situated on the South Side of Indian Creek

Valerius McGinnis.
P. M. at. Temperance.
Amherst Cty Va

MAILBAGS

Whether a mailbag was handmade by a carrier or officially designed by the Post Office, its purpose was to ensure safety, security, and efficiency in collecting, sorting, transporting, and delivering the mail. From the first colonial post riders to the Pony Express, from airmail to mail by rail, there have been many variations of mailbags.

"Mailbag" is a generic term for any bag designed to carry mail, but the Post Office uses more specific terms to illustrate a bag's function and style. A mail satchel, for example, is a shoulder bag that a mail carrier uses. Over the centuries, the Post Office has made use of all manner of sacks, pouches, and satchels—as well as unique "catcher" bags with special hooks and fasteners that allowed railway postal routes to pick up mail via cranes without having to stop at every train station.

Leather mailbag with shoulder strap and interior cotton pouches, 1859.

Satchel for city delivery and collection, mid-20th century.

Over-the-shoulder satchel with flap for letter carriers, 1920–1950.

Mailbag collected circa 2001 from the Church Street Station Post Office after the September 11, 2001, terrorist attacks.

Mail pouch used to carry first-class, domestic, or military mail, circa 1943.

Handmade cloth sorting bag used by rural letter carrier, with names on pouches for delivery, 1896.

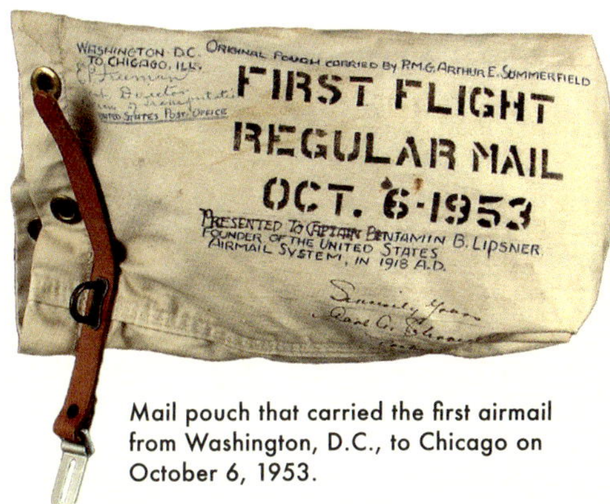

Mail pouch that carried the first airmail from Washington, D.C., to Chicago on October 6, 1953.

Mail sack for carrying magazines, circulars, and flyers, circa mid-20th century.

Canvas airmail sack, 1927–1937.

DARIEN.

Savannah

GREENSBORO
JAN
1
N.C.

JUL
12

Mail

SAWYERS AND SNAGS

On August 25, 1818, a boat christened *Walk-in-the-Water* set out from Black Rock, New York, today a neighborhood of the city of Buffalo. It was 132 feet long and rigged with two sails for days with good wind. And it had something else, something relatively new: a steam engine. A 30-foot-tall smokestack rose between the sails, and there was a pair of paddlewheels at midships. Its itinerary took it on a tour of the most important ports on Lake Erie: Erie, Pennsylvania; Grand River, Cleveland; Sandusky, Ohio; and, finally, up the Detroit River to Detroit, Michigan. It carried 29 passengers. It also carried mail.

In 1813, just six years after the first steamboat, Robert Fulton's *Clermont,* traveled upriver from New York City to Albany, Congress approved the delivery of mail by steamboat. For decades, it had proved difficult to provide efficient and reliable mail service up major rivers. All that was about to change. New steamboat designs were essentially shallow-draft barges with high-pressure steam engines and waterwheels that had enough power to counteract the swift currents of even the Missouri and Mississippi rivers. As soon as the postmaster general was authorized to sign four-year contracts with steamboat operators traveling between post towns—provided that the steamboat contracts didn't cost more than what the Post Office paid for stagecoach service between the same locations—he did. Postmaster General Gideon Granger awarded the first contract, between New Orleans and Natchez in June 1813.

Announcing the beginning of mail service on *Walk-in-the-Water,* the Richmond, Virginia, *Enquirer* assured its readers that "the mail will be received at Detroit and return to [Buffalo] in less time that is usually occupied in carrying it through a single trip by land." But it wasn't just a feat of speed; it seemed like magic. One author suggested that seeing "[a] steamboat, at that day, was to common observers, almost as great a wonder as a flying angel would be at present." In Detroit, hundreds crammed onto the wharf in anticipation

A wood engraving depicting steamboats navigating the snags down the lower Mississippi River to Baton Rouge, circa 1858.

The Richmond Enquirer, dated September 29, 1818, announced with surprise that the steamboat *Walk-in-the-Water* was transmitting mail to and from Detroit based on General Post Office orders that steamboats shall transmit mail.

BUFFALO, Sept. 8.—The steam boat arrived on Tuesday last from Detroit, and left Black Rock on Wednesday evening, for that place. She will probably occupy five or six days in a trip to Detroit and back, after her machinery has been in use a short time.

Instructions from the General Post Office have been received, for transmitting the Detroit mail by the steam boat. By this regulation, the mail will be received at Detroit and return to this village, in less time than is usually occupied in carrying it through a single trip by land.

STEAM BOAT WALK IN-THE WATER.

The arrival of this steam boat at Detroit, on the 27th August, is thus noticed in the Detroit Gazette:—

"Nothing could exceed the surprise of the sons of the forest, on seeing the Walk-in-the-Water moving majestically and rapidly against a strong current, without the assistance of sails or oars—They lined the banks above Malden, and expressed their astonishment by repeated shouts of "*Tai yoh-nichee!*"* A report had been circulated among them, that a "big canoe" would soon come from the "noisy waters" which, by order of the great father of the "*Che-me-komons*,"† would be drawn through the lakes and rivers by *sturgeon!*—Of the truth of the report they are now perfectly satisfied.

"To day she will make a trip to Lake St. Clair, with a large party of ladies and gentlemen. She will leave this for Buffalo to-morrow, and may be expected to visit us again next week."

* *An exclamation of surprise.*

† *Long knives—or Yankees.*

Under steam power, the mail was racing into the future—but there was trouble lurking under the surface.

of the boat's arrival. According to the *Detroit Gazette*, they came "to witness this...truly novel and grand spectacle."

The entire trip took 44 hours and 10 minutes.

This was a remarkable pace, but innovation was moving even faster. The average life expectancy of a steamboat was just 2.5 years. Vessels that began life steaming at eight or nine miles per hour were swiftly outpaced by newer models that moved at 12 to 15 miles per hour. (It wasn't just obsolescence—boiler explosions cut some boats' lives short.) Steamboats were making constant progress, and lucrative mail contracts enticed entrepreneurs to bid on them. At the same time, things were not as straightforwardly positive as they might have seemed; riverboat service was initially perilous. Pilots contended with sandbars, snags, and floating dead trees called sawyers. The Missouri River—the waterway Lewis and Clark explored that symbolized the growth of the new nation—was among the most perilous. So infested was it with sawyers and snags that pilots dubbed it "the river of sticks."

This was the era: Under steam power, the mail was racing into the future—but there was trouble lurking under the surface.

On April 30, 1810, the 11th Congress of the United States passed an extensive bill regulating the mail. It set out rules for employees, rules for post roads, and guidance for fees. It included a long section on penalties for stealing mail or robbing mail carriers, the latter of which could still lead to the death penalty. And deep within, it carried a highly controversial clause: "And it shall be the duty of the postmaster at all reasonable hours, on every day of the week, to deliver, on demand, any letter, paper or packet, to the person entitled to or authorized to receive the same."

Every day.

Including Sundays.

Sunday mail service had been a point of growing contention for years. It traced back to a small town, Washington, on the far western edge of Pennsylvania, and a man named Hugh Wylie. In 1803, Wylie had been named postmaster in Washington. He was often asked by people who came into town for church on Sundays if they could pick up their letters. But Wylie was also an elder at the Presbyterian Church. He was bound to keep the Sabbath as a day of rest.

During this early era, post offices and churches were often built in close proximity. With the townspeople and neighboring villagers heading to church on Sundays, it was an unofficial policy of postmasters to open up to sort as well as distribute mail on that day. This was not mandatory but a convenience for the public.

Wylie ultimately decided to open the post office before church, pause when church commenced, and then reopen after it ended.

This did not please the church.

S.W. Stanton

Walk-in-the-Water, a pen-and-ink drawing, circa 1895, by S. W. Stanton, depicts the first steamboat to run on the Great Lakes—its debut journey over Lake Erie took place on August 25, 1818.

The Postal Act of 1792 had left the hours of the post office up to the postmaster general: "That every deputy postmaster shall keep an office in which one or more persons shall attend at such hours as the Postmaster General shall direct, for the purpose of performing the duties thereof." This left open the possibility for approaches like Wylie's, which could skirt the budding conflict. But the 1810 law was more direct, putting the post in direct opposition to the Bible's decree that Sunday be a day of rest.

The 1810 law was more direct, putting the post in direct opposition to the Bible's decree that Sunday be a day of rest.

Some civic and religious communities opposed the new law. After all, the Bible afforded no exceptions. Many communities and religious groups submitted petitions to Congress. Among the most vehement protesters were the Episcopal and Presbyterian churches, which condemned Sunday mail service. Regular citizens registered their opposition, too. The residents of West Liberty, Virginia, claimed that Sunday hours were "injurious to the morals of the community" and added they were "praying that it may be abolished in the future." Religious Americans weren't just concerned about postal clerks and officers working on the Sabbath; they also worried that mail arriving on Sunday would tempt recipients to conduct business on the Sabbath or to read letters, newspapers, or political papers, a violation of holy times.

Wylie found himself in a position of having to choose: either resign as postmaster or resign from the church. Wylie opted to remain postmaster (a job that rendered him $1,000 per year, a significant sum at the time), and the church chose to expel him.

★ ★ ★

Public discontent was significant enough that it prompted Postmaster General Gideon Granger to send a dispatch to the legendary and powerful Speaker of the House, Henry Clay, in 1811—on Christmas Eve. The letter discussed the debate that was roiling, in particular, in western regions of the country. Explaining his office's position, which was intended to limit work on Sundays, he noted that he had taken great pains not to interfere with religious practice. His office even had a policy of forgoing "announcing [postal workers'] arrival or departure by the sounding of the horns or the trumpets" to avoid "[calling] off the attention of the citizens from their devotions."

With Granger drowning under the weight of the controversy, and with the election of President James Madison, Return Jonathan Meigs Jr. was appointed as the new U.S. postmaster general in 1814. Meigs, who had a dollars-and-cents approach to leading the Post Office, took the position that if mail was paused on Sundays, the whole delivery system would be delayed by two to four days. However, he also wanted to accommodate the concerns about the Sabbath. So he established in 1815 that "reasonable hours" meant

A portrait of Postmaster General Gideon Granger by Ezra Ames, circa 1820.

"where the mail arrives on Sunday, the office is to be kept open, for the delivery of letters...for *one hour* after the arrival and assorting of the mail; but in cases that would interfere with the hours of public worship, then the office is to be kept open for one hour after the usual time of dissolving the meeting for that purpose." This only partially alleviated the problem. The 1810 act also required postmasters to put up newspapers on the Sabbath, which raised some objections. Meigs argued that this took mere minutes, only momentarily interfering with postmasters' religious exercises. More important, he pointed out, the United States was at war, and the movement of the mail on Sunday was a military necessity.

Meigs's arguments pointed to the sharpening contours of the religious conflict: It pitted the moral imperatives of citizens against the business of running a nation—or perhaps just business in general: It wasn't only the federal government's interests in keeping up the flow of information or the news of war; the proprietors of stagecoach companies, who were largely responsible for

A portrait of Return J. Meigs, who was appointed postmaster general by President James Madison on March 17, 1814.

A reprint from the American State Papers of the 11th Congress, 3rd Session, Article No. 26, dated January 30, 1811, in which Gideon Granger communicated to the House of Representatives on "Remonstrance Against the Delivery of Letters, Papers, and Packets, at the Post Offices, on the Sabbath."

1812.] SUNDAY MAILS. 45

of the 9th section of the act of the 30th of April, 1810, the Postmaster General conceived himself bound to compel the Postmasters to receive letters from, and deliver letters to, the citizens, on the Sabbath day; and in comformity to that act the following instruction was given to the Postmasters, to wit:

"At Post Offices where the mail arrives on Sunday, the office is to be kept open for the delivery of letters, &c. for one hour after the arrival and assorting of the mail; but in case that would interfere with the hours of public worship, then the office is to be kept open for one hour after the usual time of dissolving the meetings for that purpose."

The Postmaster General further remarks, that, from the peculiar phraseology of the 9th section of said act, it is doubted whether he be warranted by law in limiting the right of the citizens to demand their letters to one hour on the Sabbath; and in one instance, in Pennsylvania, an officer has been prosecuted, under the section aforesaid, for refusing to deliver a letter on the Sabbath, not called for within the time prescribed by this office. Although in cases of extreme anxiety or national calamity, it may be proper for Postmasters to open their offices for the reception and delivery of letters on the Sabbath, and particularly to the officers of Government, still it is believed that the good sense of the officers is a sufficient safeguard for the delivery of letters under all such circumstances; and that compelling the Postmasters to attend to the duties of the office on the Sabbath, is on them a hardship, as well as in itself tending to bring into disuse and disrepute the institutions of that holy day.

All which is respectfully submitted.

GIDEON GRANGER, *Postmaster General.*

General Post Office, *January* 30, 1811.

BOSTON,
Plymouth & Sandwich
MAIL STAGE,

CONTINUES TO RUN AS FOLLOWS:

LEAVES Boston every Tuesday, Thursday, and Saturday mornings at 5 o'clock, breakfast at Leonard's, Scituate; dine at Bradford's, Plymouth; and arrive in Sandwich the same evening. Leaves Sandwich every Monday, Wednesday and Friday mornings; breakfast at Bradford's, Plymouth; dine at Leonard's, Scituate, and arrive in Boston the same evening.

Passing through Dorchester, Quincy, Wyemouth, Hingham, Scituate, Hanover, Pembroke, Duxbury, Kingston, Plymouth to Sandwich. *Fare,* from Boston to Scituate, 1 doll. 25 cts. From Boston to Plymouth, 2 dolls. 50 cts. From Boston to Sandwich, 3 dolls. 63 cts.

N. B. Extra Carriages can be obtained of the proprietor's, at Boston and Plymouth, at short notice.—
☞STAGE BOOKS kept at Boyden's Market-square, Boston, and at Fessendon's, Plymouth.

LEONARD & WOODWARD.

BOSTON, *November* 24, 1810.

A broadside from Leonard & Woodward, proprietors of the Boston, Plymouth & Sandwich Mail Stage, on the departures and stops along the mail route, dated November 24, 1810.

transporting the mail, also weighed in. As far back as 1808, a new stage line operating three-day trips in Virginia between Alexandria and Petersburg—spurred in part by the excessive weight and quantity of mail it delivered—announced it would operate "without regard to Sunday." The operator of a stage line between New York City and Philadelphia went further: He set Sundays as the departure days for his coaches. Meanwhile, other coach companies ceased operations on Sundays, forcing passengers to stay over at inns and taverns along the routes.

Congress issued a report in 1815 that concluded that the country's mail system had from the beginning "caused mail to be transported on the Sabbath," but it had done this only on the most important routes, and it had restricted attempts to curtail Sunday postal service. At the same time, Congress followed Granger's lead and decreed that mail carriers were to "pass quietly" during times when religious devotions were being observed.

The report did nothing to quell complaints. In January 1816, Congress received 85 petitions to abolish Sunday postal service. These appeals were all referred to the House's committee on post offices and post roads. The deluge of petitions prompted individual members of Congress to introduce multiple bills to halt Sunday mail.

All failed.

It was an important early fight over what exactly was meant by the protections of conscience, speech, and religion in the Constitution's Bill of Rights, still only a few decades old. Ultimately the House of Representatives voted 81 to 41, in 1815, that it was "inexpedient to alter the Sunday mails." Nevertheless, the debate continued, and policies around Sunday mail would continue to shift, even into the next century, and are still the subject of Supreme Court cases today. But the problem of Sunday mail wasn't the only moral quagmire buried in the 1810 law. There was something even greater, more consequential, and more pressing—something that would eventually rend the country.

★ ★ ★

"And be it further enacted," said the 1810 law, "That no other than a free white person shall be employed in carrying the mail of the United States, on any of the post roads, either as a post-rider or driver of a carriage carrying the mail."

As early as settlements were built and crops were planted in the South, mail there had operated under what was called a "plantation system." Each plantation owner would pull his mail from the mailbag and then was required to transport the bag, without delay, to the next plantation. The penalty for delaying the mail was a heavy fine of a hogshead, or barrel, of tobacco—a very valuable commodity. Plantation owners relied on enslaved people for the deliveries. Although this was technically illegal—Black people could not handle mail under a federal prohibition that began in 1802;

The two nations, so recently enemies, had agreed that slavery must come to an end.

only free whites were mandated to carry it—the government didn't object to the practice of slaveholders ordering enslaved people to transport mail. Still, it was a decades-old matter of contention.

Opinions varied from postmaster general to postmaster general, going back to the early days of the country. In 1794, the second to serve in this role under the Constitution, Timothy Pickering, wrote to Postmaster John Hargrove of Abingdon, Virginia, that "if the inhabitants...should deem their letters safe with a faithful black, I should not refuse him...I suppose the planters entrust more valuable things to some of their blacks." In April 1801, Pickering's successor, Joseph Habersham, took a slightly more reluctant tone in writing in to the postmaster of Frankfort, Kentucky, who allowed enslaved people to serve as mail carriers. The practice "was generally allowed in the Southern States by my predecessors in office," Habersham wrote. "I made no objection to it especially as it came within my knowledge that slaves in general are more trustworthy than that class of white men who will perform such services—the stages...[on] the Main Line are driven by Slaves and most of the Contractors employ them as mail carriers in the Southern States." Gideon Granger, the next postmaster general, however, agreed with prohibiting Black people from handling mail. In fact, he would make the original federal decree barring them from doing so.

By 1810, the prohibition would be codified in law. But the issue was far from settled—not simply the issue of enslaved people carrying the mail but the overall issue of slavery in the United States. Halfway through the decade, the United States and Great Britain came to an agreement to end the War of 1812. The Treaty of Ghent, ratified in early 1815, contained a remarkable article: "Whereas the Traffic in Slaves is irreconcilable with the principles of humanity and Justice, and whereas both His Majesty and the United States are desirous of continuing their efforts to promote its entire abolition, it is hereby agreed that both the contracting parties shall use their best endeavors to accomplish so desirable an object."

The two nations, so recently enemies, had agreed that slavery must come to an end.

Ironically, Gideon Granger, in an argument in favor of the racist ban on Black mail carriers, had identified precisely how the mail might help achieve this aim. "We cannot be too cautious," he wrote in an 1802 letter to Senator James Jackson of Georgia, chairman of the Committee of the Senate on the Post Office—a letter that directly preceded the ban. "...Plans and conspiracies have already been concerted by [slaves] more than once, to rise in arms, and subjugate their masters...The most active and intelligent [slaves] are employed as post riders...By traveling from day to day, and hourly mixing with people...they will acquire information. They will learn that a man's rights do not depend on his color. They will, in time, become teachers to their brethren...One able man among them, perceiving the value of this machine, might lay a plan which would be communicated by your post riders from town to town and produce a general and united operation against you."

Harper's Weekly published this wood engraving on December 11, 1869, depicting one aspect of slave life 30 years prior to the Civil War. The caption reads, "Primitive Mode of Bringing Tobacco to Market in Virginia Forty Years Ago."

For

PANIC, POTENTIAL, AND CORRUPTION

DISTRIBUTION OF POPULATION 1820
Unoccupied areas
2 to 18 inhabitants to the square mile
18 to over 90 inhabit- ants to the square mile
BRITISH POSSESSIONS
L. SUPERIOR
L. MICHIGAN
L. HURON
L. ONTARIO
L. ERIE
MICHIGAN TERR'Y
MISSOURI TERR'Y
ILLINOIS
INDIANA
OHIO
KENTUCKY
TENNESSEE
ARKANSAS TERR'Y
MISSISSIPPI
ALABAMA
GEORGIA
LOUISIANA
FLORIDA TERRITORY
SOUTH CAROLINA
NORTH CAROLINA
VIRGINIA
PENNSYLVANIA
NEW YORK
NEW JERSEY
DELAWARE
MASSACHUSETTS
CONN.
R.I.
VERMONT
N.H.
MAINE
SPANISH POSSESSIONS
ATLANTIC OCEAN
GULF OF MEXICO
Iowa Indians
Sac & Fox Indians
Pottawatomie Indians
Miami Indians
Winnebago
Menomonee Indians
Ottawa & Chippewa Indians
Chickasaw Indians
Choctaw Indians
Cherokee Indians
Creek Indians
Ohio R.
Missouri R.
Mississippi R.
Longitude 90° West from 85° Greenwich 80
75°

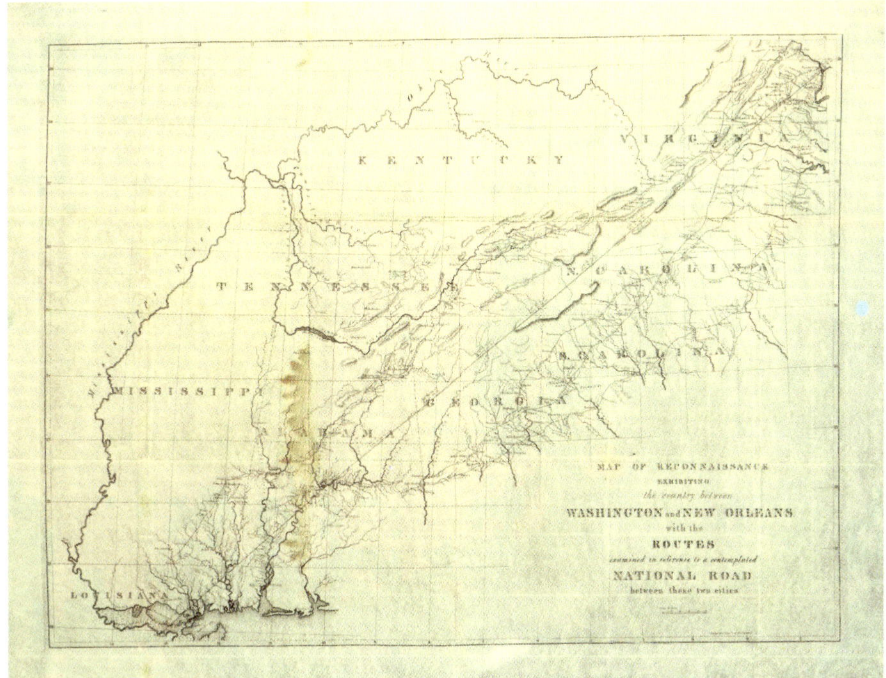

A map plotting a national road—without regard to terrain—directly from Washington to New Orleans. The map shows major cities and towns, existing roads, and military posts.

America's expansionist policies in the early 1800s were steadily growing the country, both in terms of physical territory and the creation of a rugged American identity. But in some ways it had a dark underbelly. It set up some of the forces that led to war; it expelled American Indians from their ancient homelands. After the war, it put the United States' economy on precarious footing: Between paying for the War of 1812 and purchasing the Louisiana Territory, the country had racked up major debt. The land seized from American Indians fueled a real estate bubble. Having become a major player in international trade, the U.S. was now vulnerable to economic changes in other countries, and following the war, Great Britain—seeking new markets for its products—dumped cheap wares on America, undercutting domestic businesses. Banks were not even regulated.

At the end of the 1810s, the economy came crashing down. In 1820, John C. Calhoun, the enormously influential southern politician, told John Quincy Adams, the president-to-be from the North, that "...there has been within these two years an immense revolution of fortunes in every part of the Union: enormous numbers of persons utterly ruined; multitudes in deep distress; and a general mass disaffection to the Government..."

Opposite: A map of the United States in 1820 depicting the distribution of the population across various regions.

This period came to be known as the Panic of 1819, and it was the first major economic downturn in American history.

It was clear that the country needed money, and one revenue source with potential was the Post Office. After a decade and a half without a postage increase, Congress had raised rates in 1815 to support the war effort, and the post had delivered, surpassing $1,000,000 in annual revenue for the first time. The rate increase was repealed the next year, but by 1817 revenues were again more than $1,000,000 per annum.

And yet at the start of the third decade of the 19th century, the department was facing its own panic of sorts. In the 1820s, the volume of mail in the United States began to outstrip the capacity of what could be carried on horseback, except on the most primitive backwoods postal routes. But mail revenue didn't match mail volume. There was growing debt on nonpayment of newspapers. From 1820 to 1824, the number of postage-paid letters increased by 8 percent, while the revenues from postage grew by only 3 percent—thanks to the Panic, many people could not pay. At the same time, the Post Office's expenses grew dramatically. The surpluses in the second half of the 1810s led to a post-road-building binge. But the decisions weren't strategic; many new mail routes were pet projects of members of Congress who wanted their

General Post Office,

May 1st, 1822.

Sir: In obedience to the 37th section of the act "Regulating the Post Office Establishment," I have the honor to send, herewith, for the consideration of the House of Representatives, a list of unproductive post roads for the year 1821.

With great respect,
I have the honor to be,
Your obdt. humble servt.
R. J. MEIGS, Jr

The Hon. P. P. Barbour,
Speaker of the House of Representatives.

A letter from Postmaster General Return Jonathan Meigs Jr. reporting to the House of Representatives a list of post roads that weren't profitable in 1821.

constituents to have the best mail service possible. They were often far from profitable. Miles of new road called for the issuance of hundreds of new mail coach contracts. Contract routes were expanded 47 percent, while the costs of transporting the mail were inflated by 28 percent. In Meigs's report to Congress in 1822, he stated, "... it will be perceived that, since the year 1819, the postages have diminished, while the expenses have increased, by the augmentation of post routes; and thus, increased disbursements have been made, while the means of their support have decreased."

Nothing balanced out. On May 2, 1822, Meigs published a report full of proposals aimed at covering growing deficits. His suggestions all seemed to have fatal flaws. He advised eliminating all mail contracts on routes where the post offices didn't cumulatively produce one-third of operating expenses—but many of these routes were politicians' favored initiatives. He advocated increasing the postage rates on newspapers in proportion with the cost of carrying them—but these rates had been kept low on purpose to promote the spread of the news. He sought to reduce the commissions paid to some postmasters—but often these people were not full-time employees of the Post Office and the commissions were their main source of income. And he recommended prohibiting private mail contractors from using post roads since it would take away money from the Post Office.

The report was a political and legal nonstarter. The Post Office was in need of a transformation, but this was not it. As the 1820s got under way, the American mail system was waiting for new leadership and a new way forward. Meigs's time at the helm of the Post Office would soon come to an end.

★ ★ ★

John McLean's biography seemed to trace that of the United States. He was born in the Northeast—specifically one of the 13 original colonies, New Jersey—in 1785, just before the Constitution. Then his family drifted west, following national expansion, and eventually settled in Ohio. McLean worked as a farmhand, gaining experience on the land, but used his earnings on education and eventually became a lawyer. At the same time, he operated a print shop and published the *Western Star*, a weekly newspaper in Lebanon.

McLean was also active politically. He was a proud supporter of President James Monroe. When the time was right, Monroe wanted to offer him a role in the government. It was clear what job might be a perfect fit. McLean understood the land, as well as information and education, and in the tradition of postmasters going back to Benjamin Franklin, he had been a newspaperman. In 1823, the president appointed John McLean U.S. Postmaster General, effective July 1.

Compared with Meigs, McLean was a breath of fresh air. Meigs seemed to be looking backward. He wanted to raise revenues by focusing on recouping past-due accounts. His plan for rescuing the Post Office was to oppose both extending any post roads and increasing service on existing roads. He wrote in February 1823 that he "knew of no part of the country where a new route could be established with profit." In contrast, McLean sought the future. He thought

Right: An oil portrait of the Honorable John McLean painted by Thomas Sully, circa 1831—approximately two years after he left his postmaster-general post to become an associate justice of the Supreme Court.

GENERAL POST OFFICE,
7th July, 1823.

Sir—It is believed that many of the irregularities and losses in the transmission of letters, proceed from the frequent examination of the contents of the mail, between those points at which distributing offices are established. To guard in future against such irregularities and losses, you are required to procure, with the least possible delay, if your office is not already furnished with them, *Way-bags*, made of substantial materials, and of sufficient size to contain all the letters that are required to be distributed at the intermediate offices, between your office and the next distributing office, so that the principal mail in no instance be examined, except at the distributing offices.

I am, very respectfully, your obed't. servt.
JOHN McLEAN.

Above: Newspapers were often the most expedient way to send the same information to as many people as possible. In this case, the *Lancaster Intelligencer and Journal* printed new information from the postmaster general regarding the use of "way-bags" to transmit mail to reduce "many of the irregularities and losses" along the way.

Right: Postmaster General McLean relied on newspapers to disseminate new rules to postmasters. The *Troy Sentinel* reprinted Regulation 1 from the *National Intelligencer*: "This Circular will be addressed to every Postmaster, in whose vicinity one or more newspapers are published."

that introducing smarter management, as well as tactically improving—and perhaps most of all—expanding service, would put the Post Office on firmer footing.

He made his approach apparent quite quickly. Within a week of becoming postmaster general, he sent out a notice via the nation's newspapers that he recognized "irregularities and losses" that were occurring in letter delivering, which he believed was due to mail being examined on intermediate steps along its journey. He suggested converting to sturdier bags that would keep unauthorized hands out of the mail. A few months later, one of McLean's first financial decisions came in the form of a regulation that established a new process for tracking payment for newspaper delivery. The Post Office would begin charging newspaper publishers one-quarter of the postage in advance, and each newspaper would use a new form to document the number of issues sent to the post offices in its vicinity for delivery. This introduced accountability for newspaper postage, which he believed was being collected at less than 50 percent of full freight. McClean's goal, in contrast to Meigs's, wasn't to collect old debts—though he did that, too—but rather to ensure that the real service and value the Post Office delivered was generating the proper revenue.

NEW POST OFFICE REGULATION.
[Circular.]
Post Office Department,
October 2d, 1823.

Sir: Blanks are forwarded to you, for the purpose of obtaining a statement, at the close of each quarter, of the number of Newspapers deposited in your office, to be sent in the mail.

You will furnish one of these blanks quarterly, to each publisher of a newspaper in your vicinity, and be particular in requiring him to make a return, under oath, of the number of his papers mailed in your office, for the last three months, and the Post Offices to which they were directed to be sent. The oath may be made by the person who usually folds and directs the papers, and must be as specific as the circumstances of the case will admit. You will observe, that the numbers must be placed in the columns designated as having been forwarded in the mail, either over or under a hundred miles, as may comport with the fact.

If there be two or more newspapers published in your vicinity, and mailed at your office, after you have received from the publishers the returns, as above stated, you will reduce them into one return, by stating in figures, opposite to each Post Office, the total amount of papers sent to it.

You are also required, to procure similar returns from the publishers of periodical works which are mailed at your office.

The printed form may be changed, by specifying, in the caption, the number of sheets contained in the pamphlet; or a manuscript return may be made, where the number of Post Offices to which the pamphlets may have been sent, are not numerous. A manuscript return may be made by the publisher of a newspaper, where the offices to be inserted are few, and in such cases, you can arrange the offices in alphabetical order. You will return to this department, as well the original returns, as the consolidated one which you are required to make.

This plan has been adopted from a conviction that this department does not realize much more than one half the amount that should be received from newspaper postage, and that no mode can be effectual to ensure the collection of this amount, except one that shall enable the department to raise an account against each Postmaster in the Union, for the postage on newspapers sent to his office. The above arrangement will effectually do this.

It is believed that the publishers of newspapers will most readily lend their aid, to the accomplishment of this object. They will experience from it most essential advantage, as Postmasters will be punctual to inform them, when subscribers fail to take their papers out of the Post Office.

Post-Masters are now required to charge the postage on newspapers, one quarter in advance, and to apprise printers of all papers not taken out of their Post Office; they will therefore be required to account to this department, for the postage of all newspapers sent to their offices, unless they can shew, that subscribers failed to take them, and that the printers were duly apprized of the fact.

A most rigid compliance with the duties here enjoined, will be expected and required.

I am, &c. JOHN McLEAN.

By the end of 1824, the Post Office's accounting was on firmer footing. The newspaper delivery changes alone added about $25,000 per year to the department's bottom line. It was great timing, because that year, Congress would pass a law that would represent a massive growth opportunity.

★ ★ ★

For years, there had been legislators eager to see more concerted efforts at expanding the country's transportation network. On February 4, 1817, in an address before the House of Representatives regarding a bill to set aside permanent funding for building roads and canals, John C. Calhoun, then a congressman from South Carolina, stated that he believed the government was required to "bind the republic together with a perfect system of roads and canals." He bound this to the duty to deliver mail. He argued that the mail and the press were the nervous system of the country, and that they relied on this new infrastructure. "It is thus that a citizen of the West will read the news of Boston still moist from the press," he said.

In 1824, Congress passed the General Survey Act, which authorized the president to survey routes and canals "in a commercial or military point of view, or necessary for the transportation of public mail." The act was born of a vision that connected what Calhoun enumerated as the "three distinct parts" of the United States: "the shores of the Atlantic back to the Allegheny Mountains," "the lakes and the St. Lawrence," and "that [area of land] watered by Mississippi, including its various branches."

McLean had his own vision: He saw that as long as transporting the mail was the largest expenditure of the General Post Office's annual budget, it ought to be the cornerstone of its growth—and new and improved routes were one way to achieve this. In an 1824 report to Congress, commenting on the deplorable condition of the Natchez Trace—which had fallen into disrepair, bridges collapsing and trees sprouting through the

An illustration of the Waterloo Inn, located along the route of the first stagecoach between Baltimore and Washington, D.C., from the book *Personal Narrative of Travels in the United States and Canada in 1826* by the Honorable Frederick Fitzgerald De Roos, a lieutenant in the Royal Navy.

INTERNAL IMPROVEMENTS.

Amount of moneys expended in each state and territory of the United States, upon works of internal improvement, from the adoption of the federal constitution, to the 1st day of Oct. 1828.

Maine,	$11,724 22	Tennessee,	4,200 00
Massachusetts,	104,042 46	Ohio,	390,159 03
Connecticut,	2,069 97	Indiana,	108,623 88
Rhode Island,	195 19	Mississippi,	49,385 52
New York,	68,148 45	Illinois,	8,000 00
Pennsylvania,	39,728 32	Alabama,	81,762 78
Delaware,	307,104 91	Missouri,	22,702 24
Maryland,	10,000 00	Arkansas,	44,690 74
Virginia,	150,000 00	Michigan,	48,607 95
North Carolina,	1,000 00	Florida,	79,902 91
Kentucky,	90,000 00		

The journal *Quarterly Register of the American Education Society*, Volume III, 1831, included the amount the U.S. treasury paid out to each state and territory for road improvements, as adopted to the Constitution dated October 1, 1828.

roadbed—McLean wrote that "on a good turnpike road [the mail] could be conveyed in a stage as often, and in less than half the time, at the same expense." As new settlements arose and those inhabitants petitioned for post offices, Mclean never missed an opportunity to carve a post road out of the wilderness. In 1820, the United States had 73,492 miles of post roads. By the end of the decade, that number had risen to 114,780 miles.

In some ways, the mail coaches themselves were symbolic of the flourishing of post roads in this era. Both passengers and the mail itself enjoyed certain perks on postal coaches. Passengers' fares were subsidized a modest amount by being part of the mail service, and the coaches had the right of way over other horse-drawn vehicles on post roads. They were served first at congested ferry crossings and could travel toll-free on federally financed turnpikes. And by carrying paying passengers, the coaches would potentially be more profitable.

As roads continued to improve, and with those profits up for grabs, coach companies sprang up to bid on every available contract route needed to serve the 8,401 post offices now scattered around the country. Each found a way to distinguish itself.

For some it was speed. The average pace of a mail coach with four to six horses ranged from six to eight miles per hour, accounting for stops at post offices, inns, and taverns—and this was during the summer months, if the weather was cooperative and the roads were well-maintained. On Halloween 1828, a coach raced the 40 miles from Baltimore to Washington, D.C., in just under four hours. The next year, the U.S. Mail Coach Line, the operator of one of the largest carriers in the country, transported the mail between Philadelphia and New York City, a roughly 100-mile trip, in 9.5 hours—about 10.5 miles per hour. Phenomenal, given that the coach was weighed down with 1,700 pounds of mail, six passengers, a guard, and a driver. (Of course, speed carried risks: On January 4, 1826, *The Massachusetts Spy* reported a coach obliterated by an accident on a hill descent, luckily without any loss of life. "The driver may be some to blame," the paper stated, "perhaps for driving so fast down a bad hill, but his excuse is, that the horses were restive, so that he could not keep them in the road without going fast.")

Other coach operators aimed for unmatched comfort and convenience. Service to the north of New York City was offered over what an 1826 issue of the *Literary Cadet and Saturday Evening Bulletin* of Providence, Rhode Island, called "the pleasantest route as [passengers] will arrive at Hartford [Connecticut] at so early an hour as to avail themselves to some rest before the Western Stage starts." According to the newspaper, the operator of this new stage line "pledged himself that nothing on his part shall be wanting to render the passage of travellers [*sic*] expeditiously, pleasant, and agreeable."

And, of course, companies competed on price. At the start of the decade, the sole mail coach between Philadelphia and New York City charged $10 for a seat. But soon a competing company, carrying only passengers over the same route, began charging $7. The coach operator countered by cutting its price to $5, and the competition responded by dropping to $4—a price that turned out to be unsustainable and nearly drove it out of business.

If McLean, through all this, was succeeding at growing the Post Office and expanding its offerings, he was also undoubtedly making it a target for more unsavory actors. Profits can invite competition that improves service and lowers price, but they can also incentivize bad behavior. Increased competition led to buyouts and mergers, which affected the Post Office's ability to contract out mail carriage. In 1827, for example, the Citizens' Coach Company and the Commercial Line were cutthroat competitors on the route from Boston to Providence, Rhode Island. Both reduced their fares and tried every means possible to put the other out of business, including sabotaging each other's carriages. In the end, Citizens' won the struggle and found itself with a monopoly over the route.

Right: A stipple and etching engraved portrait of Postmaster General William Taylor Barry by James Barton Longacre, circa 1833.

Immediately, the quality and value of service tanked. The *Literary Cadet and Rhode-Island Statesman* reported that "the Citizens' Coach Company then looked forward and saw a broad turnpike from Boston to Providence, completely in their possession. And what use did they make of it? They immediately raised the fare from two dollars to three and lengthened the time on the road from six to eight hours, and passengers in many instances were treated in a very rough and uncivil manner."

IMPORTANT NEWS for PASSENGERS.
GOOD ROADS AND CHEAP FARE.
Citizens Coach Fare reduced to 6 dollars.
FOR PHILADELPHIA
Baltimore, Washington City and Pittsburgh.

THE CITIZENS' COACH AND U STATES MAIL COACH. Passengers take notice. WINTER ESTABLISHMENT.

The Citizens' Coach, through in one day to Philadelphia, via Powle's Hook, Newark, E. Town, Brunswick, Princeton, Trenton, Bristol, and Frankfort.

The Citizens' Coach starts from the coach office, No. 1 Courtlandt street, every morning at half past 6 o'clock, and arrives at Philadelphia the same evening. Fare 6 dollars.

The U. S. mail coach starts from the coach office, No. 1 Courtlandt street every day at 1 o'clock, P. M. and arrives at Philadelphia next morning at 6 o'clock.

The Boston and Albany coaches starts every morning, from the coach office, No. 1 Courtlandt street, New York.

For seats apply to THOMAS WHITFIELD, at the general coach office, No. 1 Courtlandt st. first office from Broadway, New York.

N. B. Expresses and extra Coaches furnished at any hour, day or night to any part of the United States, by THOMAS WHITFIELD.

N. B. All Goods and Baggage at the risk of the owner.

LYON, WARD, BAILEY & CO.
Ja 20 Proprietors

A January 23, 1824, advertisement from Citizens' Coach, a mail stagecoach company, promoting its reduction of fares to $6 from Philadelphia, Baltimore, Washington City, and Pittsburgh.

In another case—one decided by the New Jersey Supreme Court in 1828, a ruling that lawyers would refer to in decades to come—aspiring mail deliverers Thomas Ward and Chester Bailey offered to pay their competitors, William and John Gulick, $1,000 to refrain from bidding on a contract for a route between New York City and Philadelphia. The Gulicks brought the lawsuit after they agreed to the terms but Ward and Bailey reneged on their offer to pay. The court ruled in the Gulicks' favor, but not simply because they had been wronged. Ward and Bailey's deal was illegal in the first place, the court found, because it undermined Congress' attempts to generate competition and its benefits—service, comfort, speed, low prices—for the increasingly important task of conveying the mail. Paying off competitors to secure a postal route without merit harked back to the earliest days of colonial mail service, when postmaster appointments were doled out as favors. This was a past the Post Office seemed to have left behind.

Unfortunately, this was also the exact direction in which it was heading.

★ ★ ★

One of McLean's aims in putting the Post Office on firmer footing—and in doing so by improving and expanding its offerings to *grow* into profitability, rather than cutting back, as Meigs might have done—was to increase its clout. He knew that a stronger department could stand on its own and wield greater influence in government affairs.

For McLean, this was crucial. In November 1823, he gave a full account of the Post Office since 1799, making special note of the degree to which the faithful operation of the Postal Service depended on the integrity of postmasters and receiving clerks. For this reason, he detested party patronage—officers being politically appointed for their loyalty to party, not for their merit, and subsequently making decisions out of that loyalty instead of a sense of public service. "If subserviency to the president and an ardent zeal in the promotion of his personal views shall be the passport to office, where the individual is quailed, however objectionable he may be to the people," he once wrote to Edward Everett, a congressman and governor of Massachusetts, "offices will be filled, not by high-minded and patriotic citizens, but by fawning sycophants loud in their professions, without principle, but ready at all times to execute the bidding of their master...I would scorn to hold any office, as a creature of any administration." As regards the Cabinet, the group of high-ranking advisers—typically heads of departments of the executive branch, serving at the pleasure of the president—he wrote, "The Cabinet shall never think and decide for me unless I am a member of it."

The same year President James Monroe appointed McLean postmaster general, he entertained the notion of elevating the role to greater prominence in the government. In a December 1823 address to Congress, amid a larger discussion of the state of the Post Office based on McLean's report, Monroe suggested that it might be "proper" to appoint postmasters and submit them to nomination before the Senate, like other prominent federal officers.

Six years later, McLean's successor, William Taylor Barry, would become the first postmaster general to join the Cabinet—but not at all in the way McLean might have hoped.

Western Mail Coach in Sight of Mt. Hood, an oil painting by Lloyd Branson, depicts a Concord-style coach crossing a wooden bridge set against the backdrop of Oregon's Mount Hood.

Entered according to the Act of Congress in the year 1831 by E. W. Clay in the Clerk's office of the District Court of the Eastern District of Pennsylvania.
SKOOL OF REFORM
NOTIS.
There's Clay, and this is all Clays doings.
Maine
New Hampshire
Massachusetts
Connecticut
Rhode Island
Vermont
New York
New Jersey
Pennsylvania
Delaware
Maryland
Virginia
Georgia
Kentucky
Tennessee
Ohio
Louisiana
Indiana
Mississippi
Ladder of Political Preferment
The Hickory Chair is coming to pieces at last
Famine! War! Pestilence!
ALTAR OF REFORM.
You dont get up if I can help it.
If I could only humbug that Eagle and climb up this ladder.
I'm off to the Indians.
Resignation
of the Walk fecit
,00001
The value of a unit with four cyphers going before it.
Publ.d by E. W. Clay S.E. corner of Walnut and 4th St. Philada.

Opposite: *.00001: The Value of a Unit with Four Cyphers Going Before It,* a political satire by E. W. Clay on resignations within Andrew Jackson's administration, circa 1831.

Barry's decisions caused postal operations to decline and expenditures to rise.

After John Quincy Adams won the presidency, he largely maintained the status quo. But in 1829 came the inauguration of Andrew Jackson, which changed everything. Jackson wanted to use his office to reward political friends and punish opponents. He instituted what was called the "spoils system," in which the incoming president treated government posts as the spoils of his electoral victory, appointing his preferred staffers—and, in effect, surrounding himself with only true believers in his particular brand of politics. The spoils system politicized every part of the government it touched—and, perhaps because of McLean's effectiveness at turning it into something of a power center, that included the Post Office.

As a result, President Jackson brought in Barry as his postmaster general as well as an official Cabinet member—an appointment that was a reward for his loyalty. Barry, unsurprisingly, believed wholeheartedly in the spoils system and cleaned house at postal headquarters by promptly replacing 600 local postmasters, discarding all but those faithful to Jacksonian politics. Troublemakers and critics weren't tolerated. He explained this to his daughter in a letter in May 1829, writing: "in [postal] appointments I am cautious; the government here is often deceived, and, of course, makes some bad selections...Your postmaster at New Port, and all others like him, who have acted well, are safe. But those who abused their privileges, circulated Coffin [anti-Jackson] handbills... and acted partially in their station, ought not to expect to remain in office."

Unfortunately, Barry was neither a good businessman nor tactful in his dealings with others. His rough edges irked members of Congress, as did his blind obedience to Jackson. Barry's decisions caused postal operations to decline and expenditures to rise, and members in the House of Representative and Senate began attacking him for his mismanagement of the mail service. In 1834, the Martinsburg, Virginia, *Gazette* would proclaim Barry to be "a man who has carried the art of corruption further than any man in any government." That year, the Senate unanimously voted on a motion of no confidence in Barry, and he resigned as postmaster general in 1835.

As for McLean, he *was* in fact a Jackson supporter—just one who did not support the spoils system. Nevertheless, he benefited. When Jackson brought in Barry to fill the role of postmaster general, he gave McLean an opportunity to return to the practice of law: He nominated him to serve as an associate justice of the U.S. Supreme Court. McLean was nominated on March 6, 1829, confirmed the same day, and sworn in on March 7. He would serve in the role until his death, in 1861. It would bring him perhaps his greatest brush with history.

In 1856, the Supreme Court handed down a now-infamous decision in the case of *Dred Scott v. Sandford,* which concerned an enslaved man, Dred Scott, who had lived for a time in free territory and thus believed that he should no longer be a slave. In the court's notoriously racist decision, Chief Justice Roger B. Taney held that Black people were not, and could not be, citizens of the United States. McLean saw things differently. "In the argument, it was said that a colored citizen would not be an agreeable member of society," he wrote in one of two dissents filed in the case. "This is more a matter of taste than of law." In 1856, when Taney and McLean wrote their legal opinions, the issue of slavery was about to explode and engulf the nation in civil war. In the 1820s, America was already careening down a path from which it could not veer. The conflict would arrive at the Post Office long before soldiers took up arms.

Treacherous Travel Conditions

Weather on postal routes was a liability. In the summer, clouds of dust kicked up by the horses' hooves enveloped mail coaches, turning them into stuffy, choking saunas. Perspiration soaked through passengers' clothing, making them unbearably smelly.

Winter travel was even more treacherous, and anecdotes of chaotic travel were commonplace. For example, on January 18, 1820, at 7:00 a.m., the Southern Mail line left to deliver mail to Newark, New Jersey. The next day, coming upon the causeway between Powles' (Paulus) Hook and Newark, which was choked with ice, the coach was unable to cross. A citizen named Mr. Lyon met the coach from the south near Newark in his one-horse sleigh and was able to deliver the mail to the post office at 2:00 in the afternoon.

River crossings were particularly perilous. On November 25, 1823, the United States Mail Stage was attempting to cross Mill Creek in Nashville, Tennessee. The creek was full after the previous night of rain. One horse fell into the river and drowned, though another escaped. The coach, driver, and passengers were all swept away by the force of the current. The passengers clung to a tree waiting for rescue, while the driver stayed with the coach and the mail. They floated downstream for more than half a mile when William Osmar, a 14-year-old boy, plunged into the stream and retrieved "the mail bags that had got loose from the stage, thereby preventing much loss and distress to many persons interested in their contents."

But in these situations, more often than not, the mail would be lost. In February 1827, the Baltimore-to-Philadelphia mail coach was swept downstream when the driver unwisely attempted to ford Big Elk Creek, which was swollen by floodwaters. The coach flipped onto its side during its half-mile voyage, throwing the driver and guard from the boot. Both survived by clinging to tree debris until onlookers lent a hand to pull them to safety. The coach briefly came to rest wedged against a bridge, and the temporary pause allowed locals to save some of the mail before the coach was sucked under by the surging waters and crushed beneath the bridge.

Turned over to the local postmaster, the waterlogged letters were spread out to dry before being returned to the mail stream for delivery. But the bulk of the mail was in a portmanteau chained to the

coach and was not recovered until after the waters receded. The cache of newspapers wasn't salvageable. The proprietors of this coach, Stockton & Stokes, estimated that they lost $1,000 in this accident. Fortunately, the driver was not hurt and no passengers were aboard.

A Wet Start at Daybreak, a painting by Edward Lamson Henry from Alice Morse Earle's 1911 book, *Stage-Coach and Tavern Days*.

MAIL LOCKS

Since the 18th century, postmasters and clerks have relied on padlocks to secure important mail. The clerks would collect and sort first-class, registered, and "through" mail traveling long distances, place it in a mailbag, and then safeguard it with a specially designed lock. Only authorized postal employees held keys to these brass or metal rotary locks, sometimes called pin tumbler locks—and the bags were only supposed to be opened while in postal custody to ensure secure and accurate delivery.

Brass lever pouch padlock, 1812.

Brass lever pouch padlock, 1798.

Rural Free Delivery mailbox brass padlock used to secure RFD boxes that held stamps for sale and cash, after 1896.

Rural Free Delivery brass mailbox padlock engraved with manufacturer's name, "Corbin," after 1896.

Lever pouch iron padlock by H. C. Jones with engraved with 1856 date.

Star Route registry brass padlock, circa 1880s, with front inscription reading "U.S. Star Route Mail Reg'd."

Rotary registry padlock by Smith & Egge Company made for locking registered mailbags, 1881.

Lever pouch steel padlock by Smith & Egge Company, 1882, with front engraving reading "U S MAIL."

Lever pouch brass padlock with front inscription reading "General Post Office US America 1802."

Little River L…

Ark. Ter.

MArch 9 D 1832

B…RBO…RSVILLE VA

21st June

ABOLITIONIST MAIL DEEPENS THE NATION'S DIVIDES

Alfred Huger was a lawyer and seasoned state legislator when President Andrew Jackson appointed him postmaster of Charleston. Huger had deep South Carolina roots: His father had served in the state militia during the Revolutionary War and had been the state's first secretary of state in the 1790s. Huger left South Carolina to pursue his education at Princeton but came back home to study law and was elected a state senator in 1818. He served in that role until 1833; a short time later, in December 1834, Jackson put him in charge of Charleston's post office.

It was not an easy time to be postmaster. Tensions between the North and South were rising. The abolitionist movement was growing stronger, and one way it flexed its muscle was through the mail. Antislavery pamphlets and publications were purposely being mailed to the South. Advocates viewed these mass-mailing campaigns as a right of free expression, a way to rile up the South like nothing had before and draw attention to slavery as a national curse.

In the summer of 1835, a prominent abolitionist organization called the American Anti-Slavery Society launched an immense campaign, among

Two years after the burning of the mail from the Charleston Post Office, abolitionist Elijah Parish Lovejoy's printing warehouse was attacked and burned by a pro-slavery mob. One man attempted to set the roof on fire, while the others were armed and actively shooting. Lovejoy ran outside, ready to protect his press, but was shot five times. He died a few minutes later, becaming the first white abolitionist martyr.

CHARLESTON.

THURSDAY MORNING, JULY 30.

Incendiary Publications.—The U. S. mail, brought yesterday, by the steam packet *Columbia*, from New-York, came to hand, filled with incendiary papers and tracts, intended for circulation throughout the Southern and South Western sections of the Union. It is certainly a monstrous abuse of this national convenience, that it should be converted into an instrument or means of assault on Southern Institutions; and a repetition of it will, in all probability, so influence public indignation, as to render the U. S. Mail unsafe, at least, in this quarter. If no measure of prevention be within the competency of the Post Office authorities, a remedy may, nevertheless, be found among ourselves, in the refusal of those, to whom these incendiary publications come addressed, to aid in their circulation. We understand that the South Carolina Association had a Meeting yesterday, in reference to this subject, and have issued a Circular to the Post Masters, to the South, and South West, apprising them in anticipation of the incendiary stuff of which they are to be made the official dispensers.

A notice printed in *The Charleston Daily Courier,* dated July 30, 1835, condemned the distribution of antislavery materials through mail as "Incendiary Publications."

At the time, newspapers were still paying postage at extremely low rates.

America's first mass-mailing blitzes. Huger had dutifully delivered the antislavery tracts, as was required of him as postmaster, and almost immediately was confronted by irate recipients returning them to the post office and demanding such mailings be stopped. Word of the outrage quickly spread, prompting an angry mob to form.

Huger feared that his enraged neighbors might attempt to sack his post office to get at the offending mail. On July 29, 200 to 300 citizens gathered at the office for the purpose of seizing and destroying the "incendiary pamphlets and papers." Lieutenant Brown of the City Guard confronted the crowd and persuaded them to leave. Later that night, the mob, known as the "Lynch Men," returned, broke into the unattended post office through a window, and took the offending mail. Back on the street, they emptied the mailbags, gathered some reported 300,000 pamphlets and leaflets, set a bonfire, and watched it burn.

★ ★ ★

Andrew Jackson swept into office in 1829 as an avowed advocate of freedom of the press, possessed of a clear-eyed view of the importance of the mail to maintaining such freedom. In his inaugural address, Jackson described the mission of the Post Office as being "to the body politic what the veins and arteries are to the natural body—conveying rapidly and regularly, to the remotest parts of the system, correct information of the operations of the government. Through its agency, we have secured to ourselves the fullest enjoyment of the blessings of a free press."

The Founding Fathers had believed that the dissemination of news was essential to the republic, especially as its frontier population, far from the centers of national news in the Northeast, continued to grow. And as a westerner who became a lawyer and built his estate, the Hermitage, in Tennessee, Andrew Jackson understood this in his bones.

At the time, newspapers were still paying postage at extremely low rates. At the end of the decade, assessing the conditions of the Post Office, U.S. Postmaster General John M. Niles would estimate that "printed matter contains...95 percent of the whole mails, whilst it pays but about 12 percent of the whole gross revenue." These low rates, combined with improvements in printing technology that made large print runs possible, led to the advent of mass mailings: written materials created by private organizations to be sent to as many Americans as possible.

The American Anti-Slavery Society, which was organized on December 4, 1833, by citizens

MAIL SPREADS NEWS, NOT GERMS

In addition to those who believed that many of the newspapers and periodicals in the mail at the time were tainted by abolitionist rhetoric, there were some who thought that the mail was contaminated with far worse: cholera, smallpox, and yellow fever. Many in both the North and South feared that the mail was a vector for illness and could spread germs from one house, community, countryside, and city to the next.

Yellow fever, in particular, was a serious concern. Nothing could stop the mail as predictably, or as quickly, as an outbreak of the disease. It was so common as to be a near-annual summertime event in many communities, particularly in the South, where it would strike backwater hamlets and major cities alike. Epidemics occurred in New Orleans in 1829, 1831, 1833, and 1837.

The only thing doctors knew for certain in the 1830s was that yellow fever weakened and disappeared after the first hard frosts. At the time, its origins were hotly debated. (Later it would be determined that the disease originated in Africa and was imported into the United States via the Caribbean.) The Louisiana *Planters' Banner* proclaimed, "The epidemic of 1839 was widespread and terrible in its effects." According to the newspaper, the disease first appeared in seaports and seemed to spread to interior towns and hamlets, prompting some doctors to believe it was somehow transmissible and that the mail was as likely as anything else the purveyor of the pathogen. It was also thought that there was a distinct origin for each outbreak. This reflected the point of view that it was a "strangers' disease," imported from community to community by visitors, sailors, mail, or people fleeing already infected areas. For such believers, the only reasonable defense against the disease was a quarantine. Unfortunately, for those who espoused this theory, their argument fell apart when Natchez, Mississippi, instituted a stringent quarantine and still suffered a severe outbreak.

Another outbreak of yellow fever occurred again in late 1873, mainly in Louisiana and Tennessee. The outbreak in Shreveport, Louisiana, is now ranked as the third-worst recorded epidemic of its type in the United States. In about 12 weeks, one-quarter of the population was killed by the illness. In Tennessee, about 2,000 succumbed. Then another outbreak from July to November 1878 occurred. Memphis lost more than 5,000 to the disease.

To decrease the spread, newspapers and mail were blockaded from Tennessee. The *Clarion* newspaper reported on September 4, 1878, that New Orleans had been hit with yellow fever and that "even the mail service was suspended, so fearful were the people that the deadly disease would reach them."

The Catholic Sisters of Charity tended the sick and dying during the Memphis yellow fever outbreak of 1878, which killed more than 5,000 people in the city.

from 10 free states who met in Philadelphia, saw this as an opportunity. Not only did the society believe that slavery was a heinous crime, "we also maintain," its members wrote in a declaration of their beliefs, "that there are, at the present time, the highest obligations resting upon the people of the free States, to remove Slavery by moral and political action." And so they became pioneers of mass mailings. The society sent thousands of leaflets to unsuspecting southern slaveholders. "The holders of slaves are not the just proprietors of what they claim," their principles stated. "...freeing the slave is not depriving them of property but restoring it to its right owners; it is not wronging the master, but righting the slave—restoring him to himself."

Naturally, their position was not warmly received—but this was the desired outcome. As a publicity stunt, the mailings were a stunning success, provoking anger and outrage. The *Charleston Observer* wrote that the mailings were "attempts, under the guise of philanthropy, to interfere with our domestic institutions." But there was also an undercurrent of a more primal emotion: fear. Just a few years earlier, in 1831, an enslaved man named Nat Turner had led a rebellion that killed more than 50 people in Southampton County, Virginia. Blanketed by calls for emancipation, southerners braced for more violence. After a few years of mass mailings, Congressman John Jones of Virginia would say that the pamphlets were "calculated, in an eminent degree, to rouse and inflame the passions of the slaves against their masters, to urge them on to deeds of death, and to involve them in all the horrors of a servile war."

Southern postmasters like Huger found themselves caught in the middle of a conflict they were powerless to prevent: If they refused to deliver abolitionist publications like the *Emancipator*, *The Liberator*, the *Observer*, and *Evangelist*, or the American Anti-Slavery Society's *Record*, they faced federal penalties. Yet if they delivered them, they risked the wrath of their neighbors.

So it was that abolitionist mail presented the country with a major test. Newspapers had been deemed so important that they could be mailed at a loss—the Founding Fathers had viewed this as an acceptable price for maintaining an informed electorate, even if they objected to some of the content. But now free speech was butting up against public safety, harmony, and national unity. Andrew Jackson found himself asking whether some line had been crossed.

The American Anti-Slavery Society was founded by abolitionist William Lloyd Garrison in 1833. This "Declaration of the Anti-Slavery Convention" was the inaugural document for the assemblage, held in Philadelphia on December 4 of that year. The document declared the organization's intent to publish, preach, and otherwise promote its goal: "the entire abolition of slavery in the United States."

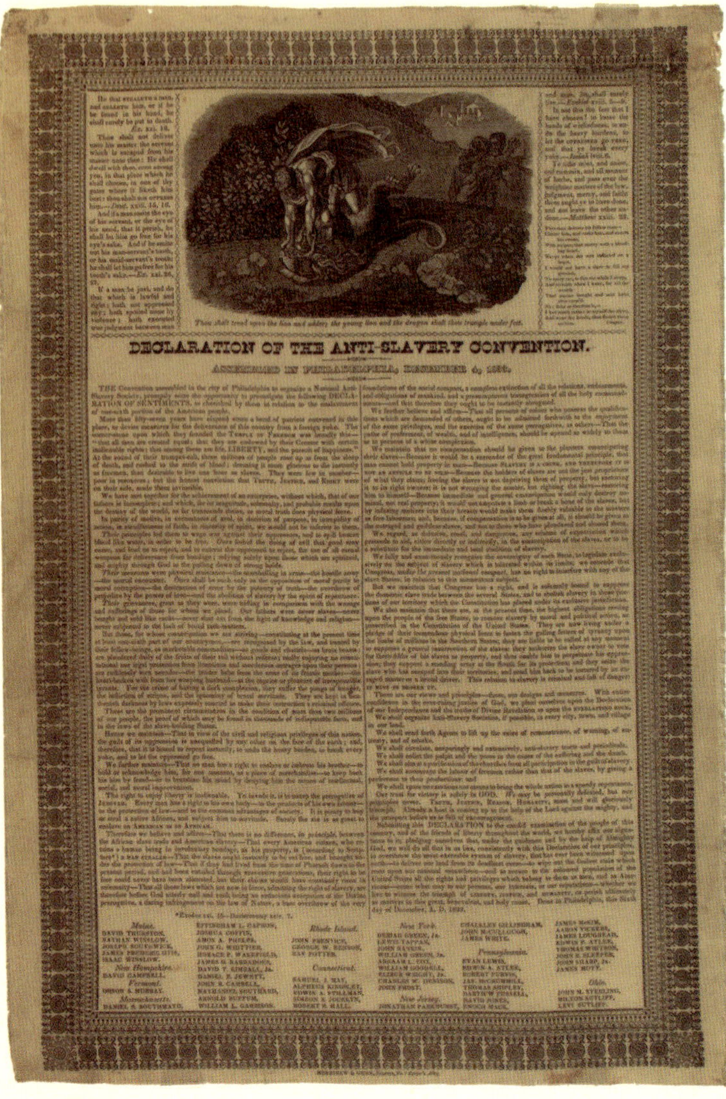

DECLARATION OF THE ANTI-SLAVERY CONVENTION.

ASSEMBLED IN PHILADELPHIA, DECEMBER 4, 1833.

THE

ANTI-SLAVERY RECORD

Vol. II. No. IX. SEPTEMBER, 1836. Whole No. 21

HOW CAN IT BE DONE?

Above: The front page of the September 1836 edition of the *Anti-Slavery Record*, published by R.G. Williams, featured a woodcut insulting the sensibilities of slave owners—a hallmark of the paper's formative issues.

Below: The October 1, 1831, edition of *The Liberator*, an antislavery publication also founded by Garrison, featuring an illustration of a market where slaves, horses, and cattle were sold.

Whether the body politic, with its veins and arteries of post roads and mailboats, had been infected by something that needed to be taken out of circulation. He and his postmasters general considered putting limits on what could be carried through the mail.

★ ★ ★

Not waiting for congressional action to forbid postmasters from delivering incendiary material, Virginia's legislature passed its own measure in 1834. The law was incredibly harsh. Postmasters were supposed to report abolitionist mailings, which would then be briefly investigated and subsequently burned. The intended recipient of the mail, were they determined to have known what they were receiving, would be sent to jail. Postmasters who failed to follow the law could be fined up to $200.

This paper was this day
received by mail—or
rather through the
post-office
John Floyd
Octo 4. 1831

THE LIBERATOR.

VOL. I.] WILLIAM LLOYD GARRISON AND ISAAC KNAPP, PUBLISHERS. [NO. 40.

Boston, Massachusetts.] OUR COUNTRY IS THE WORLD—OUR COUNTRYMEN ARE MANKIND. [Saturday, October 1, 1831.

THE LIBERATOR IS PUBLISHED WEEKLY AT NO. 10, MERCHANTS' HALL.

But none of these provisions were in fact the worst part of the law. Virginia went so far as to make local postmasters punishable even if they *unknowingly* delivered questionable publications. But since most mailings came wrapped, postmasters couldn't make the determination the law required without opening every piece of mail that might have been an offending publication. As a result, they promptly began rejecting everything but their own local newspapers.

In Lynchburg, Postmaster R. H. Glass discarded copies of the *New-York Tribune*. In

A photograph of Postmaster General Amos Kendall by Mathew Brady; prior to assuming the role, Kendall was the editor of a pro-Democratic Kentucky newspaper and part of President Jackson's "Kitchen Cabinet."

Kendall wrote: "We owe an obligation of the laws, but a higher one to the communities in which we live."

Occoquan, Postmaster L. A. Lynn went further, burning the *Tribune* rather than delivering it to its paid subscribers. But Glass and Lynn didn't stop there. They went so far as to implore out-of-state newspapers to quit sending copies in the first place. Glass wrote to Horace Greeley, the famous editor of the paper, "I shall not, in the future, deliver from this office the copies of the *Tribune* which come here, because I believe them to be of that incendiary character which are forbidden circulation alike by the laws of the land, and a proper regard for the safety of society."

In Charleston, Alfred Huger did the same. The mail that had caused him such trouble had originated in New York City, so he wrote its postmaster, Samuel L. Gouverneur, begging him to hold off on any further shipments of antislavery items. Gouverneur agreed to suspend further mailings until he received instructions from Washington, D.C.—a sign of the deeply unsettled legal status of mailing such material. Federal law was still silent on the matter.

Huger sent another letter, too. He wrote to the new U.S. Postmaster General, Amos Kendall, for permission to confiscate the American Anti-Slavery Society's publications.

Kendall had been appointed earlier in 1835. He was sympathetic to Glass, Lynn, and others like them. His letter book for that year contains several notations concerning his support, including: "I have received a letter from the Post Master at Poplar Mount, Virginia, stating his reason for returning the *New York Evangelist* to be that it 'is an Abolition paper of the deepest dye.'" Kendall's view was that destruction of such newspapers was "the only practicable remedy for evil." He also recorded that the "P. Masters in Louisiana will assuredly not be punished by me for obedience to the laws of their own state which forbids the circulation of seditionary papers." Of another dispatch referenced in his letter book, Kendall wrote: "We owe an obligation of the laws, but a higher one to the communities in which we live, and if the former be perverted to destroy the latter, it is patriotism to disregard them."

Nevertheless, Kendall, wary of the complex politics of the situation, dragged his feet. In the meantime, while Huger was waiting for a response, the situation escalated. The merchants of Charleston met on August 10 and decided to inform northern merchants "who were known to favor the views of the Abolitionists" that they

The Eastern Pony Express

Eclipsed in history by a more well-known service–the Western Pony Express of the 1860s–the Express Mail, decades later termed the "Eastern Pony Express," operated between 1836 and 1839 to rush information from New York City to New Orleans. This included financial information–mostly cotton-market price fluctuations–and breaking news of national importance between St. Louis; New Orleans; Mobile, Alabama; Charleston, South Carolina; and several other major eastern cities. The news flashes were written on small slips of paper to minimize weight and conserve space in the carrier's portmanteaux. Couriers operated in relay around the clock, some traveling by train and others by steamboat whenever possible. Elsewhere, expert riders on horseback filled in. A strict schedule was set, and the couriers strove mightily to maintain it. Service between New York City and New Orleans was to be completed within seven days, which was at least eight days faster than alternative stagecoach service.

The Express Mail was part of the 1836 Postal Act "for the purpose of convening slips from newspapers... or letters, other than such as contain money, not exceeding half an ounce in weight, marked 'express mail.'" Express postage was triple the amount for letters sent via the "ordinary mails."

The Express Mail service was seen as great postal progress. William Street Pepys wrote in 1836: "The afternoon passed pleasantly enough, aided by light chores about the shop and the posting of several letters, one bound for far away New Orleans. It is indeed a tribute to the efficiency of the blessed government under which we thrive that a letter to such an exotic distant destination as New Orleans may be posted for the comparatively trifling sum..." For a man of business like Pepys, the cost of posting a letter to New Orleans may have been trifling, but for the average American, it was expensive.

The "Eastern Pony Express" was discontinued in July 1839 when railroad routes expanded to fill most of the gaps covered by the riders, allowing the mail to bridge the distances between scheduled destinations in about 10 days.

Above: A letter sent by Eastern Pony Express from Savannah to Boston.

Right: The Post Office Department seal used from 1837 to 1970 featured a rider on horseback.

would no longer do any business with them. They encouraged Richmond, Virginia, to do likewise. Arthur Tappan, president of the American Anti-Slavery Society, became a wanted man in the South. There were real fears for his life—even talk that Governor James Hamilton of South Carolina was leading a party of assassins to put an end to Tappan, with reports of $100,000 being offered for his head.

Finally, Kendall's response arrived. He informed Huger he had "no legal authority to exclude newspapers from the mail, nor prohibit their carriage or delivery on account of their character or tendency, real or supposed." But, he added, "I am prepared not to direct you to forward or deliver the papers of which you speak." He would neither ban the papers nor make Huger deliver them. Kendall had taken the politician's way out, dodging responsibility and at the same time squandering an opportunity for the federal government to take control of the situation. It would have profound repercussions.

★ ★ ★

Realizing they had at the very least the tacit support of the highest postal official in the land, Virginia postmasters sent notices to more and more out-of-state papers: *The Republican* of Springfield, Massachusetts; the *Evening Journal* of Albany, New York; the *New York Independent*; and so on.

And other states passed legislation like Virginia's. Maryland's was particularly cruel; in certain areas, local postmasters were ordered to submit lists to their local sheriffs of subscribers receiving certain journals, treatises, and newspapers. It was a surveillance state, and those deemed to be reading offensive material could be imprisoned for 10 years or more. To ensure its act had teeth, Maryland made an example of several free Black Marylanders, charging and convicting them under the law.

In a way, it could be said that the antislavery mass-mailing campaign backfired. Access, via the mail, to the hearts and minds of everyday Americans had never been greater. The country's mail network was continuing to expand, with new contracts constantly being awarded to steamboat

Above: A portrait of Arthur Tappan, circa 1870.

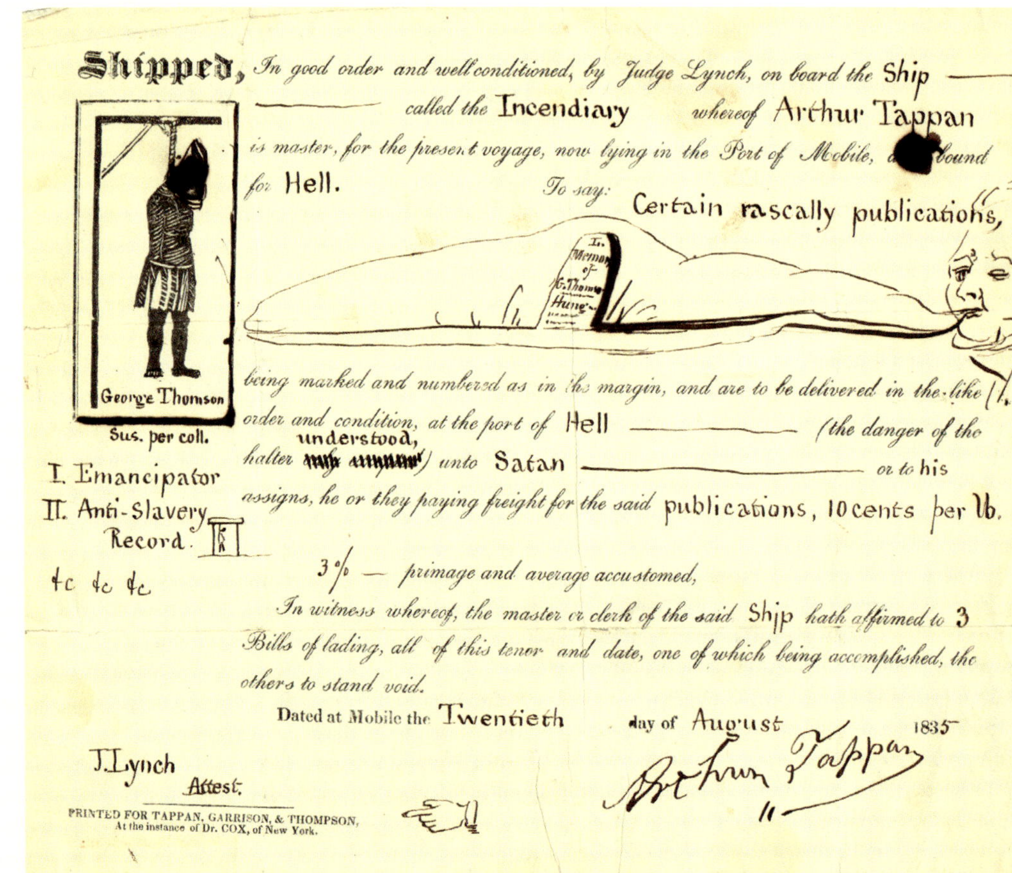

Shipped, In good order and well conditioned, by Judge Lynch, on board the Ship called the Incendiary whereof Arthur Tappan is master, for the present voyage, now lying in the Port of Mobile, and bound for Hell. To say: Certain rascally publications,

George Thomson
Sus. per coll.

I. Emancipator
II. Anti-Slavery Record. III
&c &c &c

being marked and numbered as in the margin, and are to be delivered in the like order and condition, at the port of Hell (the danger of the halter understood,) unto Satan or to his assigns, he or they paying freight for the said publications, 10 cents per lb.

3% — primage and average accustomed,

In witness whereof, the master or clerk of the said Ship hath affirmed to 3 Bills of lading, all of this tenor and date, one of which being accomplished, the others to stand void.

Dated at Mobile the Twentieth day of August 1835

J. Lynch
Attest.

Arthur Tappan

PRINTED FOR TAPPAN, GARRISON, & THOMPSON,
At the instance of Dr. COX, of New York.

Right: A caricatured shipping order dated August 20, 1835, from Tappan to British abolitionist George Thompson, mockingly confirming the mail delivery of antislavery publications like *The Emancipator* and *Anti-Slavery Record*.

"If any postmaster or deputy postmaster within this commonwealth, shall give notice to any justice of the peace, that any book, pamphlet, or other writing, has been received at his office through the medium of the mail, advising, enticing, or persuading persons of colour within this commonwealth, to make insurrection or to rebel, or denying the right of masters to property in their slaves, and inculcating the duty of resistance to such right, it shall be the duty of such justice of the peace to inquire into the circumstances of the case, and to have such book, pamphlet, or other writing, burned in his presence; and if it shall appear to him by satisfactory evidence that the person to whom the same is directed, subscribed for the said book, pamphlet, or other writing, knowing its character and tendency, or agreed to receive it with an intention of circulating it, thereby to aid the purposes of the abolitionists or anti-slavery societies, the said justice shall commit him or her to the jail of his county, to be dealt with according to law. Any postmaster, or deputy postmaster knowingly violating the provisions of this act, shall forfeit and pay a sum not less than fifty dollars, nor more than two hundred dollars, to be recovered with costs, by action of debt or information, in any court of record in this commonwealth, one moiety to the commonwealth, the other to the informer, or any person who will sue for the same."(*d*)

Southern legislation censored the circulation of abolitionist material through the mail; postmasters who violated the act were fined approximately $50 to $200. This detail is from *A treatise on criminal law: with an exposition of the office and authority of justices of the peace in Virginia: including forms of practice* by J.A.G. Davis, published in 1838.

companies on the Ohio and Mississippi rivers. It was easier than ever to spread information from northern population centers like Pittsburgh and Cincinnati to cities in slave states like St. Louis, New Orleans, and Louisville, Kentucky. But by weaponizing the mail, the abolitionists had provoked southerners into censoring the very ideas they wanted to spread. Because the mail was their principal weapon for affecting change, the movement risked being severely immobilized.

Except that the same debate was being played out, writ large, in the nation's capital. And it was being spurred there as well by mail: People were flooding Congress with antislavery petitions, often instigated by the American Anti-Slavery Society. As growing abolitionist sentiments were being expressed in the North, irritation mounted in the South. In May 1836, the House of Representatives passed a "gag rule," which automatically tabled any discussion having to do with slavery—a sort of echo of the censorship of abolitionist mailings being practiced in the southern states.

In both cases, censorship ultimately caused both sides to dig in deeper. Even as the South rejected abolitionist mailings, by the end of the decade, there was a deluge of antislavery newspapers. In 1838, an antislavery group circulated 646,000 news sheets from New York City alone, and the following year it produced 724,000.

At the end of the decade, there were so many newspapers centered on ending the barbaric institution that they were crowding one another out of the market. In April 1839, abolitionist Ann Mary Houghton of Dedham, Massachusetts, wrote to Maria Weston Chapman, an editor and publisher affiliated with the American Anti-Slavery Society, among other organizations, to report that she wouldn't be able to register many new subscribers to the abolitionist publication *Cradle of Liberty* because many locals already subscribed to *Massachusetts Abolitionist*.

All of these antislavery newspapers were still delivered—when they were delivered—at discount rates.

And yet an important and complementary part of the story of the abolitionist movement was mailed not in newspapers but in personal letters, like the correspondence between Houghton and Chapman. If newspapers could be censored, personal correspondence, luckily, could not. In personal letters, one could see the optimism abolitionists felt throughout the decade—partly because of their mail campaigns. In December 1833, Emery Brown of Augusta, Maine, wrote to the famous abolitionist William Lloyd Garrison, who published the widely read *Liberator* newspaper, that "the good cause of Anti-Slavery is steadily progressing in this region." Another Mainer, Louis O. Cowan, wrote to Garrison six months later of the "unexampled success which has attended our cause for a year past," calling it "a bright harbinger of the ultimate accomplishment of the end which abolitionists have in prospect for the elevation of their colored countrymen." To read these letters was to see that the cause of freedom would surely prevail. Unfortunately, the end game was a long way off.

In the meantime, tensions around the abolitionist mailing campaigns had another effect. They raised questions in people's minds that had nothing to do with slavery and everything to do with the mail itself: If the states and the federal government could so easily institute postal censorship, was the sanctity and reliability of the postal system at risk? Some people thought it might be wise to turn to *private* letter carriers. Over the next two decades, in the prelude to war, the country would keep expanding. And as the mail service expanded with it, it became more of a business battleground than ever.

Round dater post-mark handstamp: New York City, New York, September 11, 2001.

Postmark handstamp: Naughright, New Jersey, May 31, 1888.

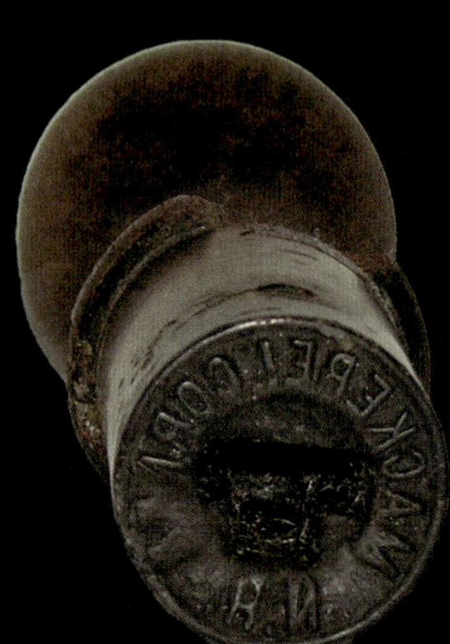

Postmark handstamp: Mackerel Corner, New Hampshire, 1840s–1850s.

Postmark handstamp used aboard the USS *Oklahoma*. The date reads December 6, 1941, one day prior to the attack on Pearl Harbor. It was retrieved from the sunken ship.

"Safety" slogan pictorial handstamp from the New Haven Safety Fair in Connecticut, October 6, 1985.

Pictorial postmark handstamp for the Branford Festival in Connecticut, June 14, 1988.

Postmark handstamp: Cleveland, Ohio, March 1, 1904. Made by the "Chambers Shop" in Lodge, Virginia.

Handstamp used by postal clerks to stamp the backs of envelopes, 1880–1913.

POSTMARK HANDSTAMPS

Often used interchangeably, the terms "postmark" and "cancellation" are not the same. A postmark–which indicates the origin, date, and time mail is received–is often used as a cancellation, but a cancellation–which is used to deface, or "kill," a stamp to prevent its reuse–is never used as a postmark. In the 20th century, both were used in tandem.

The earliest handstamps simply included a location and date. But by the 1840s, when stamps were introduced, handstamps became more uniform, with a location and year and interchangeable dates. As of December 4, 1894, the Post Office required that the time be added as well.

Many postmasters acquired commercially made stamps from the Post Office Department, while others tasked creative employees with designing stamps unique to their location. Early handstamps had printing surfaces carved from wood, although later versions used other materials, including cork, rubber, and different metals. There have even been postmark handstamps affixed to hammers–postal clerks thought the hammer motion felt more natural than a palm-held handstamp.

U
POST OFFICE
S
5
FIVE CENTS
5

U
POST OFFICE
S
X
FIVE CENTS
X

U
POST OFFICE
S
5
FIVE CENTS
5

S
X

AMERICAN MAIL GOES GLOBAL

In January 1845, a who's who of New Yorkers—politicians and private citizens alike—received an invitation to come see the "*new* post-office building." It was an old church. The Middle Collegiate Church was one of the oldest, if not *the* oldest, Christian congregations in the United States—old enough that the building in question, constructed in 1729, wasn't even its first sanctuary. The Nassau Street building down near the southern tip of Manhattan Island had been the church's home for more than a century, but the focal point of life in New York City had moved progressively farther north, so the church had followed suit, constructing a new building uptown. The New York Post Office, under the leadership of Postmaster John Lorimer Graham, saw in the vacated sanctuary a space that could accommodate New York City's ever-growing flow of mail. In 1844, he had leased the building and hired an architect and builder to turn it into a functioning post office.

The post office on Nassau Street—at its debut, and for most of its life—was a mishmash. It was still unmistakably a church, with the pulpit and religious ornamentations in place. (Luckily, the dead had been disinterred from the crypts beneath the building.) But it was also unmistakably a post office, one of great capacity. There were 15 general delivery windows and a separate window for newspapers.

New York City's secondhand post office was formerly a Middle Dutch Reform church put up for sale at $350,000; the Post Office Department offered $300,000, and local merchants covered the difference.

Yet its virtues as a post office could never quite win people over. At the time, it was part of a citywide trend of church buildings being converted to serve other purposes. New Yorkers didn't much care for this. Even more than a decade later, an 1871 issue of *Harper's New Monthly Magazine* would note that "perhaps no building could be invented more unsuited to the purposes to which it has been appropriated." And more important, people found that despite the windows upon windows for mail pickup, their letters took up to 16 hours to emerge. They wanted near-instant access—but there was simply too much mail passing through New York City.

In the month of July 1845 alone, clerks sorted 695,000 letters, plus more than two million newspapers. Part of the problem was that the increased mail volume—particularly overseas mail, as well as the local newspapers mailed to out-of-town subscribers—wasn't being offset by additional staff. In August 1846, the city's new postmaster, Robert H. Morris, reported that in a given 24-hour period he had just six newspaper-distributing clerks to handle more than 71,000 newspapers and pamphlets. Papers like the *New-York Tribune* even defended the post office's underperformance as a result of inadequate resources meeting surging mail volume.

In this way, New York City was a microcosm of the Post Office Department as a whole in the 1840s. Americans were writing more letters than ever before. In 1847, more than 124 million letters would pass through the department. There was so much material now traveling through post offices that the *Journal of Commerce* suggested that the Post Office Department could cut postage rates, still earn plenty of money, and in the process boost business interests and make life more convenient for the public. Indeed, the Post Office would focus on cost savings and innovation to make mail more affordable and more convenient.

But the new building in New York City was also a metaphor for the Post Office's attempts at that time to keep up with what *Harper's* called the voracious public's "absorbing interest in the living, active, and bustling world."

In addition, the structure was overrun with rats, and they were just as insatiable for what was *in* the mail as the public was for information. These were said to be tough old rats that could gnaw through thick leather mail pouches with ease, and when the Agriculture Bureau in Washington, D.C., began its annual mailing of choice seeds, the rats enjoyed a feast. They infested nearly every mailbag that contained seeds. To combat the great "Rat-ification," as *Harper's* called it, the Post Office Department sanctioned the use of a legion of postal cats. These four-legged carnivores became the guardians of the mail, given milk money and lodging at Uncle Sam's expense.

So it was, metaphorically, for the Post Office Department in the 1840s. Every day, like those seeds, came more mail. Then descended the rats, keeping the mail from getting to the people. Potholed postal roads. Graft on mail contracts. Robbers. New territories, with lots of new people but, as of yet, no reliable system of addresses. There was an endless tide of figurative rats, attracted to the explosive success of the mail.

An illustration in *Harper's* depicting the "Dutch-Church rats" hard at work infiltrating a leather mailbag and reading about choice seeds in the May 6 *Tribune*.

Ladies' Windows

One progressive feature of New York's Nassau Street Post Office was that it offered a separate window for ladies. This addition was well-received throughout the country. The February 26, 1845, edition of the Cadiz, Ohio, *Sentinel* marveled at this offering, informing its readers, "There is a *'Ladies' Window'* in the new New York post office. That's something like gallantry!" However, some thought such deference odd.

Visiting British novelist Anthony Trollope objected to this special treatment, writing in his 1862 travelogue, *North America*, "I confess that in the States I have sometimes been driven to think that chivalry has been carried too far; – that there is an attempt to make women think more of the rights of their womanhood than is nee'ful. There are ladies' doors at hotels, and ladies' drawing-rooms, ladies' sides on the ferry-boats, ladies' windows at the post office for the delivery of letters; – which, by-the-by, is an atrocious institution, as anybody may learn who will look at the advertisements called personal in some of the New York papers. Why should not young ladies have their letters sent to their houses, instead of getting one at a private window? The post-office clerks can tell some stories about those ladies' windows."

Left to right: A one-cent postage stamp of Henry Clay issued by Kochersperger & Co., Philadelphia, 1858; a Boyd's City Express two-cent stamp, circa 1845; a label from Pomeroy & Co.'s Express, New York, circa 1844.

In the 1840s, the Post Office Department spent lots of its time working on new solutions to the endless tide of problems—feeding and lodging cats, as it were. And as they fed those cats—better transportation, retooled postage rates, stamps, and more—the mail kept coming and coming.

★ ★ ★

Outright competition for the business of delivering mail emerged in the 1840s. In previous decades, there had been competition, but it consisted of pop-up businesses that were haphazard and that generally struggled to offer express delivery services on the same challenging routes that beguiled the Post Office Department. Not anymore. New for-profit competitors sprang up in every major urban market, intent on providing local mail services at or below what the Post Office charged. These rivals were able to offer low prices because they didn't have to bear the federal system's burden of paying to establish and maintain a long-distance transportation network across America's rugged terrain. All they had to do was provide cheap delivery in their limited, urbanized, *highly profitable* service areas—which they did, threatening the very viability of the nation's Post Office.

What these new mail companies were doing, essentially, was skimming the cream off the top of the nation's postal network, selecting the most valuable in- and inter-city service areas to operate in. So, unsurprisingly, one of the first arose in New York City. In February 1842, Alexander M. Greig and Henry Windsor established what they called the City Despatch Post. It offered better service than the local government post office, in part through the use of a secret weapon that hardly seems impressive today: stamps.

At the time, postage was collected when the recipient picked up their mail—risky for the Post Office. What if the person getting their letter couldn't pay? The City Despatch Post issued the first adhesive stamps on February 1, 1842. When attached to a letter, the stamp showed that the *sender* had already prepaid the three-cent delivery fee. This was five years before the United States issued its first official postage stamps. By July 1842, City Despatch carriers were delivering nearly twice as many local letters as the carriers for the New York Post Office.

The Post Office Department came to a simple conclusion: If you can't beat them, buy them. On August 17, 1842, New York City Postmaster Graham—who would go on to commence the ratification of the New York post—announced in the *New-York Tribune* that the Post Office Department would be buying the City Despatch. "The Postmaster General being desirous that all City Letters...should have the advantage of the most rapid delivery," he wrote, "has ordered that a United States City Despatch Post should be established with three deliveries each day." The Despatch Post was designated a separate operation of the New York City Post Office, and Graham was authorized to spend up to $1,200 to obtain furniture, pouches, and stamps for this new branch of service. A separate team of carriers was assigned to handle City Despatch letters independent from those assigned to the normal mail; Greig was the first appointed as a Despatch Post letter carrier.

Despite the fact that Graham had spared no expense, and despite its existing popularity as an independent business, the United States City Despatch Post wasn't well-received. Though people approved of the system itself—after all, they had been entrusting their letters to it for years—they found it poorly managed and not reliable enough. In 1845, the city ceased operations of the City Despatch.

Even as New York City's integration of the private carrier was failing, competition elsewhere was heating up. Other local carrier services operating around this time included A.W. Auner's Despatch Post in Philadelphia, Barker's City Post in Boston, Browne and Company's Post in Cincinnati, and Clark and Hall's Penny Post in St. Louis. Boston's Hale and Co., established in 1844, was among the Post Office's biggest competitors: The firm went beyond local coverage, focusing on city-to-city service over the most lucrative routes in New England and New York State, with service also to Philadelphia and Baltimore.

In New York City, the Post Office Department had been able to buy off its competitors. But on the national scale, that simply wasn't feasible. So instead, it used its sizable political clout to have them legislatively killed off. And the legislation that accomplished this would have huge ripple effects across the postal system.

★ ★ ★

An act of Congress passed on March 3, 1845—the last night of the administration of President John Tyler—offered the Post Office Department a rest, creating conditions that allowed it to operate better in an era of rapidly growing mail volume. Section 9 of the act established the Private Express Statutes, which gave the department a government monopoly on letter-mail service between cities, dispatching the City Despatch and its peers. It also offered an important update to how this service was handled that was designed to tackle the growing problem of transportation costs. (Importantly, the business of *package* delivery could still be taken up by anyone. That exception would have a profound effect on the Post Office Department's future, paving the way for competitors such as FedEx, UPS, and DHL—something we are all familiar with in the age of online shopping and two-day shipping, not all of it handled by the USPS.)

By mid-decade, more than two-thirds of the Post Office Department's budget was earmarked for transportation. One of the reasons costs were so high was that the department preferred to sign delivery contracts with stagecoach services—that is, services that used robust vehicles to carry both mail and passengers. But these were expensive and could be inefficient on certain routes. With the 1845 act, Congress abandoned its preference for stagecoaches. Instead, contracts were to be offered to the lowest bidder who could provide "the due celerity, certainty, and security of such transportation."

Left: A canceled six-cent stamp dated January 1, 1845, from Boston's Hale & Co., which originated its Independent Mail Service in December 1844.

Right: Alexander M. Greig's three-cent stamp, the first adhesive stamp used in the United States, was altered to reflect government ownership of the service.

Postage Stamps. Mr. White, the Postmaster in this City, has received a supply of stamps from the Department at Washington, to be used in prepaying postage on letters. These stamps will be found quite convenient to business men and others, who wish to pay the postage on their letters, as they can be attached to the letter and the letter dropped in the office at any time, without the necessity of requesting the P. M. to charge the postage, or of paying it on every letter in cash.

Between June and December 1850, the government issued about 3.6 million of the five-cent stamp from the 1847 die proofs featuring Benjamin Franklin and 892,000 of the 10-cent stamp featuring George Washington.

Postal clerks were required to write "celerity, certainty, and security" on contracts and in ledgers, a tiring task when it was repeated so frequently. As a result, in 1846, clerks started abbreviating the words by using a set of three stars (asterisks). Thus the routes became known as Star Routes. Per-mile costs on these routes dropped 38 percent, from 7.2 cents per mile to 4.5 cents per mile, as the mode of transport switched largely from stagecoach to horseback. But horseback wasn't the only method used on Star Routes; the designation would wind up being bestowed on many of the most historic, challenging, and spectacular routes in postal history, including sailing routes on Lake Erie, hovercraft routes in Alaska, and mule-train routes in the Grand Canyon.

At the same time the act was reducing transportation costs, it took a gamble on revenue, establishing a simple, more uniform system of postage rates that took effect on July 1. Whereas previously postage could work out to a wide variety of prices depending on the letter and the distance, the new system had just two pricing tiers for single letters: Those carried fewer than 300 miles were five cents; farther, 10 cents. Not only was this less complicated, but it was also much cheaper. Previously, a single letter sent more than 400 miles was 25 cents. At those rates, the average person could scarcely afford to mail a thing. The new rates made mail more accessible to everyday Americans. Indeed, with lower prices, the Post Office Department grew in popularity. By 1848, revenues equaled expenses.

Though the 1845 law would retool postage rates, it failed to give the postmaster general the authority to issue postage stamps. But with postage now simple, predictable, and affordable, stamps were even more appealing to use than when Greig's City Despatch Post was issuing them. So local postmasters, starting with Robert H. Morris of New York City, asked for permission to issue "stopgap" provisional postage stamps. Permission was granted to Morris, as well as to 10 other local postmasters. The stamps were a hit with the public. In 1847, the *North-Carolina Standard* of Raleigh summed up the benefits of stamps: "These...will be found quite convenient for business men [*sic*] and others...as they can be attached to the letter and the letter dropped off in the office at any time, without the necessity of requesting the P.M. to charge the postage, of paying it on every letter in cash."

The most widely used of these "postmaster provisional" stamps—which today are highly sought-after collector's items—was the first, from New York, designed to honor George Washington. The five-cent stamp used a printing die of Washington originally made for bank notes. It was a timeless design created by Asher B. Durand, a well-known American landscape painter who was a cofounder of the influential Hudson River School of artists and the founder of the National Academy of Design—copied from a famous unfinished portrait by Gilbert Stuart, the most prolific portrait painter of Washington. The stamps were printed by the firm Rawdon, Wright, Hatch & Edson.

Two years later, Congress finally gave the postmaster general the authority to issue stamps on behalf of the federal government. Under U.S. Postmaster General Cave Johnson's leadership, a 10-cent design and a five-cent design were provisioned. It was decided that the former should honor George Washington, the father of the nation. Rawdon, Wright, Hatch & Edson's craftmanship on the New York postmaster provisional was so highly regarded that the firm was given the federal printing job without even having to go through a bidding process. It also printed the five-cent stamp, which, according to the powers that be, ought to feature the father of the postal system.

A letter dated March 20, 1847, to William Brown, Second Assistant Postmaster General, from Rawdon, Wright, Hatch & Edson, who were under contract to design and produce the first postage stamps. While the Post Office had requested a five-cent stamp featuring Andrew Jackson, they changed it to a five-cent Benjamin Franklin stamp. They were so certain of approval that they were already "executing steel dies" in order to meet the timeline.

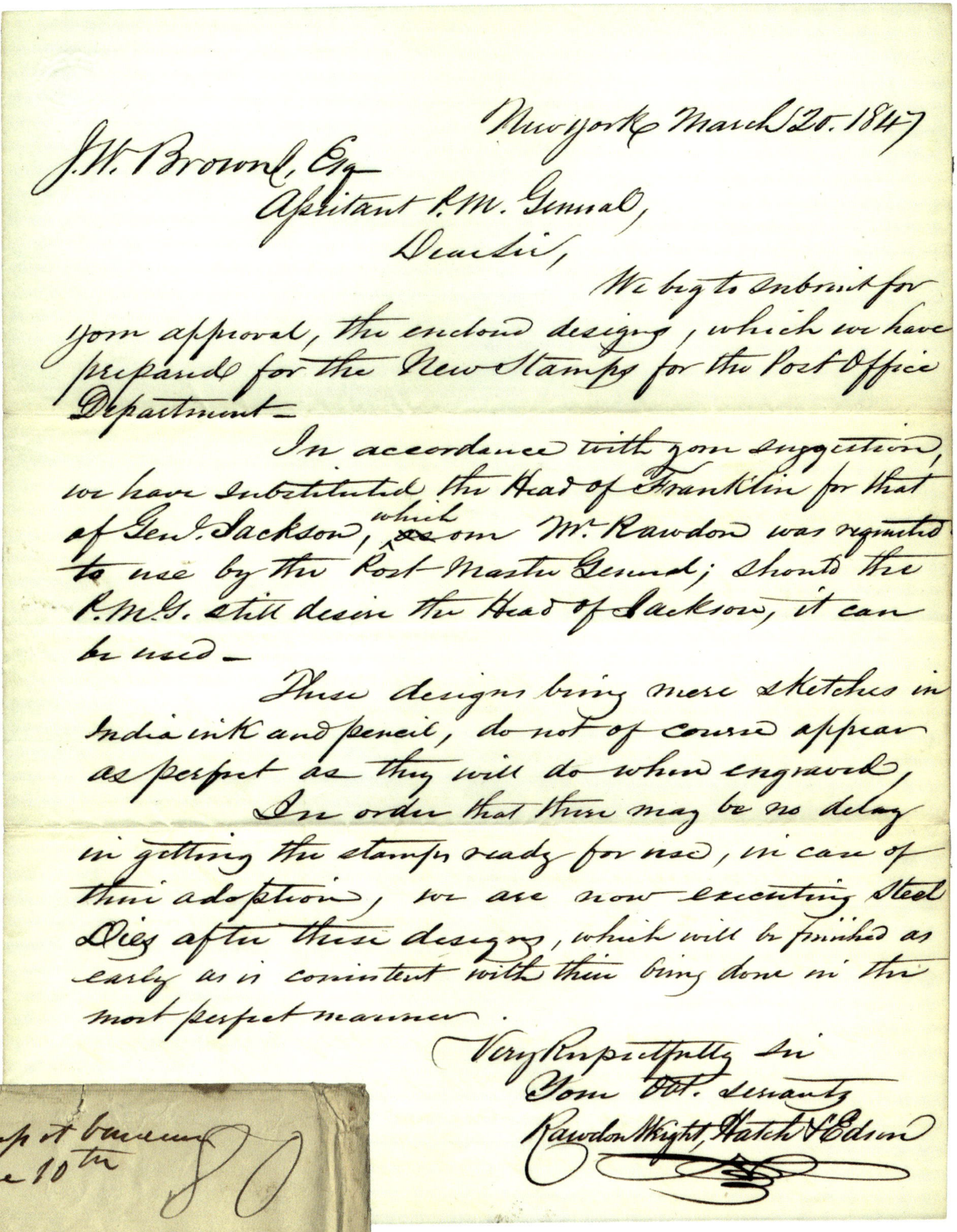

New York March 20. 1847

J.W. Brown, Esq
Assistant P.M. General,
Dear Sir,

We beg to submit for your approval, the enclosed designs, which we have prepared for the New Stamps for the Post Office Department—

In accordance with your suggestion, we have substituted the Head of Franklin for that of Genl. Jackson, which Mr. Rawdon was requested to use by the Post Master General; should the P.M.G. still desire the Head of Jackson, it can be used—

These designs being mere sketches in India ink and pencil, do not of course appear as perfect as they will do when engraved.

In order that there may be no delay in getting the stamps ready for use, in case of their adoption, we are now executing Steel Dies after these designs, which will be finished as early as is consistent with their being done in the most perfect manner.

Very Respectfully Sir
Your obt. servants
Rawdon Wright, Hatch & Edson

SAN FRANCISCO
June 20
June 10th
80
Mrs. Adelaide Talbot.
Washington City.
D. C.

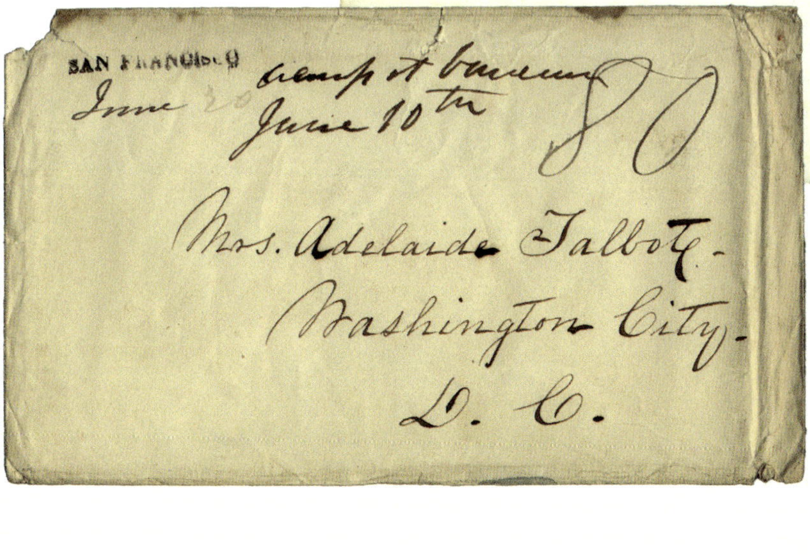

This letter was mailed from San Francisco to Washington City in 1849 with a double letter postage rate of 80 cents, as approved per a new act signed on August 14, 1848.

A Rare Postmaster's Provisional Cover

This cover (envelope) is called the Alexandria "Blue Boy" because it includes a five-cent Alexandria, Virginia, postmaster provisional stamp, mailed in 1847. It is postmarked on the left "Alexandria D.C. Nov. 25."

A "provisional cover" refers to an envelope or piece of mail that was prepared and sold by a postmaster in advance of the actual mailing, often featuring stamps or markings indicating postage paid. One of the most renowned provisionals was the Alexandria Provisional, known as the Alexandria "Blue Boy." It was found by 12-year-old Jannett Fawcett in an old sewing box in the attic of her impoverished family's home among a bundle of love letters between her grandparents. While other examples of the Alexandria Provisional are printed in black on buff paper, this example is on bluish-gray paper. The letter, written by James Wallace Hooff to Miss Jannett Hooff Brown, was mailed on November 25, 1847. The clandestine lovers were cousins with different religions, and their families opposed their affections. In this letter, James admonished his beloved to "burn as usual." Luckily, it remained unscathed. The couple married in 1853. Ultimately, the item was privately sold to renowned Cleveland philatelist George H. Worthington in December 1907 for roughly $3,000, minus a 5 percent commission. It sold again in 1917, when the Worthington Collection was broken up to pay Worthington's debts upon his death. It was acquired at a private sale by Henry C. Gibson of Philadelphia, and in 1922 it was purchased by Alfred H. Caspary.

A five-cent Alexandria Post Office postmaster provisional from 1846–1847.

J. Murray Bartels wrote the first history of the Blue Boy in the 1923 edition of *Collectors Club Philatelist* (Vol. 2, No. 1). He noted that after the sale of the cover to Mr. Worthington, "…newspaper articles invented stories about the money furnishing a trousseau for Mrs. Fawcett's daughter and other fanciful tales."

The Blue Boy has sold several times since: by auction in 1955 and 1967, by private transaction on an unknown date, and finally in 1981 for more than $1 million.

Above: A clipper-ship advertising card for the steamship *California*.

Below: A lithograph of the *California* flying the American flag. The ship was built and launched in 1848 and was operated by the Pacific Mail Steamship Company.

So Benjamin Franklin made yet another appearance in the story of American mail.

As stamps and Star Routes proliferated on the home front, mail bound to and from far-flung international locales was quickly becoming another significant aspect of the expansion of the mail system in the 1840s. The 1845 act presciently included provisions requiring the Post Office Department contract with American companies for international delivery, which was a huge business. In 1846, about a million letters flowed into New York City annually from overseas, and three million more were postmarked from there to Europe. The majority of these letters were business correspondence pertaining to imports and exports, principally for tobacco and cotton. Major foreign ports included Bremen, Germany; Havre, France; and Liverpool, England.

Another important foreign port was Chagres, Panama. Mail was shipped down the East Coast of the United States, eventually making its way to Chagres, where it would be carried over land to another ship waiting on the Pacific side of the continent, which would then deliver to ports on the Pacific Coast. And on that coast, perhaps the most important foreign destination was one that would, soon enough, be American.

★ ★ ★

On January 24, 1848, a man named James Marshall inspected a sawmill he was building in the Sierra Nevada mountains of present-day California—then Mexican territory—for his employer, a Swiss immigrant named John Sutter. The night before, he'd diverted water through the mill, and on the morning in question, he saw something shiny where loose dirt and gravel had been washed away. "I reached my hand down and picked it up; it made my heart thump, for I was certain it was gold," he would later say. This small moment in the unassuming foothills of Mexico kicked off what is considered the largest migration in American history. The Mexican-American War had been raging in the region, with California highly contested. Within months, the Treaty of Guadalupe Hidalgo, which ended the war, would make California a territory of the United States of America. The non-Indigenous population of California the day of Marshall's find was roughly 14,000. By the end of 1849, it would be nearly 100,000.

A newspaper article dated April 21, 1849, from the *Boston Evening Transcript*, announced the nearly two tons of mail bound for California aboard the ship *Falcon*. There were 226 ships sailing around Cape Horn for California at the time and another 83 headed for other locations.

CALIFORNIA. We learn from the New York Express that the California mail bags, per Falcon, weigh nearly two tons. Since the gold excitement commenced, up to the 17th inst, there have left the different ports in the United States for San Francisco, &c. three hundred and nine vessels—two hundred and twenty six of which intended proceeding around Cape Horn, and through the Straits of Magellan; about fifty for Chagres, and the remainder to Vera Cruz, Brazos, &c. These vessels took out an aggregate of nearly twenty thousand passengers.

In a matter of months, San Francisco went from a small hamlet to a raucous hotbed of 25,000 transplants from around the world.

The California Gold Rush was on.

And with it came another rush—a mail rush—and another challenge for the post office.

An estimated 90,000 people flooded the goldfields by 1850, the year California became a state. Nearly all demanded mail. The so-called "forty-niners," named for the year the flow of people west truly became a deluge, sent letters back and forth with the families they left at home, some on the East Coast, others overseas.

In a matter of months, San Francisco went from a small hamlet to a raucous hotbed of 25,000 transplants from around the world. As the population swelled, receiving a letter became a chore. Upon the arrival of a steamship with any letters, the post office closed for two or more days to put up the mail. When it finally reopened, people checking for mail queued up beginning at four in the morning and often took four to six hours to reach the window, which was manned by only a pair of clerks. Spots near the head of the line were held and sold for $5, $10, or $20 depending upon the distance to the window. And yet the miners had no way of knowing whether a letter had even been sent to them. Often, despite the long wait of elbowing, swearing, and jamming, patrons came away empty-handed.

The gold, the new territory, and the new Californians were all incredibly valuable to the nation. Congress was anxious to ensure gold-rushers could easily correspond. On August 14, 1848, when California was still a territory, Congress voted to extend all the benefits of the Post Office to the people there. The new provisions would establish post offices in California, make temporary arrangements for transportation of its mail, and set postage rates.

But Congress failed to anticipate the challenges of delivering mail to the West Coast, a far-off land that lay 3,000 miles of rugged terrain away, or even farther by sea. A land that didn't even have post roads yet. The pay for supplying service out west was calculated based upon eastern expenses, which quickly proved untenable. The high costs of transporting goods west were reflected in the prices of essentials. Flour at San Francisco cost $31 per barrel, pork $41 per barrel, cornmeal $9 per 100 pounds, eggs $1 to $3 per egg. Sugar, tea, and coffee were $4 per pound. Butter was 50 cents per pound. A pair of pants cost $20, while coats and boots each went for $30. Meanwhile, mailing a single-page letter from San Francisco to the East Coast cost only 40 cents.

The high costs made it hard to keep postmasters, too. In August 1848, Postmaster General Cave Johnson installed them in several California cities, including Sacramento, Stockton, Monterey, San Jose, and, most important, San Francisco. By October, San Francisco was already on its fourth postmaster, Samuel Y. Atlee. He quit shortly after being appointed, when his living expenses exceeded his pay. (Sometimes it was politics, not money, that made the office a revolving door in a place as important as San Francisco: In February 1849, President James K. Polk appointed war hero Colonel John W. Geary to the job; by May, he was out, likely because he opposed Zachary

Right: An illustration titled *Scene at the San Francisco Post Office showing how we get our letters* from a publication by Leland & McCombe.

The first San Francisco Post Office opened on November 9, 1848, at the corner of Clay and Pike streets. When mail steamships docked, citizens would line up for the 7:00 a.m. post-office opening. General delivery for letters and box delivery took place at the front of the building, while newspapers were picked up on the right-hand side.

Taylor, who had been inaugurated as president in March.)

Deliveries were erratic. "Can somebody tell us what has become of the U.S. mail for this section of the world?" asked the *Los Angeles Star* in 1853. "Some four weeks since it has arrived here. The mail rider comes and goes regularly enough, but the mailbags do not." The Sacramento *Placer Times* of November 3, 1849, called the conditions "certainly one of the most outrageous grievances that ever any people suffered, to be so long deprived of the receipt of regular mails from the United States."

The population kept growing, and the mail kept coming. In July 1850, the New York City Post Office dispatched 39,524 letters to California and received 40,500 in return. In September 1850, The *Alta California* estimated the rapidly growing population of California included 13,000 Californians, 62,000 Americans, and 18,500 foreigners. Those living in Los Angeles received important news in October: California had been granted statehood. Very exciting news indeed—but it was old news. California had become a state on September 9, 1850, and thanks to slow mail, word had come six weeks late.

POSTMASTERS' PROVISIONALS AND CITY STAMPS

Until the government issued the first official nationwide stamps on July 1, 1847, the payment standards for letter mail were anything but structured. Richard H. Morris, postmaster of New York City, changed this when he requested permission of then-Postmaster General Cave Johnson to issue postage stamps to prepay for mailing and delivering letters. His request was approved, and a few other city postmasters followed suit, as did all the local competition to the Post Office Department, issuing their own stamps to ensure payment up front.

This five-cent George Washington postmaster provisional by the New York postmaster was used between 1845 and 1846. It was canceled in red ink with the initials of postal clerk Alonzo Castle Monson.

In 1845, John M. Wimer, the postmaster of St. Louis, created the "Bear" provisional, which featured two bears surrounding the Missouri Coat of Arms and Great Seal.

Adams & Co's Express depicted the head of operations D. H. Haskell on this stamp for use in California. It was nicknamed the "Poker Chip," as it is believed that it was meant to be used as money rather than as a stamp.

The Striding Messenger was the symbol for D. O. Blood & Co.'s local two-cent stamp from 1847. Its motto was:

Thro' Blood's the passage,
The only way

To send a message
Three times a day.

Envelope with a local red and white Eagle Post stamp that includes a fancy cancellation. The stamp reads "at Adams' Express and 48 So 3rd."

A Providence, Rhode Island, postmaster printed sheet of 12 five-cent stamps from 1946. This stamp would have covered the cost of a half-ounce letter delivered less than 300 miles.

A very rare five-cent postmaster provisional from Millbury, Massachusetts, which was headed by Asa Holman Waters, the Millbury postmaster from 1836 to 1848.

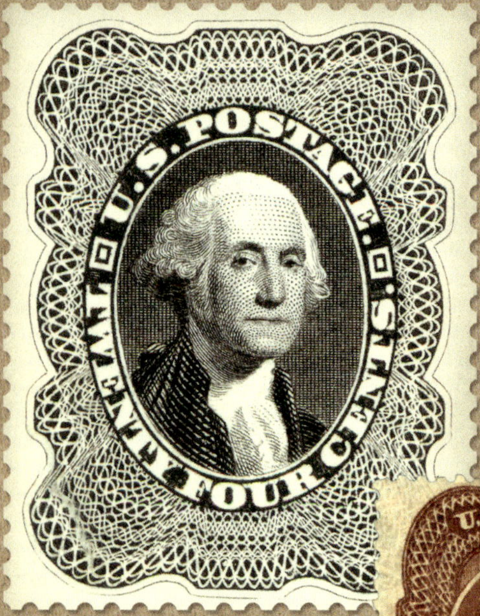
U.S. POSTAGE
TWENTY FOUR CENTS

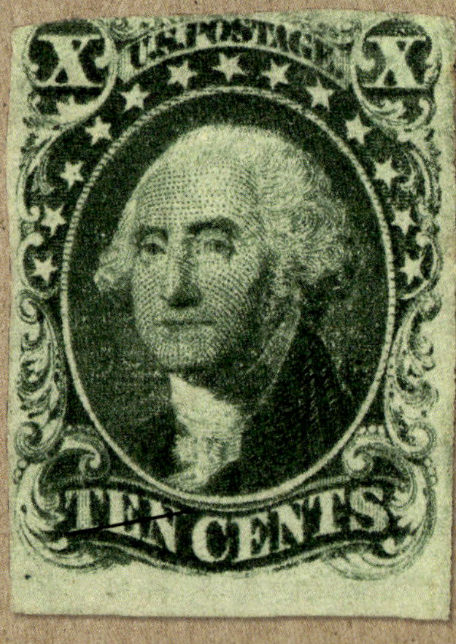

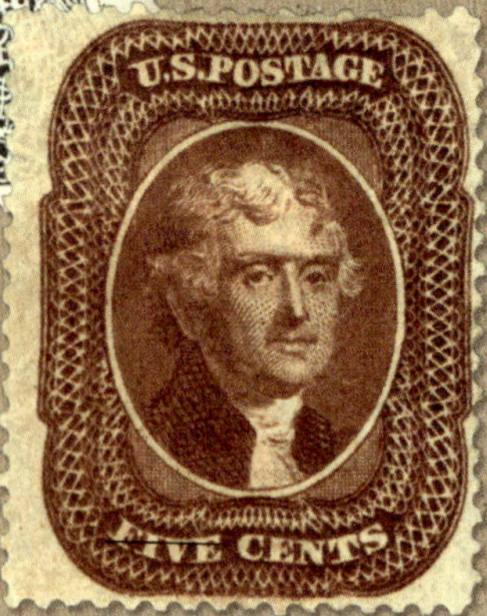
U.S.POSTAGE
FIVE CENTS

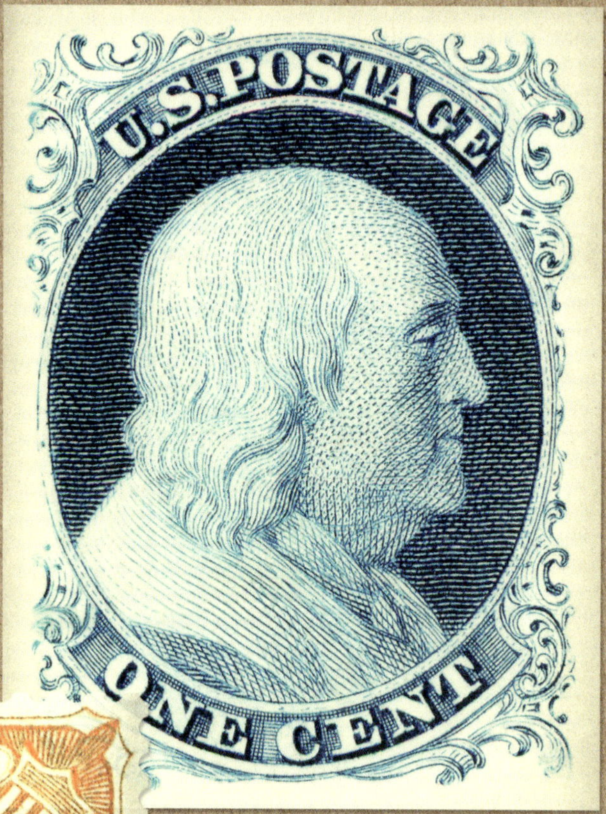
U.S.POSTAGE
ONE CENT

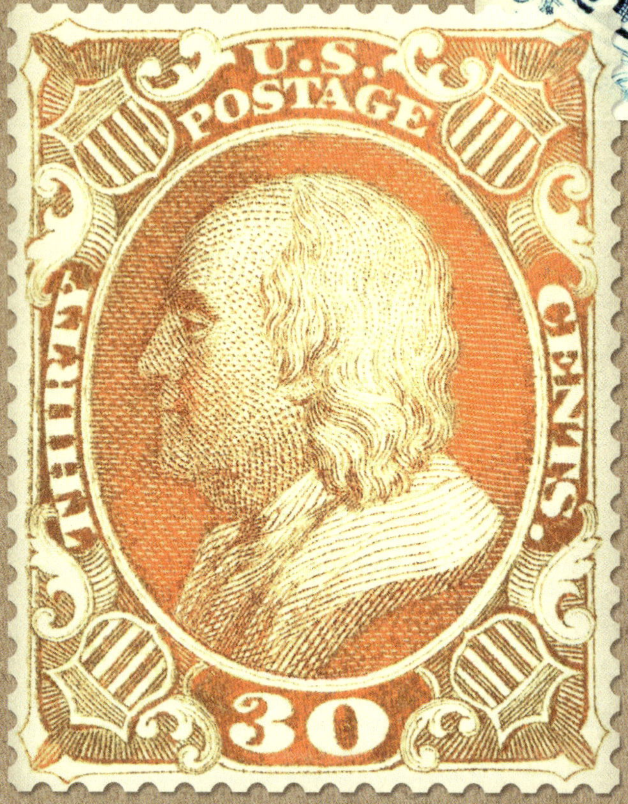
U.S.
POSTAGE
THIRTY
CENTS
30

X
U.S.POSTAGE
X
TEN CENTS

THE PROBLEM OF THE WEST

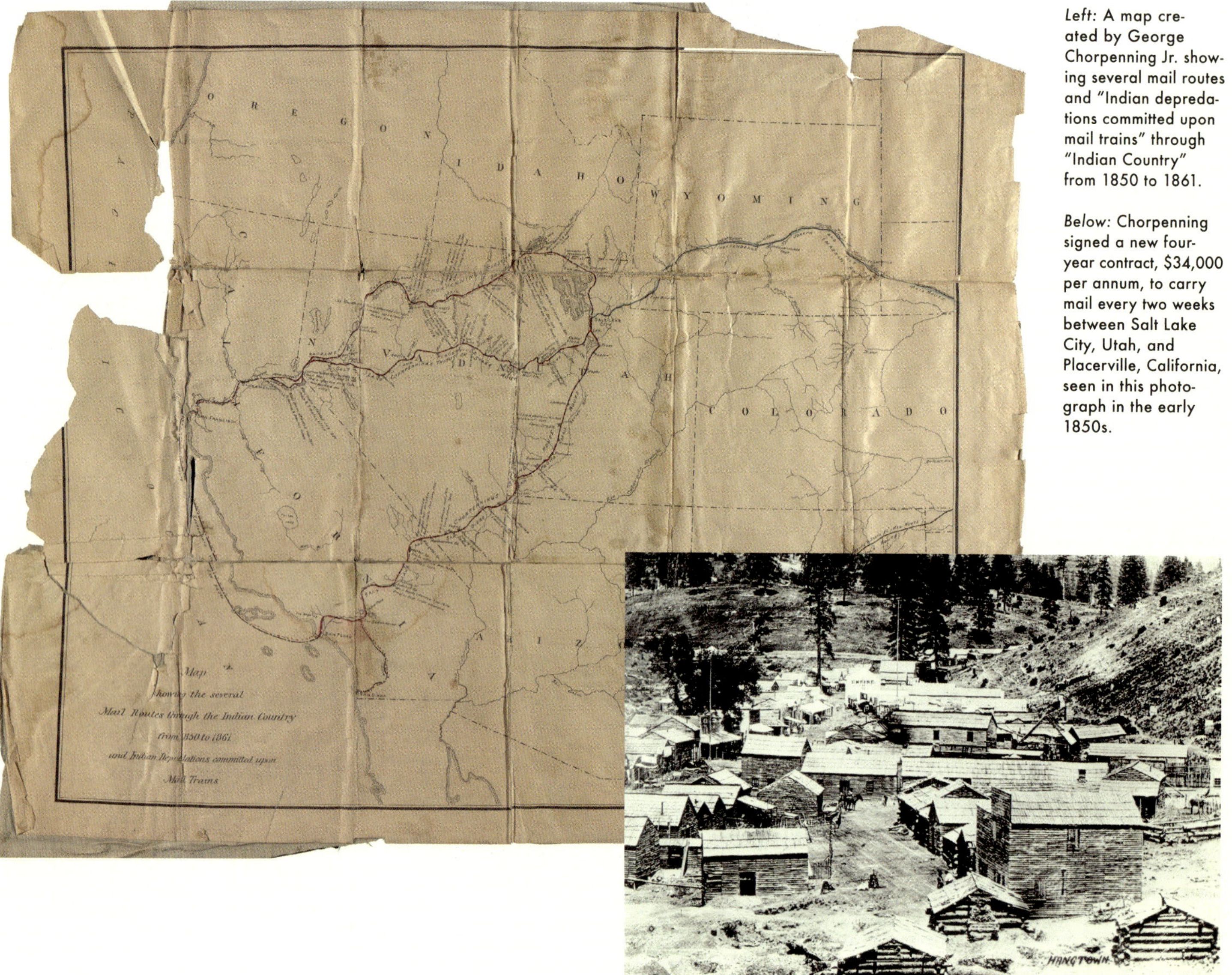

Left: A map created by George Chorpenning Jr. showing several mail routes and "Indian depredations committed upon mail trains" through "Indian Country" from 1850 to 1861.

Below: Chorpenning signed a new four-year contract, $34,000 per annum, to carry mail every two weeks between Salt Lake City, Utah, and Placerville, California, seen in this photograph in the early 1850s.

With the California Gold Rush driving a population boom on the country's new frontier, the federal government knew it needed a better way to get mail out west. Trips down to Panama, across the isthmus, and back up the Pacific Coast simply took too long.

In April 1851, U.S. Postmaster General Nathan K. Hall contracted with two Pennsylvania natives, Absalom Woodward and George Chorpenning Jr., to run the first overland mail route to the West. It was a baby step: It began with 200 pounds of mail being picked up in Sacramento in May and didn't run across the whole country but simply to Salt Lake City. Still, it would be treacherous, in terms of both the struggles they faced and the steps they took year by year to overcome them, Woodward and Chorpenning would offer a microcosm of the Post Office's story in the 1850s—one of hard-fought expansion to bring its services to the country's newest, and in some ways most important, lands.

According to the contract, Woodward and Chorpenning would leave each destination at 6:00 a.m. on the first of the month and arrive at the destination 30 days later. On an early eastbound trip, Woodward was attacked by American Indians. But he was able to outrun them and successfully deliver the mail. On later trips, his party was regularly ambushed; some mail carriers were killed. Then, in mid-November, a Woodward-led group left on a run from California to Salt Lake City and were never seen alive again. Woodward's body was found in northern Utah the following spring.

Chorpenning fared better—that is, he survived—but it would be a stretch to say that he fared well. Snow in the Sierra Nevada mountains in the winter was a huge problem. The journey took considerably longer than the 30 days the contract allotted. He struggled to find men to work with him or even to subcontract out the route. In the winter of 1852, in order to avoid the snowy passage through the Sierras, he shifted to a southern route: He sent mail down the coast to San Pedro, near Los Angeles, and from there overland to Salt Lake City on a road known as the Mormon Trail. The route worked better, but by then Chorpenning had other problems. The complaints his service was getting due to delays and mail lost en route led Postmaster General Samuel D. Hubbard to cancel the contract and award it to someone else. Chorpenning had to travel all the way to Washington, D.C., to get it reinstated. He kept the contract until 1854, when it ended.

Then he signed another four-year contract, and another after that, in 1858. He hired an experienced Norwegian skier named John A. "Snowshoe" Thompson to ensure mail made it through the mountains, and he adopted a shorter, more efficient new route in between the original northern route and the southern trek of the Mormon Trail. His pay increased dramatically. Challenges with weather, Indian attacks, and personnel never went away, but things were looking up—enough that in 1858 he cooked up a stunt to earn the overland mail some positive publicity.

At the end of that year, Chorpenning made arrangements with the carriers who brought mail into Salt Lake City to transport President James Buchanan's State of the Union address, given on December 6, to the West Coast as quickly as possible. They ran this express delivery in just 17 days.

But as happened repeatedly throughout the history of the Post Office, Chorpenning's success bred competition. People vying for his contract used underhanded tactics, spreading rumors and innuendo in the newspapers that the mail delivery was not being done properly, and that bills were not being paid. If the latter was true—and it may have been—it was actually Congress' fault, as it didn't approve Post Office appropriations in 1859, leaving postmasters without the funds to pay contracts. Nevertheless, the tactics worked. In 1860, Chorpenning was fired from his contract. It went instead to a man named William Russell, who was a partner in a series of larger enterprises, including the Central Overland California and Pike's Peak Express Company. At least one historian thinks that Russell and the Central Overland took possession not only of Chorpenning's contract but also of one of his ideas: The express route that took Buchanan's words to the country's western reaches in just 17 days may have inspired one of their routes. It would come to be known as the Pony Express.

★ ★ ★

The American population was in the throes of significant change in the 1850s. Immigrant city dwellers, runaway and former slaves, and tenant farmers were all struggling to make a living. As of 1849, they had a new and appealing option that was better than what was presented to them in the oldest part of the country: They could go west and seek their fortune. The California Gold Rush had put a new part of the country on the map, figuratively and literally. It solidified the California region as an integral part of the United States, helping it reach statehood before much of the Midwest, and in many ways, it single-handedly created San Francisco, Stockton, and Sacramento. It also created a problem for the mail. Steamship lines did the best they could, but they took a month to get from coast to coast, and they didn't have set departure or arrival schedules. With the West Coast as a new center of gravity for the country,

John A. "Snowshoe" Thompson, a native of Norway, used about 10-foot-long Norwegian skis, with one pole carried in both hands, for his mail route from Placerville, California, to Genoa, Nevada, and later Virginia City, Nevada.

On October 28, 1858, *Frank Leslie's Illustrated Newspaper* published a drawing of the overland mail on its first ride from the east, driven by John Butterfield Jr.

the Post Office Department needed to institute regularly scheduled mail service across the nation.

There was no shortage of ideas for how to do this. Hot-air balloons were becoming a fad in the 1850s, so a pianoforte maker and balloon hobbyist named John Wise launched a campaign for an early form of airmail, to little success. When the country had first begun expanding farther into desert terrain in the 1830s, U.S. Army Second Lieutenant George H. Crosman and his friend E. F. Miller had proposed the military turn to camels rather than horses for military transport, and some were turned over to the Post Office Department to deliver mail in the Southwest. It did not go well.

The dream option was, of course, the railroads. Trains could carry a seemingly infinite tonnage of mail and move it quickly, and indeed they did—east of the Mississippi River. The Great Southern Railway line claimed it could convey passengers and mail from New York City to New Orleans in four days and 17 hours, a distance of 1,285 miles. The Pittsburgh, Fort Wayne and Chicago Railroad, in conjunction with the Pennsylvania Central Railroad, maintained that it was the "shortest, quickest and most reliable route" from Philadelphia to Pittsburgh, covering the distance in six hours with only one change of cars. And the New York and Erie Railroad claimed to be the "great direct route to the western and southern states and the Canadas." But west of the Mississippi, there weren't yet rail options.

And so overland mail lines were born. These routes, traditionally served by stagecoaches, carried mail on long-distance trails through the kind of treacherous terrain that gave Absalom Woodward and George Chorpenning Jr. such trouble. There were three primary routes established over the course of the 1850s, and each had something to say about the state of mail—and about the state of the nation.

The first route was Woodward and Chorpenning's. It covered only the final third of the journey from coast to coast, yet was so challenging that it took the full decade to reach a level of predictability that the mail would need. It took a decade—but the mail persevered.

The second route arrived in 1857. Congress contracted with James Birch, who had previously been the president of a successful stage company, to carry mail along a far southern route. It began in San Antonio, which received mail from points east via New Orleans, and traversed present-day Texas, New Mexico, and Arizona to reach San Diego. On its first run, the nearly 1,500-mile route took almost two months to travel. Birch and his partner, Isaiah Woods, faced every imaginable hurdle. They had a hard time finding the number of pack mules they needed. The stagecoaches they had purchased for the route proved too heavy for the animals they *could* find. Indians attacked. Woods traveled with the mail on the inaugural trip to San Francisco, where he was to meet Birch—but when he arrived, Birch had already departed, via ship, to head back to the East Coast.

Birch's ship sank.

Birch perished.

In a cruel but fitting detail, it took two months for Woods to learn of his partner's death. He continued operating the line for a few more months before handing it off to someone else.

The San Antonio–San Diego line might have been a winner, if only because the southern route avoided the brutally difficult mountain passages and heavy snows that had made Woodward and Chorpenning's task nearly insurmountable. But as the Post Office Department would learn over and over, expanding the country's mail network wasn't just about appropriating money for new routes—it was also about hiring smart, capable, persistent, and professional people to operate them. Birch and Woods failed to meet those criteria. Though the route improved over time—the run eventually started to come in under one month—it was inconvenient for passengers, a long journey with few developed way stations along the route. In part because of the mules it relied on, but also because of these inconveniences, the route was forever known as the "Jackass Line." Congress would continue to search for alternatives.

In 1857, it awarded a contract to John Butterfield, whose overland route would share some of its path with the Jackass Line. This Star Route contract represented the longest route in the country, spanning 2,585 miles. The six-year, $600,000 annual postal contract took effect on September 16, 1858, with the promise that the mail was to be delivered within 25 days at either terminus station. Butterfield, who was the only bidder vying to secure the lengthy mail route, had a word of advice for his 800 employees at the Overland Company: "Remember boys, nothing on God's earth must stop the U.S. Mail."

This mandate guided the operation of the stage line, which was certainly designed more for the mail than for the passengers. It was an immense undertaking to create and maintain the Overland Company's route. Relay stations had to be built, wells dug, and corrals for horses created. The route required roughly 200 relay stations, spaced 20 miles apart. At each station, a well-choreographed switch took place: Usually, four men unharnessed the old team, while four others hitched the fresh horses or mules. It took a matter of minutes, with the new team typically said to be in place before the coach stopped rocking from its arrival.

This was by far the most impressive aspect of the stations. The earliest relay stations were spartan. Sir Richard Francis Burton, a British explorer who traveled on five continents, visited the American West in 1860. He described a relay station as "roofless and chairless [*sic*], filthy and squalid, with a smoky fire in one corner, and a

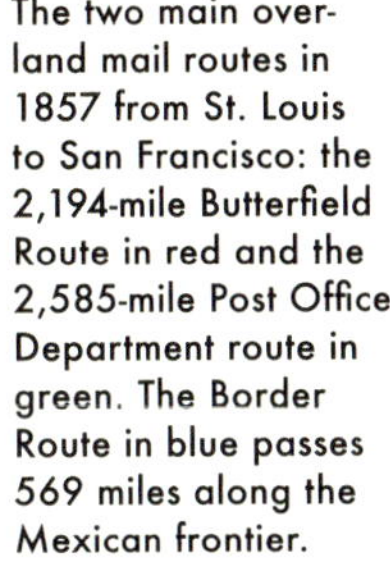

The two main overland mail routes in 1857 from St. Louis to San Francisco: the 2,194-mile Butterfield Route in red and the 2,585-mile Post Office Department route in green. The Border Route in blue passes 569 miles along the Mexican frontier.

Mail by Camel?

While John Wise attempted to fly the mail from Lafayette, Indiana, in hot-air balloons, camels were used to carry mail in the American Southwest, ambling along at about five miles an hour. The camel experiment actually began in 1836, when Second Lieutenant George H. Crosman of the U.S. Army and his friend E. F. Miller of Ipswich, Massachusetts, pitched a madcap idea to Washington bureaucrats. The gist was that the best way to deal with the environmental conditions of the Midwest and the South was to employ camels. They stated:

> *For strength in carrying burdens, for patient endurance of labor, and privation of food, water & rest, and in some respects speed also, the camel and dromedary (as the Arabian camel is called) are unrivaled among animals. The ordinary loads for camels are from seven to nine hundred pounds each, and with these they can travel from thirty to forty miles a day, for many days in succession. They will go without water, and with but little food, for six or eight days, or it is said even longer. Their feet are alike well suited for traversing grassy or sandy plains, or rough, rocky hills and paths, and they require no shoeing.*

This idea fell on deaf ears until 1848, when Jefferson Davis heard about it from Army Major Henry C. Wayne. No one in Washington gave this notion any credibility until Davis became secretary of war, and then he ran with it.

Davis believed that camels were the answer to transporting supplies to desert military facilities. In December 1854, Congress backed Davis's plan, approving $30,000 for the initiative. Wayne was assigned to obtain the animals, while Navy Lieutenant David Dixon Porter was ordered to transport them to Texas by naval warship, but it wasn't clear where the camels would come from. Wayne and Porter first approached the Bey of Tunis to acquire suitable camels, but he was willing to provide only a pair as a gift. Frustrated, the two next sailed to Turkey, where they appealed to the sultan. He was willing to oblige, but the camels he offered were Asiatic, which were considered unsuitable for use in the American Southwest. Undaunted, they sailed to Alexandria, Egypt, where they successfully acquired nine dromedaries, along with the camel pair from the Bey of Tunis. Additional animals were purchased at local bazaars at prices ranging from $100 to $400 per animal. On February 15, 1856, 33 camels and nine dromedaries set sail for the United States, arriving safely in Indianola, Texas, three months later. The initial herd was moved to San Antonio, where they were placed in service. Based upon the beasts' capabilities, Porter was dispatched to acquire additional camels. His second trip netted 41 more animals.

The Camel Corps was principally used for transporting water and supplies to military forts and for long-range scouting missions. Jefferson Davis's successor, John B. Floyd, urged Congress to increase the camel contingent to 1,000 animals: "The experiment thus far made, and they are pretty full, demonstrate that camels constitute a most useful and economic means of transportation for men and supplies through the great deserts and barren portions of our interior," he wrote. Despite Floyd's glowing summary of their service, only 45 of the original camels had survived. Congress rejected his appeal for more.

Indeed, not everyone agreed with Floyd's positive assessment, especially after about 28 of the remaining camels were turned over to the Post Office Department to transport mail, including service between Fort Mohave, New Mexico, and New San Pedro, California. Many of the post-office handlers despised the animals. The camels spat, bit, and kicked their postal handlers, who swore the creatures held grudges and relished dispensing payback whenever a back was turned, often biting the backs of the riders' heads or nipping away at loose clothing. Unlike the gallop of a horse, the camels' looping gait gave some riders motion sickness.

The arrangement wasn't easy for the animals either. The terrain of the American Southwest was rockier than the deserts of Africa, and the camels' hooves were prone to injury. Another problem was that camels caused stampedes. "You ought to see our old worn-out pack mules and team mules when we met the camels," recalled Captain William H. Hardy in March 1893. "Whew! Their heads and tails were up, although they were tired and worn out …near Soda Lake it did not take three minutes for every mule to clear itself from saddle and harness, and if there ever was whistling, snorting, and prancing notwithstanding the loud cry of the teamsters and herders we had it then."

By the 1860s, the camel mail experiment had begun to wane. The animals were sold off or simply let go to fend for themselves in the desert. Some of them went to circuses. The last surviving camel was believed to have been captured in the desert around Tucson, Arizona, in 1927. The Smithsonian's National Museum of Natural History preserves the skeleton of one of the original mail camels.

table in the corner of an impure floor, the walls open to every wind, and the interior full of dust."

The food was bad, too—unless you were an animal. Mules and horses ate better than the people they pulled. The typical relay station required 50 to 100 tons of hay each year, at $43 per ton; even so, the price didn't deter them. Food for passengers, on the other hand, was scraped together by the employees looking after the animals. It ranged from awful to inedible. Mark Twain, who described adventures in the West in his 1872 book *Roughing It*, was pitiless in describing the food. A typical breakfast consisted of "last week's bread...condemned army bacon...a beverage which pretended to be tea, but there was too much dishrag, and sand, and old bacon-rind in it to deceive the intelligent traveler," he wrote. There was no sugar or milk for the faux tea. But then there were no utensils with which to stir it in, either.

Fortunately, passengers didn't need to stay at relay stations for long. Unfortunately, time in the stagecoaches wasn't usually much better. They varied wildly in ride quality, with the standard being that they would lack it. A high-end Concord-style coach wasn't plush comfort, but it was a work of art, built by the finest craftsmen of the day. Most passengers rode in what were called "celerity wagons" or "mud wagons." Assigned to cover the beginning of overland mail service, *The New York Herald* reporter Waterman L. Ormsby deemed the inaugural westbound trip immensely painful. "Had I not just come out over the route, I would be perfectly willing to go back," he wrote. "But I know what Hell is like. I've just had 24 days of it." Twain, of course, spared no detail in his description of an experience a beleaguered air traveler today might recognize. "A through-ticket and 15 inches of seat, with a fat man on one side, a poor widow on the other, a baby in your lap, a bandbox over your head, and three or four more persons immediately in front, leaning against your knees," he wrote in *Roughing It*. On another journey, his

An illustration of "The South Pass" from the 1873 edition of Mark Twain's book *Roughing It*, first published in 1872. Twain described just leaving South Pass City, where he met the local postmaster (who was also the blacksmith, hotel-keeper, mayor, constable, city marshal, property owner, and principal citizen).

This mural by Frank Albert Mechau Jr. titled *Pony Express* was painted within the Ariel Rios Federal Building in Washington, D.C., in 1937. It depicts Pony Express riders changing horses.

So this was America in the 1850s: rough and ready at best, but making advances even in its sleep.

coach was full of 2,700 pounds of mail: "Almost touching our knees, a perpendicular wall of mail matter rose up to the roof." A hardy traveler found some things to make the trek bearable. Passengers would play cards and drink brandy or whiskey. As for the drivers, they were liable to fall asleep. Counterintuitive as it may seem, given the terrain the coach traversed, its gentle rocking motion could be like lying inside of a baby's crib. "Overland drivers and conductors used to sit in their places and sleep 30 or 40 minutes at a time, on good roads, while spinning along at the rate of eight or 10 miles an hour," wrote Twain. "I saw them do it, often."

So this was America in the 1850s: rough and ready at best, but making advances even in its sleep. Yet what was it advancing toward? The real story of the Butterfield Line was the story of its routing. Although Congress agreed to finance the creation of the line, it was unable to decide on a precise route. This was a matter of the rising tensions over slavery between the North and the South. It was widely believed that the Overland Company's mail route would set a precedent that the railroad lines would follow. As a result, the slave and non-slave states saw it as a competition for the future of the country's infrastructure.

With Congress abdicating its responsibility to make a decision, it was left up to Postmaster General Aaron V. Brown of Tennessee. He selected a route through the southern portion of the nation. It traveled across the Rio Grande in Texas, through El Paso and Fort Yuma, Arizona, and up through California to San Francisco. He defended the route on the grounds that it was the wisest way west considering northern weather conditions. He claimed that deep and impassable snows would render a northern route useless for much of the year. Perhaps Absalom Woodward and George Chorpenning Jr. would have agreed with him. Pretty much everyone else thought it was a play for southern supremacy. The *Chicago Tribune* called Brown's decision "one of the greatest swindles ever perpetrated upon the country by the slave-holders." Many northerners saw it as an attempt to get Californians to side with the South

Above: The Legends of the West stamp pane, issued in 1994, included the 29-cent overland mail stamp featuring an overland mail stagecoach driving through a California mountain pass. The inset shows a pony rider, the earliest form of mail delivery prior to coaches and express riders.

Right: John Butterfield's Overland Mail Company East and West schedules, dated September 16, 1858.

No. 1] [Sep. 16th, 1858.

OVERLAND MAIL COMPANY.

THROUGH TIME SCHEDULE BETWEEN

ST. LOUIS, MO., MEMPHIS, TENN. } & SAN FRANCISCO, CAL.

GOING WEST.

LEAVE.	DAYS.	Hour.	Distance, Place to Place.	Time allowed.	Av'ge Miles per Hour.
St. Louis, Mo., & Memphis, Tenn. }	Every Monday & Thursday,	8.00 A.M	Miles.	No. Hours	
P. R. R. Terminus, "	" Monday & Thursday,	6.00 P.M	160	10	16
Springfield, "	" Wednesday & Saturday	7.45 A.M	143	37¾	3⅛
Fayetteville, "	" Thursday & Sunday,	10.15 A.M	100	26½	3⅛
Fort Smith, Ark.	" Friday & Monday,	3.30 A.M	65	17¼	3⅛
Sherman, Texas	" Sunday & Wednesday,	12.30 A.M	205	45	4½
Fort Belknap. "	" Monday & Thursday,	9.00 A.M	146½	32½	4½
Fort Chadbourn, "	" Tuesday & Friday,	3.15 P.M	136	30¼	4½
Pecos River, (Em. Crossing.)	" Thursday & Sunday,	3.45 A.M	165	36½	4½
El Paso,	" Saturday & Tuesday,	11.00 A.M	248½	55¼	4½
Soldier's Farewell	" Sunday & Wednesday,	8.30 P.M	150	33½	4½
Tucson, Arizona	" Tuesday & Friday,	1.30 P.M	184½	41	4½
Gila River,* "	" Wednesday & Saturday	9.00 P.M	141	31½	4½
Fort Yuma, Cal.	" Friday & Monday,	3.00 A.M	135	30	4½
San Bernardino "	" Saturday & Tuesday,	11.00 P.M	200	44	4½
Ft. Tejon, (Via Los Angeles)	" Monday & Thursday,	7.30 A.M	150	32½	4½
Visalia, "	" Tuesday & Friday,	11.30 A.M	127	28	4½
Firebaugh's Ferry, "	" Wednesday & Saturday	5.30 A.M	82	18	4½
(Arrive) San Francisco,	" Thursday & Sunday,	8.30 A.M	163	27	6

GOING EAST.

LEAVE.	DAYS.	Hour.	Distance, Place to Place.	Time allowed.	Av'ge Miles per Hour.
San Francisco, Cal.	Every Monday & Thursday,	8.00 A.M	Miles.	No. Hours	
Firebaugh's Ferry, "	" Tuesday & Friday,	11.00 A.M	163	27	6
Visalia, "	" Wednesday & Saturday,	5.00 A.M	82	18	4½
Ft. Tejon, (Via Los Angeles)	" Thursday & Sunday,	9.00 A.M	127	28	4½
San Bernardino, "	" Friday & Monday,	5.30 P.M	150	32½	4½
Fort Yuma, "	" Sunday & Wednesday,	1.30 P.M	200	44	4½
Gila River,* Arizona	" Monday & Thursday,	7.30 P.M	135	30	4½
Tucson, "	" Wednesday & Saturday	3.00 A.M	141	31½	4½
Soldier's Farewell,	" Thursday & Sunday,	8.00 P.M	184½	41	4½
El Paso, Tex.	" Saturday & Tuesday,	5.30 A.M	150	33½	4½
Pecos River, (Em. Crossing)	" Monday & Thursday	12.45 P.M	248½	55¼	4½
Fort Chadbourn, "	" Wednesday & Saturday	1.15 A.M	165	36½	4½
Fort Belknap, "	" Thursday & Sunday,	7.30 A.M	136	30¼	4½
Sherman, "	" Friday & Monday,	4.00 P.M	146½	32½	4½
Fort Smith, Ark.	" Sunday & Wednesday,	1.00 P.M	205	45	4½
Fayetteville, Mo.	" Monday, & Thursday,	6.15 A.M	65	17¼	3⅛
Springfield, "	" Tuesday & Friday,	8.45 A.M	100	26½	3⅛
P. R. R. Terminus, "	" Wednesday & Saturday	10.30 P.M	143	37¾	3⅛
(Arrive) St. Louis, Mo., & Memphis, Tenn. }	" Thursday & Sunday,		160	10	16

This Schedule may not be exact—Superintendents, Agents, Station-men, Conductors, Drivers and all employees are particularly directed to use every possible exertion to get the Stages through in quick time, even though they may be ahead of this time.

If they are behind this time, it will be necessary to urge the animals on to the highest speed that they can be driven without injury.

Remember that no allowance is made in the time for ferries, changing teams, &c. It is therefore necessary that each driver increase his speed over the average per hour enough to gain the necessary time for meals, changing teams, crossing ferries, &c.

Every person in the Company's employ will always bear in mind that each minute of time is of importance. If each driver on the route loses fifteen (15) minutes, it would make a total loss of time, on the entire route, of twenty-five (25) hours, or, more than one day. If each one loses ten (10) minutes it would make a total loss of sixteen and one half (16½) hours, or, the best part of a day.

On the contrary, if each driver gains that amount of time, it leaves a margin of time against accidents and extra delays.

All hands will see the great necessity of promptness and dispatch: every minute of time is valuable as the Company are under heavy forfeit if the mail is behind time.

Conductors must note the hour and date of departure from Stations, the causes of delay, if any, and all particulars. They must also report the same fully to their respective Superintendents.

* The Station referred to on Gila River, is 40 miles west of Maricopa Wells.

JOHN BUTTERFIELD.
Pres't.

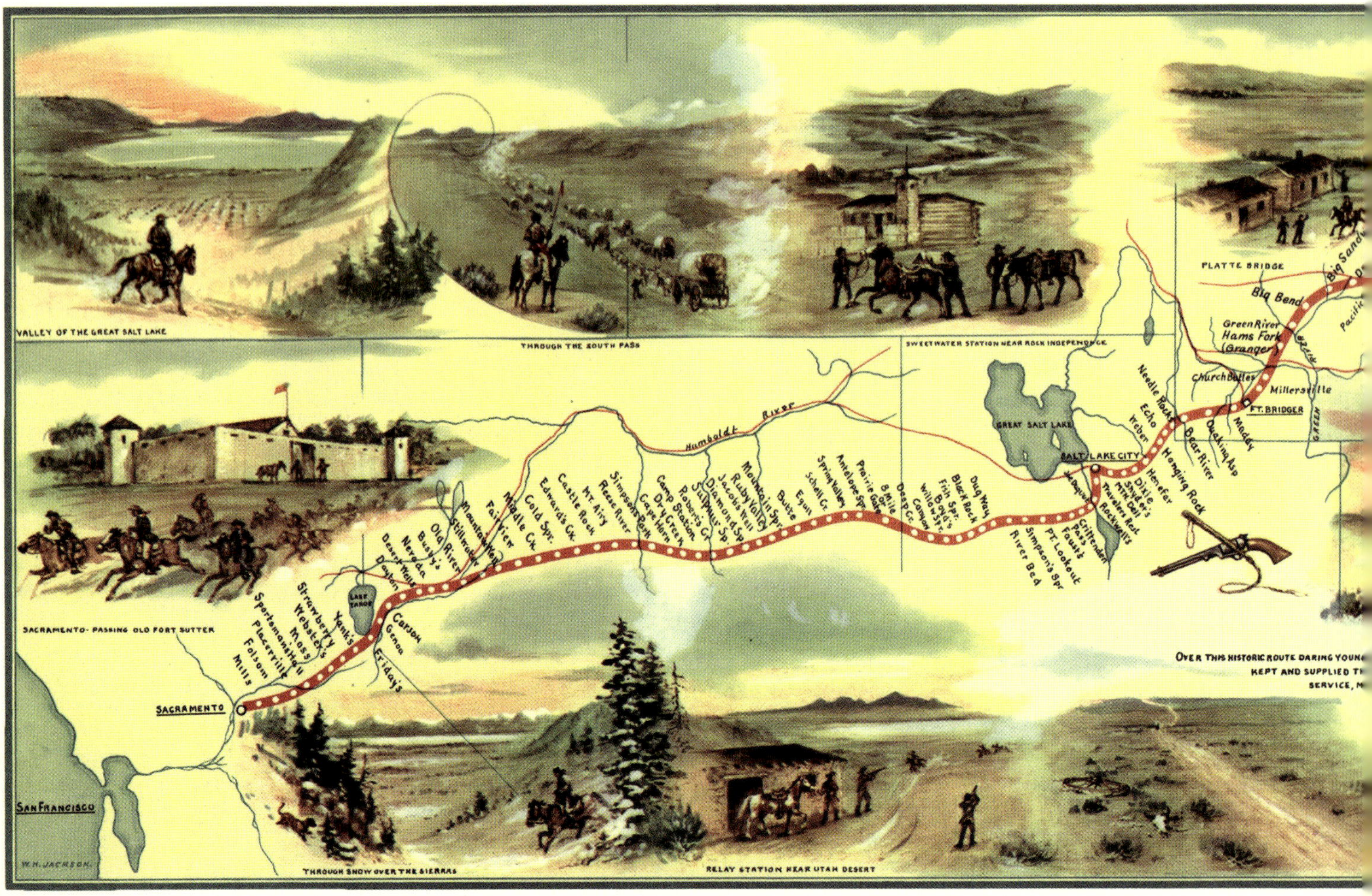

over the issue of expanding slavery—a potentially catastrophic outcome, given the state's vast gold reserves and growing population.

Butterfield, faced with these politics, opted to hedge his bets. He gave his line *two* eastern termini: one in St. Louis, contested territory home to both Union and Confederate sympathizers; and another in the southern city of Memphis, Tennessee. Traffic starting in each city met in Little Rock, Arkansas, before making the nation's longest mail run west. That run had many of the virtues of the Jackass Line and even overlapped between El Paso and Fort Yuma. Somehow, even though the Butterfield Line never earned an embarrassing name, the circumstances of its creation made it seem a bit less virtuous.

★ ★ ★

Against the backdrop of these political tensions arose an alternative to the overland coach lines. Beginning in 1860, a stable of diminutive fleet riders carried mail across the middle of the country. The route, running from St. Joseph on the western edge of Missouri to Sacramento, California, was 1,000 miles shorter than the Butterfield Line. It was faster and more efficient than any of the overland routes, meeting the needs of businessmen in California. And—important from the northern perspective—the route built for speed also skirted deep southern territory.

This was the Pony Express.

The line's operations were magnificently efficient. Relay stations were set 10 miles apart. Every third station was a home station, where extra ponies were kept. There, the saddle full of letters, called a *mochila,* would be placed on a fresh horse. Riders were small and light, often weighing less than 100 pounds. What took steamships 45 days and overland mail 20 days, these carriers were able to accomplish in 11 days. They earned $25 weekly.

Below: The Pony Express mail route from April 1860 to October 1861, stretching from St. Joseph, Missouri, to Sacramento, California, and back, with all the stops noted along the way.

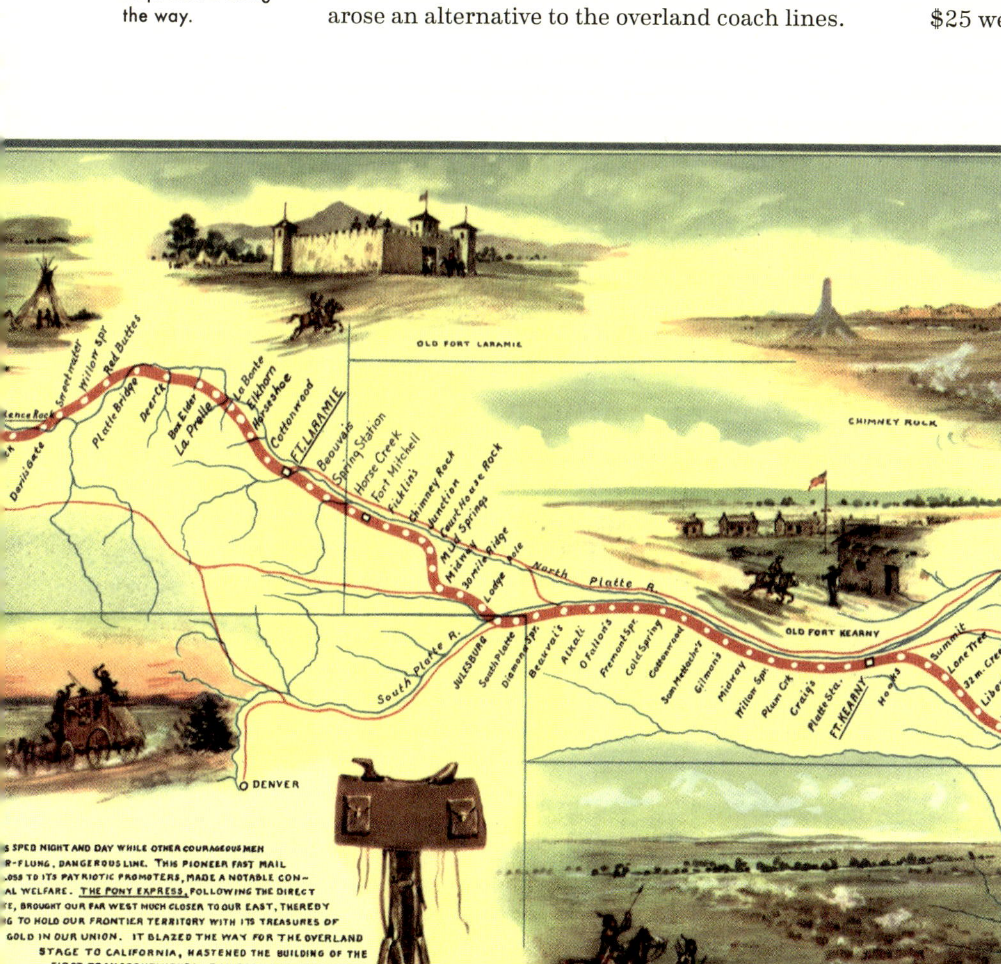

Majors insisted that his young riders take an oath on the Bible that they wouldn't cuss, drink, or misbehave in the presence of ladies.

"The pony-riders were usually a little bit of a man, brimful of spirit and endurance," wrote Mark Twain in *Roughing It*. But however high-spirited they were, riders were expected to adhere to standards every bit as exacting as those that governed the operation of the relay service itself. Alexander Majors, one of the partners who operated the line, was deeply religious. He insisted that his young riders take an oath on the Bible that they wouldn't cuss, drink, or misbehave in the presence of ladies. According to Twain, whether or not this oath actually kept the riders from carousing is another question. But they did stay prepared for what was expected of them. "No matter whether it was winter or summer, raining, snowing, hailing, or sleeting, or whether his 'beat' was a level straight road or a crazy trail over mountain crags and precipices, or whether it led through peaceful regions or regions that swarmed with hostile Indians," Twain wrote, "he must always be ready to leap into the saddle and be off like the wind!"

The price for all of this speed, glamour, and adventure was high. Pony Express postage rates weren't cheap. Letters and newspapers initially cost $5 per half-ounce (equal to about $190 today), plus normal postage. Though the price was dropped to $2 per half-ounce and then $1 per half-ounce in 1861, letters were generally written on tissue-like paper to keep costs down—and they were mostly business letters, not personal correspondence. In the words of Twain, with weight at such a premium, riders carried nothing on their person—not weapons, personal effects, or least of all letters—that could be described as "frivolous."

The Pony Express sped in and out of history like one of its riders. It was a perfect machine of mail delivery carried out by man and beast, but it couldn't turn a profit. It received only $91,404 in receipts for letters carried across the country; the expenses for horses, men, and equipment were much, much more than that. Even if prices were never lowered—which was done in an attempt to drive more business—the line couldn't have covered its costs. But what really defeated the

A Pony Express cover dated September 22, 1860, mailed from San Francisco to St. Joseph, Missouri, and stamped October 3, 1860.

This Pony Express mural study by Swedish-American artist Gustaf Oscar Dalström was designed for the St. Joseph, Missouri, post office and courthouse.

Pony Express was *actual* machines. Its riders blazed into irrelevance just as new technologies were set to eclipse the pull of horses and challenge the supremacy of written correspondence.

In 1855, railroads carried more than 19,202,469 pieces of mail. With their prodigious capacity for moving freight, they could take on unimaginable amounts of mail—volumes that made delivery cheap. The cost per mile by train was 11 cents, compared with 14 cents for stagecoaches and 16 cents for steamers. As the Gold Rush created newfound wealth out west, railroads gained another advantage: They were less susceptible to robbery than stagecoaches. But rail had deficits as well; namely, that the network simply wasn't good enough yet. In 1858, the combined mail by rail/coach service between St. Louis and San Francisco reduced delivery times—a major step up in speed and capacity. But transcontinental railroad service was still a decade away. Another transcontinental service, though, was on the verge of coming into play.

On October 24, 1861, the first telegraph line to stretch from the East Coast to the West Coast was completed. What speedy riders could do in 11 days could now be done nearly instantaneously.

The Pony Express was shut down two days later. It had delivered just 35,000 letters and left its owners in financial ruin. It was perhaps the first sign of the country's reckoning with the changes that would come in the age of railroads, in the age of new communication technology, in an age when the march of progress the post had always been part of—the literal growth but figurative shrinking of the country—would become ever faster. But that's not to say it was a failure. Both the Pony Express and the overland mail furnished the West with acceptable mail service, and more important, they played a part in the conquest and settlement of the western territories. They provided a memorable and timeless story of the building of modern America.

But before continuing that story, America had another reckoning coming its way, one that would play an even bigger role in determining what modern America would look like: the Civil War.

The First Airmail

The balloon *Jupiter* takes off from Lafayette, Indiana, in August 1859.

By the 1850s, balloonists had begun dabbling with aerial flights as a means of swiftly traveling from place to place, but it wasn't until 1859 that they considered taking officially sanctioned mail aloft with them.

John Wise, a pianoforte maker, began flying hot-air balloons in 1822, at the age of 14. More than a decade later, in May 1835, he made a hydrogen balloon that flew nine miles from Philadelphia to Haddonfield, New Jersey. Based on a succession of flights over the next seven years, Wise found that there was a current of air running in a west to east direction: the jet stream. This affirmed in his mind that above 10,000 feet, a river of air is constantly flowing, making a transatlantic flight a scientific possibility. Now he just needed backing to make his dream a reality, so he petitioned Congress for $15,000. But Congress wanted nothing to do with such a preposterous notion.

Instead, Wise accepted an offer from the United States Express Company to transport a bag of newspapers from the West Coast to the East Coast. He departed from St. Louis on July 1, 1859, in a balloon called *Atlantic*. Unfortunately, below-freezing temperatures and a storm took the balloon too far northeast; *Atlantic* was losing altitude. To remain aloft, Wise jettisoned as much ballast as he could, including the newspapers. After 19 hours and 40 minutes, he crash-landed in a tree near Henderson, New York.

The newspaper bag was recovered several days later and forwarded to New York City, leading Wise to proclaim *Atlantic*'s flight a success. He went even further, stating that regular aerial mail service was now feasible between St. Louis and Philadelphia, New York City, and Boston. To prove his point, he needed to fly mail, not newspapers.

Wise had a willing partner in Thomas Wood, the postmaster of Lafayette, Indiana. Wise convinced him that he'd receive great acclaim if his balloon successfully beat the contemporary coaches, steamboats, and trains in conveying mail from Lafayette to New York City. Wood, eager to make a name for himself with Post Office Department leadership, was intrigued and agreed to allow Wise to carry any letters that he received from an ad placed in the *Lafayette Daily Courier*. The local newspaper advertisement noted that the balloon would carry "circulars, letter bags, express mail, and charter greetings from Lafayette to her sister cities in the East."

At 2:00 p.m. on August 17, the hot-air balloon *Jupiter* ascended from the town's square. It measured roughly 34 feet in diameter and extended about 65 feet from the top of the balloon to the bottom of the suspended gondola, and its oiled cotton envelope contained an estimated 24,000 cubic feet of gas. The launch site was mobbed: Wise estimated that at least 20,000 were on hand to witness his takeoff.

After hours of drifting in the wrong direction and low on remaining ballast, Wise opted to land at Crawfordsville, Indiana, where the mail could be redirected to New York City via train. Wise's forced landing after being airborne for only five hours and seven minutes led a local newspaper to mockingly refer to his accomplishment as merely a "trans-county-nental voyage." Upon landing, Wise's mail was turned over to a Post Office Department route agent assigned to the New Albany and Salem Railroad for conveyance east. Despite contemporary cynicism, his feat has been hailed as America's first airmail flight.

Cincinnati's *Penny Press* announced *Jupiter*'s arrival: "Novel Mode of Mailing. - A letter was yesterday received at the General Land Office, from Lafayette, Indiana, which, besides having the usual postmark on the envelope, had also written on it 'via balloon *Jupiter*.' It is supposed this letter was inclosed [*sic*] with the mail bag which was dropped by Mr. Wise from his balloon during his recent ascension."

A letter mailed aboard *Jupiter*.

CLIPPER SHIP SAILING CARDS

Clipper ship cards, popular in the mid-1850s, were one of the country's earliest marketing campaigns. The multicolored advertising cards, at about 4 × 6½ inches, were delivered by the ships' crews and were useful for notifying merchants and exporters of a ship's name, captain, destination, and pier location. The lively designs and colorations were important in catching the merchants' eye—as well as any paying customers interested in booking passage west, where gold had just been discovered in California in 1848. In addition to shipping merchandise and passengers, these clipper ships often carried treasured mail to family members out west who were trying to strike it rich.

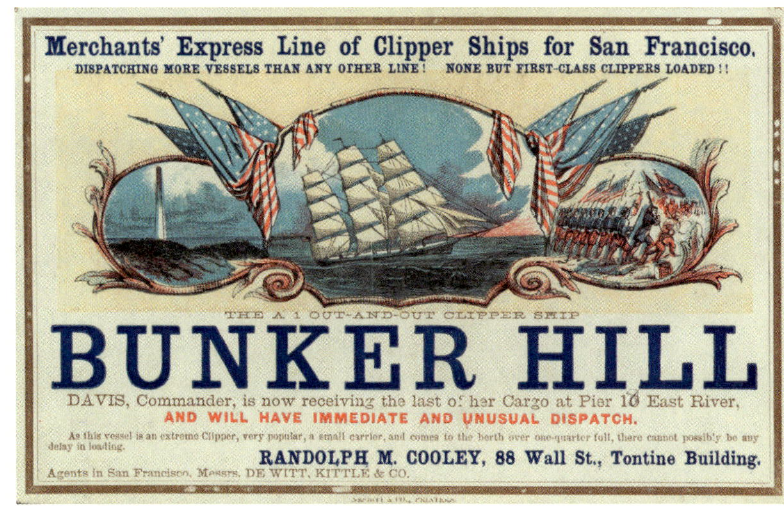

GLIDDEN & WILLIAMS' LINE
FOR
San Francisco.
FROM LEWIS WHARF.
The Beautiful, First Class, Extreme Clipper Ship
AKBAR
ELISHA CROCKER, COMMANDER.
This favorite clipper is now ready for cargo. She is sharp, fast, and all that is desirable. Shippers will oblige by the prompt delivery of their engagements.
For Freight, apply at the California Packet Office, 114 State Street.
Agents at San Francisco, Messrs. Williams, Blanchard & Co.
Watson & Clark, Prs., 60 Water St.

114 Days to San Francisco.
Coleman's California Line for
San Francisco.
THE A 1 EXTREME CLIPPER SHIP
ORPHEUS
HOLWAY, Master,
Is now rapidly Loading at Pier 15 E. R., foot Wall St.
This vessel comes to the berth with a large portion of her cargo on board, and having large engagements, will be DISPATCHED PROMPTLY.
For balance of Freight, apply to
WM. T. COLEMAN & CO.,
161 Pearl St., near Wall St.
Agents in San Francisco, Messrs. WM. T. COLEMAN & CO.

NO DELAY IN LOADING.
SUTTON & CO.'S DISPATCH LINE FOR SAN FRANCISCO.
THE SMALL SHARP A 1 FIRST-CLASS CLIPPER SHIP
JOHN TUCKER.
FRANK HALLETT, MASTER,
Is Receiving her Cargo at Pier 20 East River,
AND WILL HAVE OUR USUAL PROMPT DISPATCH.
This popular Clipper is well-known to the trade as first-class in every respect, and being of small capacity, with large engagements of Railroad material, offers inducements unequalled by any other vessel up.
SUTTON & CO., 58 South St., cor. Wall.
The Ships of this Line insure at the Lowest Rates, and dispatched quicker than any other from New-York to San Francisco.

NO DELAY IN LOADING.
115, 112, 107, 120, 116 DAYS' PASSAGE!
THE CELEBRATED A 1 FIRST CLASS SHARP CLIPPER SHIP
SEA SERPENT
Is Completing her Lading at Pier 20 E. R., Burling Slip,
AND WILL HAVE OUR USUAL PROMPT DISPATCH.
This elegant clipper has made the above short passages to San Francisco, and the fine condition of delivering her cargoes is too well known to be repeated.
SUTTON & CO., 58 South St., cor. Wall.
The ships of this line insure at the lowest rates, and dispatched quicker than any other from New-York to San Francisco.

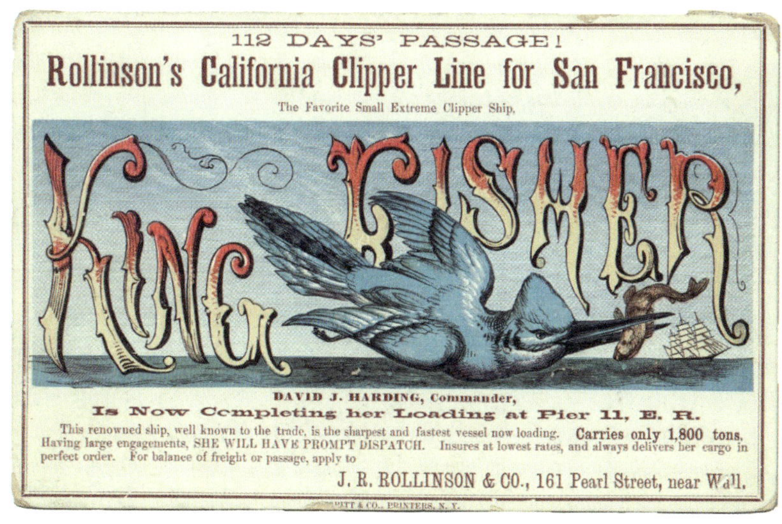
112 DAYS' PASSAGE!
Rollinson's California Clipper Line for San Francisco,
The Favorite Small Extreme Clipper Ship.
KING FISHER
DAVID J. HARDING, Commander,
Is Now Completing her Loading at Pier 11, E. R.
This renowned ship, well known to the trade, is the sharpest and fastest vessel now loading. Carries only 1,800 tons. Having large engagements, SHE WILL HAVE PROMPT DISPATCH. Insures at lowest rates, and always delivers her cargo in perfect order. For balance of freight or passage, apply to
J. R. ROLLINSON & CO., 161 Pearl Street, near Wall.

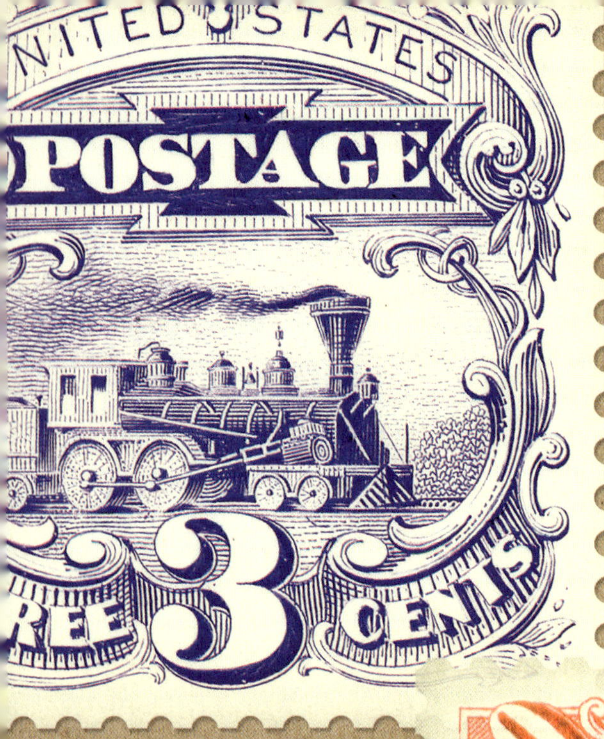
POSTAGE
3

1776
24

90
U.S. POSTAGE
90

UNITED STATES
POSTAGE
TWELVE
12

U.S.
POSTAGE
FIFTEEN CENTS

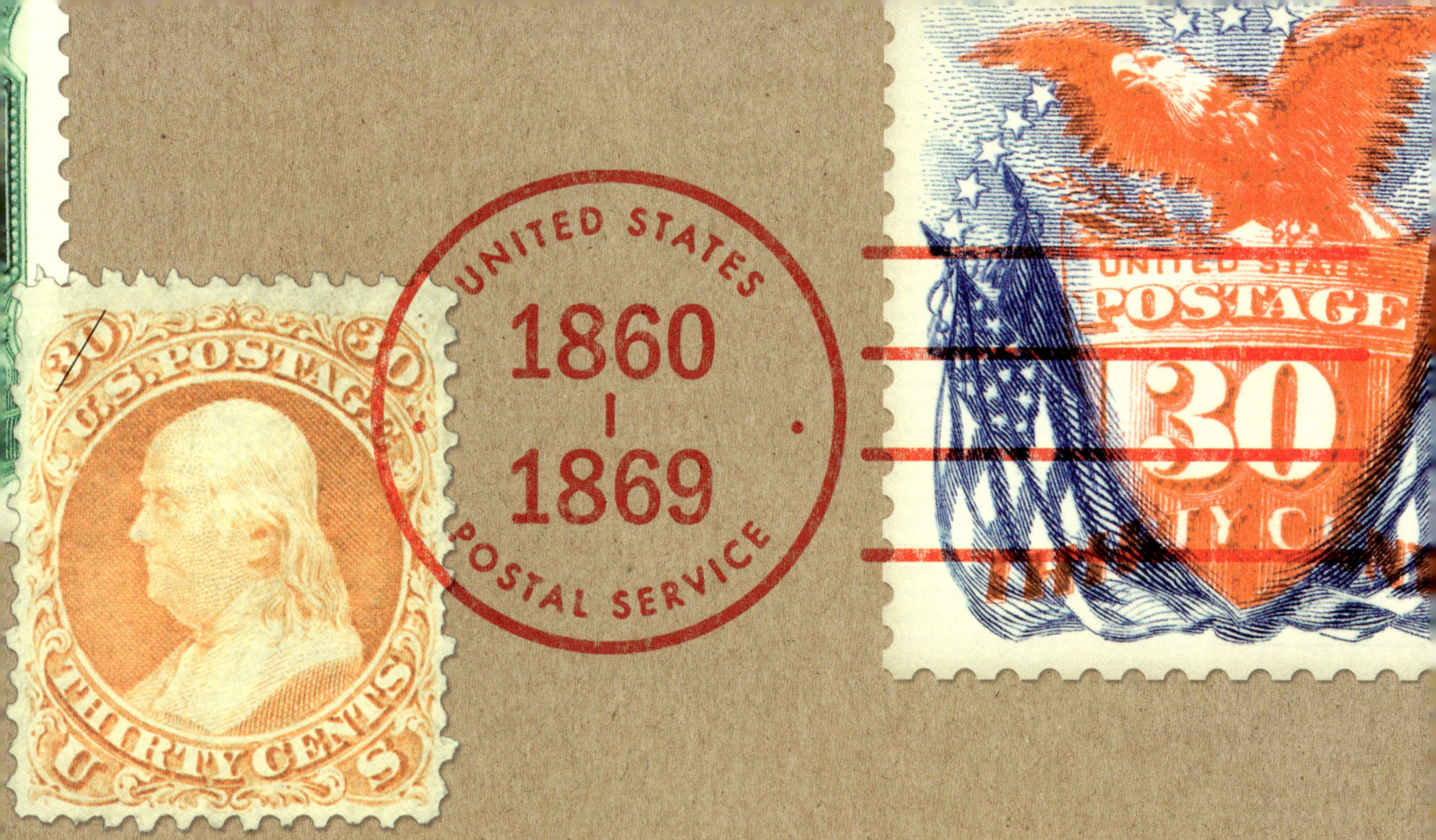
UNITED STATES
1860
1869
POSTAL SERVICE
U.S. POSTAGE
30
THIRTY CENTS
U S
POSTAGE
30

WAR

U.S. POSTAGE
2

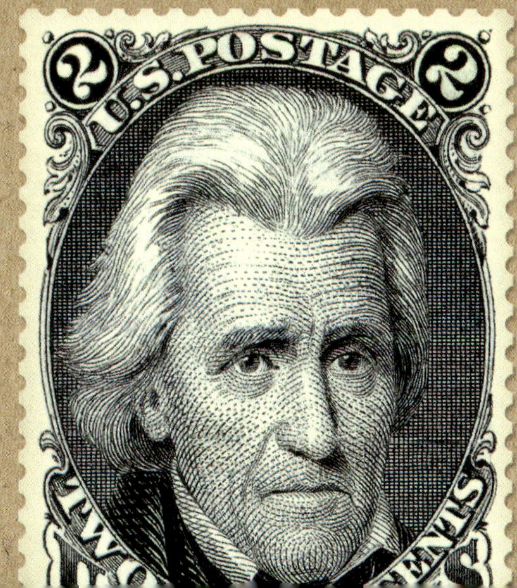

WAR BEGUN!

Ft. Sumter Bombarded!!

The Traitors Begin the War!!!

10,000 MEN AGAINST 70!!

Above: One of the many newspaper headlines announcing the beginning of the Civil War.

Opposite: Abraham Lincoln's first inauguration on March 4, 1861.

Right: A photograph of Abraham Lincoln taken circa 1846–47 when he was the congressman-elect from Illinois. Thirteen years earlier, he was appointed by Postmaster General William Barry as the postmaster of New Salem, Illinois. He held the position from May 7, 1833, to May 30, 1836.

Abraham Lincoln was elected to the presidency in November 1860. By the time he arrived in Washington, D.C., for his inauguration—March 1861—the country he was set to lead was smaller than the one that had elected him. In December, in response to the election of the antislavery Lincoln, South Carolina seceded from the Union. Mississippi followed in January 1861; Florida, Alabama, Georgia, and Louisiana took their leave later that month; and Texas withdrew in February. Before Lincoln could be sworn in, these states had drafted their own provisional Constitution and selected a Confederate president, Jefferson Davis. In his inaugural address on March 4, 1861, Lincoln declared to the aggrieved southerners that "the Government will not assail you." He called for unity, for preserving common bonds of Americans, appealing to "the better angels of our nature."

It was not to be.

A month later, on April 12, the Confederate military fired upon Fort Sumter, a Union garrison in Charleston, South Carolina. Less than two days later, the fort was surrendered to Confederate forces. The Civil War had begun. For many, the news came through the mail. Horace Greeley, the legendary editor of the *New-York Tribune*, broke the story to many in the North. "War is upon us. We are involved in war!" he advised readers. "The country even yet does not fairly realize the fact. It was surprised, bewildered, stupefied by the tidings that the rebels were cannonading Fort Sumter. Probably most of the citizens of the free States have not until a week past believed that there would be any bloodshed. The loyal States are taken by surprise."

As the realities of war set in, Lincoln's first Postmaster General, Montgomery Blair, immediately set about putting the federal Post Office Department on a wartime footing. By August 1861, mail was banned between the two belligerents: Blair had stopped mail from being transmitted from the northern states to the southern states, and John Reagan, the postmaster general for the Confederacy, reciprocated. Knowing that there was some $9 million in unused postage held in the South, the federal government demonetized all federal postage stamps issued prior to 1861. On September 12, northern postal patrons were advised that they had six days to exchange old stamps for the new issues. At that point, the older stamps and embossed stamped envelopes would all be devalued.

For the first time since the days when the Constitutional Post dueled the British Crown Post in the increasingly bellicose pre-revolution colonies, America had two distinct systems for mail. The South, postally, was on its own.

★ ★ ★

The mobile post-office headquarters for the Army of the Potomac at Falmouth, Virginia, photographed by Timothy O'Sullivan.

The fervor that accompanied the secession of the southern states, the firing on Fort Sumter, and the outbreak of the Civil War resulted in a massive breakup of families. Men on both sides flocked to join hometown regiments. Brothers, cousins, and neighbors expected to return home bathed in glory. Instead, these close-knit units were ordered farther from their homes than most had ever been before, and the war would prove to be far deadlier than any of them envisioned. Killed in battle, wounded in action as POWs, and even dying by disease; whatever the exact cause, more than 1.1 million men never returned home.

The volume of mail that resulted from this geographic separation of people was previously unthinkable. To accommodate the surge of mail from the war, the Post Office Department requisitioned 40 million more postage stamps in 1862 than it had the previous year. Print orders increased annually after that. Many military letters were sent to let family and friends know all was well; there was enough mail coming from soldiers that in the Union Army, regiments had their own postmasters—at first chaplains and later, by order of future president Ulysses S. Grant, noncommissioned officers. And if soldiers sent lots of mail home, home sent lots of mail to soldiers: It wasn't uncommon for northern regiments, typically consisting of 1,000 men, to receive as many as 600 letters a day.

From the start, the Confederate postal system was unready and unable to live up to the mammoth task before it. Reagan struggled to adapt to the new wartime reality even though he had seen it coming. In fact, Reagan had been reluctant to accept the job as the Confederacy's postmaster general, as he suspected it would be next to impossible to live up to the level of service and satisfaction offered by the Post Office Department—and he feared such failure would doom his legacy. Sure enough, when he took on the role, pretty much all Reagan had to go on was a list of southern post offices. He didn't even know whether those offices' postmasters were true secessionists and could be trusted to be loyal to a new system. But he had a plan.

Rather than simply rely on the loyalty of existing postmasters, Reagan raided officers from the Post Office Department in Washington, D.C. Targeting southern sympathizers, he asked each person of interest whether they'd accept an identical position in the Confederacy. Any official who agreed to go south was told to bring copies of every form, waybill, contract, or order they could lay their hands on. All these documents were

An unidentified Union soldier was photographed by Mathew Brady while holding a letter from home. Brady photographed many Union soldiers from the 1860s to the 1870s.

Left: This drawing appeared on a Confederate envelope cover that was mailed from Memphis to New Orleans in 1861.

Below, left: This stamp, featuring Jefferson Davis, was engraved in Europe by Jean Ferdinand Joubert de la Ferté. Twelve million of them were printed. *Right:* The Oath of Office for postmasters of the Confederate States' post offices under John Reagan as the Postmaster General.

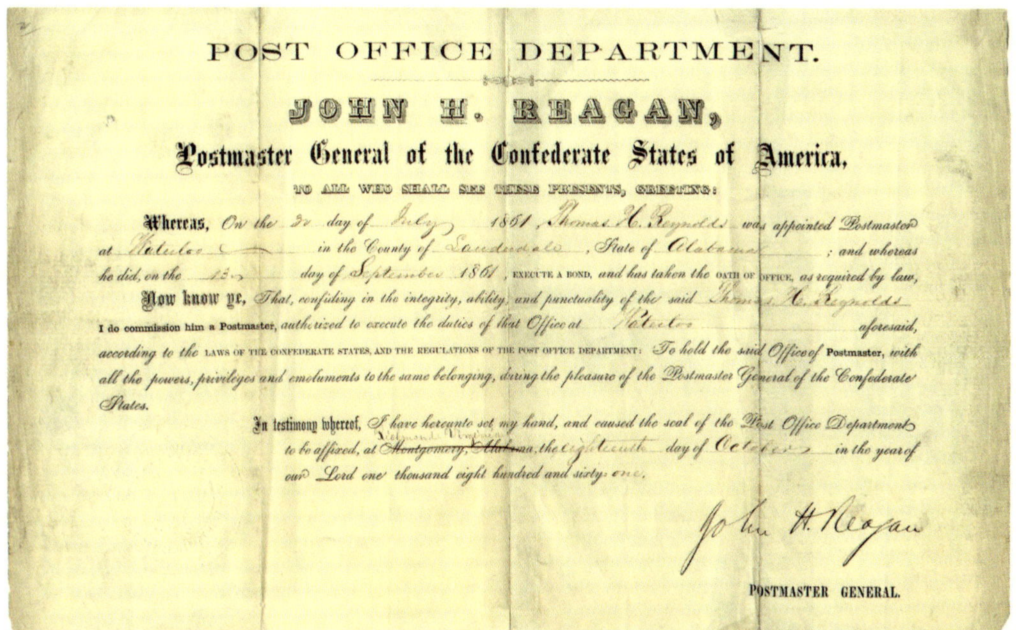

POST OFFICE DEPARTMENT.

JOHN H. REAGAN,

Postmaster General of the Confederate States of America,

TO ALL WHO SHALL SEE THESE PRESENTS, GREETING:

Whereas, *On the* 3d *day of* July 1861, Thomas H. Reynolds *was appointed Postmaster at* Waterloo *in the County of* Lauderdale, *State of* Alabama; *and whereas he did, on the* 13th *day of* September 1861, EXECUTE A BOND, *and has taken the* OATH OF OFFICE, *as required by law,*

Now know ye, *That, confiding in the integrity, ability, and punctuality of the said* Thomas H. Reynolds I do commission him a Postmaster, *authorized to execute the duties of that Office at* Waterloo *aforesaid, according to the* LAWS OF THE CONFEDERATE STATES, AND THE REGULATIONS OF THE POST OFFICE DEPARTMENT: *To hold the said Office of* Postmaster, *with all the powers, privileges and emoluments to the same belonging, during the pleasure of the Postmaster General of the Confederate States.*

In testimony whereof, *I have hereunto set my hand, and caused the seal of the Post Office Department to be affixed, at* ~~Montgomery, Alabama~~ Richmond, Virginia, *the* eighteenth *day of* October *in the year of our Lord one thousand eight hundred and sixty-* one.

John H. Reagan

POSTMASTER GENERAL.

hastily reprinted, replacing "United States Post Office Department" with "Confederate States Post Office." Just like that, Reagan had acquired the bureaucrats and much of the paperwork it took to operate a national mail system.

Of course, there was still the problem of stamps. In the South, new postage stamps had to be designed, printed, and distributed. Finding suitable printers proved difficult, as the best American engravers were in the North; the South's best engraved stamps, initially, were produced in Europe. Because Jefferson Davis, the Confederate president, was unfamiliar to many, his portrait was chosen for the first southern stamps produced overseas so those in the Confederacy would know what their president looked like. It was a sign of just how new and rudimentary the Confederate government was.

Even stamps, though, were a manageable problem. While Reagan was able to re-create the South's post office in the image of Uncle Sam's, he could not replicate the services and transportation infrastructure that had taken the United States some 100 years to develop. He had to renegotiate all stage, rail, and water route contracts amid the military's competing claims of priority. Worker shortages and service interruptions were common, due to many southern postal workers joining the military. And he couldn't simply throw money at these problems: A provision of the Confederate Constitution dictated that after March 1, 1863, "the expenses of the Post Office Department must be paid out of its own revenues."

So it was that postage became a thorny issue for Reagan and the Southern Post Office Department. On the Confederate side, the postage rate was five cents for the first 500 miles and an additional five cents per half-ounce for letters going beyond that. This compared unfavorably to the North's rate of three cents per half-ounce—even before Reagan raised the rate to 10 cents, and reduced service, in order to be self-sustaining per the constitutional requirement.

★ ★ ★

THE CIVIL WAR

The Civil War did not just divide the country—it divided the postal system. That was a challenge for many soldiers, who, upon enlisting, left home for the first time. Uncertain of when, or even if, they would return to their loved ones, they relied on the Post Office to deliver their letters home—and receive cherished missives in return.

Letters of the day contained references to loneliness, uncertainty, and the horrors observed during combat. Many were co-opted by local newspapers to provide subscribers with up-to-date descriptions of battles scattered across the country. Other communications, often notes about strategy or supply lines, were written in ciphers for fear they might be read by the opposing side.

Yet despite the fact that soldiers depended on the Post Office to stay connected to home, reliable delivery proved tricky, especially after Postmaster General Montgomery Blair outlawed service to southern states in 1861. The Confederacy's newly appointed postmaster general, John H. Reagan,

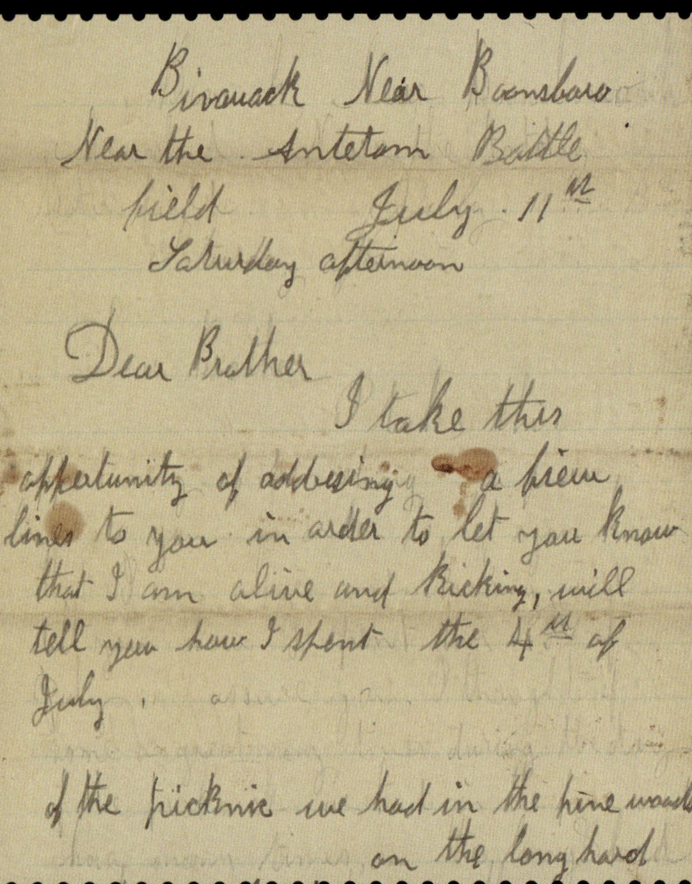

Bivauack Near Boonsboro
Near the Antetam Battle
field July 11th
Saturday afternoon

Dear Brother
I take this
oppertunity of addressing a few
lines to you in order to let you know
that I am alive and kicking, will
tell you how I spent the 4th of
July.

of the picknic we had in the pine woods
on the long hard

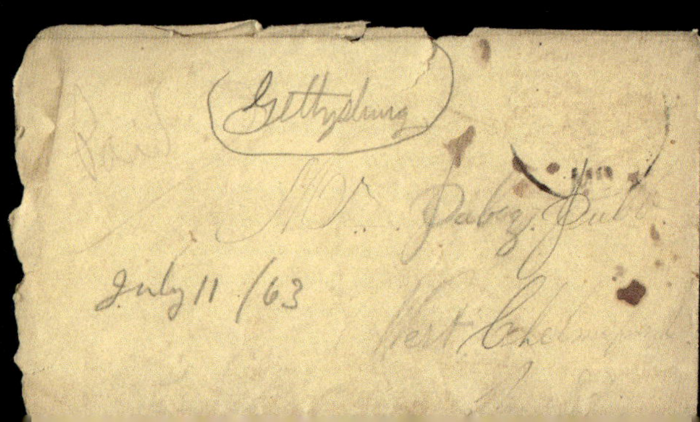

Paid

Gettysburg

July 11 /63

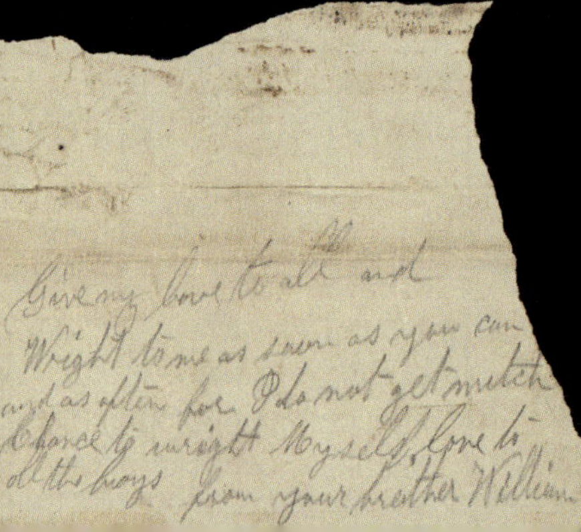

Give my love to all and
Wright to me as soon as you can
and as often for I do not get mutch
Chance to wright Myself. love to
all the boys from your brother William

Left and above, left to right: The first and last page of a letter and an envelope mailed from Gettysburg, marked "Paid" on July 11, 1863. The sender writes, "Give my love to all and wright [*sic*] to me as soon as you can..."; soldiers read their mail outside a temporary post-office tent; an unidentified soldier holding a letter and envelope; a wagon transports mail specifically for the 2nd Corps, which fought its last battle on April 7, 1865

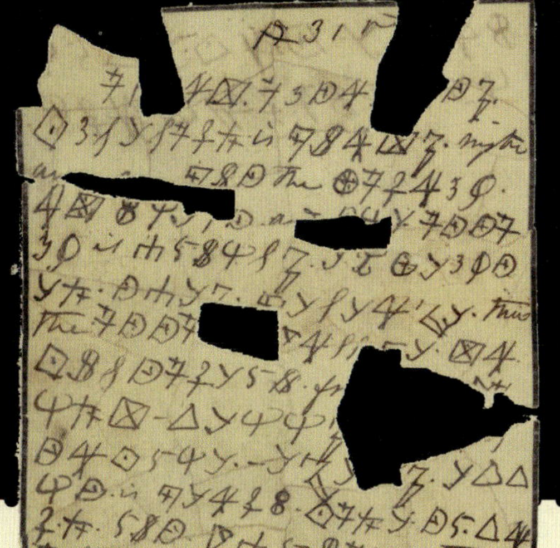

Fragments of a letter written by Rose O'Neal Greenhow, a Confederate spy, who claimed to be a southern woman. She lived in Washington, D.C., worked the political circles of the federal government, and was able to hand over secret information to the Confederacy that she wrapped in her hair. The Confederates claimed victory in the First Battle of Manassas based on her information.

quickly responded, denying delivery to the North. Soldiers with correspondents on the wrong side of the Mason-Dixon line were out of luck, unless they could find someone to smuggle letters to forbidden destinations.

Then there was the fact that soldiers were often on the move to support strategic objectives during the war. These maneuvers made it even more difficult for mail carriers to ensure letters were picked up or delivered in a timely manner. As a result, units might go for weeks without mail—and their families might not receive word of their whereabouts or well-being for even longer.

Despite these challenges, at least soldiers could rely on the Post Office to deliver letters without postage. Many fighting men did not have the ability, or the funds, to purchase stamps to carry with them. (And even if they did, billeting conditions could be excessively wet and muddy, which could render the stamps unusable.) The Post Office, however, would deliver any letters, provided that soldiers clearly noted their name, rank, and unit on the envelopes. These letters were not freebies. Each letter was marked "postage due" and expected to be paid by the recipient upon arrival.

Voting by a Pennsylvania unit in the 1864 national election. The state assigned commissioners to oversee its military voting. They were assigned 300-pound crates containing ballots and envelopes, plus hundreds of 12-cent and three-cent postage stamps. In this scene, created by battlefield artist Alfred Waud, the commissioner appears to be sitting on the ballot crate.

While the South struggled to re-create the postal system the nation had been building for more than a century, the North met the Civil War with innovation. The Post Office Department introduced a variety of services meant to fulfill the unique needs of soldiers, who had to be engaged members of their families and their country even while on the frontlines.

On May 17, 1864, a new act passed that authorized the Post Office Department to allow money orders up to $30. Soldiers regularly sent money home to their families, but transporting money by postal carrier was risky—it could be lost or stolen. Occasionally, soldiers' pay never made it home. Money orders, on the other hand, were prepaid at the post office; what was transported was a record of the money order issued by the department. There was no actual currency moved. The government assessed how much money was typically sent to families, which turned out to be $5 on average, and set a cap that was virtually assured to accommodate it. Postal money orders were offered through larger post offices and then dispensed to the smaller offices as rapidly as possible. By 1865, more than $1.3 million in postal money orders had been issued.

Mail-in balloting by soldiers and sailors in the 1864 national election was another important postal achievement. To make it happen, six northern states changed their laws to allow mail-in voting, while 14 states authorized voting at military polling places overseen by state-appointed commissioners. Not everyone approved of the idea, even within Lincoln's Cabinet. It was a former postmaster who may have tipped the balance: Gideon Welles, Lincoln's secretary of the navy, who had once served as the postmaster of Hartford, Connecticut, wasn't keen on the idea but ultimately came down in favor of it and personally ensured every sailor in the Navy could vote. This

Albert Potts designed a cast-iron letter box that was mounted onto a lamppost. While Potts hoped to convince Post Office Department officials to approve his letter boxes, his real goal was to sell quantities of his lamplights to local municipalities. The inclusion of the letter boxes gave him a competitive edge. No examples of Potts's boxes are known to have survived.

proved crucial: 78 percent of military votes went Lincoln's way. Remove them from the ballot box and it would have cost Lincoln the 1864 election.

The home front saw innovation as well. The Post Office Department expanded on a recent innovation, the use of street-corner lamppost letter boxes. These collection boxes were introduced in 1858, principally for the convenience of business and casual mailers in dropping off letters. The early boxes, developed by Philadelphia foundry owner Albert Potts, mounted to or completely wrapped around lampposts and provided a place for people to drop off letters and for postal carriers to collect them. Though Potts's approach proved ineffective, the idea persisted. Future inventors produced numerous designs, including curbside models that predate our familiar freestanding blue collection boxes. We take these for granted today, but at the time it was a revolutionary notion that mail could be dropped off at any time of day rather than only when the postal carrier came around, or during the post office's open hours. What a century earlier had been done by cutting new roads was now being done by invention: The mail was taking another leap forward in reach and accessibility.

Stamp Hobbyists Get a New Name

In the earliest years of stamp collecting, collectors were commonly called timbromanists, after a French term *timbromanie*, which translates to "stamp madness." Many collectors found the term derogatory, so on November 15, 1864, Frenchman Georges Herpin coined a new one in the publication *Le Collectionneur de timbres-poste*. Reflecting on the fact that a postage stamp's function is to indicate that payment has already been made by the sender, he combined the Greek *phil-*, meaning "loving," and *atelēs*, meaning "free from tax or charge." Philately was born, and philatelists were elated. They were no longer madmen but lovers.

The most important postal innovation to emerge from the Civil War was born of the reality that some soldiers were doomed to never send money home, and never vote, again. Prior to 1863, the Post Office didn't deliver mail to individual homes for free—people had to go to their local facility or pay an extra fee for home delivery. With all the casualities from the war, it wasn't uncommon for a woman visiting the local post office to send or receive a letter from a loved one, father, or beloved to be given a packet of previously sent missives wrapped in twine with a note from a chaplain or commanding officer telling her that he had been killed. This was the worst of all possible news for anyone to receive in public, so local postmasters insisted that something be done. On July 1 of that year, Postmaster General Blair initiated "city free delivery service" in 49 northern cities using 450 letter carriers. Under this service, carriers, who were often invalids or veteran soldiers, would deliver mail to homes within assigned delivery areas for free. They would knock on each door twice and wait until someone came to the door to accept the mail. It was time-consuming, but home-delivery service was an instant success. And while it was initially available only to city dwellers, the demand for rural equality in future decades would do much to define the *service* of the Postal Service.

★ ★ ★

Because of the ban on mail between the North and South, these two mail systems operated more or less in isolation. But a year into the war, an official exception to the embargo was established: mail for prisoners of war.

Jacob Dieter, a prisoner of war held in Andersonville, a Confederate Prison in South Carolina, wrote this two-page letter to his wife and children to let them know he was well and that there were 16 men from his unit who were captured on June 11, 1865.

Prison Camp June the 22d 1864
Dear wife and Children
I will write a few lines to you
to let you know that I am well
and hope this will find you
all in good health I cand write
but a few lines to you for
all the letters will be read before
they are sent there is sixteen of
our Company here we where taken
on the ~~th~~ eleventh of this month
there is Frank Heller W Williams
I Calady both the Geer boys H Niles
O Whipple Eli Rue Geo Dikenson
A Merit A Holt G Saville A Mccoy
Radclif D Mcarthur I dond know
how long we will have to stay
here but I hope it wand be
long I wand you to write
to me when you get this and

direct to Camp Sumter Prison
~~Andar~~ Andersonville Ga My folks
will have to try and help you
a long til I get out of this for
I cand draw any pay til I am
exchanged I sent my love to you
all let me know wether
you got that money I sent you
when I was at Saint Louis
So good Bye for this time
when I get out of this I will
all the particulars
By Jacob Dieter
to wife and Children

Opposite left: *Le Philatéliste*, a 1929 self-portrait by Swiss artist François Barraud with his wife, Marie.

Opposite right: Morning Start of the New York City Mail Carriers in Their New Uniforms, from Harper's Weekly, December 1868.

Designated points were chosen for letter exchanges. Often, boats flying a "flag of truce" to convey that they were not combatants were used to carry the mail. Letters were posted inside two envelopes. The outer envelope bore postage for the territory the letter had to travel to reach the exchange point. At the exchange, the outer envelope would be discarded. The letter would be censored, then secured in the inner envelope and affixed with postage—or a note that postage was due upon receipt—to reach its ultimate destination. (In other words, a captured Union soldier writing home would pay Confederate postage to reach the exchange point, then pay U.S. postage for their letter to get to their loved ones.)

Prisoners of war sending letters home, no matter where they were being held, were limited to just one sheet of paper. If more than one sheet was used, it would be confiscated—long letters, even from family, would not be tolerated. Confederate POWs were allowed to mail letters to relatives only—something soldiers would often fake, writing to, say, an "aunt" who was actually a girlfriend or other acquaintance. In addition, the Union's naval blockade of southern ports created a severe shortage of writing paper and envelopes throughout the Confederacy. This prompted creative southerners to use remnants of wallpaper or other scraps to create homemade envelopes and notepaper. (A homemade envelope made from other types of paper was called an "adversity cover.")

Indeed, in these exchanges, the shortcomings of the Confederate system came to the fore. The Union's more mature, better-resourced system was an advantage. The lower postage rate in the North, three cents per half-ounce, allowed Union prisoners to send and receive a great deal more mail than their Confederate counterparts, who paid 10 cents for the same privilege. And starting in July 1861, the U.S. began allowing soldiers to mail letters without including postage at all. By writing "Soldier's Letter" on the envelope, they could send letters with postage to be collected from the recipient.

The volume of mail flowing home from Union POWs infuriated the South's agent for prisoner exchange, Robert Ould. On August 5, 1863, Ould wrote to his northern equivalent, Brigadier General S.A. Meredith, complaining: "I see no reason for the appearance of your flag-of-truce boats 'daily or every other day in order that prisoners may receive their correspondence with some sort of regularity.'" If there is so much to be said, soldiers should be returned home, he argued. "It is far more important that the thousands of prisoners who are languishing in your prisons should be sent home. The best and most satisfactory message from them will be communicated with their own lips."

Mail during the Civil War attested to the aching separation that was weighing on the nation. Soldiers far from home; families separated; countrymen less than a century from winning their freedom fighting for it yet again. In his first inaugural address, Lincoln said: "Though passion may have strained it must not break our bonds of affection." People worked hard to maintain these bonds. Smuggling letters to and from the South was a crime, but stories abound of people violating the law in attempts to deliver correspondence. Many were arrested, but others made it through. Letters were hidden in hoopskirts and false-bottom trunks. Some smuggling attempts were almost whimsical. Postal lore tells of contraband letters tied into the tail of a giant kite and successfully flown across the Potomac River to Virginia—though likely this never actually happened.

The letters that did make it through convey just how painful the country's division was.

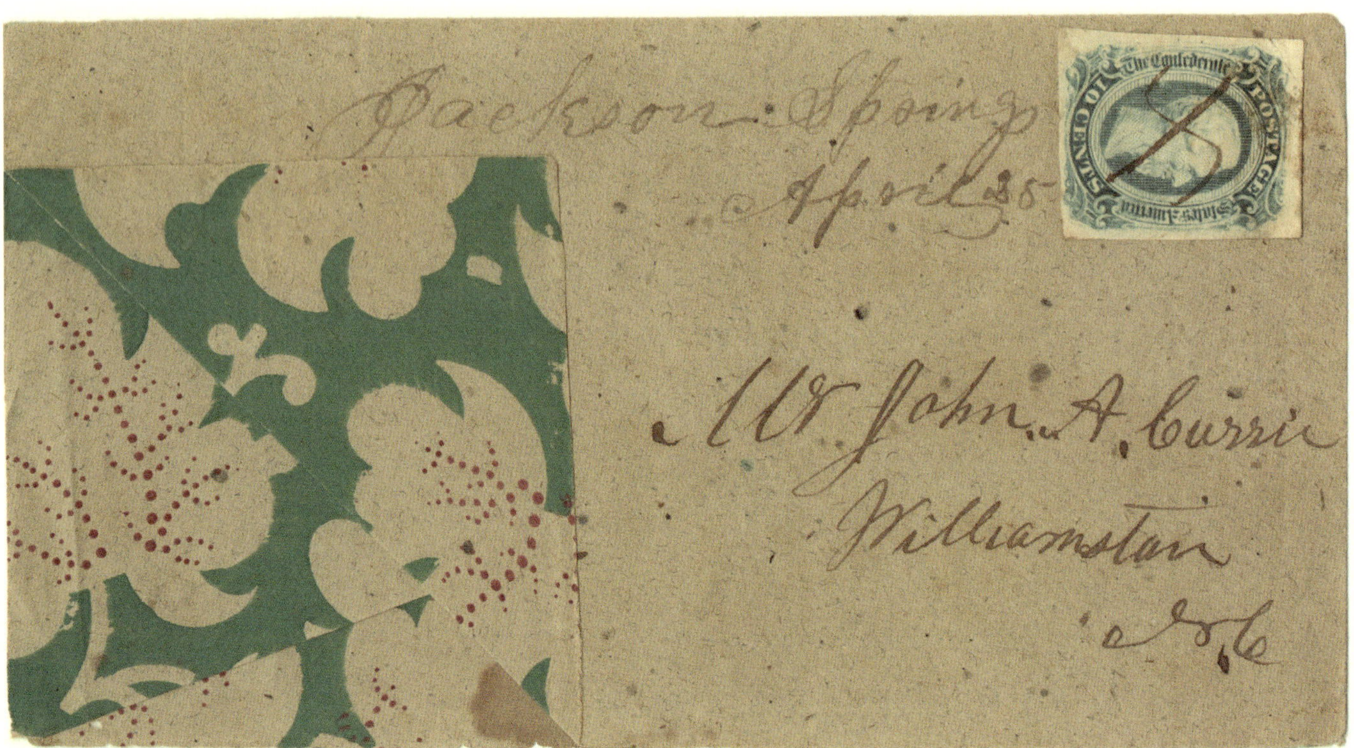

A homemade southern wallpaper envelope addressed to John A. Currie. Another common technique in the South was to steam old envelopes apart and turn them inside out for a second use.

Little by little, Union troops reclaimed United States territory.

Perhaps most poetic were the early letters from POWs: Near the start of the war, they were limited to only six lines of text. Working within these constraints, letters became blunt, visceral, and emotional. On April 2, 1863, Union Captain Charles Thayer wrote to his mother from Libby Prison in Richmond, Virginia:

> I arrived this 6 P.M. from Gordonsville (Va.)
> Wounded through fleshy part of right thigh—doing well
> 10 Privates of my reg't are with me. A Flag of truce boat is
> here & will take them off tomorrow—no chance for Officers
> to be Paroled or exchanged. 2 from my reg't are here before me I can write only 6 lines—write soon all of you—goodbye love to all.

On April 2, 1865, the Confederate capital of Richmond, Virginia, fell to Union forces. One week later, Robert E. Lee, the commander of the Confederate States Army, surrendered his troops to Ulysses S. Grant at the small town of Appomattox, some 90 miles to the west of Richmond. While other parts of the southern military would have to surrender individually and the war would not be officially declared over by President Andrew Johnson until the summer of 1866, Appomattox marked the beginning of the end of the war. (Johnson had become president upon the assassination of Abraham Lincoln, which took place the same month Richmond fell.) Little by little, Union troops reclaimed United States territory. As they did, federal mail service began to be restored to the South. By the end of 1866, nearly half of the post offices there were restored to their former allegiance. As the country worked to repair itself, so did the post.

And what of the reason the war was fought? The story of slavery in America is not one that can be told within the bounds of a book about the mail. But the Post Office Department in the 1860s was reflective of a larger project, known as Reconstruction, that was starting in the country. Its aim was to stitch the country back up, integrating now-free Black Americans into the nation's civic infrastructure. Progress was slow but meaningful. Many important Black leaders in the post–Civil War era served at least some time with the Post Office Department, starting with William Cooper Nell, who in 1863 was appointed a clerk at the Boston Post Office—thus becoming the first known Black civilian employee of the federal government. The lives of Nell and his peers convey the sweep of what was proving to be the second act of America's story.

James W. Mason was born a slave in 1841 in Chicot County, Arkansas. The son of an exceedingly wealthy plantation owner and an enslaved woman, Mason was given an elite education and placed in charge of one of the family's plantations. After the war, he became prominent in politics in Chicot County, and was appointed postmaster of the town of Sunny Side in 1867—the first Black postmaster in the nation. He went on to serve as a county judge, a county sheriff, and a state senator.

John W. Curry was a clerk and then a letter carrier in the nation's capital. He is believed to be Washington, D.C.'s first Black letter carrier—and he was much more. *The Washington Bee*, a historic Black newspaper based in the city, reported that he "[opened] the way for admission of other colored carriers" and helped Black Washingtonians secure access to public schools.

Right: John W. Curry is believed to be the first Black letter carrier employed out of the Washington, D.C., Post Office. His obituary printed in *The Colored American* on April 29, 1899, stated he was a 35-year postal veteran as a clerk and carrier and "was known as an efficient carrier, and he was well liked by those whom he served."

Clockwise from top left: William H. Carney wearing his Congressional Medal of Honor, circa 1900; photographed by John Ritchie while holding the American flag; standing on the doorstep of a New Bedford, Massachusetts, townhome in his city letter-carrier uniform.

In 1869, James B. Christian became one of the first Black letter carriers in the former Confederate capital, Richmond.

Perhaps the most remarkable story is that of William H. Carney. Carney was born into slavery in Norfolk, Virginia, in 1840. He and his family were freed early in the war when the Union Navy captured the city. They moved north to Massachusetts, and in 1863, Carney enlisted with the Union Army. He was assigned to Company C of the 54th Massachusetts Colored Infantry Regiment—the first official Black unit recruited for the Union in the North. Two of Frederick Douglass's sons served alongside him. His regiment would famously lead the charge on Fort Wagner, a Confederate fortification blocking the entrance to Charleston Harbor. Carney would nearly die in the battle. After the war, he started working as a letter carrier in New Bedford, Massachusetts. He served in that role, helping letter carriers across the country unionize along the way, from 1869 to 1901—just one year after he became the first Black American to be awarded the Congressional Medal of Honor.

Transferring Postmasterships to War Widows and Veterans' Preference

Mail service spurred one of President Lincoln's quietest yet most far-reaching wartime initiatives. It began with the arrival of two letters at the Executive Mansion on July 23, 1863. Each was written by the widow of a soldier killed in battle. Both were asking to be appointed to postmasterships. After pondering the eerie timing of the two quite similar requests, Lincoln wrote to Blair the following day: "Yesterday little indorsements [*sic*] of mine went to you in two cases of post masterships sought for widows whose husbands have fallen in the battles of this war. These cases occurring on the same day, brought me to reflect more attentively than I have before done, as to what is fairly due from us here, in the dispensing of patronage, toward the men who, by fighting our battles, bear the chief burden of serving our country. My conclusion is that, other claims and qualifications being equal, they have the better right, and this is especially applicable to the disabled soldier, and the deceased soldier's family."

Two years later, that letter brought about the first law granting veterans' preference, passed on March 3, 1865. The law stated that "persons honorably discharged from the military or naval service by reason of disability resulting from wounds or sickness incurred in the line of duty, shall be preferred for appointment to civil offices, provided they be found to possess the business capacity necessary for the proper discharge of the duties of such offices." The practice of giving veterans preferential treatment when it comes to federal employment is still in practice today.

A letter from Governor William Bebb applauding Abraham Lincoln's appointment of Melancthon Smith's widow to the position of postmaster of Rockford, Illinois. Smith's wife performed his postmaster duties while he was serving in the 45th Illinois, but unfortunately he was killed at Vicksburg.

PATRIOTIC COVERS

Between 1861 and 1865, the beginning and ending of the Civil War, citizens from both ideological sides could show their political leanings or patriotism through the patriotic covers, or envelopes, they used for mailings. These covers featured flags, eagles, soldiers, battles, portraits of esteemed leaders such as Washington, Lincoln, McClellan, and Ellsworth, and caricatures. The northern states had the advantage over the South when it came to printing and available supplies, which is why there are far more northern covers held in museum collections today than Confederate ones.

This cover includes a cancellation over a three-cent George Washington stamp; the U.S. seal in the upper left includes abbreviations for the 34 states.

An elephant labeled "Winfield Scott" holds a banner reading "I ALWAYS WIN." A cartoon figure rides a pig with a sign declaring "Jeff. Davis's Last Ride upon the SOUTH."

A cover printed with "19th Regiment Massachusetts Volunteers" and "Soldiers' Letter," along with three 1861 one-cent Benjamin Franklin stamps.

A cover featuring "Rose of Washington." Liberty stands at the right, next to an eagle holding a banner reading "E pluribus unum."

Robert Morris wrote, "We Are Coming, Father Abraham" in 1862. A portion of that poem is printed below the Union troops, pictured here.

A Union cover featuring a victorious soldier brandishing the American flag.

A Confederate cover. The 12 stars on the flag represent the number of states in the Confederacy during the war.

An unused "For the Union" cover includes the Pennsylvania state emblem in the upper right.

A cover addressed to Abraham Lincoln with a postmark from Dunkirk, New York, dated February 6, 1864. At left is an illustration of a Zouaves couple.

ENCASED POSTAGE

With limited coins in circulation during the Civil War, citizens began using postage stamps as currency. The practice became so widespread that the U.S. government authorized the monetizing of stamps by July 1862—and even printed stamp impressions on the paper used for bank notes.

John Gault, an enterprising entrepreneur and inventor, applied for a patent to encase stamps so they wouldn't be damaged in circulation. His "Design for Encasing Government Stamps," which was quickly approved by the U.S. Patent Office, allowed individuals to wrap the corners of a stamp around a cardboard circle. The addition of a transparent piece of mica, as well as a sturdy metal backing (which could also be used for advertising purposes), completed this clever apparatus. Just as soon as his enterprise began, it ended on August 21, 1862, when the government issued postage currency in five-, 10-, 25-, and 50-cent denominations.

One-cent Franklin Ayer's Sarsaparilla encased postage, which reads "To purify the blood."

Washington Ayer's Sarsaparilla encased postage.

A ten-cent Washington. The reverse reads, "Applications for advertising on this currency to be addressed to Kilpatrick Gault, No. 1 Park Place."

A five-cent Jefferson. On the reverse is an advertisement for Burnett's Standard Cooking Extracts.

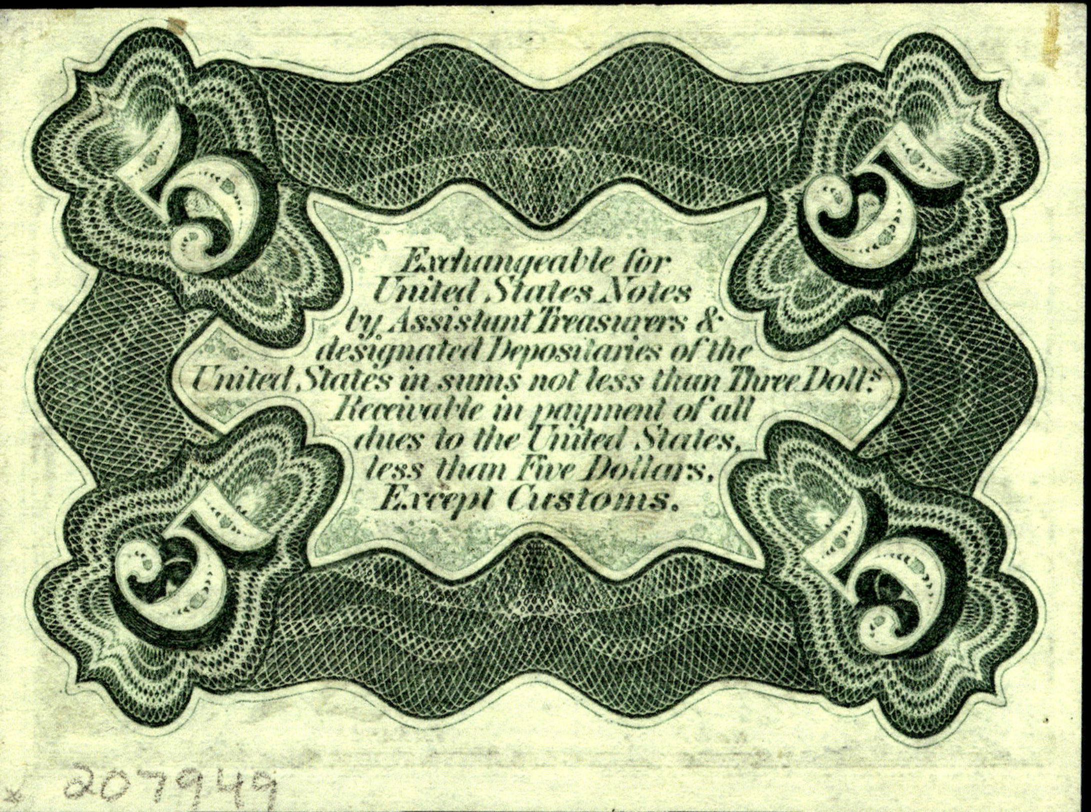

Between August 21, 1862, and February 15, 1876, fractional currency could be redeemed at the Post Office Department for face value in postage stamps. For the third issuance of fractional currency, Supervisor of the Currency Bureau Spencer M. Clark allowed his own likeness to be used on the five-cent fractional note. This act led to legislation prohibiting the depiction of any living person on U.S. currency. Denominations were issued in three, five, 10, 15, 25, and 50 cents.

U.S. POSTAGE
TWO 2 CENTS

TWELVE 12 CENTS
U.S. POSTAGE
FIFTEEN 15 CENTS

U.S. POSTAGE
24 U.S. POSTAGE 24
TWENTY FOUR
CENTS

TWELVE 12 CENTS

U.S. POSTAGE
NINETY 90 CENTS

POST OFFICE
X TEN CENTS X

U.S. POSTAGE
THREE 3 CENTS

U.S. POSTAGE
THIRTY 30 CENTS

U.S. POSTAGE

SEWED BACK TOGETHER WITH STITCHES OF RAILS AND TIES

In May 1869, a raucous crowd gathered at Promontory Summit, in Utah, near the northern reaches of the Great Salt Lake and not far off George Chorpenning Jr. and Absalmon Woodward's first overland-mail route west. For years, two railroads had been building toward Promontory. From Sacramento, the Central Pacific Railroad constructed 690 miles of track through the punishing landscape of the Sierra Nevada mountains. From Omaha, Nebraska (a connection point to the nation's eastern railroad network), the Union Pacific Railroad laid a 1,085-mile-long route. When the two railroads met, it would finally be possible to cross the entire country by train, on one transcontinental railroad from Pacific to Atlantic. May 10, 1869, was to be the day, and there was going to be a party.

An enterprising businessman named David Hewes—the brother-in-law of Leland Stanford, the former governor of California and head of the Central Pacific—thought something special ought to be done to mark the completion of this momentous project. He had a ceremonial railroad spike cast in gold. Others joined Hewes in his jubilance. More ceremonial spikes were created: an additional gold spike by Frederick Marriott, proprietor of the *San Francisco News Letter*; a gold and silver spike by the government of the Arizona Territory; and a silver spike by a representative from the state of Nevada. Merchants from San Francisco created a special hammer for driving the spikes and a final ceremonial railroad tie made of California laurelwood. Hewes's golden spike would become famous as a symbol of the completion of the railroad and of a nation that now stretched from sea to shining sea.

But for the mail, a different spike was more important. Hewes had another celebratory idea, one that would prove more symbolic for the nation's communication network. With the Western Union Telegraph Company, he worked out a plan to wire a typical railroad spike to a telegraph cable, and that cable to a ceremonial cannon in San Francisco. When this spike was struck, it would send a telegraph-like signal over the cable and fire a cannon shot on the shores of the Pacific Ocean.

Photos from that day show huge crowds, a locomotive from each railroad sitting on the rails nearly nose to nose, and at least one bottle of Champagne.

The ceremony itself did not quite live up to the hoopla. Stanford swung at the golden spike and missed, as did Thomas Durant, the representative of the Union Pacific. But no matter. When a regular railroad worker hammered in the spike

Men gather to drive the golden spike at Promontory Summit, Utah, on May 10, 1869, which marked the completion of the first trans-continental railroad. At center, Samuel S. Montague of the Central Pacific Railroad (left) shakes hands with Grenville M. Dodge (right) of the Union Pacific Railroad.

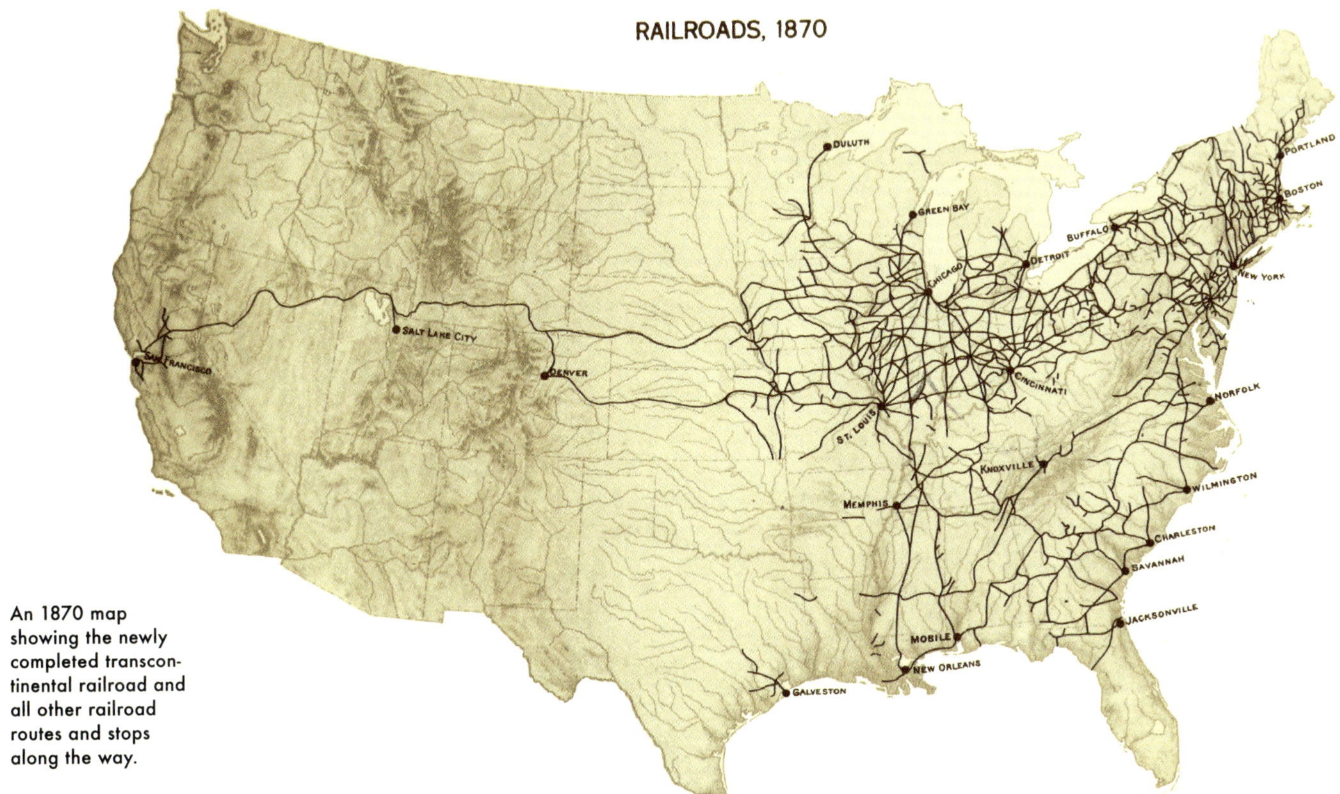

An 1870 map showing the newly completed transcontinental railroad and all other railroad routes and stops along the way.

connected to the telegraph line, the message went off with a bang over the Pacific Ocean: The nation has been connected. Minutes later, a telegrapher sent a message racing east as well: D-O-N-E.

Rail and the telegraph had brought an end to the overland mail, but they were no enemy of the Post Office Department. Together they signaled the start of a new era of communication in the United States. The Civil War had torn the country apart. When the 1870s began, socially and culturally, it was still in tatters. But in at least one way—the way that mattered for moving mail—it was knit together like never before.

★ ★ ★

The nation had always been interested in westward expansion, and after the Civil War, it became an obsession. In a century, the country had grown from a group of colonies along the Atlantic coast to a nation that straddled the entire continent. The Civil War had halted the breakneck pace of growth, but as the country emerged from the conflict, it tried to embrace a spirit of optimism. Reconstruction, as the period after the Civil War was known, was an attempt to rebuild the country's civic fabric and government institutions without discrimination against Black Americans. The United States was also approaching its centennial. And so the frenzy to expand the nation's horizons started back up. The spirit of the era was summarized in a September 1868 issue of California's *Oakland Daily Transcript*: "This is manifest destiny, which will never be fulfilled till the limits of the Union shall embrace the boundaries of the continent, and the stars that represent its States in the azure field of its emblem, shall dazzle the world by their numbers and their glory."

In practice, this meant stakes, and ties, and miles upon miles of steel track.

From the nation's first railroad, in 1830, the Baltimore & Ohio at 23 track miles, railroad expansion increased by hundreds to thousands of miles each year. The Civil War brought that to a halt—only a few thousand miles of railroad were opened, most for military purposes. But as soon as the war ended, building picked up pace. Expansion was driven not by any government impetus—with the exception of the transcontinental railroad, which benefited from federal support—but by wealthy entrepreneurs. These groups of men saw a need—and dollar signs. Earnings from the 10,982 miles of railroad in 1851 were $39.5 million. In 1870, there were 53,399 miles of railroads, and they generated upward of $450 million.

Above, left to right: Almost one month after the panic, an illustration of Wall Street at the intersection of Nassau and Broad streets depicts the mob waiting to access their money, with a view of Western Union, the Sub-Treasury, and the bank to the right; an illustration of *The Great Financial Panic of 1873—Closing the Door of the Stock Exchange on Its Members* covers the front page of *Frank Leslie's Illustrated Supplement.*

The competition for expansion and ownership was fierce. In 1870, newspapers across the country were calling this "railroad fever." The January 1, 1870, edition of Ohio's *Miami Union* printed that the fever "is now getting pretty high all over the country. Several hundred miles more will undoubtedly be made in this State within the next two or three years." Fever was an apt term. In the heat of the moment, many people made rash decisions. Individuals and companies dramatically overextended themselves financially. In 1873, railway construction costs were said to be about $3 billion, an enormous sum that led investor confidence in the profitability of the railroads to waver, causing instability that forced the New York Stock Exchange to close its doors for 10 days in September. What came to be called the Railroad Panic of 1873 was thankfully short-lived, subsiding the following month. And it had a positive side effect. Money was redirected from building trackage to improving trains themselves, something that benefited the only organization vast enough to match the scale and rapid expansion of the railroads: the Post Office Department.

In 1870, the department's patrons were served by the largest distribution network of its kind in the country. There were 28,492 post offices and 43,954 employees, including 1,419 urban letter carriers assigned to 52 major city post offices, 513 railway mail clerks and route agents, and 7,286 contractors. At the time, it was the nation's biggest business-related endeavor, and its products and services expanded the reach of every other avenue of commerce. At the dawn of the decade, it handled more than 112 million letters, 32 million newspapers and periodicals, and $8 million worth of money orders in just one year.

Rail was the perfect venue for speeding up and sizing up postal operations. Soon the Railway Mail Service (RMS), a division within the Post Office Department founded in 1862, would come to dominate the transit of mail. And the money that was not being spent on new railroads (because of the slowdown following the Panic of 1873) could now be put to use advancing ideas that had been bubbling up through the mail service for years, primarily through a lineage of three men: William Davis, George Armstrong, and George Bangs.

★ ★ ★

All the overland mail to California and the sparsely populated western territories passed through St. Joseph.

William Davis joined the Post Office Department right around the time that mail was first carried by train. In 1830, at the age of 21, he became assistant postmaster in Richmond, at Virginia's largest post office. In 1832, an outfit that carried mail by stage in Pennsylvania, Slaymaker and Tomlinson, started using trains to take some from Lancaster to West Chester. It was the first to do so. In 1838, when Congress passed legislation declaring all railroads must have the status of post roads, Davis was working his way up the ladder in Richmond, where he would serve for 25 years. But it was in St. Joseph, Missouri, where he would become postmaster in 1856, that everything would change.

St. Joseph was the starting point for the Pony Express and, like nearby Independence, was a point of embarkation for people moving into the American West. As a result, mail to the post office there was prolific—so much so that in 1858 it gained the designation of a Presidential Post Office, one whose postmaster was appointed by the country's commander in chief. That might have spelled certain doom for Davis, who was not in the same party as Abraham Lincoln, but his service had been so exemplary that when Lincoln's postmaster appointee, John Bittinger, arrived in St. Joseph in 1861, he kept Davis on as an assistant. Davis was put in charge of distribution between rail lines in the East and the overland-mail routes to the West.

This was not an easy job. All the overland mail to California and the sparsely populated western territories passed through St. Joseph, arriving principally aboard the newly built Hannibal and St. Joseph Railroad. However, the outbreak of hostilities between the North and the South, which were especially vicious in Missouri, a border state, made the timely transfer of mail at distribution points erratic at best and rendered railway operations across Missouri extremely hazardous. Nightly raids by Confederate guerrillas on the railway lines disrupted service. As a result of these conditions, westbound trains to St. Joseph were constantly running behind schedule, resulting in as much as three days' worth of mail arriving at once. This

The Hannibal and St. Joseph was the first railroad to cross Missouri as well as the first with a "post office on wheels" when, in 1862, William A. Davis modified the train car to handle mail sorting. The map, dated 1860, marks the stops and east and west termini.

The Life of a Railway Clerk

In the 1870s, as the concept of railway post offices matured and trains played a larger and larger role in mail delivery, the role of the railway clerk developed within the Post Office Department, and the life of a clerk came to embody something distinct about life in America in that time: An industrious nation was becoming more sophisticated in its pursuit of growth and advancement.

When on duty, these clerks were required to carry their travel commission, a small credential that permitted them to ride on the specific train they were assigned to; their book of instructions; copies of all special orders and schedules of mail routes; and their updated schemes. Schemes—that is, the specific plans that guide the sorting and distribution of a given set of mail—were undergoing a revolution at this time. Until the 1870s, mail clerks had to create their own schemes, and they were often full of errors. But beginning in this decade, the first printed mail schemes began to appear. What's more, just as the mail delivery system had become more complicated, schemes grew more complex and numerous: Often there were multiple types of distribution schemes that a clerk might need to know, and they were updated weekly, which meant that clerks had to constantly keep their scheme books current to avoid misdirected mail.

They also had to pass an exam to show that they'd learned post-office locations, routes, and railway schedules. The tests were high-pressure affairs that required months of studying and memorization. And frequently they involved what clerks-to-be considered a diabolical device: the sweat cabinet. It was a portable wooden box full of slotted holes corresponding to RPOs and post offices. Cards representing letters to be mailed had to be sorted into the slots until a clerk could do it to perfection. When it came time to take the exam, applicants would indeed often find themselves sweating. The feeling of dread was even put to verse by Carl Lucas in a piece called "Go-Back Pouch": "If another scheme I've got to learn / I'd rather stay right here and burn!"

As opportunities for errors among railway clerks grew more numerous, there was also an overhaul in the Post Office Department around tracking them. In 1877, Washington, D.C., hosted a conference of postal officials that included participants who had worked their way up through the ranks of the Postal Service. After considering all the ways they might try to prevent or minimize mistakes, a panel of the officials recommended the rigorous use of facing slips.

These were small paper forms that went in each mail bundle and noted key details, including the name of the postal employee who had made up the bundle. Employees were required to note errors on the slips and return them with their trip report to the local superintendent at the end of every shift. The slips had always been useful for expediting delivery, but in this way, they provided useful data for analyzing and optimizing delivery. They could also trace errors back to specific clerks, who could then face corrective actions if they repeatedly made mistakes.

There was another way in which railway clerks embodied the changes happening in America, as railways increasingly pushed into sparsely populated western territory: Their jobs took place against a backdrop of great danger. Working on the rails was a risky business. In 1872, a Christmas Eve crash near Prospect, New York, killed at least 19 people. One of the few able to be identified was Post Office Department employee Earl Douglas Bacon of Brocton, New York. The litany of such railway accidents reported in the newspaper might have dissuaded anyone from taking a job as a railway clerk. But people needed, and wanted, to work. And there was something else: Like so much at this time in America, working on the rails was dangerous, but it was also exciting and filled with purpose. And so, as ever, the mail endured.

The examination case, or "sweat cabinet," was first used in Chicago in January 1872. It was considered "the most important educational method in use" for hopeful railway mail clerks.

An illustration depicting the country's first railway post-office car. At one end was a letter case composed of four rows of 13 boxes for newspaper distribution, while at the other was a case containing 77 pigeon holes. The car also included four oil lamps, drawers, and a stove.

THE FIRST RAILWAY POST-OFFICE CAR
SHOWING PAPER AND LETTER CASES

swamped the post office and compromised its ability to distribute the mail in a timely fashion.

Bittinger later recalled Davis's breakthrough that solved this problem. "One day in the spring of 1862, Davis came into the office with a mass of drawings and asked me to look over them," he wrote. "He said he thought he knew how a [railway mail] car could be rigged up so that men could work on the mail while the train was in motion, and if it could be done it would save us a vast amount of work and delay." In other words: They could design a post office on rails. The two men got Postmaster General Blair to allow them to give the plan a try. After a brief investigation into its feasibility, the project got the green light in July.

Davis worked with the master car builder for the Hannibal and St. Joseph Railroad to design purpose-built cars made for sorting mail. The Civil War would muck up the plans, so they improvised, adding postal furniture to existing cars for initial test runs in late July and early August. They were a resounding success.

★ ★ ★

Shortly after the Railway Mail Service began at St. Joseph, Bittinger received a letter from George B. Armstrong, the assistant postmaster in Chicago, requesting information about the experimental service. His city, he wrote, was being inundated with mail. This was no exaggeration. With local populations growing and mail increasing, post offices were constantly forced to change locations to accommodate greater volumes. And in Chicago, which was a rapidly growing railroad hub, the problem was prodigious. Its first post office, established when the city was a pioneer town in 1833, was moved in 1834, 1838, 1841, and 1855. (The 1855 post office didn't stay put, either, but for a very different reason: It was destroyed by the Great Chicago Fire in 1871.) Perhaps mail sorting by rail could help the city's postal workers get out from under the heavy mail volume.

In a subsequent letter, Armstrong asked if he could personally inspect the mail cars and talk with the mail clerks about their experiences. Bittinger welcomed the opportunity to share the results of his office's success. Armstrong visited St. Joseph, leaving with a plan for similar service on the line from Chicago to Clinton, Iowa.

A few years later, in 1865, Armstrong resigned his position in Chicago to take a job at

A look at the interior of a Fast Mail train car showing the letter case at one end. Mailbags were hung within the middle of the car for ease of use by all clerks.

Post Office headquarters in Washington, D.C., as superintendent of the Railway Mail Service. That same year, he instituted a plan modeled after Davis's concept, one that significantly reduced the number of stationary distributing post offices by literally placing them aboard what were called Railway Post Offices (RPOs)—rolling distribution cars that initially were nearly carbon copies of what was being used in Missouri. The RPOs began operating in August 1864, on a route between Chicago and northern Iowa. Soon to follow were routes from Chicago to Davenport, Iowa, and to Burlington, Iowa, and routes from New York City to Dunkirk, New York, and to Washington, D.C.

In December of that year, Armstrong was commissioned to oversee all railway mail operations west of Indiana's eastern border, while a man named Harrison Park took on operations to the east. Under their shared supervision, and despite largely adverse military and political circumstances during the Civil War, the Union's railway mail system became highly successful. Once the war ended, their operations developed further. In 1867, newly designed RPOs were put into use. The cars did not have doors at either end, where the customary passenger vestibule was located. Instead, a pair of side doors were used to make more space for postal equipment and avoid accidental interruptions from passengers. The interior was fitted out much like a small-town post office, with space for sorting both letters and periodicals. There were two oil lamps, and clerks could avail themselves of a stove, a small stool, and an ice cooler. Though it may sound rudimentary today, it was revolutionary at the time. And it laid the groundwork for the next, lightning-fast leap forward, at the hands of George Bangs, who came along at the exact right time to truly take advantage of the shift in focus from rail to rolling stock that came in with the Panic of 1873.

George Bangs, who served as postmaster of Aurora, Illinois, beginning in 1861, went on to work with the Railway Mail Service (RMS). He is credited with improving the mail-sorting system on trains. In 1871, as the RMS general superintendent, he oversaw the start of the Fast Mail service, which began in 1875.

★ ★ ★

George Bangs arrived in Aurora, Illinois, not far from Chicago, as a young printer and newspaperman in 1851. While he had tried his hand at a number of occupations, including working in the boot and shoe business and as a farmer, one constant was an interest in politics and civic affairs. After purchasing the Aurora *Republican*, he worked hard to make it an important paper in the state, particularly among Republicans. In the run-up to the 1860 election, he was the state's first champion for one of its rising political stars, a lawyer and former state and U.S. representative named Abraham Lincoln. His tireless support of the candidate earned him a prize once Lincoln won the presidency: In one of his first appointments, Lincoln made Bangs postmaster of Aurora.

So it was that George Bangs, now in the mail business in Illinois, made the acquaintance of George Armstrong, who named Bangs assistant superintendent of Chicago in 1869 and, when he retired from his job at the Railway Mail Service, ceded the role to Bangs.

Bangs turned out to be a wizard of mail by rail. He had a nose for the small changes that could make the incredible volume mail workers dealt with more manageable. Among his earliest significant operational improvements was ordering the separation of mail by state before it was placed aboard mail trains. Whereas Pony Express riders would carry no more than 20 pounds of mail in a leather *mochila*, and the Overland Express carried bags of hundreds of pounds, trains were now carrying *thousands* of pounds of mail. Railway mail clerks were sorting more than 500,000 letters and papers per day. Anything that offered them a scheme for prioritization was a huge help. Loading trains by state allowed them to process this mountain of mail in the order of states they passed through, for maximum efficiency.

Bangs also oversaw the introduction of "on the fly" mail exchanges: Trains would race past hanging mail pouches suspended from trackside mail cranes. Y-shaped catcher arms attached to mail cars were able to grab the hanging mail—outgoing from the community—without the train appreciably slowing down. This was a play for speed, and it wasn't Bangs's only one. In fact, his greatest achievement was all about speed. It was called the Fast Mail.

What Bangs came to realize was that the amount of mail now being exchanged by Americans was enough to justify trains dedicated to mail, at least along certain routes. At his direction, in 1875, the Lake Shore and Michigan Southern and the New York Central and Hudson River railroads combined efforts to make the Fast Train: a train composed of four mail cars plus one coach car. It would originate in New York City and travel through Albany and Buffalo, Cleveland and Toledo, then reach its terminus in Chicago—24 hours later. Bangs's goal was to "expedite the movement of mail from the east to the west and cover the distance in 24 hours," and he secured allies among the railroads by convincing them that any railroad able to establish itself as exceptionally fast could gain dominance in the industry.

Opposite: The mail crane was introduced as a safer method for railway clerks to lift up mailbags into slowly moving trains. *Top, left to right:* A patent drawing of the crane with a hanging mailbag attached; a clerk watches for the crane. *Bottom, left to right:* The clerk uses a hook to grab the bag; the clerk removes the bag from the hook and tosses it inside the car.

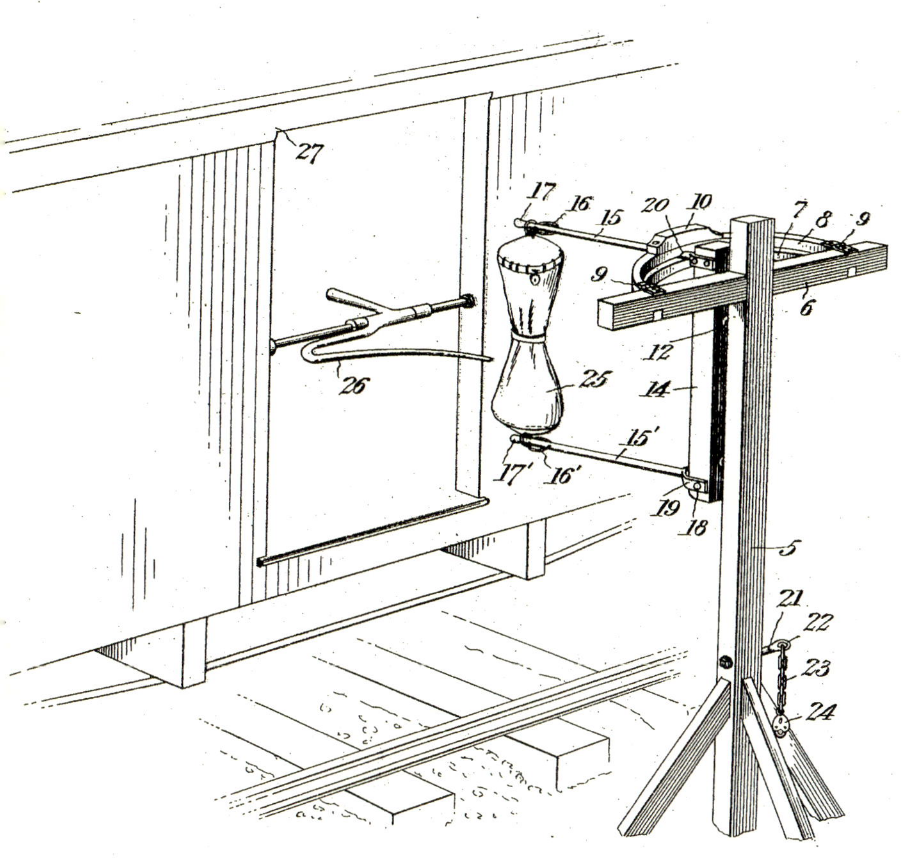
27
17
16
15
20
10
7
8
9
9
6
26
25
12
14
15'
17'
16'
19
18
5
21
22
23
24

The Post Office Delivers a Memorable Time at the United States Centennial

On May 10, 1876, a six-month-long exposition opened in Philadelphia, the birthplace of American independence. It drew 10 million visitors, one-quarter of the population of the United States at the time. Anyone who could was going to Philadelphia; there was a rush on hotel rooms, and longtime residents complained of being inundated with fairgoing "relatives" they swore they never knew existed. Railroads created special travel packages and express trains to get people to the exposition. The grounds were vast and hosted everyone from members of Congress and the Supreme Court to a variety of state governors to people seated in the Cabinet–and President Ulysses S. Grant himself. Everywhere seemed to be dripping in red, white, and blue.

It was the nation's centennial celebration.

Perhaps nowhere did the red, white, and blue blaze more proudly than at the fair's post-office building and on its letter boxes and mail wagons. The mail was a major part of the experience at the Centennial Exposition. Patrons were encouraged to purchase a variety of centennial souvenirs and mail them home, and there was no shortage of gleaming infrastructure to make that possible. Mailboxes were conveniently placed throughout the fairgrounds, and specially built red, white, and blue postal carts were used to transport mail from the grounds to the city's main post office. The building dedicated to public comfort, which contained restaurants and shops, also featured rooms of desks with paper, postcards, and postage stamps. Penny postal cards, which Congress had first authorized four years earlier, were ideal for short personal correspondence from the fair–and for advertising sales or new products and inviting business contacts to visit company displays.

There was one postal product made especially for the fair, and in a way, it told the story of the country's pride upon reaching its 100th year. Special three-cent *centennial*-embossed stamped envelopes were created for fair patrons. They were the world's first commemorative stamped envelopes, and many were even printed on-site by the Plimpton Manufacturing Company (with the permission of the Post Office Department). The beautiful envelopes were a manifestation of American innovation and ingenuity: Plimpton had perfected a machine that folded, stamped, gummed, counted,

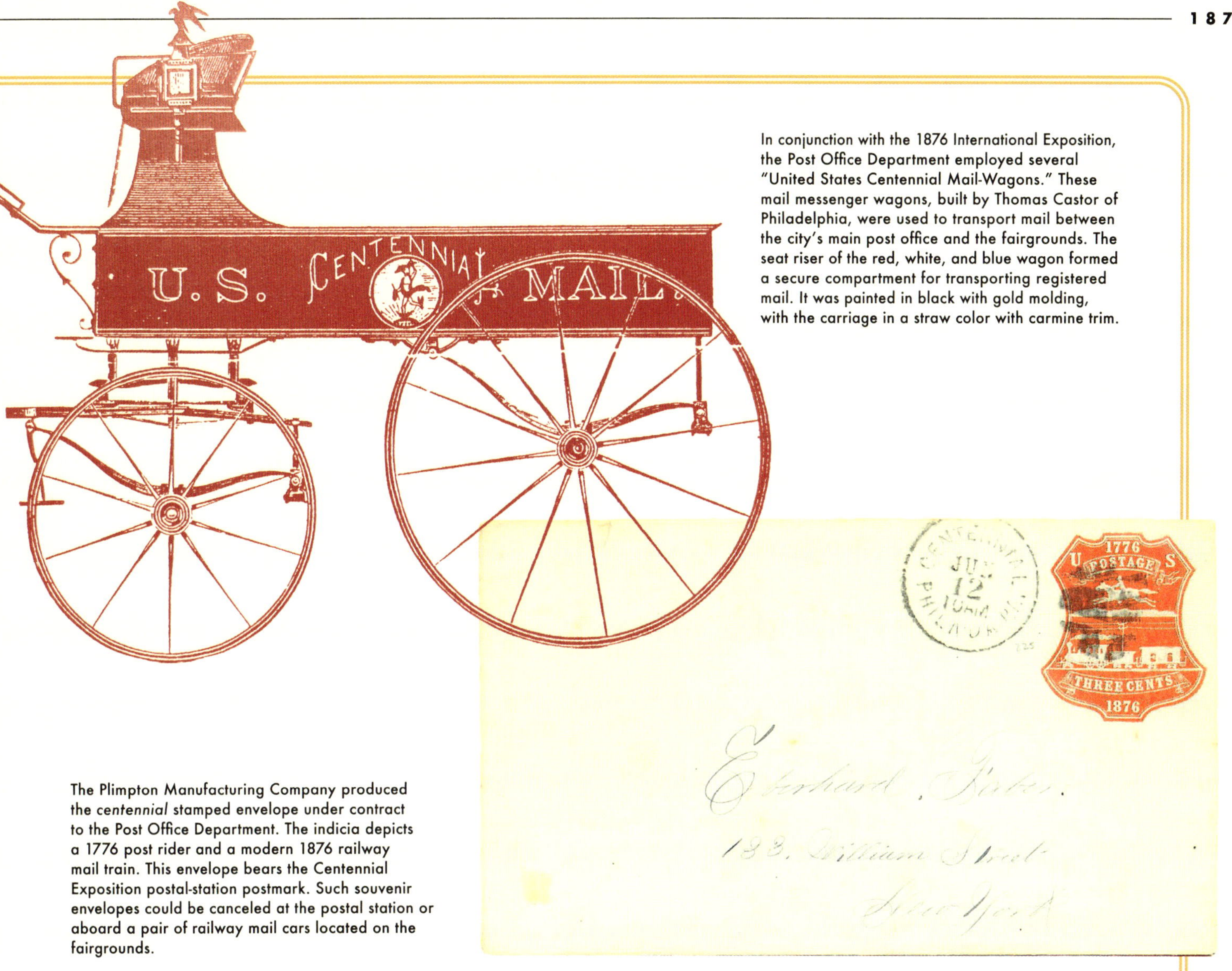

In conjunction with the 1876 International Exposition, the Post Office Department employed several "United States Centennial Mail-Wagons." These mail messenger wagons, built by Thomas Castor of Philadelphia, were used to transport mail between the city's main post office and the fairgrounds. The seat riser of the red, white, and blue wagon formed a secure compartment for transporting registered mail. It was painted in black with gold molding, with the carriage in a straw color with carmine trim.

The Plimpton Manufacturing Company produced the *centennial* stamped envelope under contract to the Post Office Department. The indicia depicts a 1776 post rider and a modern 1876 railway mail train. This envelope bears the Centennial Exposition postal-station postmark. Such souvenir envelopes could be canceled at the postal station or aboard a pair of railway mail cars located on the fairgrounds.

and packaged the envelopes, 25 to a bundle, with ribbon. They were also vastly more popular than expected. Multiple printings ultimately put into circulation 4,775,000 units of a green, letter-size version and 4,227,000 units of a vermillion commercial-size version. They were sold at post offices around the country, symbolic of the notion that the nation's advances should and would be shared with all. But there was something special for exposition attendees, a slight and subtle design tweak that, for those in the know, indicated membership in an exclusive club: Any centennial envelope with a double line under the word *postage* had been printed live at the fairgrounds, a singular souvenir of a singular moment in American history.

The railroads also prioritized quality alongside speed. The New York Central and Lake Shore Railroad went above and beyond in designing the mail cars for the Fast Mail. At a cost of $4,200 each, the cars were downright opulent. Each was painted white with cream-colored borders, gilt ornamentation, and lettering, including the phrase "the Fast Mail." Interiors included an inscription of the year 1776 in Roman numerals, MDCCLXXVI, and the motto *Novus ordo seclorum*, a Latin phrase meaning, literally, "a new order of the ages" that can also be found on the reverse side of the $1 bill and the United States coat of arms. When combined with the date, however, it suggests "the beginning of a new American era."

The single coach car attached to each Fast Train was not forgotten in this emphasis on luxury. At $3,300 each, the passenger cars were described by the Post Office as providing "superior accommodations." They were equipped with such luxuries as folding bunks, toilets, sinks, warming stoves, and water coolers. Each car was named in honor of a governor from one of the states to which the mail was transported.

The Fast Mail commenced service on September 16, 1875, beginning from the Grand Depot at New York City at 4:17 a.m. Its inaugural run to Chicago arrived a few minutes ahead of schedule. Nevertheless, clerks managed to distribute 43 pouches of letter mail and 663 sacks of papers and periodicals in this time. This initial track record became standard for the New York City to Chicago Fast Mail. The inaugural run from east to west and back was equally smooth. Based upon this enviable record, Postmaster General James N. Tyner wrote in his 1876 annual report: "These lines afforded facilities for the transmission of mails from the great commercial center of the East to all points in the West and Southwest, hitherto unknown in the history of rail transportation in this country, and enabled the Post Office Department to so completely meet the demands upon it for speedy transportation that the most sanguine expectations of the business communities

Fast Mail cars were typically painted white with red and blue trim to make them distinctive. A Fast Train generally included a set of cars consisting of at least one for sorting mail, one for mail-sack storage in conjunction with closed-pouch service, and one for newspaper distribution.

The end of the Fast Mail was in some ways the end of a golden era of mail innovation on the rails.

Fast Mail service by the Lake Shore and Michigan Southern Railroad began on September 16, 1875. On its inaugural run, the crew sorted and distributed approximately 33 tons of mail during the 900-mile run between New York City and Chicago. This later LS & MS Fast Mail car honors Governor Charles Foster of Ohio.

dependent upon them for postal supplies were more than realized."

And yet Fast Mail service between New York City and Chicago was terminated after only 10 months when the railroads asked for more money to cover the costs associated with this expedited service. Unwilling to pay more, Congress not only denied the requested increase but also cut the amount allocated to the Post Office Department for railway spending by 10 percent. In response, the railroad lines promptly suspended service on the New York City to Chicago Fast Mail on July 22, 1876. Nevertheless, the Fast Mail had proved what was possible when delivering mail with trains, at a time when the nation's train network was more expansive than ever before. And even though it ended, it did not take long for the Post Office Department to contract with other railroad lines to start moving and sorting mail again. New routes arose between major cities including New York City, St. Louis, Cincinnati, Philadelphia, Pittsburgh, Indianapolis, and Columbus, Ohio.

The end of the Fast Mail was in some ways the end of a golden era of mail innovation on the rails. George Bangs, the last of the three founding fathers of the Railway Mail Service, continued as a leader in the Post Office Department until 1876. The number of miles of RMS trackage, and the number of clerks in the service's employ, continued to grow throughout his tenure.

Bangs seemed a bit listless after he resigned. He declined an offer from President Grant to serve as U.S. postmaster general. Grant's term was nearly up, and Bangs was considered a likely Cabinet member in the administration of Grant's successor, Rutherford B. Hayes. Instead, the seats in the Cabinet went to political operatives and Bangs became an assistant U.S. treasurer. He served just over a year before dying in 1877.

But if Bangs's importance seemed an afterthought in the last years of his life, there was no question about it once he had passed. His funeral was held in Chicago. Six hundred postal clerks marched in his funeral procession. The post office was closed, and all the mail trains that came into Chicago were draped in shrouds as a sign of mourning. At Rosehill Cemetery, where Bangs was buried, there was built—and remains today—a monumental grave marker that depicts a scale replica of a mail train going through a tunnel. Whether it's entering or embarking depends on one's perspective.

The inscription on the marker tells you everything you need to know about what mail meant to the country in the 1870s. It lists Bangs's name, date of death, and age at the time he died. And then, of all the things he had done—boots and shoes, farming, newspaper, early advocacy for Honest Abe—it says: "His crowning effort, The Fast Mail."

THE LOST ART OF CANCELING

To prevent government-issued stamps from being reused, the Post Office Department required postal clerks to hand-cancel stamps on envelopes; however, until the mid-to-late 1800s, no standard equipment was available to do this. (Postmarks–hand-cancels that included the date and location next to the stamp–were available from the POD beginning in the 1860s.) To cancel stamps, clerks would use an ink slash, their initials, or a small hand-drawn piece of art. Corks, soft woods, lead, and even potatoes were used to carve designs of animals, stars, letters, leaves, and advertisements. Other designs were quite macabre, such a devil, a skull and crossbones, and even a man in a coffin. Fancy cancels were themselves canceled by POD Order Number 497 on May 19, 1904. It stated that the unauthorized use of non-POD cancels would "be considered sufficient cause for removal."

Skull and crossbones.

Cat.

Radiating V's.

Clover.

Flower.

Bee.

Advertisement for Poland's Magic Powders.

Man in the Moon.

Bucking donkey.

Devil's head.

Skull and crossbones.

U.S. POSTAGE
THREE 3 CENTS

U.S. POSTAGE
ONE 1 CENT

U.S. POSTAGE
SIX 6 CENTS

U.S. POSTAGE
THREE 3 CENTS

U.S. POSTAGE
TEN 10 CENTS

UNITED STATES POSTAGE
ONE 1 CENT

UNITED STATES POSTAGE
TWO 2 CENTS

UNITED STATES POSTAGE
4 4
FOUR CENTS

UNITED STATES POSTAGE
4 4
FOUR CENTS

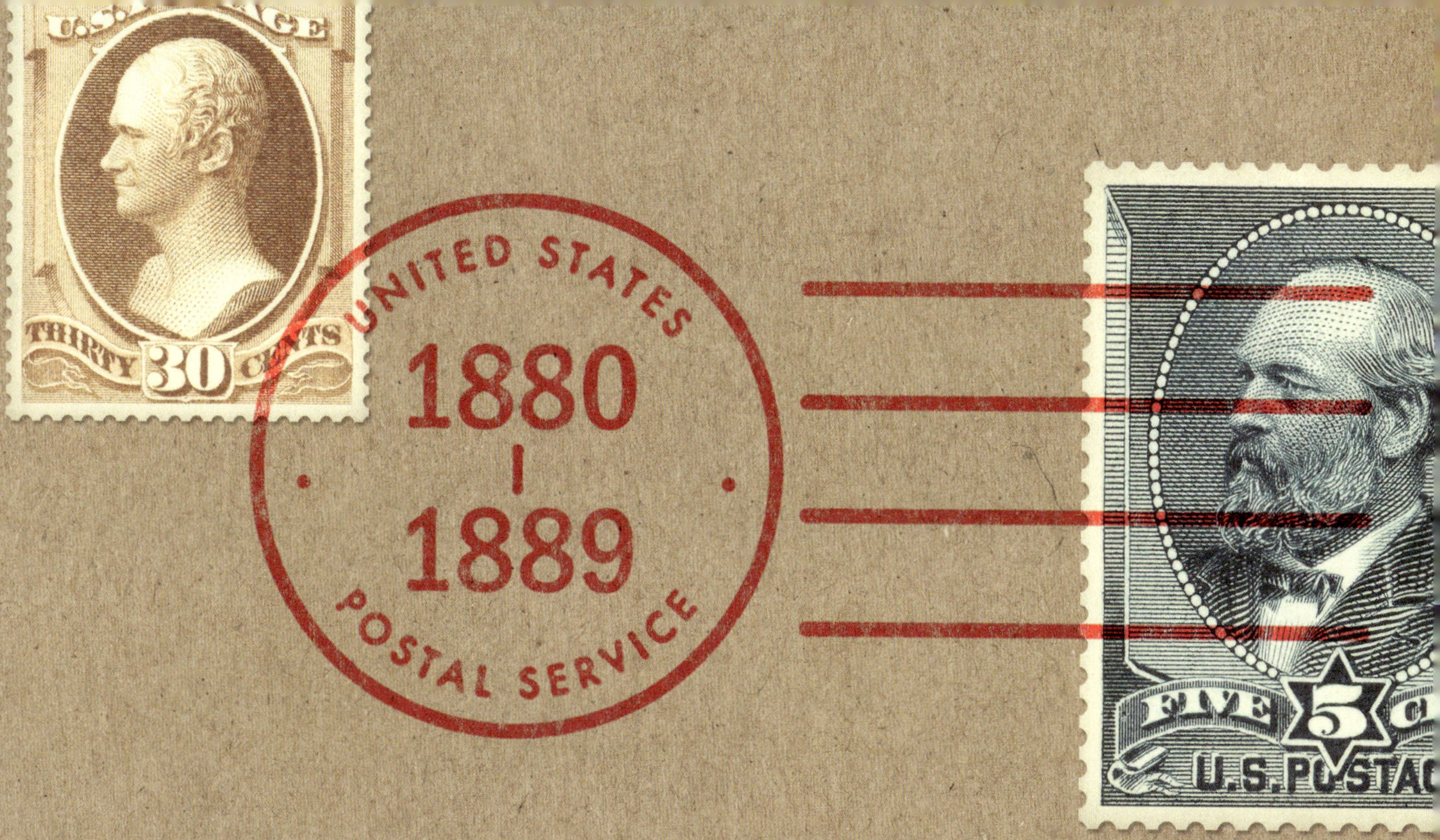
THIRTY 30 CENTS
UNITED STATES
1880
1889
POSTAL SERVICE
FIVE 5
U.S. PO STAG

IMPROVEMENTS AND EXPANSIONS, URBAN AND RURAL

U.S. POSTAGE

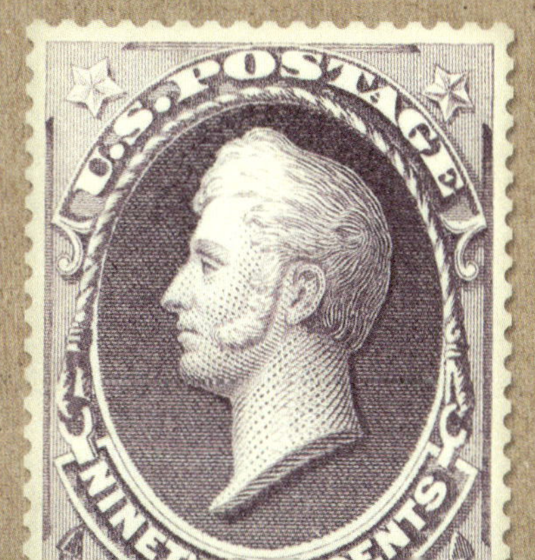

The old oak tree was already 100 years old when the people passing through Council Grove, Kansas, began using it as a place to exchange messages in the 1820s. Council Grove was a small settlement, a stop on the Santa Fe Trail that served as the last reliable place to get supplies for the arduous journey west. Wagon trains formed up in Council Grove. Travelers could leave notes about trail conditions in a cache at the foot of the tree, and wagon masters agreed to transport any letters deposited there that were addressed to a post office on their caravan route, even if it was hundreds of miles away.

For some 25 years, during the heyday of the trail, the tree was the settlement's post office.

As travelers continued to funnel through the town, and its importance grew against the backdrop of westward expansion, Council Grove matured. In 1847, a trading post was established in the town. It created a new venue for hopeful migrants to leave their letters, rendering the Post Office Oak, as it came to be known, obsolete.

Eight years later, Council Grove was assigned its first postmaster—but the town didn't have a post office. Mail was distributed from a sack on the street, or on the floor of a store. There were more and more stores, most notably the Last Chance Store, built in 1857, a place to stock up that still stands today. For a time, it also served as a post office.

People continued to settle in the West; Council Grove continued to grow. The town incorporated in 1858.

In the flush of optimism following the Civil War, seeing the railroad-building that was transforming the country, Council Grove passed a $100,000 bond measure to try to get a railroad to route its tracks through the town. In 1869, the Missouri–Kansas–Texas Railroad added a stop there. A decade later, they tried the same maneuver, and in 1881 another railroad, the Topeka, Salina and Western Railroad, came through, one that would eventually be part of the mighty Missouri Pacific Railroad.

A presentation drawing of the Springfield, Ohio, Post Office built under the direction of Mifflin Bell, supervisory architect for the U.S. Treasury, completed in 1890.

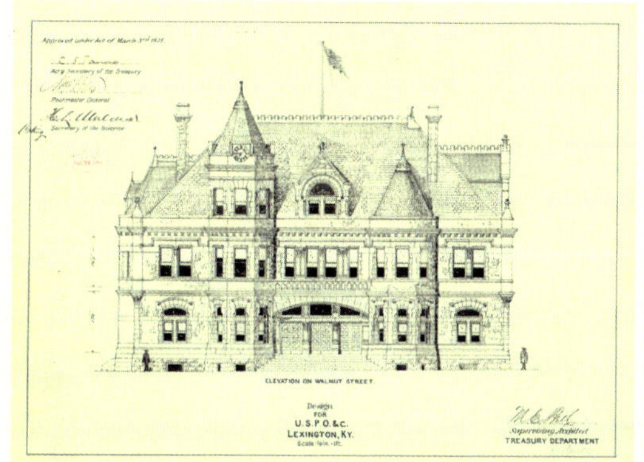

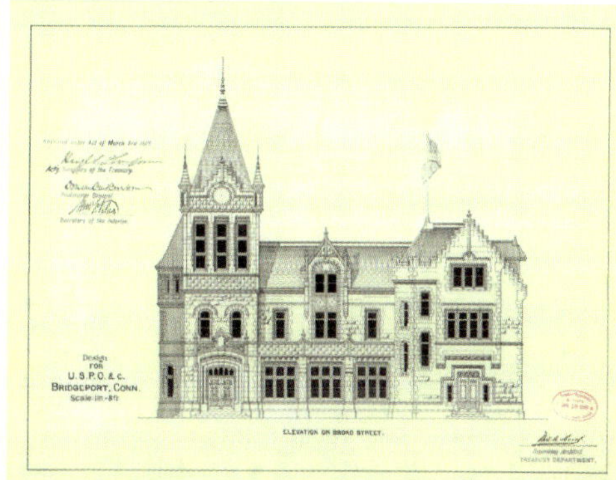

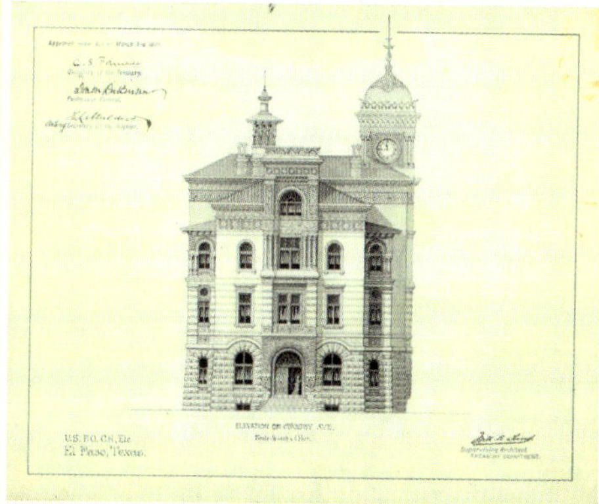

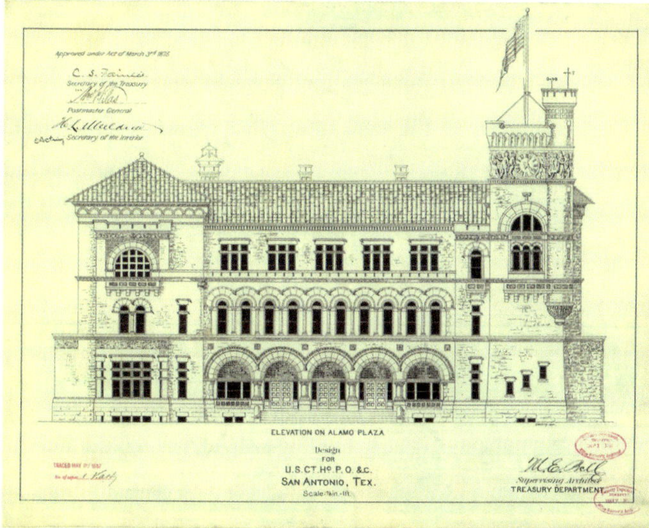

The supervisory architect for the U.S. Treasury oversaw the construction of many post offices and courthouses during the Federal Building Projects from 1852 up to the 1930s.

Top row, left to right: The post office in Lexington, Kentucky, 1886–1887; the post office on Broad Street in Bridgeport, Connecticut, 1886; the post office in El Paso, Texas, 1892.

Bottom row, left to right: The post office and courthouse in San Antonio, Texas; the post office and courthouse in Jackson, Mississippi, 1883–1907.

As time passed, the city would continue to develop, and its accommodations for the post would develop with it. By the early 20th century, the post office was housed in a handsome Italianate building on the town's main street. But the people of Council Grove never forgot about the Post Office Oak, which also continued to grow. The tree lived until 1990, and its stump is preserved to this day, accompanied by a historical marker and a small museum.

Why remember this tree? Perhaps because it played a role in the classic American story, one in full flush in the 1880s. In the railroad-building of the 1860s and 1870s, the nation—and the Post Office Department—had been spreading roots. At some point, out of those roots, cities and post offices and Americans' communication with one another would have a chance to grow up and bloom. And in the 1880s, bloom they did.

★ ★ ★

The improvements in urban mail service that originated during the Civil War, chiefly home delivery, had become highly popular in the decade and a half after the war ended. And the federal government was happy to offer them—with conditions.

To qualify for Free City Delivery service in the early 1880s, urban communities needed populations of at least 20,000 people within the proposed delivery area. If that population threshold was met, cities had to make certain infrastructure improvements. Naturally, there had to be a workable address system. Candidates had to name all their streets and install legible street signs at every intersection. The Post Office Department then insisted that municipalities assign and affix numbers to their residential and commercial buildings. On top of this, the streets had to be navigable: Cities installed sidewalks and erected streetlights. Once these conditions were fulfilled, a postal inspector would walk the hopeful city's streets, laying out potential carrier routes and identifying where curbside collection

didn't only benefit the mail. Streetlamps, sidewalks, addresses, and the like had value in and of themselves. The improvements the Post Office was demanding coincided with what was known as the Good Roads Movement, a broader progressive effort to build infrastructure that would bring *all* the advancements of urban life—not just mail—into the country's vast rural regions. The result was that while many of the settlements of the 1880s would seem rugged and uncivilized today, the allure of Free City Delivery was modernizing them fast. As they had done first with roads and wagons, and then with rail, the necessities of mail were dragging towns across the country into the future.

But there was yet another sweetener to making these changes: Uncle Sam tended to pay back the locals for their civic spending by authorizing glitzy new post offices built at the government's expense. In the 1880s, Congress authorized an array of massive federal building projects,

Operations were increasingly professionalized, complex, and, in the best cases, sophisticated.

boxes could be installed. Then, finally, service might be authorized.

Free City Delivery was a great benefit to the people of an urban area—but the required infrastructure improvements could be expensive for a small community. In Baton Rouge, Louisiana, for example, the contract it signed for the creation of a city directory called for a $150 payment to the contractor, E.F. Pope, as well as a 25-cent fee from each building owner for the job of affixing address numbers. Of course, the improvements

Opposite: City letter carriers pose in 1885 with their handcarts, which were used to collect and transport mail from the city post office to customers. The uniforms of the time were quite dapper and included round hats with a flat top and a badge indicating the route they serviced.

including the creation of grand edifices throughout the country. Every U.S. senator or member of the House of Representatives developed pet projects to try to get a piece of the action. After all, a big new project was proof of a congressman's ability to bring home the bacon for his constituents—and bacon brought ballots.

These projects (designed, overseen, and operated by the Treasury Department) represented the federal government's presence in a community. As such, they were designed to be ornate, palatial even. On the inside, they had every possible amenity. Sometimes these were beyond reason, like the multiple fireplaces in a post office in sultry south Florida. On the outside, their expression of architectural luxury rivaled that of the wealthiest residential mansions—and they frequently included features private homes never did, like clock towers. The acting mayor of Frankfort, Kentucky, James L. Sneed, remarked at the cornerstone-laying ceremony for the city's new combination post office and courthouse, in February 1884, that "the Federal Government with liberality and wisdom, has determined upon the location in our midst of a building whose spacious dimensions will afford ample and appropriate accommodations for its officials, and whose architectural beauty [will] prove a handsome ornament to the city. We fully appreciate and are duly grateful that the evidence of national prosperity has been placed within our limits." These buildings also tended to get the best real estate. A proposed combination post office and courthouse in Key West, Florida, as an example, was said to have been located in "the coolest, prettiest, healthiest and pleasantest [*sic*] place in town."

City letter carriers in the 1880s wore double-breasted long coats adorned with brass buttons. The carrier above sports a wreath-style badge on his hat, which was used from 1887 to 1922. The cap badge on the carrier at left dates from after 1922.

Typically, as in Key West, these new government palaces were joint-tenant buildings: The Post Office Department would occupy the street level, the federal court the second floor, and a lesser government agency like the Weather Bureau, Corps of Engineers, or Internal Revenue Service the top floor. This was a major promotion for the Post Office Department. For the nation's entire history so far, stretching all the way back to the one run by Richard Fairbanks out of his tavern in Boston in 1639, post offices had generally been housed in secondhand and predominantly privately owned spaces. Now their employees and their work were furnished with brand-new structures owned and operated by the government.

★ ★ ★

Operations were increasingly professionalized, complex, and, in the best cases, sophisticated. In the 1880s, city letter carriers serving Gilded Age New Yorkers had to be at least 18 years old and typically were no older than 40, unless they were honorably discharged soldiers or sailors. They were required to buy their own cadet gray-cloth uniforms tailored to department specifications and to wear them whenever on duty. While walking their routes, carriers were forbidden to engage in trivial talk with their patrons. They were also not allowed to sing, whistle, or smoke. The Post Office Department required that all carriers possess a civil tongue when addressing the public. (Some postmasters went further: The postmaster of Concord, New Hampshire, demanded his employees be "as non-committal as the Sphinx and as reticent as an Egyptian mummy on most subjects," and especially silent when it came to talk of religion or politics.)

Overcharges to Star Routes

Four decades after they were established, everything that had made Star Routes great was also making them potentially problematic. On the one hand, they brought new levels of service to underserved areas of the country, but on the other hand, the very nature of that service—it was reliant on contractors, and it was delivered in places that were hard to reach or monitor—made the system prone to being gamed. The Gilded Age was a time in American life when the country in many ways looked magnificently healthy but was in reality infected with corruption. In the 1880s, the sickness spread to the Post Office Department and settled in the Star Routes.

The way it worked was simple: Contractors would make high bids on routes, sometimes promising elevated levels of service, like expedited delivery. Then they would make their deliveries without providing the service from their bid—if they made the deliveries at all—and pocket the money from the more lucrative contract they'd earned with their empty promises. Of course, to really pull this off, you needed help from within the Post Office Department, someone who could make sure you won the contracts and that no one checked whether the service was actually delivered. For that insider, kickbacks skimmed off the top of the contracts could amount to quite a bit of money.

Though such corruption may have begun before the 1880s, this was the decade in which it exploded, thanks primarily to two men: Second Assistant Postmaster General Thomas J. Brady and former senator and secretary of the Republican National Committee Stephen W. Dorsey. Brady and Dorsey acquired Star Route contracts and then applied for enhanced payments for expedited services that were never provided. The price inflation was remarkable. In the Dakotas, a Star Route contract jumped from $2,350 to $32,000 in one year. In the Southwest, a route went from $6,330 to $150,691. The cost of service between Las Cruces and Las Vegas, New Mexico, ballooned from $14,900 to $76,311, with Brady and Dorsey splitting the profits. Given the two men's prominence, such rampant fraud couldn't go unnoticed for long. And when it did, Postmaster General Thomas L. James was livid.

James served one of the briefest tenures in the history of a U.S. postmaster general position: He took the role on March 5, 1881, as an appointee of James A. Garfield; Garfield was assassinated on September 19, and his successor, Chester A. Arthur, had his own postmaster general in office before the end of the year. Nevertheless, James was effective during his short stint. Since his time serving as postmaster of New York City under President

Ulysses S. Grant, James had been known as a reformer, and his persona as postmaster general was no different. When it came to the Star Route scandal, he wanted heads to roll. Brady and Dorsey went on trial. James also immediately started cutting back on overpayments. His first cut was $159,765 in March 1881. This was quickly followed by $80,631 in April, $288,175 in May, $127,261 in June, and $384,397 in July.

Shockingly, Brady and Dorsey escaped punishment—the government failed to secure convictions in their cases. Though the evidence was overwhelming, their high-priced lawyers were able to confuse the jury and judge by relentlessly raising legal technicalities. But even if they escaped the criminal-justice system, the two men couldn't dodge accountability in the court of public opinion. The Chicago *Inter Ocean* was representative of the day when it wrote, "It is difficult to believe that [Brady] was not in league with a set of unscrupulous contractors to defraud the Government." What's more, the Star Route scandal—and the public's perception that federal employees might be a greedy, unscrupulous bunch—contributed to the passage of the Pendleton Civil Service Reform Act, which aimed to ensure that federal employees were hired based on competition and merit rather than patronage. It was a historic pushback against President Andrew Jackson's infamous spoils system, which had introduced so many opportunities for corruption into the federal bureaucracy—the Post Office Department included.

Puck magazine published many cartoons on the Star Route frauds. On the March 7, 1883, cover, Montford Rerdell, longtime associate of disgraced Arkansas senator Stephen W. Dorsey, primes the pump to spew evidence at Dorsey and Second Assistant Postmaster General Thomas J. Brady.

By Federal definition 39 CFR § 310.3(d), a Special Delivery messenger is a person who, at the request of the sender or addressee, picks up a letter from one of them and carries it to its final destination. *Above, left to right:* A U.S. Special Delivery semicircular cap badge from 1900; a Special Delivery messenger badge, circa 1930.

At homes, the postman was to knock on the door or ring the doorbell twice and patiently wait for a reasonable amount of time until it was answered so he could properly present the mail. Without a response, the postman returned the mail to the post office to attempt delivery on the next trip. Having a household mailbox was not yet a prerequisite for service in the 1880s, so some carriers would toss mail through open windows. This practice was quickly forbidden, and residents were encouraged to install letter slots in front doors or mount personal mail receptacles at entry areas, but such actions remained voluntary. Part of the delay was due to the Post Office Department's inability to decide which official boxes to approve. It called for manufacturers to submit potential models and was deluged with more than 1,600 different designs to consider.

Away from the home, letter carriers collected mail from curbside collection boxes, which also had their pros and cons. They were simple, central collection points—but much of the mail deposited in letter boxes didn't include postage. Instead, patrons deposited stampless letters along with a few pennies for postage, expecting that carriers would purchase and affix the required stamp. Scraping for pennies at the bottom of boxes was a bother for letter carriers, especially in the winter, when the copper coins froze in place.

If there was a method of delivery that was simply without drawbacks, it was Special Delivery. Congress authorized this new service level on March 3, 1885. Letters mailed from 551 select post offices could receive accelerated service that was initially available between 7:00 a.m. and midnight. The cost was a 10-cent Special Delivery stamp that was affixed in addition to regular postage. The large size and distinctive color of these stamps made them stand out. Nine cents of the added fee went to young runners or bicyclists, who would dash the letter to its destination. The service was truly speedy: Letters were reportedly out the door within 20 minutes of arriving at post offices. Special Delivery proved so desirable that in August 1886 it was expanded to all classes of mail at every post office and made available even on Sundays and holidays.

★ ★ ★

Having a household mailbox was not yet a prerequisite for service in the 1880s, so some carriers would toss mail through open windows.

This Free City Delivery black metal mailbox was used by a household in Crown City, Ohio, in the early 20th century.

Just as Special Delivery began with only select post offices, there was absolutely a hierarchy to the level of service cities received. The biggest cities got the biggest buildings. Thanks to Chicago's rapid growth in the Railroad Age, for example, it received not just a massive new main post office but also 13 smaller postal stations and 22 substations by the end of the decade. And it wasn't just about size: Cities that made the strongest efforts could see the biggest return on their investments—often utterly transforming a city's standing in the country.

One strategy cities quickly hit upon was to host events that would attract tourists. In 1876, Philadelphia had hosted the massively successful Centennial Exposition, and that became a template for many other urban areas. Consider Atlanta. It was one of the first beneficiaries of the decade's congressional pork-barrel binge. In 1880, the city received $10,000 for new fencing, sidewalks, sodding, and roadway paving around its combination post office and courthouse. This funding was intended to gussy up its federal building in advance of the 1881 Atlanta Cotton Exposition, the first of three such world's fair–like events it was hosting to showcase its emergence as the "Chicago of the South" after the Civil War.

As a result, Atlanta earned glowing spotlights in the press. A 15-page story highlighting the city was published in *Harper's New Monthly* magazine in December 1879. The writer noted how the self-proclaimed "Capital of the New South" looked "more like a western town, since her newness and enterprise hardly affiliate her with Augusta, Savannah, Mobile, and the rest of the sleepy cotton markets, whose growth, if they have any, is imperceptible, and whose pulse beats with only faint flutter."

Other municipalities enjoyed comparable events. Cincinnati was widely promoted for hosting a National Exhibition of Industry and Art in 1883, and New Orleans was broadly publicized for holding a World's Industrial and Cotton Centennial Exposition in 1884–1885. What preceded these moments in the sun? The new $1.2 million federal building in New Orleans opened in 1881, and Cincinnati's new $4.8 million post office opened in 1882. A wave of urbanization was sweeping eastern cities, both driven by the post and driving expanded postal service. At the start of the decade, 104 cities had Free City Delivery Service, served by 2,628 letter carriers. By the decade's end, that number increased fourfold, expanding to 454 cities and 9,066 letter carriers.

Photographer Jacob A. Riis came to New York in 1870, just one among hundreds of thousands of immigrants. His photographs captured people whose daily lives were dominated by poverty, hunger, homelessness, joblessness, and hopelessness. *Above*, a peddler is seen sleeping atop two barrels in a building's cellar.

Opposite: An 1888 photograph of the New York City tenement slums titled *Bandits Roost: 59 ½ Mulberry Street* shows an alleyway called "the Bend." This alley appears to be guarded by two men at the entrance to the far right.

These were heady times in cities—but not everyone was reaping the benefits of this golden age. Far too many people lived in urban squalor. The poorest urban residents, living in privation and poverty, were often Eastern European immigrants. A New York City newspaper reporter named Jacob A. Riis—himself an immigrant from Denmark who had been in the United States only since 1870—began photographing living conditions in urban slums as part of his job as a police reporter for the *New-York Tribune*. Riis would ultimately produce a shockingly stark record of living conditions in New York City in the 1880s called *How the Other Half Lives: Studies Among the Tenements of New York*. This visual record, created by the still-new technology of photography, explains why, despite the prosperity of cities, so many people were packing up, saying farewell to the cities of the East, and striking out to find their fortunes in the West.

Many of them found themselves in places like Independence, Missouri, called the "Queen City of the Trails" because it was where the 1,600-mile-long California Trail, the 1,200-mile-long Santa Fe Trail, and the 2,170-mile-long Oregon Trail began.

Or they might have found themselves in someplace like Council Grove, Kansas.

From there, they'd move west, into sparsely populated territory where land was plentiful, fertile, and cheap—and post offices weren't more sophisticated than the Post Office Oak. But even here, in the 1880s, the country's mail system was developing.

Wherever settlements sprang up, humble post offices soon followed. Though simple, they were often the first civic structure erected in newly settled hamlets. And though they offered a higher level of service than the Post Office Oak, which was fundamentally a convenient pickup point, they were unpretentious places.

Cheyenne, Wyoming's first post office, as an example, was in a tent, the kind that sprung up in "tent towns" along many routes west.

The first post office in Guthrie, Oklahoma, established in 1889, was also in a tent. But as with many of these rudimentary post offices, while its structure was simple, its purpose was monumental: Its arrival attracted more than 3,000 anxious Americans hoping there was something in the mail for them.

Screen Wagons and Regulation Wagons

In the 1880s, the Post Office Department launched a pair of workhorses for moving urban mail: screen wagons and regulation wagons. First introduced in Sherman, Texas, in 1881, the screen wagon was as showy as the small-town post-office buildings it served. Painted red, white, and blue, it utilized wire screens to protect the mail from being pilfered. Drop-down painted sailcloth curtains protected the mail during bad weather. Three sizes of these wagons were ultimately produced, and the largest could carry up to 5,000 pounds of mail. Regulation wagons, which were initially assigned to 30 of the nation's largest cities, were similarly dressed up in patriotic colors—but they were more solidly built. The upper sides, for example, were entirely enclosed by watertight painted sailcloth. They were built by the nation's finest coachmakers and also initially came in three sizes. However, their sturdier builds were quite expensive. The largest size was eliminated in the 1890s, with its routes taken over by the more economical screen wagons.

Near right: Employees drive a No. 3 regulation mail wagon in San Francisco. *Far right:* A fully restored No. 3 city service screen wagon.

Restaurant
U.S. MAIL
U.S. MAIL
UNITED STATES MAIL. NO.3

Clockwise from above, left: The A. G. Curtis General Store and Post Office located in Granite, Colorado, circa 1885; Mose LaTray stands outside the Reedsfort, Montana, Post Office, which he built in 1880; a cedar stump was used as the Elwha, Washington, Post Office from 1892 to 1928.

Almost any structure would do. The first post office in the Upper Elwha Valley of Washington was in a huge hollow cedar stump on a property owned by William McDonald, the community's first postmaster. He added a roof to the stump to make the post office weatherproof.

For startup post offices, the federal government didn't provide much more than the basics: an eight-ounce balance scale, a stack of facing slips, a postmarking device and ink pad, plus a couple of mailbags and some postage stamps. Otherwise, the newly minted postmasters were responsible for setting up their own offices. In many cases, this meant makeshift fixtures and furnishings. Barrels and boards were commonly used as countertops. Food crates filled with empty tin cans made do as initial sorting cases until something better could be bought or built.

Some post offices were so amateurish that they didn't last long. Petoskey, Michigan, established a new one in 1880 to replace the existing postal facility: a cigar box placed on a sewing machine at the Occidental hotel, which had been in use for the previous five years.

T. Terrett Jr. Groceries and Post Office, located in Alexandria, Virginia.

The Caldwell & Bro. General Store, which also included the Spadra Post Office, circa 1880. Spadra, California, was a bustling stop on the Butterfield Stagecoach route and the Southern Pacific Railway.

★ ★ ★

Despite the humble origins of many of the new 1880s post offices, over time, many were transformed into highly professional operations. Post offices became markers of importance; their inauspicious origins and unexpected venues were no predictor of future fortunes. The nation, after all, was growing. From the start of the Civil War to the end of the 1880s, Chicago, for example, which had been a marshy outpost in what was then the West, had seen its population surge by a factor of 10 and become a metropolis of more than one million people.

What could be seen, in the improvement of mail service in the 1880s and in the spread of urban standards from east to west across the country, was no less than the maturation of the United States itself.

Another settlement with a pop-up post office that seemed unserious at best and doomed to ridicule at worst: Oklahoma Station. The Oklahoma Land Rush of 1889 led to the establishment of a post office in the small settlement. It was housed in a secondhand chicken coop. In perhaps the first indicator that Oklahoma Station was destined to be much more than a backwater location, anticipation of the mail was so high that it took 13 hours to distribute the bounty of the first mail service. Today, Oklahoma Station is called Oklahoma City, and it's the capital of the state, home to nearly 700,000 people. It's not fair to say the mail *caused* that growth. But it sure helped.

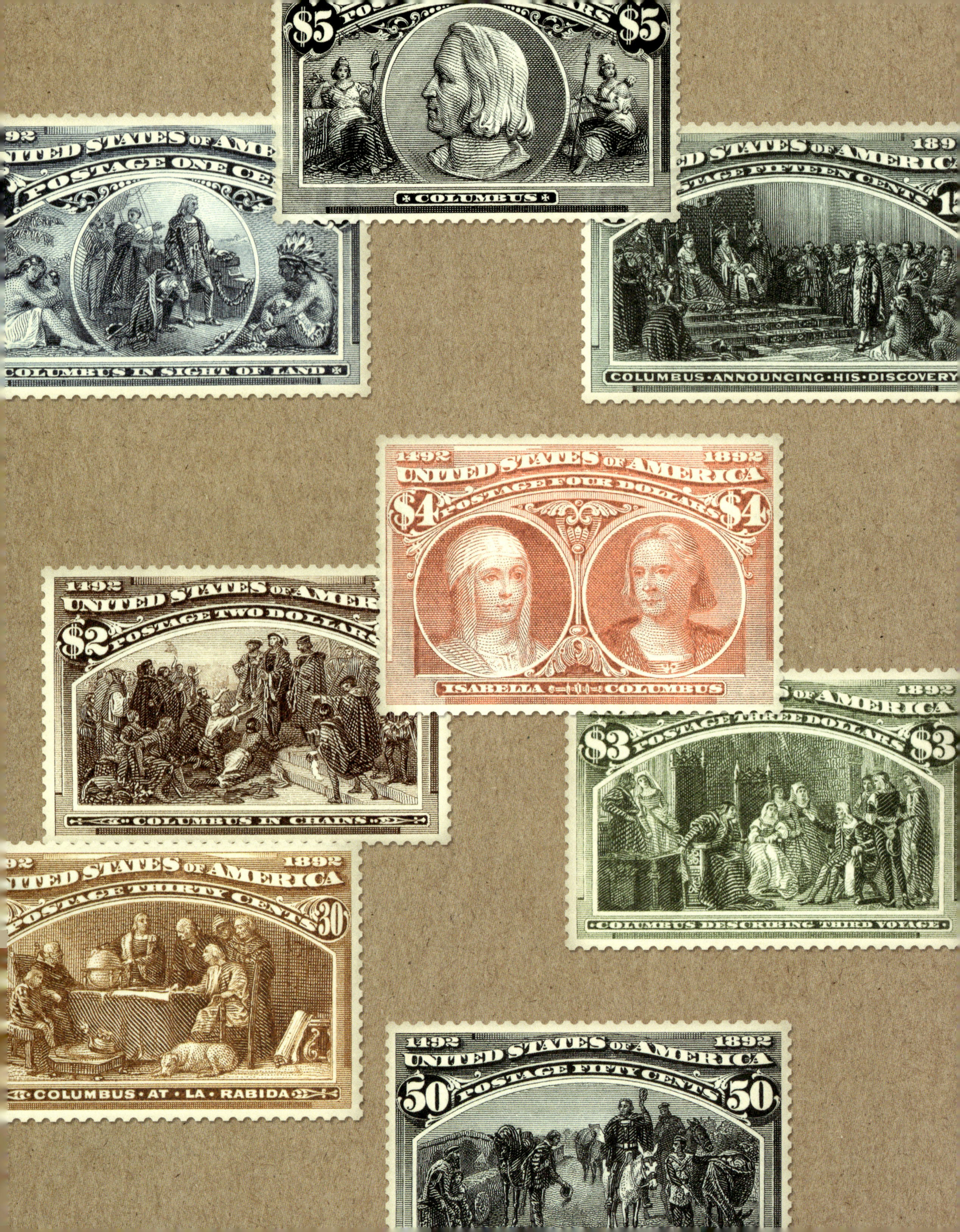

1492
1892
UNITED STATES OF AMERICA
POSTAGE FOUR DOLLARS
$4
$4
ISABELLA
COLUMBUS
$2
COLUMBUS IN CHAINS

1892
$3
$3
COLUMBUS DESCRIBING THIRD VOYAGE

1892
POSTAGE THIRTY CENTS
30
COLUMBUS · AT · LA · RABIDA

1492
1892
UNITED STATES OF AMERICA
POSTAGE FIFTY CENTS
50
50

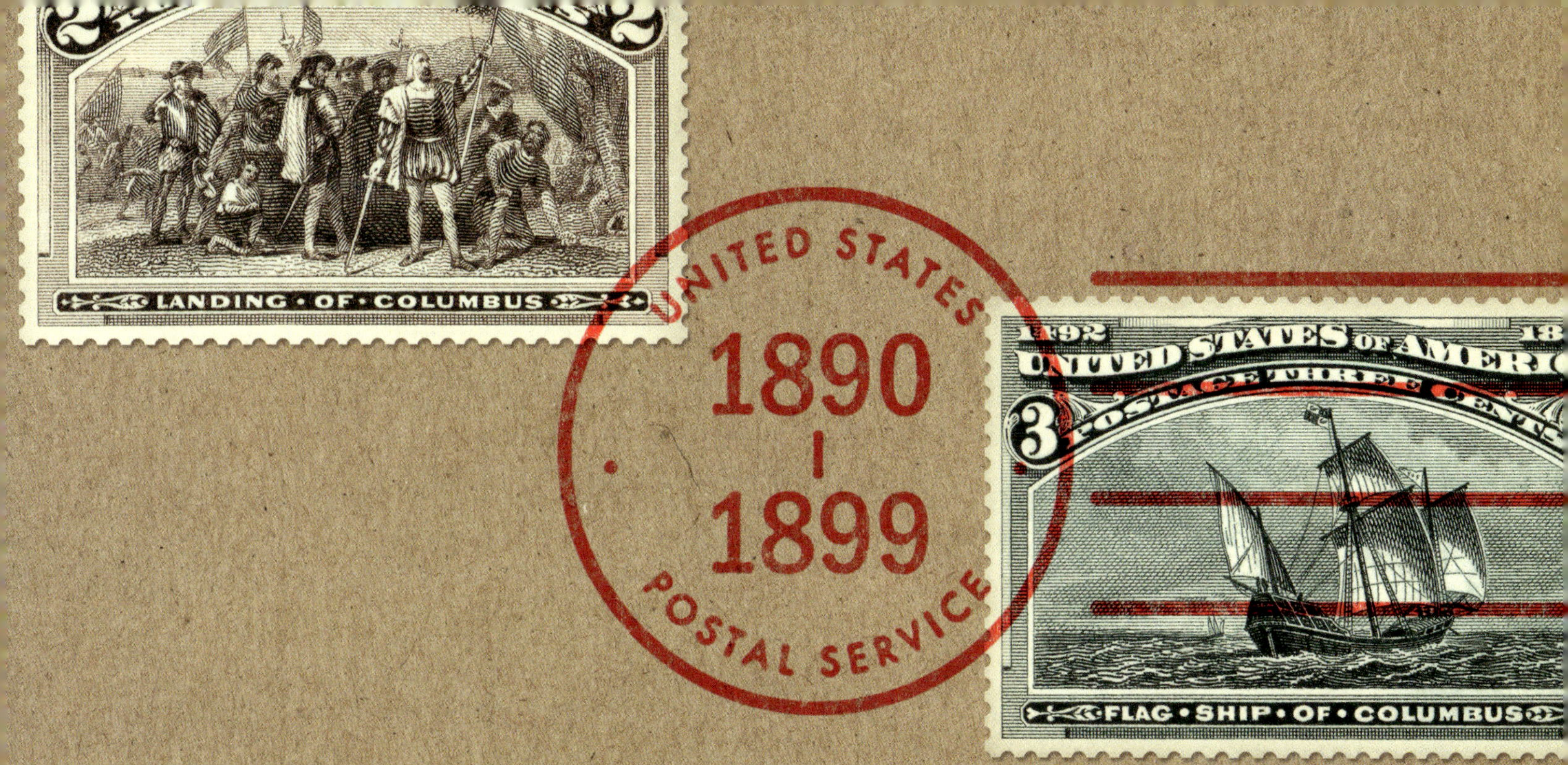

LANDING · OF · COLUMBUS

UNITED STATES
1890
I
1899
POSTAL SERVICE

FLAG · SHIP · OF · COLUMBUS

GLOBETROTTING

One autumn morning in 1888, clerks at the Albany Post Office found an unexpected visitor tucked in among the mailbags. Owney, a small mutt, must have crept in during the previous cold evening and found a warm spot among the mail. The clerks could have run Owney off, but instead, they fed him what leftovers they had. Soon they had effectively adopted the little dog, and it didn't take long for Owney to begin traveling with them.

At first his trips were short, confined to riding with the mailbags on wagons bound to the train depot a few blocks from the post office. Slowly but surely, Owney's trips grew longer. He began riding mail trains from Albany to New York City. The clerks on the trains treated Owney like one of the crew. Food and affection were in endless supply. Everywhere he followed the mailbags, he was well-received. Based upon his welcome, the dog became ever more adventurous, and his travels took him farther and farther from Albany.

The clerks in the Albany Post Office always knew when he was gone. "When the cat comes in the office, we know that Owney is away," commented one Albany postal worker in 1895. "And the dog is away from home so much that the cat is seldom obliged to move out."

Knowing that his trips were taking him far from home, the clerks fastened a note to Owney's collar asking employees of the Railway Mail Service to record his travels by adding baggage tags to it everywhere he went. The collar became a kind of measure of the incredible reach of the Post Office Department; it wasn't long before Owney's tag collection grew to a point where the collar couldn't hold them all, and he could hardly lift up his head. To lighten his load, Postmaster General John Wanamaker gave Owney a special harness-like jacket so the dog's souvenirs could be more evenly displayed. Soon this jacket was packed with trinkets, tokens, and tributes, too. On December 3, 1894, *The New York Sun* reported

Owney stands in the doorway of a U.S. Railway Mail Service car surrounded by postal-clerk friends.

An illustration of Owney sitting on top of a mailbag.

Owney "tinkles when he moves with a multitude of tin tags."

A world-class traveler, Owney journeyed around the United States and Canada, as well as through Mexico. Early on, he was caught up in an accident. Following the mishap, which happened aboard a Canadian mail train around 1890, Owney went missing and was feared dead. Months later he showed up again, without one of his ears. It seems that when he followed the mailbags into the Montreal Post Office, workers seized Owney because he had no dog license. Canadian officials learned from his collar where his home was and wrote to the Albany Post Office informing the workers there of his whereabouts, demanding $2.50 for his release. Most of the money was to pay for Owney's food bill during his brief confinement. The Albany postal workers passed the hat to pull together the money to get him released.

From then on, whenever Owney was aboard a train, it never seemed to suffer an accident or robbery. This meant a great deal to the railway-mail clerks: They had a one-in-20 chance of being hurt or killed while on duty. Mail trains were easy targets and often carried large quantities of valuables, including gold being sent from mining operations out west. Between 1887 and 1892, there were 1,610 casualties on mail trains, including 39 deaths. Owney was a beloved good-luck charm.

In the 1890s, as the century drew to a close, the Post Office Department's reach was greater than ever. Rail lines and mail boats and stages and all other manner of delivery crisscrossed the country. But even as it was a massive, professional business operation, there was also an edge of adventure to the mail. There was that chance of being killed on the rails. The excitement of pushing into new places in the sparsely populated West. In so many ways, the Post Office Department represented an exploration of the nation's frontiers. And so—especially while the country's economy could be shaky and much of its geography was still untamed—Owney had a kind of magnetism that no one had any right to expect from a scruffy little mutt. His life was one big adventure.

An original *New York Herald* piece about Owney was reprinted in the June 29, 1892, edition of Virginia's *Staunton Spectator*. "There is no one who dictates to the dog as to where he shall go, or, in fact, whether he shall go at all," reported the article, "A Traveling Dog. Owney Goes All Over the Country, But Has No Expenses." "His dogness regulates all those little matters for himself. Having made up his mind to start on a trip, Owney boards the mail car...and throws himself languidly on the mail pouches, and the engine does the rest."

Owney was more than a mascot. He might have been the spirit of the mail itself.

For two decades, while there had been wobbles, the economy of the United States had been growing steadily, driven by the expansion of the country and the prodigious upgrades in speed and efficiency that came with the railroads. Many of the massive fortunes built during the Gilded Age, especially by railroad tycoons, however, came crashing down in the early 1890s.

The financial downturn began with the failure of both the Philadelphia and Reading Railroad and the Erie Railroad amid ferocious competition on the rails. What had been a recession starting in 1891 became a full-blown financial panic by 1893. The stock market collapsed. Profits from railway shipping fell precipitously, sending one-quarter of all railroad miles—trackage valued at roughly $1 billion—into receivership.

James E. White, general superintendent of the Railway Mail Service, oversaw the Silk Train's 50-member crew and ensured the train's safe passage across the country.

What had been a recession starting in 1891 became a full-blown financial panic by 1893.

In domino fashion, banks began to fail, particularly in the southern and western portions of the country. Waves of unemployment and farm foreclosures followed. Labor unrest led to deadly strikes.

Commodity prices plummeted, with wheat leading the way to the bottom of the barrel.

Businesses closed in record numbers.

More dominoes: A widespread rejection of paper money, particularly "silver certificates," which replaced silver coins in circulation, resulted in the hoarding of silver and gold coinage. The shortage of hard money in circulation, especially high-value gold coinage in the East, required immediate attention. The Treasury Department had plenty of gold coins in California but no way to move them quickly to where they were needed most.

Treasury Secretary Charles Foster and Postmaster General John Wanamaker met in July 1892 to consider how best to resolve the problem. Wanamaker had an idea: He issued an order to immediately assemble a special mail train that would transport the overabundance of western gold coins—some $20 million worth—directly from San Francisco to New York City. The influx of coinage was expected to ease one element of the eastern panic and hopefully stabilize the economy.

In what must have been mail's greatest adventure since the Pony Express raced across the country, the Post Office Department would come

The *Chicago Tribune* welcomed the Gold Train with a front-page article on August 9, 1892. Unfortunately for those who came to watch it arrive, it departed almost immediately for New York City.

VIEW OF THE SPECIAL GOLD TRAIN AT THE LAKE SHORE DEPOT.

to the rescue. Figuratively and literally, a lot was riding on this mail train.

Wanamaker assigned his best man to the task. If anyone could accomplish a miracle it was James E. White, the general superintendent of the Railway Mail Service. White immediately set about developing the details of the operation. He code-named the vehicle the Silk Train. This moniker was used to minimize the interest of potential robbers: No self-respecting bandit would choose to hijack a trainload of silk, which would be nearly impossible to fence without being noticed.

White assembled a crew that would be in absolute control of the Silk Train until it arrived in New York City. Fifty crew members in total were required. Men who served with the military during the Civil War were preferred. Each car was to be under the supervision of an assistant superintendent from the Railway Mail Service; each of them would be assisted by nine trusted mail clerks.

Precautions were also taken in case the Silk Train did get targeted. Each crew member was given a standard military-issue Springfield carbine with 2,000 cartridges, as well as a .45-caliber Colt revolver with 1,000 rounds of ammunition. The guards in the front car, armed with Winchesters, were situated where villains wouldn't see them and charged with protecting the train's engineer and fireman. Aboard the train, a password, "Grant," was required to move between cars.

Because the train would run over tracks owned by different railroads, individual cars were to be supplied by each of the lines involved in the cross-country mission. The Southern Pacific also provided baggage cars from San Francisco for crew accommodations, food service, and baggage storage. All the various cars were marshaled at Omaha and then sent west to San Francisco.

Each of the participating railroads was to treat the Silk Train as an express run. The Union Pacific was responsible for expediting the train to Omaha, where the Chicago, Burlington and Quincy Railroad would fast-track it to the Lake Shore and Michigan Southern, which in turn would hand it off to the New York Central and Hudson River from Buffalo to New York City.

The clerks and their supervisors gathered in Omaha on July 29 for a briefing, and from there they traveled by train to San Francisco to pick up the gold. Shortly before the run began, debates within the Treasury Department ensued as to whether the gold coins should be sent in 20 smaller shipments of $1 million each. This plan became public and was abandoned. At the same time, it was determined that the impact of having the entire $20 million available for distribution all at once would be greater than infusing the coins into circulation in successive waves. The coins would be sent together.

All 80,000 pounds' worth.

The shipment consisted of $5 and $10 gold coins, packed in individual sacks containing $4,000 each. The sacks were then packed in 500 10-by-14-inch wooden boxes, eight sacks to a box. Each box weighed

"GOLD TRAIN!"

$20,000,000 For Washington.

Enroute From California Under a Special Guard of Soldiers.

The Grand Conclave at the Foot of the Majestic Rockies.

"The Jig is up; We Had Better Hustle For Our Old Places;" and the crowd Rushed into the Mills to resume Work—News Notes.

THE GOLD TRAIN.

CHICAGO, Aug. 8.—The "Gold Train" from San Francisco which is carrying twenty millions of yellow boys to the national capitol passed through this city this morning. The cars bristled with muskets and no one was allowed within smelling distance of the precious freight. The train stopped but a few moments to procuee ice water for the guards, and then the journey was resumed. The train came in over the Burlington road, arriving at 8:15 this morning. But ten minutes were cupied in switching the train fr Burlington to the Lake Shor and then the train pulled ou ington. None but guards sh selves and they looked rat tired of their jobs. Th reach Washington tomorr

Left: A newspaper article printed in the *Geuda Springs Herald* of Kansas on August 12, 1892. *Right:* Obverse of an 1888 gold coin. A shortage of these in the East prompted the Post Office Department to create the Silk Train.

160 pounds, and their tops were secured with the Treasury Department seal set in red wax. They were divided equally among the Silk Train's four transport cars and mattresses were placed atop them so clerks could rotate sleeping with the gold while others stood watch. The boxes were sent as registered mail.

The train resembled a chain of tethered war wagons. Armed clerks were posted at every possible entrance. Once the doors of the cars were bolted shut on August 4, 1892, no one was permitted outside.

Every time the train approached a watering stop, the crews went on full alert, giving it the appearance of a bristly porcupine—gun barrels protruded from every possible opening.

Vagrants often gathered at watering sites hoping to hitch rides. At the summit of the Continental Divide, a group of them awaited. The arrival of what White called "Uncle Sam's flying treasure houses" wasn't what they expected. According to White, the muzzles the would-be passengers found pointing at their faces convinced them to take the next train.

By the time the train reached Ogden, Utah, the secret was out. Much to the regret of the government, local newspapers were already broadcasting the news of the money train's arrival. Despite this, no one else attempted to board. As it passed through Chicago on the morning of August 8, a newspaper reported that "no one was allowed within smelling distance of the precious freight. The train stopped but a few moments to procure ice water for the guards, and then the journey resumed."

The Silk Train successfully completed its mission in record time. On August 9, 1892, the train arrived at Grand Central Station in New York City, at 10:46 a.m. It had traveled more than 3,000 miles in under four days. And it took less than an hour for the first batch of gold boxes to be transferred to five wagons; by 12:40 p.m., the first one was safely housed in a Treasury Department building in Lower Manhattan. Other gold shipments followed in quick succession until all $20 million was securely stored in the building's vaults. The total cost of James White's flawless run, including the expenses of the required 51 postal employees, amounted to a mere $3,500.

It's almost as if the caper had been carried out by an organization that specialized in transporting

A postcard depicting the Sub-Treasury building located in Lower Manhattan, New York City.

Travus Ross

The first thing anyone going to meet with the U.S. postmaster general in the 1890s might have noticed was an enormous gilt-framed portrait of Return Jonathan Meigs Jr., the nation's fifth postmaster general. The painting of Meigs hung alongside depictions of 19 other early officeholders in the anteroom of the postmaster general, but it stood out: It was heavy, hung oddly near the floor—and it had a propensity to fall. We know this thanks to one man: Travus Ross.

Ross was the usher and the custodian of the postmaster general. He kept a tally of all the times Meigs's painting came off the wall, which showed a distinct pattern: According to Ross's accounting, the portrait fell every time a new postmaster general came into office.

Ross himself was a remarkable individual. A Black man born in 1848 in Kentucky, he worked as a body servant for Union Colonel Roberts, and later, for General William Tecumseh Sherman during the Civil War. After the war, he spent four years working on the legendary USS *Constellation*, which had captured slave ships off the coast of Africa and assisted in the capture of at least one Confederate ship during the Civil War, the CSS *Sumter*. After leaving the *Constellation*, Ross went to work for the Post Office Department in Washington, D.C.—in the office of the postmaster general.

Over the years, Ross worked for postmaster general after postmaster general. He was an indispensable public servant who offered the department continuity in a way that his bosses, who typically served just a few years (at most), could not. Fast-forward a few decades, to the turn of the century, and Ross's loyal service was paying off: In 1901, he earned an annual salary of $1,000, nearly $40,000 in today's dollars.

In 1902, when incoming postmaster general Henry Payne (the 14th one Ross would serve) reported for duty, Meigs's portrait—which Ross had taken to calling the "Falling Picture"—fell again, right on cue. Ross dutifully tallied the occurrence. It was his 14th tick mark. When Ross died in September 1908, he had served a total of 17 postmasters general and left a mark of his own that would never be tallied again.

J. J. Millroy created this map of Alaska and the "Klondyk" gold fields in 1897. The red dotted lines mark the ship routes, while the red highlighted lines mark overland routes.

precious cargo long distances at low prices. Anyway, gold wasn't done with the United States yet. Far from it.

★ ★ ★

In 1897, shiny flecks of soft metal were discovered on the beaches around Nome, Alaska.

They were tested.

Gold.

At the direction of then-Secretary of State William Seward, the United States had purchased Alaska from Russia in 1867. Even at a cost of just $7.2 million for 586,412 square miles of new territory, the transaction was ridiculed as Seward's Folly, and in the years since, it had been a sparsely populated, barely governed afterthought on the American map. Now gold seekers called Stampeders headed to the Far North, especially to the Klondike region of Canada, which was just over the Alaskan border. (Owney, naturally, had already been to Alaska, visiting in 1895. One of the many trinkets from his travels was from "Juno, Alaska, the hottest town on earth.")

Like the forty-niners who flocked to California during that earlier gold rush, hopefuls heading for the Klondike found a treacherous journey and an even harsher landscape when they arrived. The 2,000-mile trek to California took travelers over the Plains and two major mountain ranges. The route to Alaska, however, traversed oceans and seas, river rapids, and ceaseless mountains that rivaled the Swiss Alps, with snow and ice as far as the eye could see and few natural resources for sustenance. And it was 7,000 miles long.

At the time gold was discovered, there were fewer than 30 post offices in what was called the District of Alaska. The district's governor, James Sheakley, had informed the federal government in 1896 that mail service was "shamefully neglected by those who had the contract." The responsible party, the Yukon Transportation Company, was obligated to deliver mail six times per year but had performed only half the required service by December. In addition, Sheakley complained that mail delivery was not being handled by men sworn in as mail carriers but rather by colorful characters who were non-U.S. citizens; even worse, he said, one of the characters "has been known to use language of an exceeding uncomplimentary nature in reference to American citizens."

Mail delivery was a mess all around, but the demand for it was growing quickly. In March 1897, the Alaska Steamship Company, which had been contracted to carry mail from Seattle up to towns in Alaska since 1896, brought up its first load of Stampeders. Sixty-five gold seekers brought along 400 tons of cargo, including mining equipment, dogs, dog sleds, cattle, and freight. The influx resulted in the commencement of semi-monthly winter service—previously there had been no mail delivery during the region's harsh winters—but it still typically took three months for a prospector to receive an answer to a letter from the folks in the lower portion of the country. Very quickly, the idea that Alaska could get by with three mail deliveries per year, let alone the Yukon Transportation Company's contracted six, was ludicrous: By January 1898, the Seattle-to-Alaska route was to get seven mail deliveries per *month*. Someone needed to take charge of the situation.

★ ★ ★

Above: The 140-foot steamship *Williapa*, the first boat purchased by the Alaska Steamship Company, docks at Juneau in 1897. Its first voyage, on March 3, 1895, carried 79 passengers and 23 horses.

Left: A line of gold diggers line the mountain up Chilkoot Pass, Alaska, bound for the Klondike gold fields in 1898.

Right: A carrier using a dog team and sled to transport mail in Kaasan, Alaska, circa 1900.

Postal Inspector John Philip Clum arrived in Skagway, Alaska, on March 26, 1898, with a mandate to examine a few of the state's operating post offices. He started out with Skagway and the town of Dyea, which was just five miles away. It was an inauspicious start. Despite the towns' proximity, the established mail route between them required sending mail pouches through Juneau, 100 miles away. Clum recorded his frustration in the diary he kept throughout his time in the district. "The pouch had to go to Juneau 100 miles and then return to Skagway. After traveling the 200 miles, the postmaster at Skagway brought the pouch to Dyea to have it unlocked, not having received his mail key." Among Clum's first acts was to revise the mail route.

After inspecting Skagway and Dyea, Clum left for the interior of the state and was almost immediately halted by the infamous Palm Sunday Avalanche, which killed 65 people. It wasn't going to be an easy task, fixing Alaska. But headquarters of the Post Office Department had selected Clum to straighten out service in the region because of his colorful background and experiences in the American West, including in Tombstone, Arizona, where he was mayor during the Gunfight at the O.K. Corral and became good friends with Wyatt Earp. Even an avalanche wasn't going to stop him.

Though Clum would spend a decade in Alaska, his initial mission lasted from March to September 1898. He carried everything postmasters needed to set up shop: a large supply of postage stamps, locks, mailbags, postmarking devices, and postal forms. Even more important, he was vested with the unique authority to appoint candidates as postmaster and create post offices on the spot. This was far different from the customary practice, in which settlers had to petition for a post office, identify a potential postmaster, and have the candidate approved. A postal route could take six months, or even a year, to create.

Clum would cover 8,000 miles during his five-month trip, establishing seven new post offices throughout the territory like a postal Johnny Appleseed.

He also established overland routes, operated by contract carriers, through challenging terrain. Many required dogsleds in the winter months and were manned at great personal risk to letter carriers. Ed Biederman mushed the mail between Circle and Eagle, a distance of roughly 160 miles in each direction, on a sled made of hickory lashed together by moose hide. When he was stricken with frostbite that incapacitated his hands, his route was turned over to his 16-year-old son, Charlie, who manned it for three more years. The route was so remote that if anything would have happened to Charlie while out on the trail—luckily, it didn't—he likely would not have been found until the spring. But this was what it took to deliver mail in the Far North.

Below: Prospectors line up outside the "Mail Office" in Dyea, Alaska, circa 1898.

A stereoscopic view of Postal Inspector John Philip Clum riding a mule during his inspection of Alaska post offices.

Despite these challenges, under Clum's direction, the post was moving faster and with increasing frequency during the summer. Five steamers would make two trips each month from Seattle to various locations. In the winter, new contracts had been signed to use reindeer and dogs to move mail.

On June 21, 1899, roughly one year after completion of Clum's initial mission, a front-page story in *The Seattle Star* announced that "one of the largest Alaska mails which has ever been received at the local post office was brought down this morning on the steamer *City of Topeka*...mail consisted of 14 pouches of letters, seven pouches of registered letters, and 10 sacks of papers." Whereas local papers had previously publicized many of the miners' complaints about mail in the region, now they celebrated records. And even these quickly became old news. In the same paper, five days later, word that an even larger shipment of mail had been delivered only made page four.

★ ★ ★

Alaska was a distant frontier in the 1890s, but leading up to the turn of the century, much of America was still a distant frontier—in terms of infrastructure and amenities, if not miles. Rural areas in the contiguous United States could also feel intensely isolated, even if they weren't 7,000 miles away. Alongside the far-flung travels of mail dogs and gold rushers, the 1890s saw a persistent fight over mail back home.

More and more people outside cities could read news and opinions from home and from afar, as evidenced by the amount of mail going to Alaska. By 1890, the literacy rate in America was 86.7 percent. In 1891, rural voters were beginning to mobilize as a political force under the new People's Party. Farmers living in the South and Midwest had been hard hit by past events such as the Civil War and droughts, and they felt abandoned by the Republican and Democratic parties. Populists, as they were called, wanted lower tariffs, an increased supply of money, and better government support, including a subtreasury for crops that they could borrow against. By the 1896 election, the Democratic Party had absorbed the Populists' platform and incorporated a plank in its own platform that called on politicians to woo farm voters. A big part of doing that effectively was understanding what the rural-urban divide looked like at that time. Often, families were keen to keep their kids on the farm, but urban living had a great attraction that was enticing them away. "When we can have all the conveniences of city life in our country homes," wrote E. A. Wheeler, a country-dwelling resident of Santa

A lone ranch mailbox near Farson, Wyoming.

Roughly four in every five Americans lived in rural areas in 1890, and for them, postal service was substandard.

Clara County, California, in 1898, to his postmaster and assistant postmaster—meaning, among other things, free postal delivery—"there will be less desire for city life."

Mail service wasn't the only divide, but for the increasingly literate American populace, it was certainly one that mattered. Roughly four in every five Americans lived in rural areas in 1890, and for them, postal service was substandard. They had to travel to the nearest town post office to collect mail, a journey that might take all day—and they had to undertake it without even knowing for certain whether there were letters to collect.

Some forward-looking officials, including Postmaster General Wanamaker, understood this problem early in the decade. Wanamaker was a major proponent of Rural Free Delivery—in other words, offering the same service of home-delivered mail to rural Americans that city dwellers were accustomed to—as he tried to "never forget the country." In November 1891, in a report to the president, Wanamaker reported that a $10,000 pilot of such a program, which Congress had funded earlier in February, seemed too small. There was a business case for the program, Wanamaker argued, having to do with allowing for correspondence between rural entrepreneurs and their potential customers. But there was also a deeper reason, he suggested, something core to the philosophy of the mail system for decades: It was important to help rural citizens keep up on current affairs, and it was right to treat everyone, urban or rural, the same.

Two months later, Congressman James O'Donnell of Michigan introduced a bill that would extend Rural Free Delivery, often simply known as RFD. As the country was sliding from recession to panic, it was rejected by the House Committee on Post Office and Post Roads over its high estimated price.

In a letter dated April 30, 1892, to the Senate, Wanamaker wrote that "the extension of the free-delivery postal service to the rural districts, in any form, would be appreciated by the rural dwellers as the greatest boon of modern terms." He attached to his letter 472 articles from 258 newspapers that wrote favorably on continuing the service.

It took a year, but on March 3, 1893, Congressman Tom Watson of Georgia proposed an amendment to the annual Post Office appropriations bill to extend RFD for $10,000, and it passed. Unfortunately, a new president was sworn in the next day. Grover Cleveland's ascension to office included sweeping out Wanamaker and bringing in his own postmaster general, Wilson S. Bissell. The position of the Cleveland administration was that rural service was a "crazy scheme" that made no financial sense for a nation already under economic stress. Watson's amendment never stood a chance.

But rural legislators kept trying. In 1896, Congress managed to up the total to $40,000 to test Rural Free Delivery. Postmaster General William L. Wilson, Bissell's successor, proved more amenable to championing it. Bissell was an Ivy Leaguer from the big city of Buffalo, New York; Wilson grew up in West Virginia and dedicated his life to public service there. He conducted the required test of the new delivery among his neighbors in Jefferson County. The test sites included Charles Town, served by three mail carriers; Halltown, served by one carrier; and Uvilla, also served by a single rural letter carrier. The experimental service was launched on October 1, 1896. The first five West Virginia routes, each about 20 miles in length, proved extremely popular: During the

The "Oaken Bucket"

One of the odder pieces of Post Office history is a nine-inch-deep bucket known as the "Oaken Bucket." In May 1895, in an attempt to promote the Atlanta Exposition that would be held that year, the bucket was mailed from Atlanta to destinations, in theory, around the globe. The exposition was designed to signal the reemergence of the South as a player on the American stage, and to usher in the vision of Atlanta as a cultural and commercial center of the "New South." The bucket could hold the aspirations of the world–but it miscarried from the start. It scarcely made it out of the United States, spending most of its time in the mid-Atlantic and Midwest before making it to Great Britain, the only foreign nation it would visit. Along the way, postal clerks were asked to attach a shipping tag with their trip postmark or a personalized note. When the bucket got back to Atlanta in September 1895, it had dozens and dozens attached. Alas, at least one may have indicated that the bucket didn't quite achieve the recognition, or the spirit of wonder, or even the spirit of fellow feeling it had been aiming for. "I sincerely hope," wrote one British clerk, "that the fellow who started this infernal bucket on its trip has kicked it before now."

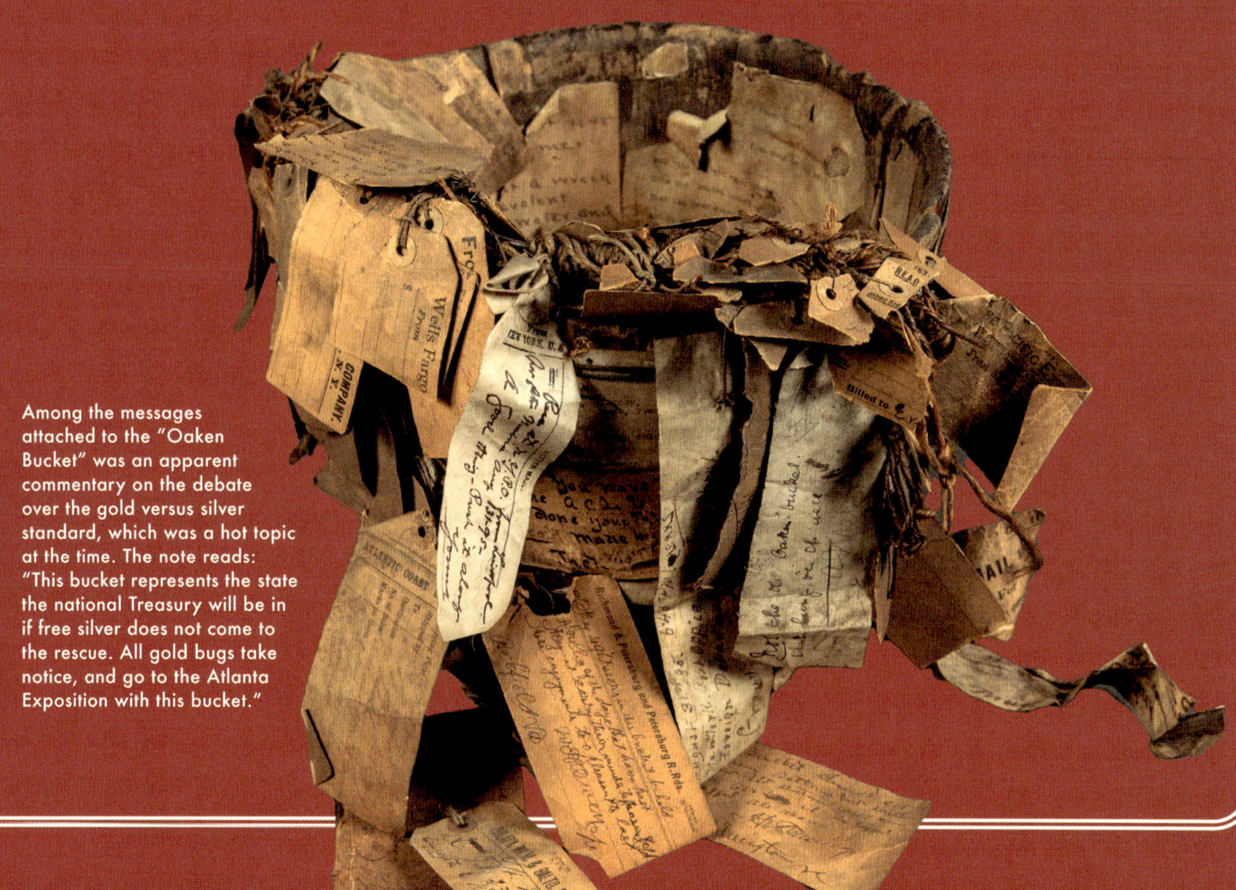

Among the messages attached to the "Oaken Bucket" was an apparent commentary on the debate over the gold versus silver standard, which was a hot topic at the time. The note reads: "This bucket represents the state the national Treasury will be in if free silver does not come to the rescue. All gold bugs take notice, and go to the Atlanta Exposition with this bucket."

Above: An unidentified woman delivers along the Rural Free Delivery (RFD) No. 1 Route in Kansas, circa 1899. It was not unusual for a wife to fill in for her ill husband or be an employee of the Post Office Department.

Left: RFD carriers were required to use their own vehicle and horse (or other animal) for transporting mail. This one-man wagon would have cost about $100 at the turn of the century. It was built by the L.C. Graves Company of Springboro, Pennsylvania.

first month of service, the three Charles Town carriers, Harry Gibson, Frank Young, and John Lucas, delivered 2,226 pieces of mail to 87 rural families. Keyes Strider, the Halltown carrier, and Uvilla's carrier, Melvin Strider, did about the same amount of business. Thrilled with the glowing success of the West Virginia service and eager to expand the experiment, Wilson asked members of Congress to nominate counties where they would like to see RFD tested. By the end of 1896, there were 44 routes in 29 states.

Wilson was a savvy tactician when it came to building support for Rural Free Delivery. Amid bleak economic times, he knew it was crucial that grassroots desire for the service be undeniable. To apply, the Post Office Department required that at least 100 families along the proposed route sign a petition requesting service. Petitions were then forwarded to that district's congressman, or to one of the senators from the state, for their recommendation. Congressmen and senators, eager to hold on to their seats, rarely refused to endorse a route. The number of RFD routes quickly grew. By June 1900, there were 1,214 nationwide, serving an estimated 879,127 people. By the start of 1901, the number of routes and the number of Americans served had doubled—and there were applications pending for 2,258 additional routes.

★ ★ ★

Melvin T. Strider, who had served as the first rural mail carrier in Uvilla at just 15 years old, recounted to the Washington *Evening Star* in 1959 that "when I started, there weren't even any mailboxes...There were plain homemade wooden cartons, cigar boxes, cans, and just about anything that would hold mail." Just as it had in virtually every other place it touched in American life, the Post Office Department helped bring rural America into the future. When the government approved 14 different commercially available boxes for rural service in 1901, it became a requirement that rural homes have a mailbox to receive service. After years of resisting permanent mailboxes, farm families now displayed them with pride.

But there was a much bigger change born out of the rapid spread of RFD: Roads were improved.

The vision of a nation tied together by adequate roads was as old as the republic itself, but in recent

The vision of a nation tied together by adequate roads was as old as the republic itself.

decades a coalition of farmers needing to get goods to market and bicyclists needing to avoid crashing had been advocating for quality roads as part of the Good Roads Movement. Prior to 1900, less than 10 percent of America's roads were hard-surfaced in one form or another. Most were dirt roads that had to be kept reasonably smooth—but that was impossible much of the year. In rainy weather, backwoods roads became rivers of gumbo-like mud. It was not uncommon for rural mail carriers to clean the mud out from between the spokes of their wagons several times on some sections of the road. One Missouri carrier swore that the muck on his route was so deep and sticky it would break the wheels clean off his vehicle if he wasn't careful.

Rural mail carriers received $1,200 in salary a year. From their pay, they had to purchase a suitable wagon and feed and care for their horses. The pay was simply not enough—especially if the roads of their mail routes were destroying their wagons and harming their animals. So in addition to usable mailboxes, the Post Office Department demanded of local, state, and federal governments serviceable and accessible roads. Without them, routes were rejected or suspended. This didn't just help the Good Roads crusaders—it also prepared the Post Office Department for what was coming next: an utter revolution on wheels.

But before we look ahead to the new century and what it would bring, we should consider what the century coming to a close had brought to the post. And there may be no better way to do that than to hear the rest of Owney's story.

Frugal farm families were hesitant to invest in buying rural mailboxes—although they were required to have one to receive service. As a result, lidless lard cans, old barrels, empty soap boxes, and discarded horse-feed crates appeared along roadsides as makeshift receptacles. For those who could afford a box, advertisements ran in newspapers and magazines for the best, biggest, sturdiest, and most weatherproof models.

After all, his most remarkable trip took him all the way around the world. What a thing for the Post Office Department to be able to do! With the help of a postal clerk, Owney, along with his tiny suitcase containing a soft sleeping blanket, a comb, and a brush, set off from Tacoma, Washington, on August 19, 1895.

Aboard the steamship *Victoria*, Owney found plenty to do. His favorite shipboard activity was chasing rats. The ship's crew regarded him as a first-class "rat dog."

He began by visiting several cities in China and Japan. He was sent by registered mail part of the way. Postal clerks were not quite sure what to call Owney, so they created a special classification just for him: "Registered Dog Package."

When he arrived in Japan, officials were perplexed. The impressive collection of tags on Owney's custom harness led them to believe that he belonged to someone of great importance. He was also adorned with a sailor's hatband from the USS *Detroit*, which was operating in Asian waters, giving him the appearance of a military official. As if that weren't enough, he had an official passport, issued on October 2, 1895, by America's consul at Hiogo, the Japanese prefecture containing Kobe, which gave Owney the freedom to travel anywhere in the country.

Owney's Trip

Owney's world adventure was generously written up in *St. Nicholas*, an illustrated magazine for young people, in November 1896.

After visiting Japan, he sailed on as a kennel passenger to China, and then returned briefly to Japan.

A fellow passenger, Herbert Flood of San Francisco, recalled his introduction to Owney: "When I entered the office of the steamship's agent at Kobe, Japan, to book passage, I inquired if there were any other passengers, and was informed that there was one other, who was all ready to leave on the ship, which would sail in two hours. On the agent's books the passenger's name was entered as 'Mr. Owney' and his residence [was listed as] 'America.' I asked for an introduction to my fellow-passenger, and the clerk whistled. A large-sized Irish terrier...who had been sleeping on a pile of mailbags in the corner, trotted to the front. It was Owney, the traveling dog and protégé of the postal clerks of America."

Once he left for a second time, Owney sailed to Singapore, Suez, Algiers, and the Azores, before

READY FOR THE JOURNEY AROUND THE WORLD.

AROUND THE WORLD

landing in New York City aboard the British steamer *Port Phillip*. Postal clerks sent him by train back to Tacoma, Washington, to complete his journey. He arrived on December 29, 1895, none the worse for wear and with more badges, reportedly about six pounds heavier. Hundreds of his friends turned out to welcome him back. Owney's trip set no speed record—it took 132 days—but it added to his reputation as a world traveler. In all, he traveled more than 143,000 miles. His token collection now included mementos from Yokohama, Kobe, Hong Kong, Shanghai, Foochow, Singapore, Perin, and St. Michael in the Azores.

A postal service that was struggling to open its national headquarters in 1800 had sent precious cargo clear around the world.

By 1897, Owney was getting too old to travel. He had lost sight in one eye. He reportedly had a hard time eating anything other than soft foods and milk. For his own protection, he retired to the place where he'd first caught the itch for riding with the mail: the Albany Post Office.

But Owney hated the idea of being grounded. He had lived a life of wanderlust. In June 1897, he ran away from the post office. He apparently boarded the first available train—a mail train bound for Toledo, Ohio. It was the last one Owney would ever take. He died in Toledo in June 1897.

The little mutt had found the mail at exactly the right time, when decades and decades of road-building and rail innovation and professionalization had extended its reach across a continent and beyond. But the era of hopping mail trains and seeking his fortune had come to an end for Owney. For America, the reality wasn't quite so dramatic. The railroads would remain important, and still do today. But the era of the train was ending. A new method of transportation was about to start its engines. As the 1800s drew to a close, adventure on the rails was crystallizing into memory.

As for Owney? James E. White, the superintendent of the Railway Mail Service who had overseen the Silk Train operations, led a nationwide campaign for the preservation of his body. A Toledo taxidermist ensured Owney would live forever. In 1911, his remains were transferred to the Smithsonian Institution, which has cared for the dog ever since.

SHEET MUSIC

In the popular World War I ballad "Bring Me a Letter from My Old Town," the protagonist, a soldier at war, sings his request for jokes from his old pal, words of romantic longing from his girl, and a note of pride from his father. Given the importance of the mail system in helping absence make the heart grow fonder, you can find the mail celebrated in many popular songs. Letter writing and mail carriers have been commemorated from the 1860s through modern times, in musical styles ranging from polkas to pop songs.

"The American Stamp Polka" was written by Maria Seguin in 1864. The cover features one-cent Franklin stamps and three-cent Washington stamps with fancy hand cancellations so they could not be cut out and used.

"Don't Forget to Drop a Line to Mother" was written by Harry Williams and Egvert Van Alstyne in 1908.

"The Man Who Brings the Mail" is a march from 1923 featuring words by Pitt Parker and music by Frank Barone.

"Bring Me a Letter From My Old Home Town" was a 1918 ballad with words by A. G. Delamater and music by Will R. Anderson. The lyrics tell of a wounded soldier wanting to hear news from home.

"The Letter That Never Reached Home," from 1916, features words by Edgar Leslie and Bernie Grossman, with music by Archie Gottler.

"Good Mister Mailman," from 1898, features words by George F. McCann and music by Joseph E. Howard.

"The Postman's Knock" features words by L. M. Thornton and music by W. T. Wrighton. The first line begins "What a wonderful man the Postman..."

"Love Letter Waltzes" was composed in 1897 by H. Engelmann. The collection of popular waltzes was dedicated to his wife.

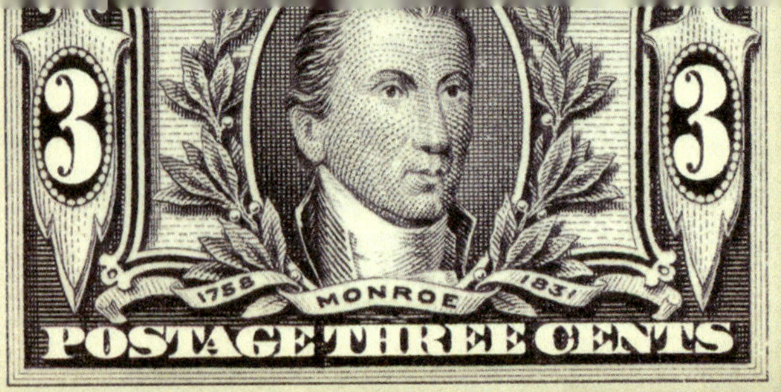

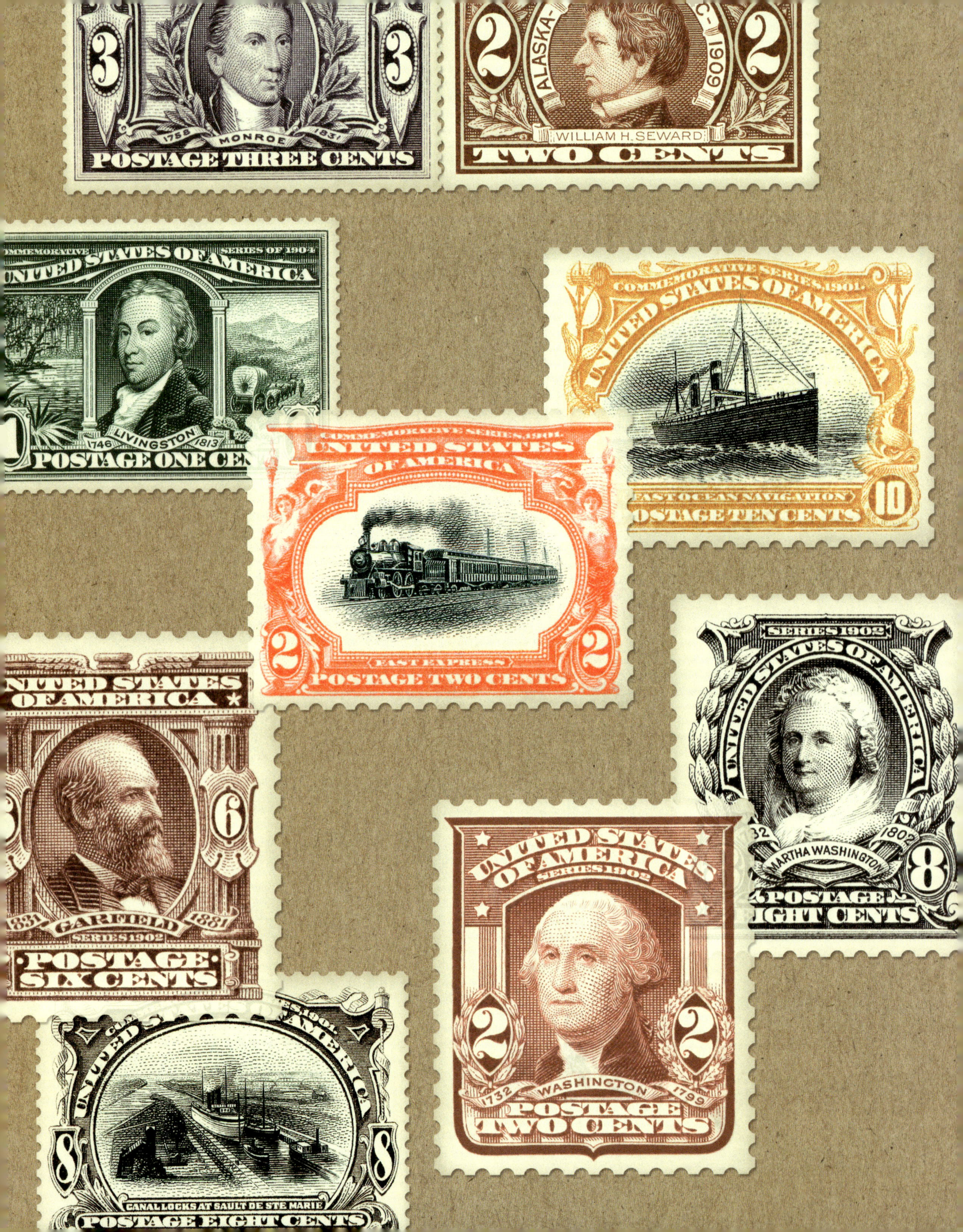
3
MONROE
1758
1831
POSTAGE THREE CENTS
2
ALASKA-
1909
WILLIAM H. SEWARD
TWO CENTS
COMMEMORATIVE
SERIES OF 1904
UNITED STATES OF AMERICA
LIVINGSTON
1746
1813
POSTAGE ONE CE
COMMEMORATIVE SERIES, 1901.
UNITED STATES OF AMERICA
FAST OCEAN NAVIGATION
POSTAGE TEN CENTS
10
COMMEMORATIVE SERIES, 1901
UNITED STATES
OF AMERICA
FAST EXPRESS
POSTAGE TWO CENTS
2
SERIES 1902
UNITED STATES OF AMERICA
MARTHA WASHINGTON
1802
8
POSTAGE
IGHT CENTS
NITED STATES
OF AMERICA
6
GARFIELD
1831
1881
SERIES 1902
POSTAGE
SIX CENTS
UNITED STATES
OF AMERICA
SERIES 1902
WASHINGTON
1732
1799
POSTAGE
TWO CENTS
8
CANAL LOCKS AT SAULT DE STE MARIE
POSTAGE EIGHT CENTS

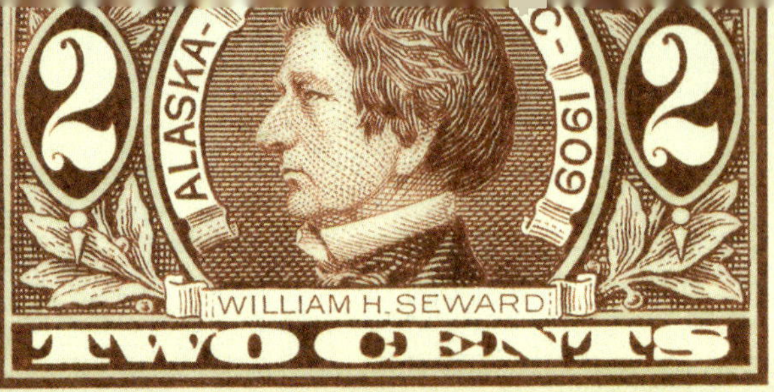

THE MAIL GAINS TRACTION

At the start of the new century, one type of mail delivery was by far the newest, most popular, and fastest growing. You've probably never heard of it.

Approaching the year 1900, streetcars were the perfect form of transportation for the post. With long-distance railroads facing financial difficulties, urban street rail lines were becoming popular people-movers. And since they went where the people were, in the population hubs of the country, they tended to have exactly the kind of network the mail needed. Before long, they were adapted for mail service.

The first streetcar successfully put to postal use was in St. Louis in 1891. Brooklyn, New York, added streetcar mail in 1894, and the following year, Washington, D.C., Philadelphia, Cincinnati, Chicago, Boston, and New York City joined the club. That same year, streetcar mail officially became a part of the Railway Mail Service.

After a brief stint operating streetcars that combined mail service and passenger service, which proved inefficient, the Post Office Department searched for full-size streetcars that solely carried mail. They were handsome vehicles, often painted white with gold striping and the department's intertwined USM (U.S. Mail) logo. The streetcars were driven by motormen and conductors under the employ of private companies contracted to provide the vehicles, but they were manned by mail clerks who made pickups and deliveries at the train depots and substations on each route as well as sorted and canceled mail while in transit. Seventy-five clerks in total staffed streetcars, with as many as four per car.

In 1896, San Francisco and Rochester added streetcars. Baltimore in 1897. Pittsburgh in 1898.

Then, in 1900—just five years after it had adopted streetcar mail—New York City killed it. San Francisco followed in 1905. Rochester in

A United States Mail trolley car #215, circa 1895. This trolley car only carried the mail, but later cars would transport both mail and passengers.

The Boston Elevated Railway streetcar #642 carried both mail and passengers. It traveled on Malden, Broadway, and Ferry streets between Charlestown and Post Office Square.

1908. Many more cities would shutter the service within the next 10 years.

Streetcars weren't particularly speedy, but they worked. Their demise wasn't because of their effectiveness. It was because just as fast as they'd become the future, they'd become the past.

Ten days into the century, in what would soon be known as the Motor City, a test took place. Detroit Postmaster Freeman Dickerson sent a new vehicle on a delivery route from the city's main post office to its stations. It was an electric vehicle made by the Wood Motor Company. A little more than one month later, on February 14, a gasoline-powered vehicle made by the Detroit Automobile Company ran the same route. Each run took less than half the time the routes took with horse-drawn transportation. Both were great, but "an automobile operated by gasoline will be far preferable," because it required no downtime for charging, Dickerson told his superiors.

It really didn't take much more than that: The motor car killed the streetcar and claimed the 20th century for itself.

★ ★ ★

Detroit wasn't the only city to test automobiles, and it wasn't the first. There'd been tests in Buffalo and Cleveland in 1899. But the symbolism couldn't be overlooked in Detroit. David Dunbar Buick had started the company that would be the foundation of General Motors in Detroit in 1899, and within just a few years of the tests, Henry Ford had established Ford Motor Company in the city. For more than 100 years, the Post Office Department had been building the infrastructure to get people their mail and newspapers. Postal officials were constantly looking for faster and more efficient methods of delivery. Now, at the turn of the 20th century, the Post Office was getting in on the ground floor of a new kind of transportation in the place that was to be, effectively, transportation's world headquarters. Post offices were skeptical at first but soon were won over by the potential speed and efficiency of cars and became open to testing the machines. Car manufacturers, in turn, were more than happy to offer models for testing in hopes of landing lucrative sales down the road. Consider how much mail railroads carried; there would soon be many, many carloads to go around.

So testing in major cities commenced. Detroit continued its trials; Dickerson secured several freebie Oldsmobiles to use in experimental Christmastime runs between 1902 and 1905. "The machines were given a very severe test, inasmuch as during the two days that they were in operation we had a very heavy snowstorm," he told Post Office Department headquarters. "The results

Top: Although the Post Office Department was reluctant to spend money on experiments, in 1906 this pair of Columbia Mark 3 touring cars was placed under contract to test their value in collecting mail in Baltimore.

Bottom: A six-horsepower Knox mail car transported mail six times a day to and from numerous locations on the St. Louis World's Fair grounds in 1904. About 800 letters were carried five times per day and about 1,000 pounds of newspapers per day.

Opposite: Postal clerks and carriers at the Buffalo Post Office with a 1901 Columbia Mark XI electric delivery wagon. It transported mail between the post office and a temporary postal station at the nearby Pan-American Exhibition from May through October 1901.

of the trial of these three machines were simply surprising. They accomplished so much more than we anticipated they would."

There was a kind of one-upmanship in the tests. In St. Louis, the postmaster placed a single-cylinder gasoline-powered Knox waterless truck in service to collect the mail at the 1904 World's Fair, which the city hosted. The truck was said to be capable of hauling 1,000 pounds of mail. It never wound up carrying much mail, but it was a show-offy stunt for a city under the spotlight.

Hoping to outdo his colleagues, Baltimore's postmaster employed a pair of modified Columbia Mark 3 touring cars in 1906. Each was outfitted with a mail collection cart body and could do the work of two mail wagons.

The postmaster at Norfolk in 1907 used a pair of eight-horsepower buckboard service cars called Orient Surreys, from Waltham Manufacturing Company, to bridge the gap between land and sea. The two cars made round trips between Norfolk's main post office and the steamship landing that hosted an expo celebrating the 300th anniversary of the founding of the colonial settlement of Jamestown. One of the cars managed to complete the 10-mile round trip nine times each day.

In a bid to one-up the others, the mail service in Milwaukee in July 1907 decided not to use an affordable existing vehicle but tested a pair of small railway-car-like bodies mounted on Johnson Service Company steam-powered cars. A mail clerk in each vehicle would sort mail into in-town and out-of-town destinations, which the vehicle delivered to the main post office and the railway depot, respectively. The test was so successful that Johnson received a four-year contract, among the first placed with a car company. It was extended in 1911.

★ ★ ★

Postmaster General Frank Hitchcock approved of testing the myriad makes and models available—but success could be elusive. Cars were a new technology that postal workers were figuring out along with everyone else.

For one, the Post Office Department was particularly interested in using electric vehicles rather than gas or steam. They had fewer moving parts and were easy to maintain and operate. As the famous inventor Thomas Edison had said, "Vehicle transportation in cities and suburbs will

Postal workers had no clue what kind of weight the new vehicles could handle.

ultimately be done by electric storage battery vehicles. There is no escape from the fact that an electric motor has but one moving part, that rotates, where all other motors have hundreds of parts, mostly reciprocating." But though the Post Office Department tested many electric models, including vehicles from Adams, Argo, Columbia, Rauch & Lang, General Vehicle, Walker, and Waverley, many simply didn't have the "juice" to last for the long distances the post required or to carry the weight of mail.

Overloading, in fact, was another major issue: Postal workers had no clue what kind of weight the new vehicles could handle. It turned out that most cars simply were not equipped to carry a large load of mailbags. Breakdowns on congested city streets were not uncommon.

Tires and road conditions, too, thwarted postal workers. Management preferred to use solid rubber tires, rather than tires with air in them, whenever possible—it was believed they cut down on accidents and couldn't pop. But solid tires were hard on roads and drivers' bodies, and they had poor traction in the snow. In places like Boston and New York City, it was not uncommon to see stranded mail trucks abandoned after a snowstorm. Eventually, the mail service made a switch to solid rubber tires that had holes around the sides to provide some degree of cushioning and ride quality.

Dinkeys, Doodlebugs, and Ding-Dongs

Mail-carrying electric interurban rail systems came into use shortly before 1900 and would reach a peak in the 1920s with hundreds of short lines linking large cities, particularly in the Northeast and Midwest. The self-propelled railcars drew their power from overhead electrical lines and typically included a passenger compartment, baggage section, and mail compartment. They were known by a wide variety of outlandish names, from "puddle jumpers" to "hoodlebugs" to "doodlebugs" to "ding-dongs."

Then there was the "dinkey," a small four-wheeled car that could be used for an array of purposes. Some had donkey engines–an extremely loud variety of steam engine that at the time was replacing horses for hauling heavy loads–and four wheels, while others were simply passive trailer cars. Many were designed for narrow gauge tracks. Though dinkeys were looked down upon by many railroad men in the 1900s (perhaps this is why they were given such an embarrassing name), they performed first-class work for the Post Office Department. Though they also caused occasional accidents. One of the first dinkey-related accidents occurred on November 19, 1886, when a Louisville and St. Louis railway mail train at New Albany, Indiana, ran into a dinkey backing off a bridge. Although the dinkey was small, it was heavy, and the impact telescoped the mail car. Luckily, the lone mail clerk was not seriously injured.

For the most part, a mail route aboard a doodlebug or dinkey was a coveted job. It was usually staffed by only one man, so a clerk could be his own boss. Nevertheless, in an era of vulnerable, lighter-weight ding-dongs and doodlebugs, it's no surprise that the heavy dinkey could also be a bugaboo.

The St. Louis Car Company built car #376 as an interurban baggage and passenger car for the Indiana Service Corporation in 1926. In 1935, the car was transformed into a railway post office.

The Columbia Mark 3 truck was tested in Baltimore, in 1906. It was built to carry two mailbags and a few parcels; however, this truck is overloaded, with barely enough room for the driver.

Accidents were not uncommon, either. The root cause was the same thing that made cars so alluring: speed. Mail carriers could get going much faster than they ever could with horses. The Post Office Department ended up limiting maximum speeds to 12 miles per hour on major streets and installed governors on its motor vehicles that would prevent them from going faster than necessary. The department established a classification for accidents based on the dollar value of damage done to the vehicle. An accident was anything that cost less than $150 to repair, and a wreck was an accident that cost $150 or more. In New York City, it wasn't uncommon for there to be 12 accidents and one wreck each month.

Still, all of these problems were solvable—especially if cars kept delivering results. In many ways, the biggest hurdle to the Post Office Department's adoption of the new technology was economics. In the early days of automobiles, lots of manufacturers popped up and lots of manufacturers went bankrupt. That was a sure way to end a contract for postal use.

★ ★ ★

Though many urban postmasters were motivated to try out motor vehicles at least in part because of the notoriety and bragging rights they could win, rural carriers were interested in testing cars for a much simpler reason: profitability. They saw that with cars they might be able to complete their routes quicker and cheaper. Carrier pay was based on the length of the route, so everyone wanted the longest route possible: A 50-mile route earned the carrier $1,800 per year, compared with just $480 per year for a four- to six-mile route. The catch, of course, was that longer routes took much more time. Cars stood to make even the longest routes short.

Two early adopters in southwest Missouri showed the potential. In July 1902, a local entrepreneur named H. C. Greip chauffeured a postal carrier along his route from the post office in Carthage, Missouri, out into Jasper County. The Carthage postmaster had worked out a deal: Greip would provide the vehicle for a test, and the postmaster would provide free advertising for Greip. At the end of the test, Postmaster T. B. Tuttle told the *Carthage Evening Press*, "I expect that the carrier with the auto will be able to make

Between November 1902 and January 1903, the "Murray" car, manufactured by the Church Motor Company, was tested along one mail route in Adrian, Michigan. This was the earliest known use of an automobile for Rural Free Delivery mail service in the country. The vehicle failed to complete its first run due to high snow drifts and frozen, muddy roads; however, subsequent tries successfully showed that it could cut delivery times in half.

More important, the car consumed only 15 cents' worth of gas each trip, which was less than the cost of horse feed.

the run of 25 miles, more or less, deliver and collect his mail matter, and be back at the office within two or three hours." A test in Belleville, a short drive away, later that year had essentially the same result. The 25-mile route took a team of horses about four hours. The car took fewer than two hours. Plus, Tuttle told the paper, "We might find [cars] cheaper than horse feed, and we have to feed our own horses at present."

Motor cars at the time could cost anywhere between $390 and $650, roughly twice the price of the best of the best horse-drawn wagons. But horses themselves were pricey. For a horse-drawn wagon, a carrier would typically need to own three horses. Two pulled the wagon at a time, but they would be rotated to allow for rest. Feeding horses was expensive, and the pay for a mail route didn't fluctuate with the cost of hay. In 1906, one young carrier tallied the costs, finding that of his $50 monthly salary, harnesses and blankets cost him $20, blacksmith fees cost him $3, veterinary services cost him $2, and feed bills cost him $17. What's more, he had to pay loans on his wagon and rent for the roof over his head. Carriers tried to cut corners whenever they could, doing their own shoeing and growing their own feed. But at a certain point, purchasing a car would just make sense.

What about bad weather? A test in Adrian, Michigan, in the winter of 1902–1903 saw the automobile stymied on its first run by freezing conditions—but every successive run was a success. More important, the car consumed only 15 cents'

Mail by Tube

Almost in parallel to the advent of mail carried by automobile, another system was developed for carrying mail in pneumatic tubes. It proved to be expensive, inefficient, and not very adaptable, but there was a certain cachet to it–plus, it had perhaps the coolest official name of all mail services: pneumatic tube service.

In this system, up to 600 letters at a time were crammed into canisters roughly 21 inches long and seven inches in diameter. The canisters were placed into a network of tubes and then pumped to their destination. At peak mail volume, canisters could be sent every six to 15 seconds. The appeal was clear: With the tube network installed underground, mail delivery could avoid traffic jams and inclement weather. The first system began in Lynn, Massachusetts, in 1887. New York City started a network in 1888. Boston, Philadelphia, Chicago, and St. Louis were soon to follow. (Urban legend has it that the first pneumatic canister in New York City contained a cat that arrived safely without expending any of its nine lives.)

Unfortunately, downsides quickly became clear, too. Tubes weren't as congestion-proof or weatherproof as they seemed. With so much mail to move, the system could get backed up. And though no one needed to go outside to deliver tube mail, the pipes could get clogged with ice in the winter. And there were other ways for things to go wrong. With hundreds of curves in the system, coins, ball bearings, and bolts broke through packages, becoming shrapnel inside canisters. Glass containers were often smashed, including perfume bottles, dousing all the mail packed in with them.

But price was the deciding factor. Tube mail was expensive, and over time, Congress appropriated less and less money, making it impossible to fund the systems. A full pause in the service during World War I nearly brought pneumatic mail to its end, but the companies that maintained the system pulled political strings to keep it going for another few decades. Nevertheless, when New York City finally emptied its tubes in 1953, America's experiment with tubular dispatch was over.

A view of one of New York City's pneumatic tube stations. The postal workers who manned these stations were nicknamed "Operators" or "Rocketeers"; 136 worked there in total.

Go-to Guys Lead Far-flung Mail Service

At the turn of the century, Frank W. Vaille earned a plum assignment. Go to the beautiful, tropical Hawaiian Islands, he was told, and set up mail by rail. It was a coveted job, but Vaille deserved it. Before being assigned to Hawaii, he put in good work in another island nation, far from home, as the director general of the Philippines' postal administration. Vaille was what you might call one of the Post Office Department's "go-to guys." These were loyal, capable employees who could be trusted with critical jobs. In the 1900s, Vaille and another go-to guy took mail service thousands of miles around the globe.

The other go-to guy, G.W. Carr, was actually even more important to mail in Hawaii than Vaille. He'd also been sent to the islands in 1900, but he was in charge of all mail service there, not just rail. Thanks to Vaille, the first railway mail route in Hawaii was established on June 14, 1900, running 71 miles from Honolulu to Kahuku, six days per week. Thanks to Carr, by 1904, Hawaii was served by 27 Star Routes, covering 561 miles, and four railway mail trains, operating more than 108 miles of track.

But it wasn't a competition. The two men were great collaborators, and they would both go on to deliver for the Post Office Department in other far-flung locales. In 1902, with progress in Hawaii well under way, Carr was reassigned to oversee the establishment of the U.S. Mail Service in American Samoa. Vaille would become the head of the Railway Mail Service in Alaska and several states in the Northwest. With their help, the Post Office Department would do for territories around the globe what it had done for the United States: promote the development of physical infrastructure and increased capacity to communicate. It's no fluke that Hawaii would already have an automobile mail route by 1907, when the car was barely just invented–and statehood was still more than five decades away.

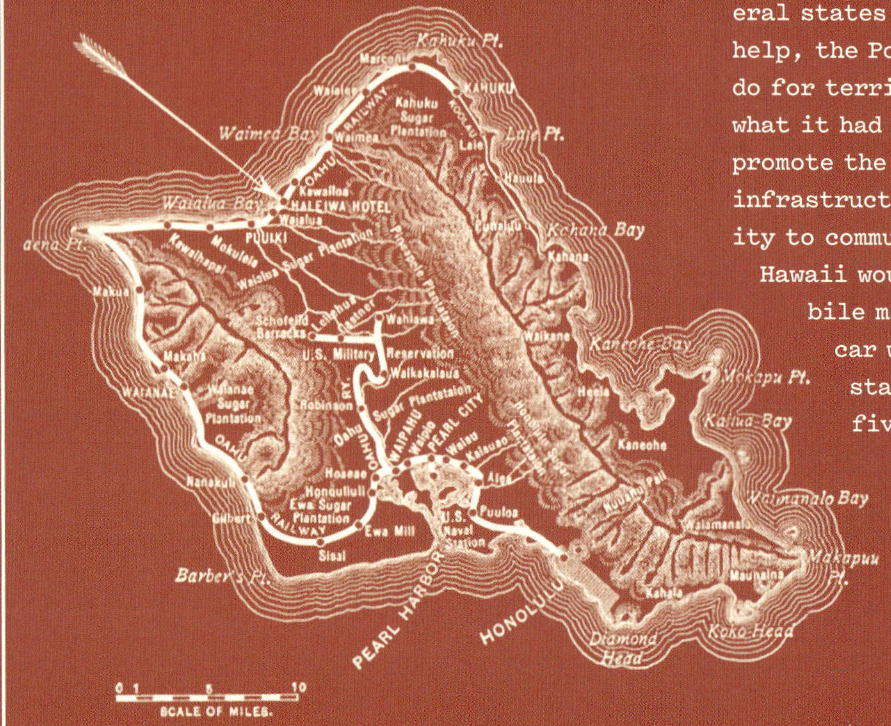

The Oahu Railway (thick dotted line) traveled daily to and from Kahuku and Wahiawa and Schofield Barracks. The route passed through pineapple and sugar fields with a stop at the North Shore's first hotel, the Haleiwa Hotel.

Model B B $400

Government Tests of

ORIENT BUCKBOARD

Result in a Perfect Score

Under the auspices of the Post Office Department, two Orient Buckboards were operated for six consecutive days over Rural Mail Routes in Maryland, Virginia and the District of Columbia, selection being made of the roughest and hilliest roads available. The tests were conducted under the personal supervision of a Post Office Department official, who occupied one of the cars.

Although roads, lanes and grades (some of 40 per cent. or more) were encountered, many regarded as practically impassable to motor cars, both Buckboards completed a perfect record without a single failure.

And The Remarkable Part Was

Not a single repair or adjustment was made, either during the tests or at garage.

The expense of operation on Rural Mail Routes was estimated at seven-eighths of a cent per mile, based on 123 stops on a route of 24½ miles.

The above tests demonstrate the utility, durability and economy of the Orient Buckboard as a car for rough and ready service in all sections of the country, no matter what the road conditions may be.

Energetic agents are desired in unassigned territory.

Write for our business proposition. Catalog free.

Model B B with Top. $425

Waltham Mfg. Co., Waltham, Mass.

Members A. L. A. M.

An advertisement from *Automobile Trade Journal and Motor Age* in 1906 announcing the Orient Buckboard's "perfect score" after two of the vehicles were tested over rural mail routes in Maryland, Virginia, and Washington, D.C.

worth of gas each trip, which was less than the cost of horse feed. Tuttle's instincts had been true; rural carriers were slowly becoming convinced that the time was right to give automobiles a try.

The only question that remained in the minds of rural carriers—and it would last for a few years—was whether postal headquarters would approve of the use of automobiles on rural routes. In 1906, the Post Office Department decided to conduct a month-long trial over a 24-mile rural route outside Washington, D.C., using a pair of four-horsepower Waltham Orient Buckboards.

The results of the test prompted the Post Office to conclude that "the adaptability of motor transportation to rural service having thus received favorable demonstration, the question of its practicality as applied to all sections of the country remains a matter of consideration." That wasn't outright approval, but it was all that rural carriers needed to hear. More and more started buying cars. When they did, they were ecstatic to discover how cheap, economical, and fast they were. They could complete their routes in half the time and for four-fifths the cost.

As carriers made the switch, newspaper accounts across the country began to trickle in. Reporters were finding the same story pretty much everywhere they looked. After a 24.5-mile route in Indianapolis was covered in one hour and 50 minutes by carrier Louis J. Kline, the *Indianapolis Journal* offered a report that summed it all up: "Mr. Kline thinks his experience of to-day indicates that the automobile ultimately will be used very generally for the delivery of mail."

For a while, there was talk of the government requiring rural carriers to buy a standardized mail delivery truck, but such talk fizzled out when everyone realized how expensive it would be. Instead, carriers were left to their own devices to decide what vehicle made sense for them. Touring cars—vehicles that either were convertibles or lacked roofs and had seats for four or more people—proved to be the most popular because the mail could conveniently be piled in the back seat. They were great family cars for going to church or on joy rides when not being used for mail duty. But for most carriers, it was all about affordability. And once you'd gotten past switching from horse to machine, there was another, cheaper option than cars.

Postal management had long liked the idea of motorcycles. In 1899, Postmaster General Charles Emory Smith told Congress: "In view of the prominence which these vehicles have recently attained in the development of the means of general transportation, it is believed that the time has come for utilizing them in connection with the carrying of the mails."

For carriers, motorcycles could deliver time savings, in some cases even greater than automobiles', at a lower cost. The two-wheeled conveyances were dubbed the "bachelor's automobile" because they were an affordable entry point into horseless travel: A motorcycle came in below $300, whereas cars started at almost $400.

motorcycle to collect mail from letter boxes mounted on lampposts to stunning success.)

The Atlanta Journal-Constitution proclaimed, "The use of motorcycles by a few carriers is but one of the signs of a new era in rural life." And indeed, in many ways, it was. Despite the risks, motorcycle sales to rural mail carriers skyrocketed—so much so that it caught postal leaders off guard. And they had a peculiar reaction: They worried carriers were completing their routes too fast.

"The use of motorcycles by a few mail carriers is but one of the signs of a new era in rural life."

Of course, there were drawbacks. If a carrier didn't have a sidecar, there was no natural place for the mail on a motorcycle. And even if one did have a sidecar, capacity was limited. A commercial sidecar topped out at 250 pounds of mail. Carriers often improvised in response, affixing urban letter carrier mailbags to the motorcycle's steering fork, or mounting saddlebags. Some added poles that held columns of tied packages like pretzels on a stick.

And that great advantage, speed, was a double-edged sword, just as it was with cars—except accidents on motorcycles were much more dangerous and could easily be fatal. When James Melton, a rural carrier in Oklahoma, hit a dog, the head of the Rural Letter Carriers' Association, Thomas Drew, reported to fellow members that the motorcycle was in the shop, Melton was in bed recuperating, and the dog was dead. "Rather expensive way to kill a dog," he said. At least Melton survived. In another early accident, John Schutjer, a carrier in South Dakota, died when the front wheel of his motorcycle came off as he was traveling at a high rate of speed.

But there were also benefits beyond cost and (potentially dangerous) speed. One carrier reported carrying a prodigious load of Christmas Eve mail in snow with no difficulties. When floodwaters made it impossible to ford a California river, carrier "Spud" Nordstrom pushed his two-wheeler onto a railroad bridge and rode bumpety-bump over the ties to complete his route. No other vehicle could have accomplished that feat. (Even in cities, motorcycles had great value. In 1908, the Washington, D.C., Post Office tested a three-wheel

★ ★ ★

Postmaster General Frank Hitchcock hated the idea of using motorcycles, believing them unseemly for the Post Office Department. But what really irked him was that carriers could complete their routes so quickly that they were effectively getting paid the same amount as before, but for less work. He proposed a ban on them, leading fledgling motorcycle makers, who had banded together in 1908 to form the Motorcycle Manufacturers Association, to use their newly established clout in Congress to fight back against limitations on their products. Hitchcock was told to back off. That led Hendee Manufacturing Company, maker of Indian Motorcycles, to boast, "Now that the ban on motorcycles for RFD has been lifted, there is offered unlimited opportunity for RFD men to increase their earnings."

Those earnings were increased with the addition of time for carriers to do other things that made them money. They found they could freelance on the side, using their automobiles for doing errands or providing taxi services for paying customers. This prompted Fourth Assistant Postmaster General James I. Blakslee to tell Congress that rural carriers were enjoying joy rides each day and getting $1,200 per year for doing so.

Blakslee fudged a good deal in his testimony on the matter. He gave the impression that there was a huge number of motorized routes, while in truth fewer than one-tenth of carrier routes at the time were gasoline-powered. He also told Congress that those motorized rural mail routes were being completed in two hours, which was never the case, even under ideal conditions, let alone during the winter months. But his exaggerations had the intended effect: Congress believed him. When Rural Free Delivery was primarily conducted on horseback, the lengthiest routes topped out at 25 miles. For motorized delivery, routes were standardized at no fewer than 50 miles.

The effect of that change? It created an extraordinary burden for the mail carriers who were still using horse-drawn wagons. And remember: Despite Blakslee's insistence to the contrary, that constituted nine-tenths of all rural carriers. They had to bow out, work longer hours than ever before, or—the opposite of the intention—buy cars.

From the beginning of the post in the United States to this time, the mail service had mostly been expanding. Technology was improving; routes were multiplying. Yes, steamboats had replaced horses and wagons on some routes, and railroads had replaced others. But there was still a role for horses alongside boats and for boats alongside trains, and with the country growing, the service was only getting bigger and bigger. With the turn of the century and the dawn of the automobile era, the Post Office Department would have to face a new question, the exact same one considered by those horse-bound rural carriers: When do we change technologies? And who will be affected by that change, and how?

But before that question came up again in earnest, another one arose: What does mail look like in the midst of a 20th-century war?

Left: According to an article in the *Hebron Journal* dated January 1, 1909, RFD carrier L. D. Whittaker of Belvidere, Nebraska, purchased his own Excelsior motorcycle for his rural mail route.

Right: Many companies began manufacturing and selling motorcycles to rural mail carriers, including the New Era Gas Engine Company.

PARCEL POST
MAIL TRAIN
5
CENTS
5

1 CENT

U.S. POSTAGE
CENTS
24

U.S. POSTAGE
3
CENTS
3

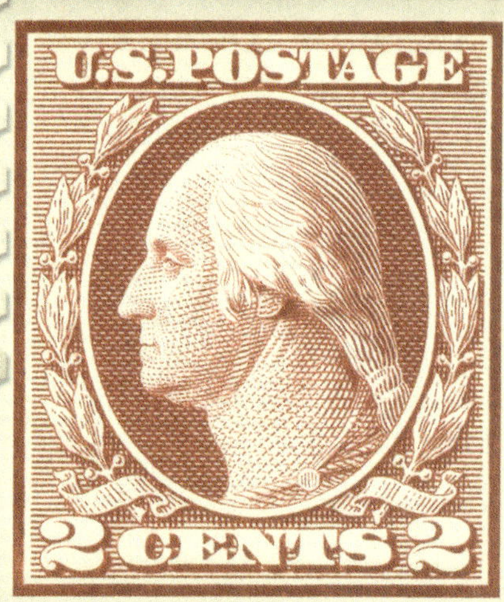
U.S. POSTAGE
2 CENTS 2

U.S. POSTAGE
SAN FRANCISCO, 1915
GOLDEN GATE
5
CENTS
5

POSTAGE

U.S. POSTAGE

U.S. POSTAGE

U.S. POSTAGE

THE GREAT WAR

On the first day of 1913, around midnight, workers in the St. Louis Post Office carefully prepared a very precious parcel. It required special new packaging, capable of protecting six delicate, identical objects. If they broke, they might leak and could potentially damage other goods. Just a few minutes after midnight, the package went out the door.

A half-dozen eggs were on their way to Edwardsville, Illinois.

It was the first day of domestic parcel service and all kinds of things were being mailed in celebration.

Postmaster General Frank Hitchcock mailed a small silver loving cup to the postmaster of New York City, Edward M. Morgan.

Morgan reciprocated by sending Hitchcock a much larger silver trophy, contributed by former Postmaster General John Wanamaker, who initially proposed the creation of Parcel Post.

The Princeton Woodrow Wilson Club mailed an 11-pound package of apples to New Jersey's governor, Woodrow Wilson himself, who would soon be president.

The eggs came back to St. Louis from Edwardsville with the 7:00 p.m. mail—in the form of a cake.

Parcel Post was a game changer. It proved immensely popular, extraordinarily versatile, and highly profitable. It was a boon to rural Americans, especially farmers, who could use it—in combination with Rural Free Delivery—to get their products to market much more cheaply than before. Parcel Post initially allowed packages up to 11 pounds to be delivered through the post office, but in the first year, the limit had already been raised to 20 pounds. It would soon be 50. Forty million packages were sent in the first month of service; within six months, the total was 300 million.

Despite the speed at which it grew, not all the nuts and bolts of Parcel Post had been worked out prior to launch. For one, none of the then-existing 759 post offices in government-owned buildings, or any of the additional 410, had been designed with extra room for parcels. So Parcel Post developed in fits and starts. Every few months, there was a new tweak to the service.

Six months in, the Post Office Department instituted collect-on-delivery (COD). Under COD, postage would be paid by the package's recipient. Letter carriers hadn't been ready for the physical

Parcel Post carriers loaded with packages during the Christmas season.

Postmaster General Frank Hitchcock mailing the first official parcel from the Washington, D.C., Post Office at midnight on January 1, 1913, to Postmaster Edward M. Morgan in New York City.

Her Household Goods Sent by Parcel Post; Stove One of Articles

Seattle, April 24.

MRS. ANNIE OLSON is believed to be the first housewife in the United States to "move" by parcel post.

Postoffice clerks were astounded when she appeared at the parcel post window demanding stamps for conveyance of her household goods from this city to Quinault.

"I figured it would be cheaper this way," said Mrs. Olson, handing in a barrel containing her kitchen stove.

Other articles of furniture were forwarded, weighing in all 337 pounds, and including kitchen utensils, a rocking chair, and a dining room table. They cost her $4.62 in stamps. They cost her $20 the old way, she said.

An article in *The Washington Post* dated April 25, 1915, about Annie Olson, who used Parcel Post to mail her household goods from Seattle to Quinault, Washington.

toll of the onslaught of parcels, and now they had to deal with customer-service headaches, too. What if someone ordered a product through the mail, then opted not to pay when it arrived? The Post Office Department, under this system, was to act as the debt collector.

In March 1914, the department piloted a farm-to-table program that matched farmers with customers in cities. It picked up steam over the next few years.

At the same time, the department was scrambling to obtain enough trucks for the mass of parcels now flying around the country. In July 1915, it established its own Motor Vehicle Service. At that time, the government owned a mere 32 motorized mail vehicles, all located in the nation's five largest cities. Within five years, the postal-truck fleet had grown to nearly 2,500 vehicles in 134 cities.

In 1914, responding to confusion over what could or could not be legally mailed, the Post Office Department had to declare live animals (except queen bees) and children unmailable.

Amid the confusion, people found clever ways to use Parcel Post to their advantage. In April 1915, Seattle housewife Annie Olson arrived at the Parcel Post window with 337 pounds of household

In 1916, a bank in Vernal, Utah, was built with bricks that were mailed via Parcel Post. Packs of ten bricks each were individually wrapped and packed into 1,500 wooden crates, for a total of 15,000 bricks. The bank opened in February 1917.

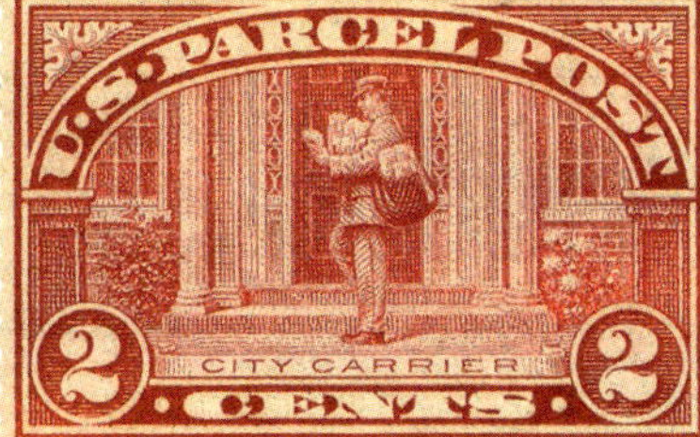

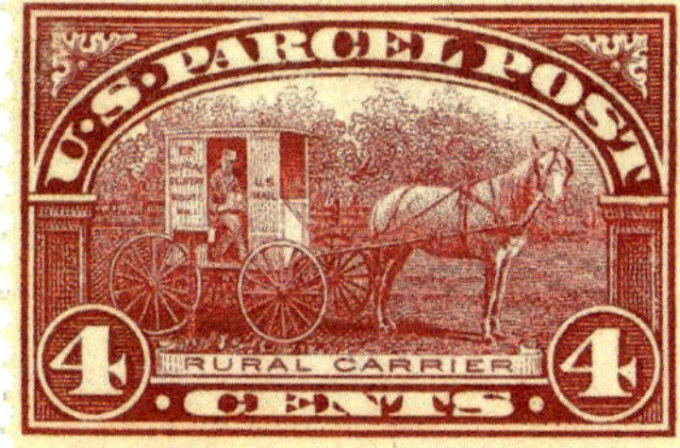

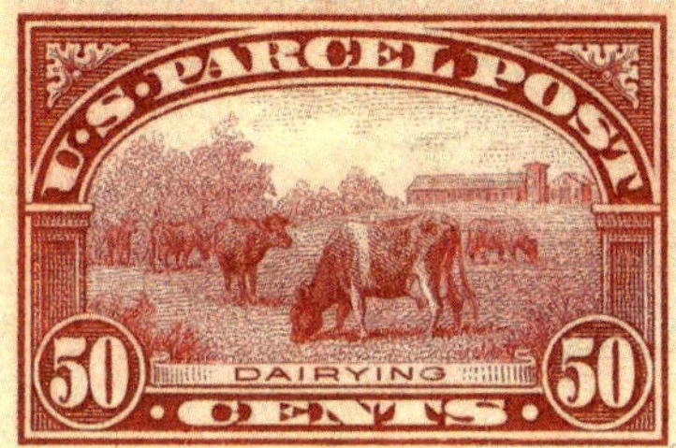

Above: Effective January 1, 1913, the Post Office Department required that Parcel Post stamps be purchased and affixed to all parcels. The carmine-rose stamps were issued in three sets of four stamps each between November 27, 1912, and January 3, 1913. The sets depict, in order of release, postal workers, methods of postal transportation, and users of Parcel Post.

goods in tow, including her stove in a barrel. She was moving. She sent everything 147 miles to Quinault, Washington, at a total cost of $4.62.

To build a bank in Vernal, Utah—a city a considerable distance from the nearest rail line—businessman William Horace Coltharp had bricks sent by post. He dutifully followed the 50-pound limit for packages: The bricks required some 1,500 crates. The new bank, delivered brick by brick, is the largest object ever sent by Parcel Post. It prompted Postmaster General Albert Burleson to institute a limit, per customer, of 200 pounds per day and remark that "it is not the intent that buildings be shipped through the mail."

Right: To transport the sudden avalanche of Parcel Post deliveries, the Post Office hastily received an array of trucks like this one, furnished by different contractors.

Then came Christmas 1917. Religious holidays were extremely trying for the postal system as a whole, but this one was particularly challenging. Hundreds of thousands of packages were sent. Many were poorly wrapped and damaged in transit. Some found their way to the "Christmas box hospital" in Hoboken, New Jersey, for repairs. Others contained contraband, like alcohol, which postal inspectors had to detect.

Of course, most of these weren't domestic Parcel Post packages. They were part of the Military Postal Service. Americans were trying to reach their boys abroad: The nation was at war.

There were a number of innovations in the post in the 1910s. Some were bound for relevance, but not until future decades. Others were stalled by World War I and faded into obscurity. Then there were those, like Parcel Post, that in some ways found their purpose *during* the war. Whatever the case, the story of the 1910s is easiest to see through the prism of a war that engulfed the globe just as the Post Office Department was perfecting its ability to send almost anything anywhere.

★ ★ ★

Precious Cargo

What is loud, unruly, expensive to travel with, and usually lighter than the 50-pound Parcel Post limit?

In the early days of the Post Office Department's new shipping service, some people found reasons to mail children, even though it was inadvisable and, after a declaration in 1914, not permitted. In 1915, six-year-old Edna Neff was mailed by a Florida child welfare officer. The destination? Her father's home in Christiansburg, Virginia, following a Pensacola court ruling transferring custody of Edna to him from her mother. The reason? Edna's postage was just 15 cents. Sure beats the cost of food and gas and hours and hours in the car.

Other kids got packaged up because families were working the system. Among the first was the Pierstorff family, who sent their daughter Charlotte May–just four or five years old, according to contemporary newspaper accounts–from Grangeville to Lewiston, Idaho, on February 19, 1914. The Pierstorffs couldn't afford the price of a train ticket, and Charlotte May weighed 48.5 pounds. Fifty-three cents in postage was affixed to her coat,

Top: A studio photo of a letter carrier with a baby in his mailbag.

Bottom: Charlotte May Pierstorff, who was sent by her parents from Grangeville to Lewiston, Idaho, via Parcel Post.

Little Girl Sent By Mail As Parcel Post Package

MAY PIERSTORFF, FIVE YEARS OLD, TO VISIT GRANDMOTHER BEDECKED WITH POSTAGE STAMPS BY UNCLE SAM.

Little May Pierstorff, age five years, was sent from Grangeville to Lewiston on today's train as parcels post mail. The postage bill for the little girl and her suitcase was 53 cents. The entire "package" weighed 49 pounds.

The postage stamps were affixed to a small suitcase carried by the child and she was taken to the depot along with the regular mail. She was consigned or addressed to C. G. Venniger-holz in whose home her grandmother awaits her and who has doubtless received the "package" from the mail carrier ere this hour. Little Miss Pierstorff is the daughter of Mr. and Mrs. J. E. Pierstorff of this city. Her uncle, Leonard Mochel, is one of the mail clerks assigned to the run from Lewiston to Grangeville.

This is thought to be the first instance where a child has been sent through the mails since the inauguration of the parcels post system. On a short run like this from Grangeville to Lewiston which can be made in a few hours the stunt is doubtless unique and novel, thought it is hardly probable that this mode of transportation will become universally popular.

A news article from the *Idaho County Free Press*, February 19, 1914.

and the girl was sent to Lewiston. She traveled the entire distance in the mail compartment of the Camas Prairie train. She arrived safely at her destination but will forever be remembered for the indignity of being mailed as, officially, a chicken.

If there is a lesson from the era of mailing kids–aside from the obvious–it's that mobility is important. The story of American independence is in some sense the story of people wanting the freedom to move. The story of the Post Office is in some sense the story of things needing the freedom to move. The story of mailing children may be that if it's much cheaper to move things than it is to move people, well, some folks will find a way to get people passed off as things–including their children.

America tried to stay out of the war, which began in 1914. But German hostilities and attacks on American soil and at sea increased. After repeated affronts to America's neutrality and sovereignty, President Wilson asked Congress for a declaration of war on Germany on April 2, 1917. Congress responded by declaring war on April 6.

European leaders doubted the United States would be capable of fielding a modern military in anything less than a year, but that was a miscalculation. Selective conscription was adopted on May 18, 1917. The first adult males between the ages of 21 and 30 were registered on June 5, and the first of the 50,000 troops representing the American Expeditionary Force were safely transported to France by the end of that month.

The United States had succeeded at quickly setting up a modern military. But how fast could it get the Post Office Department transformed into a wartime asset?

As with previous armed conflicts, the Post Office needed to adapt to the new political and logistical landscape. On April 5, the day after the declaration of war, mail to all the Central Powers—Germany, Austria-Hungary, the Ottoman Empire, and Bulgaria—was suspended. The first Army Post Office (APO) was established in Saint-Nazaire, France, on July 12, 1917. The Post Office Department ultimately established 169 APOs overseas, but, owing to complaints about poor service and friction between civilian workers and military personnel, the government sought a new approach.

Passover parcels for Jewish members of the 77th Division of the American Expeditionary Force arrive at Saint-Denis, France, on April 9, 1919.

During World War I, overseas and even local soldiers had special "writing rooms" such as this that provided a quiet space and included everything needed to write letters home. Soldiers were forbidden from disclosing their locations, activities, and planned operations. While the banned subjects didn't leave much to write home about, anyone who forgot these rules would have their letters cut apart by censors.

A contingent of postal officials was dispatched to England to study how the British were handling their wartime mail. The 10 highest-ranking civilian employees from each of the Railway Mail Service's 15 regional divisions, plus representatives from the money-order and registry divisions and other specialized branches of the Post Office Department, were all given special State Department travel authorizations. The following year, on May 9, 1918, the Military Postal Express Service (MPES) was inaugurated in France, and the military took over control of APO operations.

The MPES was the first postal system in the world to be established independently of any existing civilian postal system. It combined foreign and U.S. services: The leadership of the agency consisted of the heads of the Post Office's Divisions of Foreign Mails stationed in Europe, plus the Railway Mail Service, which brought mail from across the United States to New York City, from where it would be sent to Europe by ship.

To expedite military mail service on the home front, a distribution terminal was established in New York City and a processing facility was created dockside in Hoboken, New Jersey, for shipping and receiving overseas mail. Wartime expenditures led to increased costs for nonmilitary mail; effective November 2, 1917, the cost of mailing a one-ounce first-class letter in the United States was raised from two cents to three cents. It wasn't actually a rate increase but rather a one-cent war tax.

In 1918, the Post Office Department reported that the volume of military mail handled in the previous year exceeded any other period in its history. By the end of that year, more than 131,900 sacks of mail were shipped from the States to doughboys overseas and, in addition, 25,532 sacks from France were received and sorted for the French soldiers. Within the next 12 months, more than 50 million letters were sent to those serving in the military and approximately 28 million letters were sent to those back home from camps and trenches. At one point, the overall volume outstripped all the mail carried by the French civilian postal system.

The massive volume led to shortages of writing paper and envelopes. Organizations such as the YMCA and Jewish Relief Board stepped in to provide free notepaper and envelopes, along with coffee, chocolates, and cigarettes, to any penniless service member as part of their mobile canteens and stationary post exchanges. (The YMCA was also famous in France for its "Doughnut Factories," serving "doughnuts for doughboys.") Though the organizations donating paper came from a variety of religions, a soldier's denomination or faith had nothing to do with the letterhead he wrote home on. Any paper was good paper, whether provided by the Knights of Columbus, Jewish Relief Board, YMCA, or Red Cross, although occasionally a soldier would offer an explanation to assure the folks back home that they hadn't converted to another faith.

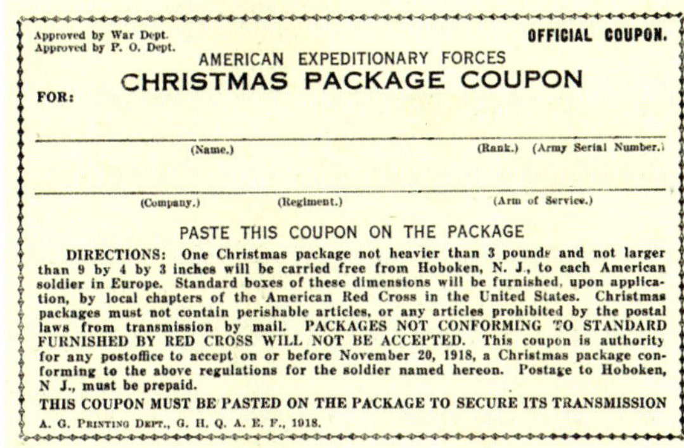

Approved by War Dept.
Approved by P. O. Dept.

OFFICIAL COUPON.

AMERICAN EXPEDITIONARY FORCES

CHRISTMAS PACKAGE COUPON

FOR:

(Name.) (Rank.) (Army Serial Number.)

(Company.) (Regiment.) (Arm of Service.)

PASTE THIS COUPON ON THE PACKAGE

DIRECTIONS: One Christmas package not heavier than 3 pounds and not larger than 9 by 4 by 3 inches will be carried free from Hoboken, N. J., to each American soldier in Europe. Standard boxes of these dimensions will be furnished, upon application, by local chapters of the American Red Cross in the United States. Christmas packages must not contain perishable articles, or any articles prohibited by the postal laws from transmission by mail. PACKAGES NOT CONFORMING TO STANDARD FURNISHED BY RED CROSS WILL NOT BE ACCEPTED. This coupon is authority for any postoffice to accept on or before November 20, 1918, a Christmas package conforming to the above regulations for the soldier named hereon. Postage to Hoboken, N J., must be prepaid.

THIS COUPON MUST BE PASTED ON THE PACKAGE TO SECURE ITS TRANSMISSION

A. G. Printing Dept., G. H. Q. A. E. F., 1918.

The military required that all Christmas packages include this coupon to ensure they were delivered. Various chapters of the Red Cross were instrumental in getting these packages to their correct destinations.

WORLD WAR I

After Congress decided to join World War I on April 6, 1917, the Post Office Department had to find a way to support the receipt and delivery of what would quickly amount to tens of millions of letters between the United States and Europe during the entirety of the conflict. At first the Post Office Department took the lead on establishing overseas offices. Yet as the number of U.S. service members grew—and the War Department became increasingly concerned about soldiers sharing sensitive information that might benefit the enemy—they took over mail-service duties in 1918. In doing so, they created the first official U.S. Army Post Office, which worked independently of the Post Office Department, as well as the first all-military mail service, the Military Postal Express Service. These were not run by postal employees but rather by military personnel (often recruited directly from the Post Office) and are still in use today.

A United States Marine Corps recruitment and enlistment poster stating that the postmaster has the authority to accept applicants from the St. Louis area.

The U.S. Mail train from Paris to Coblenz (now spelled Koblenz), a German city on the banks of the Rhine, unloads mail for those stationed there. The city was occupied by Allied Forces during the demilitarization of Germany in 1915.

Not only did the War Department's actions help streamline the delivery of mail to soldiers, sailors, and Marines, especially as the volume of military mail dramatically grew, they allowed military brass to take a firmer hand in controlling what information was being shared via post. The War Department's Military Intelligence Division created a formal censorship program that worked to stop the spread of sensitive information through newspapers, telegraph, radio, and photographs, and letters sent home from the Western Front.

Above, left to right: Members of the Military Postal Express Service sort through newly arrived mail at Saint-Pierre-des-Corps, France, on October 23, 1918; soldiers writing letters home shortly before sailing to France from Newport News, Virginia, on August 22, 1918; the Army established a Christmas box hospital so soldiers could repair boxes for shipment to American soldiers serving in France; three American soldiers open their Red Cross Christmas boxes, which would have included tobacco, candy, playing cards, chewing gum, cigarettes and pipes, handkerchiefs, and other necessities.

This March 5, 1918, envelope addressed to Denver, mailed via the U.S. Army Postal Service overseas, was censored and marked as "passed." It was sent by an officer, per the pencil marking, and mailed for free.

During World War I, it became necessary to obscure and protect certain information.

Based on one month's stamp sales, mail volume peaked in January 1919, when a record 28 million letters were processed. Besides personal and military mail, industries and the government were also now sending lots and lots of mail. Transportation companies, financial institutions, and agricultural concerns produced a large volume of correspondence. The government, expanded by the addition of scores of new bureaus and commissions, generated thousands of tons of letters.

★ ★ ★

Amid that incredible amount of mail, the Post Office Department was forced to face questions and challenges it had never encountered before. Though many changes would be temporary, they would plant seeds for policies that would reverberate throughout the 20th century, as new technologies and changing social mores found their way to the Post Office Department.

For one: censorship. As we've seen, the history of the mail in the U.S. to this point was in some sense the story of the government's desire to spread *more* information to *more* people. But during World War I, it became necessary to obscure and protect certain information.

At first, the government was resistant. Up through June 1917, the United States hadn't considered the necessity of mail censorship. It was the only country in the war not to exercise absolute censorship on mail matter. But that month, the legislature passed the Espionage Act. It contained many provisions, but one of them was to make letters—especially those written home by American military personnel—subject to censorship, under the direction of the Central Censorship Board.

At larger military training camps, censorship committees of 30 readers or more were established to examine all incoming and outgoing letters. This process delayed mail by at least a day. Additionally, 11 censorship stations were established, with more substations set up along the Mexican border. By 1918, more than 1,600 personnel were engaged in reviewing as many as 125,000 pieces of mail per day.

Because of the threat of espionage by mail, all censorship stations were also made to test letters selectively for invisible writing and to examine suspect mail for secret codes. This became a tedious challenge. In 1918, the Central Censorship Board issued instructions to its letter snoops describing how they were to combat methods of avoiding censorship. Some spy letters were discovered, including a pair of letters sent to pro-German sympathizers, Eric and Albert Matthes, in San Francisco. One of the letters contained writing on the margin in invisible ink.

But for American soldiers, the biggest impact of censorship was its limits on what they could write home. Military personnel were told that they were forbidden from mentioning where they were, what was happening, where they were going, how they got there, and what the weather was like, as all this information might disclose their location, troop concentrations, or planned operations. Any offending information was cut out of a letter. Because many of these letters contained highly personal information, a number of the military censors were chaplains. But even chaplains can use scissors, and anyone who forgot these rules would have their letters cut apart. Some arrived home looking like doilies.

In addition to questions about what could be in the mail, there were questions about who would

The government authorized the Espionage Act and the Central Censorship Board during World War I to stop the dissemination of sensitive or harmful information from the enemy, at home and abroad. The Post Office Department's censorship board in its Washington, D.C., office enforced the postmaster general's idea of blocking mail that interfered with the war effort as well as morale.

Parmlee Campbell delivering mail to Nellie McGrath. Both women were temporary wartime letter carriers in Washington, D.C.

carry it. The war created dramatic labor changes within the Post Office Department. Within three months of the declaration of war, more than 2,278 postal clerks entered the military or transferred to jobs related to war production work. From April 1917 to September 1918, nearly a quarter of all Railway Mail Service clerks enlisted or switched to war-related work. Because of their expertise, most of these men were assigned to Army or Fleet Post Offices overseas or to other military facilities that processed the mail. By the end of 1917, the first calendar year of America's involvement in the war, the total number of clerks lost to the armed forces, transferred to war production work, or dismissed exceeded 9,000. In 1918, City Delivery Service alone lost 3,618 of its letter carriers. Those inducted into the military were placed on leave without pay so that they might return to the Post Office following the war.

Who would fill the gaps? Women, for the first time, took on major roles in the business of the nation's mail. They entered the Post Office workforce in a variety of positions.

On November 6, 1917, Parmlee "Permelia" Campbell and Nellie McGrath became temporary letter carriers in Washington, D.C. Both had family ties to the mail service already: Campbell was the widow of a letter carrier, while McGrath's husband, who had been a letter carrier, was currently in uniform. At the insistence of First Assistant Postmaster General John C. Koons, more soon followed. As a wartime contingency, on November 23, 1917, Koons instructed the postmasters of eight of the largest post offices to conduct a 15-day trial of female letter carriers. December was selected as the test period because hundreds of extra carriers were normally brought on then anyway to help handle the Christmas rush. As a result, dozens of women delivered mail experimentally in Chicago, New York City, and St. Louis during the 1917 holiday season. Though this was a modest test, it demonstrated that women were exceptional at the job.

Effective April 27, 1918, when an eligible male could not be found, a woman was appointed as letter carrier. This led to 25 women taking the civil service carrier exam in Washington, D.C., in August 1918. On September 5, Irma G. Craig, who received the highest exam score, became the first female letter carrier in Washington, D.C., appointed through the regular process used for all letter carriers. That same year, women began provisionally delivering mail in other cities as well, including Detroit and Portland.

Most of the wartime female letter carriers relinquished their jobs when the veterans returned, but a few continued to serve well after the war. In Anaconda, Montana, Anna McDonald was still delivering mail in late 1938—the eve of another conflict that would press women across the country into service.

★ ★ ★

World War I famously ended on the 11th hour of the 11th day of the 11th month of 1918. As it was on its way out, Spanish influenza was on its way in. The Spanish flu was first seen in military personnel in the spring of 1918, but at the time the virus proved relatively mild. In the fall, it returned with a vengeance, spread by the movement of troops around the world. Ultimately, it infected an estimated 500 million people and killed 10 percent of them before subsiding by the end of the decade.

The Post Office Department ordered all postal employees who dealt with the public to wear gauze masks to protect patrons and contain the pandemic. Around the country, post-office hours were curtailed and services were suspended. Spittoons were installed in post offices so that patrons and workers wouldn't spit on the floors. The postal system, in other words—fresh off the experience of World War I—kept moving.

The war had taught the nation that even amid great conflict, the mail was of exceptional importance. After all, the volume of mail from the folks back home to soldiers overseas had been staggering. Everyone with a pen or pencil became a willing "pen pal" to someone in the service. Those at war encouraged this, of course. "Keep my letters coming, please, and tell my friends that they might write to me once in a while too," wrote Sergeant Bill Snyder to his father from France on July 26, 1918.

Postmaster General Albert S. Burleson, in his annual report for the fiscal year ending on June 30, 1918, noted that the safe and prompt delivery of military mail added significantly "to the contentment and happiness of our officers and soldiers." This was perhaps the most important function of the Post Office during the war years, and it was one that would not be forgotten even when, as Burleson stated in the following year's report, "the department promptly began to bring about readjustments to a peace basis."

Ultimately, the Spanish flu infected an estimated 500 million people and killed 10 percent of them.

A New York City letter carrier wearing a mask to protect himself against influenza in October 1918. From 1918 to 1920, the Spanish flu, as it was called, caused about 50 million deaths worldwide.

U.S.POSTAGE
1624
1924
HUGUENOT-WALLOON TERCENTENARY
5
5
CENTS

VERMONT SESQUICENTENNIAL
1777
U.S.POSTAGE
1927
BENNINGTON
2
CENTS

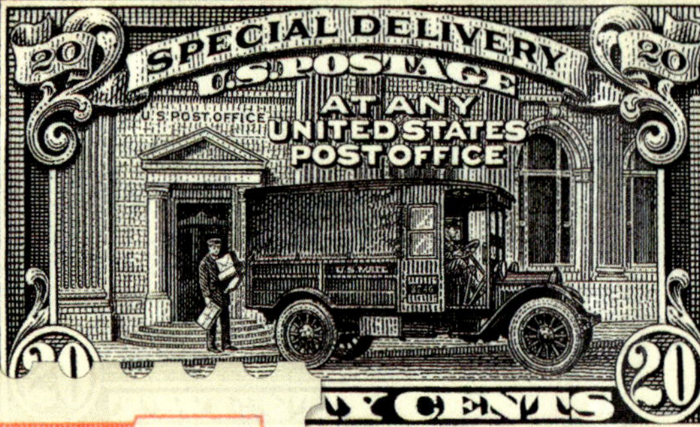
20
SPECIAL DELIVERY
20
U.S.POSTAGE
AT ANY
UNITED STATES
POST OFFICE
20

1779
UNITED STATES POSTAGE
1929
MAJ.GEN.SULLIVAN
2
CENTS
2

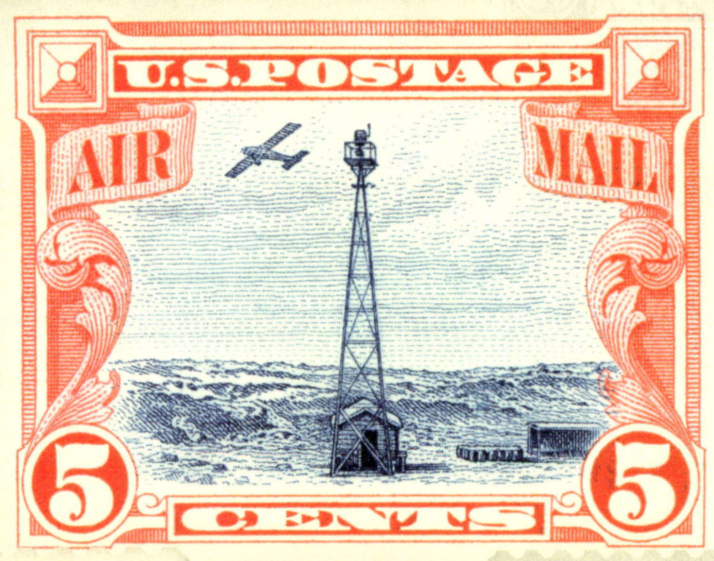
U.S.POSTAGE
AIR
MAIL
5
CENTS
5

UNITED STATES POSTAGE
SPECIAL
DELIVERY
AT ANY
UNITED STATES
POST OFFICE
15

CENTENNIAL
1925
UNITED STATES
POSTAGE
FIVE CENTS
5

UNITED STATES POSTAGE
1775
1925
WASHINGTON AT CAMBRIDGE
LEXINGTON-CONCORD
1
ONE CENT
1

U.S.POSTAGE
1803
1889
JOHN ERICSSON
MEMORIAL
5
CENTS
5

GETTING ROBBED IN THE ROARING 20S

Whether as foresight or folly, the Post Office had always embraced attempts to incorporate new technology into its work. Trains delivered. Electric cars lagged. Experiments continued.

As the war in Europe began to die down and pilots and planes returned from Europe, the Post Office Department set its sights on its next frontier: airmail service. Having no planes of its own, the Post Office turned to the military to get what it needed to test the feasibility of taking to the air. An inaugural flight test left the ground on May 15, 1918, between Washington, D.C., and New York City, with a relay point in Philadelphia. The test actually included multiple pilots and multiple planes—one team traveled the route in each direction.

On the Washington, D.C.-bound route, execution was flawless. The New York City plane, piloted by Lieutenant Torrey Webb, departed precisely on time from Belmont Park raceway on Long Island. In Philadelphia, Lieutenant James Edgerton was waiting to transport the mail to the nation's capital. Without incident, Edgerton delivered it to Washington.

In the other direction, the D.C. departure was delayed. Prior to the flight, Major Ruben Fleet thrilled onlookers with an extravagant aerial show in the same plane that would be used to transport the mail, draining it of gas. When the young pilot assigned to transport Washington's mail to Philadelphia, Lieutenant George Boyle, climbed into the cockpit and attempted to start the engine, it wouldn't turn over. Workers scurried to drain gasoline from vehicles at the temporary airfield, which was located at Washington's polo fields (today's Potomac Park). Finally, they secured enough fuel for the flight, the engine caught, and Boyle eased the throttle forward and took off.

Unfortunately, George Boyle was a bigger problem than the lack of gasoline.

He had been picked to pilot the mail to Philadelphia at the urging of his future father-in-law, who was a member of the Interstate Commerce Commission. But Boyle had little actual flying experience. During the flight, he got lost. He decided to land in a field in southern Maryland

Mail is loaded onto a Curtiss JN-4H "Jenny" biplane on May 15, 1918, at Bustleton Field in Philadelphia, with U.S. Army personnel observing. This was the midpoint stop on the New York City–Washington airmail route.

For the Post Office, the 1920s were not a joyous time.

to get directions—but unfortunately his landing turned out to be a crash landing.

The Post Office trucked the mail back to Washington, D.C., where Boyle had started.

To placate his future father-in-law, Boyle was given a second chance. This time the Post Office Department and the Army hedged their bets, assigning a seasoned pilot to fly on Boyle's wing and shepherd him in the right direction. Before the flight, the expert pilot gave him some parting advice: Keep the Chesapeake Bay on your right. Boyle took the instruction literally, too literally, and flew himself nearly all the way around Chesapeake Bay, in a big circle. When he realized he was heading south, not north, he decided to land and get his bearings.

He crashed. Again.

The mail was trucked to Philadelphia. Boyle was sent back to flying school.

For most of the country, the transition from World War I into the 1920s was one of delight, joy, and excess. The decade following the Great War was a break from the past—a break from financial failures, cultural and social chasms, and Victorian sensibilities on morals and manners. The decade infamously came to be called the Roaring Twenties.

For the Post Office, it was not to be a joyous time. It was challenged, tried, snakebit, making the 1920s a dangerous decade. The Post Office, in the 1920s, was George Boyle. The department would work through three great challenges over the course of the decade: one born from its failures, one born from its success, and one born from its embrace of the future.

★ ★ ★

After World War I ended, what has been called the First Great Migration was under way. Black Americans, driven by lingering racial resentments and Jim Crow laws in the South, were moving north, primarily to major cities. Hundreds of thousands of African Americans were on the move, and manpower shortages caused by the war meant job openings in the North, including at the Post Office Department.

The problem? The department had spent a decade establishing a horrifyingly unwelcoming, segregated work environment. This was its great failure.

The election of Woodrow Wilson early in the previous decade had shepherded in a dark

Lieutenant George Boyle, photographed on May 15, 1918, at the Polo Grounds in conjunction with the inauguration of airmail service between Washington, D.C., and New York City.

The Post Office Department was one place where African American men could find steady, valuable jobs. While there was little room for advancement, the positions were coveted and eventually led to the emergence of the Black middle class. This young African American clerk, photographed in 1922, is testing the Gehrig Mail Distribution Machine, with automatic "pigeonholes" that represented cities or states.

age at the department, one of draconian work demands, cost cutting, and, worst of all, racism. The watershed moment was on March 4, 1913, when, almost immediately upon taking the helm of the Post Office Department, President Wilson's nominee for postmaster general announced sweeping changes.

A staunch segregationist, Postmaster General Burleson supported Jim Crow laws in the South and wanted them in force everywhere. He would set back race relations on a national scale by at least a half-century.

It took Burleson only a month to make his first dramatic, racist proposal: segregating railway mail clerks on the grounds that he didn't believe white workers should have to share towels, eating spaces, and lavatory facilities with Black clerks in the close quarters of a railway mail car. (Of course, they had been doing so for nearly 50 years without difficulty.) But this was just Burleson's starting point. During his tenure, every aspect of the Post Office Department was ultimately segregated. He implemented his plans with the full blessing and support of a segregationist president—Wilson asked only that his efforts be carried out without undue public upset.

Burleson's steps in segregating the postal system pervaded every level of operations, from Post Office headquarters to the smallest government-owned post offices. Supervisors began separating railway mail crews and shifts at post offices based on color. In some cases, Black workers were physically separated from white colleagues by fencing or cages. Segregated restrooms and break rooms were created in larger postal facilities throughout the country. Black employees received the worst assignments and used the oldest and most dangerous equipment. Some were fired outright or assigned to miserable positions with the goal of making them quit. For new openings, a photograph was required with every job application, allowing Black applicants to be automatically weeded out before they could even be hired.

So when Warren G. Harding was elected in 1920 and came into office in 1921, there was much work to be done to repair race relations at the Post Office Department—and they certainly wouldn't be repaired in one decade. Far from it. But when Harding's third postmaster general, Harry S. New, promised that "federal hiring would be color-blind," it was at least an improvement, and there were good-faith attempts at change under way. In 1925, the Washington, D.C., postal workforce was 24 percent African American; by the beginning of the following decade, that had increased to 35 percent. In Philadelphia and Baltimore, by 1928, the Post Office Department's workforce was almost 20 percent and 24 percent Black, respectively. But there was still racial discrimination within small and large post offices across the country. Perhaps the clearest indication that the road to justice would be long was the fact that the percentage of low-level, low-salaried positions held by African Americans was roughly 20 times higher than that of higher-paying ones. The story of Black Americans at the Post Office—and the role of the Postal Office in their lives—would go on to be one of the most important aspects of postal history in the 20th century.

★ ★ ★

Ashland and Gerber mail train Number 13, in Oregon's Siskiyou Mountains, 1923. Hugh, Roy, and Ray DeAutremont have designs on robbing the train of valuables that are being sent through the mail. They think the Number 13 includes a large shipment of gold, but it does not. The DeAutremont brothers attempt to get the train's lone mail clerk to give them access to the mail car, and when he refuses, they go to plan B: dynamite. They don't know what they are doing and use far too much. One end of the car is blown to pieces. The bungling brothers leave the scene—though not without leaving just enough evidence, including a pair of coveralls containing a registered mail receipt and a .45-caliber weapon with a traceable serial number, for the authorities to identify them. What remains on the tracks is ghastly.

Most of the mail on the car is incinerated (though, to the Post Office Department's credit, where addresses were still legible, the mail was dutifully delivered). The interior of the mail car is gutted by fire. Sydney L. Bates, the engineer; Marvin Sent, the fireman; Coyle A. Johnson, the brakeman; and postal clerk Elvyn Dougherty are all dead. The DeAutremont brothers are ultimately tracked down, arrested, convicted, and given life sentences. But none of that can change one incontrovertible fact: The mail is now so valuable that it is a target, and people are losing their lives because of it.

This was the problem born of the Post Office Department's success: Mail workers spent much of the Roaring Twenties getting robbed.

Kindly Post in a Conspicuous Place

United States of America

POST OFFICE DEPARTMENT

ON OCTOBER 11, 1923, A SOUTHERN PACIFIC RAILWAY TRAIN WAS BLOWN UP NEAR SISKIYOU, OREGON, U. S. A. THE MAIL CLERK WAS KILLED AND HIS BODY BURNED, AND THREE TRAINMEN WERE SHOT AND KILLED. CONCLUSIVE EVIDENCE OBTAINED SHOWS THAT ROY, RAY AND HUGH DE AUTREMONT, THREE BROTHERS, WHO LIVED IN EUGENE, OREGON, COMMITTED THE CRIME.

$15,900 REWARD IN GOLD!

ROY A. A. DE AUTREMONT.

RAY CHARLES DE AUTREMONT.

HUGH DE AUTREMONT.

$5,300 Reward For Each Man!

REWARDS TOTALING $15,900 WILL BE PAID FOR INFORMATION LEADING TO THE ARREST AND CONVICTION OF THESE MEN. THE UNITED STATES OFFICERS HAVE CONCLUSIVE EVIDENCE AND WILL TAKE CARE OF THE PROSECUTION.

ANY INFORMATION CONCERNING THE WHEREABOUTS OF THESE MEN SHOULD BE COMMUNICATED IMMEDIATELY TO THE NEAREST POLICE OFFICER. IF CONVINCED THE SUSPECTS ARE THE MEN WANTED, NOTIFY THE PERSONS NAMED BELOW BY WIRE.

C. RIDDIFORD,

D. O'CONNELL,

The last great Western-style mail-train robbery was committed by the DeAutremont brothers in 1923. The detonator they used to blow open the mail car killed the lone clerk aboard and set fire to much of the mail.

During the first half of the decade, five mail robberies stood out as million-dollar jobs.

By this point, mail volume was high, being carried on networks crisscrossing the country, using many modes of transportation. Neither registered mail nor postal workers were safe. Post offices and mail trucks were held up and mail trains were robbed with abandon. Most of the robberies were committed in the Midwest and all the way out near the Pacific, in places known for gold.

Following a large post-office robbery in New York City, every postal employee there was fingerprinted—which led to the discovery that some of them had police records. They were immediately discharged of their duties. Postmaster E. W. Morgan is seen here having his fingerprints taken.

Postmaster General William H. Hays reported to Congress in 1921 that there had been "a sudden and unusual increase in crimes committed in the 'hold-up' of railway mail trains, mail messengers, etc., and arrangements were made for the arming of large numbers of postal employees..."

It wasn't that there were no robberies prior to the 1920s. There were. But the ferociousness and magnitude of robberies in the 1920s were new and remarkable. During the first half of the decade, five mail robberies stood out as million-dollar jobs. The losses were astronomical. In 1921 alone, the Post Office Department lost $6 million to crooks. Of that sum, only half was recovered. In the first six months of 1922, the department lost $2.3 million from 10 major robberies. One of those grabs was a $1.5 million heist in New York City by an organized band of thieves. Only $500,000 was recovered. In 1923 and 1924, more than $11 million was stolen and $4 million was never recovered. The losses were too much for Uncle Sam to swallow.

So Uncle Sam fought back.

In 1921, the Post Office Department began utilizing distinctive burglar-proof containers mounted on special flatbed piggyback railcars to move closed-pouch mail between New York City and Chicago. The steel containers were like giant mail safes filled with mailbags that could be loaded onto flatcars in about 20 minutes. The department also became more mindful that its own employees, who handled the mail, could be in on the thievery. In 1922, after completing the investigation of a 1921 truck robbery as well as disrupting a plot to rob the City Hall Post Office, the New York City department announced in newspapers around the country that it would begin fingerprinting all employees. Matches with police records led to between 400 and 500 men being discharged. Fingerprinting is still in place today.

At the same time, the department also made it worth good mail clerks' while to fight back. In late 1921, Postmaster General Hays established a $5,000 bounty for the capture of any railway mail bandits. The first person to collect was clerk Herman F. Inderlied, who nabbed a notorious criminal on November 15, 1921, just as his train was about to leave the Santa Fe station for Los Angeles.

The crook expected the railway mail car of the Atchison, Topeka and Santa Fe train to be holding $15,000 in registered mail. He was wrong, just as the DeAutremont brothers had been. He snuck onto the mail train and put a gun to the head of

Mail Clerk Tells How He Captured Notorious Bandit

Phoenix, Ariz., Nov. 16.—Roy Gardner, captured mail bandit, was bound over to the federal grand jury here late Wednesday and his bond fixed at $100,000.

After the bond had been announced, Commissioner Henke asked Gardner if he thought he could make the amount. The prisoner answered:

"Oh yes, sir. I can make it all right."

The complaint charged him with attempting to rob the United States mails and with assaulting a United States mail clerk.

The prisoner acted as his own attorney at the hearing and questioned all but one of the prosecution witnesses. He said he did not want to offer any evidence in his own behalf.

Herman F. Inderlied of Phoenix, the mail clerk who was in charge of the car and who captured Gardner, was the first witness.

About 10 minutes before the train was due to leave for Los Angeles, he got out of his car to get the mail from a drop box at the station, leaving his revolver on the table, he testified.

When he returned to the car, he said, he was confronted by a masked man who pointed a revolver towards his head and ordered him to hold up his hands and to back into the corner.

"I started backing but did not hold up my hands," he said. "All the time I was trying to convince the masked man that there was nothing of value in the mail in my car.. I don't know why I didn't hold up my hands."

When he got into the corner, he said, the bandit ordered him to lie down on his stomach, and he started to do so. As he started to get down, he said, the bandit put his hand at the back of Inderlied's head and shoved him. Then, he said, he started to straighten up but only got high enough to see the gun held in the other's hand.

"I made a grab for it and got his wrist," Inderlied testified. "Then we started scuffling and wrestling."

Finally, he testified, the bandit changed the gun from his right hand to his left, and tried to club the clerk with it, but Inderlied caught that hand. At last, he said, both fell down and continued wrestling but finally he got on top of the bandit and got possession of the gun. About that time, he testified help arrived in response to his calls.

In reply to questions asked by Gardner, Inderlied admitted that the bandit had numerous chances to shoot him both before and during the scuffling.

Inderlied said he kept the gun he took away from the bandit until he returned from his run Wednesday, when he turned it over to the officers. He identified five bullets as those he had taken from the gun. Two of the bullets had wooden noses and the two others had lead noses.

J. E. Wilke, special agent of the department of justice, who followed Inderlied on the stand, said Gardner told him that the bullets were so arranged that in case he had to fire, the wooden nosed ones would go first. Gardner explained, according to Wilke, that the wooden nosed bullets contained small shot that probably would stop a man without killing him.

Gardner was under two sentences of 25 years each when he escaped from McNeil Island, 71 days ago.

Roy Gardner—known as "the King of Escapes"—was one of the most extraordinary outlaws of modern times. He committed a number of train robberies and led officers on a series of spectacular escapes, culminating in a remarkable getaway from McNeil Island federal penitentiary, which was supposed to be inescapable. Policeman Louis Sonny, below, finally caught him and returned him to prison.

Inderlied, who was changing into work clothes. The mail clerk instinctively spun around and knocked the gun to the floor. A scuffle ensued, and Inderlied gained the upper hand. He subdued the would-be robber and sat on him until two U.S. Marines arrived from another car to help. The criminal turned out to be none other than Roy Gardner, alias R.P. Nelson, also known as the "Smiling Bandit." Gardner had been convicted twice before of mail robbery—he'd made off with nearly $200,000 in total! —but had twice escaped from custody. He would escape again, be recaptured, and sent to the infamous Leavenworth penitentiary. "Sometimes prisoners escape from Leavenworth," he told reporters. This three-time mail thief did not.

Some officials started to think of postal employees as the first line of defense. It was suggested that mail clerks be issued bulletproof vests and even recommended that some postal personnel, especially those carrying registered mail, be armed with submachine guns. Instead, the department acquired a fleet of armored mail trucks and armed all railway mail clerks. Initially, in 1921, mail clerks and mail handlers were issued .45-caliber revolvers, but they were large and heavy weapons with long barrels, which hampered the clerks' ability to work. They were soon replaced with smaller .38-caliber pistols, which were less accurate and had far less stopping power but afforded an increased range of motion while working. Many mail clerks considered their Colt "Bankers Specials" to be little better than "bean shooters," but arming them had the desired effect. A number of clerks were willing to mix it up with would-be robbers, and it did in fact serve to stanch some of the department's losses.

A group of workers makes mailboxes at the Navy Yard in Washington, D.C., in November 1922.

Mailboxes Are a Must

In 1922, it became mandatory for urban citizens to have a mailbox or mail slot to receive services. The official edict of the postmaster general was "No Mailbox–No Mail!"

Many newspaper publishers capitalized on the new requirement by offering suitable receptacles for new subscribers. *The Washington Times*, for example, provided free see-through glass mailboxes to readers willing to subscribe to a three-month trial of the daily and Sunday editions.

Another 1920s breakthrough in mailboxes was the introduction of pairs of die-stamped, sheet-metal curbside letter boxes. Manufactured at the Naval Gun Factory at the Washington Navy Yard, one box was labeled "Local" while the other was designated "Out-of-Town." Letter mail was now separated before it ever got to a post office. The test was successfully tried in the business district in Washington, D.C., in September 1922, using 27 of the unique box sets. This innovation helped gain public support for separating letter mail prior to its post-office destination; in all, 100 of these so called "double-barreled" sets were manufactured.

Postal guard John Belt displays his revolver in Washington, D.C.'s first armored mail truck. The bulletproof cab was fabricated at the Baldwin Locomotive Works and delivered to the Post Office Department on November 19, 1925.

As robbers got more daring, and their ploys more ingenious, the Post Office had to keep up. On June 12, 1924, the six-man Newton Gang pulled off the largest mail-jacking in U.S. history. Their plunder included $3 million—equivalent to $48 million in today's dollars—in cash, bonds, and valuables taken from 63 mailbags on the Chicago, Milwaukee, and St. Paul Fast Mail train. The robbers had incapacitated the mail clerks with gas bombs, which prompted the Post Office Department to supply its railway mail clerks with surplus military gas masks. The new regalia was an awkward fit with the job of working the mail; it was the case over and over that the tools clerks were given to fight off robbers interfered with the actual tasks of the Post Office.

Perhaps this—plus the fact that they were mailmen, not policemen—is what led the Post Office Department to enlist the military's help. At the request of Postmaster General Will Hays, 2,100 Marines were assigned to protect mail trains and mail trucks transporting valuable registered mail, as well as guard post-office workrooms and entrances (on a temporary basis). New York City, Washington, D.C., Chicago, San Francisco, and other major cities received deployments in late 1921.

The Marines were intended as a stopgap, to remain only until a postal guard force could be organized—but that would require authorization from Congress, and it was slow in coming. This idea of creating a postal police force was nevertheless popular. In 1921, the New York City paper *The Evening World* wrote, "The Post Office should lose no time in organizing a guard force to do the work the Marines are now doing." The paper wanted them to be specially outfitted, like the Royal Canadian Mounted Police.

Instead, on and off over the decade, Marines would provide muscle for the mail. Navy Secretary Edwin Denby stated, "When our Marine Corps men go as guards over the mail,

Due to the number of train robberies in the 1920s, RPO clerks were required to learn how to shoot and carry .38-caliber pistols. The pistols were to be used more to deter would-be thieves than to actually hurt someone.

Right: An article from *The Evening World* dated December 19, 1921.

Below: In 1926, President Coolidge sent 2,500 Marines to stand guard over the mail at Union Station in Portland, Maine. This was the second time the Marines were called to mail duty by a president. The first was in 1921 by order of President Warren G. Harding.

NO PERMANENT JOB FOR MARINES.

CONTINUED use of the marines as mail guards is stirring up opposition in Congress and out. The longer the marines are employed in this way the stronger the opposition will become.

Many of the objections raised are not sound. The strongest is that the marines are marines and should be kept available for their regular service. When a command is scattered it loses the very things that distinguish the marines—esprit de corps and perfect preparation for duty.

In the emergency it was wise to employ the marines. But the Post Office should lose no time in organizing a guard force to do the work the marines are now doing. In addition to the regular inspection service, a guard organization modelled on the general lines of the Canadian Northwestern Mounted Police ought to do the work even better than the marines.

It is always bad to put a soldier on a civilian job. Normally the soldier is under the discipline of officers chosen with a regard for their good judgment. Free the soldier from this disciplined leadership and he is likely to fail when judgment is needed.

that mail must be delivered or there must be a dead Marine at the post of duty." After the 1921 request, Marine guards were gradually reduced beginning in January 1922—but they'd be called back in October 1926 following another outbreak of banditry.

That year, the Post Office Department calculated that it lost more than $1.4 million in 14 major robberies. Of those losses, only about $760,000 was recovered. But if the bulk of money wasn't found, at least most of the thieves were: The sleuths of the Postal Inspection Service never gave up on their search for mail crooks. In 1926, 65 of them were convicted, with the average sentence being 16 years in prison. The conviction rate prompted Arizona's *Douglas Daily Dispatch* to write: "Robbing Uncle Sam's mail is a poor way of attempting to get money, for seldom if ever do the guilty persons escape."

★ ★ ★

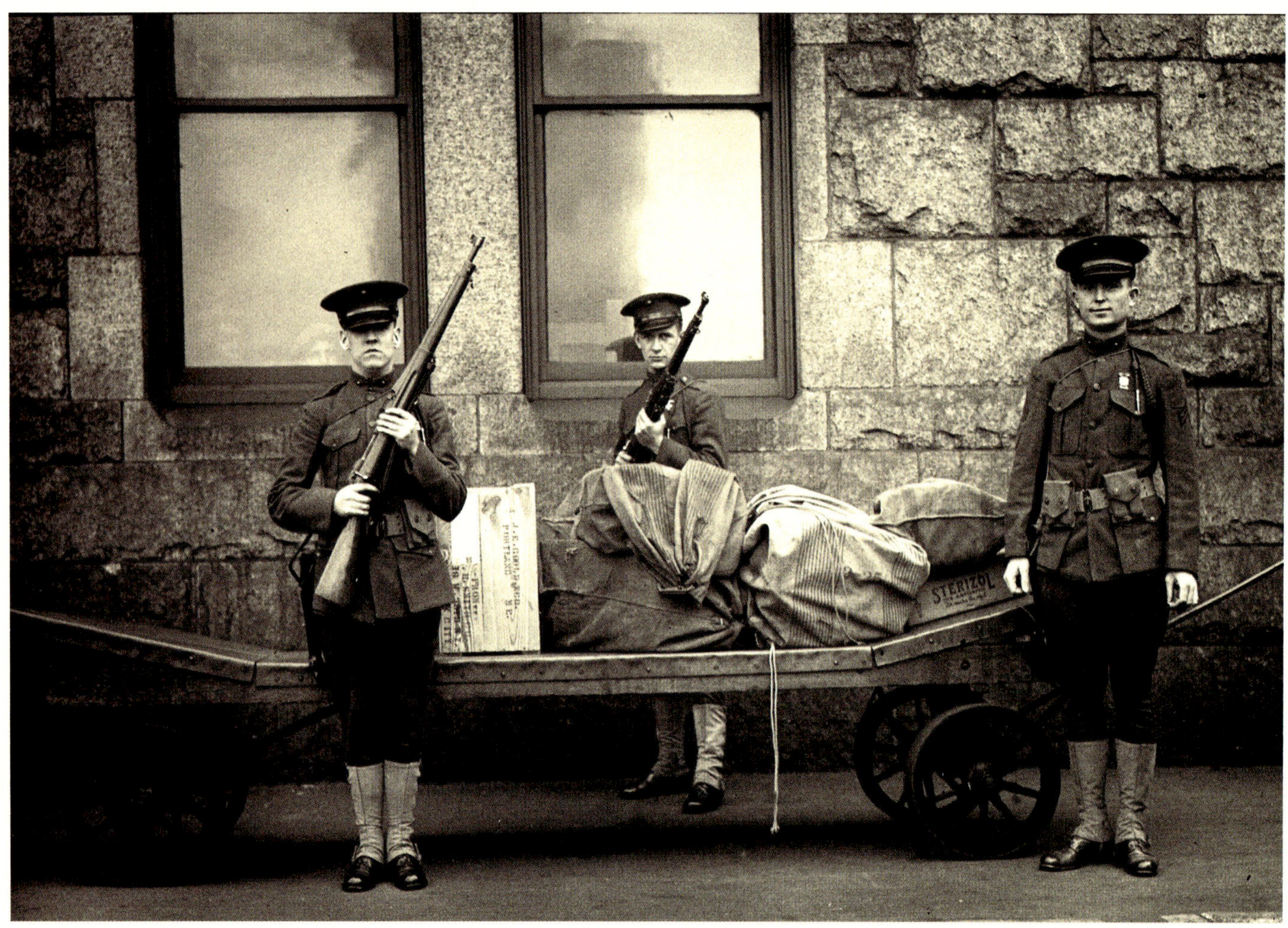

Airmail Service Superintendent Benjamin Lipsner grabs an airmail bag from a U.S. Mail truck to load into pilot Max Miller's airmail plane on his pathfinding flight between New York City and Chicago on September 5, 1918.

In the 1920s, flying may have been great for mail, but it was potentially deadly for pilots.

The last of the decade's challenges to the Post Office takes us back to George Boyle, and to airmail. The Post Office Department saw that transporting mail through the air was indisputably a part of its future. The problem? In the 1920s, flying may have been great for mail, but it was potentially deadly for pilots. The Post Office was driving forward into the future, but it meant a high level of risk for the airmen who were carrying the work.

After flights between New York City and Washington, D.C.—the route Boyle couldn't figure out—became commonplace, the next task was to fly the mail to Chicago. To prove it could be done, postal management turned it into a healthy competition between Max Miller and Eddie Gardner, two of the first four postal pilots (along with Robert Shanks and Maurice Newton). Each would fly in separate planes, with the winner aiming to complete the feat in under 10 hours.

Neither pilot arrived in Chicago on time. On the return trip, Gardner was forced to fly at night, because a mechanic in Cleveland had locked the gasoline tanks and left the airfield, believing the pilot wasn't coming, causing a huge delay.

Night flying was certain death in those days, when planes lacked modern instruments.

It didn't seem that way to Gardner, though. "The metropolis was wonderful," he said. "Lights everywhere. Manhattan, the Bronx, Brooklyn, and to the back of us, Staten Island, Queens, and far out on Long Island." Unfortunately, the lights he needed *weren't* shining brightly. The landing field at Belmont Park raceway wasn't as illuminated as it should have been.

Frantically searching for a safe place to land, Gardner spotted what he thought was a field lined by small trees. He descended in a pair of successive 15-foot drops that he expected would glide him gently into a safe touchdown. Except what he believed were 30-foot-tall trees were three-foot-tall shrubs—so he bottomed out. Gardner was woozy and bleeding, but he was alive. More important, the mail was safely on New York soil in under 10 hours.

Early aircraft had few instruments. For pilots of that era, the best indicator of the angle of their wings was said to be an open bottle of whiskey strapped to the instrument panel of their cockpit. If nerves needed to be steadied, the bottle was an instrument for that, too.

Gardner continued flying the mail until November 1918, when he was ordered to fly in dense fog. He refused. Postal management at the time rigidly insisted that its planes were to fly under any weather conditions. The rule was "Fly or be fired." Thus Eddie Gardner was fired, likely preserving his own life. (He later rejoined the service, then left of his own accord in April 1919.) His fellow airmail pioneers fared less well. Max Miller died in a flaming mail-plane crash, and Maurice Newton quit after sustaining a wreck

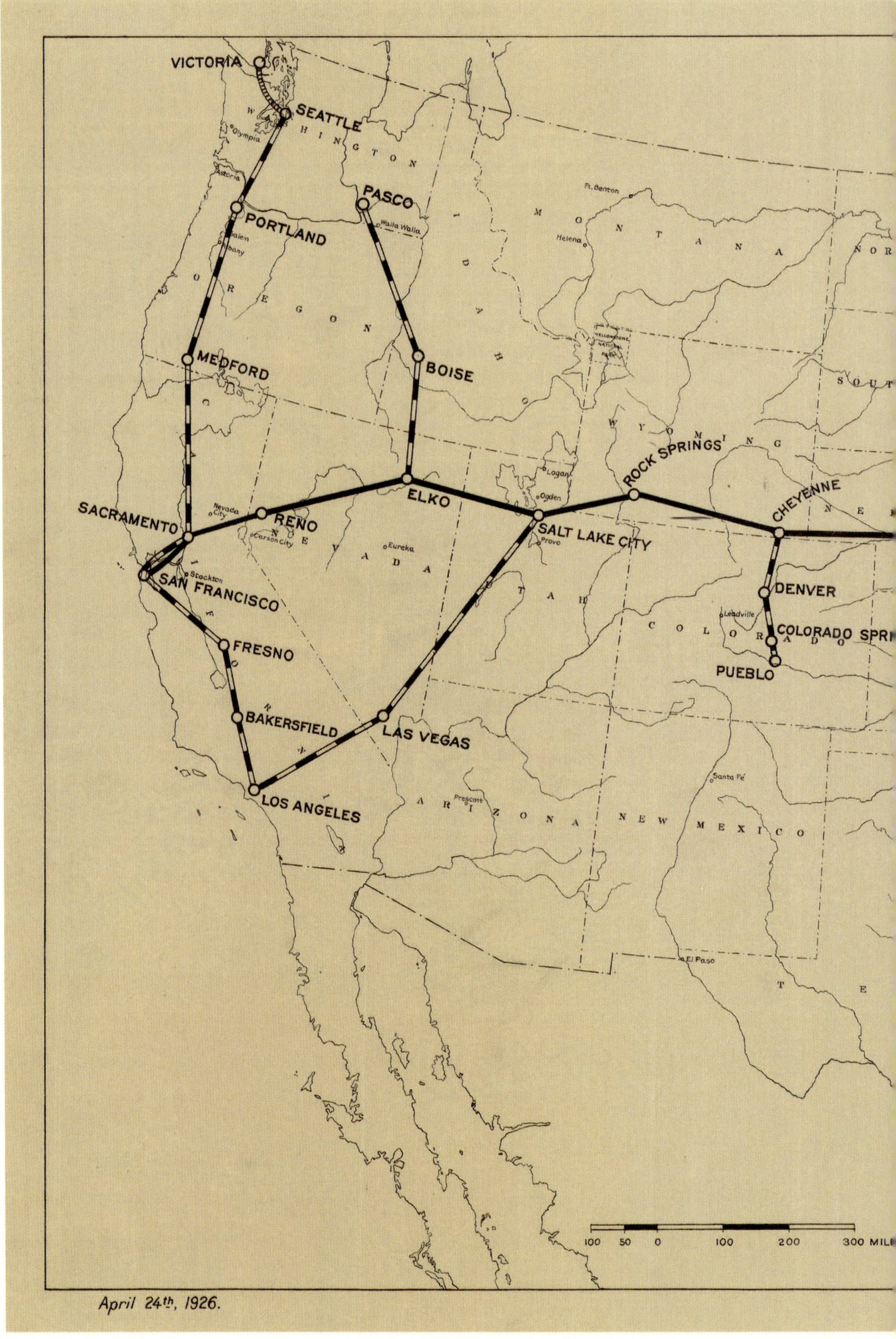

The domestic web of airmail routes—transcontinental, overseas, and contract—and landing fields was constantly expanding. This map shows the system as of April 24, 1926.

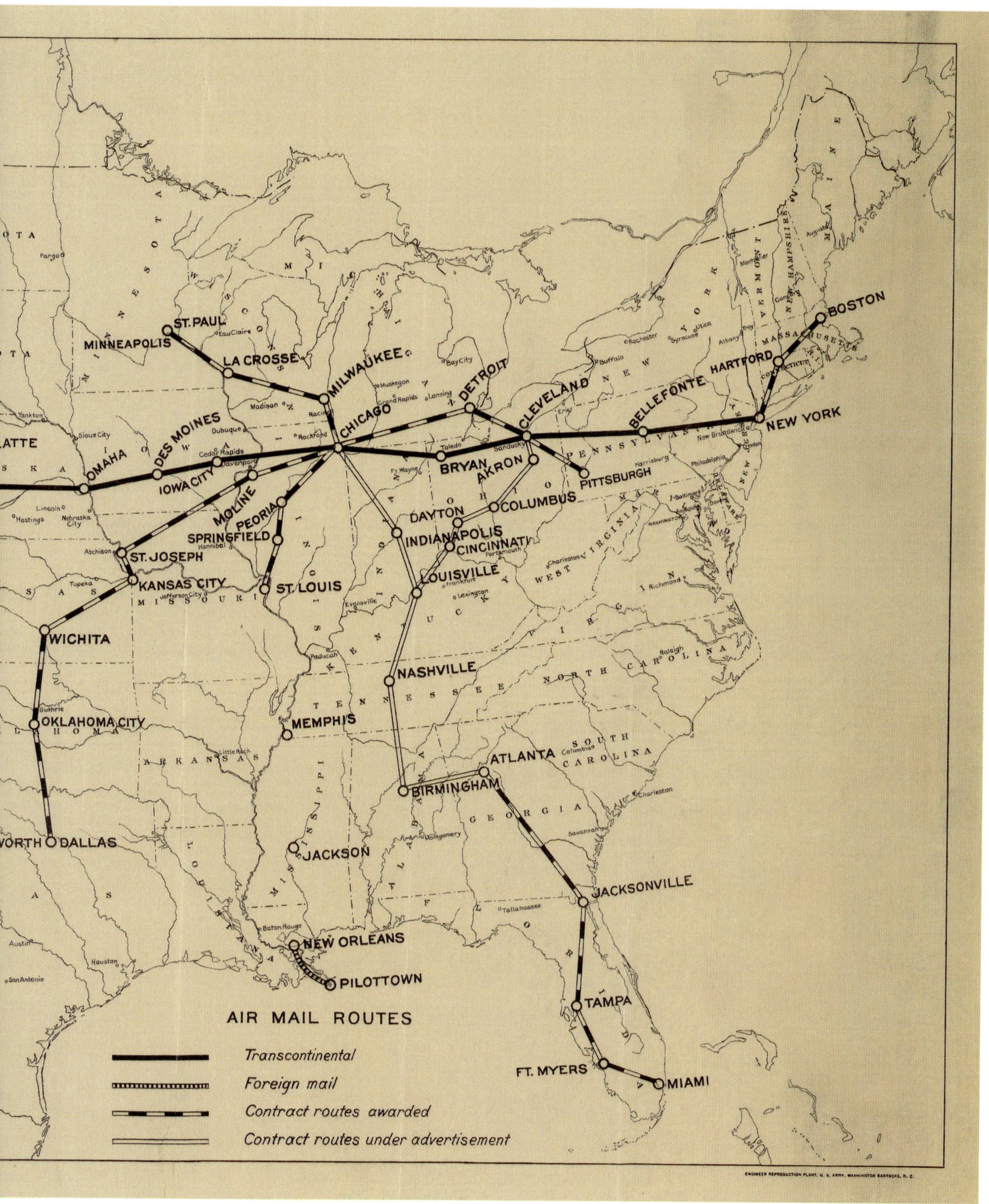
AIR MAIL ROUTES
Transcontinental
Foreign mail
Contract routes awarded
Contract routes under advertisement
BOSTON
HARTFORD
NEW YORK
BELLEFONTE
CLEVELAND
PITTSBURGH
DETROIT
CHICAGO
MILWAUKEE
LA CROSSE
ST. PAUL
MINNEAPOLIS
BRYAN
AKRON
COLUMBUS
DAYTON
INDIANAPOLIS
CINCINNATI
LOUISVILLE
NASHVILLE
BIRMINGHAM
ATLANTA
JACKSONVILLE
TAMPA
FT. MYERS
MIAMI
IOWA CITY
DES MOINES
OMAHA
MOLINE
PEORIA
SPRINGFIELD
ST. LOUIS
ST. JOSEPH
KANSAS CITY
WICHITA
OKLAHOMA CITY
DALLAS
MEMPHIS
JACKSON
NEW ORLEANS
PILOTTOWN

This letter, measuring 8½ by 6 feet, required total postage of $11.50. It was sent to Postmaster General Harry S. New from the Chamber of Commerce of Muskegon, Michigan, thanking him for establishing airmail from Chicago to their town.

The story of airmail took a turn in March 1929, when President Herbert Hoover chose Walter F. Brown as postmaster general. If George Boyle, the wayward early postal pilot, had gotten preferential treatment because he was the son of an important bureaucrat, Brown had the sense of entitlement Boyle might have had—but purely out of arrogance and self-absorption. Brown acted like a postal prince during his time in office, from 1929 to 1933. He had to have the most opulent office in Washington and to be ferried around town in nothing but the flashiest limousines.

He was also a visionary.

Brown believed that what the railway industry had done for both passengers and mail in the 19th century would be done by planes in the 20th. They were capable of carrying people across the country, and mail, too, making the service accessible to more Americans. He was prepared to use mail contracts to transform the industry, single-handedly. But he went too far. Through a series of laws and policy changes, as well as a propensity for working only with the largest airlines in fulfilling contracts—to the unfair detriment of the country's nascent small airlines—he kicked off an airmail scandal. When Franklin Delano Roosevelt became president, he brought in a new postmaster general, James Farley, who would undo much of Brown's work. In fact, Farley would give airmail service over to the Army Air Corps—which proved to be its own debacle.

The point is this: The Post Office Department at the time, in reaction to rapid changes of the early 20th century, was chaotic and reactionary. Things could be counterintuitive. Throughout the Roaring Twenties, a time of legendary wealth and excess in the United States, the Post Office Department's pilots were dying in crashes, its trucks and trains were getting robbed, and its Black employees were trying to gain the respect they had been robbed of by the department itself. But things could turn on a dime.

After all, much of Brown's sordid airmail scandal is lost to history, because seven months into his term, one of the most shocking events in American history took place. On October 24, 1929, known as Black Thursday, the bottom dropped out of the stock market.

The Great Depression was beginning.

And wouldn't you know it, the 1930s would actually be a pretty good decade for the Post Office. Experiencing the highs and lows of one of the most challenging decades in American history would be a little bit like landing a plane in a field, blind, and coming to a stop in one piece—six inches from a stump wrapped in dynamite.

National Air Mail Week

By 1928, airmail was booming. Sixty-three of the nation's largest cities were linked by 9,916 miles of flyways, and five more routes were under consideration. Pilots were flying an average of 22,110 miles daily, transporting on average 5,700 pounds of mail per day. That year, in May, National Air Mail Week was first observed. It marked the 10th anniversary of the first regular airmail service between New York City and Washington, D.C., and celebrated the expansion of the service since then. In the words of Postmaster General Harry S. New, the service had grown from a "crawling babe" to "the modern equivalent of the Pony Express." The primary purpose of Air Mail Week activities was to promote the speed, efficiency, and value of airmail. The celebration would return a decade later for the 20th anniversary. As was its custom, the Post Office Department issued a distinctive and highly collectible two-color, six-cent airmail stamp to mark the occasion. At that point, airmail had grown to a volume unimaginable in 1928: 62,826 miles of routes crisscrossing the country, with planes covering 70,000,000 miles annually—all at speeds undreamed of in 1918.

This six-cent airmail stamp, designed by President Franklin D. Roosevelt, was issued in 1938 to celebrate the 20th anniversary of the first government airmail.

Postal Inspector "Raid" badge, issued to the wearer by the United States Postal Inspection Service, 1973–1999.

National Star Route Carriers' Association chest badge worn by contractors who delivered mail, 1932–1950. Star Route carriers did not wear uniforms, so this badge, bestowed by the NSRCA to the wearer, was a sign of authority.

Postal Inspector chest badge with the shield of the United States in the center, circa 1940.

City Letter Carrier chest badge specific to the Cleveland area, early 20th century.

Railway Mail Service postal clerk's shield-design chest badge, mid-19th century to early 20th century.

BADGES

In the earliest days of the Post Office, if you saw a man on a horse with a leather satchel or saddlebags, blowing a bugle as he galloped into town, he was most likely the mailman. In 1887, badges were issued as part of a standard uniform. By the early 20th century, they were available for the different service groups: the Rural Free Delivery Service, Railway Mail Service/Railway Post Offices, Star Routes, Motor Vehicle Service, Postal Police, Postal Inspectors, and more. In early days, postal inspectors preferred anonymity and carried a pocket-size paper "credential" to show their authority, only taking it out upon request. However, in the 1970s, all inspectors received badges and were instructed to wear them on their left lapel.

A city delivery service cap badge with the number 1822, reflecting a route number, before 1887.

Rural Free Delivery letter cap badge, early 1900s.

U.S. Post Office Department Motor Vehicle Service oval-style cap badge, 1920s.

Concept design for the U.S. Post Office Department collections service badge #855. This badge was never issued.

U.S. Post Office Department Christmas Assistant chest badge, 1959.

★GOLDEN GATE★
UNITED STATES POSTAGE
INTERNATIONAL EXPOSITION
19
3
CENTS
39

KAMEHAMEHA I
3¢
U.S. POSTAGE
HAWAII

UNITED STATES POSTAGE
XTH OLYMPIAD-LOS ANGELES 1932
5

BOULDER DAM-1935
U.S. POSTAGE

U.S. POSTAGE
THREE
CENTS
N.R.A.
3¢
IN A COMMON DETERMINATION

ARBOR DAY
2
2
1872-1932
TWO CENTS

1839
1939
3
CENTS
CENTENNIAL OF BASEBALL
UNITED STATES POSTAGE

U.S. Postage
IN MEMORY
AND IN HONOR
OF THE MOTHERS
OF AMERICA
THREE
CENTS

U S POSTAGE
GRAND CANYON
2¢
2¢

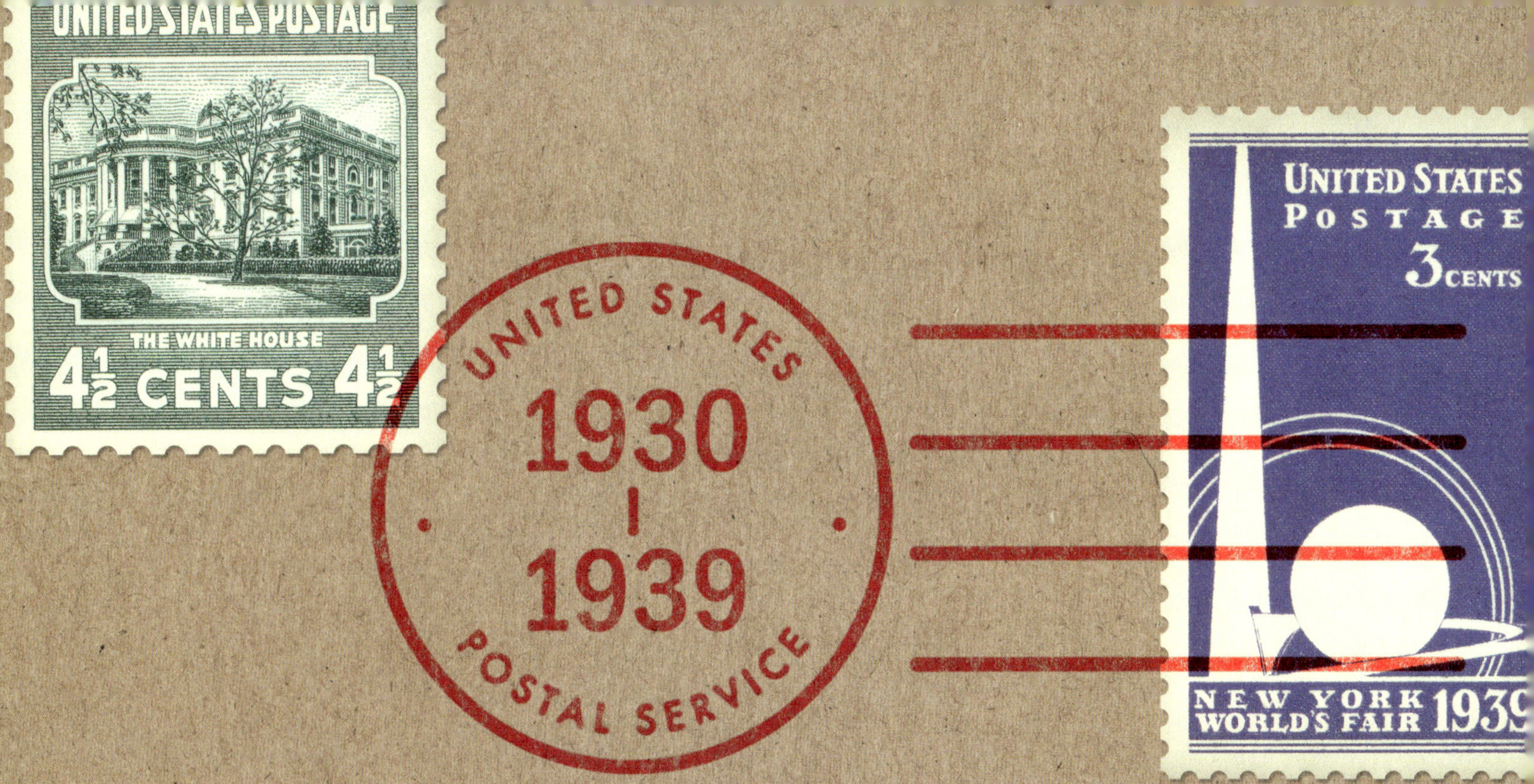
UNITED STATES POSTAGE
THE WHITE HOUSE
4½ CENTS 4½
UNITED STATES
1930
1939
POSTAL SERVICE
UNITED STATES
POSTAGE
3 CENTS
NEW YORK WORLD'S FAIR 1939

THRIVING IN THE GREAT DEPRESSION

BYRD ANTARCTIC
EXPEDITION II
1926
1927
LITTLE AMERICA
1929
1933-4
U.S. POSTAGE
3
3
CENTS

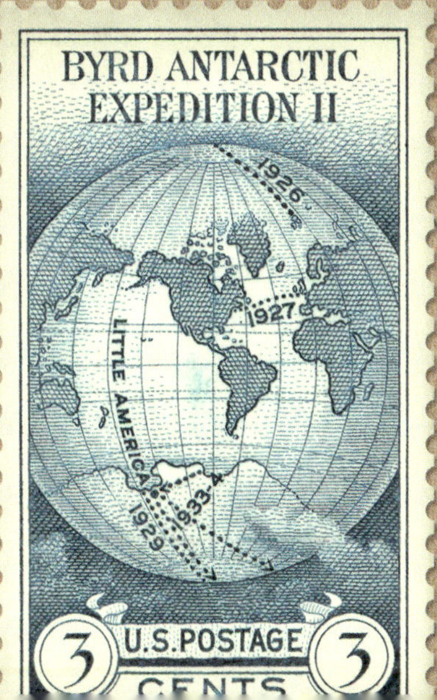

The post office due to be built in Dutchess County, New York, would be special. The Depression was in full swing, but the construction or improvement of government buildings was being used as a form of stimulus. Which meant there was a building boom for post offices. And though most were clones of one another, built on common designs for efficiency and affordability's sake, the Dutchess County building was designed to be a replica of the first house in Rhinebeck, New York, a town in the county. The order to make the new post office so distinctive came from one of the county's native sons: President Franklin Delano Roosevelt.

For the American people, post offices were the most visible face of the government. They touched every community and family practically every day. So new postal facilities weren't just about replacing old and outdated country-store post offices, though they would do that; they were also about showing struggling Americans what the government could do for them. The creation of new post offices became a linchpin in the government's efforts to return the country to prosperity.

Perhaps this was why, rather than insisting that the new Dutchess County Post Office be built in Hyde Park, the town that was home to his estate—which is what everyone expected— FDR insisted on Rhinebeck. It wasn't about him.

That said, Roosevelt was deeply involved in the project. The stones for the project were salvaged from the ruins of the historic house of Henry Beekman, one of Roosevelt's ancestors, which had burned down in 1910. "I never knew anyone to take as much interest in the public buildings of the neighborhood as my husband," Eleanor Roosevelt

The post office in Rhinebeck, New York (left), did not follow supervising architect Louis A. Simon's "Starved Classical" design in the way that Fort Lauderdale's did (below).

United States Post Office, Fort Lauderdale, Florida

On November 7, 1930, three locations of the Bank of Tennessee closed: Nashville, Knoxville, and Louisville. News of the closings spread via newspapers, and panicked crowds were rushing banks. Such was the case outside the Bank of the United States (above), the fourth-largest in the U.S., after its failure in New York City, December 1931.

said. "He has watched every step...of the building in Rhinebeck." Roosevelt became known as "...the nation's No. 1 'unlicensed architect.'"

The Rhinebeck Post Office, which still stands today, is symbolic of the Post Office's role in the 1930s. Though the country was mired in the Depression, the Post Office Department managed to be a sturdy rock. While no clerk or carrier would have wished the Depression on anyone, in some ways it was a good decade for the mail. Because of its role in American life, the Post Office got special attention, as did the post office in Rhinebeck when it was dedicated on May 1, 1939: The sitting U.S. president showed up, and he brought a few of his friends: The Crown Prince and Crown Princess of Denmark and Iceland enjoyed a lovely day.

★ ★ ★

When the Roaring Twenties came to a screeching halt with the stock-market crash in October 1929, almost overnight farm values fell from $5.7 billion to $1.7 billion, worker salaries dropped from $50.8 billion to $29.3 billion, and unincorporated business incomes plummeted from $8.1 billion to $2.9 billion. More than 1,000 privately owned banks failed.

This was a Depression on a scale never seen before. People with savings in failed banks lost everything. Companies closed; workers were let go. Property taxes weren't paid. Consumer spending plummeted and business investments disappeared. At its worst, in 1933, the country's gross domestic product was roughly half what it had been in 1929, and one-quarter of the nation's workforce was jobless. Most of the unemployed had no safety net.

If there were any lucky Americans, they were the ones who held funds in the Postal Savings System, a banking program the Post Office Department had established nearly two decades earlier.

The idea had come about after another financial calamity that shook public confidence in private banks: the Panic of 1907—which modern-day experts compare to the financial crisis of 2007–2009. Coming out of the panic, it was estimated in 1909 that at least 25 percent of the country's currency and coinage was hidden under mattresses, stashed in socks, or buried in backyards, especially in areas where banks were few and far between, like the South and the West. President William Howard Taft's administration wanted to find a way to get that money back into circulation. The trusting and high-touch relationship Americans had with the Post Office seemed like it might offer an opening to do so—not to mention the fact that the public reportedly had access to only 1,453 savings banks around the country but 61,000 post offices.

On January 3, 1911, the Post Office Department initiated the Postal Savings System on a trial basis at 48 post offices, designating one in each state and territory in the country. For as little as the cost of a 10-cent savings stamp, people could sock away money and earn 2 percent on their deposits, which the Post Office would in turn place in banks at a 2.5 percent interest rate. (The half-percentage-point difference paid for the operation of the system.) Customers eventually had the option to convert their savings into U.S. bonds that delivered slightly higher interest rates, backed by the full faith and credit of the federal government.

A Works Progress Administration worker receives his paycheck in January 1939.

Most deposits were modest. In Chicago, the average individual yearly deposit was $130. In New York State—excluding the very wealthy denizens of New York City—the average was $98. (New York City averaged a staggering $60,000 in new deposits every *day* in 1915.) And yet, by 1916, the Postal Savings System held savings totaling more than $80 million. It had proved especially popular with foreign-born wage earners, many of whom came from countries with government-backed banks also often operated out of post offices.

But this was nothing compared to the popularity the system would achieve during the Great Depression, when many Americans would turn to the Postal Savings System as the safest place to save.

"While banks were failing all over the country and a veritable avalanche of funds came out of other banks," said Representative Emanuel Celler of New York, "it was the Postal Savings System that salvaged much of the money withdrawn by the frightened and the timid." In the first six months of 1930, the amount of money deposited was 104 times higher than that of the same period in the program's initial year, 1911. The number of depositors in the service grew from around 674,000 the year of the crash to 770,000 in 1932 to *2.5 million* by 1935, when there was $1.2 billion on deposit. Many of the new depositors came from the Midwest, where the Depression hit the hardest.

Around the middle of the decade, deposits finally began to slow. It wasn't because of an improved economic outlook—the Depression continued to drag on. Rather, it was because the federal government passed a law in 1933 that made one of the virtues of the Postal Savings System available to banks more broadly. On January 1, 1934, the newly created Federal Deposit Insurance Corporation (FDIC) began insuring deposits, overseeing the sound operation of banks, and sorting out bank failures. In other words, the FDIC gave many banks the same ironclad federal backing the Postal Savings System had been enjoying for years. With the creation of the FDIC, deposits to the Post Office slowed, but the system still catered to smaller investors through the end of the 1930s and beyond.

Left: The Post Office Department published a special booklet on purchasing U.S. savings bonds beginning on July 2, 1935. The booklet's illustrations were created by artist Franklin Booth.

Below: A Postal Savings System depositor's numerical reference card printed in 1935 for new customers. This specific card was issued by the West End Station in Washington, D.C., in 1941.

Form PS 301-A
April 1935

POSTAL SAVINGS SYSTEM

DEPOSITOR'S NUMERICAL REFERENCE CARD

The number of your postal savings account is 10297

Please keep this card in your purse and refer to your account by number when making deposits or when writing concerning it.

POSTMASTER

Washington (West End Sta.) D. C.
(City) (State)

GPO 5—11765

★ ★ ★

Of course, saving mattered only if you had a job, and far too many Americans were out of work. Putting the country back to work was a national priority. With an executive order issued on May 6, 1935, President Roosevelt created the most famous jobs program of the Great Depression: the Works Progress Administration (WPA). Over the course of its existence, the WPA—which would be renamed the Work Projects Administration in 1939 before winding down in 1943—spent about $10.5 billion putting 8.5 million people to work. Even just its initial appropriation, $4.9 billion, was gigantic. In its first year, it accounted for 6.7 percent of the country's GDP. The focus was on construction projects. Over the course of the Great Depression (including before the start of the WPA) about 40,000 new public buildings were built, and more than 85,000 government-owned structures were enhanced. As for WPA projects, think mainly of public facilities—schools, parks, roads, and bridges, for example.

And post offices.

Diesel Trains Pull into the Station Too Late

The romance of the rails may have reached its peak in the 1930s. Rail lines introduced some of the most iconic trains of the era, and newspapers treated each new line as newsworthy, often providing front-page coverage. In November 1936, the *Red Lodge Daily News* in Montana announced the inauguration of the Burlington Railroad's newest Zephyr, the Mark Twain, which offered service between St. Louis and Burlington, Iowa, with a stop at the writer's hometown of Hannibal, Missouri. The Mark Twain consisted of four cars, including a full-size railway post-office car. For railway mail clerks, serving on a stylish train like the Mark Twain was considered a plum assignment.

This was also the dawn of the diesel era in rail transportation. Diesel was cheaper and allowed trains to run faster. When the Burlington Zephyr completed the 1,017-mile run between Denver and Chicago in November 1936, it required just $15.36 in fuel and set a speed record: 12 hours, 12 minutes. In a series published in *The Indianapolis Times* in 1935, David Dietz wrote: "Like glittering streaks of silver or gleaming arrows released from the gigantic bow of some god, the stream-lined, articulated, Diesel-powered trains rush across the countryside." He claimed that the diesel engine was going to pull America out of the Depression.

Alas, it was not to be. The economic downturn had all but bankrupted many of the smaller railroad lines just as an affordable alternative–the car–had become commonplace. Every year after 1929, railroads posted losses on passenger revenue. The Post Office Department had the same experience as everyday Americans. In 1931, an official noted that railroads were curtailing their service–which meant cutting some mail trains–but that it was okay, because Star Route service using automobiles could fill the gap without costing more. So it was that the 1930s constituted the last gasp of the beautiful, adventurous golden age of mail on rails in the United States. No matter how fast diesel trains could race down the tracks, they couldn't outrun reality.

The Burlington Zephyr train was unveiled at Exposition Park in Los Angeles in 1934, with huge crowds lined up to see the streamlined, futuristic-looking locomotive.

Burlington
Route

The "Starved Classical" design was adopted to standardize architectural plans for new post offices built in the mid-to-late 1930s. At left is the Caldwell, New Jersey, Post Office and at right, the post office in Gleason, Tennessee.

Every member of Congress insisted on having new post offices in their state or district. Enabling legislation flowed. The allotment from Congress reached more than $44 million to build more than 400 new post offices.

The government's supervising architect, Louis A. Simon, found himself in charge of an overwhelming amount of work. His office was responsible for designing and building government offices, including government-owned postal facilities. There was simply no way they could keep up with the demand if they treated each new building as its own separate architectural assignment. Instead, Simon and his colleagues came up with sets of cookie-cutter building designs that could be used in any part of the country, perhaps with minor tweaks to the facades to keep nearby post offices from looking too similar.

This building style was dubbed "Starved Classical." Lacking massive porticos and opulent exterior embellishments, the structures that resulted were architecturally suited for frugal times. Members of Congress were known to grumble that a proposed new government building might not blend in with their local surroundings, but Simon's designs cleverly dodged these complaints. Their classical and Art Deco details, hewn from terra cotta or concrete, could harmonize with nearly any surroundings. And besides, they often replaced shabby post offices that had seen far better days. In fact, in many remote hamlets, a new post office was instantly the newest and fanciest building in town.

The designs were also cheap, quick, and easy to build. Most were competitively bid and typically constructed within nine months at costs between $75,000 and $100,000. Each project was assigned to a Post Office Department construction engineer, who provided project management and worksite supervision and furnished postal headquarters with periodic progress reports. The laborers who built the buildings weren't paid much, but they were thankful to be working at all.

When each post office opened, it was usually received as a crown jewel of the community. The opening and dedication were a big deal. Cachet post-office covers, decorative stamped envelopes designed to celebrate a new opening, were cheap

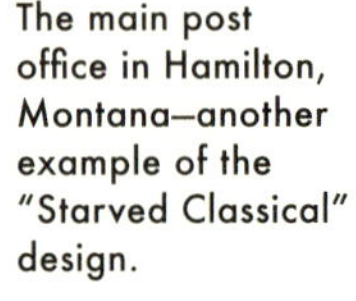

The main post office in Hamilton, Montana—another example of the "Starved Classical" design.

Above: The post office in Mount Union, Pennsylvania, built in 1936, was enhanced with a partial stone facade and window iron-work. Otherwise, it was identical to other buildings of this size and layout.

Right: Hundreds of citizens of Whiting, Indiana, gather to celebrate the dedication of their new post office on July 21, 1933.

but beautiful souvenirs. Almost every postal facility built in the 1930s, regardless of the building's size or renown, was commemorated with such localized cachets. The opening festivities would be attended by an array of luminaries, including state leaders, postal officials, and local politicians. Often a parade would follow the dedication ceremony—an excuse to issue new uniforms to postal employees and feature those with musical talents. In 1939, the local newspaper in Weldon, North Carolina, reported on the opening of the town's addition. "The new Post Office Building is a beautiful structure, modern in every respect," the paper said. "The citizens of Weldon have received the new building with just pride."

Air Mail by Daniel Rhodes, completed in 1941 and located in the Piggott, Arkansas, Post Office.

Texas Immigrant by Gordon K. Grant, completed in 1939 and located in the Brady, Texas, Post Office.

Turning a Corner by Joe Jones, completed in 1939 and located in the Anthony, Kansas, Post Office.

A study for a mural titled *Scene in Poughkeepsie, 1850*, by Gerald Sargent Foster. The mural was never installed, but the study resides in the Smithsonian American Art Museum.

Winter Landscape by Jessie Hull Mayer, completed in 1940 and located in the Canton, Missouri, Post Office.

The Leisurely Native Tempo by Stevan Dohanos, completed in 1940 and located in the Charlotte Amalie Post Office in the U.S. Virgin Islands.

The Army Enlists in the Post Office

In 1934, a branch of the military briefly took on the challenge of flying the mail around the country. The unexpected intersection of two very different parts of the federal government feels like an experiment that should have worked perfectly. After all, the military had great pilots, an expansive network of bases around the country, and experience dealing with the stress of war—certainly, it could handle the mail. Right?

The story begins at the dawn of the decade, when Postmaster General Walter F. Brown co-drafted the Air Mail Act of 1930, also called the McNary-Watres Act. It gave the Post Office Department the freedom to dole out contracts to private businesses to provide airmail. In other words, it gave Brown near-dictatorial power over airmail contrators—power that would have far-reaching consequences.

Almost as soon as the law passed, on April 29, Brown canceled all existing airmail contracts, changed the revenue formula, and held secret meetings called the "Spoils Conference" in Washington, D.C., to award new contracts. The invitees? Basically, only the major airlines; smaller airlines that had previously held contracts were hung out to dry. Brown envisioned a new world with three routes—northern, southern, and central—each serviced by one of the big three airlines: American Airlines, Northwest Airlines, and Transcontinental & Western Air. Brown's approach caused a major outcry: By taking contract opportunities away from smaller airlines, it was essentially killing a huge portion of the aviation industry.

People didn't much care for Brown's tyrannical approach. In 1934, when Franklin D. Roosevelt swept into office and named his own postmaster general, James Farley, the two men decided it was time for a reset. They canceled all existing contracts again. To continue delivering the service while they decided what to do, they had a novel solution: The Army Air Corps would step in.

It might sound like a brilliant idea, but the military was given just 10 days' notice to prepare to take over 17 airmail routes covering 11,000 miles. It was to be responsible for major routes servicing New York City, Boston, Chicago, Atlanta, San Francisco, Dallas, Denver, and Salt Lake City. Major General Benjamin Delahauf Foulois, the commander of the Army's Air Corps, assured President Roosevelt that the Army was ready for the challenge. Its airmail flights began on February 19, 1934.

It was a practical and public-relations disaster.

Above: An Army Air Corps Keystone B-6 twin-engine biplane lands in the middle of a snowstorm in 1934 ready for refueling.

Left: A cachet cover celebrating the Army Air Corps' first flight on February 19, 1934.

The roughly 150 airplanes that were used weren't meant to fly mail; neither were the Army's pilots, who were trained to fly combat and reconnaissance missions. Much of the flying required for airmail was "blind flying": flying at night and often in inclement weather, using instruments. Military planes could carry heavy loads, but some simply weren't designed to handle the particular distribution of weight that came with mail. In the first three weeks, 10 Army pilots died. Billy Mitchell, the wartime assistant chief of the Army Air Corps, blamed the military's miserable showing on "poor equipment, lack of flying experience by pilots and bad weather." The reasons didn't matter: By May, a devastated Roosevelt had restarted commercial contract airmail. It took several years for commercial aviation, not to mention the Army Air Corps' reputation, to fully recover from the episode. But the public's desire for airmail itself was seemingly unscathed. By the 1936 fiscal year, more than 15,000,000 pounds of mail were being flown around the country.

Twenty-eight American artists spent three years, from 1935 to 1938, creating artworks to match the building's grandeur.

Perhaps no one was ever prouder of these openings than Postmaster General James Farley, who crisscrossed the country attending dedications throughout his time in office, which lasted through the end of the decade. He was often the principal speaker, and according to *The Washington Evening Star,* he commanded "immediate respect for his forthrightness, his disarming frankness, and the conviction of sincerity he radiates." By all accounts a spirited speaker, Farley was said to have another gift as well: He could remember a person's name long after he met them. Here was another way in which the Post Office could fortify the country. After all, the effect was to remind people that they were alive, that life would go on, that they had communities, that there were some things they could count on. Having the postmaster general—an official from high up and far away—remember your name was almost like receiving a letter from an old friend.

★ ★ ★

Though the new post offices—Rhinebeck's and other exceptions set aside—were largely similar on the outside, and even on the inside, there was one key differentiator: art. Murals or other embellishments executed by artists for the Section of Painting and Sculpture (later called the Section of Fine Art, often just called "the Section") adorned many of the buildings. The Section was a jobs program, not unlike the WPA itself, but aimed at artists and administered by the Treasury Department's Procurement Division. Over its nine-year history, it awarded some 1,400 contracts for artworks—including murals in 1,300 post offices.

The works, usually individualized murals focused on unique aspects of each community's colorful culture and history, were the result of a rigorous process. Artists were chosen through competition, their identities kept anonymous so that committee members would be impartial. Mural artists were provided with guidelines and themes. Once an artist was awarded a commission, they engaged in lengthy negotiations with the Post Office Department, the town, and the Section before beginning their work. To alleviate any discord with the community, artists were constantly reminded that the community members were the patrons. They were the ones who had to be satisfied if the artist was to keep their commission. (Not that there were never issues—Rhinebeck's murals depicted countless scenes of slavery, ruffling community feathers.)

Even big-city post offices built in the 1930s, though not part of WPA projects, received special attention and had opulent edifices and interiors. The grand project of the era was the Post Office Department's new building at the southwest corner of 12th Street and Pennsylvania Avenue in Washington, D.C. The building was designed by the architectural firm Delano & Aldrich, whose primary commissions had previously been extravagant homes—a business that dried up as the Depression took hold. In their new circumstances, William Delano and Chester Aldrich aimed for the magnificent. Taking inspiration from the Place Vendôme, a prominent public square in the historic core of Paris, they designed a seven-story neoclassical structure with an unusual footprint: Two semicircles placed back to back, with sweeping side wings, created a dramatic facade. Twenty-eight American artists spent three years, from 1935 to 1938, creating artworks to match the building's grandeur. On the inside were numerous murals and sculptures. And on the outside, in a gesture that in its way acknowledged the significance of the Post Office in the lives of everyday Americans—so apparent in this decade—the artists, through sculpture and bas-relief panels, depicted the history of the postal system.

★ ★ ★

It's important to point out that despite its relatively privileged position as a cornerstone of the federal government during a trying time, the Post Office Department certainly did not have it easy during the Great Depression. Mailing decreased during the decade-long economic struggle—aside from the fact that they had no money to spare for postage, many Americans were on the move, living in cars, tents, and migrant camps, looking for work. They were not preoccupying themselves with mail.

It was also a period of change. The Railway Mail era was coming to an end. Not only did the economic downturn all but bankrupt many of the smaller railroad lines, but the affordability of automobiles also made train travel practically a thing of the past. The decreasing supply of mail trains affected the profitability of the Post Office Department; its streak of operating profits since 1916 vanished in 1931, and for the next few years there was a steady stream of sizable annual deficits.

Postmaster General James Farley pledged to restore reduced wages and end layoffs once business conditions improved, but in the meantime, he was forced to make some tough choices. There were $30 million in reductions in 1933. Farley froze hiring and introduced unpaid furloughs.

But there was still work to be done. Postal employees who may have felt moved to complain about their pay in the 1920s were thankful to still have steady jobs in the 1930s.

A strange thing had been happening for two decades now: The Post Office's fortunes had been flipped from the country's. In the Roaring Twenties, the Post Office struggled through challenge after challenge. Then, in the Great Depression, it was a point of strength for the ailing nation. Maybe the Post Office was a kind of ballast—risk-taking when times were flush, solid as a rock when times were hard. Whatever the case, in the decade that was coming, the entire United States would be snapped back into sync.

Something so fresh in the country's memory that many hadn't imagined it could happen again so soon was on its way: war.

Left: Postmaster General James Farley speaks at the dedication of the new Post Office Department headquarters in Washington, D.C., on June 11, 1934.

Below: Constructed between 1935 and 1938, the new building featured a sweeping Neoclassical Revival design by architectural firm Delano & Aldrich.

Philatelist-in-Chief

James Farley was one of Franklin Delano Roosevelt's greatest teammates long before he became his postmaster general. Farley always seemed to know what the president needed. One interesting example: During a Cabinet meeting, if there was a lull in the conversation, or if discussions became heated, Farley would fish around in his pocket and produce something all but guaranteed to calm FDR down—a future stamp model prepared by the Bureau of Engraving and Printing. The president loved stamps. When Farley would take out a model, time would stop and tempers would cool. The president's assent was not required to approve a new design, but he always enjoyed seeing the latest proposals and would typically write "Okay FDR" on the covers of those designs he liked—which happened to be most of them.

Roosevelt understood design principles and was keenly aware of the promotional value of postage stamps. The first one he is known to have had an actual hand in designing was the 1933 three-cent stamp promoting Rear Admiral Richard E. Byrd's second Antarctic expedition. The president's sketch depicted the eastern coasts of the United States and South America and the western areas of Europe and Africa, with the routes of Byrd's transatlantic, North Pole, and South

Left: The title of this stamp, "Toward United Nations," is attributed to Roosevelt in commemoration of the United Nations Conference on International Organization.

Below: Monaco issued a commemorative stamp in honor of Roosevelt one year after his death.

Pole flights. The stamp was notable for another reason: It was canceled at America's first post office in Antarctica. Roosevelt saw to it that the Post Office Department carried mail bearing the new stamp to the Byrd expedition base in Little America, located on the Ross Ice Shelf about 800 miles from the geographic South Pole, for canceling and return. FDR's stamp actually helped fund the expedition: Collectors had to pay 53 cents per cover to get the Little America postmark—three cents for the stamp and 50 cents to finance Byrd's endeavor. Byrd was, of course, deeply appreciative; Roosevelt's sole request of him was "a letter for my stamp collection."

In 1929, when the postal policy of recognizing the 50th anniversaries of states' admittance to the Union became complicated because both Dakotas, Montana, and Washington were all up for stamps, Roosevelt stepped in and advocated for a single-stamp approach. On another sheet of White House stationery, he sketched out a design captioned "50 Years of Statehood" and arranged the four states side by side, with the specific dates of admission directly below. This was, in all probability, the worst of the president's sketches. The states, depicted in a geographically correct fashion along the border with Canada, looked like laundry hanging from a clothesline. Stamp collectors have dubbed this the "Washline" commemorative.

On April 12, 1945, Roosevelt was sitting for a portrait with painter Elizabeth Shoumatoff when she praised the recently issued "Florida Statehood" stamp. When she asked if he had had anything to do with the stamp, he reportedly replied proudly, "I certainly did." Minutes later, he complained of a severe headache, collapsed, and died of a cerebral hemorrhage. The United Nations Conference commemorative stamp was due out in less than two weeks. Nevertheless, the Post Office Department ordered the Bureau of Engraving and Printing to revise the design. "Franklin D. Roosevelt" would appear in the field, below the date, and above a flat laurel branch. It was the nation's first memorial to the fallen leader.

THE WHITE HOUSE
WASHINGTON

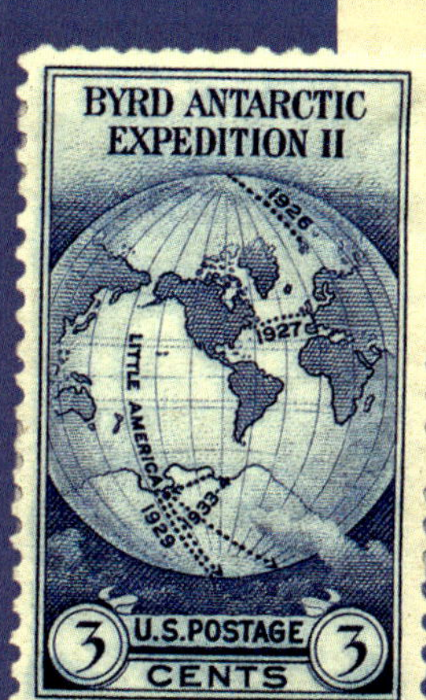

FDR's sketches for a "50 Years of Statehood" stamp and the "Byrd Antarctic Expedition" stamp.

U.S.POSTAGE
1848
1948
AMERICAN
TURNERS
OF HEALTH
CENTS
3

UNITED STATES POSTAGE
U.S. NAVY

These IMMORTAL CHAPLAINS ...
INTERFAITH IN ACTION
3¢ UNITED STATES POSTAGE 3¢

DR. GEORGE WASHINGTON CARVER
UNITED STATES POSTAGE
3¢

US ARMY
US POSTAGE
3¢

ORT BLISS CENTENNIAL
3¢
3¢
EL PASO TEXAS
1848 1948
U.S. POSTAGE

"OUR REPUBLIC AND ITS PRESS WILL RISE OR FALL TOGETHER"
1847 1947
JOSEPH PULITZER
3¢ UNITED STATES POSTAGE

ALOMAR MOUNTAIN OBSERVATORY
1948
UNITED STATES POSTAGE

EVERGLADES NATIONAL PARK
3¢
TATES POSTAGE

FOR THE INCREASE AND DIFFUSION OF KNOWLEDGE AMONG MEN
1846 · SMITHSONIAN INSTITUTION · 1946
3¢ UNITED STATES POSTAGE

MAIL

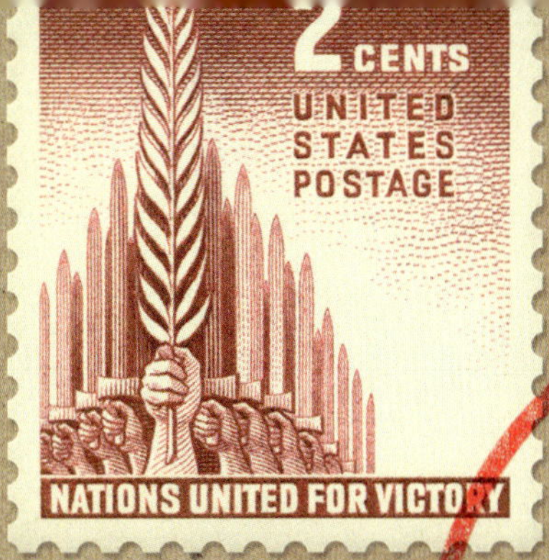
2 CENTS
UNITED STATES POSTAGE
NATIONS UNITED FOR VICTORY

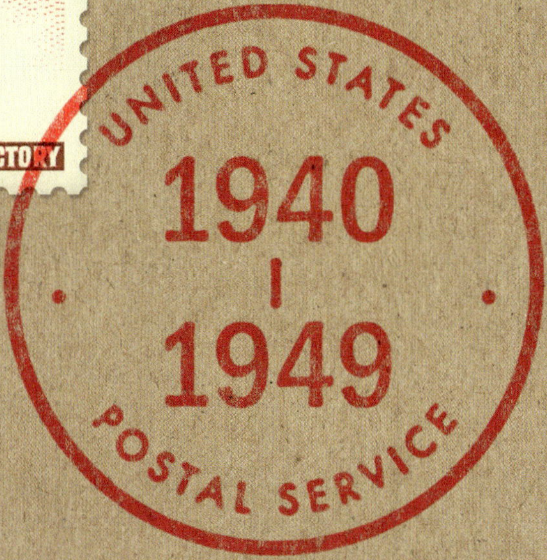
UNITED STATES
1940
1949
POSTAL SERVICE

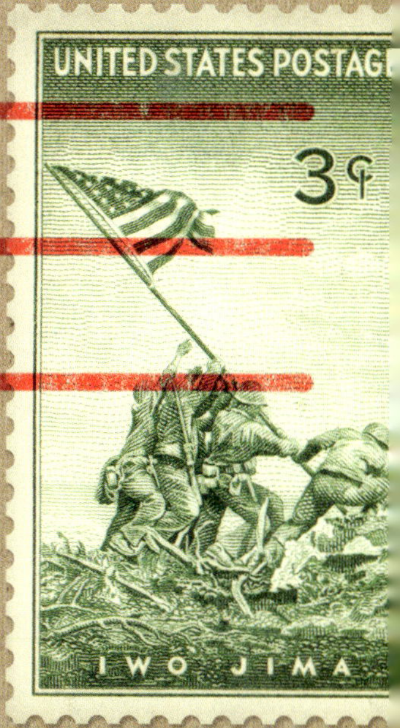
UNITED STATES POSTAGE
3¢
IWO JIMA

THE GREAT WAR: THE SEQUEL

WIN THE WAR
3¢ 3¢
UNITED STATES POSTAGE

"TOWARD
UNITED NATIONS
APRIL 25, 1945"
FRANKLIN D. ROOSEVELT
5¢ UNITED STATES POSTAGE

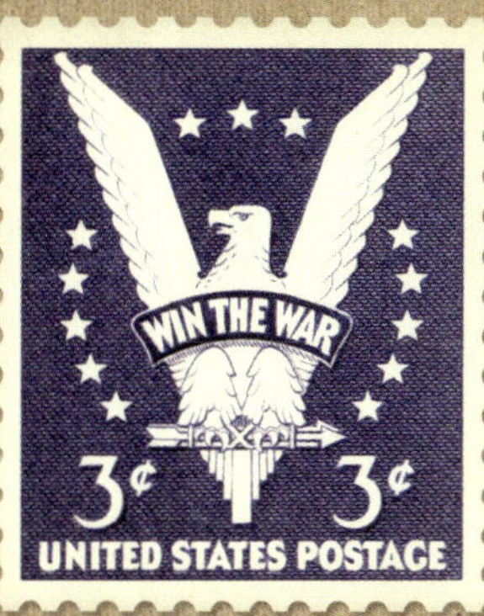

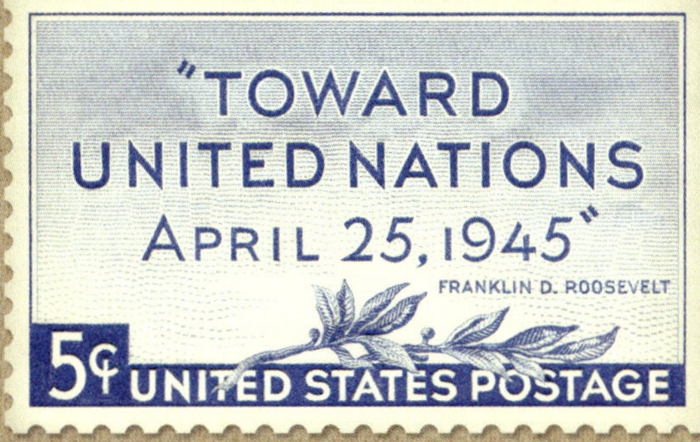

In the first few minutes of the attack at Pearl Harbor, the USS *Oklahoma* was torpedoed five times and capsized. The event was forever memorialized by this simple registered mail handstamp that was recovered from the *Oklahoma*. Worn and rusted from being submerged in seawater for many months, the stamp bears the date "Dec 6 1941," its last date of use.

Christmas 1942. It brought to mind the holiday exactly 25 years earlier. What would have been a challenging time in any case—holiday mail was always grueling—pushed the Post Office Department to its limits, thanks to something beyond its control. Something that happened on Sunday, December 7, 1941.

On that morning, 353 planes from six Japanese aircraft carriers attacked the U.S. Navy base at Pearl Harbor, in Hawaii. More than 2,400 Americans died and more than 1,100 were wounded. The next day, at 12:30 p.m., President Roosevelt spoke before Congress, famously calling December 7 "a date which will live in infamy," and requested a declaration of

war on Japan. Congress gave it to him within hours, and the United States entered World War II.

By the time of the attack on Pearl Harbor, there were already more than 175,000 temporary Post Office Department employees on duty to handle holiday and military mail. But immediately, everything changed. Within days, transpacific airmail service to the Far East was suspended. On March 17, 1942, Congress authorized free mail service for the military, creating a tidal wave of mail. An increase in volume of about 30 percent came almost immediately, and the flow only increased as the war effort ramped up. Within months the average warfighter was writing five letters a week to those back home.

Christmas 1942 was not unlike Christmas 1917, during World War I—except, symbolic of the difference in impact of the two wars more broadly, everything was happening on a much grander scale. Several single months of World War II saw the mail system handle more than the 35 million letters and 15 million parcels it handled during all of World War I.

During what was essentially the nation's first wartime Christmas of the new conflict, parcel shipments set records. There were 84 percent more packages going out in 1942 than in 1941, and 15 percent more coming in. This mass of Christmas parcels filled more than a million mail sacks.

Above: Corporal Albert Franczaki of Kensington, Pennsylvania, passes out mail to fellow soldiers in France, somewhere west of Saint-Lô. The Signal Corps released this photo on August 4, 1944, with the title "The Mail Gets Through—Even to the Fighting Fronts."

Opposite: Many of the Post Office Department's plans for modernization had to be put on hold because of the Japanese attack on Pearl Harbor on December 7, 1941.

At the same time, the Post Office Department faced a major challenge: Everything was in shortage.

Between December 1941 and November 1942, the Post Office lost 25,000 experienced employees to military service.

In 1941, rail lines provided nearly 22,000 freight cars to haul holiday mail, but in 1942, military needs meant they had only 500 to offer.

In 1941, the department borrowed about 2,500 trucks from the military and other government agencies, plus rented nearly 10,000 more from private firms to handle the Christmas mail rush; in 1942, they weren't available. The military needed its vehicles, and contractors were reluctant to lend theirs out because wartime tire rationing made them more valuable than ever before.

Time and again, the Post Office Department has stepped up for the country to keep families, communities, states, and the nation connected. The 1940s were no different. The war effort would bring out the best of the Post Office—urgency, grit, innovation. The nation's postal employees would once again roll up their sleeves for the American people. And they would deliver something more than mail. In his annual report just months after the attack on Pearl Harbor, Postmaster General Frank C. Walker wrote about the value of a simple letter. It "strengthens fortitude, enlivens patriotism, makes loneliness endurable," he said. It "inspires to even greater devotion the men and women who are carrying on our fight far from home and from friends."

★ ★ ★

Parcel Post mail bound for Germany being bagged up and prepared for dispatch overseas to American troops still stationed there on July 19, 1947.

The Military Post Offices of the U.S. Army and Navy issued this poster so that families at home could prepare early for the holidays in order for their loved ones to receive some holiday spirit oversesas during World War II.

On the home front, the Post Office Department became the ultimate jack of all trades.

The 1942 holidays symbolized just what a massive effort the war would entail. When President Roosevelt asked Congress to declare war on Japan the day after the attack on Pearl Harbor, the Post Office Department—America's biggest business—was already doing its part.

Two years earlier, amid growing unease at the way the war was going in Europe, Congress had passed the Selective Service and Training Act of 1940. This instituted the first peacetime draft in U.S. history, requiring men between 21 and 45 to register for potential military service. (The age range later expanded.) The Post Office Department was a key player in registering men. Many signed up at their local post office, and later, that office would announce the draft numbers that notified them of their status.

Additionally, there was already a military postal system that in 1941 was furnishing mail to 517 military camps around the country, and to three Army Post Office installations that transmitted military-related mail overseas. Of course, this system stood to greatly expand.

As the war developed, the Post Office Department found its involvement growing. With American troops increasingly embroiled in the war's two great theaters, Europe and the Pacific, the department found its workers on the frontlines of two theaters, too: the home front, and the battlefield.

On the home front, the Post Office Department became the ultimate jack of all trades. For the same reasons the mail service was lavished with such attention during the Depression a decade earlier—it was one of the few federal institutions present in virtually every community—it was called upon to put into action many necessary government activities during the war. By 1942, in addition to collecting, processing, transporting, and delivering the mail, the department was relied upon to do jobs of such variety that you might expect they'd be performed by a number of other federal departments.

The Treasury? The Post Office Department sold war savings bonds, and on July 1, 1942, it became a temporary tax collection agency for the Internal Revenue Service. It collected the mandatory $5 use tax from the nation's 32 million motor vehicle and motorboat owners.

The Department of Justice and the Department of Labor? The Post Office helped register alien nationals—anyone entering the country after December 26, 1941, had to register—earning a 60-cent reimbursement for every person it registered, which was a lot of people: Ultimately, three million foreign workers registered at post offices nationwide. They also had to notify the government any time they moved. This was a way to keep an eye out for enemies within, but most turned out to be migrant workers from Canada; very few, less than 8 percent, were from countries that were opponents in the war.

The Post Office Department also helped with another surveillance activity: censorship. Military and civilian mail alike was opened, screened, and if necessary blackened or cut away. This was deemed critical to prevent the dissemination of sensitive information across enemy lines.

The Department of Commerce? Mail workers conducted an ongoing census of women who could potentially serve as war workers—something with which the department itself had experience. Just as in World War I, women filled in as short-term mail handlers and postal clerks in many major cities and small towns. By 1943, the postal system was short some 40,000 male employees—shortages were especially pronounced in New York City and Chicago, the nation's two largest postal centers—but the mail moved smoothly thanks to the legions of women who stepped in to keep things going.

At the same time, the Post Office had a great deal of work to do to maintain its operations, and that meant finding new ways to do things. Innovation was afoot. The home-front ideas that came out of the 1940s didn't always hit right away, but they were harbingers of postwar service.

With most of the men overseas during World War II, women were accepted for jobs that normally weren't available to them. For the Post Office, this meant putting them to work in back-breaking areas that required muscle and stamina, such as sorting rooms.

WORLD WAR II

During World War I, the U.S. Post Office Department had to deal with dramatic increases in overseas mail. Yet after Congress authorized free mail service for military personnel in 1942, the department had to manage an almost immediate 30 percent jump in letters from soldiers, sailors, and Marines stationed in the European and Pacific theaters. The introduction of V-mail, which allowed friends and family members to send letters to warfighters via airmail, also helped escalate delivery burdens.

To manage these increases, as well as maintain strict operational security, the Postal Service instituted new rules for mail. Letters were routinely examined by censors, who blacked out potentially sensitive information about troop movements or battle plans. In addition, the military, at

Above, left to right: Fifteen nurses from the 268th Station Hospital in Australia receive their first batch of mail from home; a photograph taken on December 21, 1944, in England shows the Army's 20th Fighter Group as they get ready to unload a massive quantity of mailbags, then sort and deliver their contents as quickly as possible before Christmas; after returning to Pearl Harbor from the Makin Island raid of August 26, 1942, crewmen take time to read their mail.

A photograph taken on March 28, 1944, near San Giovanni, Italy, shows how popular the 455th Bomb Group mail clerk was when handing out Christmas packages that had been delayed.

times, had to suspend mail service due to ongoing battles or infrastructure damage that interrupted delivery routes.

It didn't take long for Europe to see a seemingly impossible backlog of 17 million pieces of undelivered mail. In February 1945, the 6888th Central Postal Directory Battalion, the only Women's Army Corps unit of color to serve overseas during World War II, came to Birmingham, England, to take this problem in hand. The battalion, affectionately known as the Six Triple Eight, managed to sort and ship letters and parcels addressed to nearly seven million American service members and government personnel stationed across Europe in approximately three months. With the motto "no mail, low morale," they repeated this incredible feat during missions in Rouen and Paris, France. Members of the Six Triple Eight received a Congressional Gold Medal for their work 80 years later.

On December 26, 1944, in India's War Theater #20, soldiers crowd the small military post office on base to retrieve their mail.

NC 2110

Opposite: A Stinson Reliant skyhooking the mail.

Skyhooking

Serving remote communities presented a special challenge for airmail. It wasn't dropping off a town's incoming mail, for that was simple: Any low-flying airplane could easily drop a sack of mail to the ground. Picking up a community's outgoing mail? That was much harder. Most rural hamlets had no space for a suitable runway. Throughout the 1940s, this problem was solved with a technique called skyhooking.

It was a dentist who came up with it. Lytle Adams dreamed of an airmail pickup system he wanted to roll out to North and South America, inspired by the Railway Mail Service's successful "on the fly" method of mail exchange, which had been in use since the 1870s. The system involved flying a specially outfitted Stinson Reliant aircraft low over a pair of 14-foot-high posts. The mail was suspended between the posts on a rope; the Reliant would grab the rope and reel it in as it flew by. In 1927, Adams started the All American Aviation company to commercialize the process. It quickly ran out of money, but the wealthy du Pont family swooped in to offer financial backing.

All American Aviation was originally awarded a pair of one-year experimental postal contracts to test the idea in 54 of the most remote and isolated communities in the Allegheny Mountain region of the United States. Eventually, over the course of the decade, skyhooking was successfully used on experimental routes in Ohio, New York, Pennsylvania, Kentucky, and West Virginia. Altogether, All American Aviation served more than 150 post offices in flight patterns that covered more than 1,000 miles. During the first year alone, more than 23,000 successful pickups took place and more than 75,000 pounds of mail were exchanged. Unfortunately, the war sucked resources from the Post Office Department, so there were fewer contracts to go around. Skyhooking service ended in 1949. It was fun while it lasted, though, especially for the crews running the routes: They took advantage of the specially designed skyhooking mail canisters to put together sky feasts on their flights, reeling in everything from Coca-Cola to slices of warm apple or peach pie to, in one case, a pair of turkey dinners.

Highway Post Offices were designed to make up a distribution network that could sustain rapid pickups, sorting, and dispatch to key points between major cities.

Right: A poster reminder to add the zone number to all letters and packages.

Among the Post Office's major goals was making delivery more efficient. On May 1, 1943, it inaugurated "postal zone numbers" for 124 of the nation's largest postal regions. Under this scheme, each carrier's delivery district was given a distinct number corresponding to the station where the carrier was assigned, allowing even the most inexperienced postal clerks to sort mail by the numbers. The goal was to aid in separating mail and expediting deliveries, and it was so successful that it led to a transformative innovation two decades later—ZIP Codes (more to come on that).

The other big efficiency play in the 1940s predated the war effort—but the war had a major impact on it, and vice versa. On July 11, 1940, President Roosevelt had signed legislation creating Highway Post Offices (HPOs), which would be modeled on the Railway Post Offices that had been effective for decades.

Like the RPOs, the HPOs were designed to make up a distribution network that could sustain rapid pickups, sorting, and dispatch to key points between major cities. A committee that was established to figure out how to put the idea into practice narrowed the potential service areas to about 200 routes, each limited to a range of around 150 miles—a distance dictated by the gas capacity of the vehicles under consideration to serve the routes. They usually covered roughly 20 small-town post offices twice per day.

Three vehicle options were selected: a converted White Motor Company passenger bus, a refitted Mack International passenger bus, and a reconfigured International Harvester Company semi-tractor and trailer fitted out with windows. These were all "off the assembly line" vehicles that were hastily modified for postal purposes. None was ideally suited for mail service, but each was tested on a different route in 1941.

The Post Office Department purchased this 1941 Mack CM3G for experimental use in California. Because it was a gas guzzler, it proved only marginally acceptable. Despite that, Mack furnished 15 additional Model C45GTs in 1948.

The White Motor Company bus entered service first, on February 10, 1941, traveling a route between Washington, D.C., and Harrisonburg, Virginia. On August 4, 1941, the Mack CM3G Special ran from San Francisco to Pacific Grove, California. And finally, on May 3, 1941, the International Harvester took on a route from Peru, Indiana, to Indianapolis.

The International Harvester was a complete disaster from the very beginning. Its springs broke, its compressor failed, and its lighting system shorted out before the semi could even be put into service. Of the other two, the White Motor Company vehicle worked out better. It weighed less than the Mack truck and used less fuel, allowing it to cover its route with fewer stops for gas.

By the time this assessment had been made, of course, the United States had joined the war. Though the three HPO routes were allowed to keep operating, expansion was out of the question. It would simply pull too much money and manpower away from the war effort. The expansion of the highway post was postponed until after the war, and it didn't truly reach its potential until the 1950s, when purpose-built vehicles were created using Post Office specifications. Like postal zone numbers, the HPO system would be a trailblazer that inspired new ideas. Unlike postal zone numbers, it wouldn't take decades for those ideas to see the light of day. A

The inaugural HPO clerks sort mail inside the White Motor Company Highway Post Office in 1941 on its route between Washington, D.C., and Harrisonburg, Virginia. The interior layout was based on the RPO car it was replacing.

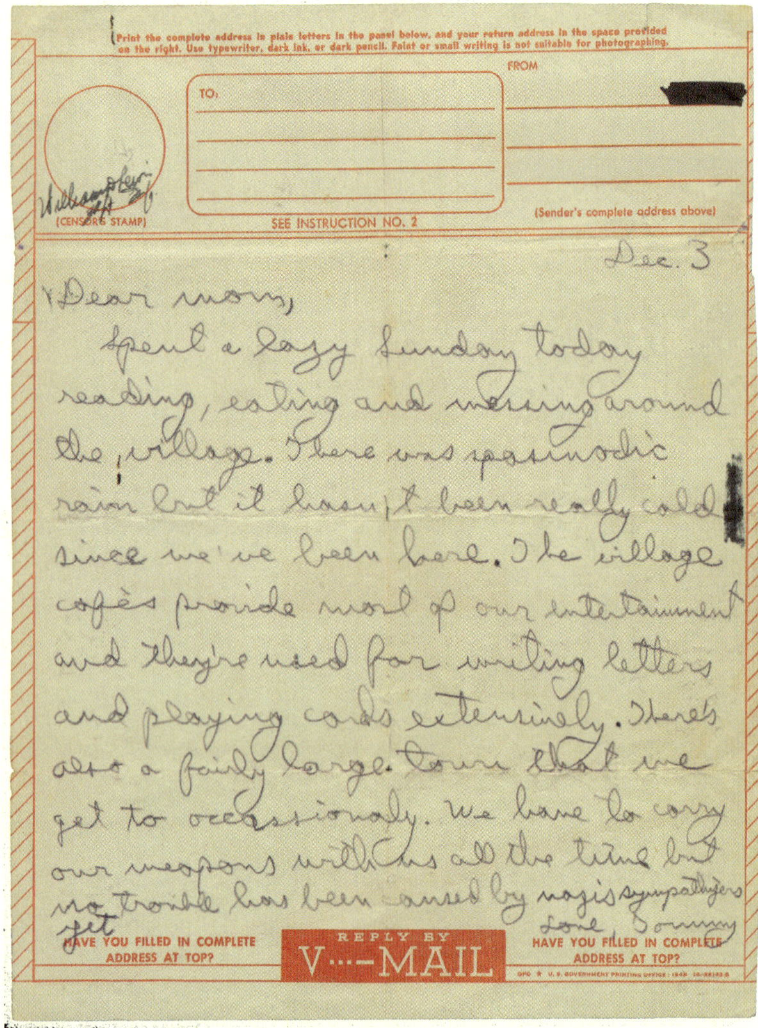

Print the complete address in plain letters in the panel below, and your return address in the space provided on the right. Use typewriter, dark ink, or dark pencil. Faint or small writing is not suitable for photographing.

TO:

FROM

(CENSOR'S STAMP)

SEE INSTRUCTION NO. 2

(Sender's complete address above)

Dec. 3

Dear mom,

Spent a lazy Sunday today reading, eating and messing around the village. There was spasmodic rain but it hasn't been really cold since we've been here. The village cafés provide most of our entertainment and they're used for writing letters and playing cards extensively. There's also a fairly large town that we get to occasionally. We have to carry our weapons with us all the time but no trouble has been caused by nazis sympathizers yet

Love, Sonny

HAVE YOU FILLED IN COMPLETE ADDRESS AT TOP?

REPLY BY V···–MAIL

HAVE YOU FILLED IN COMPLETE ADDRESS AT TOP?

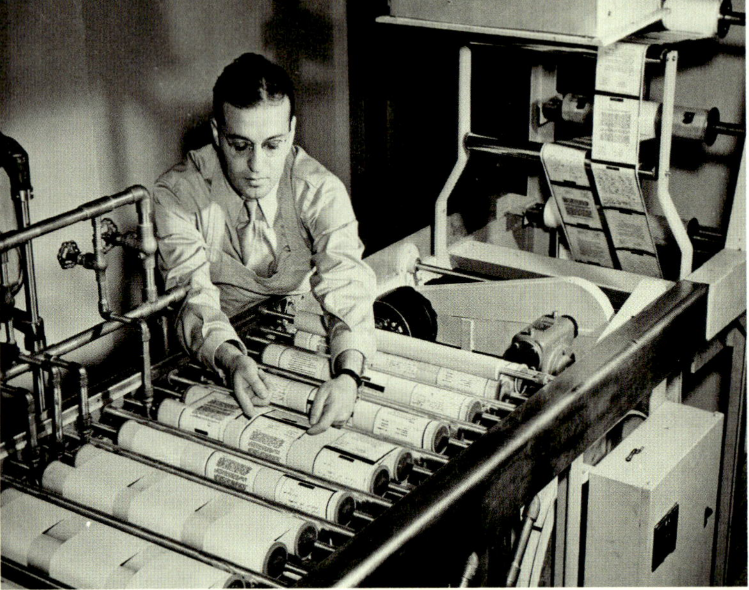

Top: A V-mail letter, dated December 12, 1944, sent to a mother in Washington, D.C., from her son serving overseas during World War II.

Bottom: One of the steps in processing V-mail was to reproduce it from microfilm to paper at the Pentagon. V-mail was 1/65th the weight of ordinary mail and saved 98 percent of cargo space required for ordinary letters.

memo from the Department of Defense reveals that the military studied the Post Office Department's efforts to convert buses for other uses and was able to do something similar for its own purposes: Its buses became transport vehicles for troops.

★ ★ ★

Just months into the war, mail volume was clearly becoming a real problem. The three Army Post Office installations that existed in 1941 quickly become 202. By July 1943, the U.S. Navy had 1,326 postal facilities of its own. By the time the war was over, even those numbers would be dwarfed: In April 1945, the Army had more than 800 APOs and the Navy had more than 4,800 fleet post services—not to mention 700 domestic military post offices. At maximum mobilization, these facilities were serving more than 11.5 million men and women in uniform.

The challenge, principally, was mail's physical bulk. Lugging large sack after large sack of mail over long distances, across oceans, and through terrestrial war zones simply would not do.

The clever technique that solved this problem was called microfilming. The British had been using the technology since 1940, and U.S. leadership took its cues from that to design its own system, with the help of photography pioneer Eastman Kodak Company. Letters written to overseas personnel were photographed, and then a device designed by Kodak put the photo negatives onto rolls of film. Each roll was smaller than a pack of cigarettes and could contain an astounding 1,600 letters. They would then be flown to their destination, where the letters would be "blown up" to their original size, reproduced on photographic paper, or written out by hand. That reproduced copy was then delivered to the recipient, and originals were saved at home until delivery, in case something went wrong along the way.

Some of the Last Letters to Make It Home

In 1944, the troopship *Caleb Strong* departed Newport News, Virginia, for a 21-day voyage to the Mediterranean port of Oran, Algeria. While at sea, the 92 soldiers and airmen aboard wrote letters to loved ones back home. These missives were entrusted to one of the ship's sailors. He was supposed to mail the letters as soon as the *Caleb Strong* returned to the United States in May 1944. For whatever reason, he didn't. Instead, he stashed a duffel bag containing 235 letters from the 92 servicemen in the attic of his aunt's house, in Raleigh, North Carolina. And there it remained for more than 40 years, until, in February 1986, an exterminator discovered it. He turned the bag over to the Raleigh postmaster, Ross Garulski, who knew what he had to do.

Garulski had to deliver them.

By law, the Postal Service is obligated to deliver mail as originally intended, even if there's a delay of years—or decades. And if the intended recipients can't be found, the letter remains the property of the sender, so in some cases the veterans themselves were due to get their letters back. Garulski and his compatriots got to work researching the whereabouts of the relatives of those 92 World War II servicemen. Just a few months later, some were ready to be returned. One of the letter writers had become a professional baseball player. Another, a POW. One moved back home and lived in a place called War, in West Virginia. Raul Alvarez got back the letter he had written for Terry Espinosa. He assured her in his letter that "I love you with all my heart and no one will come between us." By the time the letter was delivered, the couple had been married for 36 years. After leaving the military, Alvarez became a letter carrier.

The last of the 235 letters to be delivered went to Norman T. Smith of Henderson, Maryland, in 1989. They had been written by Smith's brother, Sergeant Clarence F. Smith, and were handed over by the postmaster general, Anthony Frank, himself. Frank told the *Arizona Republic* that these letters had been the most challenging because Smith is a common last name, and pertinent military records had been destroyed by a fire at the Federal Records Center in St. Louis. But even after nearly half a century, the Post Office had to deliver. It was a small measure of gratitude for all that the men onboard the *Caleb Strong* had given to their country.

Reach Your Boy
OVERSEAS
by
Vmail
the letters
that travel on film
EASY TO USE
SUREST—
FASTEST—
and MOST
PATRIOTIC
Your Stationer and Post Office have
V...—MAIL LETTER FORMS

Opposite: More than a billion V-mail letters were delivered between June 1942 and November 1, 1945, when V-mail service ended.

The system debuted on June 15, 1942. It was called Victory Mail, or V-mail for short.

"The easiest, fastest, and best way to send [letters] to them is to use V-mail," claimed the Navy. "Your letters are then microfilmed, flown overseas, and distributed in a much shorter time than they would be if you used regular mail. By using V-mail when writing to Americans on the fighting fronts, you not only save time in transportation, but you also save space on merchant ships." The difference was significant. In their original form, 150,000 one-page letters weighed 1,500 pounds and filled 22 standard mailbags. When microfilmed, they fit in a single mail sack weighing approximately 45 pounds. Approximately 98 percent of space was saved.

To work, the V-mail system relied upon tight cooperation among businesses, the Post Office Department, and the military. The public purchased standardized V-mail letter forms from local stationery stores or other vendors, wrote their letters, and folded the forms as directed. These were addressed as usual, with postage affixed, and distributed to designated Army Post Office or Fleet Post Office addresses at one of three sorting facilities: New York City, San Francisco, or Chicago. Before leaving the United States, the letters went to a private business—Kodak put them on film. Finally, the military was responsible for transporting the film and converting it into letters, which happened at a variety of facilities in the European and Pacific theaters.

This cooperation wasn't just successful—it worked like gangbusters. According to the Annual Report of the Postmaster General for 1945, mail dispatched to the Army that year exceeded 2.5 billion pieces, compared with 1.4 billion pieces during the previous year and only 570 million items the year before that. The Navy witnessed similar growth. Sailors, Marines, and their families

The Office of War Information created a campaign called "Send 'em V-mail and keep 'em smiling," encouraging families to send V-mail overseas as morale boosters. Look how happy it has made this U.S. Coast Guard ensign.

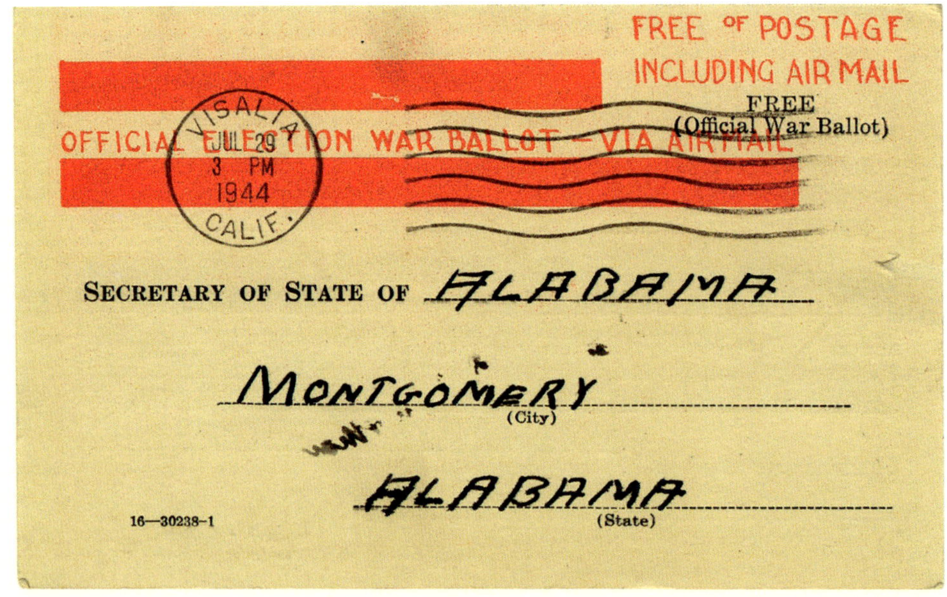

FREE OF POSTAGE INCLUDING AIR MAIL

FREE
(Official War Ballot)

OFFICIAL ELECTION WAR BALLOT — VIA AIR MAIL

VISALIA JUL 29 3 PM 1944 CALIF.

SECRETARY OF STATE OF ALABAMA

MONTGOMERY
(City)

ALABAMA
(State)

16—30238—1

July 7-25-44.
(Date)

Secretary of State of: ALABAMA

Being on active duty in the armed forces of the United States and desiring to vote in the coming election, I hereby apply for an official war ballot.

My home address is ________ (Number and street), in the city, town, or village of MONTGOMERY, in the county of MONTGOMERY, in the State of ALABAMA, and my voting district or precinct to the best of my knowledge is ________

I desire that the ballot be sent to me at the following address ________

VISALIA CALIF.
(Signed)

Signature certified by:
Nathan B. Kaufman 1st Lt.
(To be signed by any commissioned officer)

W. D., A. G. O. Form No. 560
September 17, 1942

GPO 16—30238—1

2002.2013.90

The Presidential election of 1944 between Franklin D. Roosevelt and Thomas E. Dewey was the first time that the Federal Government had sought to address absentee voting on a national level. This is official war ballot request going to the Alabama Secretary of State.

exchanged nearly 840 million pieces of mail in 1945, nearly double the volume of the year prior.

As far as the Post Office Department was concerned, V-mail was the great miracle of World War II.

In fact, the most famous problem with it was nothing more than a consequence of how much Americans wanted to reach their boys abroad. Women would often seal their letters with a kiss, and the lipstick they used tended to clog the Kodak machines that did the letter-to-film conversion. Additionally, when microfilmed, the lipstick reproduced as a black lip imprint on the film, obliterating any writing below it, and sometimes obscured the addressee's name. In the Post Office, it was known as the Scarlet Scourge. As scourges of war went, it was far from the worst.

★ ★ ★

In at least one major way, the Post Office Department's theaters of the home front and the battlefield would overlap: troop voting. It presented an opportunity to reestablish a service that had been in operation during the Civil War—and it would need to progress beyond the continental U.S. to far-off stations around the world.

The ability to vote by mail during World War II was a point of pride for most. More than 16 million Americans served in uniform during the war,

Efforts to allow members of the military to vote in the 1942 congressional elections were bogged down by voting requirements in southern states.

and it is estimated that at least 11 million of them successfully cast absentee ballots by mail in the 1944 national elections. Mail-in voting was a great morale booster for America's troops during World War II.

But the road to getting there was not easy. Efforts to allow members of the military to vote in the 1942 congressional elections were bogged down by voting requirements in southern states. Black voter suppression was common in much of the country, and in the South, many states required voters pay fees, called poll taxes, that most African American voters could not afford to pay. This was the intended effect—to keep Black Americans from being able to vote. Should the poll taxes apply to African Americans fighting for their country? After much debate and arm-twisting, Congress finally passed a bill that guaranteed "every individual absent from the place of his residence and serving in the land or naval forces of the United States was entitled to vote in elections for federal offices." Additionally, the legislation provided that "no person in military service in time of war shall be required, as a condition of voting in any election...to pay any poll tax."

The new law opened the path for African Americans abroad to vote. It was also a just outcome for the Post Office, which had been fighting its dark history of segregation under Woodrow Wilson and was still fighting it even as some of its most important wartime operations were carried out by Black Americans. The 6888th Central Postal Directory Battalion was a predominantly Black battalion of women serving in Europe during World War II. This group, based in England and France in 1945, broke all records for distributing mail to frontline troops. Upon its initial arrival overseas, the battalion was confronted with a warehouse full of unprocessed mail, some items dating back two years. Under less-than-ideal conditions—namely, a rat-infested aircraft hangar that lacked heat and adequate lighting—they set about processing the pileup. Working around the clock, the women cleared the backlog in just three months. They functioned like a well-tuned dynamo, accurately sorting and sending, on average, 130,000 pieces of mail a day, even as troops were constantly on the move.

And yet the actions of the 6888th were not going to change things for African Americans back home after the war. When World War II came to a conclusion, halfway through the decade, troops returned home and found an America rife with change—some for the better, some for the worse. The Post Office would be a touchstone in the lives of many Black Americans as they fought for equal rights. But before we see how the mail fit into the civil rights era, we have to take a detour, for the Post Office needed to confront something that was gaining power, ubiquity, and capability in the flush years after the United States and its allies won World War II: the automobile.

The swift delivery of letters later in the war in Europe and North Africa was due to the efficiency and accuracy of the 6888th Central Postal Directory Battalion. The unit also redirected mail for missing, hospitalized, and deceased servicemen.

U.S. POSTAGE 3¢
BENJAMIN FRANKLIN
250TH ANNIVERSARY

THE INFRASTRUCTURE DECADE

If you want to understand what happened to the mail system in the 1950s, you have to go back. Back before the end of World War II, back before the start of the Great Depression.

At the end of World War I, a young soldier was worried about his career. He was a military man through and through, but he'd failed to see action in the war. He graduated from West Point in 1915 and served in a variety of roles on the home front before finally being commissioned to go overseas in October 1918. Weeks later, before he could deploy, the war came to an end. He was 28 years old and felt as if his role in the world might have passed him by. All he wanted was to serve his country overseas, to go create the future he saw for himself.

Then the future came to him. His name was Dwight Eisenhower.

In 1919, Eisenhower was tasked with observing the first transcontinental motor convoy. The military was sending 79 vehicles and 297 personnel on a 3,200-mile trip, from Washington, D.C., to San Francisco. The purpose was to study the infrastructure required to move troops around the country. The route mostly followed the Lincoln Highway, today U.S. Route 22, the most well-known long-distance route at the time—an era when many roads in the western states were often little more than the dirt paths the Post Office had encountered in the Northeast a century earlier. U.S. Route 22 had been designed specifically to spur imagination about the potential for road building. Its creator, Carl G. Fisher, hoped it would "stimulate as nothing else could the building of enduring highways everywhere that will not only be a credit to the American people but that will also mean much to American agriculture and American commerce."

Eisenhower reported back to his superiors about the condition of roads across the country, about the challenges they presented, about their importance to national security. And after that, whether he liked it or not, Eisenhower never seemed to be able to get away from roads.

Of course, his military career took the turn he wanted it to—in fact, it took turns almost no one could have imagined. Eisenhower became Supreme Allied Commander in World War II, leading the Allied powers to victory. And key to that victory, he saw, were the roads. Though the German Army continued to rely on its tried-and-true methods of transporting supplies and men by trains and even bicycles, the autobahn, Germany's system of highways, made it possible to get American troops and supplies exactly where they needed to be.

At the end of the war, Eisenhower was a national hero. His renown on the battlefield—the arena he so narrowly missed his opportunity to enter decades earlier—propelled him to the presidency in the election of 1952. He would serve as commander in chief from 1953 to 1961, and his careful attention to the underlying infrastructure that makes a nation work would be one of the defining features of the 1950s.

And infrastructure, of course, meant roads.

Eisenhower spearheaded the creation of America's Interstate Highway System. He had one of his most important deputies from the D-Day invasion, Lucius Clay, come up with a plan for a network of roads that would crisscross the country. There were many reasons why it needed this kind of infrastructure upgrade. One was simply to make driving safer for drivers and passengers. A second was to make the country safer in a larger sense: Another defining feature of the 1950s was the start of the Cold War with the USSR, and with the omnipresent fear of nuclear war, the nation's leaders had to plan for the potential wide-scale evacuation of Americans from their homes. And finally, Clay and Eisenhower understood that an interstate highway network would supercharge the nation's economy by bolstering the flow of money, goods—and information.

With the passage of the Federal-Aid Highway Act of 1956, which funded interstate construction, the road network was under way. There was extensive testing of road construction. Unsurprisingly, given the president's background, it was carried out with military vehicles. Army trucks drove 17 million miles on test roads.

But they might as well have tested them with mail trucks. In a way, what is today officially known as the Dwight D. Eisenhower National

Opposite: The Richmond-Petersburg highway (Interstate 95), photographed on March 28, 1958.

Inset: The Public Roads Administration, part of the Federal Works Agency, approved the official route numbering for the National System of Interstate and Defense Highways. The green dots designated the east to west routes with Interstate Route 90, while the red dots designated the north to south routes with Interstate Route 95.

OFFICIAL ROUTE NUMBERING FOR THE NATIONAL SYSTEM OF INTERSTATE AND DEFENSE HIGHWAYS
AS ADOPTED BY THE AMERICAN ASSOCIATION OF STATE HIGHWAY OFFICIALS. AUGUST 14, 1957
AMERICAN ASSOCIATION OF STATE HIGHWAY OFFICIALS
917 NATIONAL PRESS BUILDING
WASHINGTON 4, D. C.
E-W ROUTES
N-S ROUTES
RECOMMENDED:
Commissioner, Public Roads Administration
APPROVED:
Administrator, Federal Works Agency
PUBLIC ROADS ADMINISTRATION
FEDERAL WORKS AGENCY
NATIONAL SYSTEM OF INTERSTATE HIGHWAYS
SELECTED BY JOINT ACTION OF THE SEVERAL STATE HIGHWAY DEPARTMENTS
AS MODIFIED AND APPROVED
BY THE ADMINISTRATOR, FEDERAL WORKS AGENCY
AUGUST 2, 1947

Mailsters Inspire Patriotism

Mailsters proved exceptionally popular when participating in Fourth of July parades, where their red, white, and blue coloring served as a patriotic mood maker. As part of this transformational decade, all newly purchased postal vehicles were furnished with tricolor paint jobs. The new color scheme was more than cosmetic. The white top was said to reduce heat inside the vehicle, the blue lower portion was believed to reduce cleaning costs, and the red reflective strip was envisioned to increase visibility for other drivers, resulting in fewer accidents. Older olive-colored postal vehicles from the 1930s and 1940s were repainted over time. This paint pattern was applauded by former GIs who, having seen far too much olive drab during the previous decade, had come to detest the color. On the Fourth of July, 1955, the postmaster general announced that all large curbside collection boxes and lamppost letter boxes would also be repainted to match the patriotic red, white, and blue pattern. This news was well-received by a nation swept up in patriotic fervor following World War II and the armistice in Korea.

System of Interstate and Defense Highways was the logical conclusion of what had started when postal riders first began transforming game trails and Indian paths into proper post roads in the colonial era. It was a recognition that the infrastructure of the country was what enabled information to flow, and that the flow of information was what enabled the country to flourish. Eisenhower saw that in war and then put it into practice at home, and whether he was thinking specifically of the mail or not, one thing is for certain: In the 1950s, the decade of infrastructure and the decade of the automobile, there were many, many mail trucks on the nation's roads, far more than ever before.

As soon as troops started coming home in 1945, the United States was set on a course of utter and dramatic transformation. So many children were born that they would come to be known as baby boomers. Car ownership jumped from 55 percent in 1950 to about 75 percent by the end of the decade. Families were using their newfound mobility to change where they lived: People were moving to the suburbs.

As all of this happened, Americans continued to send more and more mail.

Between 1950 and 1960, mail volume rose by more than 18 billion pieces. To deal with such tremendous growth, the postal system added approximately 150 contract highway post-office routes. To avoid the costs of ownership and maintenance, these vehicles and their drivers were furnished by contractors, while the mail crews were postal employees.

The makeup of those mail crews changed. War veterans returned and rejoined the ranks of the Post Office Department. These were prosperous jobs. Throughout the Depression and until the end of World War II, basic postal pay rates had remained the same. Starting in July 1945, a series of pay increases boosted incomes; by 1950, postal workers were making $3,420 per year, compared with an average household's $3,300.

But the real challenge of the 1950s wasn't how to pay workers better; it was how to make sure postal crews reached the people that mail was destined for. As the country had grown bigger and more complex, the Post Office Department had needed to as well. And just as Eisenhower focused on roads and infrastructure, the Post Office looked

Letter carriers leaving a New York City post office with mailbags and arms overflowing with mail, newspapers, and packages. The maximum load they could carry was 35 pounds.

The 1952 Henry J, manufactured by Kaiser-Frazer, was a Special Delivery vehicle for transportation of mail to and from airports. The back seat folded down, allowing 58 cubic feet for mail.

The Post Office Department was the kind of car-buying customer Summerfield Chevrolet would have loved to see walk through its doors.

to its vehicles. In the 1950s, it completely remade the fleet of cars that moved the mail, built new buildings for them to move mail to, and dramatically upgraded the technology in those buildings.

★ ★ ★

It's one of the more satisfying random details of history that for his postmaster general, Eisenhower selected a car salesman. Arthur Summerfield had done more than sell cars, of course—by the time he assumed the role in 1953, he'd been a prominent player in Republican politics for at least a decade—but just as Eisenhower couldn't avoid roads, he couldn't avoid cars. He started factory work at age 13, and by 19 he was an inspector at a Chevrolet plant in Flint, Michigan. Not long after that, he'd put together a business that made him the biggest independent motor-oil distributor in Michigan. But all that was just the prelude to opening Summerfield Chevrolet, a car dealership that was one of the largest in Michigan by the time he accepted Eisenhower's appointment to lead the Post Office.

Naturally, a big part of Summerfield's tenure would be buying postal vehicles.

The Post Office Department was the kind of car-buying customer Summerfield Chevrolet would have loved to see walk through its doors. It was desperate. At the end of World War II, its vehicle fleet was in immediate need of upgrades. The department hadn't put much money into the fleet during the Great Depression, for obvious reasons, but had anticipated that in the 1940s it would finally be able to replace its aging workhorses, most of which were purchased more than two decades earlier. With the attack on Pearl Harbor, that hope faded. War took precedence. By 1941, more than 90 percent of the postal system's trucks were considered obsolete. A small number of International Harvesters and Fords acquired in the 1930s were new enough to not be considered completely hopeless, but that was about it. In 1941, when driver Larry Clark boasted that his 1931 Ford Model AA was the "best maintained in the fleet," its front right fender was held on with baling wire and its running boards were barely attached to its chassis. But it ran. On some mornings, as many as one-third of the mail trucks in certain cities had to be coaxed into just starting, let alone running.

When the war came to an end, the hope was that the decline of the vehicle fleet could be halted and reversed. An ambitious plan was initiated to replace all mail trucks purchased before 1947 in a buying blitz, but the Post Office Department ran into a problem: With so much mail being sent, it simply couldn't stand to lose too many serviceable trucks. The blitz became a gradual phase-out, stretched over six years. The Post Office slowly started replacing aging vehicles from the 1920s and early 1930s with newer Ford Model F-3 and Dodge Series B-1 trucks to the tune of about 1,800 vehicles per year.

But the Post Office Department's new fleet began to take shape in earnest as of 1952. That year, the department started a decade-long buying binge that reflected the pent-up needs and remarkable change of two decades of dramatic American history. The number of vehicles purchased, and the array of styles selected, was astounding.

Summerfield oversaw vehicles created specifically for letter carriers and collection-box drivers. The experimentation was worthwhile if not always successful. One test involved a pair of Henry Js, odd, compact economy cars built by the Jeep brand's owner at the time, Henry J. Kaiser. The Henry J was so focused on cost savings it didn't even have a trunk door—you had to get to cargo from the inside, behind the rear seat. The department also tried out the Nash Rambler, a station wagon, in a right-hand drive configuration that had the steering wheel next to the curb. These in-between-sized cars were not the way to go. The most interesting models of the era were either much bigger—or much smaller.

Until the 1950s, one type of vehicle that had not been tried was a van or truck in a

Left: Postal officials inspect the newly purchased 1953 Nash Airflyte Rambler wagon.

Below: The white-top 1950 International Harvester included the Civil Defense emblem on the door.

configuration called "forward control." In this design, the driver sits as far forward as possible, with the driver's seat and windshield essentially above the engine. Pushing everything forward creates a maximum amount of cargo space in the back. Today, this design might most be associated with bread trucks and other old-fashioned delivery vans.

Drivers appreciated that forward-control vehicles gave them great sightlines for spotting errant children or dogs running into the street. Thousands of left- and right-hand drive, forward-control models from Chevrolet (Summerfield's specialty), International Harvester, and Dodge were acquired over the course of the decade.

At the other end of the scale was a rather peculiar vehicle, the Mailster. This was a three-wheeled mini mail buggy that came in different configurations but generally looked like a cross between a proper delivery vehicle—a pickup or bread truck, say—and a golf cart or Vespa scooter. (Mailsters were manufactured by at least seven different companies across the country.) Each was powered by a 7.5-horsepower engine and could hold 500 pounds of mail. Whereas once upon a time, mail vehicles would drive carriers to the beginning of the routes they would walk, with the maneuverable Mailster, they could zip along their routes with the mail, spending most of their shift behind the wheel. The time saved allowed the Post Office to consolidate some routes, serving more people with fewer workers.

Decatur, Georgia, was among the first jurisdictions to receive a fleet of Mailsters, in March 1957. The Washington, D.C., suburbs quickly followed, with 29 allotted to Bethesda, Maryland, in May 1957 and 39 assigned to Chevy Chase, Maryland, in June. By 1959, approximately 5,000 carrier routes were covered by Mailsters.

Letter carriers initially liked that these cut down on the time they spent lugging around heavy leather mailbags. "This has saved my back a whole lot," said newly assigned Chevy Chase Mailster driver Christopher C. Hall in 1957. Before he had one, Hall walked a seven-mile route, periodically stopping at relay boxes to refill his satchel. With

Several Mailsters parked outside a post office, ready to take on mail for delivery. The front apron could be unzipped in warmer weather to provide ventilation, while side curtains could be closed in colder weather.

Carriers quickly realized it was safer to drive Mailsters on sidewalks than on busy city streets where they had to compete with bigger and faster vehicles.

The 1955 Cushman Mailster had easy access for the carrier to grab the mail from the back. These vehicles were best suited for temperate climates—as few as three inches of snow could immobilize the three-wheeler.

the Mailster's capacity, he didn't need to repeatedly return to the relay box. Mailsters also eliminated the need to deliver parcels separately from letters, which was more efficient for the Post Office Department and better for patrons: Now they could receive all their deliveries at once.

But the three-wheelers were far from perfect. They worked best in mild climates and on flat terrain, which is why the majority were initially used in Florida and across the South. In sandy soil, they tended to spin out and dig themselves into tiny dunes. In hilly areas, they were underpowered. In colder climates, they were immobilized by mere inches of snow.

Carriers quickly realized it was safer to drive Mailsters on sidewalks than on busy city streets where they had to compete with bigger and faster vehicles. But even that posed problems. The vehicles' ground clearance was so shallow that they often got hung up on curbs. Less stable than four-wheeled vehicles, Mailsters were also prone to tipping, for almost any reason: going in or out of curves or while being passed by large trucks on the highway. One carrier swore his Mailster was tipped over by a large dog. And when they were tipped, their fiberglass bodies tended to shatter. Over time, letter carriers came to realize that Mailsters, though incredibly useful, could also be incredibly dangerous when traveling on anything busier than a side street. They started calling the otherwise beloved little vehicle "the Traveling Coffin."

The sea change in mail transportation, from the utter dominance of rail in the 1850s to the rapid ascent of the automobile in the 1950s, meant that the Post Office Department had to completely rethink what kinds of post offices were needed, and where. First were the smaller post offices in newly growing suburban areas, close to good roads. The second was a mail-sorting facility called a "Sectional Center" that would funnel mail to the suburban offices. Sectional Centers represented an all-new design for the Post Office Department. They would be concentrated in high-population metropolitan areas—but outside congested city centers—and each would feature a dozen or more large, open loading bays for processing truckloads of mail.

Building these new post offices would be a significant undertaking. The Eisenhower administration built 2,700 new post offices between 1953 and 1958. In 1958 alone, construction began on 634 postal projects—the largest number of new starts ever taken on by the Post Office Department up to that time, adding 25 million square feet of space—at an approximate cost of $26 million. And yet the department estimated it would still need at least 12,000 new facilities over the following three years. What made the project doable was the even steeper cost of the alternative. The administration looked into repairing the nation's older downtown post offices, built between 1900 and 1920. The expected cost was $2 billion—more than the buildings themselves were worth.

This page, opposite, and following spread: Pages from a building-designs brochure issued by the Post Office Department on April 1, 1959, served as a guide for the construction of small "Thousand Series" post offices around the country. These facilities were typically located on the fringes of town centers and featured ample parking spaces. They were comparatively small, uniformly one-story structures with consistent interior specifications. Most important, they were privately financed through lease-purchase agreements.

UNITED STATES
POST OFFICE
UNITED STATES
POST OFFICE
ARIZONA

UNITED STATES POST OFFICE
TOWN
STATE
UNITED STATES
POST OFFICE
MISSISSIPPI

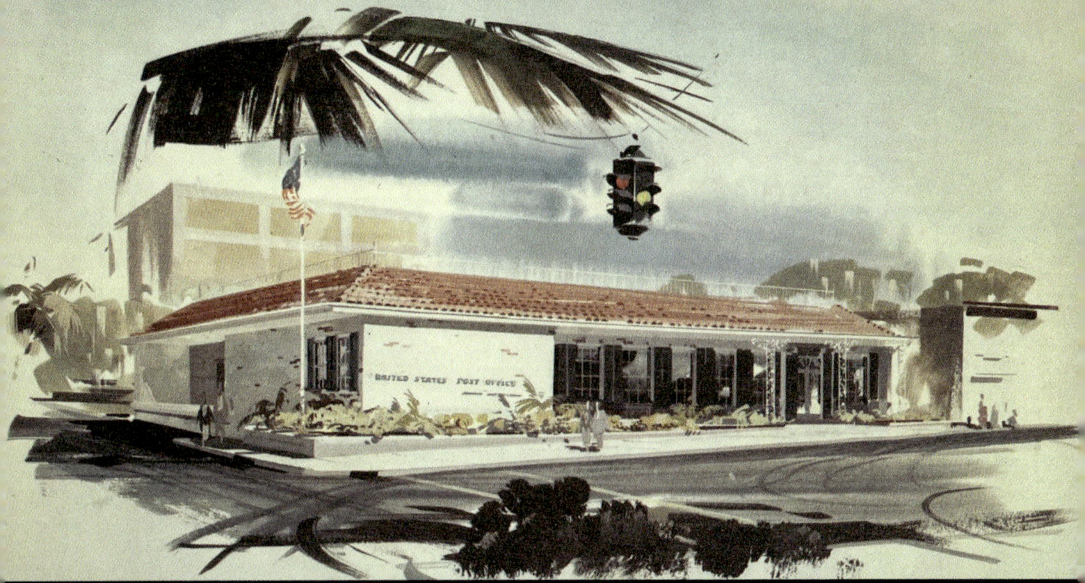
UNITED STATES POST OFFICE

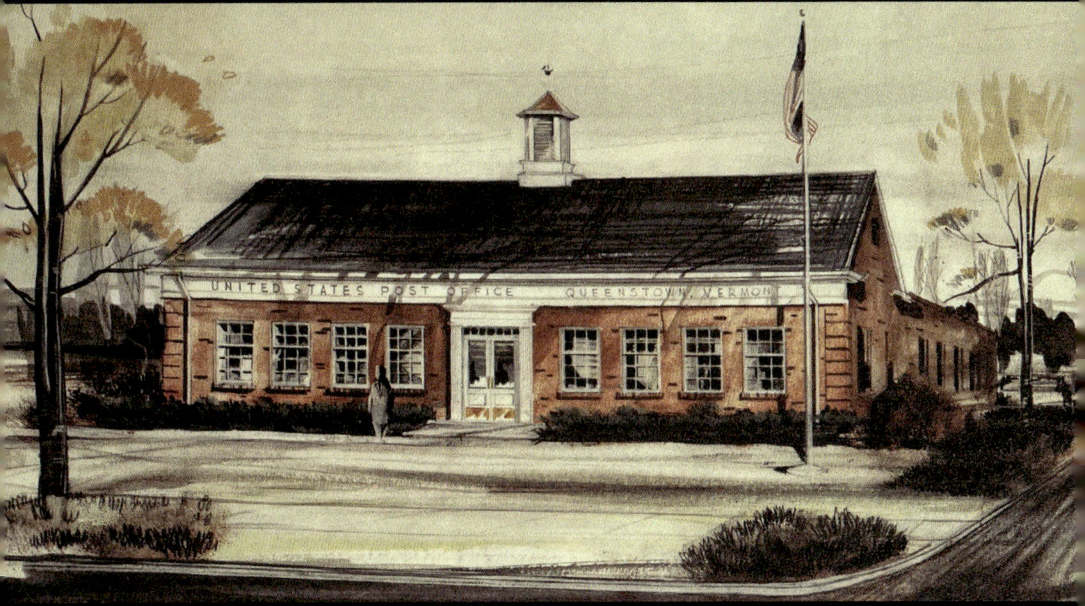
UNITED STATES POST OFFICE
QUEENSTOWN, VERMONT

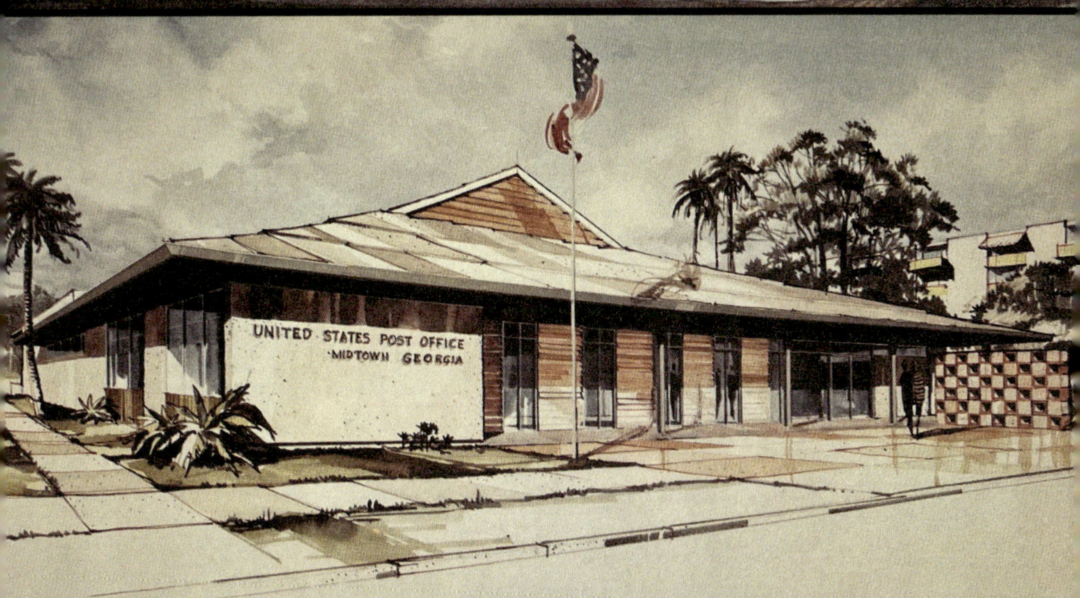

UNITED STATES POST OFFICE
MIDTOWN GEORGIA

The Transorma quickly became the backbone of letter-sorting operations, a status it would hold for the next two decades.

Opposite: Five operators are seen working on the top platform of the Transorma letter-sorting machine while one operator works below, at the Blair Post Office in Silver Spring, Maryland, in 1957. The machine stood 13 feet high, 50 feet long, and 20 feet deep.

But that didn't mean the government thought it was best to have taxpayers foot the entire bill for thousands of new buildings. So rather than spend the money to construct government-owned Post Office Department buildings, as had always been the practice in the past, the administration decided to allow private developers to pick up the tab. In return, the government promised to sign on to long-term leases to use the buildings if the development measured up.

To facilitate the process, potential investors and builders were provided with designs and specifications. Fifty suitable facades were furnished as typical examples of what an acceptable exterior might look like for each of eight different-sized buildings. The support allowed developers to move extremely fast. The branch station in Wheaton, Maryland, was standard: The 14,000-square-foot facility was built in 92 days at a cost of $292,000. It was owned by the Northwest Ridge Corporation, which leased it to the government for roughly $21,000 per year.

Before long, ribbons were being cut on as many as two new postal facilities per day.

★ ★ ★

As these buildings were being built, the technology that lived inside them was changing. In 1952 the postmaster general reported that "many phases of mail-handling operations inherently depend upon the eye, the brain, and the foot, and as yet no robot has been invented to learn 'schemes,' decipher addresses, or sort and effect the delivery of mail."

Within five years, that assessment would change.

The first breakthroughs were in sorting. A semiautomatic parcel-sorting machine was introduced in Baltimore in 1956. The following year, the first viable letter-sorting machine, which had been invented in Europe, was tested in the United States. Called the "Transorma," it ushered in the era of postal automation.

Previously, each of the 50 billion pieces of mail sent in a year was handled an average of 11 times. The amount of labor involved in collection and delivery was enormous. Then the Transorma arrived. The 13-foot-tall machine required five operators. A conveyor belt brought each letter to an operator, who examined it and keyed in a numerical code that indicated its destination. From there, the machine would automatically transport the letter to the appropriate box for that destination. It was capable of sorting 15,000 letters per hour, twice the number of letters five clerks could have processed working by hand. The Transorma quickly became the backbone of letter-sorting operations, a status it would hold for the next two decades. About 600 of these machines were ultimately used; they and other automated sorting technologies would eventually make manual sorting obsolete. But more important than any one new mechanized mail aid was a combination of devices. As far back as the 1870s, inventors had found ways to help mail workers. (A canceling machine was patented in 1875.) In the late 1950s, all the various inventions up to that point were combined: automatic cancelers; culling machines, which sorted letters by size; edger stackers, which stacked all letters in the same direction; facer cancelers, which put all letters in the same orientation and canceled them; and Mail-Flo, a system of conveyor belts that moved letters from machine to machine without a clerk having to lift a finger.

Fittingly, the test case for the potential of combining these various tools was the nation's capital. By early 1959, the Washington, D.C., office had been retooled to use a multitude of machines to handle its mail. With more than six

TRANSORMA

During the Cold War, in the event of a nuclear attack, food and water rations were stored in numerous underground federal buildings, including post offices. By 1977, rations had deteriorated to a point where they were no longer safe for human consumption.

Above: A woman demonstrates the five-destination "Outgoing Mail Sorter," where a ZIP Code is entered and turned into a barcode for the automated scanning system.

Right: President Roosevelt established the Office of the Civil Defense in 1941. A decade later, President Truman signed the Federal Civil Defense Act of 1950, which formally established a system to focus on U.S. defense against any attacks from foreign countries. Postmaster General Arthur Summerfield released the Post Office Civil Defense plan in 1955.

miles of conveyor belts operating in the facility, the Post Office Department touted it as the "World's Most Mechanized Post Office." In just a few years, new studies of the setup would find it to be less economical than originally suspected and bring the expansion of systems like that in D.C. to a halt—but the trend toward replacing some of the most traditionally human elements of mail work with machines would never go away.

The 1950s saw the economy grow, the population grow, the country's ambitions grow. It was the same for the Post Office Department: new vehicles, new buildings. But underneath it all was a lurking menace. No sooner had World War II ended, with American families settling into comfortable postwar routines, than the Cold War began to ramp up, solidified by the Soviet Union's detonation of its first atomic bomb, in 1949. Two years later, President Harry Truman created the Federal Civil Defense Administration to prepare for the worst. At the same time Americans were celebrating the dawn of the post-WWII era, a defensive mindset began to pervade every aspect of American life. Some people built bomb shelters in basements. Others stockpiled survival rations in preparation to endure until radiation levels dropped. Schoolchildren everywhere practiced for an attack they all hoped would never come.

Yet again, the Post Office Department offered what it had to help.

Under the nation's civil defense program, certain public and commercial buildings were designated as fallout shelters. This included post offices, which took on a new, pivotal role during the Cold War era. Basements and storage areas were stocked with 17.5-gallon drums of water, each expected to sustain five survivors for two weeks. Postal buildings were also provided with boxes of canned food rations and first-aid supplies, collapsible cots, paper blankets, and radiological survey instruments, which included pen-sized dosimeters, a small device used to measure the amount of radiation. Geiger counters were furnished to larger post offices. Sanitation kits, each stuffed with toiletries for 50 occupants, were also supplied. Empty water drums were to be used as privies. In fact, at the dawn of the 1960s, Congress would allocate $2 million in the department's budget specifically for the building and provision of fallout shelters in 31 existing big-city postal facilities around the country, including Boston, Chicago, New York City, and Washington, D.C. Congress also allocated nearly $208 million in military money for the eventual construction of fallout shelters in smaller post offices throughout the country.

And the Post Office Department did even more.

THE KOREAN WAR

The sheer amount of mail processed by the Post Office during World War II helped the military create a global network of distribution centers overseas. In fact, the U.S. Navy quintupled the number of post offices it ran by 1945. Other services saw similar growth. Together, they helped manage the more than 11 tons of mail delivered each day for multinational forces in the Korean theater.

The military mail service stopped Free Mail and Victory Mail in 1947. Yet once service members began to deploy to Korea in 1950, these beloved programs started back up. This was a huge morale booster for soldiers, sailors, and Marines who wanted to stay in touch with their loved ones while overseas. The onslaught of letters and parcels was proving to be too much for aircraft cargo bays. As a result, the military implemented new restrictions on the size and weight of airmail being sent to the troops.

Above, left to right: Soldiers receive mail on the front line in 1951; mail from home is sorted for various locations in South Korea at the military post office, circa 1951; the 1st Marine Division gets a mail call and a big morale boost, having just come out of heavy fighting in the Nakdong River area, August 22–23, 1950; a helicopter mail guard delivers the mail to a convoy of soldiers headed

Still, the efficiencies gained in the mail system during WWII proved to be a boon for those stationed in Korea. There are even accounts of soldiers receiving letters less than an hour after arriving in the country, thanks to improved delivery logistics. This became more important, as warfighters relied on their post offices not just to stay connected with loved ones but also to receive special entitlements like combat pay.

On November 15, 1951, a soldier from the 5th Cavalry Regiment takes a moment to write home during a break in fighting Chinese Communist forces.

The New York City Post Office, under the supervision of Postmaster Albert Goldman, produced this poster for Letter Writing Week in 1950 encouraging people to write letters to the troops in South Korea.

Postal workers were trained in radiation monitoring and first aid.

Displaying the Civil Defense decal pledge card on a postal vehicle indicated that it could be commandeered by the government during an enemy attack on the country or during peacetime for emergencies such as natural disasters.

Post offices became nationwide distribution centers for a free publication, *Fallout Protection: What to Know and Do About Nuclear Attack*, a 48-page booklet containing survival information for nuclear winter. Every post office facility also received bundles of preprinted refugee identification cards that were to be distributed to survivors following a nuclear attack as a means of keeping track of displaced persons. Though that was the principal purpose of the refugee cards, they were to be used in the event of a natural disaster, such as a hurricane, tornado, or flood, as well.

Postal workers were trained in radiation monitoring and first aid, and many with personal ham radios formed a postal radio network to augment the civil defense radio system.

Postal vehicles were designated for important potential poststrike roles. Larger vehicles were to become mobile first-aid stations, people movers, or roving food-and-water distribution centers. Even the little Mailster had a role, impractical as it may have been—it was to be used as a police patrol vehicle in the aftermath of an attack. Mailsters' limitations made the effectiveness of this plan dubious, but they nevertheless patrolled New York City in countless air-raid drills.

As we know today, it went no further than drills. The nuclear attack whose possibility so consumed Americans starting in the 1950s never actually happened. But it's hard not to think that the specter of nuclear disaster always lurking just below the surface was the universe reminding the country that it had another problem festering under the shiny surfaces of growth, success, and superpower: racism and segregation. It was no different for the Post Office, which was still climbing out of the hole of its dark days of segregation earlier in the century. In the decade to come, social ferment would bring these issues to the fore—and it would not be a drill.

Above: Post offices nationwide distributed free copies of *Fallout Protection*, a 48-page booklet containing survival information in the event of a nuclear attack.

Left: Beginning in 1956, postal vehicles bore decals signifying their use as Civil Defense units. By March 1971, when the use of the decals was terminated, more than 25,000 postal vehicles had been identified in this way.

The first official letter sent via missile mail was written by Postmaster General Summerfield to announce the historic milestone in communication. The envelope was canceled on June 8, 1959, from the submarine USS *Barbero*.

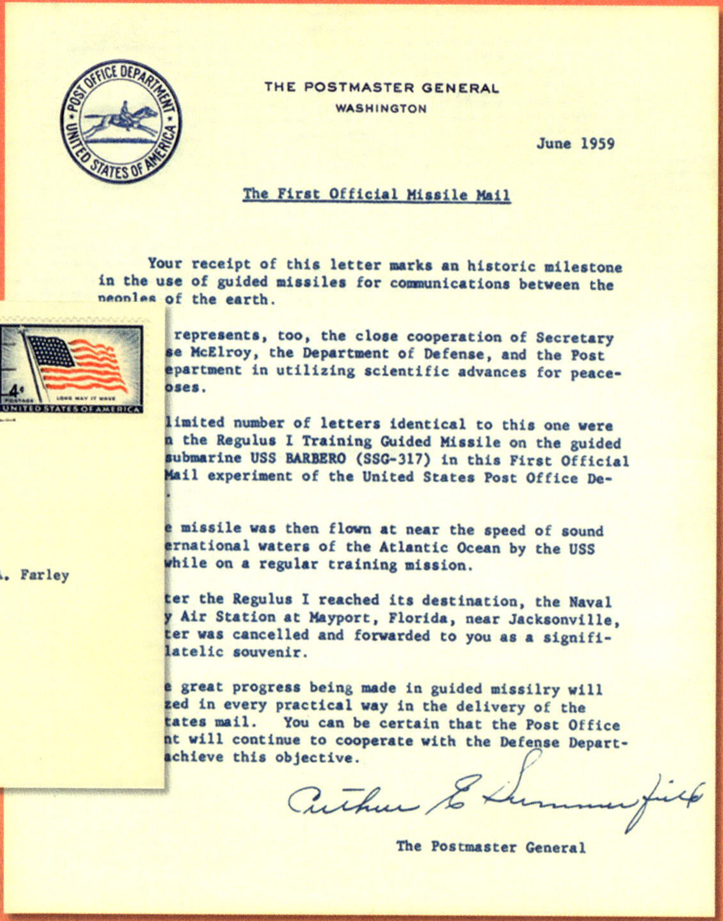

THE POSTMASTER GENERAL
WASHINGTON

June 1959

The First Official Missile Mail

Your receipt of this letter marks an historic milestone in the use of guided missiles for communications between the peoples of the earth.

represents, too, the close cooperation of Secretary se McElroy, the Department of Defense, and the Post epartment in utilizing scientific advances for peace-oses.

limited number of letters identical to this one were n the Regulus I Training Guided Missile on the guided submarine USS BARBERO (SSG-317) in this First Official Mail experiment of the United States Post Office De-

e missile was then flown at near the speed of sound ernational waters of the Atlantic Ocean by the USS while on a regular training mission.

ter the Regulus I reached its destination, the Naval y Air Station at Mayport, Florida, near Jacksonville, ter was cancelled and forwarded to you as a signifi-latelic souvenir.

e great progress being made in guided missilry will zed in every practical way in the delivery of the tates mail. You can be certain that the Post Office nt will continue to cooperate with the Defense Depart-achieve this objective.

Arthur E Summerfield

The Postmaster General

THE POSTMASTER GENERAL
WASHINGTON

U S S BARBERO
JUN
8
9.30AM
1959
(SSG-317)

4¢ POSTAGE
LONG MAY IT WAVE
UNITED STATES OF AMERICA

The Honorable James A. Farley
515 Madison Avenue
New York City, N. Y.

MISSILE MAIL

As part of the nation's defense during the Cold War, in 1957 the Navy deployed five nuclear-powered submarines with nuclear-tipped Regulus I cruise missiles. The initial variants of the remotely controlled Regulus I missiles were equipped with retractable aircraft-like landing gear so that they could be tested and retrieved. This fact set off lightbulbs in the minds of postal planners, who saw a service potential in this type of missile technology. Was high-speed missile mail service possible? The Post Office Department convinced the military to try it. Among the agreed-upon details of the mission: The test would be covert, announced only after the fact, in order to shock adversaries into realizing the nation's ballistic capabilities...and if it failed, no one would be any the wiser.

While the USS *Barbero* was docked at Norfolk, Virginia, Postmaster General Summerfield placed two red, white, and blue metal "mailboxes," holding 3,000 letters between them, inside the missile's nose.

At sea, *Barbero* launched its Regulus I missile off the coast of Florida, directing it to land at the Naval Auxiliary Air Station in Mayport, roughly 100 miles away. The missile, which was fired shortly before noon, covered the 100 miles in about 20 minutes.

For the Post Office Department, this was more than a publicity stunt. The 3,000 letters inside the missile's nose were identical, except for the addresses. They extolled the virtues and possibilities of using missile mail in the future. Each was intended for an important dignitary, including President Eisenhower and members of Congress.

In subsequently promoting the success of the missile mail mission, Postmaster General Summerfield optimistically forecast the potential uses of such missile technology, predicting: "This peacetime employment of a guided missile for the important and practical purpose of carrying mail, is the first known official use of missiles by any Post Office Department of any nation. Before man reaches the Moon, mail will be delivered within hours from New York to California, to Britain, to India or Australia by guided missiles." Unfortunately, Summerfield's predictions exceeded guided missile technology at the time. Mail volume surpassed the capacity of Regulus missiles. The cost of flying a few hundred letters by missile was prohibitive. As a result, regular missile mail service never materialized.

This mail container was one of two placed within the nose of the Regulus I missile, which was fired from the *Barbero* and landed at the Naval Auxiliary Air Station in Mayport, Florida.

COLLECTION-BOX POST OFFICES

Collection boxes were iconic symbols of the Post Office Department, so much so that oversized replicas were transformed into temporary post offices in areas around New York City from the mid-1950s to the 1970s. Wall Street, Bryant Park, and Times Square were just a few of the places around the city where customers could purchase stamps and drop off their holiday mail.

Customers line up to buy holiday stamps at a temporary Christmas station across from Radio City Music Hall in New York City in 1977.

Post Office Department employees paint the giant mailboxes in preparation for setup around New York City.

This oversized collection box was used as a temporary post office at Rockefeller Plaza in New York City during the 1954 Christmas rush. It was one of five such giant mailboxes set up in Manhattan and the Bronx to enhance holiday service.

Customers sending their holiday mail or purchasing holiday stamps could beat the regular post-office crowds and stop at the collection-box post office during lunch or after work.

Acting New York City Postmaster Robert K. Christenberry mails a letter in one of the giant mailboxes on December 8, 1958.

U.S.POSTAGE
5c

50c
U.S.POSTAGE
LUCY STONE

HIGHER EDUCATION
UNITED STATES POSTAGE
4¢

4c

U.S.
POSTAGE
5c
ERIE CANAL
1817 1967

JOHN F. KENNEDY
13c
UNITED STATES

Christmas 1962

5c

5
CENTS
US
POSTAGE
Sixth International
Philatelic Exhibition
Washington D.C. 20008

US
5c

1910 1960
CAMP FIRE GIRLS
UNITED STATES
POSTAGE
4c

to
the
fine
arts

ALLIANCE FOR
PROGRESS

UNITED STATES
1960
|
1969
POSTAL SERVICE

WHEN THE MAIL STOPPED MOVING

The nation's largest mail-processing facility was at the crossroads of the Midwest: Chicago. In the 1960s, the main post office in Chicago, built about 30 years before, was actually the largest postal facility in the world. With 60 acres of floor space—the size of 45 football fields—it could handle 35 million letters per day. More than half of America's first-class mail passed through the facility as it crisscrossed the country.

The problem? All of this processing was done by hand.

Though the 1950s had seen the introduction of all manner of new technologies to the processing of mail, those technologies mostly hadn't made it to Chicago—but the postwar boom in mail volume certainly had. And in 1966, after years of mail coming in faster than it could be processed, the Chicago Post Office was having a processing meltdown. *Ten million* pieces of mail froze in place.

Attempts to dig out set in motion a cascading avalanche that tumbled through the system's predominantly manual operations. When the breakdown in Chicago came on October 13, 1966, mail had to be diverted to other postal facilities around the country to avoid a further catastrophe. Some midwestern mail was transferred as far away as Florida for processing. There was a panic that the failure in Chicago might trigger a system-wide shutdown.

Chicago's main post office, built in the 1930s, was the nation's largest and most congested postal facility by the 1960s. Designed to predominantly handle railway mail, it had few loading docks for big trucks. As trucks replaced trains as major mail movers, this limitation led to delays in unloading trucks in the 1960s and created a massive logjam of mail that temporarily collapsed the system.

Packages pile up at New York City's General Post Office.

The unraveling of the Chicago Post Office wasn't a problem of 1966 alone. It was the culmination of decades of decisions about leadership, real estate, and labor issues. Postmaster General Lawrence O'Brien testified to the House Appropriations Subcommittee on Departments of the Treasury and Post Office that "enough did not happen in the previous 33 years." The Post Office Department had been slow to adapt the designs of processing centers and post offices to the modern era, whether that be the ascendancy of the automobile or the breakthrough of sorting technologies. Employees were underpaid and overworked. Even business practices were behind the times. "We are trying to move our mail through facilities largely unchanged since the days...when our mail volume was 30 percent of what it is today," O'Brien said.

Something would need to be done to rescue the mail system from the failures epitomized by the disaster in Chicago. And figuring out what it might be meant working to understand the forces that dominated the Post Office in the 1960s, when technology continued to advance but the humans at the heart of the system fell behind.

★ ★ ★

In October 1960, halfway across the country from Chicago, a new post office is dedicated in Providence, Rhode Island. It's not simply a new building; it's a new approach to post offices. The so-called "automated post office" was a showpiece, a state-of-the-art mail-handling facility featuring equipment developed under a $15 million research contract with Intelex Systems, a subsidiary of the International Telephone and Telegraph company. The post office at Providence included three miles of conveyor belts to carry mail between automatic sorting, facing, and canceling machines. The machines could process about 25,000 pieces of mail an hour, including 18,000 letters and 4,800 packages. Though this was impressive, it was nothing compared with what was being processed by hand in Chicago—but then again, the Providence facility was 13 acres to Chicago's 60, and Chicago had 28,000 employees, which was more than one-tenth of Providence's *entire population*.

Until the 1960s, collecting, sorting, canceling, and delivering America's mail were almost exclusively manual processes. Canceling machines were among the most sophisticated technology in widespread use at the time, and by then many of those machines were up to 40 years

Above: The Post Office Department publicized the creation of its "First Automated Post Office" in Providence on October 20, 1960, with the issuance of a stamp to commemorate the event. Unfortunately, the machines installed in this showcase facility couldn't match the precision and speed of human hands.

Opposite: President Lyndon B. Johnson designated October 10–15, 1966, as National ZIP Code Week and called upon everyone "to contribute to a stronger and more efficient Postal Service...by learning and using the ZIP Code...and encouraging others to do so as well." New York City letter carriers also reminded customers of the new system when they rallied on the steps of the New York City Post Office.

old. In 1959, the Post Office handled a staggering 63 billion pieces of mail. Between being dropped into a mailbox and being delivered, almost every piece of that mail was handled 17 times. Not so in Providence.

The tension between the Chicago school of post offices and the Providence school of post offices would characterize the 1960s. On the one hand, the postal labor force remained immense, but the volume of work they took on was racing ahead of their compensation. On the other hand, new technologies were making it possible to do more with fewer humans. Those technologies weren't yet in wide adoption, but it was clear which version of the post office the department saw as the future: A rendering of the Providence facility was featured on a 1960 stamp that was the first design ever to celebrate the Post Office Department itself.

★ ★ ★

The most important innovation of the decade, though, wasn't a piece of physical machinery at all. On July 1, 1963, the "Zone Improvement Plan," which assigned every region of the country a number for easier sorting, made its debut. The idea of zone codes wasn't new; they had been successfully used before, but not with the level of granularity the new system provided. The first digit of each number indicated one of 10 national service areas. The second and third digits indicated the sectional center that served the recipient, while the last two digits identified their post office. We still rely on these five-digit codes today; of course, rather than talking about the "Zone Improvement Plan," we simply call them "ZIP Codes."

Prior to the creation of ZIP Codes, manual sorting by state and city addresses slowed the mail process and increased the opportunity for errors. With a ZIP Code, even an inexperienced clerk could swiftly sort by the numbers: They only needed to glance at the code to know immediately which of the 553 sectional distribution centers a piece of mail was bound for. Postal officials estimated that using ZIP Codes could reduce delivery times by up to 24 hours and cut down the number of times a piece of mail was handled by an average of six touches.

But even if the benefits were obvious to postal workers, the department still had to sell the system to the people who would use it, and it was never going to work without the business community. After all, 75 percent of the country's mail

Nearly three-quarters of those surveyed liked the idea of using ZIP Codes because they could precisely target deliveries to specific destinations.

came from business mailers. To find out whether they'd have a problem, the Post Office conducted a pre-rollout survey among 21,000 of the biggest mailers. Support was overwhelming: Nearly three-quarters of those surveyed liked the idea of using ZIP Codes because they could precisely target deliveries to specific destinations.

When the Post Office Department was finally ready, the rollout of ZIP Codes was exceptionally well-choreographed. Every postmaster was given talking points and preprinted announcements for local newspapers explaining the value of ZIP Codes. Additionally, the department sent information cards to 72 million mailboxes detailing the system. But even more vital than all those mailings was an endearingly childlike drawing of a smiling, quick-moving letter carrier named Mr. ZIP. Introduced on January 10, 1964, as part of a national media campaign, Mr. ZIP could be found on four-foot-tall plywood cutouts in more than 35,000 post-office lobbies, on decals applied to 45,000 postal vehicles and 400,000 street mailboxes, and in newspaper and television ads. Invariably, he appeared alongside a message: "Use ZIP Code."

MAIL
MOVES THE COUNTRY
ZIP CODE
MOVES THE MAIL
THE POSTAL SERVICE DELIVERS WELL OVER
80 BILLION
MESSAGES EACH YEAR
MAIL IS THE BLOOD THAT SURGES THROUGH THE ARTERIES OF COMMERCE...
ORDERS
ORDERS
ORDERS
ORDERS
PRODUCTS
PRODUCTS
...THE TIE THAT BINDS FAMILIES AND FRIENDS
Dear folks, I Passed. Send money. Love, your son
AND MR. ZIP'S MODERN POST OFFICE DEPARTMENT MAKES IT POSSIBLE
U.S. POST OFFICE DEPARTMENT
POD Publication 127 May 1968
1

THEN IT'S ON ITS WAY...
ZIP CODED MAIL GOES IN A STRAIGHT LINE TO THE SECTIONAL CENTER OR LARGE POST OFFICE NEAREST ITS DESTINATION
U.S. POST OFFICE
NEXT STOP, THE LOCAL POST OFFICE WHERE A LETTER CARRIER PICKS IT UP FOR DELIVERY...
U.S. MAIL
...TO THE PROPER ADDRESS
REGULAR POSTAGE PLUS ZIP CODE... THAT'S ALL IT TAKES
MRS GEORGE ZOT
120 GLOBE AVE.
DULUTH, MINN. 55801
MISS BETTY BROWN
12 HURD ST.
CHICAGO, ILL. 60635
Don't tie up mail service
U.S. MAIL
MAIL EARLY IN THE DAY AND USE
ZIP CODE
4
GPO : 1968 O - 298-667

TODAY, NEARLY ALL LONG DISTANCE FIRST CLASS MAIL GOES BY AIR
U.S. MAIL
U.S. MAIL
THERE IS A FIVE NUMBER CODE FOR EVERY ADDRESS
20260
THIS IS THE ZIP CODE FOR THE POSTMASTER GENERAL'S ADDRESS IN WASHINGTON, D.C.
POST OFFICES CAN SORT MAIL WITH MORE SPEED BECAUSE OF ZIP CODE
YOUR ZIP CODE GOES IN THE RETURN ADDRESS. THE CODE OF THE PERSON GETTING YOUR MAIL GOES IN THE MAILING ADDRESS
MRS GEORGE ZOT
120 GLOBE AVE.
DULUTH, MINN. 55801
MISS BETTY BROWN
12 HURD ST.
CHICAGO, ILL. 60635
HERE'S HOW ZIP CODE WORKS
SUPPOSE THE ZIP CODE IS 60635
THE "6" SAYS IT GOES TO THE MIDWEST.
THE "06" NARROWS IT DOWN TO CHICAGO.
"35" PINPOINTS A LOCAL POST OFFICE... THIS ELIMINATES MANY HANDLINGS. THE LETTER IS SORTED FASTER AND SENT MORE DIRECTLY TO ITS DESTINATION.
9
5
0
1
6
CHICAGO
4
8
2
7
3
2

REMEMBER TO MAIL EARLY IN THE DAY BEFORE PLANES, TRAINS AND TRUCKS LEAVE
U.S. MAIL
YOUR LETTER GOES FROM HERE...
U.S. MAIL
...RIGHT TO THE POST OFFICE
WHERE IT IS CANCELLED, SORTED AND SACKED...
U.S. MAIL
...WITH OTHER MAIL GOING TO THE SAME ZIP CODED AREA
U.S. MAIL
60635
IN SOME LARGE POST OFFICES, EQUIPMENT READS AND SORTS MACHINE PRINTED ZIP CODED ADDRESSES ON LETTERS
LARGE VOLUMES OF BUSINESS MAIL ALREADY PRESORTED BY THE CODES BYPASS THE POST OFFICE AND GO STRAIGHT TO THE TRANSPORTATION TERMINAL
U.S. MAIL
POST OFFICE
AIRPORT
3

Opposite: The Post Office Department created this comic magazine in 1968 to educate readers about the new ZIP Code system.

Right and below: Just by looking at the first digit of a ZIP Code, postal workers could immediately tell where in the country a letter or package was going.

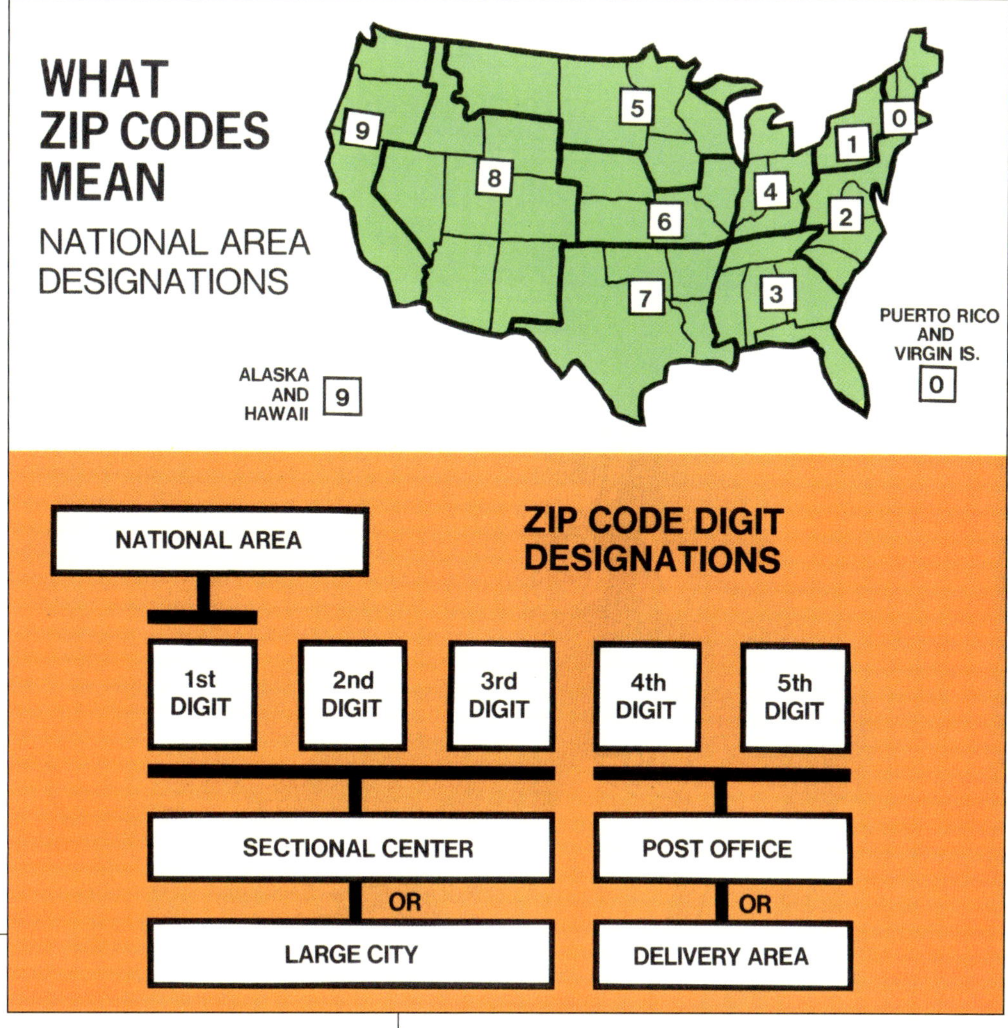

EXAMPLES

NEBRASKA

STATE

693 ■ 692 ■ 687 ■ 691 ■ 686 ■ 688 ■ 680 ■ 681 ● 683 ■ 684 ■ 685 ● 690 ■ 689 ■

■ SECTIONAL CENTER ● LARGE CITY

SECTIONAL CENTER AREA

6 8 0 7 1

SECTIONAL CENTER POST OFFICE

71 680 681

■ SECTIONAL CENTER

○ POST OFFICE

● LARGE CITY

LARGE CITY AREA

OMAHA

12 42 22 52 64 34 04 11 10 54 14

CITY POST OFFICE DELIVERY AREA

6 8 1 4 2

Here's why: The ZIP Code system is a series of standard geographic units. The United States is divided into 10 large areas. Each area is given a number between 0 and 9—the first digit in a ZIP Code number. Key post offices in each area are designated sectional centers—the next 2 digits. Each sectional center serves a series of associate post offices—the last 2 digits (the same system applies to major cities and delivery units within these cities). This entire system is based on local transportation and trade—the hubs of commerce throughout the United States.

It's either cruel or comic, depending on how you look at it, that as the employees of the Post Office were facing a crisis about their value to the postal system, the department's most famous innovation of the decade was identified not with a living, breathing person but with a cartoon character.

★ ★ ★

ZIP—which you probably didn't even realize was an acronym—wasn't the only jumble of letters the Post Office Department introduced in the 1960s. There was a whole alphabet soup of new technologies aimed at making the processing of mail more efficient.

ABCD, or Accelerated Business Collection Delivery, was a same-day delivery service that operated within cities' central business districts.

NIMS, or Nationwide Improved Mail Service, was a joint business and government effort introduced in 1961, at 300 of the largest post offices, that called for business mailers to deposit the bulk of their mail well before the peak mailing period between 4:00 p.m. and 9:00 p.m. It was a solution to the havoc wreaked when mail came late in the day, clogging the system, creating a nightmare for postal workers, and costing the Post Office Department a fortune in overtime pay.

VIM, which stood for Vertical Improved Mail, addressed problems associated with serving high-rise apartments and large office buildings, where an army of letter carriers had to go from apartment to apartment or from office to office delivering mail: In 1967, more than 1,400 carriers had to be employed to service 645 buildings in 60 cities. Under VIM, buildings were given communal lobby lockbox areas and corporate mailrooms, reducing the cost of delivery to high-rises by 85 percent.

Of course, not every new service bore an acronym. One of the decade's first, for instance: Instant Mail, also called Speed Mail, was essentially a government-operated fax system. It made

ABCD assured business mailers of same-day delivery services within a community's business district. Post offices identified specific ABCD collection boxes and assigned ABCD mail trucks to serve local business mailers located in downtown areas.

With this ad campaign, Postmaster General J. Edward Day, at left, encouraged customers to make mailing part of their daily routine rather than waiting for the 5:00 p.m. rush.

Left: Postmaster General John A. Gronouski demonstrates the new VIM mail-delivery system for high-rise buildings.

Below: The Hartford Building in San Francisco had the VIM system installed, as outlined in this Post Office Department pamphlet.

its debut on November 1, 1960. Instant Mail was far ahead of its time—and it previewed some of the challenges innovation would create by putting jobs at risk and majorly disrupting the status quo.

The service began harmlessly enough, when the Post Office Department bounced a message by satellite from the main Washington, D.C., post office to the Chicago office, and back again, in a matter of seconds. At the receiving end, the first electronically transmitted letter was instantly printed out and delivered to President Eisenhower. The president was at the White House with the note in his hands within 15 minutes of its transmission back from Chicago. Additional messages were sent to Vice President Richard Nixon, members of Congress, and other government officials. They weren't just simple test messages; they aimed to curry favor for the service. "Your always available support of worthwhile projects dictates an immediate report to you of the most recent development in improved mail service Speed Mail..." said the note to Nixon. It was personally signed by Postmaster General Summerfield.

The process was simple and, in some ways, reminiscent of V-mail. A standard sheet of paper with the message was scanned, electronically transmitted, and printed, with the resulting identical copy placed in a window envelope for immediate delivery. The test equipment could receive and fold letters at a rate of one every 10 seconds. But that exceptional speed and automation undermined literally centuries of the postal service's infrastructure and politics. As officials at the department discussed an approach to getting Congress to authorize this new class of

Right: Postal management demonstrating how a message could go from a Washington, D.C., office to a postmaster's office in Newark, New Jersey.

Below: One of the steps involved in Speed Mail was the use of satellite dishes to transmit customers' letters from local telephone-company offices in Washington, D.C., to the Washington Post Office, which would receive the transmission and print it out.

ZIP Codes: The Ultimate Sorting System

The Zone Improvement Plan was developed to make sorting mail more efficient. But one man, Jonathan Robbin, showed that ZIP Codes could be used for sorting people, too. They were novel at the time, and from today's vantage point, Robbin's techniques are clear forerunners of the data-driven targeting that now affects so many facets of our lives.

A Harvard-educated computer whiz, Robbin linked ZIP Codes with demographic data from the U.S.Census: things like ethnicity, mobility, and housing style. His company, the Claritas Corporation, used 34 census characteristics in total to develop 40 different neighborhood "types," each with a snappy name like "Young Influentials" or "Bohemian Mix." America's wealthiest neighborhoods, where one in 10 was a millionaire, were called "Blue Blood Estates." The nation's poorest rural settlements were labeled "Hard Scrabble." In between were clusters named "Towns & Gowns," "Emergent Minorities," and "Grain Belt." Within each of these neighborhood types, Robbin believed he could reasonably predict what people ate, drank, drove, and even thought. In other words, given one of the nation's 36,000 ZIP Codes, with Robbin's system direct-mail marketers or entrepreneurs or politicians could predict whom they would encounter there–and determine how to target them.

Of course, this sounds almost quaint today, in the age of hyper-targeting with the far greater troves of data available online. But back then, it was revolutionary. In 1974, Robbin launched a marketing system called PRIZM, for Potential Rating Index for ZIP Markets. In 1983, the Post Office introduced the ZIP+4 system, which added four digits that specified a recipient's city block, their apartment building, or a post-office box. PRIZM evolved to match and was also adapted over time to account for the fact that a ZIP Code's population is not static–people move in and out, earn more or less, die and are born. Reflecting the increasing diversity of American society, the 40 PRIZM clusters of 1974 grew to become 68 distinct lifestyles by 2022. The system is still in use today.

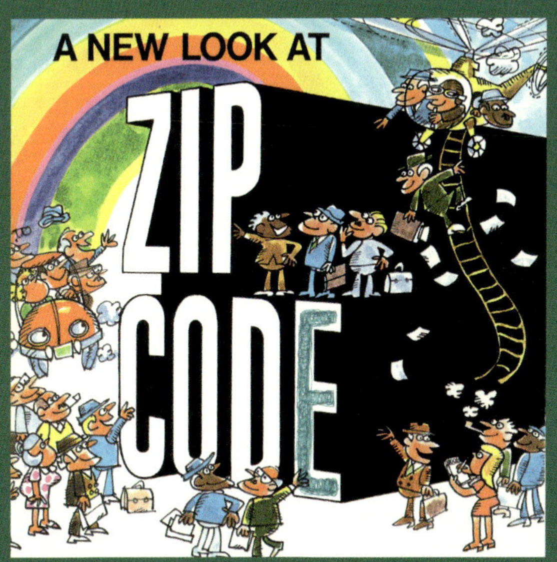

THE VIETNAM WAR

Logistical advances across the postal system helped support mail sent to troops serving in the Vietnam War. Mail was no longer competing with people and supplies for space in military aircraft. Instead, the combination of commercial airlines, military airlift, and chartered aircraft helped shoulder the burden as part of a postal program called Parcel Air Lift, which is still in use today. New innovations in cargo containers and automated location tracking were also a boon to soldiers waiting on word from home. Most mail sent from the U.S. could arrive in Vietnam in as few as three days.

But there was a difference between a letter arriving in-country and being delivered into the hands of the service member it was addressed to. Postal units started to be assigned to theater-level commands to help with delivery

MAIL FOR SERVICEMEN ...A POSTAL GUIDE FOR SPEEDING SERVICE

"More than 75 percent of all packages, letters and other mail is now airlifted overseas as a result of new legislation and actions by President Johnson."

Lawrence F. O'Brien
Postmaster General

POD Publication 118, Feb. 1968

HELP AMERICA'S SERVICEMEN RECEIVE THE BEST POSTAL SERVICE IN THE WORLD

Be familiar with the many new postal services for speeding letters, packages, books and other articles to the military men and women stationed in Southeast Asia, Europe and other distant lands. With a few minor exceptions, the rates and regulations in this pamphlet apply to mail addressed to all servicemen with an Armed Forces Post Office Address.

Mail sent through Armed Forces Post Offices must include the full five-digit APO or FPO number.

SEATTLE
SAN FRANCISCO
NEW YORK
Mail delivered to port cities for onward distribution to serviceman's unit.

CORRECTLY ADDRESSED MAIL .. can be immediately sorted to planes flying over seas.

Pvt. John J. Doe 14032214
Co. A 3rd Bn. First Bgd.
Fourth Infantry Division
APO San Francisco 96262

Can't be delivered.

Smn. John J. Doe 140221
Naval Air Station
FPO New York

Letters and gift packages must be addressed to a specific serviceman.

"SERVICEMEN VIETNAM"

NONMAILABLE MATTER

Some items cannot be mailed to military post offices. These include matches, lighter fluid, magnetic materials and radioactive matter. If in doubt about the mailability of an article, ask your local postmaster.

SECURITY
CIGARETTES

Above, left to right: USMC military postal clerks stand on either side of Major General George S. Bowman Jr., all holding up the Post Office Department flag presented to them by Postmaster General Blount; it was a morale-booster for soldiers in Vietnam to receive letters from home, as well as entertainment like magazines; mail arrives to the 1st Marine Division in Vietnam in November 1968; The U.S. Marine Corps released this press photograph taken on November 12, 1969, with the headline: "Neither rain nor sleet nor Qua Son Mountains stop Lance Corporate W. G. Wright of Iowa from delivering the mail."

Instructions for customers sending packages to soldiers stationed overseas.

oversight. Thirteen of these units, scattered across the Vietnam theater, operated 24 Post Offices. Because of the country's humid and rainy weather, the Army adopted the use of green, waterproof mailbags that could be dropped from helicopters mid-flight into remote locations. (This practice didn't last long, however—far too many bags were lost in the jungle, leaving soldiers, sailors, Marines, and airmen without morale-boosting letters and packages.)

Privates First Class Edward, Falls, and Morgan of the U.S. Marines, 1st Battalion, 7th Regiment, spend some down time eating rations and writing letters home.

A U.S. Marine CH-46 helicopter loaded with mail, food, water, and other supplies lifts off en route to companies in the field in Ca Lu in Quan Tri Province.

"We were treated like unwanted stepchildren," recalled former railway mail clerk John McClellan.

mail, they realized the problems they would face. Instantaneous electronic delivery would mean that thousands of postal jobs were lost or never created. And there were real questions about how electronic mail delivery would affect the private sector. For one, it would put the Post Office Department in direct competition with a vaunted communications company, Western Union, which was already in the business of using some 40,000 machines scattered across the country to transmit facsimiles. Opinion pages across the country cried foul on this point. "Why shouldn't these facsimile letters be carried by the private agencies best qualified to transmit them?" argued the New York *Daily News*. Delaware's *Milford Chronicle* argued that "it will mark another retreat from the concept of government doing for the people only what the people cannot do for themselves."

For many members of Congress, all of this added up to a no-go. The service was effectively dead on arrival. There wasn't a huge downside to axing the instant service: At the time, letters were being transported by air from the West Coast to the East Coast in roughly six hours—not instant, but certainly exceptionally speedy service.

Of course, it wasn't only newfangled Instant Mail that challenged the postal service's legacy infrastructure. New approaches to sorting, largely centralized in buildings, were causing the last era of mail to fade, fast.

In 1945, there were 528 railway mail routes. By 1965, the number of railway routes was down to 190 and falling as more and more were cut. In-transit sorting on magnificent RPOs had once been on the cutting edge, but now sorting was moving to massive factory-like complexes. Sometimes they were staffed by a city's worth of employees, as in Chicago, and other times with innovative new technologies, as in Providence. (Highway post-office routes were equally affected, going from 170 in 1960 to 147 by 1965.)

These changes had a deeply human impact, one that involved the rancorous assimilation of former railway mail clerks into other postal positions. The majority of these clerks were absorbed into other slots, but the transition wasn't always easy. Local postmasters thought of former rail staffers as unreliable workers who had too much wanderlust in their blood or were too independent in nature to follow the processes at their new jobs. "We were treated like unwanted stepchildren," recalled former railway mail clerk John McClellan. That reasoning was silly, but there was another reason their absorption upset other mail workers: They disrupted the existing seniority structure within local post offices.

The disruption—be it by technology directly or by other postal workers—goes a long way toward explaining the rapidly growing prominence of the labor movement within the Post Office in the 1960s. But to fully understand it, we have to consider the larger picture of the decade in the United States. We have to talk about the civil rights movement.

★ ★ ★

Early in the 20th century, during the presidency of Woodrow Wilson, the Post Office Department was undeniably a horribly segregated institution. But in the time since, it had been working hard to make amends—and in the 1960s, as the civil rights movement was forcing America to reckon with racism in its past, many of the department's efforts were paying real dividends. Under the New Deal and during the labor shortages of World War II, more and more African Americans were hired by the Post Office Department. Once they were employed, civil service rules made their jobs far more secure than they would have been

President John F. Kennedy signs Executive Order 10988, which gave federal employees the right to organize and engage in collective bargaining.

in the private sector. During the first half of the 1960s, the department became the largest employer of African Americans in the country; nearly 10 percent of postal workers were Black. At one point, New York City, Chicago, and Los Angeles—cities responsible for an annual volume of more than 10 billion pieces of mail—each had an African American postmaster.

Complementing the department's own efforts to do better by Black postal workers was the organizing prowess of these workers. In 1913, 35 Black railway mail clerks founded the National Alliance of Postal and Federal Employees (NAPFE). The reason? In 1913, Black mail workers were experiencing what *all* postal employees would experience five decades later: They were being cut out of the Railway Mail Service. The NAPFE and other unions would become important forums for Black postal workers to fight for fairness, for themselves and for their profession.

And indeed, railway mail clerks, in the years to come, would be some of the postal employees who most clearly saw the tie between the two. In the 1950s, serving principally between New York City, Scranton, and Buffalo, Walter Bell couldn't stay overnight just anywhere. There was a Black-owned hotel near New York City's Grand Central Terminal where the clerks could find room and board, but "in Scranton it was hard to find a place that would allow a Black person to check into a short-term hotel for the four- or five-hour layover," he told the Smithsonian Institution in a 2007 oral history interview. Instead, Bell would typically stay in his rail car, sleeping on mailbags. Because he was never certain where or if he would be able to get a meal, Bell's "grip"—a small travel case used by every railway mail clerk—always included extra food.

And this was on a northern route. In the South, things could be much worse. Southern routes often took Black clerks through "sundown towns," which were white-only towns that set curfews or prohibited Black people from being on the streets after a certain time. In these instances, sleeping in a railway mail car may well have been the safest way for a Black clerk arriving late to spend the night. Prescribed sentences for violating these ordinances included fines and jail time, but vigilante punishments included beatings and lynchings. The combined circumstances of the job and prejudice based on skin color gave people like Bell incentive to organize. And just as he and his peers were feeling this, so were other African Americans and exploited workers across the country. In the 1960s, the architects of the civil rights movement were increasingly finding common cause between them and using these aligned interests to grow their movement.

Interestingly, early in the decade, President John F. Kennedy made a decision that explicitly tied the causes together. In 1962, he issued Executive Order 10988, which for the first time gave federal workers—which included Post Office Department employees—the right to collective bargaining through labor organizations, or unions. The National Association of Letter Carriers, a postal union that dates back to the 1880s, was part of a coalition that pressured Kennedy to act. And within that executive order was a provision that no labor organization would be recognized that "discriminates with regard to the terms or conditions of membership because of race, color, creed or national origin." Racial prejudice and labor representation were legally linked. Within months of the executive order, the first postal labor agreement would be negotiated. Labor's power across the country, including in the mail service, was as strong as it had been in some time. But the conditions that would unleash its real power within the Post Office Department wouldn't be apparent until October 1966. When Chicago ground to a halt, it was clear that something about the department had irrevocably changed. Workers needed to be respected.

By 1967, President Lyndon B. Johnson had decided that his administration had to do something about the gridlock in Chicago. That year he created an independent commission, composed of some of the most astute businesspeople and labor leaders in the country, to recommend how to get the system unstuck—and make sure it didn't get stuck again.

The 10-man commission and its resulting report were both named after its leader, Frederick R. Kappel, the retired chairman of the American Telephone and Telegraph Company. The Kappel Commission Report, officially titled "Towards Postal Excellence," came out in June 1968. It was a truly radical document.

The report called for the establishment of a government-owned corporation to operate the Post Office Department, one that would be free from congressional oversight and could replace patronage and petty politics with sound business practices. This new corporation would undergo significant modernization, adding automation and mechanization that would loosen its reliance on outdated manual processes. In other words, the idea was to run the Post Office Department the same way the nation's most successful private enterprises were run. By the same token, and perhaps in acknowledgment of the decade's victories for labor, the report also concluded that postal workers deserved the same collective-bargaining rights afforded to private-sector workers under the National Labor Relations Act.

Was the report too radical? Perhaps. Congress opted not to act on the commission's recommendations when they were first proposed. Seven months later, President Johnson was out of the White House, having chosen not to run for reelection against the backdrop of the Vietnam War. By January 1969, the Kappel Commission Report seemed to be as good as dead.

But when President Richard M. Nixon was sworn into office that month, one of the first things he did was appoint Winton Blount as his first postmaster general. And one of the first things Blount did was dust off the report.

Following the 1968 election, Nixon had zeroed in on Blount when he was still just president-elect. From the very beginning, Blount was like a dog with a bone when it came to postal reform. As he recalled, "I got a message the President wanted

Postmaster General Winton Blount sells a first-day cover to S. Dillon Ripley, secretary of the Smithsonian Institution, at the official opening of the reconstructed Headsville General Store Post Office, located inside the National Museum of American History, in July 1971.

The president himself would lose as many as 1,800 appointments.

to see me, and I came to New York. He asked me to be the Postmaster General. I asked him how in the heck did he come up with that idea...And I said, 'Well, I'm not interested in being Postmaster General as they have operated in the past. But if you want postal reform, I'd be honored to do it.'"

That was exactly what Nixon wanted. The White House maintained two lists of things to be accomplished: The green list included those things that the president wanted done now, and the red list those that could be done eventually, maybe. Blount got postal reform on the green list, making it a priority that sat alongside ending the Vietnam War. Starting practically the moment he was sworn in, on January 22, 1969, Blount got to work.

And work it was. "We announced 15 days after being sworn in in 1969 that we were no longer going to appoint postmasters by the congressional system," Blount recalled. "Well, it created a firestorm in Congress, building up from all of the counties and cities around the nation." Eliminating patronage had always been a non-starter with certain members of Congress, perhaps even a grave insult. During the Johnson era, a senior Post Office Department official's attempt to fire an underperforming political appointee led powerful senator James Eastland to go straight to the president and promise to make sure none of his judicial appointees would ever again see the light of day. And at the time Blount was trying to do away with patronage, it meant taking away as many as 60,000 appointment opportunities from members of Congress. The president himself would lose as many as 1,800 appointments, which meant there were pockets of resistance even within the White House.

But Blount was undeterred. He twisted every arm he could. He had breakfast with multiple legislators every single day. He submitted himself into the jaws of his enemies. The Republican Party on the Hill was angry at him, and after being in office for little more than a month, Blount met with congressional Republicans in an unprecedented, two-and-a-half-hour closed-door meeting.

TOWARDS POSTAL EXCELLENCE

The Report of The President's Commission on Postal Organization

June 1968

In a message written by President Richard M. Nixon to Congress on May 27, 1969, in response to "Towards Postal Excellence," he stated that "traditions die hard and traditional institutions are difficult to abandon. But tradition is no substitute for performance, and if our postal system is to meet the expanding needs of the 1970s, we must act now."

"They blistered the tar off him," claimed Paul Carlin, Blount's assistant postmaster general for planning. And that was only round one. "They hadn't had enough, so five days later or so, they called him back for another hour and a half." Throughout, Blount wasn't fazed. He calmly, logically, and convincingly explained the benefits of a properly run postal system. He had a reasonable fact-based retort for every criticism. He disposed of objection after objection. In the end, "they didn't know what to do with somebody like that," said Carlin. Everything Blount said made sense.

But it still wasn't enough. All of Blount's powers of persuasion, and all of his calm airing of grievances, and all of his logical reasoning made inroads but couldn't carry postal reform across the finish line. It happened, though. Eventually. All it took was a shocking event that no one saw coming. One day very soon, Winton Blount would get his way—and the Post Office Department would come to an end.

IT ALL DEPENDS ON
ZIP
CODE
10c

8¢
UNITED STATES
POLAR BEAR

USA
10c
INTERNATIONAL WOMEN'S YEAR

UNIT
Prevent
drug abuse
8c

Family Planning
UNITED STATES 8c

THE BOSTON TEA PARTY
8c U.S.
BICENTENNIAL ERA

U·S
LaGuardia/14c

ENERGY
CONSERVATION
UNITED
10¢
STATES

26c
AIRMAI
Shrine of Democracy
USA

WILDLIFE CONSERVATION
UNITED STATES 6c

8c
U.S.
ANTARCTIC
TREATY
1961·1971

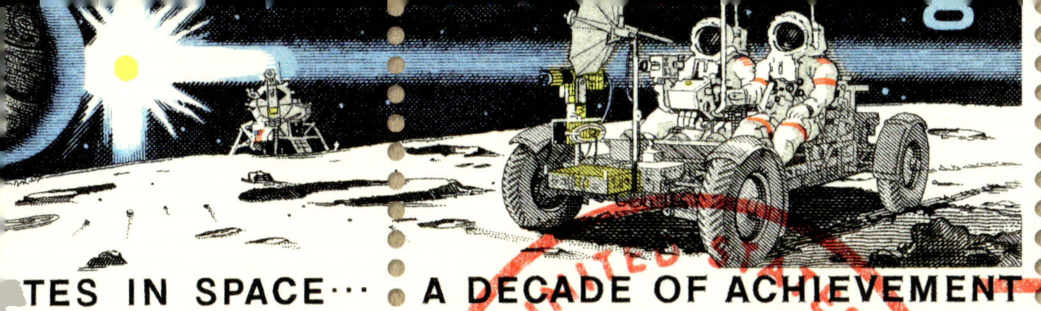

GOODBYE, POST OFFICE DEPARTMENT. HELLO, U.S. POSTAL SERVICE.

As the 1970s began, the Post Office Department was the object of national ridicule. It was plagued with problems that short-term operational and administrative patches couldn't fix. Most postal operations were still manual, with workers doing their jobs the same way they had been done 100 years earlier; Congress had allocated little money for postal automation and mechanization. The department faced a $5 billion backlog in capital repairs. Pay was inadequate; working conditions were archaic; political patronage hampered career growth, leading to high employee turnover; and in major city post offices, mail volume was outpacing processing capabilities. Real postal reforms were needed, beginning with better pay.

The fact was that Post Office jobs were labor-intensive and often strenuous—workers spent long days and long hours on their feet—and without better pay, the department was losing out in the labor market to the private sector. The department's vacancy rate in 1970 was reportedly 23 percent. When it did manage to hire someone, due to training requirements, it took an average of 13 weeks to bring new hires on board. At most postal facilities, at least a few shifts were perpetually shorthanded—and, as usual, mail volume was increasing.

Congress was responsible for setting postal workers' wages. At the time, they were historically low. In 1970, the starting annual salary for a full-time postal worker was $6,176, about $43,000 in today's dollars. After 21 years of service, a postal employee could expect to make on average only $8,442 a year, or $56,000 in today's dollars—still $2,000 to $3,000 less than what other workers servicing homes, like municipal garbage collectors, were earning.

For workers residing in rural areas, where the cost of living was relatively low, the pay *may* have been adequate. Still, those with families often had to take additional jobs to make ends meet. And in urban areas like New York City, San Francisco, Boston, and Chicago, the pay amounted to poverty-level wages or worse. As many as 65 percent of New York City railway mail clerks were in debt, while in Boston, about 45 percent of them reportedly owed money to loan sharks or pawn shops. Some postal employees qualified for public assistance. Others went without meat for meals even though they worked full-time.

After years of poor pay, averaging less than a 2 percent raise per year, postal employees had had enough. They demanded a real raise—10 to 15 percent. On March 12, 1970, Congress responded: a measly 4 percent. At the same time, they voted for a 41 percent increase in their own salaries. This the postal workers simply could not abide.

Strikes by federal workers were illegal, but on March 17, Bronx and Manhattan postal employees went on strike anyway. This was called a "wildcat" walkout—it was a spontaneous action of New York–area leaders of the National Association of Letter Carriers rather than an organized, union-led effort.

Within a matter of days, the seemingly leaderless strike spread, crippling areas of the country that were linchpins of the postal system. To quell

Right: Chicago *Today* covered the mail strike by comparing the average salary for patrolmen and firemen ($12,120) and police sergeants and fire lieutenants ($14,184) to that of letter carriers (just $6,176 per year for new hires).

Opposite: Brooklyn postal workers celebrate after voting down a proposal by their union's president to go back to work during the nation's major postal-work stoppage on March 22, 1970.

22 Chicago today, Friday, March 20, 1970 ★★

Mailmen protest 'poverty' pay

POSTOFFICE LETTER carriers claim they have been promised wage scales comparable to private industry, but top pay stands at only $8,442 a year.

The carriers are angry and many, including 77 in Berwyn, have violated federal law by calling a strike. To dramatize their complaint, they risk a $1,000 fine, a year in federal prison, and loss of jobs.

A young person who joins the postoffice as a letter carrier earns $6,176 a year to start. If he remains with the department for 22 years he will receive the top scale.

Officials of the National Association of Letter Carriers point out that their men are underpaid even when compared with municipal workers.

IN CHICAGO, for example, patrolmen and firemen receive $12,120 annually; police sergeants and fire lieutenants get $14,184; street sweepers and garbage men are paid $9,214; laborers at sanitary department incinerators receive $9,214, and garbage truck drivers get $9,776.

Local government building trades union workers not only have the same tenure guarantee as the postal workers, but earn the same union scale that is paid seasonal skilled craftsmen.

And the postal workers, who say their salaries have left them near the poverty line, will help pay the taxes that will go for wage increases won by Chicago teachers in their illegal 2-day strike last year. The teachers, pay scale ranges from $8,400 to $15,015.

POSTAL WORKERS say they were promised pay increases 16 months ago, but no action has been taken. The pay package has been delayed in Congress.

"The President and Congress are fighting over whether they should make this a semi-public corporation," said a Berwyn letter carrier. "The reform sure sounds good, but they haven't given us a dime. And then they turn around and vote themselves pay raises."

The carriers are upset about other issues. They want the postoffice to stop its policy of dropping a man one notch in pay when he is transferred from substitute to regular employe status.

"THEY GIVE YOU a promotion, but they take pay from you," said Dennis Brodie, president of local 1545 of the letter carriers union in Berwyn.

The carriers also want paid health and life insurance, a pension plan, and full retirement benefits after 20 years of service.

Critics often point out that the postal employes receive generous vacation benefits. Carriers receive 13 days' vacation during the first 3 years, 4 weeks from the 4th year thru the 14th year, and 26 days after 15 years.

"It sure sounds nice," said Brodie, "but what does all that vacation mean if you can't afford to go anywhere?"

BRODIE was critical of supervisors in the Berwyn postoffice.

"They don't follow set rules and regulations," Brodie said. "I was suspended for 5 days a while back for being late 4 times in 90 days. My supervisor was late 6 times in 14 days but nothing happened to him."

Outside the Berwyn postoffice, local police waved to the pickets and firemen dropped off a coffee cake for them.

Industry feeling pinch of walkout

★ from page 3

affected upstate New York and was spreading among cities of Connecticut.

A bomb scare brought work to a halt briefly this morning at a postoffice in Wash-

word on service men in Viet Nam to pensioners depending on the postman for their checks to corporate presidents involved in million dollar deals.

In New York City, banks, brokerage

HIGHER PAY NOW!
HIGHER PAY NOW!
NIXON GETS 100% WE'LL SETTLE FOR 50%
GOVERNMENT SHOULD PAY... FULL BENEFITS
LET MR. ZIP DELIVER THE MAIL !!!
TOP PAY RIGHT NOW
1st CLASS MAIL
1st CLASS PAY!

CB-22
SEARS, ROEBUCK AND CO. U.S.A. (7-2216)
MFG. INC

Above: Baltimore postmaster Warren Bloomberg placed "HOLD" signs on mailbags bound for New York City that were beginning to reach more than half-way to the ceiling.

Opposite: On March 19, 1970—two days into the strike—millions of pieces of mail in New York City alone simply stopped moving. Nationwide, hundreds of millions of pieces of mail, such as these parcels in Philadelphia, froze in place.

Right: In the Bronx and Manhattan, some postal facilities' entire shifts failed to report to work, resulting in massive backlogs of mail.

the uprising, court injunctions were served against officers of the Brooklyn and Manhattan-Bronx letter-carrier unions. In response, uniformed letter carriers stopped picketing—but members of the clerk and mail-handlers craft unions immediately took their places on the picket lines. Restraining orders were then issued against postal-clerk unions and individual picketers, but by then the entire system was shutting down: Solidarity with the New York strikers spread widely and quickly, with postal workers voting for walkouts at major mail facilities, local post offices, and substations around the country. Before long, 210,000 workers at more than 670 postal facilities in more than 30 major cities across 13 states ultimately would join the strike. Workrooms were deserted. Sorting facilities were ghost towns. Chicago's meltdown in 1966 was one thing; this was something else. Almost overnight what was thought impossible had become a national crisis: The Post Office had shut down.

On March 19, the second full day of the strike, millions of pieces of mail in New York City alone simply stopped moving. Wall Street stood still. Hundreds of mailbags bound for the city were sidetracked in the Midwest until workers became available to properly process them.

In Philadelphia, postal drivers heckled a coworker who dared to bring collected mail to a sorting facility empty of staff.

In Chicago, a lone supervisor found himself attempting to do the work of 74 employees.

By March 20, almost all of Milwaukee's 1,500 letter carriers marched on leaderless picket lines in front of local post offices.

In Parma, Ohio, a suburb of Cleveland, postal workers demonstrated their solidarity with their brothers in big-city New York, voting "no" to staying on the job.

On March 23, back in New York City, only 347 of its 10,729 employees reported to their shifts at the General Post Office. Most were supervisors and managers. Instead of walking the workroom floors, the rank and file were walking the picket lines.

Up to this point, the public had been oblivious to the plight of the postal workers, but they couldn't ignore the sudden breakdown of one of the nation's most important systems. The strike was front-page news across the country. *Time* magazine reported that mail "began piling up by the ton." Hundreds of millions of pieces of mail froze in place. Without skilled postal workers, the movement of letters, business mail, financial transactions, and government mailings ground to a halt. Shipments of live animals, including chicks, bees, ladybugs, and frogs, were also caught up in the paralyzed mail stream, with reluctant supervisors and managers left to tend to them. Perishable food and fruit shipments spoiled on workroom floors.

In Washington, D.C., millions of 1970 census questionnaires languished on the Government Printing Office's loading dock, immediately across the street from the capital's main post office, because no one was on duty to accept them. Elsewhere, newspapers and other periodicals piled up at publishers. Mortgage and utility bills weren't mailed, and payments had to be postponed. Bank statements stopped. Year-end tax filings were late. College admission letters were stuck in limbo. Any pension, Social Security, or welfare payments not already delivered were delayed.

That March, for a lucky few, draft notices to report to Vietnam weren't delivered.

The bulk of the mail in most major cities wasn't being collected, processed, or delivered. For the first time in 200 years, America's mail wasn't moving.

President Richard M. Nixon vowed to turn things around. The president would deliver. His first idea, if not a good one at the very least a provocative one, was to use the military. In a tactic dubbed "Operation Graphic Hand," Nixon sent almost 30,000 regular and reserve federal troops and the National Guard to New York City to move the mail. In publicity photos from the time, the Guard appeared diligent and effective.

They weren't fooling anyone.

The public expressed little confidence in the Guard's ability to restore mail service, and they were right. The reality? Soldiers and reservists were no substitute for career postal workers. In fact, though some of the activated Guardsmen were postal workers who could easily step into the job, most needed training—to put it lightly. They were clueless when it came to postal practices and procedures, and so were their superiors. The military's usual chain of command was no help. It took them extraordinary amounts of time to figure things out. Fittingly, as training led Guardsmen to realize the demanding nature of postal work, many signaled their solidarity with postal workers.

Using the military had quickly been revealed as a bandage at best and a publicity stunt at worst. But there was one silver lining: Although mobilizing the military failed to move much mail, it did provide a brief pause during which the strikers and government officials could meet to try to resolve their differences. And that allowed Winton Blount to spring into action.

★ ★ ★

Though some government officials were arguing for harsh retribution against the striking postal workers and their leaders, including injunctions, fines, and other punitive measures, Postmaster General Blount had kept a cool head from the beginning. He wisely treated the interruption as a "work stoppage" rather than a strike, making discussions between the two sides less contentious, and the possibility of reaching an agreement more likely. His instincts served him well: Though workers in places including New York City and St. Paul continued to hold out, by March 24, many had begun to return to their jobs at the urging of

Most of the National Guardsmen who were brought in to help move the mail were clueless when it came to postal practices and procedures. Their superiors were of little help.

WEATHER
Hazy sunshine today and Tuesday. Some fog and low clouds along the coast late night and early morning hours. Little temperature change. High today 78. Low tonight 54.

Citizen News

HOLLYWOOD
FINAL
LATE NEWS ★
COMPLETE SPORTS

Vol. 65 No. 299 | Established in 1900 | MONDAY, MARCH 23, 1970 | 24 | 10 Cents

TROOPS MOVE N.Y. MAIL

Today

mothers Brothers Go to ABC

"The Smothers Brothers Comedy Hour," a comedy-variety mmer series signaling the return of the celebrated-singer medians to network television, will premiere on the ABC levision network Wednesday, July 8, it was announced today
Please Turn to Pg. 9, Col. 1

opulation in County Up 19 Pct.

Population of Los Angeles County reached 7,207,556 on Jan. a gain of 1,164,800 or 19 per cent during the last decade, the unty Regional Planning Commission estimated today.

The growth rate during the early years in the decade was

EDITORIAL

Let's Pay A Living Wage!

What a contrast! Postal workers in the United States are on strike because they seek wages which will lift them from poverty to respectability.

The U.S. Federal Government is providing billions of dollars for foreign aid.

President: 'Work or No Talks'

President Nixon has ordered troops to begin the restoration of essential mail service in New York City.

The President said the supplementary military work force will be withdrawn as

Left to right: The first bicentennial stamp released in 1971, designed by Bruce N. Blackburn.; a block of four 10-cent bicentennial stamps issued on July 4, 1974, commemorating the First Continental Congress.

RINGING IN THE BICENTENNIAL

While the early 1970s were dotted with troubling events such as the postal workers' strike, an oil embargo causing huge lines at gas pumps, Watergate, and Vietnam, by the middle of the decade a shift started taking place. It was finally time for fireworks, picnics, and parades to celebrate America's bicentennial. Festivities began in April 1975 and continued through July 4, 1976. To contibute to the festivities, the Postal Service released an unprecedented number of commemorative stamps solely dedicated to America's 200 years of history–114 in total over a six-year period beginning in 1971. The first issuance was an eight-cent American Revolution bicentennial stamp highlighting a newly approved logo specific for the events. Bruce N. Blackburn designed the stylized five-pointed star in red, white, and blue that adorned souvenirs and was added to a flag flown on many government buildings.

This bicentennial issuance combined four stamps to form one image—in this case, John Trumbull's painting of the signing of the Declaration of Independence in Philadelphia on August 2, 1776.

Postmasters general surround President Nixon after the signing of the Postal Reform Act of 1970. From left: John A. Gronouski (1963–1965), J. Edward Day (1961–1963), James A. Farley (1933–1940), Nixon, Blount (1969–1972), Arthur E. Summerfield (1953–1961) Lawrence F. O'Brien (1965–1968), and W. Marvin Watson (1968–1969).

labor leaders, who saw there was now an opportunity to negotiate.

Obviously, Blount faced a daunting challenge: He'd known all along that the strike was about wages, but he didn't have any control over what employees were paid. Congress set federal wages, and at the last opportunity had delivered that measly 4 percent, and now, less than two weeks later, they weren't of a collective mind to do anything different. But Blount had to give the postal workers something, so he promised them that he'd find a way to negotiate a fair pay package once a significant number of workers returned to work. By March 25, even more of them were back on duty, and Blount kept his word. Good-faith negotiations got under way.

"And one night about three o'clock in the morning," Blount later remembered about April 2, 1970, "we reached a general agreement with the unions." The postal workers were granted an immediate 6 percent pay raise, including retroactive wage hikes. An additional 8 percent increase was pledged once effective postal-reorganization legislation was enacted. That extra 8 percent would put the total raise in the range postal employees had originally asked for. This was great news, but it was also terrible news. Blount still had no authority to set federal wages, and he hadn't secured authorization from the president to make any promises. And this was a big promise: The raises he'd agreed to amounted to billions of dollars.

The next morning, Blount went to the Oval Office to explain to President Nixon what he'd done. By 10:00, seven hours after reaching the agreement, he was acknowledging his error in judgment—promising money he wasn't allowed to promise—to the president. But he also made his case. Then all he could do was wait anxiously for the response.

When President Nixon made a decision, this is what he said: "I'll support what you did."

The pay hikes were going to stick. But now the Nixon administration had to push through legislation to reorganize the Post Office Department.

★ ★ ★

When Winton Blount had taken the job as postmaster general in January 1969, he'd set out on an exhaustive campaign to win over lawmakers with a plan to completely reform the Post Office Department, to make it into, essentially, a government-run corporation that took good ideas from the business practices of private industry but offered its wares to all Americans. Back then, of course, he had failed. But the strike had shaken something loose—now, finally, the reforms Blount was campaigning for, whose origins stretched back to the Kappel Commission Report following the Chicago meltdown in 1966, had a real chance at being put in place.

The reforms were sorely needed. The strike may have been the thing that got legislators to consider real change, but it was a symptom, not the underlying illness. The underlying illness, in the words of President Nixon, was obsolescence. "Our present postal system is obsolete," he had said a year earlier. "It has broken down; it is not what it ought to be for a nation of 200 million people."

In the 1970s, once you caught a glimpse of the Post Office's obsolescence—and the strike had certainly brought that to light—you started to see it everywhere.

The Post Office Department had come to be managed by an unwieldy conglomerate of governmental entities and committees that included the General Services Administration, the Civil Service Commission, the Interstate Commerce Commission, the Civil Aeronautics Board, the Bureau of the Budget, and the Government Accountability Office. These unlikely partners each had a hand in controlling various aspects of the department, such as finance and transportation.

Leadership was subject to the wild swings of the presidential spoils system: Because the postmaster general was presidentially appointed, the person holding the position could change with each newly elected president—which snowballed into extensive changes to upper management.

Personnel issues regarding pay, promotions, performance, and training had been long neglected. Years of mounting debt had grown to more than $1.4 billion by the end of 1970.

If Congress could pass a postal reform bill and get Nixon to sign it, for the first time in its history the Post Office Department would be an autonomous agency, theoretically able to address or avoid the systemic issues that had made it outdated.

Blount leaned hard on legislators, much as he had before, but the strike gave him leverage he hadn't previously had. On August 12, 1970, five months after the strike broke out, Congress willingly signed into law the Postal Reorganization Act.

The first paragraph of the act reads: "The United States Postal Service shall be operated as a basic and fundamental service provided to the people by the Government of the United States, authorized by the Constitution, created by Act of Congress, and supported by the people. The Postal Service shall have as its basic function the obligation to provide postal services to bind the Nation together through the personal, educational, literary, and business correspondence of the people. It shall provide prompt, reliable, and efficient services to patrons in all areas and shall render postal services to all communities. The costs of establishing and maintaining the Postal Service shall not be apportioned to impair the overall value of such service to the people."

While the basic mission of the mail service remained as before, so much else was different.

Under the new structure, oversight of the mail shifted from Congress to an 11-member Board of Governors, nine of whom were to be appointed by the president by and with the advice and consent of Congress, with the final two slots being filled by the postmaster general and the deputy postmaster general. These latter two roles were no longer appointed by the president but hired by the Board of Governors. Members were to have nine-year staggered terms.

The act granted postal unions the right to negotiate with the new management over wages, benefits, and working conditions. It allowed the new agency to address inefficiencies in operations.

At a news conference, Postmaster General Blount introduces six of the 11 members of the Board of Governors, from left to right: Theodore W. Braun, George Johnson, Crocker Nevin, Charles H. Codding, Patrick E. Haggerty, and Myron A. Wright.

In a day, Postmaster General Winton Blount went from a Cabinet-level postal official to the head of a large, corporation-like independent agency, with an official monopoly on mail delivery in the United States.

And, of course, the Post Office Department ceased to exist. It had had a good run, from 1795 to 1970. In its place was the United States Postal Service, with a new seal developed by the firm of famed industrial designer Raymond Loewy. It was a stylized bald eagle, poised to take flight.

With the passage of the 1970 Postal Reorganization Act, which transformed the United States Post Office Department into the United States Postal Service, a new seal was developed by the famed industrial designer Raymond Loewy. The design featured a stylized bald eagle, poised to take flight.

★ ★ ★

In the end, Blount got almost everything he wanted. *Almost*. One of the many things that needed to change did indeed change—but not in the fashion he'd hoped. He had no ability to set postage rates. "[We] never lost a thing except how to set rates," he noted on the 25th anniversary of the creation of the Postal Service. The approval of postage rates was placed in the hands of a brand-new Postal Rate Commission created by the Postal Reorganization Act that would receive rate-adjustment requests from the Postal Service and have 10 months to review them before approving or dismissing the request. But the process took even longer than that, as the rate adjustments themselves required the agency to build a full legal case, which itself took months. The process was meant to provide ample opportunities for the public to weigh in on the proposed rate changes, but in practice it hamstrung the Postal Service's ability to operate competitively. "We all knew that was a price we paid for getting postal reform," said Postmaster General Blount. Later postmasters general viewed it as perhaps too high a price. Benjamin Franklin Bailar, who served from 1975 to 1978, believed the Postal Rate Commission was a "major failure." "It's an impediment to the things the Postal Service has to do to be competitive," he said. But that's a story for later decades. The brand-new United States Postal Service would spend the rest of the 1970s figuring out how it worked.

After all, until 1970, postal workers had to beg Congress for every benefit they could get. But the Postal Reorganization Act enshrined into law the right to collective bargaining, covering everything from wages, health benefits, leave policies, and working conditions to safety issues, work schedules, grievance-resolution procedures, and cost-of-living adjustments. On January 20, 1971, the new USPS leadership participated in the first collective-bargaining session with seven postal unions, including those representing letter carriers, clerks, maintenance employees, motor vehicle service workers, special-delivery messengers, rural letter carriers, and mail handlers. Exactly six months later, on July 20, 1971, the USPS signed a two-year contract with the unions. It was the first collective-bargaining agreement in the history of the federal government, and the first to include cost-of-living adjustments and a no-layoff clause.

The Postal Reorganization Act also allowed for binding arbitration. Under this process, if the two sides can't reach an agreement under normal negotiations, a neutral third party listens to their arguments and comes up with a resolution that they must follow. Binding arbitration was invoked in 1972 to resolve a proposed hiring freeze, and in 1975 over the Postal Service's contribution to employee health insurance, which ultimately was increased from 65 percent to 75 percent. These were contentious negotiations—in 1975, members of the New York Metro Area Postal Workers Union marched in front of USPS headquarters in Washington, D.C., threatening another nationwide strike—but the infrastructure of the Postal Reorganization Act held.

The biggest test for the new agency came late in the decade, as an issue that had been growing for years came to a head. Going back to at least the 1950s, postal workers had been in a kind of

The first collective-bargaining session between representatives of the major postal unions and the United States Postal Service took place on January 20, 1971.

cold war against an enemy whose forces were constantly growing: technology. The sorters, edger-stackers, facer-cancelers, and the like that had by the 1970s been making postal workers more efficient for decades were also making them more dispensable. Though no automated system could completely obviate the need for human involvement in processing the mail at that time, in the 1970s the Postal Service had consolidated its high-speed equipment in 21 bulk mail centers located across the country. These "bulkers" symbolized the tension between man and machine, and in 1978, their workers very visibly joined demonstrations.

During that year's heated contract negotiations, the Postal Service sought to limit pay increases and increase mandatory overtime, as well as eliminate the no-layoff clause, which was hamstringing its ability to cut costs amid the rampant inflation that seized the nation near the end of the decade and an oil embargo that was making the fleet of postal vehicles more and more expensive. The unions, naturally, opposed these measures. Workers at the bulk mail center in Richmond, California—as well as other locations—staged wildcat walkouts. Eventually, Postmaster General Bill Bolger, who had taken the role that very same year, refused further negotiations

THE WORKER

10¢

AUGUST 1978 VOL. 1, NO. 5

Wildcats Kick Off P.O. Battle

Dump the Pact, Amnesty for all Fired Strikers

New York--At midnight, July 20, the 1975 postal contract expired. At the negotiations in Washington D.C. the clock was stopped while US Postal Service (USPS) officials and union big shots hammered out the final details of a settlement. Over 5½ hours later they announced to the waiting press that there would be no strike. All that remained was to push the new pact through.

But in front of the Bulk and Foreign Mail Center in Jersey City, NJ, a group of Tour 2 workers stood outside at shift change. They were angry and not at all ready to go back inside and start three years under a new contract which first reports suggested was a sellout. They were met by workers leaving the night tour, who added their anger at the stopped clock and at being made to work without a pact all night. The crowd grew, arguing and talking. Members of the NY-NJ Good Contract Committee took the lead in denouncing the sellout.

Tour 2 did not go into work. Tour 3 stayed out, too. The wildcat was on!

Three thousand miles away the Postal Workers and Mailhandlers locals at the San Francisco bulk in Richmond voted to strike. They were joined by the Meadows Facility near the Jersey Bulk. At each, the walkout was at least 75% effective.

Although the three wildcats were all over by the night of Tuesday, July 25, with both union hacks and Postal Service inspectors on the rampage against strikers, the walkouts had broken the situation wide open. Instead of the relatively smooth sellout those on top were hoping for, talk in stations from coast to coast was of the contract's shortcomings, the possibility of a national strike, and amnesty.

THE BATTLE LINES ARE DRAWN

even though prices are rising almost twice as fast.

The postal contract was very important to this program. The miners' strike had won them wage and cost of living increases totalling almost 40% over the next 3 years. To avoid a strike and sugarcoat some attacks, the railroad bosses gave up 37% over a 3 year contract. The government was desperate to

continued on page 6

The 1970s brought the final death knell for both railway and highway mail routes.

and called for binding arbitration. The final agreement proved largely beneficial to the postal workers, but layoff protections were modified: Employees on the job as of September 15, 1978, would continue to be protected from layoffs, but newer hires would gain such protections only after six years on the job. It was an agreement, but in some ways an uneasy one. At the end of a decade that had begun with a massive strike, seen the creation of a new postal agency, and unfurled amid labor unrest, postal workers were perhaps better off than they had been in decades. But it didn't feel that way; things still seemed shaky. They still saw themselves as having to fight for every gain. It was only in retrospect, in light of the challenges the new Postal Service would face in decades to come, that one might say that workers at the end of the 1970s were, yes, fortunate.

Opposite: With contracts set to expire at midnight on July 20, 1978, the postal union and the Postal Service said they had reached a new agreement. However, New Jersey bulk mail center's tour 2 and 3 shift workers were ready to put up a fight. "The Battle of the Bulk" ensued, resulting in the firing of 200 strikers and jeopardizing the renegotiation of future contracts.

★ ★ ★

The Post Office Department rode off into the sunset in the 1970s, and so did something else: The decade brought the final death knell for both railway and highway mail routes. More and more mail sectional sorting centers—facilities to sort and deliver between local post offices and network distribution centers—were created, making the routes unnecessary. A decline in train ridership and the construction of some 41,000 miles of interstates, plus a postwar boom in automobile sales, hurt the railways. Long-haul Star Routes, airmail, and mechanization—all led to highly accurate, high-speed postal automation, leaving the old routes high and dry. By 1971, only eight railway mail routes remained, and by 1974 only one HPO route was in service. That route, between Cleveland and Cincinnati, was terminated on June 30, 1974. Three years later, the lone surviving railway route, between New York City and Washington, D.C., was discontinued, on June 30, 1977.

Winston Lark, one of the crew members on that last railway mail run, was saddened by the loss. Years later, it still made him emotional. "1977, that was the last time that a working mail train rode the rails," Lark remembered in 1992. "It was a glorious affair, full of tears and all that.... I think that if the trains were still running today, I would still be on them, and I think almost everybody else would be too."

Bernie Bernstein, another railway worker, didn't work the last runs, but he went along for the ride anyway. The trains, he noted during a public symposium on the rise and demise of Railway Mail, "were loaded with postal officials, trainmen, and reporters." Everyone wanted to be along for the ride. With a smile, he added, "Most of the activity was in the club car, where people were feeling pretty good by the time the train rolled into Union Station."

The labor-centric focus of the 1970s could perhaps obscure exactly what was happening on this last ride of the rails. It wasn't just about the end of certain kinds of jobs, or certain internal processes, or certain ways of doing things. This was the end of an era of history. The end of a colorful, dangerous, swashbuckling, invigorating chapter of the story of mail in America.

John Kay was the supervisor aboard the last mail train run. As usual, he wore his .38-caliber Colt "Bankers Special" revolver—the gun issued back when mail trains were so valuable, they were prime targets for the most daring robbers—but he wasn't sure why. "I don't think the bandits knew we were around anymore," he joked. After that trip, like many other railway mail clerks, he retired.

Supervisor John Kay's last crew aboard the New York City to Washington, D.C., mail train on June 30, 1977.

UNIFORMS

When the Post Office was first established, carriers were not required to wear specific uniforms. In 1892, however, Postmaster General John Wanamaker asked for uniforms to be regulated across the country, as "good discipline requires a more strict enforcement of [the Post Office's] provisions."

The resulting uniforms were blue-gray in color, to differentiate them from the dark blue used by police, firemen, and other uniformed services. At that time, each carrier was required to wear a sack coat in the Postal Service's blue-gray color–specifically tailored to extend between the hip and the knee–and matching pants.

Postal-uniform hats have also evolved with time (and popular fashion trends). In the 1800s, you might have seen a carrier wearing a police-style helmet in the winter and a straw hat in the summer. As the century turned, the Post Office adopted a military-style hat much like those worn by Teddy Roosevelt and his Rough Riders during the Spanish-American War. Since then, bell-crown caps have come and gone, to be replaced by safari-like pith helmets and official USPS baseball caps.

A letter carrier's sack coat featuring two silver stars at the cuffs to denote 30 years in the city delivery service, 1906–1956.

A letter carrier's uniform jacket, reminiscent of President Dwight D. Eisenhower's World War II waist-length Army jacket, 1947–1948.

A female letter carrier's uniform jacket from 1968–1970 with gold-toned buttons, maroon braid at the cuffs, and a patch on each shoulder featuring the Post Office Department seal with "Letter Carrier" written above.

Women's Rainwear

SHORTY RAINCOAT
Waterproof nylon fingertip raincoat with hood. Fabric is coated both sides, stronger yet softer. Snap front, patch pocket. Postal Blue, Sm. (8-10), M (12-14), L (16-18), XL (20-24).
No. 11435 with hood $43.50

MATCHING PANTS
Postal Blue Nylon. Elasticized back with side snap adjustment. Waist sizes Sm., Med., Lrg., X-Large.
No. 11436 pants $20.95

RAINCOAT
Fabric of silky soft nylon twill. Coated inside and silicone treated outside so water runs off. Snap front. Two slash pockets. Postal Blue. Sizes 8-20.
No. 11432 .... $54.50

HOOD
No. 11433 (One size fits all) $15.50

Galoshes and Boots

Stretch rubber pocket boot. Non-skid soles. Lightweight, black. Sizes: Sm. 5-6, Med. 6½-7½, Lrg. 8-9, XL 9½-11.
No. 11357 .... $11.50

100% waterproof "leather-like" vinyl "over the sock" boots. Fluffy nylon fleece lining and insole. Black. Sizes: M 5-11. (No half sizes).
No. 11366 (10" boot) $16.95

Stretch rubber knee high boots that fold. Black. Sizes: Sm. 5½-6½, Med. 7-8, Lrg. 8½-9½, XL 10-11.
No. 11364 .... $11.50

26

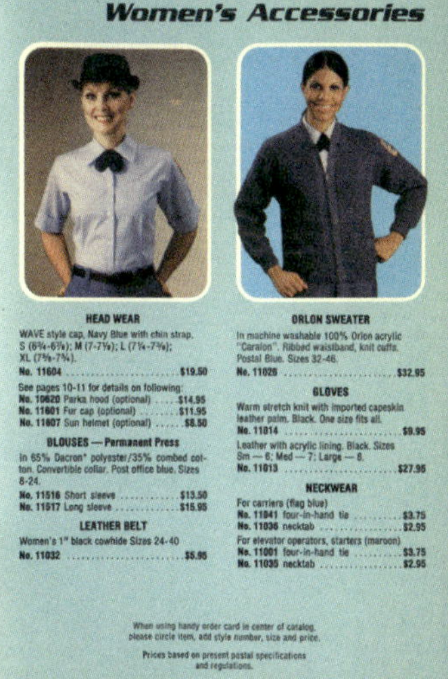

Women's Accessories

HEAD WEAR
WAVE style cap, Navy Blue with chin strap. S (6¾-6⅞); M (7-7⅛); L (7¼-7⅜); XL (7½-7¾).
No. 11604 .... $19.50

See pages 10-11 for details on following:
No. 10620 Parka hood (optional) $14.95
No. 11601 Fur cap (optional) $11.95
No. 11607 Sun helmet (optional) $8.50

BLOUSES — Permanent Press
In 65% Dacron* polyester/35% combed cotton. Convertible collar. Post office blue. Sizes 8-24.
No. 11516 Short sleeve $13.50
No. 11517 Long sleeve $15.95

LEATHER BELT
Women's 1" black cowhide Sizes 24-40
No. 11032 .... $5.95

ORLON SWEATER
In machine washable 100% Orlon acrylic "Caralon". Ribbed waistband, knit cuffs. Postal Blue. Sizes 32-46.
No. 11026 .... $32.95

GLOVES
Warm stretch knit with imported capeskin leather palm. Black. One size fits all.
No. 11014 .... $9.95
Leather with acrylic lining. Black. Sizes Sm — 6; Med — 7; Large — 8.
No. 11013 .... $27.95

NECKWEAR
For carriers (flag blue)
No. 11041 four-in-hand tie $3.75
No. 11036 necktab $2.95
For elevator operators, starters (maroon)
No. 11001 four-in-hand tie $3.75
No. 11035 necktab $2.95

When using handy order card in center of catalog, please circle item, add style number, size and price.

Prices based on present postal specifications and regulations.

27

DOUBLE-KNIT DRESS
In easy, flattering A-line design with darts. Ponte di Roma 100% Dacron* keeps its good looks. Short sleeves. Two side pockets. Back zipper. Dark blue with crisp white trim. 3" hem. Shoulder emblem.
No. 12160 .... $35.50
Sizes: Junior/Missy 5/6 to 15/16
Missy only — 18, 20
Half sizes — 14½ to ?4½

SWEATER
Attractive bulky knit, in machine washable 100% Orlon "Caralon". Two pockets, knit cuffs and two inch ribbed waistband. Postal Blue. Size 32-46.
No. 11026 .... $32.95

30

*DuPont Reg. TM

Women's Clerk Uniforms

POINTED-COLLAR BLOUSE
Fashionable, comfortable permanent press broadcloth 65% Dacron* and 35% combed cotton. 3¼" pointed collar. Roll up sleeves. Shoulder emblem. Colors: white, gold and blue.
No. 13570 gold $13.50
No. 13571 white $13.50
No. 11516 blue — half sleeve $13.50
No. 11517 blue — long sleeve $15.95
Sizes: 8 to 24 (size 12 equals 34)

SLACKS
Neatly tailored in smart looking, cool wearing Dacron*/ Orlon*/mohair. Side pocket. Easy waist-alteration feature. Regulation dark blue. Unfinished bottoms. Give waist size.
No. 12285 .... $27.50
Sizes 8-24

SKIRT
Smart, one-pocket skirt in wrinkle-resistant tropical cloth of 68% Dacron*, 25% acrylic and 7% mohair. Split waistband for easy alteration. Six gore styling with darts front and back. Dark blue. 2½" hem.
No. 12280 .... $27.50
Sizes: 8 to 24 (size 12 equals 26" waist)

When using handy order card in center of catalog, please circle item, add style number, size and price.

31

Fechheimer- the quality surcoat

The surcoat with the famous Fechheimer fit and an unmistakable look of quality. Finest Postal Blue fabric with regulation braid on sleeves. Finger-tip length, full cut for ease of movement. Single breasted design with buttons and full zipper. Permanent body and sleeve lining of quilted nylon. Insulated with Dacron* polyester fiber fill. Knit wristlets. Snap open side vents. With emblem and tab. Sizes: Reg. (34-50), Short (36-46), Long (36-50).

16 oz. Venetian gabardine 55% Dacron, 45% wool
No. 80903 .... $106.95

18 oz. serge, 55% Dacron and 45% wool
No. 80904 .... $109.95

Motor Vehicle Service surcoat. Same as 80903 but Ultramarine Blue sleeve braid with Vehicle Service tab
No. 32964 .... $106.95

- Double zipper lets you get at pants pockets easily. Zip up top zipper — then zip up bottom one to open coat from bottom.
- Snap open side vents insure greater freedom of action and comfort. Rugged, long wearing, sure-acting snaps.
- Knit elastic wristlets fit tight to wrists. Keep out cold air.
- Two deep, handy slash pockets plus two roomy breast pockets. Two additional pockets inside lining.
- Warm quilted lining of insulated thermal Dacron* polyester throughout body and sleeves.
- Drawstring inside surcoat lining can be drawn tight for increased warmth and comfort.
- Arm holes taped to prevent sagging.

Made-to-measure surcoats — see page 21.

Dickey & Chest Protector

Fits comfortably over chest to protect chest & neck from wind & cold. Heavy weight, bulky, top quality acrylic stretch knit. Washable — Postal Blue
No. 11022 One size fits all $7.50

6

*DuPont Reg. TM

Sweaters

BULKY KNIT SWEATERS
Favorite bulky-knit sweater. In machine washable 100% Orlon acrylic "Caralon". Postal Blue. Knit waist and cuffs. Wear as an outer garment or under coat or jacket. Sizes 36-50.
No. 11029 (Zip front — Orlon) $32.95

SCARF STYLE / **ZIP FRONT**
Zip front sweaters in machine washable 100% Orlon "Caralon" or 100% wool. Postal Blue. Two set-in pockets, double elbows, interlocking stitches for longer wear. Sizes 36-50.
No. 11028 (Scarf — Orlon) $30.50
No. 11023 (Scarf—wool: 36-46) $32.50
No. 11027 (Zip front — Orlon) $28.50

7

Pages from the 1981 Spring/Summer uniform collection for postal clerks and carriers.

A pillbox hat worn by a female letter carrier from Illinois, circa 1971.

A letter carrier's uniform cap and a Post Office Department cap badge, 1956–1970.

A 1980s uniform cap featuring the 1970s Post Office Department logo.

A Post Office Department pith helmet for use in the sun and rain, 1970s–1990.

Science & Industry
USA 20c

OBSTACLES, SCANDALS, POLITICS, AND NEW BEGINNINGS

In the early morning hours of May 18, 1980, Mount St. Helens was 9,677 feet tall, the fifth-highest mountain in Washington State. One of the crown jewels in the necklace of summits making up the Cascade Range in the Pacific Northwest, the symmetrical, snow-capped peak was so lovely that it was known as the Mount Fuji of America, in reference to the famous Japanese mountain that has captivated people for centuries. On clear days, people in Portland, Oregon, could see Mount St. Helens looming on the horizon, less than 60 miles to the north-northeast, not far from the Washington–Oregon border. But from the inside, Mount St. Helens is far less lovely. It's a volcano, filled with heat and plumbed with magma. In the early days of the 1980s, pressure was building.

A series of small earthquakes began on March 16. Hundreds took place over a series of days. On March 27, for the first time in more than 100 years, Mount St. Helens erupted. A crater nearly as wide as a football field was formed in the peak.

A week later, the mountain was topped by a lava dome the size of four football fields, and earthquakes were a constant. But then, on April 22, the mountain went quiet.

May 7: earthquakes, again. Over and over. After 10 days, a 450-foot bulge had formed on the north side of the mountain. Lots and lots of lava.

A towering ash plume erupted from Mount St. Helens over a period of nine hours on May 18, 1980.

Postal janitor Mox Simmerman shovels ash in front of Washington's Ephrata Post Office on May 19, 1980. He said the ash fallout from Mount St. Helens reminded him of the Dust Bowl.

The air intakes of postal Jeeps located within a 12-mile radius from the volcano were choked by volcanic debris in the air.

At 8:32 a.m. on Sunday, May 18, a 5.1-magnitude earthquake rocked the mountain. The bulge shook loose in a massive avalanche of dirt and debris. The pressurized magma inside the mountain was unleashed in an explosion that pushed the avalanche down its slopes at 300 miles per hour, flattening everything in its path. Soon this chain reaction freed the main chamber of the volcano, and ash shot straight up into the sky, a classic eruption. It blew the top off the mountain; the new crater was 1.8 miles across. Mount St. Helens spewed for nine hours. Take a football field and pile it 150 miles high with ash, and that's how much ash came out. Five hundred forty million tons worth. It fell on an area of 22,000 square miles. The eruption was the most destructive in North America's historical record.

At the end of May 18, 1980, Mount St. Helens was some 1,300 feet shorter than it had been at the start of the day.

The eruption created a major nightmare for the public, for government, for schools and businesses. And for the United States Postal Service.

But as usual, the Post Office's fortitude shone through, even when ash dimmed the sun.

The air intakes of postal Jeeps located within a 12-mile radius from the volcano were choked by volcanic debris in the air, but local postmasters used pantyhose as secondary air filters and kept moving. There were numerous closures and road restrictions, but by Tuesday, May 20, post offices were back open and serving customers who wanted to purchase stamps or mail letters. Incoming mail was diverted to Seattle until it could be delivered to points near the mountain. On May 22, Postmaster Mark M. Fuller stated that mail delivery in Spokane would resume along 192 mail routes and carriers would deliver "as much as we can" until all of the 3.5 million pieces of mail that had been stockpiled over four days were eventually sent to the people who were waiting for them.

Two days after the eruption, a curious headline appeared in Washington's *Tri-City Herald*, the newspaper serving the cities of Kennewick, Pasco, and Richland, 150 miles west of the mountain. "Cancel that ash," the front page blared. The ensuing story explained that people were mailing envelopes full of ash to one another, and it was clogging the cancellation machines. Bill Helm, postmaster at the Pasco Post Office, said six letters had already scattered ash all over other mail and machines. "It's a serious problem and really could damage equipment," he said. "If people want to mail ash I suggest they put it in a plastic bag and mail it in a small package."

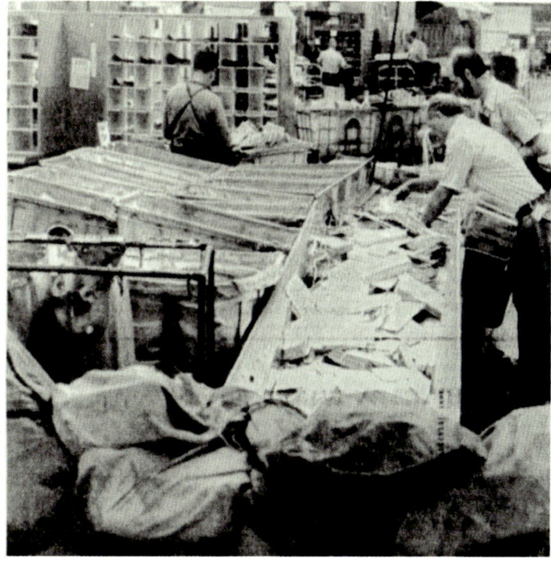

Right: Spokane's postal annex experienced a three-day backup of mail due to the eruption of Mount St. Helens.

The early 1980s saw a five-cent postal rate hike due to inflation and the rising cost of covering the USPS's expenses.

It was an inauspicious start to what would be a challenging decade—a challenging series of decades, really. The Postal Service was bigger and more complex than ever, still incredibly capable of moving a shocking volume of mail from person to person around the country. Throughout the 1980s and beyond, it never failed to take innovative approaches to the new technologies, like the computer, which would rapidly change the way people communicated with one another. But there was pressure building inside the system, even during the 1950s and 1960s. The reorganization in the 1970s that turned the Post Office Department into the Postal Service was an earthquake. But just as with Mount St. Helens, the earthquake wasn't the main event; it simply signaled an eruption to come. And erupt the U.S. Postal Service would, for decades to come, starting in the decade that began, so memorably, with a bang.

In October 1981, Postmaster General William Bolger spoke at the stamp-dedication ceremony commemorating James Hoban, the architect of the White House.

★ ★ ★

William F. Bolger had taken over as postmaster general in March 1978, and in 1979 the Postal Service turned a profit of nearly $300 million. Hopes were high. But they came down, fast. Bolger declared 1980 a "banner year." The reason? The USPS had run a $306 million deficit—just half of the $600 million that had been anticipated.

This wasn't just a Post Office issue. The economy in the United States was facing major challenges. Inflation reached an all-time high of 14 percent. But people seemed to be especially upset when Bolger took actions to help the Postal Service keep up. Newspaper editorials and the public were in a frenzy over rumors that a postage increase was coming. To respond to the rumors and quell fears of an immediate price hike, Bolger warned people that the next increase would happen in the spring of 1981. In June 1980, the New York *Daily News* asked six citizens: "Would a postage rate increase to 20 cents next year be a little too much for you?" The "yes" responses won out at a rate of 5 to 1. One person asked why the Postal Service should "be rewarded for the poor service and inefficient way in which it handles mail?" while a retiree stated "Absolutely...I have to live within a budget. Why can't the Postal Service...?" A high school student who didn't think it would be too much said, "It's still a bargain...the cheapest means of communication between distant points."

In March 1981, a three-cent postage rate increase was indeed approved, bringing the cost of a stamp to 18 cents. Yes, that was less than the 20-cent bump mentioned in the *Daily News* survey—but word of an additional two-cent hike came just seven months later. The Postal Service essentially had no choice. In an interview with *The Washington Post*, Robert L. Hardesty, chairman of the USPS Board of Governors, said about the increase, "Your local supermarket cannot sell you milk and bread and groceries at 1978 prices because it has to pay more for its goods, its wages, and its utilities...For the same reasons, the Postal Service cannot continue to deliver your mail at 1978 prices."

It didn't help that every rate change the postmaster general wanted came with a lag. Recall the one thing Winton Blount wanted but couldn't get when the Post Office Department was reorganized: the ability for the USPS to set its own rates. It took time to request and get approval from the Postal Rate Commission, and that was a problem as the country faced a challenging economic reality. Lacking the ability to nimbly adjust pricing, Bolger took the savvy approach of developing technology that could make the Postal Service more efficient, saving money. That worked like gangbusters. But he also looked for ways that technology, combined with the vast scale of the USPS, could create opportunities to *bring in* money. Every time he did that, he would inevitably find ash in the machine.

Three major initiatives that took shape on Bolger's watch illustrate the possibilities and the perils the Postal Service faced in the 1980s. Bolger would remain postmaster general only until 1985, so he never saw any of the three come fully to fruition. But by the time he left office, one thing was clear: The Postal Service was mired in an impossible situation, one in which it was now expected to run like a business but unable to freely innovate and compete.

In 1982, its computers began to read. Computer-powered single-line optical character readers (OCRs) could read the bottom line of the address on a piece of mail—the key part was the ZIP Code—and print a corresponding barcode that would allow automatic sorting into carriers' routes. With OCRs, a letter needed to be handled only once at the originating post office. This was the beginning of Bolger's first initiative, which aimed to make the Postal Service's sorting operation far more efficient.

With the introduction of ZIP+4 in 1983, the targeting of barcodes became even more precise, and the entire delivery operation took another leap. But *multiline* optical character readers were the true marvel. Multiline OCRs could read several lines of an address, meaning that most of the time, they could read the entire address on an envelope. A multiline OCR would look up the address in its internal directory and print the exact barcode for the piece of mail. Assuming the address was in the machine's directory, a piece of mail didn't even need to have a ZIP Code on it.

In 1986, the Postal Service accepted delivery of 106 second-generation single-line OCRs for use at 57 locations around the country. Each one processed an average of 857 pieces of flat mail

In the 1970s, most postal workers were still doing their jobs the same way they had 100 years earlier, including hand sorting. By the 1980s, however, this was starting to change with the introduction of new technologies like the optical character reader (OCR).

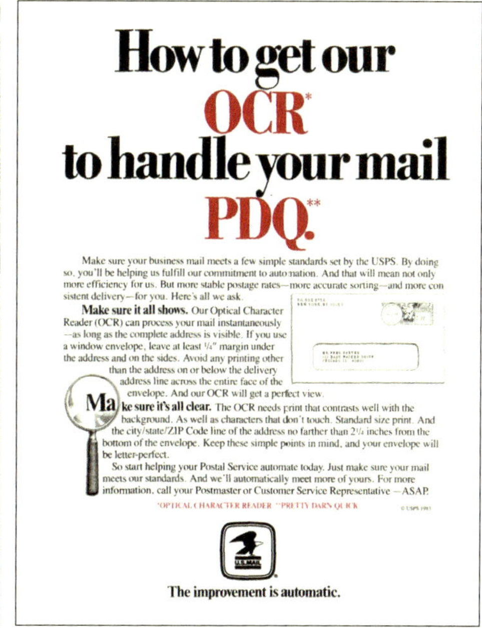

per work hour, versus 550 pieces per work hour processed manually. The goal was to continue installing OCRs at a rate of a dozen a month. (That same year, the Postal Service also installed 71 new barcode sorters.)

With these improvements, there were effectively three types of sorting being done by the USPS. The first was the old-fashioned version: fully manual. By 1986, that accounted for just 23 percent of the mail stream. Fifty-seven percent was being sorted mechanically, a process in which machines required human intervention. The final 20 percent of America's mail required no people at all. It was sorted automatically, with programmed robots like OCRs and barcode sorters. Two years later, automatically sorted mail had already cannibalized a good portion of the mechanical sorting: 34 percent was automated, and 48 percent was mechanized. Automation efforts would only continue to grow. In the late 1980s, a team in Fort Lauderdale, Florida, created a computer program that allowed for the processing of 30,000 letters per hour.

There was a simple and very good reason for the Postal Service to invest in these new machines: price. By the end of the decade, mechanical sorting was five times as expensive as automated sorting, and manual sorting was *nine times* as expensive. It cost 2.8 cents to sort a single piece of mail manually. That may not sound like a lot—until you multiply it by billions of pieces of mail per year. If he could save 2.5 cents per piece on sorting mailables, maybe Bolger and the USPS could survive the glacial pace of getting postage rates changed.

★ ★ ★

At the same time OCRs were making inroads in sorting, the USPS was also thinking about delivery. In the early 1980s, the service was in desperate need of a new delivery vehicle, one that could take it into the 21st century. The 1950s Jeep DJs that letter carriers had been using for years were far past their prime. They had been able workhorses, especially on unpaved roads, but now they were showing their age. Literally: They still bore the markings of the U.S. Post Office Department rather than the U.S. Postal Service.

Management wanted a vehicle that had longevity, one that wouldn't rust in the punishing conditions letter carriers braved to deliver the mail. Instead of going through the typical competitive bidding process that looked at off-the-shelf vehicles, the USPS decided to conduct competitive tests of new vehicles designed from the ground up. The USPS offered specifications, and manufacturers would offer test vehicles. On order: a weather-tight aluminum alloy body, with easy entrance and exit, that could accommodate a carrier standing six-foot-two and weighing about 230 pounds, as well as run 20 hours a day, seven days a week, month after month, year after year. In short, a Life Long Vehicle, or LLV, that would last at least a quarter of a century.

Three teams submitted models for testing: one led by aerospace contractor Grumman Allied Industries; one from American General, best known today as the maker of the military's Humvee; and a joint venture between trailer company Fruehauf and the General Automotive Corporation (not to be confused with General Motors,

The Jeep DJ (Dispatcher), painted in postal red, white, and blue and adorned with the new standing-eagle seal, was first added to the postal fleet in 1975 and was in use through 1984.

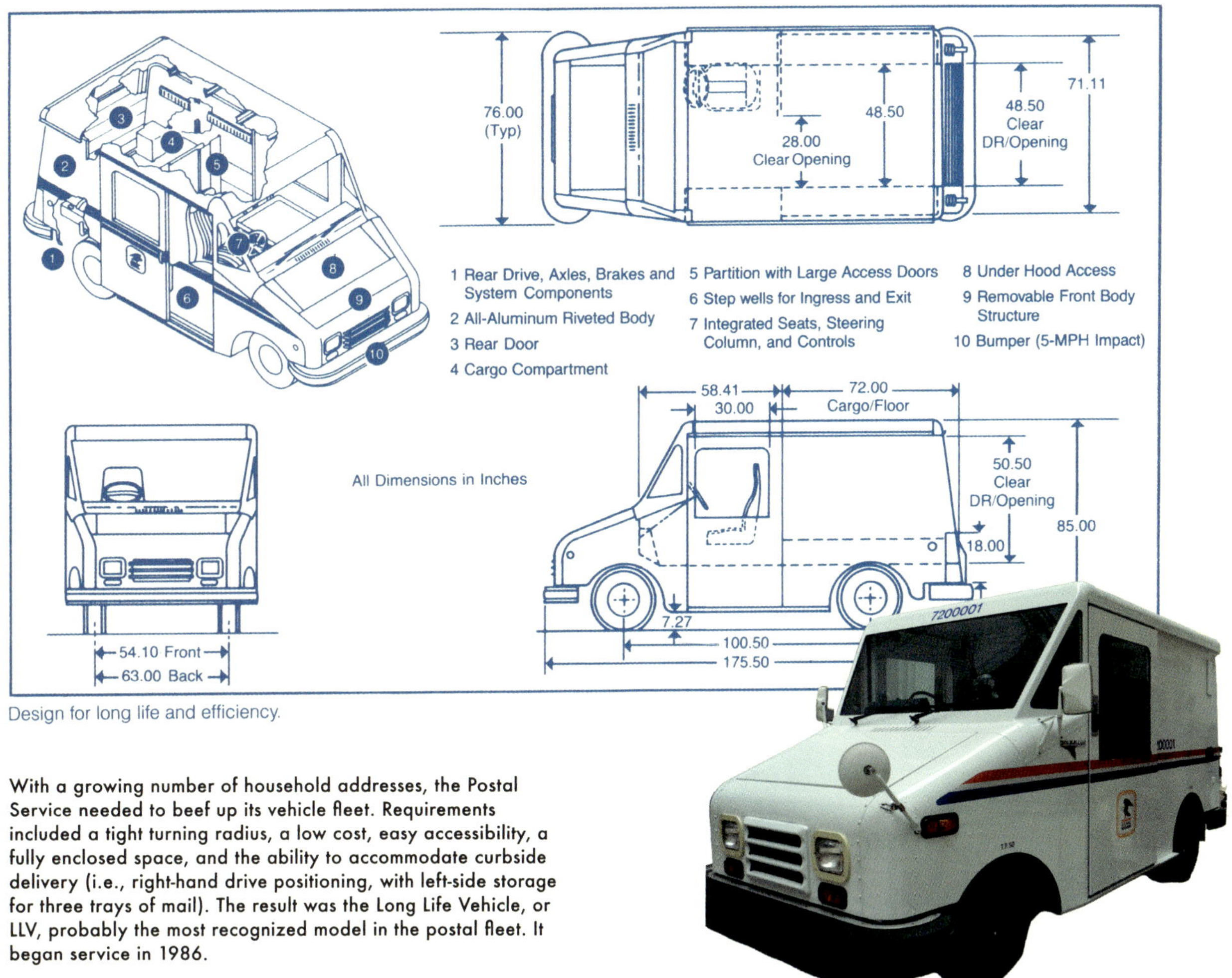

Design for long life and efficiency.

With a growing number of household addresses, the Postal Service needed to beef up its vehicle fleet. Requirements included a tight turning radius, a low cost, easy accessibility, a fully enclosed space, and the ability to accommodate curbside delivery (i.e., right-hand drive positioning, with left-side storage for three trays of mail). The result was the Long Life Vehicle, or LLV, probably the most recognized model in the postal fleet. It began service in 1986.

maker of, among others, Chevy and Cadillac vehicles). The testing was authorized in 1983 as a winner-take-all competition. At stake: contracts worth about $1 billion for 100,000 LLVs.

The vehicles were showcased in December 1984, and testing commenced in March 1985 at the Uniroyal Test Facility in Laredo, Texas. Each vehicle would perform a series of road durability trials for about 24,000 miles. There were nearly 1,000 miles of potholes, nearly 1,000 miles of cobblestones, more than 5,000 miles of pavement at highway speeds, and more than 11,000 miles of gravel. Bad weather did not delay the tests—in fact, it offered a chance to further prove endurance and maneuverability in rain and high winds.

Occasionally, cattle would wander onto the test track to liven things up.

After four months of grueling testing, only one vehicle remained running: the Grumman. Grumman's prize? The USPS purchased 99,150 vehicles for $11,651 each in April 1986—the largest vehicle order ever placed by the service. The LLVs went into production at Grumman's Montgomery, Pennsylvania, factory, where at the height of production, 100 mail trucks rolled off the line every day. Each was painted white with a beltline of red, white, and blue stripes running horizontally from front to back, directly under the side-door windows. The 1970 seal was placed on each door; the eagle would always face forward.

The LLVs began to appear on the streets a year later, on April 29, 1987. Over time they proved to have a few limitations: The lack of windows in the cargo area restricted visibility, and the placement of the side mirrors was a constant complaint among letter carriers. The pins in the door locks wore out quickly and enabled almost any key to unlock the vehicle, requiring the Postal Service to frequently replace lock cylinders. Because they rode low, snow was their mortal enemy. Nevertheless, the LLVs proved to be long-lived indeed: It was almost three decades before ProMaster vans began replacing them.

★ ★ ★

HOW E-COM WORKS

Customer transmits messages through private common carriers

Message received, printed, inserted into E-COM envelope, processed as First-Class Mail

Message delivered to home, office, or post office box

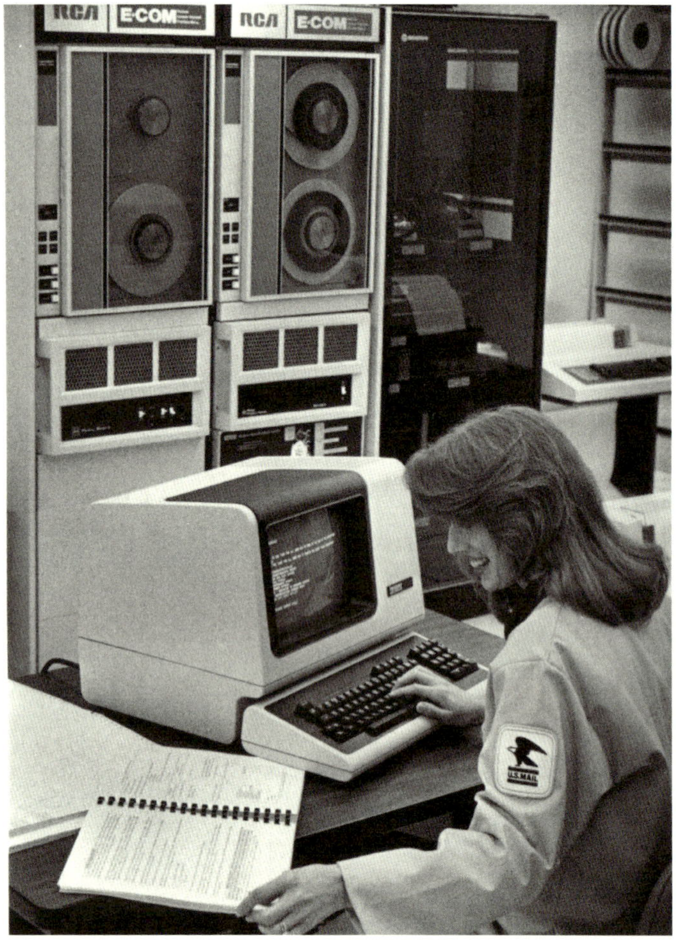

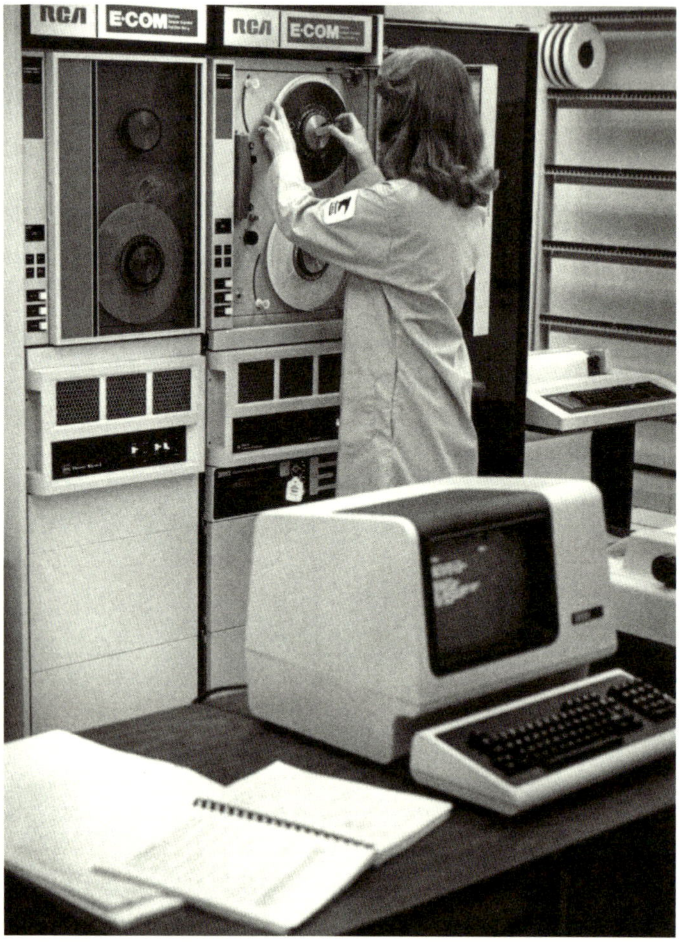

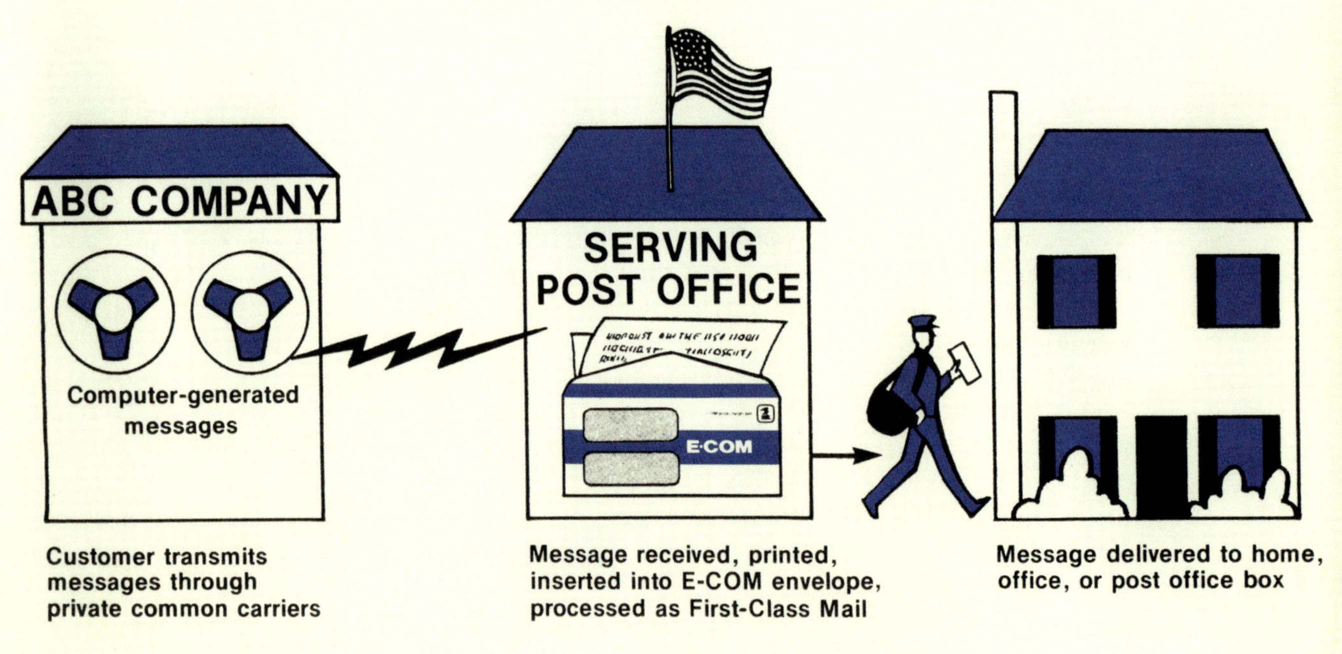

Opposite: The Postal Service continued innovating with Electronic Computer Originated Mail, or E-COM. It debuted on January 4, 1982. The RCA Government Communications System, under contract, would automatically print the message, put it in an envelope and seal it, and then add it to the first-class mail—all within two business days.

E-COM was a cross between an email and a letter.

Electronic Computer Originated Mail, or E-COM—a whole other kind of delivery—debuted on January 4, 1982. In today's terms, it was a cross between an email and a letter. The Postal Service transmitted electronically generated messages to one of 25 designated receiving facilities, where they were printed and placed into traditional envelopes for delivery. Aside from speed, E-COM offered the following benefit: The message was date-stamped by the Postal Service, which meant that it could be used to confirm delivery in court proceedings and to validate business transactions. Postmaster General Bolger sent out the first transmission: "We are very proud of this milestone in the history of the Postal Service and pleased to share this occasion with you through this message."

Just three months earlier, it had been unclear if the E-COM system would even see the light of day.

The Postal Service had always been interested in improving technology, whether that meant adopting the automobile or testing out rocket delivery. LLVs and OCRs were both technological improvements in that tradition. Optical character readers, in particular, were truly cutting-edge. But they were both bread-and-butter upgrades for the Postal Service: vehicles and mail handling, delivery and sorting. These are the Post Office's core functions. In 1982, under Bolger, the USPS made another technological leap. This one was in line with the agency's mission, in the sense that it was about moving information from person to person. But it also represented expansion into a new field. And that would portend its doom and foreshadow fights the Postal Service would find itself in for years.

If the USPS were to offer E-COM, Philip M. Walker of GTE Telenet told a hearing of the Subcommittee on Government Operations, "it would have accomplished a result which the Postal Rate Commission, the Federal Communications Commission and I believe the Congress have all sought to avoid; namely the Postal Service would have bootstrapped its way into direct competition with the private sector." It was October 1981, and GTE Telenet and another telecommunications company had come forward to formally protest the USPS getting involved in anything other than "hard-copy" mail. Electronic mail services, Walker argued, were really telecommunications services.

The October hearing wasn't the first protest but rather one in a series. E-COM surmounted every hurdle but always lost something along the way. In the late 1970s, when the idea for E-COM was first proposed, industry heavy hitters like AT&T raised objections. The Postal Rate Commission had the power not only to set the price for the service but also to approve it in the first place, and it took an exceptionally long time to review the proposal, ultimately ruling that the Postal Service had to contract out the actual electronic transmission of messages to telecom companies—raising E-COM's price. The Justice Department conducted an antitrust review, which prevented the USPS from lining up customers. Only when the Court of Appeals for the District of Columbia ruled that the service was in the clear, in April 1982, was Bolger able to get the offering off the ground.

Right: The cover of the new E-COM program asked, "What's blue and white and read all over?" Within three years, the service was discontinued.

INTELPOST

Another Experiment in Digital Mail

E-COM wasn't the only USPS service started this decade to transmit mailings digitally. INTELPOST, short for International Electronic Post, began in September 1980, offering services between Toronto, Washington, D.C., and New York City. It used facsimile scanners to convert letters, documents, graphics, and other messages into digital form, then had computers transmit them abroad. By late 1982, INTELPOST was available in Chicago, Houston, and San Francisco, and by 1984, American customers could reach people in the United Kingdom, the Netherlands, Argentina, West Germany, Switzerland, Hong Kong, France, Japan, Bangladesh, and Singapore.

It took the USPS an investment of more than $6 million to get to that point. Unfortunately, revenue over the same period amounted to just $58,080. When Herbert H. Schiller, assistant postmaster general, said in 1984 that "our traffic has been trivial," it marked the beginning of the end. That same year, the House Committee on Government Operations proclaimed it "a complete failure" and recommended it be shut down "as soon as practical." Because it involved a variety of international posts that still found the service useful, "as soon as practical" turned out to be 20 years later. In 2004, INTELPOST was finally and officially terminated.

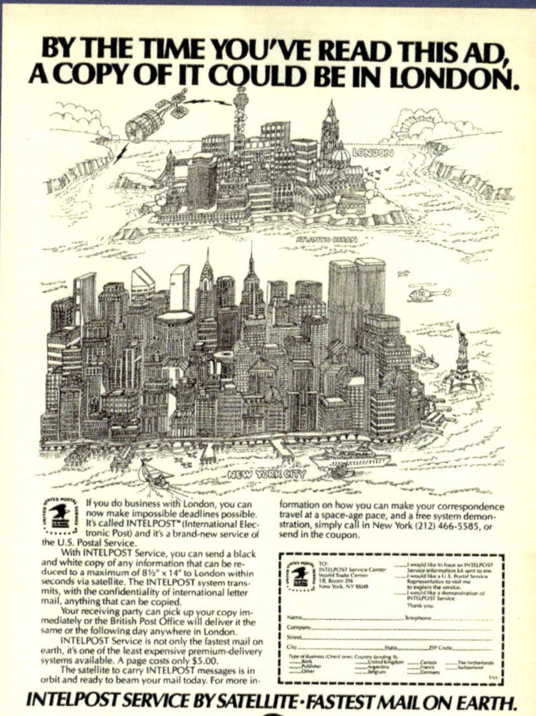

The "Fastest Mail on Earth" is what the USPS called its new invention, INTELPOST (International Electronic Post). The impossible became possible when, at just five dollars per page, customers could send a letter from New York City to London in record time.

A very young Paul N. Carlin began his career at the Post Office Department in 1969, when President Richard M. Nixon made him a liaison with Congress on postal issues. He became postmaster general on January 1, 1985.

Of course, there was still the problem of price.

Initially, the Postal Service had hoped to send E-COM messages for the same 15-cent price as a first-class stamp. But it quickly became clear that was not going to work. The Postal Rate Commission's ruling to force the USPS to contract out transmission was said to increase costs by 60 percent. E-COM was introduced with a two-page limit. The first page cost 26 cents, and the second cost five cents. In addition, there was an annual $50 fee for the service. In its first year, 3.2 million E-COM messages were sent. According to a study by the Cato Institute, each one lost the USPS $5.25.

In 1983, the USPS handled 15.3 million E-COM messages and requested a rate change to 31 cents for the first page and nine cents for the second. It took a year for the PRC to respond, and when it did, it approved higher rates: 52 cents for the first page and 15 cents for the second. The USPS Board of Governors declined—those rates would price the service right out of the market. When the PRC came back with 49 cents for the first page and 14 cents for the second, the board again declined, and this time suggested selling off or leasing the service to a private company.

There were no buyers.

Opposite: On Carlin's second day as PMG, he wrote a memo requesting a meeting of top managers to discuss operational and service performance. The meeting would never take place.

Bolger himself wasn't the one to shut E-COM down. This only seems fair; in a way, his push to get E-COM running was vindicated by the fact that the service helped the USPS stay out of the red during its years of operation, which also turned out to be Bolger's final years in office. He retired in 1985. It was his successor, Paul N. Carlin, who discontinued E-COM on September 2 of that year.

With the benefit of hindsight, it's hard not to see the end of E-COM as symbolic of something bigger. The end of a dream of the Postal Service, scarcely more than a decade after its birth, as a new, fresh, and vibrant organization. A dream of a Postal Service freer to experiment and innovate, and less encumbered by bureaucracy. Certainly, the end of E-COM coincides perfectly with the beginning of the USPS's slide, in the back half of the decade, into scandal, institutional failure, and violence. Fittingly, Carlin, the man who dropped the ax on E-COM, would soon meet an ax himself.

★ ★ ★

Carlin became the new postmaster general on January 1, 1985. The challenges began immediately: The day he took over, he had to deal with the merger of second-class mail—periodicals like newspapers, magazines, journals, and newsletters—into first-class mail, which raised delivery costs. He had to deal with an incredibly complex issue when the airlines were deregulated and consequently cut late-night flights, wreaking havoc on long-distance air transportation of mail. Overall, he was tasked with streamlining the Postal Service while investing in new technology, speeding up delivery, and cutting costs—no small task.

The Board of Governors was initially happy to have Carlin. He'd been with the USPS since 1969, before it was even the USPS. He arrived full of confidence, certain he understood the business, bureaucracy, and obstacles. What he may have failed to anticipate was that his greatest obstacle would be the Board of Governors itself.

The board had it out for Carlin, and it had nothing to do with job performance. He actually had a remarkably effective approach to running the USPS. He assembled roughly 800 key field managers in Chicago and tasked them with devising strategies to bring service performance standards up to acceptable levels while cutting unnecessary spending, a risky plan that no other postmaster general had tried before him. He

THE POSTMASTER GENERAL
Washington, DC 20260-0010

January 2, 1985

MEMORANDUM FOR J. KENNEDY

As my first act as Postmaster General, I have sent a copy of the book In Search of Excellence to each member of our management team who presently holds a position level 20 and above.

My purpose in doing this is to begin the process of developing our organization to the point that we will collectively become the model for not only the rest of the public sector, but also for the business community we serve.

We have made significant progress since postal reform. I believe we now have the mechanisms in place which will enable us to achieve greatness. Toward that objective, a good starting point is to acquaint our key managers, postmasters, and supervisors with the basic principles on which most excellent organizations are founded. This highly acclaimed study of management practices provides a fine beginning.

As a senior manager, I am asking that you make a further contribution to this effort. Take the time to set up an informal session with the level 20 and above members of your management team, preferably in a non-postal environment, to discuss the findings of this book and how the basic concepts presented can be applied to further improve the operational and service performance of your organizational unit. I suggest that this discussion session be in-depth and that it, therefore, be scheduled separate and distinct from normal operational meetings.

If you feel that your staff is too small to hold a meaningful discussion, it is suggested that you combine your session with a neighboring PCES manager. I ask that these sessions be completed by the end of April.

Thanks for your help. I am counting on you!

Paul N. Carlin

Paul N. Carlin

No, the Board of Governors had it out for Carlin because, to put it simply, they—or some of them—were corrupt and Carlin was not.

swore to not sacrifice service to reduce costs. During his term, Carlin implemented a labor law paying new workers less than those hired earlier, providing a cheaper workforce. At the same time, he, along with 33 top headquarters officials, took a 3.5 percent pay cut and had more than 700 postmasters from New York, Washington, D.C., Los Angeles, and other major cities forgo a 3.2 percent pay raise. The USPS had been running a $3 million-per-day deficit, but Carlin's engineering took it from a projected $750 million loss for the year to a profit of $250 million.

No, the Board of Governors had it out for Carlin because, to put it simply, they—or some of them—were corrupt and Carlin was not.

Almost everything could be traced back to a hotel-room meeting in March 1986. In attendance: Peter Voss, the vice chairman of the Board of Governors; John McKean and Ruth Peters, two other members of the board; and John Gnau of the public-relations firm John Gnau Associates. Before Carlin had become postmaster general, the USPS had been in the process of updating its mail-sorting equipment, and Voss had a company in mind. He'd told Recognition Equipment Incorporated (REI) to apply for the contracts with the help of Gnau's firm, and he intended to make sure they'd win. He and Peters had been pressuring Carlin to accept REI's bid. In the hotel room, the four conspirators hammered out a plan to direct the USPS deputy postmaster general to halt all contracts that extended old mail-sorting equipment, putting REI on a fast track.

On July 10, 1985, special legal counsel to the board, Gerald Rosberg, visited Carlin to inform him that the REI contract "could send someone to jail." Carlin halted the REI purchase four days later and requested help from the General Accounting Office and the Postal Inspectors to review the entire transaction.

And that was pretty much it for Paul N. Carlin.

A few months later, the board—including Voss and McKean—set in motion a review of Carlin's performance. Unsurprisingly, they decided a new postmaster general was required. The official reason given for Carlin's firing—surprising given his financial success—was a "changing environment that required a different marketplace perspective."

Despite the fact that Carlin was on his way out, the investigation he'd initiated continued. In April 1986—three months after Carlin officially left the job—an employee of Gnau's firm told investigators about a scheme of bribes and kickbacks. A month later, Voss pleaded guilty to three counts of bribery and embezzlement and resigned from the board. He admitted to taking $20,000, and that he stood to gain $600,000 in kickbacks if he helped REI win a $250 million Postal Service equipment contract. Court filings put it in much starker terms: One of the kickbacks was for a contract that, if allowed to go forward, would have cost the Postal Service $8 billion over a decade. Voss was sentenced to four and a half years in prison. Gnau and another employee of GAI pleaded guilty to conspiring to conceal their relationship with Voss as well as paying him thousands of dollars in kickbacks to win a postal contract for REI.

As for Carlin? He spent years trying to get his job back. He argued, in court, that he was removed "by a vote which was fraudulently procured by a corrupt postal governor." But the courts didn't want to get involved, and Carlin's crusade came to an end in 1988. The Board of Governors never offered any kind of settlement or apology. If there is any solace to be had for Carlin, it might be this: For the rest of the 1980s, postmaster general would be a pretty tough job. After Bolger held it down for the first five years of the decade—having already been there for the last two of the 1970s—Carlin was out in just one year, and there would be three more postmasters general before 1990.

Albert Casey, the president of American Airlines, was sworn in as the next postmaster general on January 7, 1986. He said he would serve at most nine months, only until a candidate could be found. He lasted seven, resigning on August 15. His successor seemed far more promising.

Preston R. Tisch was already a billionaire and widely respected business leader. He was appointed the day after Casey resigned and took his hiring as "license to overhaul the only federal bureaucracy with the capacity to operate like a Fortune 500 company." The board was excited to have Tisch and ready for vigor and creativity; as one contemporary report said, they "seemd to like [his] propensity for shaking up the status quo." They got another premature retirement.

Tisch announced he was through on January 5, 1988, 16 months after he took the job. Congress and the White House had required him to cut $430 million from the USPS budget. When his replacement, Anthony Frank, was announced a month later, part of the news was that the Post Office's budget would be cut $2 billion in 1988 and 1989. The frustration behind Tisch's retirement was unmistakable when he was quoted as saying, "The consequences of that are clear...We have been forced to defer virtually all new facility construction contracts and reduce planned expenditures for new equipment and customer convenience services." The post-office hours, sorting hours, and part-time employees' hours would all be cut. Small post offices would be closed. To add insult to injury, Congress also denied a three-cent postage increase that had already been approved by the PRC and would have taken effect in April 1988.

Frank had left his position as chairman and CEO of First Nationwide Financial Corp. to be the next postmaster general. He would bridge the 1980s and 1990s. Postal officials described his approach as "an aggressive program of cost management, revenue generation, and staff training designed to extend the time between rate increases, [and] improve employee relations." Frank had a lot of priorities, but one of the biggest was controlling labor costs. He stated, "Our employees have a right to expect personal respect, job security, good working conditions and wage comparability...But they also have a responsibility." He "[expected] postal labor unions to contribute by allowing greater flexibility in future contracts."

Frank's plan was sensible on paper, but he may have underestimated the extent to which all of the cost cutting, the scandal, and the generally insulting attitude toward the USPS's level of service was taking a toll on postal employees. Pressure. Pressure. Pressure. Just like Mount St. Helens. Inevitably, some of them were going to blow. The continuity between the 1980s and the 1990s was, unfortunately, to some extent about an aura of violence that surrounded the mail.

Left to right: Postmasters General Albert Casey, Preston R. Tisch, and Anthony Frank.

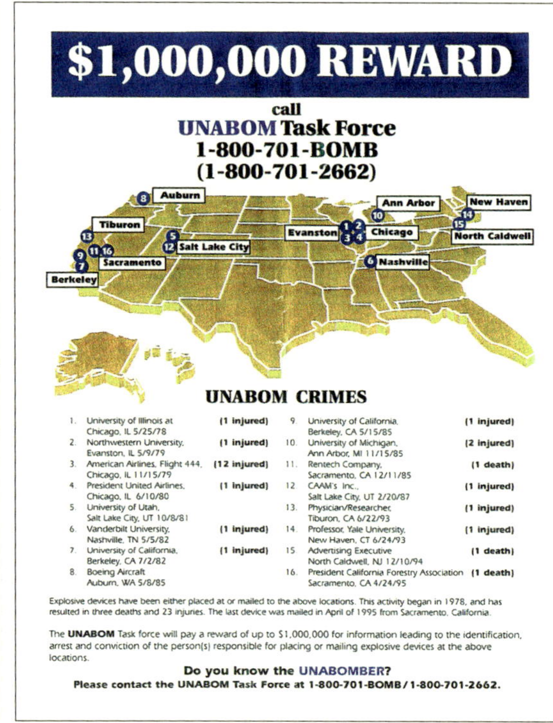

A 1987 sketch, left, of the Unabomber based on one witness's description as he was placing an explosive device behind CAAMS Inc., a computer rental store in Salt Lake City. The UNABOM Task Force—a joint effort of the FBI and the U.S. Postal Inspection Service—offered a $1 million reward in a 1995 poster (right) outlining the Unabomber's activity and asking for the public's help identifying him.

Throughout the 1980s, there was an unwanted intruder in parcel delivery: primitive, homemade bombs. The first actually showed up in May 1978, when an unmailed package with a return address from a professor at Northwestern University was found by a passerby and returned to the apparent sender. The professor in question had no knowledge of the package and notified the campus's security department. It exploded upon opening, injuring a security officer. Over the course of the 1980s, the bomber would mail four bombs, injuring four people. Because he initially seemed to target universities and airlines, he was known as the Unabomber. But the randomness of his attacks made the mail a source of fear in a way reminscent of past scares about letters spreading disease. It would be years before the Unabomber was caught.

But at least the Unabomber was unaffiliated with the Post Office; he was simply a random individual exploiting the mail's ability to deliver anything, anywhere, to the worst possible ends.

On August 20, 1986, at 7:00 a.m., Patrick Henry Sherrill, a part-time Postal Service employee in Edmond, Oklahoma, pulled two .45-caliber pistols and one .22-caliber handgun out of a mailbag and shot his coworkers, killing 14 and wounding six others. He then turned the gun on himself and died. It was not the first act of violence carried out in a post office, but it was, until then, the deadliest. Of those killed, two were supervisors, five were letter carriers, and seven were mail clerks. It was felt that Sherrill had retaliated against management for being verbally reprimanded the previous day for poor performance.

This would not be the last time tragedy would strike the USPS from the inside. The weight of decades of challenges would come down on the Postal Service with full force in the 1990s. Postal employees would not be spared, and all too often, they would turn their anger and despair on one another. Like the end of E-COM, the violence in Edmond would prove to be not a blip in history but a harbinger.

Pipe debris retrieved by the FBI from the Unabomber's February 1987 bombing at CAAMS Inc.

The Eagle Takes Flight

As the world shrunk in the 1980s, with new forms of communication–especially digital forms–making the planet feel smaller than ever, an experiment from the 1970s really took off: Express Mail. The service guaranteed 24-hour delivery out of 3,000 post offices in 1,200 cities. Express Mail drop-off used special blue collection boxes, and delivery required a recipient's signature, allowing the verification of the date and delivery time. It also had its own special stamp bearing a photograph, taken by NASA, of an eagle in flight in front of the Moon. In 1983, a major advertising campaign was launched to promote next-day service for packages up to two pounds.

The key to Express Mail was the "Eagle Air Network," an overnight air system for transporting First-Class, Express, and Priority Mail. The Postal Service assembled a partially branded fleet of 73 contracted cargo aircraft, operated by a variety of private airlines and based at an operations hub in Indianapolis. When mail arrived at the hub, it was triaged to ground transportation or outbound flights and departed fewer than four hours later. The fleet flew six nights per week to 46 cities.

How popular was Express Mail in the 1980s? Popular enough that during the 1985 holiday season, keeping up with demand required that USPS ally itself with one of its greatest rivals. In November 1985, newspapers across the country announced that the Postal Service had contracted for "15 days of mail transport with none other than its 'absolutely, positively overnight' foe Federal Express." FedEx was the lowest bidder to operate four routes, over which it would carry more than 200,000 pounds of mail per night. The contract lasted only through the Christmas rush, from December 3 to December 21. (The USPS and FedEx would join forces again 16 years later.) Despite the incredible volumes that had to be moved, the Eagle Air Network achieved exemplary service. In the last year of the decade, when the Postal Service's branded aircraft were transporting an average of 380,000 pounds of mail nightly–about 125,000 pounds of which were Express and Priority Mail–they boasted a 97.9 percent on-time performance.

32 USA
CINCO DE MAYO
USA 32
1998
32 USA
SPECTACLE REEF, LAKE HURON
USA 29 1992
Jan E. Matzeliger
Shoe Lasting Machine No.274,207
Patented March 20,1883
29
Black Heritage USA
Organ & Tissue Donation
Share your life...
USA 32
USA 22
1998
29 USA
ANNIE OAKLEY
USA 29
CIRCUS
HAPPY NEW YEAR!
USA 29
The Integrated Circuit
HANUKKAH USA 32
1996
1991 USA
32 USA

IS THE USPS THE GOVERNMENT OR A BUSINESS?

It happened so quickly.

On August 2, 1990, Iraq invaded its small neighboring country of Kuwait. On August 5, U.S. President George H. W. Bush famously vowed that "this aggression will not stand, this aggression against Kuwait." On August 7, Operation Desert Shield, a buildup of military forces from the United States and a large coalition of allied nations, kicked off. In January of the following year, after Iraq had blown through withdrawal deadlines set by the international community, combat operations commenced. Desert Storm, as this phase would be called, ended on February 28, 1991, with Kuwait liberated.

The Gulf War took just five days to begin and a little more than six months to come to an end.

As fast as it had come and gone, the Gulf War represented a major campaign for the United States Postal Service.

For one, the way the USPS served the military had evolved. Much earlier in the military's history, it had been established that each branch would manage its own mail program. That all changed in 1980, when the Defense Department and the Postal Service created a joint postal-service entity for all branches of the Armed Forces. The Military Postal Service Agency (MPSA) acted as an extension of the Postal Service beyond the boundaries of U.S. sovereignty, providing full postal services, where possible, for all Defense Department personnel overseas.

On top of that, the force the Post Office was serving had changed. For the first time, women were fully integrated into the war effort, deployed to combat zones as fighter pilots, rangers, Navy SEALs, and generals. Mothers, daughters, sisters, and nieces were fighting alongside those whose positions had predominantly been male. About 660,000 men and 40,000 women served in combat zones. Of course, past wars had mobilized all of society one way or another; but in the Gulf War, pretty much anyone of age could be overseas—and in dire need of mail service.

Is it any wonder, then, that the number of military post offices grew dramatically? During the Vietnam War, there were 24 MPOs delivering some 11 tons of daily mail. During the Gulf War, there were 203 MPOs, delivering 170 tons daily.

A sailor aboard the aircraft carrier USS *John F. Kennedy* (CV-67) on January 1, 1991—just four months into the war. More than 40,000 pounds of mail were delivered on the carrier during Operation Desert Shield.

THE GULF WAR

Even as telephone calls became less expensive, mail calls remained a critical morale booster during Operations Desert Shield and Desert Storm. The 4401st Air Postal Squadron, which had been stood up in 1986, deployed to Saudi Arabia on August 1, 1990, in order to run military post offices in the Persian Gulf region.

Like past wars, the Gulf War presented considerable logistical difficulties for mail service. More than 690,000 troops were deployed in support of the mission—approximately the population of the state of Wyoming—and were spread across an area the size of Alaska. The Free Mail program was reactivated and a new public letter-writing service campaign called "Any Serviceman," which allowed any citizen to write letters of appreciation to any member of the military, was launched.

Above, left to right:
A postal clerk sorts packages for Operation Desert Storm soldiers in the mailroom of the battleship USS *Missouri* (BB-63) on January 12, 1991; U.S. Navy crewmen carry mail sacks delivered by a Sea King helicopter from Helicopter

This pen-pal mailbox was located in Kay York's first-grade classroom at Stewardson-Strasburg Elementary School in Illinois in 1991. Her students exchanged letters with military personnel serving in the Persian Gulf. The box housed outgoing mail to members of the 8th Special Operations Squadron and also served as the repository for newly arrived letters from the servicemen and -women, who wrote the students during Operations Desert Shield and Desert Storm.

This ultimately led to Military Airlift Command being responsible for moving 150 to 170 tons of mail daily.

During the height of the Gulf War, the Postal Service operated more than 200 MPOs in Southwest Asia, with 1,300 full-time postal specialists helping support mail call. Due to potential terrorist threats, the Federal Aviation Administration started using X-rays, bomb dogs, decompression chambers, and parcel inspections to make sure nothing dangerous was being sent through the mail. Those screening techniques are still in use today.

The USPS faced increasing competition from companies such as FedEx, UPS, and DHL.

The surge in mail volume posed logistical challenges to postal operations across the country. But the mail endured. Facilities went into overdrive in the five processing locations for dispatching mail to Desert Shield and Desert Storm (Dallas, Chicago, New York City, San Francisco, and Dulles, Virginia). The MPSA expanded work shifts and operational schedules to expedite services. The automation readability team in Fayetteville, North Carolina, designed and printed pre-barcoded, machine-readable envelopes and distributed them to thousands of military families to help expedite mail to their loved ones overseas.

Military personnel abroad played no small part. Staff Sergeant Douglas Jarvis Jr.'s mail unit was processing more than 300,000 pounds of mail daily. He wrote to his local postmaster back in the States (Milton, Washington), Connie Methven, and asked her for official Postal Service gear that could make his outpost look authentic. "We are keeping your tradition alive," he wrote her, "but now you must add 'sandstorms' to your motto of 'Neither snow nor sleet nor gloom of night...'"

But the more important story the Gulf War told about the mail was a different one. In the military, the Postal Service's centuries-old monopoly on mail was intact, but everywhere else it was fading. The USPS faced increasing competition from companies

The Evansville Courier and Press covered the first-ever postmaster-general visit to the area on July 24, 1990. Anthony Frank was met by 75 union postal workers protesting changes in mail-service standards and plans to contract with private companies to hire up to 12,000 people to operate a new barcode system.

Courier photo by KEVIN SWANK

Postal workers march outside Downtown post office.

Postmaster general's visit picketed by postal workers

Mail service changes, private pacts protested

By PATRICK W. WATHEN
Senior staff writer

The first Evansville visit by a postmaster general came Tuesday at a time when postal authorities are seeking to cut manpower costs, increase revenue and alter service — goals that rile union postal employees.

Anthony Frank, postmaster general since 1988, was in town at the request of Evansville Postmaster Larry Howell to speak to the Rotary Club.

Frank

When he stopped briefly at the main post office Downtown, he was met by about 75 union pickets from throughout Indiana and parts of Kentucky.

Mark Greenwell, president of American Postal Workers Union Local 347, said union workers were protesting changes in mail service standards and a plan to contract with private companies that would hire up to 12,000 people to operate a bar code system the Postal Service hopes to use to process all of the mail by 1995.

"To us, this is the first step toward privatization," Greenwell said.

The postal workers union was joined by members of the National Association of Letter Carriers and Laborers International Union of North America.

As Frank's car left the post office for the Rotary meeting at the Executive Inn, protesters began chanting, "Frank must go."

During a news conference at Evansville Regional Airport, Frank said the automation program is going "extremely well." The postal service has test sites in Louisville and Nassau County, N.Y.

"It's saving money the American people expect us to save. It's saving money by replacing people with machines," Frank said.

But, he said, it is saving money without laying off postal employees and no layoffs will occur. During the past year, Frank said, 21,000 postal jobs have been eliminated through attrition.

"We're going to protect their jobs and give the American people what they want: lower and slower rates of increases," Frank said.

The Postal Service has proposed raising the price of a first-class stamp from 25 cents to 30 cents. Frank said the Postal Service will have to try to hold down costs.

"If our costs go up too high, major mailers will figure out how to do things more efficiently," he said.

Frank discounted privatization talk. "We're going to make ourselves so efficient, there will be no talk of privatization," he said.

He told Rotarians that about 2 percent of the mail that receives overnight delivery in the Evansville area now will take two days to arrive under service standard changes to go into effect later this month.

A survey of postal customers found that they expect local overnight service, but their definition of local was much narrower than the Postal Service's. "Some places, we were trying to go overnight 150 miles away," he said.

Nationally, 51 percent of the mail will be overnight, down from the current 55 percent, Frank said.

Labor negotiations, which begin Aug. 20, are going to be difficult, Frank predicted. But, he said, "we need labor restraint and I'm going to push for it, but not to the detriment of our people." Labor contracts expire in November.

When he became postmaster general in 1988, operating expenses were twice the rate of inflation, he said. In 1990, the Postal Service is operating 2 percent less than the inflation rate, a level Frank wants to maintain.

However, he said, postal rates must be increased from time to time. "Everyone is subject to inflation."

A postal clerk sorts mail in the post office aboard the battleship USS *Missouri* (BB-63). The military estimated that each soldier deployed during Operation Desert Shield would receive approximately 1.88 pounds of mail.

such as FedEx, UPS, and DHL. (Though Amazon started in 1994, it did not deliver its own packages until 2014 with the launch of "Fulfilled by Amazon.") Meanwhile, the world was embracing computer technologies, including a new way of communicating: email, no stamps required. As the decade began, about three million people worldwide were using internet services; at its end, the number was upward of 10 million. In the whirlwind war that kicked off the decade, the USPS was masterful and unchallenged, delivering exemplary service. In a home country that was changing faster than ever, the 1990s would evince a much different record.

★ ★ ★

In the early 1990s, one journalist called U.S. postmaster general "the most thankless job in America." This might as well have been incorporated into the oath each new officeholder spoke as they were sworn in.

Anthony Frank almost certainly agreed with the journalist's assessment. Since its reorganization as the U.S. Postal Service, the mail was supposed to be run as a business, and Frank wholeheartedly believed in that idea. It was both his greatest strength and his greatest weakness. He was praised for cutting costs and bringing efficiency to mail distribution. Mailings increased by more than five million pieces per year over his tenure, and the USPS turned a profit two of the years he was in office.

On the other hand, the costs of those cost savings were great. Take one of Frank's most notorious cost-cutting plans: He aimed to eliminate 47,000 jobs by 1995—the size of a small town! When Frank visited Evansville, Indiana, in January 1992, he was met with about 75 picketers from the American Postal Workers Union Local 347, the National Association of Letter Carriers, and Laborers International Union of North America. "Frank must go!" they chanted.

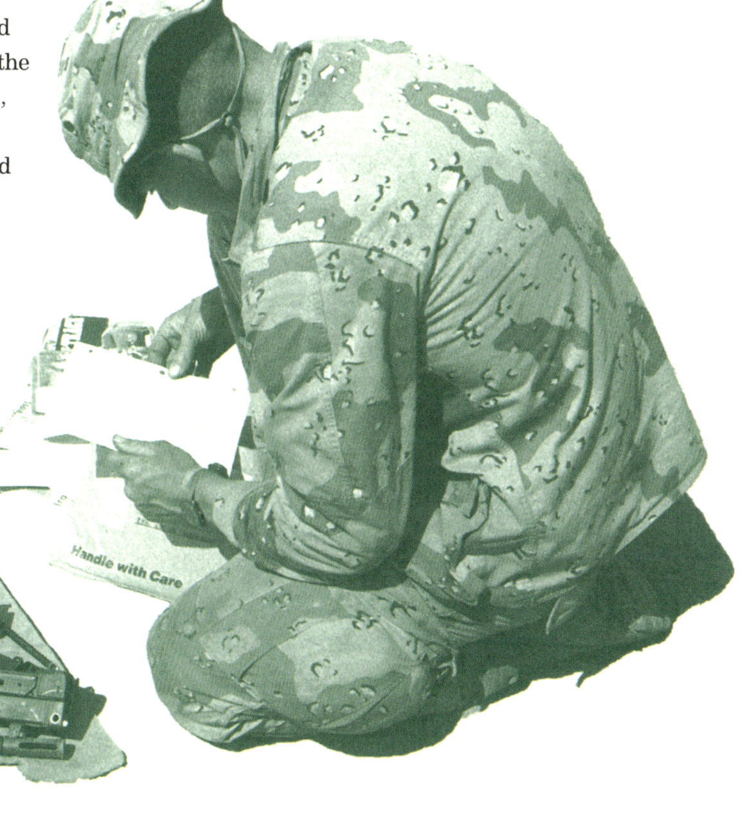

First Lieutenant Timothy Harryman of the 1st Marine Division pauses while cleaning his rifle to read his mail. This was the first mail call since his unit was deployed to Kuwait during Operation Desert Storm.

The Elvis Stamp

In 1983, Pat Geiger, the head of the Elvis Postal Stamp Campaign, began petitioning for the Postal Service to issue an Elvis Presley stamp. But she confronted a problem: The USPS had a rule that no one could appear on a stamp before the 10th anniversary of their death, and Elvis had died just six years earlier, in 1977. By the time 1987 rolled around, there was a groundswell of support for the stamp. But there was also a group of people who, believing Elvis to be a flawed figure, were staunchly opposed–and their ranks included Postmaster General Anthony Frank. When Frank took office in 1988, he declared that there would be no Elvis stamp.

Geiger, however, persevered. She marshaled devotees of the King of Rock and Roll to send letters to the Postal Service pleading for a stamp. "I don't think we've ever been pushed harder on a subject than we were on Elvis," Frank said. "We've got over 60,000 letters on the topic. I get people badgering me on the street..." The pressure was on. And despite his professed opposition to an Elvis stamp, Frank was somewhat sympathetic to the idea–one of his goals was to bring cultural relevance to the postage-stamp program.

So in the early 1990s, a process commenced like no other in the Postal Service's history. The USPS commissioned eight artists to develop potential Elvis stamp designs. There were no restrictions on era, career, or approach. Out of that commission came 60 artworks that ranged in style from watercolor to abstract modernism. These were whittled down to two, and then, between April 6, 1992, and April 24, 1992, the American public voted. Each of the roughly 1.2 million participating voters submitted their ballot on a 19-cent postcard that was available at all post offices. The choice came down to a simple question. Did Americans want to remember the young, svelte Elvis with slicked-back hair from the 1950s? Or the older, heavy-set, mutton-chopped Elvis who embodied a certain era of Las Vegas?

In the end, the voters' choice of which to celebrate was clear: More than 75 percent preferred the young Elvis design. On January 8, 1993–what would have been the singer's 58th birthday–the new stamp was dedicated at his home, Graceland, in Memphis, Tennessee. Geiger had gotten her way. But Frank, who stepped down just a few months before the stamp was released, and the Post Office had gotten something, too: They'd been the center of the cultural conversation, the source of a joyful diversion for millions of Americans. "It's important to have fun," Frank stated in 1992. "The American people are not having a lot of fun right now, so if this adds to fun, that's good."

The USPS commissioned eight artists to develop potential Elvis stamp designs in a wide range of styles.

ive more information in 1993
ıe Elvis stamp please fill in
me and address below:
al)

Mrs Ms

Address

City

State ZIP Code

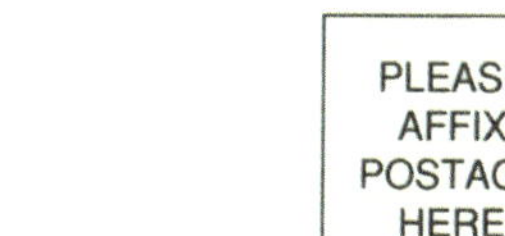

ELVIS POLL
PO BOX ELVIS
MEMPHIS TN 38101-1001

The USPS designed this 19-cent postcard for Americans to cast their vote for the new Elvis stamp. Roughly 1.2 million of the postcards were submitted.

The USPS released this $1 stamp on September 29, 1991, for the 1992 Winter and Summer Olympics, for which USPS was a worldwide sponsor.

But all business leaders face tough decisions. For every time they get the business to grow, there's a point when they need to let people go. The difference, as Frank saw it, was that the postmaster general had a handicap. In 1988, the year he was sworn in, he voiced his displeasure with how the USPS was run in an interview with *The New York Times*. "Can you believe it, we have no say over what we can charge for our services," he said. "When our competition cuts its prices or changes its price structure, it takes us almost a year to get some kind of change through. The USPS's competitors like UPS and FedEx can turn on a dime to adapt to market changes, whereas the Postal Service has to wait almost a year to clear all changes through the independent Postal Rate Commission."

One of Frank's strategies for getting around this was to innovate in areas not reliant on the commission. He oversaw the introduction of an Elvis stamp, which was a huge success and brought new cultural relevance to the USPS. But many of his other projects faced criticism. He initiated an Olympic sponsorship program that included the creation of an Office of Olympic Marketing. Twenty-three employees attended the Winter Olympics in Albertville, France, and "Touch the Torch" ceremonies delighted postal employees around the country. Unfortunately, the $5.5 million the office raised went directly to the Olympics. He also made plans to broaden the reach of the USPS by putting a post office in every Sears store—but was met with hostility from unions and organizations such as the New York City Central Labor Council, which represented 1.5 million workers.

It all proved to be too much, and in January 1992, Frank resigned. His initial assessment of the job had been right. He simply couldn't be as nimble as his competitors, and too often the ways left to him to keep costs in check were killing morale.

The same month Frank left office, he spoke with *The Washington Post*. One of his greatest regrets, he said, was "his inability to overhaul the 'corporate culture.'" This was about more than just the structure and operations of the USPS; by this time, postal employees had already begun shooting one another. But even setting that aside for the moment, the business of the place didn't look like it was about to get any better. After all, Frank's successor was known as "Carvin' Marvin."

★ ★ ★

Marvin Runyon was the sixth postmaster general in fewer than eight years. He was known for his time leading the Tennessee Valley Authority, an electric utility that also blurred the line between the public and private sectors. Famously, he had slashed 40 percent of the TVA's workforce, including 7,000 people in a single day, earning his gruesome nickname. Postal workers weren't expecting much better. Runyon's mantra was "messages, merchandise, and money," by which he meant new technology, new businesses—and a reduction in labor costs.

Right: The commemorative Elvis Presley stamp went on sale in Memphis in 1993, on Elvis's birthday, January 8. One day later, it was released nationwide.

Runyon felt that the USPS needed to act and run more like a business than a federal agency.

Within his first 90 days at the helm of the Postal Service, he summarily wiped out middle-management positions and offered incentives to USPS employees for early retirement. The cumulative effect was the loss of about 30,000 positions from the 729,000 it had in early 1992. The remaining employees had to reapply for their jobs, a first for the Postal Service.

But if Runyon was somewhat brutal, it is only fair to say that he was also strategic. Coming into the position, he was combatting the bloated, bureaucratic mindset of the agency, which had become imbued with an "autocratic management style." Runyon saw people, including workaday employees and customers, as crucial to the Postal Service's success. In a 1993 speech, he argued for a "shift...from operation-driven, cost-driven, authoritarian, and risk-averse to one that is success-oriented, people-oriented, and customer driven." He felt that the USPS needed to act and run more like a business than a federal agency. Runyon also had a vision. From the very beginning of his term as postmaster general, he predicted—correctly—that a "rapid shift to electronic communications will radically alter the Postal Service's mail mix and put increased competitive pressure on the organization." Runyon thought the only way the Postal Service could remain competitive was to build highly automated postal plants, where high-tech capabilities like scanning, tracking, and tracing would keep costs down and quality up. So that is what he set out to do.

The development and installation of high-speed letter-sorting equipment, started during Frank's tenure, was continued. From 1993 to 2001, letter delivery productivity improved by nearly 50 percent. This new proficiency allowed the Postal Service to reduce the number of city delivery routes by 4,100 from 1995 to 2001 while simultaneously absorbing an approximate 4 percent increase in the number of delivery points.

In addition to the high-speed sorting, a nationwide, delivery-point-specific coding system was instituted in 1993: Postal Service equipment and large-volume mailers began applying 11-digit barcodes that allowed barcode sorters to sort mail into the order in which carriers deliver it. (This built on the nine-digit ZIP+4 system that had been introduced in the 1980s.)

The delivery barcode sorter (DBCS), an automated letter-sorting machine used for barcoded letter-size mail, was introduced in 1990. This machine can sort between 35,000 to 40,000 letters per hour with about 99 percent accuracy.

More than nine out of 10 Americans gave the USPS the highest rating of confidence.

But Runyon knew even that wasn't going to be enough. Per his mantra, new lines of business were needed if the Postal Service was to make more money without sending the price of stamps to the moon. (This would have required the highly unlikely approval of the Postal Rate Commission, anyway.) Runyon approved of selling merchandise in the 40,000 USPS locations across the country—everything from notecards to stuffed animals. Far more important than selling merch, though, were Runyon's efforts to get the Postal Service a piece of the rapidly growing pie that was online retail.

★ ★ ★

The proliferation was astounding. In 1995, the internet boasted approximately 23,000 websites. A decade later, there were more than 55 million. With the introduction of search engines such as Yahoo in 1994 and Google in 1997, and the appearance of e-commerce sites like Amazon in 1994 and eBay in 1995, the internet provided near-instantaneous and inexpensive access to buyers and sellers. Though these sites did reduce the volume of some traditional advertising mail, the Postal Service's losses were more than offset by increased package and parcel business resulting from content searches and online sales.

At about the same time, in the early 1990s, the USPS became aware that mechanical postage meters, which private companies used to charge postage for all that online buying and selling, were being tampered with. A call for private-sector proposals for online postage solutions that might be more secure led two entrepreneurs to suggest duplicating the meter functionality with a home computer and printer. And so was born a service that came to be called PC Postage® or Smartstamp, in a nod to the personal computer.

Testing began in March 1998, just months before Runyon would step down from his role. Approved vendors would create digitally encoded, two-dimensional postage barcodes that patrons could print directly onto envelopes or address labels using personal computers and the internet. The first provider to hit the market, E-Stamp, launched nationwide in August 1999.

The Postal Service was surprised by the positive impact of providing convenient postage and mailing solutions on facilitating the growth of online markets and auction websites. In combination with some of Runyon's other improvements, USPS profits rose from just under $1 billion to more than $3.5 billion in 1998. The same year, a well-regarded survey found that the Postal Service held the topmost favorability rating of all federal agencies. More than nine out of 10 Americans gave the USPS the highest rating of confidence. (The Postal Service continues to be rated highly today.) Unions may have disliked him for his modernization and automation efforts—and yes, many postal employees had lost their jobs—but what Carvin' Marvin was doing, at least from a business standpoint, was working.

But what is that worth if people are losing their lives?

★ ★ ★

The mail bombs that had begun appearing all the way back in the late 1970s and continued throughout the 1980s remained a problem in the 1990s. The Unabomber was still at large; there were four attacks in the decade, and two of the three people who died from his bombs were killed in 1994 and 1995. The public was so terrorized by the possibility that they could reach for their mail and open up a deadly weapon that the Postal Service had been forced to launch a major mail-bomb-awareness initiative focused on telltale signs of explosive devices, such as a missing return address, overpaid postage, or chemical staining of the package's outer wrappings. All the while, the Postal Inspection Service, the FBI, and other agencies were racing to discover the Unabomber's identity.

As the decade dawned, investigators knew very little about the bomber. It seemed likely that he had lived at some point in Chicago and spent time in Salt Lake City and San Francisco. The bomber also appeared to be somehow associated with academia, but that link was uncertain because the victims seemed to have been selected using a library search of academic publications. Investigators were also thwarted by the bomber's use of common components in making his explosive devices.

Then, in 1995, there was a break in the case.

Writing anonymously, the Unabomber began contacting major news publications requesting that they publish what would come to be known as "the Unabomber Manifesto," officially titled "Industrial Society and Its Future." In exchange, he said the bombings would end. Federal law-enforcement leaders including Attorney General Janet Reno agreed to publish the suspect's 35,000-word essay in *The Washington Post* and *The New York Times*. When a man named David Kaczynski read the manifesto, he thought he recognized the prose and some of the themes. They reminded him of his brother, Ted. David decided to inform investigators. When he told them about his older brother's past, all the pieces clicked into place. Ted had grown up in Chicago, entered Harvard at age 16, graduated with a PhD in mathematics, and began teaching at age 25 at the University of California at Berkeley, where two of the bombings occurred. He had also spent time in Salt Lake City. David provided handwriting samples and gave investigators his brother's likely whereabouts: Ted lived like a hermit in a primitive 10-foot-by 14-foot plywood and tar-paper cabin the brothers had built near Lincoln, Montana.

Theodore "Ted" Kaczynski was arrested at the cabin on April 3, 1996. A subsequent search of the hut, which lacked running water and electricity, revealed bomb-making materials, including a pair of explosive devices he was about to mail, and other incriminating evidence. Kaczynski pleaded guilty in January 1998 and was sentenced to four life sentences plus 30 years without the possibility of parole. (He died in prison in 2023.) The Unabomber's decades of mail-bound terror had come to an end.

But there's something else important to be said about Kaczynski. At a time when Postal Service employees were becoming known for shocking acts of murder and suicide, it's hard not to feel that Kaczynski may have unwittingly shed light on some of the most deep-seated underlying causes. In "Industrial Society and Its Future," Kaczynski argued that technological advances have been a "disaster" for humankind, that they offer meaningful benefits but "have destabilized society, have made life unfulfilling, have subjected human beings to indignities." New technologies, he wrote, "will probably lead to greater social disruption and psychological suffering, and it may lead to increased physical suffering." He wrote of the long-term outcome of technological advancement in terms that, sadly, Postal Service employees—who'd had their prestige reduced, their pay suppressed, and their jobs automated into oblivion—might have recognized: "permanently reducing human beings and many other living organisms to engineered products and mere cogs in the social machine."

★ ★ ★

A number of the postal inspectors who worked the case were at the scene of Kaczynski's arrest, left to right: Robin Shipman, John Burkhardt, Tom Berthiume, Brad Reeves, Gary Bridgewater, and Paul Wilhelmus.

These posters are required to be displayed in postal work areas for every employee to review. The USPS initiated a zero-tolerance policy against violence and behavior in the workplace in 1992 that was signed by the unions and management representatives. The policy has been refined and updated each year since then.

For Joseph Harris, the 1990s got off to a terrible start. In February 1990, he was fired from his job at the Ridgewood, New Jersey, Post Office after his supervisor, Carol Ott, wrote him up for harassment. More than a year later, in the early morning of Thursday, October 10, 1991, Harris walked into his former place of work and shot two mail handlers to death. He'd come from Ott's house. Police officers found Ott there, stabbed to death; her boyfriend had been murdered, too. Harris had apparently planned to wait in the post office and ambush more employees, but thankfully, law enforcement got to him first.

Thomas McIlvane, too, had been fired from a postal job in 1990. He worked at a post-office facility in Royal Oak, Michigan, outside Detroit. A month after the Harris killings, McIlvane took a .22-caliber rifle into the Royal Oak Post Office and killed four employees, injured four others, then turned the weapon on himself.

These were just two of the more infamous incidents; during the 1990s, there were 12 post-office shootings by current and former employees.

The phrase "going postal" was coined a few years later, on December 17, 1993, as part of an article titled "Violence at Work Tied to Loss of Esteem," published in the *St. Petersburg Times*. It came from a symposium sponsored by the USPS in response to the rising cases of employees becoming violent. Another phrase, "toxic work environment," showed up as well. That phrase had originated four years earlier in a written guide to nursing leadership and showed up again in the *Times* article. A toxic work environment, it was thought, was another ingredient of violent outbursts. A workplace violence consultant, Dennis Johnson, reported that the toxicity came from bosses being "overbearing, authoritarian, secretive and confrontational."

The Post Office had known this was one of its big problems.

When Anthony Frank was leaving office and told *The Washington Post* that he regretted failing to overhaul the USPS's corporate culture, he added that he believed the Postal Service had "a paramilitary character." If an employee asked why they had to do something, far too often the response was "Because I told you to." Supervisors' attitudes, Frank said, amounted to: "I ate dirt for 20 years; now it's your turn to eat dirt."

The solution to this problem was simple to state but hard to execute. It was suggested to the Postal Service that it should reform its "military-style" management approach and appreciate that employees were assets. But aside from years of entrenched culture, the business challenges Frank and Runyon and the revolving door of postmasters general before them had been fighting were huge obstacles. It was hard to treat employees as assets when they were expensive and machines could increasingly do their jobs.

The Postal Service couldn't stand the phrase "going postal," but it spread too fast for it to be quashed. In 1998, it was statistically proved that postal employees were not disproportionately violent, but by that time, "going postal" had transcended its use for post-office shootings and become

Emergency Services arrived at Oklahoma's Edmond Post Office on August 20, 1986, shortly after letter carrier Patrick H. Sherrill entered the building and killed his supervisor, 14 coworkers, and finally himself. Six employees were also injured during the incident.

A New Corporate Look

When the Postal Reorganization Act transformed the Post Office Department into the USPS in 1970, the Postal Service adopted a new logo: a bald eagle standing atop a red, white, and blue treatment of the words "U.S. Mail." It was a classic logo, emblazoned on the thousands of Long Life Vehicles that brought most Americans their mail. But in the 1990s, many questioned the implications of using a stationary eagle when there was nothing motionless about America's Postal Service. Something more dynamic was needed to evoke the image of revolutionizing mail service. The 1970 design would remain the official seal of the Postal Service, but in 1993 a new logo debuted to change the image of the mail that met everyday Americans. It depicts the head of an eagle slicing through the air, moving decisively forward. Known as the Sonic Eagle, it's still in use today.

The First Semipostal Stamp

In 1997, a law was passed that allowed the Postal Service to become a fundraiser for other governmental agencies. The Semipostal Authorization Act, Pub. L. 106-253, granted the USPS discretionary authority to issue and sell semipostal stamps to advance causes it considered to be "in the national public interest and appropriate." Semipostal stamps are priced higher than standard-issue stamps: They cover the price of sending first-class mail, and what's left over is transferred to another agency as a donation for work on a specific issue (minus some money to pay for program costs).

The first semipostal stamp, which also indicates the initial impetus for the program, was the 1998 Breast Cancer Research stamp. Every time one of these stamps is purchased, 70 percent of the price above first-class postage goes to the National Institutes of Health and 30 percent to the Medical Research Program at the Department of Defense. The stamp is still on sale today; in nearly 30 years, more than 1.1 billion have been sold, raising more than $97.5 million for the cause.

Under the law, one semipostal stamp could be issued and sold for two years. In addition to breast cancer, stamps have supported conservation, Alzheimer's research, and treatment for PTSD, bringing in more than $12 million in total for the NIH, U.S. Fish and Wildlife Service, and the Department of Veterans Affairs.

USPS art director Ethel Kessler turned to artist Whitney Sherman to design this semipostal stamp for breast-cancer awareness and research.

In essence, the Postal Service was vying to become the infrastructure of online ordering and delivery.

a term used to describe any employee or person overcome by rage who acts out through violence, especially in the workplace. Despite the fact that shootings became more sporadic in the 2000s—there was a 15-year reprieve from 2006 to 2021—the repeated acts of violence remain a black eye for the Postal Service and an awful reminder of how bad things can get if it doesn't solve its challenges.

★ ★ ★

If the Postal Service were a private corporation, by 1996 it would have been by revenue the ninth largest in the country. A big reason why was PC Postage, which helped grow the USPS package business. Runyon had been right about the increasing importance of the digital sector. There were about 20 million online shoppers in 1999, spending about $3 billion, and research suggested that in a year, as calendars turned over to a new century, that figure could increase seven times over. Digital was it.

In the last year of the decade, the Postal Service launched numerous initiatives to bolster its electronic appeal. In March 1999, a new website, USPS.gov, helped businesses enhance their sales and marketing by direct mail. In August, a national advertising campaign, "What's Your e-Priority?" positioned the Postal Service as the preferred shipper from the internet to residential homes. In November, the Return@Ease service debuted to make it easier for customers to return goods purchased online from participating retailers like Eddie Bauer and Amazon.

In essence, the Postal Service was vying to become the infrastructure of online ordering and delivery. Two centuries after the American mail system began by cutting roads through wilderness, it was trying to become the conduit of online commerce. Of course, this was a vastly different project. Unlike in the 1700s, the Postal Service was now a legacy organization, a huge, slow bureaucracy trying to ride an information superhighway that was still traversed mainly by young, nimble, technically advanced companies. And so it was perhaps inevitable that at the same time computerization was giving the USPS a lift, it also gave it a hassle.

What was being called the "Millennium Bug" had the potential to crash all kinds of computerized systems, especially data and banking systems. Computer programs had been programmed to record years by the final two digits—"99" rather than "1999"—so the year 2000 was going to register as "00." What would a computer think? That the year had gone backward? The Millennium Bug was going to be a problem for every business and government agency, but it stood to be an especially big problem for the Postal Service. This was its prize for being a massive institution. It had to Y2K-proof 15,000 suppliers, 153 software applications, 50 computer systems in 250 facilities across the United States, and 10,000 personal computers, plus mainframes and other hardware and software. And it had to get it right: Other government agencies and private-sector organizations were looking to the USPS as a potential backup delivery system in the event of computer malfunctions. The cost to the Postal Service? Between $500 million and $700 million. This in an agency that, remember, had just managed to grow its profits to a few billion dollars.

At this point it was William J. Henderson's problem. He had taken over as postmaster general on May 16, 1998, and he would carry the Postal Service into the 21st century. Runyon had lasted nearly six years on the job, a longer and more effective tenure than probably anyone expected out of Carvin' Marvin. He'd turned out to have more vision than the hatchet man many had perceived him to be. But his accomplishments had been hard-fought. Just a few months into the job, he made an assessment: "Next to being President the position of Postmaster General is the most challenging management job in the country." Runyon's message was something Henderson would do well to heed—indeed, something every postmaster general to come would do well to heed. What could be learned from observing Runyon, and Frank, and their predecessors back into the 1980s was that as the century came to a close, the Postal Service was fully on the other side of a fundamental shift: What had once been an organization sure to harness and direct new technologies—roads, horses, trains, cars—was now trying desperately to keep up with them.

MAILBOXES

After the Post Office Department issued its first stamps in 1847, it also introduced mailboxes on sidewalks around cities and on lampposts, so if you had already purchased a stamp, you affixed it to the envelope and dropped it into the nearest collection mailbox or handed it to your letter carrier.

In 1863, mail services expanded to include collection and delivery at residential addresses. At that time, postal carriers were required to knock on each door and wait for someone to answer. The inefficiency proved to be too much. So by 1923, households were required to have a mailbox or letter slot in order to receive mail. This provided a remarkable opportunity for new businesses to sell mailboxes of various sizes and shapes—often featuring whimsical elements. As some mailboxes were more practical than others, the Post Office Department ultimately had to release specific design criteria. Not only did they have to easily fit letters, papers, and magazines, but they needed to be strong enough to withstand inclement weather and simple enough for carriers to open (while still deterring mail thieves). The department also mandated that each box have a signaling device to notify carriers when mail was ready for pickup.

This mailbox was said to have been used on the USNS *General Simon B. Buckner* during the Korean and Vietnam wars.

An 1880 street lamppost letterbox manufactured by the Orr and Painter Co. of Reading, Pennsylvania.

A Corbin Lock Company street-lamppost letterbox, 1889.

This six-sided street-pillar mailbox, with a schedule card that could be affixed to the front, was used near Dooner's Hotel in Philadelphia, circa 1880.

James G. Cutler manufactured this collection box, which would sit at the bottom of a mail chute, 1920.

One of the most recognizable mailbox designs, approved by the Post Office Department in 1915.

A handmade wooden Rural Free Delivery mailbox, 1896–1900.

"Please send this Letterbox to the Post Office Honolulu" was painted on this tin-can mailbox, which was soldered shut. In the early 20th century in Niuafo'ou, an island between Samoa and Fiji, people used these types of tin cans as mailboxes.

This gold-painted metal street collection box, with a brass letterbox lock, was used between 1850 and 1899.

KWANZAA
34
USA
Spay
Neuter
USA
37
Spay
Neuter
US
37
39
USA
AMBER ALERT
saves missing children
JURY DUTY
SERVE WITH PRIDE
37
USA
Adopting a CHILD
Shaping a LIFE
Building a HOME
USA
33
LUNAR NEW YEAR
37
USA
ChildHealth
SPACE ACHIEVEMENT AND EXPLORATION
WORLD STAMP EXPO 2000
TAKE ME OUT TO THE
BALL GAME

STATE OF EMERGENCY

It didn't take long for the 2000s to enter a state of emergency. In March 2001, the Postal Service Board of Governors wrote a letter to the president and to Congress asking for a comprehensive review of postal laws. The reason? "We believe that regulatory reform is needed for the preservation of universal service," they wrote. The USPS's fundamental promise, to provide every American with reliable, regular mail delivery, was at risk.

What followed was twofold. First, the USPS was added to the Government Accountability Office's annual high-risk watch list, which highlighted those government agencies "vulnerable to waste, fraud, abuse, or mismanagement, or in need of transformation." Second, the Senate required the Postal Service to submit a comprehensive transformation plan by year's end that would outline how it would meet current and future challenges around revenue, resources, technology, and competition—and this had to be a realistic plan, one that would appease all of the mail's various stakeholders, from Congress to unions to customers.

This is what John E. "Jack" Potter walked into when he took the job of U.S. postmaster general on June 1, 2001. He was a legacy employee who had worked for the USPS since 1977, and whose father had been a 40-year postal employee. Potter had already proved his mettle by filling a congressionally created position in 1998 to oversee the aggravatingly slow mail delivery plaguing the Washington, D.C., metropolitan area.

When he started the postmaster-general job, he was expecting a loss of more than $2 billion in the coming year and had no blueprint on how the belt-tightening would come about. So he and his team got to work figuring it out. They started piecing together a plan to submit to the Senate. Intended to explain how the Post Office could maintain its standard of "Everyone, Everywhere, Every Day" in the 2000s (and beyond), the plan had two parts. The first was all about the Postal Service of the present—increasing revenue,

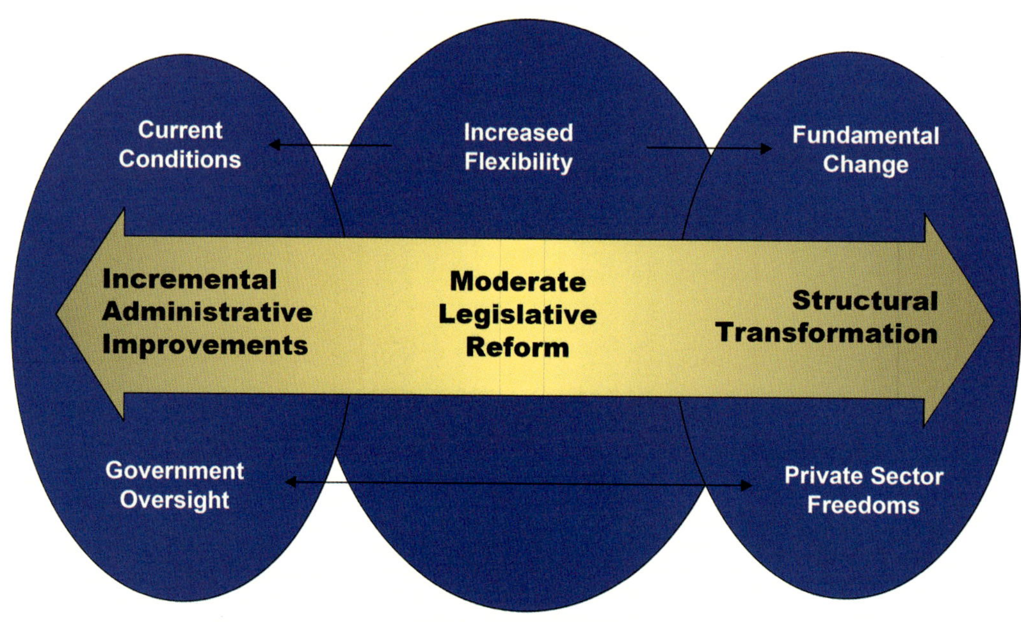

In October 2001, Postmaster General John E. "Jack" Potter sent the "Comprehensive Transformation Plan" for the future of the USPS to Joseph Lieberman, the chairman of the Committee on Governmental Affairs. This graphic visualizes the challenges and opportunities for change.

The Canal Street Post Office was about a mile north of the Church Street Station Post Office and took over some of the mail processing when Church Street had to close. It wouldn't reopen until August 2004.

efficiency, and employee performance—and the second was all about the Postal Service of the future. In particular, Potter was ready to propose a fundamentally new legislative framework for the USPS, just a few decades after it was created. The way Potter's team saw it, there were three choices: The USPS could remain a government agency that provided only services *not* provided by the private sector; it could become a private corporation; or it could remain a commercial government enterprise but operate in private markets. Its preference was that final choice—one that would have given the USPS a chance to prove it could be the company to bring an innovation like E-COM, early email, to the masses. It was both the practical recommendation and a somewhat shocking one. The Postal Service, reorganized again and in direct competition with private American companies? Nevertheless, Potter was ready to make it happen. The Postal Service had to end its state of emergency once and for all.

Then, as the USPS was finalizing the report, a real, nationwide emergency intervened. Actually, two of them.

★ ★ ★

The Church Street Station Post Office has been a mainstay of Lower Manhattan since it was built in the 1930s. It takes up a whole city block and stands topped by two Art Deco limestone towers. From its location far downtown, near the tip of the island, this post office had by the 2000s, for decades, been serving the titans of New York City's financial district. But at the dawn of the new century, its charge was more grandiose than ever: It handled all the mail for an office complex directly across the street, the World Trade Center, a cluster of seven buildings so massive it had two ZIP Codes all to itself: 10047 and 10048.

Ten letter carriers worked at Church Street Station sorting and delivering the mail to that complex, and on September 11, 2001, some of them witnessed the planes strike the Twin Towers. Some saw their patrons leap from high windows. Some saw the buildings fall. All saw the white powder, tiny pieces of the World Trade Center that, like snow, filled the air and coated everything it touched.

Letter carrier Rafael Feliciano served floors 78 through 110 of the South Tower. "If I live to be 90, I will never forget what I saw that day," he remembered.

The first hijacked plane struck the North Tower, ZIP Code 10048, at precisely 8:46:40 a.m. One minute later, a postal clerk recorded the last transaction of the day. It was for $87.54. At 9:02:59 a.m., a second hijacked flight struck the South Tower. The New York State government had its own ZIP Code in that building: 10047. Debris fell directly on the Church Street Station Post Office. Windows were broken and everything inside and out was covered with a thick coating of dust.

Thanks to the diligence of the postal workers, miraculously, no one inside Church Street Station or on any of the other floors of the building was physically injured. By 10:00 a.m., less than an hour after the second plane struck, postal workers had been ordered to evacuate, and station supervisor Jennifer Boykin, along with the building's safety officers, went from floor to floor to ensure that no one was left behind.

The phrase "United We Stand" underscored the feelings of unity, courage, and confidence citizens felt after the 9/11 attacks. Clerks and carriers who had to move from the Church Street Station across from the World Trade Center to a Midtown Manhattan post office carried this sentiment with them as they sorted and delivered mail.

Nearby, at the Jersey City postal station across the Hudson River, stunned survivors were transported to shelters and train stops in postal trucks. People who stumbled past the Brooklyn Post Office across the East River were offered a cool drink of water.

Within 48 hours, all the mail in the Church Street Station Post Office had been moved to Midtown Manhattan, where it was distributed out of the city's main post office—the old Farley Building on 33rd Street. The Church Street Station's 10 letter carriers and customer-service representatives were reassigned to the Farley Building so they could personally distribute any mail addressed to ZIP Codes 10047 and 10048, which had once been home to 16,000 super-active mailboxes and now were smoldering ruins. Letters continued to arrive addressed to occupants of the World Trade Center. The Postal Service held them for nearly three months before returning them to senders, one of the longest time periods the service has ever held on to unclaimed mail. The hope was that somehow claimants would appear. Sadly, many never did.

Letters arrived, too, for the people doing search and rescue at the World Trade Center—as many as 80,000 per day.

Employees from the Church Street Station who processed mail and were considered "back of the house" clerks were sent to the nearby Morgan Processing Center until the Church Street Station facility was rehabilitated. The letter carriers and customer-service representatives from that branch, on the other hand, were assigned to greet and embrace those customers who did survive the attack, and to receive news of those who were missing or known to have perished.

Just after September 11, the Federal Air Administration suspended all air transportation. Airmail had to find another way to be delivered. The USPS transported more mail by truck; some 700,000 vehicles were conscripted to the effort.

Potter had, of course, expected none of this. He surveyed the disaster-stricken landscape, a man who had the mail in his blood, and made a simple pronouncement: "The best thing we can do for America right now is to keep the mail moving."

Excepting portions of New York City, mail was collected and delivered as usual. By September 21, the other post offices in Lower Manhattan, Bowling Green and Wall Street, had reopened. It would take three years, but the Church Street Station would reopen, too. On Monday, August 2, 2004, it would once again serve the neighborhood.

ZIP Codes 10047 and 10048 would never be used again.

MANAGER OPERATIONS PROGRAMS SUPPORT
NEW YORK DISTRICT

UNITED STATES POSTAL SERVICE

October 11, 2001

Dear Postal Customer

Enclosed please find mail that was recently retrieved by relief workers at the World Trade Center disaster site. As the addressee of record, I am sure whoever sent you this correspondence would want you to have it.

Sincerely,

Jeffrey C. Wilensky

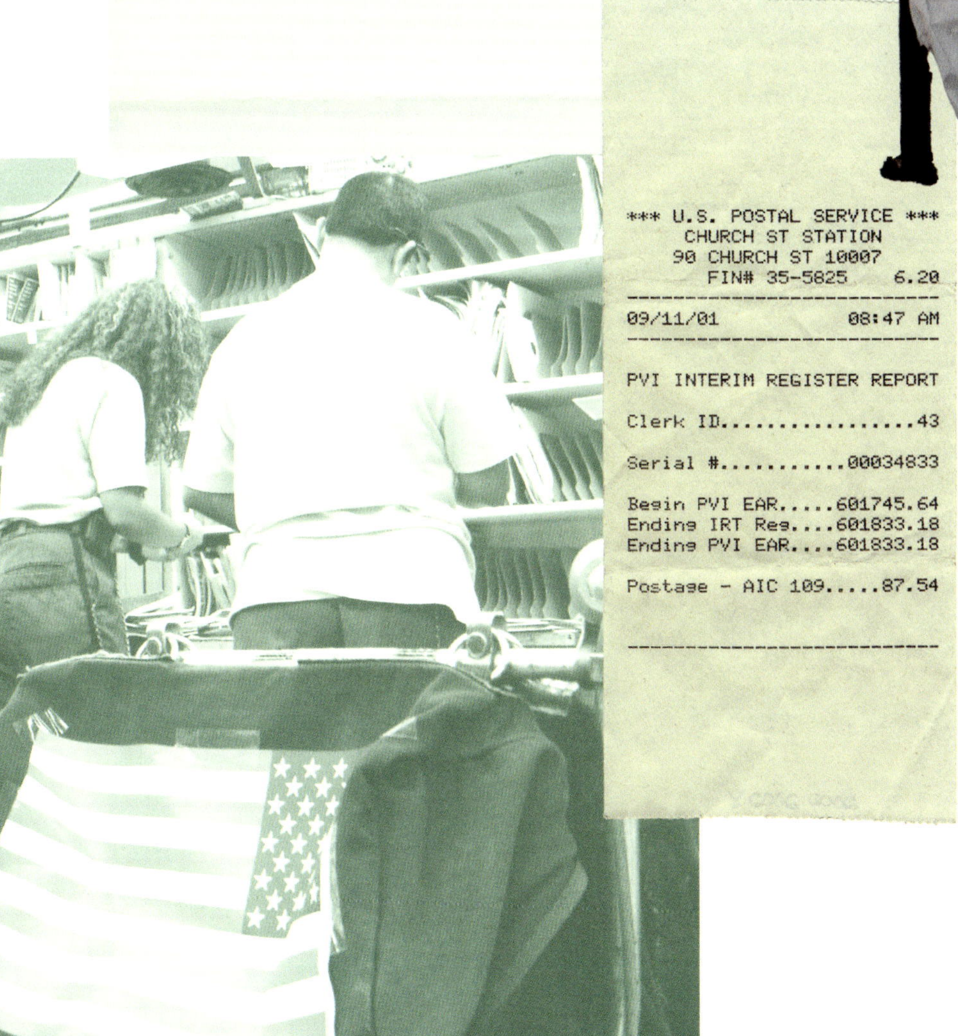

*** U.S. POSTAL SERVICE ***
CHURCH ST STATION
90 CHURCH ST 10007
FIN# 35-5825 6.20

09/11/01 08:47 AM

PVI INTERIM REGISTER REPORT

Clerk ID.................43

Serial #...........00034833

Begin PVI EAR.....601745.64
Ending IRT Reg....601833.18
Ending PVI EAR....601833.18

Postage - AIC 109.....87.54

Clockwise from top left: Mail was found a little over a month after the 9/11 attacks on the World Trade Center. It was then delivered to the addressee of record with this note; notices and photographs affixed to a post-office relay box near Ground Zero by loved ones of the missing; a registry receipt from the Church Street Station Post Office showing the last transaction conducted that day at 8:46:40 a.m.—just after the first plane hit the North Tower; after the Church Street Station had to shut down, postal clerks were sent to a Midtown Manhattan post office.

THE GLOBAL WAR ON TERRORISM

Two years after the 9/11 attacks, the United States entered into a war with Iraq that lasted for eight years. At its peak, in 2007, there were 170,300 troops overseas. And of course, they needed mail service.

For the USPS, Operation Iraqi Freedom, as the engagement was called, was a considerable test. Men and women were deploying to a region, the Persian Gulf, slightly smaller than the state of Oregon—and it was 8,000 miles away from home. Despite these Herculean challenges, 65 million pounds of military mail were delivered to deployed personnel in 2003. In April alone, more than 11 million pounds of mail were delivered—the equivalent of about forty 40-foot-long trailers full of mail every day. That number rose above 40 million by July.

Camp Leatherneck in Afghanistan receives a truck carrying more than 10,000 pounds of mail to the postal detachment, 2nd Marine Logistics Group, on November 18, 2011.

Moving this volume of mail was not accomplished without incident. In the summer of 2003, the Postal Service was subject to explosive accusations from an Army inspector general official. Mail was moving too slowly from the Persian Gulf to the United States, the official alleged, and moreover they believed the Postal Service was giving a lower priority to military mail, which generated no revenue because it was free for military personnel to send letters home. A review by the Postal Service's inspector general

Sailors unload a pallet of mail aboard the USS *New Orleans*, deployed as part of the Boxer Amphibious Ready Group.

ultimately vindicated the USPS. The delivery time was based on the amount of returned mail from the Army back to the USPS for processing. The war was over in less than six months, and troops were being sent home. The mail was basically chasing them halfway around the world and back. The Department of Defense did not provide forwarding addresses, so when the USPS received the undeliverable mail from the Persian Gulf, it still didn't have any instructions on how to deliver. This miscommunication yielded lessons the Postal Service can apply should the country enter another global conflict.

Above, left to right: Sailors aboard the aircraft carrier USS *Theodore Roosevelt* (CVN 71) sort mail in the hangar bay on August 5, 2015; the U.S. Marine Corps lands an MV-22 Osprey on the flight deck of the USS *Bataan* to deliver the first mail to be received by soldiers on deployment as part of the Navy's scheduled mission of security and crisis response on February 20, 2014; pallets of mail are transfered from the USS *New York* to the USNS *Rappahannock* while on deployment.

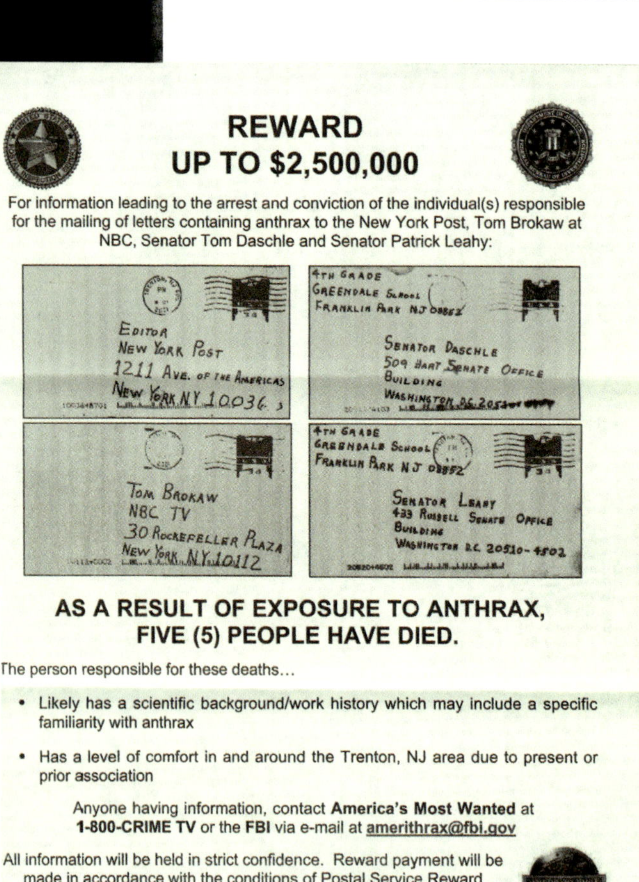

REWARD
UP TO $2,500,000

For information leading to the arrest and conviction of the individual(s) responsible for the mailing of letters containing anthrax to the New York Post, Tom Brokaw at NBC, Senator Tom Daschle and Senator Patrick Leahy:

AS A RESULT OF EXPOSURE TO ANTHRAX, FIVE (5) PEOPLE HAVE DIED.

The person responsible for these deaths…

- Likely has a scientific background/work history which may include a specific familiarity with anthrax
- Has a level of comfort in and around the Trenton, NJ area due to present or prior association

Anyone having information, contact **America's Most Wanted** at **1-800-CRIME TV** or the **FBI** via e-mail at amerithrax@fbi.gov

All information will be held in strict confidence. Reward payment will be made in accordance with the conditions of Postal Service Reward Notice 296, dated February 2000. Source of reward funds: US Postal Service and FBI $2,000,000; ADVO, Inc. $500,000.

Clockwise from top left: A biomedical lab technician at the U.S. Army's Fort Detrick holds up an anthrax-laced letter two months after it was mailed to Senator Patrick Leahy. The letter to Leahy and another one sent to Senator Tom Daschle killed five people and infected 17 more; the USPS printed and mailed out this letter regarding anthrax and the reward for information to more than 141 million addresses; the USPS also designed this poster about how to detect suspicious mail and packages to better ensure postal workers' safety.

Within a month of the attacks, artifacts from New York City, including from the Church Street Station, were packaged up and mailed to the National Postal Museum. On the way there, they passed through the Brentwood Mail Processing and Distribution Center in northeast Washington, D.C. As the artifacts of possibly the worst tragedy perpetraded on U.S. soil processed through, a killer stalked Brentwood. Letters being passed through were shaken and jostled by automated machinery, culled, canceled, and sorted. A small handful of them, as they were agitated, released something deadly: anthrax spores.

More anthrax-laced letters passed through a facility in Trenton, New Jersey, and in both locations, postal workers were on the frontlines of the attack simply because they processed the mail. Though media coverage focused on the prominent targets of the letters, like senators Tom Daschle and Patrick Leahy, newscaster Tom Brokaw, and the *New York Post*, it was mail workers who were exposed. At least 22 inhaled anthrax. Seventeen workers fell ill, including Postal Inspector William Paliscak, and several had to be hospitalized. Five died, including postal employees Joseph Curseen Jr. and Thomas Morris Jr.

The Brentwood and Trenton facilities were immediately closed, and decontamination protocols were implemented. All the mail at the Brentwood facility was embargoed—including the pair of packages addressed to the National Postal Museum that contained artifacts from the 9/11 terrorist attacks—until they were judged safe to deliver.

If the Postal Service was going to be attacked, it was also going to do what it could to deliver justice. The U.S. Postal Inspection Service joined forces with the Federal Bureau of Investigation and created the Amerithrax Task Force to discover the source of the deadly poison. A nine-year investigation involving a slew of experts in microbiology, chemistry, and bioweapons interviewed 10,000 witnesses spanning six continents, recovered more than 6,000 pieces of possible evidence, issued 5,750 grand jury subpoenas, gathered 5,730 environmental samples from 60 locations, and scrutinized more than 1,000 possible suspects. Government researcher Bruce Edwards Ivins became a prime suspect in April 2005, even though the contaminated mailings stopped in October 2001. Ivins died by suicide in 2008 before charges were filed against him. On February 19, 2010, the Amerithrax Task Force concluded its investigation and submitted its summary findings of Ivins's culpability as the perpetrator.

It took until 2003 for an independent environmental clearance committee to declare the Brentwood facility decontaminated and ready to be put back into service. When it reopened, it had a new name: the Curseen-Morris Mail Processing and Distribution Center.

A memorial plaque was installed outside the Brentwood Post Office in Washington, D.C., after two postal clerks died from coming in contact with the anthrax-laced letters mailed to senators Patrick Leahy and Tom Daschle. Thomas Morris, Jr. died on October 21, 2001, and Joseph Cursee, Jr. died one day later. A third coworker, Leroy Richmond, eventually succumbed to his exposure and resulting cancer on October 1, 2019.

Forever Stamp Issued

For years, one of the challenges of using postage stamps was figuring out what to do when the postal rates increased. If postage went up to 37 cents, all of a sudden, your old 35-cent stamps flipped from convenience to inconvenience. What was the least annoying way to fill the two-cent gap? So, on April 12, 2007, the USPS tried something new, introducing the first "Forever" stamp. This stamp would suffice for one-ounce first-class mail no matter when it was used. If the postage went up, your unused Forever stamps would be valid even though you'd paid less for them than you would for one-ounce first-class mail now. Perhaps because they freed customers from a distinctly postal hassle, the first Forever stamps bore the image of the Liberty Bell. New batches were printed in 2008 and 2009. In 2011, it was decided that all new commemorative stamps would be Forever stamps. Denominations are left to those stamps that are not commemorative. In 2024, 23 non-commemorative stamps were issued.

Mail that was located in the same post offices where anthrax was found had to be irradiated. This resulted in a backlog of about 1.8 million pieces that would require X-raying and e-beaming to kill off the anthrax spores.

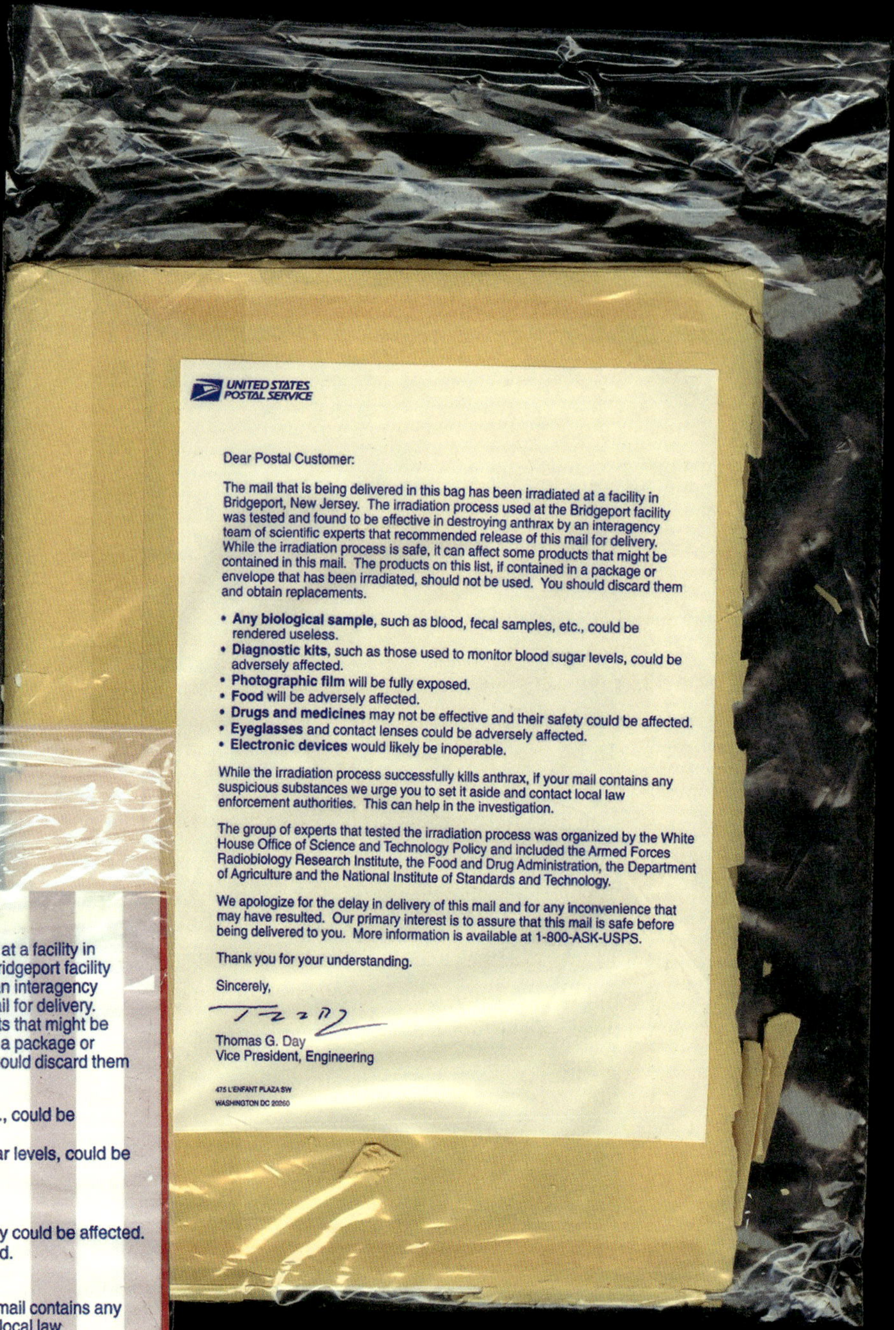

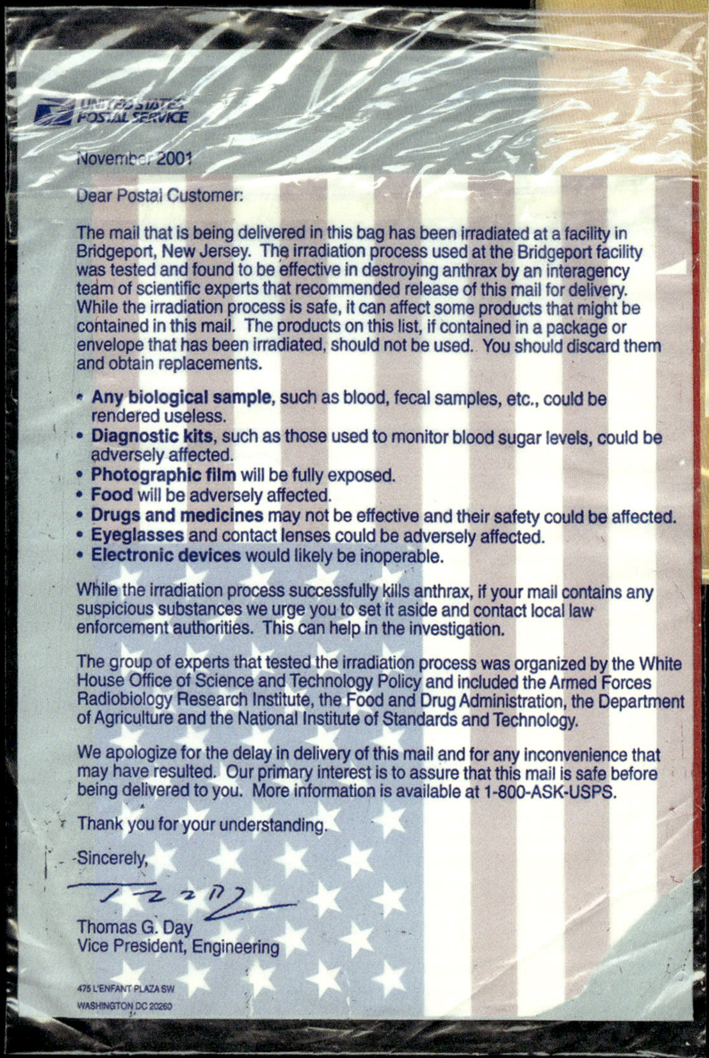

UNITED STATES POSTAL SERVICE

Dear Postal Customer:

The mail that is being delivered in this bag has been irradiated at a facility in Bridgeport, New Jersey. The irradiation process used at the Bridgeport facility was tested and found to be effective in destroying anthrax by an interagency team of scientific experts that recommended release of this mail for delivery. While the irradiation process is safe, it can affect some products that might be contained in this mail. The products on this list, if contained in a package or envelope that has been irradiated, should not be used. You should discard them and obtain replacements.

- **Any biological sample**, such as blood, fecal samples, etc., could be rendered useless.
- **Diagnostic kits**, such as those used to monitor blood sugar levels, could be adversely affected.
- **Photographic film** will be fully exposed.
- **Food** will be adversely affected.
- **Drugs and medicines** may not be effective and their safety could be affected.
- **Eyeglasses** and contact lenses could be adversely affected.
- **Electronic devices** would likely be inoperable.

While the irradiation process successfully kills anthrax, if your mail contains any suspicious substances we urge you to set it aside and contact local law enforcement authorities. This can help in the investigation.

The group of experts that tested the irradiation process was organized by the White House Office of Science and Technology Policy and included the Armed Forces Radiobiology Research Institute, the Food and Drug Administration, the Department of Agriculture and the National Institute of Standards and Technology.

We apologize for the delay in delivery of this mail and for any inconvenience that may have resulted. Our primary interest is to assure that this mail is safe before being delivered to you. More information is available at 1-800-ASK-USPS.

Thank you for your understanding.

Sincerely,

Thomas G. Day
Vice President, Engineering

475 L'ENFANT PLAZA SW
WASHINGTON DC 20260

UNITED STATES POSTAL SERVICE

November 2001

Dear Postal Customer:

The mail that is being delivered in this bag has been irradiated at a facility in Bridgeport, New Jersey. The irradiation process used at the Bridgeport facility was tested and found to be effective in destroying anthrax by an interagency team of scientific experts that recommended release of this mail for delivery. While the irradiation process is safe, it can affect some products that might be contained in this mail. The products on this list, if contained in a package or envelope that has been irradiated, should not be used. You should discard them and obtain replacements.

- **Any biological sample**, such as blood, fecal samples, etc., could be rendered useless.
- **Diagnostic kits**, such as those used to monitor blood sugar levels, could be adversely affected.
- **Photographic film** will be fully exposed.
- **Food** will be adversely affected.
- **Drugs and medicines** may not be effective and their safety could be affected.
- **Eyeglasses** and contact lenses could be adversely affected.
- **Electronic devices** would likely be inoperable.

While the irradiation process successfully kills anthrax, if your mail contains any suspicious substances we urge you to set it aside and contact local law enforcement authorities. This can help in the investigation.

The group of experts that tested the irradiation process was organized by the White House Office of Science and Technology Policy and included the Armed Forces Radiobiology Research Institute, the Food and Drug Administration, the Department of Agriculture and the National Institute of Standards and Technology.

We apologize for the delay in delivery of this mail and for any inconvenience that may have resulted. Our primary interest is to assure that this mail is safe before being delivered to you. More information is available at 1-800-ASK-USPS.

Thank you for your understanding.

Sincerely,

Thomas G. Day
Vice President, Engineering

475 L'ENFANT PLAZA SW
WASHINGTON DC 20260

In response to the anthrax attacks, the government began irradiating mail to prevent further anthrax threats and commenced conducting routine anthrax attack drills.

★ ★ ★

Potter couldn't afford to view September 11 and the subsequent anthrax crisis purely through the lens of human tragedy. The comprehensive Transformation Plan had been completed in their immediate aftermath, and in the months to follow, the reverberations of the attacks would be a drag on the USPS's quest to find its future.

In March 2002, the Government Accounting Office reported that "the USPS's financial outlook is becoming increasingly dire." Around the same time, Potter spoke before members of the House Appropriations Subcommittee and estimated that the overall costs to the USPS from both the September 11 and anthrax attacks were estimated to be around $50 million—with about half for the repairs required for the Church Street Station. In addition, the Postal Service had spent an extra $150 million on transportation costs stemming from new federal rules that, for security reasons, prohibited anything heavier than 16 ounces on commercial airliners.

Similarly, in response to the anthrax attacks, the government began irradiating mail to prevent further anthrax threats and commenced conducting routine anthrax attack drills. The president and Congress released $675 million to the Postal Service to aid in cleaning up the two affected post offices and enforce security measures to thwart future attacks. In 2003, the Postal Service would go on to install state-of-the-art biohazard detection systems at 15 locations nationwide. Deployed in 2004, these provided a new level of protection—but, of course, they were not free.

Potter at one point estimated that the USPS would need an extra $1.5 billion per year over the "next few years" to increase security.

The cataclysmic emergencies were the immediate cause of the dwindling Postal Service coffers, but Potter made a point of tying the agency's underlying ill financial health to its business structure. "The basic economic assumption of the business model—that continuing growth in mail volume and revenue would support continued infrastructure growth—is no longer valid," he said in a speech. "In fact, volume growth is at risk from competition and technology, while the number of delivery points is increasing. Without postal reform, the widening divergence of volume growth and delivery point expansion will make it impossible to continue the long-term successes that have been achieved since postal reorganization."

Given that the USPS had to foot the bill for expenses associated from the attacks, its management felt that the financial future looked uncertain; however, the final results stated otherwise. By the end of 2003, Potter and the USPS reported a $3.9 billion surplus with a net income of $900 million, despite declining mail volume and about 1.8 million new addresses. A postage increase brought in almost $1 billion, and Congress appropriated $500 million to enhance mail security, thereby reducing expenses. The USPS also had its smallest career employee total (729,000) since 1994, yet it ended up delivering 24 billion more mail pieces overall. The 2004 financial plan also predicted a surplus of about $2.1 billion, and 2005 was anybody's guess, depending on the economy.

From the 1970s through 2005, the Postal Service was in its best financial position. With a 95 percent rate of overnight delivery on first-class mail, 2006 was also a banner year.

★ ★ ★

For the first half of the decade, Potter had been asking for a legislative overhaul to the Postal Service. At the start of the second half, he got it. In 2006, the Postal Accountability and Enhancement Act (PAEA) was signed into law. It had been more than 35 years since Congress signed the Postal Reorganization Act of 1970; perhaps an update was overdue. PAEA made more than 150 sweeping changes to postal law. For better or for worse, the act modernized price regulation and service standards; it increased the authority of what had been the Postal Rate Commission to become the Postal Regulatory Commission (PRC) and required a variety of reports and evaluations for transparency. It also ended the previously mandated break-even business model and allowed

Without the money to do the prefunding, the Postal Service would find itself in dire financial straits.

for profits or losses, encouraging retained earnings to be reinvested into the business.

Contrary to Potter's hopes for *more* leeway to innovate even if it meant competition with private companies, the act also *restricted* the Postal Service's authority to provide non-postal services. It changed the definition of "postal service" to not allow for any potential profit-making businesses that fell outside of delivery, acceptance, collection, sorting, and transportation of mail. This was not, ultimately, a surprising change: The Postal Rate Commission had requested that "interested parties" give recommendations for the new definition, and the parties included major competitors like Pitney Bowes and the United Parcel Service. For the past decade, each time the USPS had tried to enter into a new business, its competitors pushed back, through legal action or lobbying on Capitol Hill to curb the USPS's efforts to go beyond the business of the mail. Now that was over—but not for the reasons the USPS had hoped. There was no longer any question. The Postal Service simply could no longer make such forays into other promising money-making ventures.

But the most damaging provision in the PAEA was actually something far drier and more bureaucratic. The act established an accelerated schedule for the funding of Postal Service retiree health benefits and required the USPS to *prefund* future retiree health benefits by establishing the Postal Service Retired Health Benefits Program (PSRHB). This prefunding required a transfer of $3 billion from a USPS escrow account to the new PSRHB. If the surpluses of the first half of the decade had continued, this might have been fine. But in 2007, as the "Great Recession" was just beginning to affect the economy overall, the Post Office began posting losses—big ones. Without the money to do the prefunding, the Postal Service would find itself in dire financial straits. The ramifications of this 2006 reform would have devastating consequences for more than a decade and a half.

Three years after the PAEA was passed, Potter ended up testifying before the Senate, for which he'd put together the transformation report at the beginning of the decade. What he was sharing was a far cry from that report's admonition to serve "Everyone, Everywhere, Every Day." Potter testified that he might be required to eliminate Saturday mail delivery to save money. The Great Recession, in full swing by 2008, saw a drop of more than nine billion pieces of mail, which led to a $2.9 billion loss that year; 2009 was not expected to look much better. Potter argued for a change to the retirement benefit rules. He noted that the USPS is "the only public or private entity required to prepay health benefit premiums at these extremely high levels," which in 2008 represented 10 percent of the agency's operating budget.

After some three decades in service of the mail, Potter understood that the USPS was "a vital economic engine in our national economy." So he argued passionately for a way to keep the service healthy. He believed that "legislative relief [was] necessary to preserve the nation's mail system." But if Congress would deliver change, he wouldn't be around to see it. Patrick R. Donahoe, Potter's successor, took over on December 6, 2010. Potter had served essentially the full decade. He'd seen the devastation of September 11 and anthrax, ridden high with surpluses and been brought low by recession and deficits. Through it all, he'd fought for the mail, something he believed in, something that was his family's life's work.

Even so, when Potter left office, he felt a responsibility to offer a warning. He estimated the USPS would cumulatively lose more than $238 billion by the end of the decade to come.

Right: President George W. Bush signed the Postal Accountability and Enhancement Act (PAEA) on December 20, 2006. Attending the signing were, from left: Postmaster General Jack Potter; Senator Thomas Carper (DE); Rep. Tom Davis (VA); Senator Susan Collins (ME); James C. Miller III, Chairman of the Postal Service Board of Governors; Rep. Danny Davis (IL); and Rep. John McHugh (NY).

New Set of Wheels Fails to Strike the Right Balance

In the summer of 2002, the Postal Service agreed to test the two-wheeled transport scooter known as the Segway, at the urging of its inventor, Dean Kamen. Though electric personal-mobility devices are common today, the Segway was novel for its time—and it seemed to have potential as a mail mover. It was capable of traveling 12.5 miles per hour, much faster than the 2.5 miles per hour mail carriers did on foot. And though the 40 off-the-shelf units the USPS purchased for the pilot couldn't carry much more than a letter carrier's standard satchel, modified Segways released later could roughly triple a letter carrier's capacity.

The device was tested for use on "park and loop routes," in which carriers park their vehicles, do a loop through a several-block area on foot, then return to their vehicle to drive to the next loop. Testers took Segways on hilly routes at six locations around the country.

Unfortunately, the results were disappointing. Trucks had to be retrofitted with special lifts for transporting the 80-pound test Segways to and from their assigned routes, carriers had to bring extra batteries, and there was a fear that fall-related injuries would climb. Plus, no carrier really wanted to use the Segway in inclement weather, as they afforded no protection.

What sealed its fate, though, may have been when postal officials realized that adequate charging stations would be required at every carrier-based postal facility—and that most of them lacked the space. The barriers were simply too high; the Postal Service sold off its used Segways in a 2006 public sale.

FOREVER * USA
2016

USA FOREVER
2016

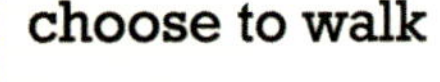
choose to walk

2011
USA GO GREEN
forever
GO GREEN
reduce our
environmental
footprint usa
forever
step by step

USA
BONSAI
SIERRA
JUNIPER

USA
14
FOREVER

USA
44

FOREVER
Heart Health
usa
2012

FOREVER USA
LANT for more BEAUTIF

2011
FOREVER

Pluto
Forever
USA
2016

New Horizons
Forever
USA
2016

TUMN FERN

Forever
USA
DIE'S WOOD FERN

USA
NTED FERN

Forever
USA
FORTUNE'S HOLLY FERN

T SHIELD FERN
USA

UNITED STATES
2010
|
2019
POSTAL SERVICE

GOING GREEN, SEEING RED

Patrick R. Donahoe, Jack Potter's successor, took over as postmaster general in December 2010. His main task, like that of Potter and the revolving door of postmasters general of the past few decades, was to figure out how to make the post-reorganization Postal Service operate as a business while still fulfilling its mission of providing reliable, every-single-day service to all Americans. But he had at least one new element to his job: Starting in the early 2000s, the USPS had added the goal of being a greener and more sustainable business. Donahoe knew that would be challenging. He stated that becoming "leaner, greener, faster, smarter" meant "right-sizing our delivery network and our workforce to better meet the needs of 21st-century America." The policies put in place that strove for the pursuit of leaner, faster, and right-sizing usually led to labor strife and deadly violence. Accomplishing them without those horrible side effects would require rethinking how the Postal Service operated, inwardly and outwardly.

Donahoe, like Potter, was a long-term postal employee. So he at least had a chance to see what was coming—to see the challenges that would bring the Post Office to within four days of utter collapse. After all, early in pursuit of its green initiatives, the Postal Service had had a front-row seat to an incident that might have been instructive.

Under Potter, the Postal Service had embarked upon an effort to test and acquire an array of green and alternative-fuel vehicles to reduce emissions. This effort had begun in earnest back in early 2000s with the deployment of 21,275 flexible-fuel vehicles (FFVs) powered by a mix of ethanol and gasoline called E85. Then, in 2002, the Postal Service acquired 500 fully electric delivery vehicles called Ford-Utilimaster FFVs. They were made by Ford Motor Company, in collaboration with Baker Electromotive. The USPS hoped these could be, if not outright replacements for the LLVs, a part of its fleet of the future. These electric vehicles were emissions free, and their batteries' life span was estimated at three to five years. It seemed like a perfect plan—except that, before the year was even over, Ford announced it was canceling its electric-vehicle program. The producer of the FFV's battery pack, East Penn Manufacturing Company, said it was ending production of the batteries. No replacements would be available when the FFV batteries reached end-of-life, and to make things even worse, the estimated life span was reduced to just two years.

The Post Office had to scramble. It decided in August 2003 to return all the FFVs, its onetime

Approximately 35,000 solar panels line the carport canopies of the USPS's Los Angeles Processing and Distribution Center, covering 23 acres. The shade these panels provide lowers the temperature about seven degrees as compared with the open-air temperature.

In 2011, five electric-vehicle suppliers—Autoport, Bright Automotive, EDAG, Inc., Quantum Technologies, and ZAP—worked with the USPS to convert one each of the Grumman LLVs (Long Life Vehicles) into an electric vehicle. All five vehicles were tested in the Washington, D.C., area, but only one, the Autoport eLLV, was still in service in 2014.

vehicles of the future, in exchange for gasoline-powered Ford Windstar vans. In 2007, around the time the FFVs theoretically would have had to replace their batteries, the Postal Service purchased thousands of new vehicles, including nearly 6,000 flexible-fuel Chevy Uplanders and some hybrid two-ton Eaton Corporation box vans—neither of which was emissions free.

So what happened? It was simple, really. Ford had been trying to go electric, realized it had the wrong business model, and got out.

By the end of the 2010s, people would be wondering the same thing about the Postal Service. Did it have the right business model? Could it make things work? Except it wouldn't be talking just about going green—it would be talking about delivering mail.

★ ★ ★

As the decade began, Donahoe had major issues beyond being *environmentally* sustainable. Finances were a major problem, too. He had to draft a plan to overcome liquidity issues amid rising costs. With the continued shift to electronic communication via the internet, letter mail had dropped 3.5 percent in one year, from 2009 to 2010—which contributed to a loss of $8.5 billion. And the losses kept coming; from 2011 to 2014, the average loss was more than $5 billion. In 2012, the loss was *$15.9 billion*. This was largely a legacy of 2006's PAEA. The USPS had defaulted on its requirement to prefund retiree health care benefits, and that resulted in a payment in 2012 of $11.1 billion. At one point that year, the USPS had fewer than four days' worth of cash available.

Donahoe, like so many postmasters general before him, wanted legislative change. And just like his predecessors, he was unable to get it. Instead, he was forced to fall back on "aggressive cost reductions" and "pursuing revenue-generating opportunities."

These did not go over well.

A strategy called the Retail Access Optimization Initiative sought to shutter about 3,700 post offices and processing plants that had been rendered unprofitable and no longer necessary due to the decline in mail volume. Four out of five of these were in rural areas, places where a post office was more than just a building for getting mail—it was a hub of social and civic life. The communities set to lose their post offices erupted in protest. In the face of backlash, in May 2012 the plan shifted from closures to reduced operating hours. This was far more palatable to the small towns that were affected, but it meant that the initiative saved the Postal Service some $163 million less than expected.

The next big piece of the plan was to eliminate Saturday delivery, which was expected to save the service $2 billion to $3 billion per year. This, too, was met with a remarkable measure of outright hostility. Citizens, members of Congress, union leaders, direct-mail marketers, and even Hallmark began lobbying Congress against reduced delivery. Some people told Donahoe to start selling T-shirts and mugs in the post offices, but that venture had already been tried once and lasted just two years, from 1989 to 1991, when Congress criticized the USPS for venturing outside its postal responsibilities.

SUSTAINABILITY
LEANER | GREENER | FASTER | SMARTER
2010 REPORT
UNITED STATES
POSTAL SERVICE ®

Opposite: The 2010 fiscal year report on sustainability was released in July 2011; it highlighted many of the energy-saving achievements the USPS had made, including reducing more than 1.06 metric tons of CO_2 from the 2008 baseline—equaling the annual emissions of almost 204,000 passenger vehicles.

So the cost-cutting measures largely failed. What about "revenue-generating opportunities"? In 2013, Donahoe took a bold path: He made postal services available at Staples stores. Under the USPS's agreement with the office-supply company, a counter that looked like a miniature post office would be added to stores, and it would offer all the same services available at USPS locations. A pilot location opened in Boston in November 2013, and by year's end, 500 more locations nationwide would roll out the new counters.

Labor revolted.

The American Postal Workers Union didn't like this arrangement, because the Staples locations were staffed by its employees instead of unionized postal workers. The union called for a nationwide boycott of Staples, arguing that its employees were not adhering to USPS rules for mail and even potentially lowballing mailing fees. Four years later, a National Labor Relations Board judge killed the USPS-Staples deal. The mini post offices were dismantled; another of Donahoe's big ideas had been scuttled.

Also in 2013, the USPS signed an agreement with Amazon Fulfillment to deliver parcels on Sundays. By the end of April 2014, the Sunday service was operating out of 459 Postal Service hubs in 22 districts around the country. In just the first four months of that year, more than 2.7 million parcels were delivered to customers on Sundays from these hubs, and the USPS expanded the service to 786 additional hubs in 24 more districts across the country. Though the service was great for customers, it actually cost the Postal Service 17,446 more hours in labor expenses in a single month due to poor management and operations inefficiencies by some hubs and a lack of, or inconsistent, supervisors.

To make the deal with Amazon work, the USPS negotiated labor contracts requiring new employees to work on Sundays and early mornings, for rates far below the premium pay career employees would have received for these hours. It was a subtle but significant symbol of the gulf between the constraints on the Postal Service and the competitive practices of the companies it found itself up against.

★ ★ ★

Luckily, as all else was going badly, the Postal Service's efforts to go green were going great. After getting its start in the previous decade, by the time the 2010s began, the USPS was ahead of the curve among government agencies. It was the first federal agency to have a sustainability officer, the first federal agency to publish a third-party-verified greenhouse gas (GHG) emission inventory and to commit to absolute GHG reductions at the 2009 United Nations Climate Conference in Copenhagen, and one of the first federal agencies to issue rigorous and public sustainability performance reports. It compiled its targets into a USPS-wide dashboard that rated progress on each one with a red, yellow, or green light.

For the first time in what seemed like a long time—after decades of talk of "right-sizing" to cut costs—the size of the Post Office was proving to be an asset. Find a way to make vehicles more efficient, and you'll multiply that efficiency by the massive 220,000-vehicle fleet. (And the Postal Service had a big head start with its initial electric and flexible-fuel vehicles.) Make an energy-saving change to how facilities are run, and you'll have 34,000 facilities to amplify that effect. Find a great way for humans to be green, and you'll have more than half a million employees to carry it out.

Right: In August 2014, protesters headed to the 500 Staples stores where the USPS had set up its mailing-station pilot program. Employees there would be paid less than union postal employees, and this was seen as a step toward privatization.

Below: USPS customers, as well as union postal workers, began a "Save the Postal Service" movement. As talk of privatizing the USPS continued to be tossed around, another campaign was launched letting everyone know that the U.S. mail was not for sale.

U.S.
NOT FOR SALE
MAIL

"We Deliver."

From June to August 2011, the Missouri River crested over 19 feet in the Bismarck area due to thawing winter snow and more than a foot of rain. Some mailboxes were submerged completely underwater. Mail delivery slowed until the waters receded and postal vehicles could return to residential areas.

The year 2010 arrived as the worst on record for 100-year weather events, dramatic occurrences so powerful that meteorologists said they should occur only once every 100 years. There were 79 of these events in 2010. Usually, the annual total was roughly half that. A February storm called "Snowmageddon" dropped 32.4 inches of snow at Washington Dulles International Airport and just a few days later was followed by "Snoverkill," a second crippling blizzard. Deadly floods and tornadoes in Tennessee, Mississippi, and Kentucky killed dozens in April, the same month that a 7.2-level earthquake struck Southern California. A severe tornado outbreak caused widespread damage in Oklahoma City in May; a hailstorm in South Dakota in July produced nearly two-pound hailstones; and a freak tornado hit New York City in September, the same month Los Angeles experienced its hottest day on record. Even the tropical paradise of Hawaii wasn't spared: The Kilauea volcano continuously spewed out lava that threatened houses and roads.

Through all these disasters, the United States Postal Service played a vital role as part of the federal government's national emergency response network. The service delivered food, medicine, and other necessities to affected communities. Within hours, postal employees were hard at work along with other first responders and electric and gas repair crews to reestablish service. Mail, after all, is vital infrastructure: It ensures people can contact friends and relatives when cell-phone service fails. That's why, in times of crisis, the Postal Service more than ever emphasizes its mantra: "We Deliver."

Left: When Hurricane Sandy hit the East Coast in the fall of 2012, it stretched 800 miles to the Great Lakes region, causing destruction and flooding. In Toms River, New Jersey, a postal vehicle had to navigate obstacles like this boat on the roadside that was relocated by the storm's high winds and record-setting storm surges.

Below: In Baton Rouge in 2016, storms dumped more than 30 inches of rain, causing major flooding. As soon as the area was given the all-clear, mail clerks were back making deliveries. They would deliver what they could and hold on to the rest until it was claimed.

USPS BlueEarth

In 2010, President Barack Obama called for a task force to establish a sustainable electronics waste strategy. Ever the leader on going green, the USPS established the BlueEarth Federal Recycling Program in 2012, which made it the e-waste recycler of choice for the federal government. Under the program, agencies and their employees were able to recycle unwanted electronic devices free of charge, preventing them from going to landfills. This is especially important with e-waste, as it can be particularly dangerous to both the environment and human health. Unwanted and obsolete small electronic devices and ink cartridges recycled through the program were shipped to a certified third-party recycling facility, which ensured they were either securely recycled or remanufactured for resale opportunities. By 2013, there were about 973,000 federal employees and contractors eligible to participate in the BlueEarth program.

With all those employees—618,000, to be exact—a whole bunch of minds were coming up with new, good ideas. The Postal Service worked hard to build a conservation-based culture. It invited mail facilities, distribution centers, and post-office employees to join "Lean Green Teams" tasked with helping reduce operational costs and carbon footprints. Members collaborated across functions to identify and implement low- and no-cost ways to conserve natural resources, purchase fewer consumables, and reduce waste across a variety of aspects of how mail was handled.

Employee brainstorms often unlocked solutions that were beneficial for the USPS—and for customers. In 2012, there were about 22,000

Opposite: In 2010, T3 three-wheeled electric vehicles were tested in Florida, California, and Arizona. They could travel for about 40 miles before needing a recharge. By 2014, only 13 vehicles were still in use, as they provided little protection from the weather and could reach a maximum speed of only five miles per hour.

secure recycling bins in nearly 12,000 post-office lobbies, which made it easier for customers to read, respond to, and recycle their PO Box mail year-round, diverting more than 30,000 tons of paper from landfills. A few years later, the employees of the Clatskanie, Oregon, Post Office realized they could take this even further. In small rural towns like Clatskanie, curbside recycling wasn't available. All customers—not just PO Box customers—would see a benefit from being able to recycle rather than bringiing home or discarding their mail. So, the USPS employees decided to make even more recycling bins available. As the bins filled up, costs for trash hauling went down. The Clatskanie Post Office was able to reduce garbage pickup to every other week instead of weekly. It was good for the environment—and for the community.

In fact, the Postal Service's recycling programs tended to pay off in a big way. In 2010, reductions in energy usage, water and petroleum fuel usage, and solid waste sent to landfills helped the USPS save more than $5 million. The following year, recycling efforts generated more than 222,000 tons of material and $13 million in revenue, with $9 million saved in landfill fees.

Compared with other postal administrations worldwide, the USPS was a leader. Canada Post was down almost 3 percent in GHG emissions—but the Postal Service was down 13 percent. Though the U.K.'s Royal Mail diverted 79 percent of waste and the USPS diverted only 38 percent, the Royal Mail reduced water use by just 1 percent, while the USPS managed 35 percent.

But these successes weren't enough to retain Patrick Donahoe. In November 2014, he announced his retirement. To succeed him, the USPS Board of Governors hired the first female postmaster general and the third consecutive career postal employee to take the job, Megan J. Brennan. Her first day was February 1, 2015.

Brennan continued the green efforts, including a long-term project to find potential successors to the LLV. But as she did that, she ran into the same buzzsaw that all the previous postmasters general had. The Postal Service's business structure simply wasn't working. Case in point: Even as the USPS was losing money, in her first year Brennan faced a mandatory *reduction* in pricing. A past pricing bump that had been approved by Congress to help alleviate some of the multiyear declines in revenue was expiring. Most of the reductions were just one or two cents per piece of mail—but they applied to particularly voluminous categories of mail and added up to a loss of about $2 billion per year. Brennan's analysis: "Our current pricing regime is unworkable and should be replaced with a system that provides greater pricing flexibility and better reflects the economic challenges facing the Postal Service."

In support of its green initiatives, at the beginning of 2010, the USPS began a new program called the Three Rs—Read, Respond, Recycle—adding recyling bins to all post-office lobbies. The bins were placed near post-office boxes so customers would recycle as much of their mail waste as possible. In fiscal year 2014, the USPS diverted about 30 percent of total waste for recycling.

Brennan announced a preference for centralized delivery of mail via "cluster boxes"—mailboxes for multiple addresses clumped together into one unit.

Brennan was unwittingly caught in a much bigger bout of organizational dysfunction than perhaps anyone before her. Since the Postal Reform Act of 1970, the president had been charged with appointing nine of the 11-member USPS Board of Governors, with the advice and consent of the Senate. (The final two members are the postmaster general and the deputy postmaster general.) On December 8, 2016, for the first time in USPS history, the board had zero members.

The problem wasn't that President Obama had not nominated anyone. It was that the Senate was playing politics with the nominations. Bernie Sanders, the Democratic senator from Vermont, blocked two of Obama's nominees. In retaliation, Mitch McConnell, the Republican senator from Kentucky, blocked the rest. It's beyond the scope of this book to judge the politics. But it's easy to say, objectively, that no organization is going to operate well if its leadership and governance is a political football.

The USPS was able to keep operating—barely—because before their terms expired, the last five governors had adopted a resolution delegating the board's authority to a temporary emergency committee. The board needed four or more governors to reach a quorum and conduct business; with literally no governors, the committee kept things running.

A quorum was finally reached in August 2019 under President Donald Trump. But Trump wasn't exactly making life easier for Brennan. According to reporting from *The Washington Post*, in May 2018, he pressured her to double the rate charged to Amazon for shipping and delivering packages. She refused.

But without good ways to generate more revenue, Brennan was yet another postmaster general reduced to using cost-cutting measures that alienated customers and clients. She announced a preference for centralized delivery of mail via "cluster boxes"—mailboxes for multiple addresses clumped together into one unit (which might be some distance from the homes it served). The appeal for Brennan was the fact that a mail carrier could deliver to an entire group of people at once instead of going door-to-door. Cluster boxes were

Apartments and new residential developments, especially in the suburbs, were mandated to use Cluster Box Units, or CBUs, instead of individual mailboxes. These reduced the time it took postal carriers to deliver their mail and thus were a cost savings.

more efficient in time and cost for mail carriers, especially in newly built subdivisions. Customers, however, found the boxes inconvenient. The National Association of Home Builders expressed concerns for its builders of subdivisions, arguing that cluster boxes could negatively affect sales. Even worse, the USPS Office of Inspector General found that cluster boxes decreased the "read and response" rates for donation mail and advertising mail from 12 percent to 4 percent. The Nonprofit Mailers organization stated: "It is clear that operational cost savings are taking precedence over value creation, marketing, and listening to customers."

In October 2019, as the decade was nearing its end, Brennan announced her retirement. Like her recent predecessors, she saw she was playing a game she could not win. The situation had become especially dire since the PAEA had added the immense cost of the retirement system to the service's books. The net financial losses since that legislation was passed in 2006 amounted to $92 billion, $66 billion of it in the 2010s.

At this time, many of the world's postal services had become privatized. The U.K., Germany, Portugal, the Netherlands, and even Japan were all run this way. Some people were starting to think that maybe the USPS should follow. The agency simply had the wrong business model, the thinking went. When Ford found itself in that position years earlier with its electric-vehicle unit, it got out. What about the Postal Service?

Was becoming a private corporation the way to go?

In the ensuing public-policy debate, there were strong arguments that only this kind of shift would be enough to help the USPS keep up with the fast-changing communication environment. On the other hand, policymakers recognized that the Postal Service, with its national infrastructure reaching every household and business six days a week, makes contributions to society that are not strictly limited to mail delivery.

To see this, one only needed to look at some of the casualties. Some of the now-closed post offices had opened in the early 19th century: Leon, Virginia, established June 5, 1810, and closed September 3, 2011; Plessis, New York, established September 16, 1823, and closed March 26, 2011; Mitchellville, Tennessee, established March 11, 1828, and closed October 10, 2011. Others dated back to the postwar glory days of the American Century. The majority were in rural areas, where their closures left citizens feeling cut off from the rest of the world—and cut off from one another. These were the places where people gathered, swapped stories, and heard the news from around town. A post office, these people would tell you, offers a special kind of community building just by being open.

And as the decade came to a close, those people indeed did say that. Customers, and even some of the USPS's longtime adversaries, like the American Postal Workers Union, fought to keep the Postal Service public. "Save the Post Office," their protest signs said. "U.S. Mail Not for Sale."

Informed Delivery

A test run of the Informed Delivery service was initiated in 2014 and launched to 42,000 ZIP Codes three years later. It's not email; however, it is a way to electronically view the physical mail that you get in your mailbox or delivered to your address. The Postal Service scans the front of the mail piece and then sends you a notification that you have mail to preview. The service allows up to 10 mail images in the daily email for free.

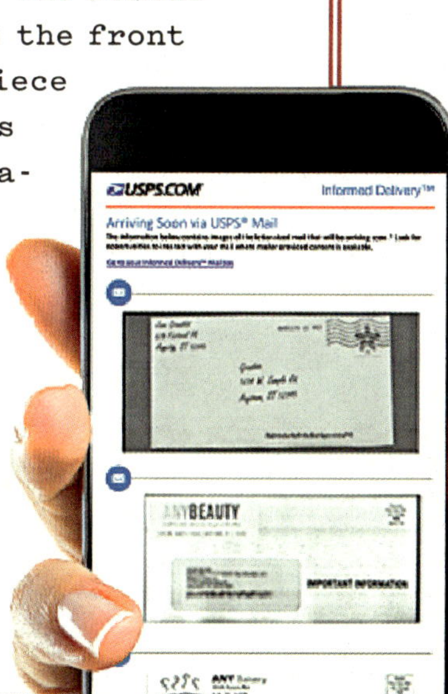

FOREVER / USA
USA
TAP TAP TAP
forever usa
MARIACHI
2022
MANATEE
2024
USPS/FOREVER/USA
FOREVER/USA
HIPHOP
B-BOY
2020
IGH LONESOME SOUND
BLUEGRASS
USA
YES!
FOREVER
2024
USA FOREVER
2021
FOREVER
USA
ART OF THE SKATEBOARD

THE PATH TO PROSPERITY

Louis DeJoy took the oath of office as the nation's 75th postmaster general on June 16, 2020. He was the fifth to join the USPS from the private sector since the Postal Reorganization Act of 1970. Board chairman Robert M. "Mike" Duncan administered the oath, while John M. Barger, chair of the selection committee, held the Bible.

The Postal Service, its Board of Governors, Congress, and the American people needed a Hail Mary. Since 2007, the USPS had been in a downward spiral. Financial losses were deepening. Investment and even just basic repairs were sorely lacking at most postal facilities. The delivery vehicle fleet was oftentimes older than the carriers driving them. The organizational structure was redundant, and there was an unacceptably high rate of employee turnover. Innovation had stalled out. And worst of all, overall performance was declining and the organization was at the brink of collapse.

And these were just the internal issues.

Externally, the mail had entered a new era. There were more places than ever for it to go, but there was less of it to go around. New addresses were constantly being added—1.7 million in 2023 alone—further stretching a misaligned and outdated network, bringing the total to 2.6 million businesses and 154 million residences. But the total mail volume had plummeted more than 42 percent since fiscal year 2007, and to make things worse, the cost of actually delivering it, thanks to inflation, was still on the rise. Customer confidence was declining.

The truth is that the USPS had been running in place for years. Previous leadership teams tried to hold the system together. But resistance to change came from all sides—Congress, presidential administrations, the Postal Regulatory Commission, unions, and key players in the mailing industry. Since 2009, the Government Accountability Office had had the Post Office on its high-risk watch list due to the major losses. And another thing the Board of Governors had to reckon with, when Postmaster General Brennan announced her retirement on January 31, 2020,

For years, there had been a tug of war between people who thought it should remain a public service and those who thought it should be a private company.

was that in all that time, the postmaster general had been a career USPS employee. It might be time to look outside the service for its next leader.

Enter Louis DeJoy.

DeJoy hadn't built a career inside the Postal Service—instead, he'd been just outside. His last job had been as chairman and CEO of New Breed Logistics, a contractor to the Postal Service for more than 25 years—and a distinguished one at that, receiving Quality Supplier Awards from the USPS four separate times. DeJoy retired from New Breed in 2015, then served on the company's board until 2018. By 2020, after a couple years off, the USPS Board of Governors suspected he might be ready for a new challenge.

On May 3, 2020, the eight members of the board unanimously selected DeJoy as the next postmaster general. After Senate confirmation, he took office on June 15, 2020.

What a job he was about to embark upon: His responsibility would be no less than securing the future of the Postal Service. For years, there had been a tug of war between people who thought it should remain a public service and those who thought it should be a private company. If it were to remain the former in 2020s America, well, it was going to have to be Louis DeJoy's doing.

Some things were beyond the organization's control. Less mail but more addresses? Beyond USPS control. Inability to control prices? Beyond USPS control. Coffers being drained by the requirements of the Postal Accountability and Enhancement Act? Beyond USPS control. The Postal Regulatory Commission, the Board of Governors, postal unions, private lobbyists, Congress? All beyond USPS control.

But DeJoy could control how the USPS worked. He could cut costs, as everyone before him had aimed to do, and he could also sniff out new revenue streams, update systems, improve the work environment to make employees more effective, and foster innovation.

One of the first things DeJoy did was order that mail trucks be filled to capacity with mail when leaving the loading docks. The current practice was to distribute mail immediately, even if there was only a tiny amount to move. Mail trucks would leave loading docks carrying barely any mail, incurring the full cost of gas, wear and tear, and time for just a few letters or packages. It was incredibly inefficient. If there wasn't enough mail to fill them up, DeJoy reasoned, it could wait. Facing a projected $9.7 billion loss in his first year, he had to start somewhere.

And so he did.

Unfortunately, before DeJoy could make his move, history made its own.

★ ★ ★

On the last day of 2019, the World Health Organization's country office in China was alerted to a cluster of people with a mysterious pneumonia-like illness in the city of Wuhan. Five days later, the U.S. Centers for Disease Control and Prevention began its own investigation, and on January 17, 2020, it started screening passengers who flew to the United States from Wuhan for the new virus. The first confirmed case in the United States, in Washington State, came just three days later. From there, it was a cascade: Confirmed spread within the country. Quarantines. Enhanced measures on flights from China. Testing kits developed for the virus. In February, the number of deaths worldwide from the new illness surpassed 1,000. On the last day of that month—February 29, Leap Day—the first death was confirmed in the U.S. On March 11, the World Health Organization declared the illness a pandemic.

COVID-19 had officially arrived.

It would become the third-worst worldwide spread of a disease since the Spanish flu of 1918.

That epidemic killed more than 100 million people over three years; the HIV/AIDS epidemic killed about 33 million from 1981 to 2022; COVID-19 has killed some 27 million since 2019, and the numbers continue to rise.

As the disease spread, one by one countries closed borders, ordered employees to work from home, and shut down businesses. The American public was introduced to the concept of "essential workers"—those whose jobs absolutely could not be halted, as they were necessary to keep the country going. These included grocery clerks and food-delivery people, utility workers, transportation workers, and, of course, employees of the United States Postal Service.

The unfolding of COVID-19, just like the Spanish flu, would leave an indelible mark on the mail. Or maybe it's more accurate to say that the mail left an indelible mark on the pandemic: Not only did delivery carry on, but many of the most crucial American efforts to help the country weather the pandemic required it.

On March 20, 2020, Postmaster General Brennan created the USPS COVID-19 Response Command Team to give full-time focus to the pandemic. One of its first initiatives: coordinating delivery of "President Trump's Coronavirus Guidelines for America" postcards, which set out basic rules to help stop the spread of the virus, to 138 million residential addresses. The postcards reminded people to use the 15-day rule—staying isolated for that long if they had COVID or felt ill—to slow the spread; what to do if someone within their household tested positive; and to practice good hygiene.

Did hygiene need to include special treatment of the post? As with the Spanish flu, customers were concerned the virus could be transferred through contact with mail. Though people were soon assured that the risk of transmission was low, some took precautions anyway, including waiting to touch packages and disinfecting them along with any surfaces they touched. The USPS helped with information on alternate delivery options.

The pandemic highlighted the Postal Service's key place in the nation's critical infrastructure. In fact, growing package volume accelerated beyond all expectations, by more than 30 percent. No matter what, mail would still be delivered six days a week.

On March 27, 2020, the president signed the Coronavirus Aid, Relief, and Economic Security Act, which authorized the USPS to receive a $10 billion loan from the U.S. Treasury if the Postal Service found that it would not be able to fund operating expenses due to the pandemic. That lifeline proved crucial: COVID-19 brought much of the world to a halt, but the Postal Service's financial troubles could not be stopped. On April 9, 2020, Brennan, "who would be leaving USPS in mid-June," advised the House Oversight and Reform Committee that the USPS would run out of funds by the end of September. Suffice it to say that in July 2021, DeJoy was able to secure the full $10 billion loan.

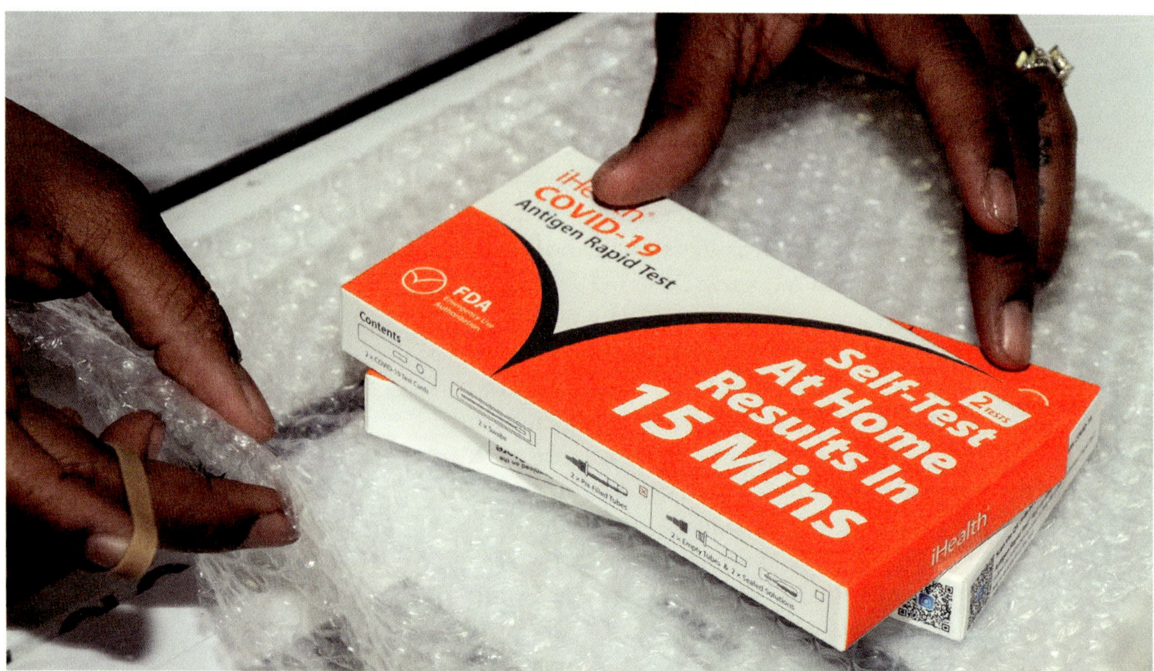

In 2024, the USPS was on its seventh round of delivering free at-home COVID-19 test kits. The kits were a collaboration with the White House and the Administration for Strategic Preparedness and Response within the U.S. Department of Health and Human Services.

In order to slow the spread of the COVID-19 virus, President Donald Trump issued the "15 Days to Slow the Spread" card, which the USPS delivered to every household and business by the USPS. Less than one month later, the card was updated to "30 Days to Slow the Spread."

THE PRESIDENT'S **CORONAVIRUS GUIDELINES** FOR AMERICA

15 DAYS TO SLOW THE SPREAD

Listen to and follow the directions of your **STATE AND LOCAL AUTHORITIES.**

IF YOU FEEL SICK, stay home. Do not go to work. Contact your medical provider.

IF YOUR CHILDREN ARE SICK, keep them at home. Do not send them to school. Contact your medical provider.

IF SOMEONE IN YOUR HOUSEHOLD HAS TESTED POSITIVE for the coronavirus, keep the entire household at home. Do not go to work. Do not go to school. Contact your medical provider.

IF YOU ARE AN OLDER PERSON, stay home and away from other people.

IF YOU ARE A PERSON WITH A SERIOUS UNDERLYING HEALTH CONDITION that can put you at increased risk (for example, a condition that impairs your lung or heart function or weakens your immune system), stay home and away from other people.

For more information, please visit
CORONAVIRUS.GOV

But the USPS wasn't the only entity that needed money. With millions of Americans out of work, the federal response to the pandemic also included direct payments, known as stimulus checks, to Americans. In April 2020, the USPS began delivering checks from the U.S. Treasury to about 60 million households.

But this was all a prelude to what was perhaps the most important and impactful task in the Post Office's history. In January 2022, the USPS began fulfilling and delivering COVID-19 rapid test kits to homes, in partnership with the White House and other federal agencies. The first orders were taken on January 18. With that, the country's COVID readiness underwent a dramatic transformation. When the pandemic began, no test kits existed. Months later, they had been invented but weren't widely available. Fast-forward, and on just one day, February 22, 2022, the Postal Service delivered *six million* test kits. By March 2, in total, more than 68 million packages had been processed and delivered to American households.

DeJoy cited test-kit delivery as "a major point of pride throughout our organization." He didn't say this, but COVID provided one vision of what the Post Office could be in the 21st century: the physical plumbing of government service delivery. It wasn't quite the same as being the plumbing of the country's information system, but it was no less noble—which is what DeJoy *did* point out. "There are few assignments the Postal Service has received," he said, "that better exemplify our public service mission than the request of the Biden administration to deliver America's COVID-19 test kits."

By the end of May 2022, 380 million had been delivered. In September 2024, COVID-19 was resurgent and the initiative was extended to provide a seventh round of free test kits. During the program (which was suspended in March of 2025), the USPS had successfully delivered more than 900 million tests.

★ ★ ★

The USPS named this green tag "Tag 191" to identify trays and sacks that contain ballot mail. The tag is optional; however, its use provides great visibility to containers of ballot mail as they go through the Postal Service's processing and distribution operations.

The 2020 presidential campaign began long before DeJoy even took office. But as Election Day, November 3, drew closer, it was clear to DeJoy and the USPS that this was going to be an election like none before it. In the throes of the pandemic, facing fears of spreading or contracting the virus, more Americans than ever before were interested in voting by mail. Indeed, when the dust settled, 43 percent of tallied votes would be on mail-in ballots, a huge jump from roughly 25 percent in the 2016 and 2018 elections. It would be the first election in which most voters had not cast their ballots in a voting booth on Election Day. But that was to come. In the middle of 2020, the USPS was just working on figuring out how it was going to smoothly deliver millions of blank ballots to voters and millions of filled-out ballots back to elections officials.

Unfortunately, the concrete details of how the Postal Service planned to fulfill its duty quickly proved irrelevant. People began listening to rumors, rather than facts. Rumors, for example, from inside and outside of the Post Office, of mailbox removals and of sorting machines being taken out of commission. These rumors, in the minds of some, added up to a purposeful slowing of mail service driven by partisan politics.

Observing the prevailing public sentiment, in mid-August, DeJoy announced he would halt any changes in mail service until after the election. He was still hauled before the Senate on August 21, 2020, and the House of Representatives on August 24, 2020—virtually, of course—to address the rumors.

He was just two months into the job, but DeJoy had an answer to virtually every concern. Regarding mailbox removals, he stated that it has long been USPS policy to remove blue mail collection boxes that have low mail volumes. In fiscal year 2017, more than 6,000 boxes were removed; in fiscal year 2019, it was about 1,600. In 2020, there were still more than 140,000 boxes available.

What about the sorting machines? DeJoy told the Senate that in April 2020, before he'd joined the service, a report on the utilization of letter- and flat-sorting equipment showed that neither type of machine was utilized even 40 percent of the hours it was available. In other words, even if machines were removed, there would still be plenty of capacity left to efficiently sort the mail.

So there was no truth to the rumors. There was no purposeful slowing of the mail. In fact, during his short time in office, DeJoy had already made significant improvements to mail processing. After he coordinated with numerous employees in sorting and distribution centers and management, the number of daily trips had increased from 35,000 to more than 39,000, and the on-time dispatch rate improved from 89.4 percent to 97.0 percent. But people were afraid. What if seniors didn't get their Social Security checks on time? What if prescription drugs failed to show up? What if veterans missed services?

Members of the public and of Congress started calling for DeJoy's firing. Not even three months after his hiring and only two weeks after the Senate hearing, a letter appeared in the *Fresno Bee* on September 4, 2020, headlined "Fire DeJoy, restore Postal Service."

The rumors about the USPS's pre-election performance may not have been true, but people had a good reason to direct anger toward it: The service was continuing to struggle. After all, that's why DeJoy had been hired—because service wasn't great. In the congressional hearing, he offered some contrition. "We all feel bad about the dip in our service level," he stated. "We serve 161 million people. We still deliver at 99.5 percent of the time...Everybody's working feverishly to get that right...We're considering dramatic changes to improve the service to the American people."

All DeJoy could do was take the hits and explain his plan. And in fact, he had a plan—one of growth and sustainability—that had been in the works practically since he'd set foot in the door. In early 2021, he spoke to the House about this plan but also about the necessary actions to right the USPS ship. These did not differ wildly from what his predecessors had suggested: changing the PAEA's crippling funding rules, requiring retirees to get on Medicare, and modernizing the rules for setting postal rates.

Some of these things would soon happen. But first, the USPS would get a report card for its work during the election. In March 2021, a federal assessment found that 135 million ballots had been mailed out and returned in an average of just 3.7 days—2.1 days from election officials to voters and 1.6 days for completed ballots to be delivered to vote counters. The number of mailed ballots doubled, but the rejections of those ballots declined from 1 percent to 0.8 percent. All told, the Post Office had delivered 97.9 percent of them on time within three days.

Given that the USPS excelled during the election *and* during a pandemic, DeJoy quickly learned the commitment to service from the men and women of the Postal Service and the difficult path ahead. No one could blame him for being dismayed by the rumors and the unwarranted criticism his agency suffered during the campaign. But all through the pandemic and the election, he'd been working diligently on a plan to secure the Post Office's future.

"Delivering for America" was only the second 10-year plan in the long history of the American mail service—which in a way was precisely the problem: The USPS was supposed to operate like a business, but it wasn't doing the kind of forward-looking planning that it needed to succeed. And so here it found itself, writing a plan that needed to quickly reverse projected losses of $200 billion over the following 10 years.

Dear Postal Customer,

If you vote by mail, we're committed to providing you a secure, effective way to deliver your ballot. Use this checklist to prepare:

- ☐ Start today. Give yourself and your election officials ample time to complete the process.
- ☐ Rules and dates vary by state, so contact your election board to confirm. Find links at **usps.com/votinginfo**.
- ☐ Request your mail-in ballot (often called "absentee" ballot) at least 15 days before Election Day.
- ☐ Once received, follow the instructions. Add postage to the return envelope if needed.
- ☐ We recommend you mail your ballot at least 7 days before Election Day.

We're ready to deliver for you. Make sure you're ready, too.

Your United States Postal Service

©2020 United States Postal Service®. All Rights Reserved.
The Eagle Logo is among the many trademarks of the U.S. Postal Service®.

475 L'Enfant Plaza SW
Washington, DC 20260

PRESORTED
STANDARD MAIL
POSTAGE & FEES PAID
USPS
PERMIT NO. G-10

Please Recycle

At the height of COVID-19, voting by mail for the 2020 election was a matter of health safety. Any voter could request a ballot by mail if they filled out this USPS election-information circular and returned it by the 11th day prior to an election.

If you plan to vote by mail, plan ahead.

Please read this important information for U.S. citizens.

The Next Generation Delivery Vehicle

The newest vehicle added to the USPS's fleet of vehicles is the NGDV, which stands for the Next Generation Delivery Vehicle. Oshkosh Defense has been tasked with making 66,000 electric NGDVs, and all the vehicle's new features are outlined in this spec sheet.

The last Grumman Long Life Vehicle, that stalwart of the USPS delivery system since the 1980s, was built in 1994. Which means that by the start of the 2020s, the newest LLV was 26 years old, having lasted far longer in service than anyone had any right to expect. The USPS needed a new delivery fleet, and it couldn't come fast enough.

Luckily, the Postal Service's next vehicle had been in development for some time already. In 2015, the USPS had released the specifications for an LLV successor. The vehicles needed to feature a larger cargo capacity, at least 155 cubic feet, to meet the demands of the growing parcel business. They had to be able to maintain a speed of 60 miles per hour on a 1 percent grade, at an altitude of 3,000 feet. They had to manage hundreds of stops and starts, even with the air conditioner running at maximum to keep the mail carrier cool. (This was something the LLVs lacked.) And the vehicles had to be able to do all this for a life span of no fewer than 12 years, with a target of 20.

An official request for a proposal from manufacturers interested in building the new fleet went out in October. Six companies were ultimately awarded the opportunity to test prototypes. It took more than five years and another postmaster general to winnow the field down to one. In 2021, Oshkosh Defense signed an agreement to make its Next Generation Delivery Vehicle (NGDV) the new mail van. It was a large, ungainly

vehicle with a high boxy cab and a low snoutlike hood that was referred to in the media as a "duck bill." In December 2022, Postmaster General Louis DeJoy announced plans to purchase more than 60,000 of them by 2028, a significant portion of the 106,000 vehicles the USPS aimed to buy in a $9.6 billion investment in fleet upgrades that was part of Delivering for America. Many of the new vehicles would be electric, as the Post Office continued to work hard at being a leading government organization when it came to going green.

The first NGDVs rolled onto routes in the fall of 2024. They got the expected (mocking) reviews for their appearance–but they also quickly won over mail carriers. The prevailing opinion might best be summed up by Athens, Georgia, postal worker Avis Stonum, who told the Associated Press, "You can tell that [the designers] didn't have appearance in mind"–but also that when she got to experience air conditioning on her route for the first time, "it felt like heaven blowing in my face."

Long may they run.

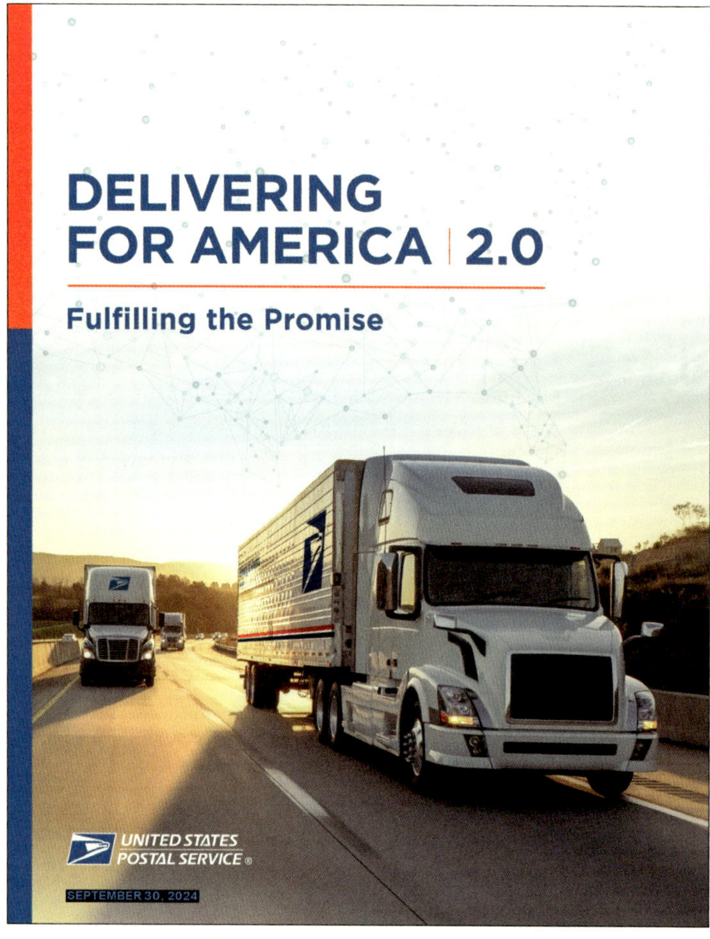

Delivering for America 2.0, released in 2024, was a progress report following the initial 2021 Delivering for America, a 10-year plan to transform the Postal Service from an organization in financial and operational crisis to one that is self-sustaining and high-performing.

Delivering for America was released on March 23, 2021, the work of a team that included the postmaster general and a newly established officer corps that he selected, as well as the Board of Governors. Everyone was utterly crucial, because the profound change the plan called for required everything from pricing freedom to updated management processes to new legislation.

The numbers in Delivering for America were all big, starting with that $200 billion. Seeing how the plan divvied up efforts to eliminate the projected shortfall made clear how wide-reaching they had to be. The biggest amount, $58 billion in savings, would require legislative and administrative action—the action that postmasters general had been calling for for decades, and that DeJoy had outlined to the Senate: eliminating the PAEA's prefunding requirement and getting retirees on Medicare, among other things. Then, $44 billion depended on the Postal Regulatory Commission, which would need to provide more pricing flexibility. Improved efficiency in sorting and processing was due to bring costs down by $34 billion, and growth in the package-shipping business, plus innovative new products, aimed to boost revenue by $24 billion.

Improving efficiency, delivering more packages, and finding new projects aren't simply a matter of will. They don't happen just by trying harder. They require investment. Delivering for America also outlined a plan for upgrading IT, modernizing post offices, and finally buying a new fleet of vehicles. It specified a new network structure, designed to streamline mail processing, that comprised regional processing and distribution centers (RPDCs), local processing centers (LPCs), and sorting and delivery centers (S&DCs), which would bring a kind of hierarchical coherence to the work of handling mail. The price tag for this was $40 billion. And investment of any real kind hadn't happened at the USPS in a very long time.

★ ★ ★

A plan is only a plan until the elements of it begin to happen, and for Delivering for America, the big one happened on April 6, 2022. On that day, President Joseph R. Biden signed the Postal Reform Act. This legislation included a slew of operational changes aimed at efficiency and accountability: It kept mail delivery at six days a week; required the USPS to disclose and publish performance metrics on its website every six months; required its website to deliver operational reports to the PRC, president, and Congress; allowed it to use the most cost-effective modes of transportation; and more. It also included perhaps the single most important postal reform since reorganization in the 1970s.

It repealed the PAEA payment requirements.

Biden's signature on the bill, one single signature, would save billions of dollars per year. It was a tremendous piece of progress, hope, and forward momentum.

But the Postal Reform Act wouldn't make delivering the whole package of changes outlined in Delivering for America a sure thing—not by a long shot. There were still all kinds of challenges,

Delivering for America outlined a plan for upgrading IT, modernizing post offices, and finally buying a new fleet of vehicles.

some of which were under the control of the USPS and some of which were not.

In 2023 and 2024, RPDCs and LPCs began to open, but there were some serious kinks to work out before they would be fully operational.

An unexpected surge in inflation, which in May 2022 reached 8.6 percent—the highest it had been since the early 1980s—decreased mail volumes. Especially affected were marketing mail and volume packages, two of the Post Office's most lucrative and essential business lines.

Even worse, inflation made it essential for the USPS to borrow money to finance the changes it was undertaking.

And then another election rolled around. With memories of 2020's partisan hullabaloo around election mail still fresh, DeJoy aimed to get ahead of things, saying that "we're trying to calm everybody down." But like clockwork, as the election grew closer, some in Congress argued the USPS threatened to "disenfranchise voters." Once again, DeJoy announced he would pause changes—this time, Delivering for America's reform efforts—until after the election.

But around the same time, DeJoy did something else, too. In September 2024, he released Delivering for America 2.0: Fulfilling the Promise, an update on the original plan. The new missive pointed out that the initiatives in the original plan were putting the USPS on a "positive trajectory" as it was "built for 21st century realities, not one that maintains the vestiges and nostalgia of bygone business models and antiquated ways of working." And this was crucial, the plan said, because the USPS, as ever, "plays a vital and valued role in the daily life of the American public, and in the life of our nation."

★ ★ ★

The USPS operates one of the largest vehicle fleets in the world.

U.S. POST OFFICE
PENLAND N.C.
28765

Opposite: The Penland Post Office in North Carolina flooded during Hurricane Helene when the Toe River waters crested and flooded the area. The building still stands today.

Natural Disaster, Unthinkable Devastation, Uncommon Devotion

In early fall 2024, there was a day when letter carrier Jason Kimmel's first delivery caused a woman to break down in tears. The package was a birthday present for the recipient's son, and, as she told Kimmel, she never imagined as she'd be getting it anytime soon.

Kimmel serves Hendersonville, North Carolina, a town that was devastated by Helene, one of the strongest and deadliest hurricanes of the 21st century. Kimmel returned to work soon after the storm to try to do his part in helping people's lives get back to normal. And he was not alone. "Some people are still without power and clean water and they're coming to work this whole time," he told *Government Executive* about his fellow postal workers. "It's pretty incredible."

Letter carriers in regions affected by Helene reported to work after their own homes were damaged and their own cars destroyed. They sorted mail by headlamp. They deviated from their usual routes as needed. They sweated out delivering the mail even when they had no running water at home and couldn't shower at the end of the day. Why? "Seeing the mail truck come by, bringing the catalogs, even junk mail, it's the first sign that we're digging out and getting back to normal," Kimmel said.

Accounts in the aftermath of the hurricane were not unlike reports from the Church Street Station Post Office after the events of September 11, 2001. When people were at their lowest, the mail could provide familiarity, comfort, and connection. The difference with Hurricane Helene was that it was a natural act rather than a human one. As the climate continues to change, such events may become more common. In their aftermath, the uncommon devotion of postal employees will make them frontline workers—and will make it more important than ever for the USPS develop a culture that supports its carriers.

On July 26, 2025, the United States Postal Service, successor to the United States Post Office Department, successor to the General Post Department, will celebrate its 250th anniversary.

When the United States of America was not yet a nation, when it hadn't even yet declared independence from Great Britain, the Second Continental Congress founded the mail system with a modest remit, as reported in Secretary Charles Thomson's notes:

> ...the Congress resumed the consideration of the report of the Committee on the post office; which being debated by paragraphs, was agreed to as follows:
>
> That a postmaster General be appointed for the United Colonies, who shall hold his office at [Philadelphia], and shall be allowed a salary of 1000 dollars per [year] for himself, and 340 dollars per [year] for a secretary and Comptroller, with power to appoint such, and so many deputies as to him may seem proper and necessary.
>
> That a line of posts be appointed under the direction of the Postmaster general, from Falmouth in New England to Savannah in Georgia, with as many cross posts as he shall think fit...

From that decree evolved the USPS of today, in which the number of "deputies as to him may seem proper and necessary" has become 640,000 employees. In which the "line of posts... with as many cross posts as he shall think fit" has become more than 33,000 post offices, 12.7 million business addresses, and 167 million residential addresses. The USPS of today operates the world's largest civilian vehicle fleet—more than 246,000 vehicles—and processes more than 116.2 billion pieces of mail per year, six days a the week. It is responsible for 44 percent of the world's mail volume.

How does such a vast operation grow from such humble beginnings? It takes will, the kind of will that maps out potential post roads and clears them of rocks and stumps. It takes ingenuity, the kind of ingenuity that put a whole post office inside a railcar. It takes foresight, the kind of foresight that was testing automobiles—electric and gas—from the very earliest days of their invention. It takes a sense of adventure, the kind that drove young men to hop on horses and race express mail across the challenging frontier of the West.

It takes the spirit of Benjamin Franklin, who so believed in the power of mail that all the way back in 1764 he bragged to the British, his soon-to-be enemies, that his mail service had sped up communication between New York City and Philadelphia

The Postal Service travels everywhere and in all weather to deliver mail and packages. Here, an LLV travels through the small, unincorporated community of Rocky Fork, West Virginia, with its retro-looking red covered bridge over the Pocatalico River.

USPS's 250th anniversary identifier is called "Eagle in Flight" and symbolizes the Postal Service's past, present, and future.

by "making the travels by night as well as by day, which had heretofore not been done in America." Mail between New York City and Boston would be next, Franklin had promised.

Indeed, for the first 175 years of its existence—at least—the Post Office was focused on conquering the physical space of America. The way to connect Americans was to cut post roads through wilderness that could be traveled from growing city to growing city, night and day. It was to push into untamed territories as the nation expended. It was to race across the desert and two mountain ranges with news of gold in a new power center on the continent's West Coast; and to ensure that Hawaii and Alaska, the noncontiguous states, could feel no farther away than the first 48.

But somewhere along the way, something changed. The map had been filled in. The roads had been cut. Stagecoaches had been supplanted by cars. Trains had been supplanted by planes.

The Post Office Department had been supplanted by the Postal Service.

The speed at which a letter or package could get from any one place in the United States to any other plateaued. The connections between Americans increasingly moved from physical space to cyberspace.

What is the Post Office in this new world? The first decades of the fourth century in which it has existed offer some clues. In the catharsis of meeting longtime customers after the terrorist attacks of 9/11, in the bolstering of Americans' recycling efforts, in the delivery of COVID-19 kits and the transmission of ballots, one can glimpse a Post Office that functions as our nation's civic glue. For so long, in building the postal network, the mail service was making the country smaller. It can bring us closer together.

This has, of course, always been part of the Postal Service's job. Just look at the letters home from wars, from the American Revolution through the Civil War, two world wars, Korea, Vietnam, Iraq, and countless others. Look at how post offices were places of emotional refuge during the Great Depression and physical refuge during the Cold War.

Yes, this has always been a part of the mail's *job*, but maybe now, with the swashbuckling eras of the Pony Express and the Fast Train and World War I pilots flying airmail without instruments firmly in the past, it can be the mail's *purpose*.

This will require no less transformation, modernization, or innovation than it took to build the postal network. Above all, the impulse to look forward, to survey the untamed frontier of the country—no longer mountains and desert and prairie but a frontier nonetheless—and work diligently and ingeniously to connect Americans across it is what will carry the United States Postal Service for another 250 years.

All the way back in 1639, the forefathers of today's Americans could pick up their mail at Richard Fairbanks's tavern at Washington and State streets in Boston. In the 1740s, if you lived in Benjamin Franklin's Philadelphia, the mail might have come right to your home. In the 1850s, in Council Grove, Kansas, people gathered their mail under the boughs of the Post Office Tree. In the 1930s, struggling, out-of-work citizens kept their chins up thanks to ornate new post offices, built with the largesse of the New Deal. In the 1980s, Americans could get mail from abroad electronically through INTELPOST. No one knows how Americans will receive their mail 25 years from now, let alone 250 years from now. But we can bet that it will have something in common with the mail service of the past: It will be person-to-person. It will start with the deeply human need to tell someone else about something of import, to reach out and connect.

As Americans, if the past 250 years have taught us anything, it's that we will always need to connect with one another, and as long as Americans need to connect, we'll need the Post Office.

And the Post Office will be there, draped in red, white, and blue.

An eagle, always facing forward.

LIST OF ALL POSTMASTERS GENERAL

Dates prior to 1900 are the dates the postmasters general were appointed or commissioned; dates after 1900 are the dates they took office. Appointments by the U.S. president were made with the advice and consent of the Senate.

POSTMASTERS GENERAL APPOINTED BY

THE CONTINENTAL CONGRESS

BENJAMIN FRANKLIN
Appointed July 26, 1775

RICHARD BACHE
Appointed November 7, 1776

EBENEZER HAZARD
Appointed January 28, 1782

POSTMASTERS GENERAL APPOINTED BY

THE PRESIDENT UNDER THE CONSTITUTION

SAMUEL OSGOOD
Appointed September 26, 1789
by George Washington

TIMOTHY PICKERING
Appointed August 12, 1791
by George Washington

JOSEPH HABERSHAM
Appointed February 25, 1795
by George Washington

GIDEON GRANGER
Appointed November 28, 1801
by Thomas Jefferson

RETURN J. MEIGS JR.
Appointed March 17, 1814
by James Madison

JOHN McLEAN
Appointed June 26, 1823
by James Monroe

WILLIAM T. BARRY
Appointed March 9, 1829
by Andrew Jackson

AMOS KENDALL
Appointed May 1, 1835
by Andrew Jackson

JOHN M. NILES
Appointed May 19, 1840
by Martin Van Buren

FRANCIS GRANGER
Appointed March 6, 1841
by William Henry Harrison

CHARLES A. WICKLIFFE
Appointed September 13, 1841
by John Tyler

CAVE JOHNSON
Appointed March 6, 1845
by James K. Polk

JACOB COLLAMER
Appointed March 8, 1849
by Zachary Taylor

NATHAN KELSEY HALL
Appointed July 23, 1850
by Millard Fillmore

SAMUEL D. HUBBARD
Appointed August 31, 1852
by Millard Fillmore

JAMES CAMPBELL
Appointed March 7, 1853
by Franklin Pierce

AARON V. BROWN
Appointed March 6, 1857
by James Buchanan

JOSEPH HOLT
Appointed March 14, 1859
by James Buchanan

HORATIO KING
Appointed February 12, 1861
by James Buchanan

MONTGOMERY BLAIR
Appointed March 5, 1861
by Abraham Lincoln

WILLIAM DENNISON
Appointed September 24, 1864
by Abraham Lincoln

ALEXANDER W. RANDALL
Appointed July 25, 1866
by Andrew Johnson

JOHN A.J. CRESWELL
Appointed March 5, 1869
by Ulysses S. Grant

JAMES W. MARSHALL
Appointed July 3, 1874
by Ulysses S. Grant

MARSHALL JEWELL
Appointed August 24, 1874
by Ulysses S. Grant

JAMES N. TYNER
Appointed July 12, 1876
by Ulysses S. Grant

DAVID M. KEY
Appointed March 12, 1877
by Rutherford B. Hayes

HORACE MAYNARD
Appointed August 26, 1880
by Rutherford B. Hayes

THOMAS L. JAMES
Appointed March 5, 1881
by James A. Garfield

TIMOTHY O. HOWE
Appointed December 20, 1881
by Chester A. Arthur

WALTER Q. GRESHAM
Appointed April 3, 1883
by Chester A. Arthur

FRANK HATTON
Appointed October 14, 1884
by Chester A. Arthur

WILLIAM F. VILAS
Appointed March 6, 1885
by Grover Cleveland

DON M. DICKINSON
Appointed January 16, 1888
by Grover Cleveland

JOHN WANAMAKER
Appointed March 5, 1889
by Benjamin Harrison

WILSON S. BISSELL
Appointed March 6, 1893
by Grover Cleveland

WILLIAM L. WILSON
Appointed March 1, 1895
by Grover Cleveland

JAMES A. GARY
Appointed March 5, 1897
by William McKinley

CHARLES EMORY SMITH
Appointed April 21, 1898
by William McKinley

HENRY C. PAYNE
Appointed January 15, 1902
by Theodore Roosevelt

ROBERT J. WYNNE
Appointed October 10, 1904
by Theodore Roosevelt

GEORGE B. CORTELYOU
Appointed March 7, 1905
by Theodore Roosevelt

GEORGE VON L. MEYER
Appointed March 5, 1907
by Theodore Roosevelt

FRANK H. HITCHCOCK
Appointed March 6, 1909
by William H. Taft

ALBERT S. BURLESON
Appointed March 5, 1913
by Woodrow Wilson

WILL H. HAYS
Appointed March 4, 1921
by Warren G. Harding

HUBERT WORK
Appointed March 4, 1922
by Warren G. Harding

HARRY S. NEW
Appointed March 5, 1923
by Warren G. Harding

WALTER F. BROWN
Appointed March 6, 1929
by Herbert Hoover

JAMES A. FARLEY
Appointed March 6, 1933
by Franklin D. Roosevelt

FRANK C. WALKER
Appointed September 11, 1940
by Franklin D. Roosevelt

ROBERT E. HANNEGAN
Appointed June 30, 1945
by Harry S. Truman

JESSE M. DONALDSON
Appointed December 16, 1947
by Harry S. Truman

ARTHUR E. SUMMERFIELD
Appointed January 21, 1953
by Dwight D. Eisenhower

J. EDWARD DAY
Appointed January 21, 1961
by John F. Kennedy

JOHN A. GRONOUSKI
Appointed September 30, 1963
by John F. Kennedy

LAWRENCE F. O'BRIEN
Appointed November 3, 1965
by Lyndon B. Johnson

W. MARVIN WATSON
Appointed April 26, 1968
by Lyndon B. Johnson

WINTON M. BLOUNT
Appointed January 22, 1969
by Richard M. Nixon

POSTMASTERS GENERAL APPOINTED BY

THE USPS BOARD OF GOVERNORS

WINTON M. BLOUNT
Appointed July 1, 1971

E. T. KLASSEN
Appointed January 1, 1972

BENJAMIN F. BAILAR
Appointed February 16, 1975

WILLIAM F. BOLGER
Appointed March 15, 1978

PAUL N. CARLIN
Appointed January 1, 1985

ALBERT V. CASEY
Appointed January 7, 1986

PRESTON R. TISCH
Appointed August 16, 1986

ANTHONY M. FRANK
Appointed March 1, 1988

MARVIN T. RUNYON
Appointed July 6, 1992

WILLIAM J. HENDERSON
Appointed May 16, 1998

JOHN E. POTTER
Appointed June 1, 2001

PATRICK R. DONAHOE
Appointed December 6, 2010

MEGAN J. BRENNAN
Appointed February 1, 2015

LOUIS DeJOY
Appointed June 15, 2020

INDEX

C

D

E

Q

R

S

ABOUT THE AUTHOR

JAMES H. BRUNS followed his father—a renowned philatelist and postal historian—as Smithsonian's curator of U.S. Philately and Postal History in 1983. After rising to the position of Deputy Director of the National Philatelic Collection, he became project manager for the Smithsonian's newest museum. He assisted with planning the museum's building, facilities, and exhibits. The success of such planning led to Jim being appointed as the Founding Director of the Smithsonian's National Postal Museum.

The museum, created in cooperation with the USPS, opened in 1993 and is located within the historic City Post Office next to Washington, D.C.'s Union Station. This sophisticated and highly interactive museum is the United States' first major museum devoted to postal history and philatelic exhibitions.

Jim is the author of 15 books and over 150 articles pertaining to postal history and philately.

An exterior view of the Smithsonian National Postal Museum in Washington, D.C.

AUTHOR ACKNOWLEDGMENTS

This work is the product of many minds and hearts, and I am indebted to all those who contributed mightily to its publication. I owe special thanks to Ellen Espinoza-Hale, the United States Postal Service's project manager for this publication. Special gratitude also goes to Jennifer M. Lynch, the former Historian of the United States Postal Service, for reviewing portions of this work and suggesting so many fine additions and thoughtful revisions.

I am also indebted to Dr. Frank Scheer, who heads up the Railway Mail Service Library, for his invaluable assistance in fact-checking some of this work and in furnishing several of the photographs of important artifacts highlighted here that are not part of the National Postal Museum's collections.

Recognition also goes to many of my former colleagues at the Smithsonian Institution, including Nancy Gwynn, the late former head of the Smithsonian's Library and her staff, most particularly Baasil Wilder, the branch librarian at the Smithsonian's National Postal Museum, for his thoughtful and dedicated assistance in selecting and assembling the historic photographs used to illustrate these pages; and Erin Clements Rushing, the former Smithsonian's Libraries outreach librarian. I am also deeply indebted to Elliot Gruber, the Director of the Smithsonian's National Postal Museum, and his staff for their help in showcasing the remarkable manufacts and artifacts that accompany this work. This includes Manda Kowalczyk, preservation specialist, and Elizabeth Heydt, collections manager, for their assistance in selecting and photographing many of the artifacts depicted here. Assistance was also furnished by National Postal Museum Specialists Patricia Raynor, James O'Donnell, and William Lommel. I am grateful for their continued friendship and support. In addition, I'm extremely grateful to the various institutions, agencies, firms, and individuals that have furnished historic documents and photographs of the artifacts and rarities highlighted in this book, including the Library of Congress, the National Archives and Records Administration, the United States Postal Service, the Smithsonian Institution, United Press International, Pioneer Press, Charles E. Young Research Library/UCLA, Casper College Library, Carnegie Library of Pittsburgh, Knox College Seymour Library, Wyoming State Archives, Seth Kaller Auctions, Robert A. Siegel Auction Galleries, Cole Woodbury, Suzi Taylor, George Barrowclough, Robin Everett, and Matthew Liebson.

USPS ACKNOWLEDGMENTS

The USPS would like to express their sincerest gratitude for the assistance and guidance of the following in bringing to light the story of the Postal Service:

Melcher Media: Charles Melcher, Megan Worman, Lauren Nathan, Bonnie Eldon, Susan Lynch, Madison Brown, and Christopher Steighner.

James H. Bruns, author, for agreeing to take on such a huge historical task.

USPS: Stephen Kochersperger, Historian; Karen Marks, former librarian, June Brandt, Senior Research Analyst on Postal History; Jennifer Lynch, former Historian; Amity Kirby, Manager, Licensing; Alicia Marlatt, Manager, Creative Art; Dino Omerovic, Licensing Analyst; Loren Clark, Licensing Analyst; Daniel Afzal, Photographer; Chelsea Rebro and Jared Carlson from Purchasing and Supply Management Specialist.

National Postal Museum, Smithsonian Institution: Toby Mensforth, Deputy Director; Marty Emery, Manager, Public Relations and Internet Affairs; Baasil Wilder, Librarian.

Architect of the Capitol; Becky Davis; Boston Public Library; The Cabinet Card Gallery; California Historical Society; California State Parks; The Civil War Philatelic Society; Columbia Historical Society; Defense Visual Information Distribution Service; Federal Bureau of Investigation; Georgia Historical Society; The Gilder Lehrman Institution of American History; Howard University; Idaho State Museum; John F. Kennedy Presidential Library and Museum Archives; John Glancy; Johns Hopkins Sheridan Libraries & University Museums; Library of Congress; *Los Angeles Times* Photographic Collection; Maine Historical Society; Matt Abruzzo; Minnesota Library; Missouri State Archives; National Archives and Records Administration; National Park Service; Nebraska State Historical Society; New York Historical Society; Ohio Statehouse; Oklahoma Highway Patrol Collection; Oklahoma Historical Society; Peabody Essex Museum; Pennsylvania Academy of Fine Arts; Records of the U.S. Senate: Center for Legislative Archive; Richard Frajola; Smithsonian American Art Museum; Smithsonian American History Museum; Smithsonian Libraries and Archives; Smithsonian National African American History & Culture Museum; Smithsonian National Portrait Gallery; *Spokane Chronicle*; Temple University Libraries; Tennessee State Library and Archives; Toledo Museum of Art; U.S. Marine Corps Archives & Special Collections; Uintah County Library; United States Geological Survey; United States Olympic & Paralympic Committee: Karen Hays; United States Maritime Administration; University of California, Berkeley, Bancroft Library; University of Chicago Library University of Florida: George A. Smathers Libraries; University of Michigan; University of Pennsylvania; University of Texas at Arlington Library; University of Washington; The White House; Whiting-Robertsdale Historical Society; Yale Library: The Beinecke Rare Book and Manuscript Library; Ypsilanti Historical Society Photo Archives.

Elementary schools would have children make posters focusing on Post Offices. This poster was completed by a fourth-grader in Tucson, Arizona, in the mid-1980s. The motto reads: "No matter where you are [we'll] get it to you. Merry Christmas." This fourth-grader has now been a USPS employee for almost two decades.

PHOTO CREDITS

All images courtesy of USPS, except for the following:

From *A Life Span and Reminiscences of Railway Mail Service*, James E. White, 1910: 190 (top); Amity Kirby: 447; Architect of the Capitol: 55; From *Atlas of the Historical Geography of the United States*, 1932; Charles O. Paullin and John K. Wright, Washington, D.C., plate 140: 155; From *The Automobile*, July 2, 1904: 210 (bottom), From *Automobile Trade Journal and Motor Age*, 1906: 217; From the *Baltimore Sun*, 1970: 343 (top); Bancroft Library at the University of California, Berkeley: 110 (bottom); Courtesy of Becky Davis, Postmistress of the Penland Post Office: 430; Beinecke Rare Book and Manuscript Library at Yale: 22; Courtesy of Bentley Historical Library at the University of Michigan: 214; Boston Public Library: 93 (bottom), 96 (right), 260 (bottom) The Cabinet Card Gallery: 227; California State Parks: 124 (top right); From *Chicago Today*, March 20, 1970: 340; From the *Chicago Tribune*, August 9, 1892: 190 (bottom); From *Citizen News*, March 23, 1970: 344 (bottom); Courtesy of The Civil War Philatelic Society: 137 (bottom right); Columbia Historical Society: 51 (top); Combined Military Service Digital Photographic Files: 377 (top), 378 (bottom); From the *Daily News*, July 6, 1922: 251; Defense Visual Information Distribution Service: 398–399; From the *Evansville Courier and Press*, July 25, 1990. Used with permission: 378; From *The Evening World*, December 19, 1921: 246 (top); Courtesy of Fairfax County Library 691: 184 (bottom); Federal Bureau of Investigation: 370, 385 (right); George A. Smathers Libraries at the University of Florida: 189; Courtesy of the Georgia Historical Society: 47 (bottom), 434 (third row, left); Gettysburg College, Special Collections and College Archives, Musselman Library: 88; From the *Geuda Springs Herald*, August 12, 1892: 191 (top); The Gilder Lehrman Institute of American History: 40; From the *Great Falls Tribune*, November 17, 1921: 243 (middle); HathiTrust: 62, 97; From *Harper's Bazaar*, volume XVII, no. 52, p. 836, December 27, 1884: 52; From *The Herald*, June 22, 1922: 242; From *History of the Ordinance of 1787 and the Old Northwest Territory*, Federal Writers' Project, Marietta, OH, Northwest Territory Celebration Commission, 1937: 34 (left); Howard University: 146 (top left); From *The HUB*, Vol XVIII: 165 (top); Courtesy of Huntington Library: 185; Idaho County Free Press, February 19, 1914: 227; Idaho State Museum: 226; From the collection of James H. Bruns: 212, 260 (top), 314 (left); John Carter Brown Library at Brown: 16; John F. Kennedy Presidential Library and Museum Archives: 335; Courtesy of the John Glancy Collection: 301 (bottom); Johns Hopkins Sheridan Libraries & University Museums: 204 (top and bottom), 205 (top left, bottom left, middle right, and bottom right); Justin Sullivan/Getty Images: 405; Library of Congress: 2, 6 (top), 14, 42–43, 46, 47 (bottom left), 51 (bottom), 67 (bottom), 72, 76, 80, 92, 96 (left), 111, 123, 124–125 (bottom), 134, 135 (bottom), 136 (top), 139 (left), 140, 141, 144, 147, 148 (second from bottom), 154, 156, 166, 177, 180, 181, 194, 195 (left), 196–198, 201 (left), 205 (top right), 215, 223, 225 (bottom), 228, 231, 233, 234, 239, 244, 245 (top), 254, 261, 266 (top left, bottom), 267 (top), 273, 274 (middle), 288 (bottom), 290, 297, 299, 310, 311 (bottom), 348–349 (bottom), 353 (right bottom), 397 (top right), 434 (first row, left; fifth row, middle), 435 (first row, second from left; first row, third from left; second row, left; second row, left; second row, third from left; second row, right; third row, second from left; third row, right; fourth row, left; fourth row, second from left; fourth row, third from left; fourth row, right; fifth row, left; fifth row, third from left; fifth row, right; sixth row, second from left; sixth row, third from left; sixth row, third from left; sixth row, right), and 436 (first row, left; first row, second from left; first row, third from left; second row, second from left; second row, third from left; second row, right; third row, left; third row, second from left; third row, third from left; third row, right; fourth row, left); Maine Historical Society: 246 (bottom); From *Mid-Pacific Magazine*, 1914, Vol. XVI, No. 4: 216; Mildred Lane Kemper Art Museum at Washington University in St Louis: 47 (top); Courtesy of the Minnesota Library: 143; The Miriam and Ira D. Wallach Division of Art, Prints and Photographs: Print Collection, New York Public Library: 25; Missouri State Archives: 157 (top); National Archives and Records Administration: 12, 13, 17, 20, 57, 94, 172, 173, 229 (bottom), 230 (left and right), 235, 238, 252-253, 262, 278 (bottom), 279, 282–283, 288 (top), 291, 293, 313 (top and middle left), 332 (top left and top right), 333, 344 (top), 374–376, 377 (bottom), 378 (top), 434 (fourth row, right), 435 (second row, third from left), 435 (third row, second from left), and 435 (third row, right); National Gallery of Art: 45; National Museum of African American History and Culture: 146 (right); National Museum of American History: 151 (top and bottom), 191 (bottom), 230 (middle); National Park Service: 53; Newspapers.com: 31, 63, 75 (top left), 78 (left), 89, 106 (top), 110 (top), 135 (top); New York Historical Society: 15 (right); New York Public Library: 18 (bottom), 26, 28, 30 (top), 35, 44 (top), 68, 93 (top), 102, 103 (bottom), 119, 128, 142 (right), 192, 434 (first row, right and second row, left); From the *Niles National Register* (St. Louis, Missouri) 9 May 1829, page 8: 77; The NYS Historic Newspapers: 75 (top right); The Ohio Statehouse: 67 (top); Oklahoma Highway Patrol Collection: 386 (bottom right); Oklahoma Historical Society: 44 (bottom); Peabody Essex Museum: 130–131; Pennsylvania Academy of Fine Arts: 74 (bottom), 78 (right), 434 (fourth row, middle); Courtesy of Postal Record, National Association of Letter Carriers, AFL-CIO: 145; From *The Railway Mail Service, Its Origins and Development*, Clark Ezra Carr, 1909: 160, 162; Records of the U.S. Senate, Center for Legislative Archives: 54; From *RFD News*, June 1909: 219; Courtesy of Richard Frajola: 95 (top), 126, 165 (bottom), 201 (right); From *Roughing It*, Mark Twain, American Publishing Company,1886, page 100: 122; Save our Heritage Organisation: 118; Smithsonian American Art Museum: 32, 127, 269 (top); Smithsonian National Postal Museum: 15, 18 (bottom), 21, 29, 34 (right), 41, 58–59, 66, 79, 83, 84–85, 98–99, 104 (middle and right), 105, 106 (bottom left and right), 107, 109 (top), 112, 113 (top left, top right, and middle left), 129, 136 (bottom), 137 (top and bottom left), 138, 139 (right), 148 (topmost, second from top, and bottommost), 149 (top, middle left, middle right, and bottom right), 150, 161, 163 (bottom left and right), 167, 168–169, 174, 178–179, 182–183, 188, 199, 200 (left), 208, 213, 225 (top), 229 (top), 232, 241, 245 (bottom), 247–250, 255–257, 263 (right), 271, 274 (top and bottom), 275, 278, 284, 286 (bottom), 287, 292, 316 (left and right), 317, 324 (bottom), 352, 353 (right top and right second from top), 381, 390–391, 397 (top left and bottom), 400 (top right), 402, and 434 (first row, middle; third row, middle; and third row, right), 446; Special Collections Research Center, Temple University Libraries: 342; Courtesy of *Spokane Chronicle*: 357 (bottom); From *Stage-Coach and Tavern Days*, Alice Morse Earle, New York, The Macmillan Company, London, 1900: 23; From *St. Nicholas*, Volume XXIV, Part I, November 1896: 202–203; Courtesy of the Tennessee State Library and Archives: 91, 266 (top right); Toledo Museum of Art: 18 (top); Courtesy of Uintah County Library, all rights reserved: 224; University of California: 109 (bottom); University of Chicago Library: 434 (fourth row, left); University of Michigan: 74 (top); University of Pennsylvania: 69, 103 (top), 120; University of Southern California Libraries, California Historical Society: 116 (bottom); University of Texas at Arlington Library: 73; United States Geological Survey: 356; U.S. Marine Corps Archives & Special Collections: 312, 313 (middle right); U.S. Presidential History: 434 (fifth row, left); U.S. State Department: 434 (second row, right); Courtesy UW Special Collections (TRA787): 195 (right); From *The Washington Post*, April 25, 1915: 224 (top); The White House: 404; Courtesy of the Whiting-Robertsdale Historical Society: 267 (bottom); From *The Wide World Magazine*, Volume 49, 1922: 243 (left and right); Wide World Photos: 322 (right); Wikimedia Commons: 64–65, 142 (left, sidebar); World File Photo: 357 (top); Yale University Archives: 116 (top); York University: 204 (middle); Ypsilanti Historical Society Photo Archives: 300